MICROSOFT®
VISUAL BASIC® .NET
PROGRAMMER'S
COOKBOOK

Microsoft®
.net™

Matthew MacDonald

PUBLISHED BY
Microsoft Press
A Division of Microsoft Corporation
One Microsoft Way
Redmond, Washington 98052-6399

Library of Congress Cataloging-in-Publication Data
MacDonald, Matthew
    Microsoft Visual Basic .NET Programmer's Cookbook / Matthew MacDonald.
       p. cm.
    Includes index.
    ISBN 0-7356-1931-X
    1. Microsoft Visual BASIC. 2. BASIC (Computer program language) 3. Microsoft .NET. I. Title.

    QA76.73.B3M285   2003
    005.2'7--dc21   2003046416

Printed and bound in the United States of America.

3 4 5 6 7 8 9   QWT   8 7 6 5

Distributed in Canada by H.B. Fenn and Company Ltd.

A CIP catalogue record for this book is available from the British Library.

Microsoft Press books are available through booksellers and distributors worldwide. For further information about international editions, contact your local Microsoft Corporation office or contact Microsoft Press International directly at fax (425) 936-7329. Visit our Web site at www.microsoft.com/mspress. Send comments to *mspinput@microsoft.com*.

Acquisitions Editor: Danielle Voeller
Project Editor: Dick Brown
Technical Editors: Mark Bukovec and Marc Young
Interior Graphic Designer: James D. Kramer

Principal Compositor: Daniel Latimer
Interior Artists: Joel Panchot, Rob Nance
Principal Copyeditor: Lisa Pawlewicz
Indexer: Ginny Bess

Body Part No. X09-39101

For Faria

Table of Contents

Acknowledgments

Writing this book was great, albeit tiring fun. The unique format of the "cook-book" is surprisingly rewarding, as it gives the author an unusual chance to create chapters filled with dense, practical examples that specifically deal with the issues raised by professional programmers. I look forward to finding out what recipes are the most useful—and what interesting techniques or tricks I might have overlooked.

I owe a heartfelt thanks to many individuals at Microsoft Press, including Danielle Voeller, who sold me on the idea of a cookbook, and Dick Brown, who guided it through the editorial process. Marc Young and Mark Bukovec provided the tech review for this book (along with many invaluable suggestions), and Lisa Pawlewicz added polish with her expert copyediting. I'm also indebted to the principal compositor Dan Latimer and electronic artist Joel Panchot, as well as numerous others at Microsoft Press who have worked tirelessly behind the scenes to ensure that indexing, figures, and page setting were successful. In addition, I'd like to extend a special thanks to those individuals who contributed tips, insight, or tools that I used in creating the recipes in this book, including Lutz Roeder, Francesco Balena, Mike Krueger, Lance Olson, and many more. Any remaining mistakes or omissions are purely my own.

Finally, I would like to thank my parents (all four of them) and my loving wife.

Introduction

The Microsoft Visual Basic .NET language now spans more programming tools, concepts, and application programming interfaces (APIs) than ever before. With the Microsoft .NET Framework, your Visual Basic code can go to work in a Microsoft Windows service, a Web application, an XML Web service, a Windows client, or a remote component. It can use robust multithreading, manipulate relational data and XML, harness COM+ services, and more. With all this functionality comes a price—even the most experienced developer can have trouble isolating a useful feature buried somewhere in the enormous .NET class library!

The *Microsoft Visual Basic .NET Programmer's Cookbook* is designed to share some of the best practices, tips, and undocumented secrets that help programmers master all aspects of .NET. This book doesn't intend to replace the many excellent tutorials that describe .NET basics and explain the foundational concepts for programming various types of applications. Instead, this book aims to fill the knowledge gaps of a professional programmer. In other words, you shouldn't turn to this book to learn how to create your first multithreaded program. However, when you need a reference that can give you an at-a-glance look at several different asynchronous programming patterns and provide you with a recipe for deriving your own custom thread class, this book will be invaluable.

The best way to think of this book is as a cross between an "FAQ on steroids" and a library of templates that show best practices. It would be impossible to list all the useful snippets of code I've come across as a .NET programmer (and even if I did, the resulting book would be too large and disorganized to be much help to anyone). Instead, this book includes recipes that respond to the questions developers ask again and again on message boards, discussion lists, at conferences, in my .NET courses, and in direct-to-author e-mails. One of the reasons that a book like this works so well is that developers *do* run into the same problems time and time again, and the right solutions are often universal.

This book not only focuses on how to *do* things, but also how to do them *right*. For example, it's easy enough to create a custom *Exception* class, but developers won't necessarily know the recommended constructors they should include, or the steps they should take to make the exception serializable so that it can be thrown across application domains in a remoting scenario. You'll find a similar theme when using threads, implementing common design patterns in .NET code, or creating custom objects that support the standard interfaces for copying, cloning, and comparing.

Another difference with this book and many other .NET titles is that it's relentlessly practical. Many books about .NET cover only what the .NET platform encompasses. They might describe its limitations, but they rarely go beyond them. This book, on the other hand, covers everything developers need to get their work accomplished, even if it stretches into an area where the .NET class library hasn't caught up yet. Here are some examples:

- **The Win32 API**   As comprehensive as the .NET Framework is, it doesn't duplicate the entire Windows API. Some reasons you might turn to the API include playing a WAV file, logging in as a new user, getting Web connectivity information, and shutting down Windows programmatically.

- **Windows Management Instrumentation (WMI)**   WMI is a framework you can use to retrieve a wide array of hardware-specific and operating system–specific information. We'll use WMI to find out about currently installed printers, and retrieve lists of Windows users and groups for the current computer.

- **JavaScript**   In Microsoft ASP.NET Web applications, all code executes on the server. If you want to set control focus on the client, show a client-side message box, or just tailor the appearance of the rendered page, you need to enhance your pages with a twist of JavaScript.

- **Legacy COM Components**   The .NET Framework supplants the Component Object Model (COM), but there are still a number of tasks that can be greatly simplified with legacy COM components. One example is the Windows Script Host, which allows you to create shortcuts and send keystrokes to other applications. We'll use other examples when showing a Web page, using a masked text box, playing video, sending e-mail messages with Messaging Application Programming Interface (MAPI), and automating Microsoft Office applications.

- **Your Own Custom Components**   Some of the missing pieces of .NET can be easily filled in with your own custom components. For example, this book includes completely developed classes for accessing a File Transfer Protocol (FTP) site, contacting a Post Office Protocol (POP) mail server, reading MP3 headers, creating a salted password hash for storage in a database, and working with vectors, fractions, and complex numbers.

- **Third-Party Components**   The .NET component market is alive and well, with many professional components for sale that can save hours of programming effort. We won't cover any of these in this book, but we will feature a few components that are open source or completely free. This includes components for reading ZIP files, writing PDF documents, and showing menus in ASP.NET.

Feedback

This book is largely driven by the questions and interests of the programming community. So, if you have an unanswered question or found that a recipe didn't completely answer a question, feel free to e-mail me at VBCookbook@prosetech.com. Reader feedback will be used to enhance the recipe set in future editions of this book.

Code Samples

The recipes in this book are designed to illustrate a particular concept by isolating only the essential details. Many of the code samples use simple Console applications, and often the complete code is provided in the recipe. Other times, only code snippets will be shown. Mundane details, like the designer code Microsoft Visual Studio .NET adds automatically to any Windows application, are not shown.

The complete code is available online at *http://microsoft.com/mspress/books/6436.asp* (click the Companion Content link in the More Information box on the right side of the page) and *http://www.prosetech.com*. The code is organized by chapter and recipe number. For example, to find the complete code for recipe 7.4, you would look up the code in the project directory "Chapter 07\Recipe 7-4". Some additional steps are required to install the two virtual directories used for the ASP.NET Web page and Web service examples. These are described in a readme.txt file provided with the download code. You can also find an updated list of all the hyperlinks featured in this book at *http:// www.prosetech.com.*

> **Note**   The code in this book has been tested with versions 1.0 and 1.1 of the .NET Framework. In most cases, these two platforms work almost exactly the same, although .NET 1.1 (which is a part of Visual Studio .NET 2003) includes a slew of minor bug fixes and performance enhancements. In the rare cases where the Visual Studio .NET 2003 behavior differs from that of the original Visual Studio .NET, the text makes special mention of the differences. Code shortcuts that are not available in .NET 1.0 code are not used in this book.

System Requirements

You'll need the following software to work through the samples in this book:

- Microsoft Visual Studio .NET or Visual Studio .NET 2003

- Microsoft Windows 2000, Windows XP, or Microsoft Windows Server 2003

The minimum hardware specification for development is a 450-MHz Pentium II-class processor, with a minimum of 128 MB of RAM if you're running Microsoft Windows 2000, and 256 MB of RAM if you're running Windows XP, Windows 2000 Server, or Windows Server 2003. You'll need about 5 GB of free hard-disk space to install Visual Studio .NET 2003. These values are bare minimums, and your development life will be much easier on a system with ample RAM and free disk space.

Variable Naming

In the past, Microsoft favored a variation of Hungarian notation when naming variables. That meant, for example, that a Visual Basic integer variable would start with the prefix *int* (as in *intCount*). But in the world of .NET, memory management is handled automatically, data types can change without any serious consequences, and the majority of variables are storing references to full-fledged objects. Hungarian notation is starting to show its age.

The new Microsoft standard is to avoid variable prefixes, especially for properties and methods visible to other classes. This style is similar to the standard used for COM components and controls, and it makes a great deal of sense for code transparency. Data types no longer pose the problems they once did because Visual Studio .NET will spot invalid conversions and refuse to compile.

In this book, data type prefixes are not used for variables. The only significant exception is with control variables, for which it is still a useful trick to distinguish between different types of controls (such as *txtUserName* and *lstUserCountry*) and with some data objects. Of course, when you create your own programs, you are free to follow whatever variable naming convention you prefer, provided you make the effort to adopt complete consistency across all your projects (and ideally across all the projects in your organization).

Other Books

As explained in the introduction, this books deals with the programming challenges faced by working developers. It is *not* the best place to learn the basics of programming or the fundamentals of .NET. That said, programmers of almost any level will be able to learn something useful or have a question answered from the recipes in this book.

If you're looking for a top-down tutorial that leads you through a particular aspect of .NET programming, you might be interested in one of the books in the following list. This list is by no means comprehensive, but it does include some useful resources (all of which I endorse fully).

- For a thorough introduction to almost every aspect of Visual Basic .NET programming, refer to Francesco Balena's excellent book *Microsoft Visual Basic .NET Core Reference* (Microsoft Press, 2002).

- For an introduction to Visual Basic .NET from the perspective of the Visual Basic 6 programmer, you can read my own *The Book of VB .NET* (No Starch, 2002).

- For an exhaustive look at Microsoft ADO.NET, try David Sceppa's insightful *Microsoft ADO.NET Core Reference* (Microsoft Press, 2002).

- For a comprehensive look at building distributed applications that use Web services and .NET Remoting, along with the best practices needed to thread safely and scale successfully, refer to my own *Microsoft .NET Distributed Applications* (Microsoft Press, 2003).

- For a complete introduction to ASP.NET for Visual Basic programmers, consider Stephen Walther's *ASP.NET Unleashed* (Sams, 2001) or my own *ASP.NET: The Complete Reference* (McGraw-Hill, 2002).

- For detailed information about the .NET code access security model, check out Eric Lippert's *Visual Basic .NET Code Security Handbook* (Wrox, 2002).

Microsoft Press Support

Every effort has been made to ensure the accuracy of the book and its companion content. Microsoft also provides corrections for books through the World Wide Web at the following address:

http://www.microsoft.com/mspress/support/

In addition to sending feedback directly to the authors, if you have comments, questions, or ideas regarding the presentation or use of this book or the companion content you can send them to Microsoft using either of the following methods:

Postal Mail:

Microsoft Press
ATTN: Microsoft Visual Basic .NET Programmer's Cookbook Editor
One Microsoft Way
Redmond, WA 98052-6399

E-Mail:

mspinput@microsoft.com

Please note that product support isn't offered through the above mail addresses. For support information regarding Visual Studio .NET 2003, go to *http://msdn.microsoft.com/vstudio/*. You can also call Standard Support at (425) 635-7011 weekdays between 6 a.m. and 6 p.m. Pacific time, or you can search Microsoft Product Support Services at *http://support.microsoft.com/support*.

1

Strings and Regular Expressions

Strings are a fundamental ingredient in almost every application. You'll use string processing to validate user-supplied input, search a block of text for specific words or recurring patterns, and format numbers, dates, and times.

In the Microsoft .NET Framework, strings are based on the *String* class. The *String* class is far more than a simple array of characters—it also comes equipped with a full complement of methods for searching, replacing, and parsing text. The early recipes in this chapter (1.1 to 1.10) show how you can use this built-in functionality to accomplish common string manipulation tasks. Later recipes consider some slightly more involved techniques, including the *StringBuilder* class, which greatly increases the performance of repetitive string operations, and *regular expressions*, which provide a platform-independent syntax for specifying patterns in text. Regular expressions can be a daunting subject, and crafting your own expressions isn't always easy. To get a quick start, you can use recipe 1.17, which includes an indispensable set of premade regular expressions that you can use to validate common types of data such as passwords, phone numbers, and e-mail addresses.

Finally, the last four recipes demonstrate how you can deal with specialized forms of string data, such as file system paths and Uniform Resource Identifiers (URIs). Using the techniques in these recipes can save pages of custom code and remove potential security holes from your applications.

Before you begin using the recipes in this chapter, you should understand a few essential facts about strings:

- Strings are immutable, which means they can't be changed. Operations that appear to modify a string actually create a new string. For that reason, if you need to perform several repetitive string manipulations in a row, it's almost always faster to use the *StringBuilder* class, which is described in recipe 1.14.

- A string is a reference type that behaves like a value type. For example, when you compare two strings, you are comparing the content contained in the string, not the object reference. This allows strings to be allocated efficiently in memory, while ensuring that they still work the way programmers expect them to work.

- All string methods use zero-based counting. This means that the first character is located at position 0. This is in contrast to the Microsoft Visual Basic 6 string processing functions, which use one-based counting.

> **Note**   Visual Basic .NET also supports legacy Visual Basic string manipulation functions such as *Len*, *InStr*, *Left*, *Right*, and so on. However, using these methods is discouraged. The *String* class methods enable you to write code that can work in any .NET language (including C#) with very little modification. Using these methods also ensures better consistency. If you mingle Visual Basic language functions and .NET Framework class library functions, you might introduce unexpected bugs, because the Visual Basic functions use one-based counting with strings, while the class library functions use zero-based counting.

1.1 Combine Strings

Problem

You need to join two strings or insert a string into another string.

Solution

Use the *&* operator to add one string to the end of another. Use the *String.Insert* method to insert a string in the middle of another string.

Discussion

You can join strings together using the *&* or + operator.

```
Dim FirstName As String = "Bill"
Dim LastName As String = "Jones"
Dim FullName As String

FullName = FirstName & " " & LastName
' FullName is now "Bill Jones"
```

> **Note**   Although the + operator can be used to join strings in the same way as the *&* operator, it's not recommended. If you use the + operator for concatenation and one of the values in your expression isn't a string, Visual Basic .NET will attempt to convert both values to a *Double* and perform numeric addition. However, if you use the *&* operator, Visual Basic .NET will attempt to convert any nonstring value in the expression to a string and perform concatenation. Thus, the *&* operator is preferred for concatenation because it's unambiguous—it always does string concatenation, regardless of the data types you use.

Strings also provide an *Insert* method that enables you to place a substring in the middle of another string. It requires a *startIndex* integer parameter that specifies where the string should be inserted.

```
Dim FullName As String = "Bill Jones"
Dim MiddleName As String = "Neuhaus "

' Insert MiddleName at position 5 in FullName.
FullName = FullName.Insert(5, MiddleName)
' FullName is now "Bill Neuhaus Jones"
```

Incidentally, you can also use the complementary *Remove* method, which enables you to delete a specified number of characters in the middle of a string:

```
FullName = FullName.Remove(5, MiddleName.Length)
' FullName is now "Bill Jones"
```

1.2 Retrieve a Portion of a String

Problem

You need to retrieve a portion of a string based on its position and length.

Solution

Use the *String.Substring* method.

Discussion

The *String.Substring* method requires two integer parameters, a *startIndex* and a *length*. As with all string indexes, *startIndex* is zero-based (in other words, the first character in the string is designated as character 0).

```
Dim FullName As String = "Bill Jones"
Dim FirstName As String

' Retrieve the 4-character substring starting at 0.
FirstName = FullName.Substring(0, 4)
' FirstName is now "Bill"
```

Optionally, you can omit the *length* parameter to take a substring that continues to the end of the string:

```
Dim FullName As String = "Bill Jones"
Dim LastName As String

' Retrieve the substring starting at 5, and continuing to the
' end of the string.
LastName = FullName.Substring(5)
' LastName is now "Jones"
```

Visual Basic .NET includes the legacy *Left* and *Right* functions, but they're not recommended. Instead, you can use the *Substring* method in conjunction with the *Length* property to provide the same functionality. The code snippet below outlines this approach.

```
' Retrieve x characters from the left of a string.
' This is equivalent to Left(MyString, x) in VB 6.
NewString = MyString.SubString(0, x)

' Retrieve x characters from the right of a string.
' This is equivalent to Right(MyString, x) in VB 6.
NewString = MyString.SubString(MyString.Length - x, x)
```

1.3 Create a String Consisting of a Repeated Character

Problem

You need to quickly create a string that consists of a single character repeated multiple times (for example, "------------").

Solution

Use the overloaded *String* constructor that accepts a single character and a repetition number.

Discussion

The following code creates a string made up of 100 dash characters. Note that in order to use the nondefault *String* constructor, you must use the *New* keyword when you declare the string.

```
Dim Dashes As New String("-"c, 100)
```

When specifying the character to repeat, you can append the letter *c* after the string to signal that the quoted text represents a *Char*, as required by this constructor, not a *String*. This is required if you have *Option Strict* enabled, which disables implicit conversions between *Char* and *String* instances.

You could also perform the same task by using string concatenation in a loop. However, that approach would be much slower.

1.4 Change the Case of All Characters in a String

Problem

You want to capitalize or de-capitalize all letters in a string.

Solution

Use the *ToUpper* or *ToLower* method of the *String* class.

Discussion

ToUpper method returns a new string that is all uppercase. The *ToLower* method returns a new string that is all lowercase.

```
Dim MixedCase, UpperCase, LowerCase As String
MixedCase = "hELLo"

UpperCase = MixedCase.ToUpper()
' UpperCase is now "HELLO"

LowerCase = MixedCase.ToLower()
' LowerCase is now "hello"
```

If you want to operate on only part of a string, split the string as described in recipe 1.2, call *ToUpper* or *ToLower* on the appropriate substring, and then join the strings back together.

1.5 Perform Case-Insensitive String Comparisons

Problem

You need to compare two strings to see if they match, even if the capitalization differs.

Solution

Use the overloaded version of the shared *String.Compare* method that accepts the *ignoreCase* Boolean parameter, and set *ignoreCase* to *True*.

Discussion

The *String.Compare* method accepts two strings and returns 0 if the strings are equal, -1 if the first string is less than the second (*StringA* < *StringB*), or 1 if the first string is greater than the second (*StringA* > *StringB*). Optionally, the *Compare* method can also accept a Boolean parameter called *ignoreCase*. Set the *ignoreCase* parameter to *True* to perform a case-insensitive comparison.

```
If String.Compare(StringA, StringB, true) = 0 Then
    ' Strings match (regardless of case).
End If
```

Alternatively, you can just put the strings into a canonical form (either both upper case or both lower case) before you perform the comparison:

```
If StringA.ToUpper() = StringB.ToUpper() Then
    ' Strings match (regardless of case).
End If
```

1.6 Iterate Over All the Characters in a String

Problem

You want to examine each character in a string individually.

Solution

Use a *For…Next* loop that counts to the end of string, and examine the *String.Chars* property in each pass, or use *For Each…Next* syntax to walk through the string one character at a time.

Discussion

Iterating over the characters in a string is fairly straightforward, although there is more than one approach. One option is to use a *For…Next* loop that continues until the end of the string. You begin at position 0 and end on the last character, where the position equals *String.Length* - 1. In each pass through the loop, you retrieve the corresponding character from the *String.Chars* indexed property.

```
Dim i As Integer
For i = 0 To MyString.Length - 1
    Console.WriteLine("Processing char: " & MyString.Chars(i))
Next
```

Alternatively, you can use *For Each…Next* syntax to iterate through the string one character at a time.

```
Dim Letter As Char
For Each Letter in MyString
    Console.WriteLine("Processing char: " & Letter)
Next
```

Performance testing indicates that this approach is actually slower.

> **Note**   With either technique, changing the individually retrieved characters won't modify the string because they are copies of the original characters. Instead, you must either use a *StringBuilder* (see recipe 1.14) or build up a new string and copy characters to it one by one.

When you retrieve a character from a string using these techniques, you aren't retrieving a full *String* object—you are retrieving a *Char*. A *Char* is a simple value type that contains a single letter. You can convert a *Char* to an integer to retrieve the representative Unicode character value, or you can use some of the following useful *Char* shared methods to retrieve more information about a character:

- *IsDigit* returns *True* if the character is a number from 0–9.

- *IsNumber* returns *True* if the character is a valid hexadecimal number from 0–F.

- *IsLetter* returns *True* if the character is a letter from A–Z.

- *IsLetterOrDigit* returns *True* for any alphanumeric characters (A–Z or 0–9).

- *IsLower* and *IsUpper* return *True* depending on the case of the character.

- *IsPunctuation* returns *True* if the character is classified as Unicode punctuation.

- *IsSymbol* returns *True* if the character is classified as a Unicode symbol.

- *IsWhiteSpace* returns *True* if the character is classified as Unicode whitespace (typically a space, tab, line break, etc.).

As an example, the next function iterates through a string and returns the number of alphanumeric characters using the *Char.IsLetterOrDigit* method.

```
Private Function CountAlphanumericCharacters( _
    ByVal stringToCount As String) As Integer

    Dim CharCount As Integer = 0

    Dim Letter As Char
    For Each Letter In stringToCount
        If Char.IsLetterOrDigit(Letter) Then CharCount += 1
    Next

    Return CharCount

End Function
```

1.7 Parse a String Into Words

Problem

You want to analyze a string and retrieve a list of all the words it contains.

Solution

Use the *String.Split* method. Depending on the complexity of the task, you might need to take additional steps to remove unwanted words.

Discussion

The *String* class includes a *Split* method that accepts an array of delimiter characters. The *Split* method divides the string every time one of these delimiters is found, and it returns the result as an array of strings. You can use this method with the space character to retrieve a list of words from a sentence.

```
Dim Sentence As String = "The quick brown fox jumps over the lazy dog."
Dim Separators() As Char = {" "c}
Dim Words() As String

' Split the sentence.
Words = Sentence.Split(Separators)

' Display the divided words.
Dim Word As String
For Each Word In Words
    Console.WriteLine("Word: " & Word)
Next
```

The output from this code is as follows:

```
Word: The
Word: quick
Word: brown
Word: fox
Word: jumps
Word: over
Word: the
Word: lazy
Word: dog.
```

Unfortunately, the *Split* method has a number of quirks that make it less practical in certain scenarios. One problem is that it can't collapse delimiters. For example, if you use a space character as a delimiter and attempt to split a string that contains multiple adjacent spaces (such as "This is   a   test") you will end up with several empty strings. A similar problem occurs if you are trying to handle different types of punctuation (like commas, periods, and so on) that are usually followed by a space character.

You have several options in this case. The simplest approach is to ignore any strings that consist of a delimiter character. You can implement this approach with a custom function that will wrap the *String.Split* method, as shown on the following page.

```
Private Function EnhancedSplit(ByVal stringToSplit As String, _
  ByVal delimiters() As Char) As String()

    ' Split the list of words into an array.
    Dim Words() As String
    Words = stringToSplit.Split(delimiters)

    ' Add each valid word into an ArrayList.
    Dim FilteredWords As New ArrayList()
    Dim Word As String
    For Each Word In Words
        ' The string must not be blank.
        If Word <> String.Empty Then
            FilteredWords.Add(Word)
        End If
    Next

    ' Convert the ArrayList into a normal string array.
    Return CType(FilteredWords.ToArray(GetType(String)), String())

End Function
```

This code eliminates the problem of extra strings. For example, you can test it with the following code:

```
Dim Sentence As String
Sentence = "However, the quick brown fox jumps over the lazy dog."

Dim Separator() As Char = {" "c, "."c, ","c}
Dim Words() As String = EnhancedSplit(Sentence, Separator)

Dim Word As String
For Each Word In Words
    Console.WriteLine("Word: " & Word)
Next
```

The output correctly removes the comma, spaces, and period:

```
Word: However
Word: the
Word: quick
Word: brown
Word: fox
Word: jumps
Word: over
Word: the
Word: lazy
Word: dog
```

Alternatively, you can use a lower-level approach, such as iterating through all the characters of the string searching for delimiter characters. This is more common if you are performing multiple string operations at the same time (such as splitting a string into words and stripping out special characters). Recipe 1.6 explains how to iterate through characters in a string. If you want to use multi-character delimiters, you can also use regular expressions and the *Regex.Split* method. See recipe 1.17 for more information about regular expressions.

1.8 Find All Occurrences of Specific Text in a String

Problem

You want to count how many times a certain word or sequence of characters occurs in a string.

Solution

Call the *String.IndexOf* method multiple times in a loop, until you reach the end of the string.

Discussion

The *String* class provides an *IndexOf* method that returns the location of the first match in a string. Fortunately, there is an overloaded version of *IndexOf* that enables you to specify a starting position for the search. By stepping through the string in a loop, specifying greater and greater start positions after each match, you can retrieve a list of all matches. (Another overload enables you to limit the number of characters the search will examine.)

Here's a function that simply counts the number of matches:

```
Private Function CountMatches(ByVal stringToSearch As String, _
  ByVal searchFor As String) As Integer

    Dim Position As Integer = 0
    Dim Matches As Integer = 0

    ' This loop exits when Position = -1,
    ' which means no match was found.
    Do
        Position = stringToSearch.IndexOf(searchFor, Position)
        If Position <> -1 Then
            ' A match was found. Increment the match count.
            Matches += 1
```

```
                ' Move forward in the string by an amount equal to
                ' the length of the search term.
                ' Otherwise, the search will keep finding the same word.
                Position += searchFor.Length
            End If
        Loop Until Position = -1

        Return Matches

End Function
```

Here's how you might use this function:

```
Dim Text As String = "The quick brown fox jumps over the lazy dog. " & _
    "The quick brown fox jumps over the lazy dog. " & _
    "The quick brown fox jumps over the lazy dog. "

Console.WriteLine(CountMatches(Text, "brown"))
' Displays the number 3.
```

If needed, you could enhance this function so that it returns an array with the index position of each match:

```
Private Function GetMatches(ByVal stringToSearch As String, _
    ByVal searchFor As String) As Integer()

    Dim Position As Integer = 0
    Dim Matches As New ArrayList()

    ' This loop exits when Position = -1,
    ' which means no match was found.
    Do
        Position = stringToSearch.IndexOf(searchFor, Position)
        If Position <> -1 Then
            ' A match was found. Store the position.
            Matches.Add(Position)

            Position += searchFor.Length
        End If
    Loop Until Position = -1

    ' Convert the ArrayList into a normal integer array.
    Return CType(Matches.ToArray(GetType(Integer)), Integer())

End Function
```

Notice that this technique is fundamentally limited—it can only find exact matches. If you want to search for a pattern that might contain some characters that vary, you will need to use regular expressions, as discussed in recipe 1.19.

1.9 Replace All Occurrences of Specific Text in a String

Problem

You want to replace a certain word or sequence of characters each time it occurs in a string.

Solution

Use the *String.Replace* method.

Discussion

The *String* class provides a *Replace* method that replaces all occurrences of text inside a string, and returns a new string:

```
Dim Text As String = "The quick brown fox jumps over the lazy dog. " & _
  "The quick brown fox jumps over the lazy dog. " & _
  "The quick brown fox jumps over the lazy dog. "

Dim ReplacedText As String = Text.Replace("brown", "blue")
' ReplacedText is now "The quick blue fox jumps over the lazy dog."
' repeated identically three times.
```

If you want to replace the occurrence of a pattern in just a portion of the string, you will need to write additional code to divide the string into substrings. You then call *Replace* on only one of the substrings. Here's a function that automates this task based on a supplied *stopAtIndex* parameter:

```
Private Function ReplacePartial(ByVal stringToReplace As String, _
  ByVal searchFor As String, ByVal replaceWith As String, _
  ByVal stopAtIndex As Integer) As String

    ' Split the string.
    Dim FirstPart, SecondPart As String
    FirstPart = stringToReplace.Substring(0, stopAtIndex + 1)
    SecondPart = stringToReplace.Substring(stopAtIndex + 1)

    ' Replace the text.
    FirstPart = FirstPart.Replace(searchFor, replaceWith)

    ' Join the strings back together.
    Return FirstPart & SecondPart

End Function
```

For more flexible options replacing text, you're encouraged to use regular expressions, as discussed in recipe 1.20.

1.10 Pad a String for Fixed-Width Display

Problem

You need to align multiple columns of fixed-width text, perhaps in a Console window or for a printout.

Solution

Pad the text with spaces using *PadLeft* or *PadRight*, according to the largest string in the column.

Discussion

The *String.PadLeft* method adds spaces to the left of a string, whereas *String.PadRight* adds spaces to the right. Thus, *PadLeft* right-aligns a string, and *PadRight* left-aligns it. Both methods accept an integer representing the total length and add a number of spaces equal to the total padded length minus the length of the string.

```
Dim MyString As String = "Test"
Dim NewString As String

' Add two spaces to the left of the string.
NewString = MyString.PadLeft(6)

' You can also pad with other characters.
' This adds two dashes to the left of the string.
NewString = MyString.PadLeft(6, "-"c)
```

String padding is only useful when you are using a fixed-width font (often named Courier, Monotype, or Typewriter), where each character occupies the same display width. One common example is the Console window.

If you attempt to align text in a Console window using tabs, any text that stretches past the required tab stop won't be lined up properly. Instead, you must use padding to make sure each string is the same length. In this case, it's often useful to create a custom function that determines the maximum required string width and pads all string accordingly. Here's an example that uses strings in an array:

```
Private Sub PadStrings(ByVal stringsToPad() As String, _
  ByVal padLeft As Boolean)

    ' Find the largest length.
    Dim MaxLength As Integer = 0
    Dim Item As String
    For Each Item In stringsToPad
```

```
        If Item.Length > MaxLength Then MaxLength = Item.Length
    Next

    ' Pad all strings.
    ' You can't use For Each…Next enumeration here, because you must
    ' be able to modify the strings, and enumeration is read-only.
    Dim i As Integer
    For i = 0 To stringsToPad.Length - 1
        If padLeft Then
            stringsToPad(i) = stringsToPad(i).PadLeft(MaxLength)
        Else
            stringsToPad(i) = stringsToPad(i).PadRight(MaxLength)
        End If
    Next

End Sub
```

To test this function, you can use the following example. First, try displaying two columns of data without padding and only using a tab:

```
Dim Fruits() As String = _
  {"apple", "mango", "banana", "raspberry", "tangerine"}
Dim Colors() As String = {"red", "yellow", "yellow", "red", "orange"}

Dim i As Integer
For i = 0 To Fruits.Length - 1
    Console.WriteLine(Fruits(i) & vbTab & Colors(i))
Next
```

The output looks like this:

```
apple    red
mango    yellow
banana   yellow
raspberry        red
tangerine        orange
```

If you use the custom *PadStrings* function, however, the situation improves.

```
Dim Fruits() As String = _
  {"apple", "mango", "banana", "raspberry", "tangerine"}
Dim Colors() As String = {"red", "yellow", "yellow", "red", "orange"}

PadStrings(Fruits, True)
PadStrings(Colors, False)

Dim i As Integer
For i = 0 To Fruits.Length - 1
    Console.WriteLine(Fruits(i) & "    " & Colors(i))
Next
```

Here's the new output:

```
    apple  red
    mango  yellow
   banana  yellow
raspberry  red
tangerine  orange
```

Keep in mind that Microsoft Windows applications rarely use fixed-width fonts, and when printing it's usually more convenient to explicitly set coordinates to line up text.

1.11 Reverse a String

Problem

You need to reverse the order of letters in a string.

Solution

Convert the string to an array of characters and use the *Array.Reverse* method, or use the legacy *StrReverse* Visual Basic 6 function.

Discussion

The functionality for reversing a string isn't built into the *String* class, although it's available in the *Array* class. Thus, one basic strategy for string reversal is to convert the string into an array of *Char* objects using the *String.ToCharArray* method. Then, you can reverse the array using the *Array.Reverse* shared method. Finally, you can create a new string using a special constructor that accepts a character array.

```
Dim Text As String = "The quick brown fox jumps over the lazy dog."

Dim Chars() As Char = Text.ToCharArray()
Array.Reverse(Chars)

Dim Reversed As New String(Chars, 0, Chars.Length)
' Reversed is now ".god yzal eht revo spmuj xof nworb kciuq ehT"
```

If you aren't concerned about creating generic .NET code, you can use a somewhat undocumented shortcut: the *StrReverse* legacy function from Visual Basic 6, which is included in Visual Basic .NET for backward compatibility:

```
Reversed = StrReverse(Text)
```

1.12 Insert a New Line in a String

Problem

You need to insert a line break or tab character in a string, typically for display purposes.

Solution

Use the *NewLine* property of the *System.Environment* class, or use the global *vbTab* and *vbNewLine* constants.

Discussion

Visual Basic .NET provides three equivalent approaches for inserting line breaks. It's most common to use the *System.Environment* class, which provides a *NewLine* property that returns the new line character for the current platform:

```
Dim MyText As String
MyText = "This is the first line."
MyText &= Environment.NewLine
MyText &= "This is the second line."
```

However, the *System.Environment* class doesn't provide a property for tabs. Instead, you can use the traditional Visual Basic-named constants *vbNew-Line* and *vbTab*, which also results in slightly more compact code. Here's an example that formats Console output using tabs:

```
Console.WriteLine("Column 1" & vbTab & "Column 2")
Console.WriteLine("Value 1" & vbTab & "Value 2")
```

Of course, this code isn't guaranteed to properly align information, because the text varies in size, and some values might stretch beyond a tab position while others don't. To improve on this situation in tabbed output with fixed-width formatting, you need to use padding, as explained in recipe 1.10.

Finally, another equivalent approach is to use the *ControlChars* enumeration, which includes *NewLine* and *Tab* constants.

```
Dim MyText As String
MyText = "Description:" & ControlChars.Tab & "This is the first line."
MyText &= ControlChars.NewLine
MyText &= "Description:" & ControlChars.Tab
MyText &= "This is the second line."
```

Some other languages, such as C#, include fixed string literals that can be used to represent special characters such as a tab. Visual Basic .NET doesn't use this convention.

1.13 Insert a Special Character in a String

Problem

You need to use an extended character that can't be entered using the keyboard.

Solution

Determine the character code for the special character (possibly using the Character Map utility [charmap.exe]), and convert the number into the special character using the *ToChar* shared method of the *System.Convert* class.

Discussion

To insert a special character, you must first determine its Unicode character number. One useful tool that helps is Character Map, which is included with all versions of Windows. Using Character Map, you can select a font, browse to a specific character in its character set, and determine the character code. Figure 1-1 shows an example with the copyright symbol selected.

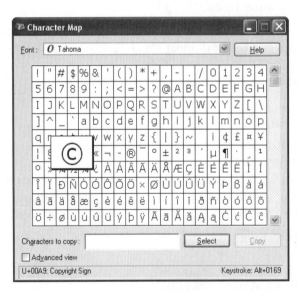

Figure 1-1   Using Character Map to view character codes.

The number at the bottom left (00A9) is the hexadecimal code using the Unicode standard. The number at the bottom right (0169) is the equivalent decimal code.

You can now use this character in any type of application. Windows applications fully support Unicode characters, and all Windows fonts (which means you can use special characters from fonts such as Symbol, Wingdings, and Webdings, if they are installed). Console applications might not display special characters, depending on the display font you have configured.

Here's an example that displays a special character in a label by converting the character's Unicode decimal value to a *Char*.

```
Dim CharCode As Integer = 169
Dim SpecialChar As Char = Convert.ToChar(CharCode)
Label1.Text = SpecialChar.ToString()
```

The result is the copyright symbol shown in Figure 1-2.

Figure 1-2   Displaying a special character.

> **Note**   You must use the *System.Convert* class. You can't convert a number to a *Char* directly using the *CType* function.

If you want to use a hexadecimal Unicode value, you must add the characters *&H* before the value to indicate that it is hexadecimal. Here's an example that uses the hexadecimal value for the copyright symbol:

```
Dim SpecialChar As Char = Convert.ToChar(&HA3)
```

1.14 Manipulate Strings Quickly with *StringBuilder*

Problem

You need to perform a repeated string manipulation, and you want to optimize performance.

Solution

Use the *System.Text.StringBuilder* class to perform your string operations, and convert the final result into a string by calling *ToString*.

Discussion

Ordinary .NET strings are immutable. Changing just a single character causes the whole string to be thrown away and a new string to be created.

The *StringBuilder* class represents a buffer of characters that can be directly modified. These direct modifications are faster than repeatedly generating a new *String* object. However, using the *StringBuilder* might introduce a small overhead because you need to copy the string into the *StringBuilder* before performing any work, and copy it out when you are finished. In general, if you need to perform more than two string manipulation tasks in a row, the *StringBuilder* approach will be faster.

To start using a *StringBuilder*, you must first create an instance and supply the string you want to use:

```
' Copy MyString into a StringBuilder named Builder.
Dim Builder As New System.Text.StringBuilder(MyString)
```

You can then use various *StringBuilder* methods to modify the buffer, including:

■ *Append*, which adds a string to the end of the buffer. You *cannot* use the *&* operator to add a string to a *StringBuilder* buffer.

■ *Insert*, which works like the *String.Insert* method described in recipe 1.1.

■ *Remove*, which works like the *String.Remove* method described in recipe 1.1.

■ *Replace*, which works like the *String.Replace* method described in recipe 1.9.

Unlike the *String* object, you can also modify an individual *Char* through the *Chars* property, as shown here:

```
' Replace every even character with a dash.
Dim i As Integer
For i = 0 To Builder.Length
    If (i + 1) Mod 2 = 0 Then
        Builder.Chars(i) = "-"c
    End If
Next
```

When you have finished all your manipulation, call *ToString* to retrieve the string representation.

```
MyString = Builder.ToString()
```

It's important to understand that the *StringBuilder* initially reserves a certain amount of size for the buffer. If you supply a string of less than 16 characters, the *StringBuilder* initially reserves 16 characters in the buffer. If the string is larger than 16 characters, *StringBuilder* tries to double the capacity (in this case, to 32). If that's still too small, it tries the next highest capacity—64, 128, and so on. If your modifications cause the string in the buffer to grow beyond its allocated capacity, the buffer will be automatically relocated in memory and the data will be copied. This operation is completely transparent, but it hurts performance. Thus, you should always ensure that you use a maximum capacity that has room for the finished string so that no copy operations will be required.

You can also specify the number of characters to allocate for the buffer in the *StringBuilder* constructor. In this case, if the string content in the *StringBuilder* exceeds this buffer, the buffer will be doubled. In other words, if you exceed a 50-character buffer, a new 100-character buffer will be created.

```
' Reserve 50 spaces in the buffer.
Dim Builder As New System.Text.StringBuilder(MyString, 50)
```

Here's a sample *StringBuilder* interaction from start to finish:

```
Dim MyString As String = "The"
Dim Builder As New System.Text.StringBuilder(MyString, 44)

' Modify the buffer.
Builder.Append(" quick brown fox")
Builder.Append(" jumps over")
Builder.Append(" the lazy dog.")

MyString = Builder.ToString()
```

1.15 Convert a String into a Byte Array

Problem

You need to convert a string into a series of bytes, possibly before writing it to a stream or applying encryption.

Solution

Call the *GetBytes* method on one of the encoding objects from the *System.Text* namespace.

Discussion

There is more than one way to represent a string in binary form, depending on the *encoding* you use. The most common encodings include:

■ **ASCII** Encodes each character in a string using 7 bits. ASCII encoded data can't contain extended Unicode characters. When using ASCII encoding in .NET, the bits will be padded and the resulting byte array will have one byte for each character.

■ **Full Unicode (or UTF-16)** Represents each character in a string using 16 bits. The resulting byte array will have two bytes for each character.

■ **UTF-7 Unicode** Uses 7 bits for ordinary ASCII characters and multiple 7-bit pairs for extended characters. This encoding is primarily for use with 7-bit protocols like mail, and it isn't regularly used.

■ **UTF-8 Unicode** Uses 8 bits for ordinary ASCII characters and multiple 8-bit pairs for extended characters. The resulting byte array will have one byte for each character (provided there are no extended characters).

.NET provides a class for each type of encoding in the *System.Text* namespace. To encode a string into a byte array, you simply create the appropriate encoding object, and call the *GetBytes* method. Here's an example with UTF-8 encoding:

```
Dim MyString As String = "Sample text."

Dim Encoding As New System.Text.UTF8Encoding()
Dim Bytes() As Byte

Bytes = Encoding.GetBytes(MyString)
Console.WriteLine("Number of encoded bytes: " & Bytes.Length.ToString())
' The byte array will contain 12 bytes.
```

You can also access a pre-instantiated encoding object through the shared properties of the base *System.Text.Encoding* class, as shown here:

```
Dim Bytes() As Byte
Bytes = System.Text.Encoding.UTF8.GetBytes(MyString)
```

You can retrieve the original string from the byte array by using the *Get-String* method of the encoding class.

> **Note**   In .NET, UTF-8 is the preferred standard. Not only does it support the full range of Unicode characters, it uses an adaptive format that reduces the size of the binary data if you aren't using extended characters. When encoding ordinary ASCII characters, UTF-8 encoding is identical to ASCII encoding.

By default, higher-level .NET classes such as *StreamReader* and *Stream-Writer* use UTF-8 encoding when reading or writing from a stream. For example, consider the following code snippet, which encodes a string into a byte array and then writes it to a file.

```
' Encode the string manually.
Dim Encoding As New System.Text.UTF8Encoding()
Dim Bytes() As Byte = Encoding.GetBytes(MyString)

' The only way to write directly to a file stream is to use a byte array.
Dim fs As New System.IO.FileStream("test1.txt", IO.FileMode.Create)
fs.Write(Bytes, 0, Bytes.Length)
fs.Close()
```

The following code shows an identical approach that writes the same string data using the same encoding, except now it relies on the *StreamWriter* class.

```
' Encode the string using a StreamWriter.
Dim fs As New System.IO.FileStream("test2.txt", IO.FileMode.Create)
Dim w As New System.IO.StreamWriter(fs)

' You can write strings directly to a file stream using a StreamWriter.
w.Write(MyString)
w.Flush()
fs.Close()
```

Chapter 5 presents more recipes that work with files.

1.16 Get a String Representation of a Byte Array

Problem

You need to convert a byte array into a string representation.

Solution

If you are creating a string representation of arbitrary binary data, use *BitConverter.ToString* or *Convert.ToBase64String*. If you are restoring text stored in binary format, call the *GetString* method of the appropriate encoding object in the *System.Text* namespace.

Discussion

There are several solutions to this time-honored problem, depending on the task you need to accomplish. The quickest approach is to use the *System.BitConverter* class, which provides shared methods for converting basic data types into byte arrays and vice versa. In this case, you simply need to use the overloaded *ToString* method that accepts a byte array.

```
Dim Bytes() As Byte = {0, 120, 1, 111, 55, 255, 2}
Dim StringRepresentation As String

StringRepresentation = BitConverter.ToString(Bytes)
' StringRepresentation now contains "00-78-01-6F-37-FF-02"
```

In this case, the string contains each value of the byte array in hexadecimal format, separated by a dash. There is no automatic way to reverse the conversion and determine the original byte array using the string.

Another approach is to use Base64 encoding through the *ToBase64String* and *FromBase64String* methods of the *System.Convert* class. In Base64 encoding, each sequence of three bytes is converted to a sequence of four bytes. Each Base64 encoded character has one of the 64 possible values in the range {A-Z, a-z, 0-9, +, /, =}.

```
Dim Bytes() As Byte = {0, 120, 1, 111, 55, 255, 2}
Dim StringRepresentation As String

StringRepresentation = Convert.ToBase64String(Bytes)
' StringRepresentation is now "AHgBbzf/Ag=="

' Convert the string back to the original byte array.
Bytes = Convert.FromBase64String(StringRepresentation)
```

Both of these approaches are useful for creating arbitrary representations of binary data, which is sometimes necessary if binary data isn't allowed. For example, XML files usually use Base64 encoding to include binary data. Using one of the text encodings in recipe 1.15 wouldn't be appropriate, because you aren't dealing with text data. Furthermore, these encodings will use special extended characters that aren't displayable and can't be safely included in an XML file.

However, if you are working with a byte array that contains real text information, you'll need to use the correct encoding class to retrieve the original string. For example, if UTF-8 encoding was used to encode the string into binary, you need to use UTF-8 encoding to retrieve the original string:

```
Dim Bytes() As Byte = {72, 101, 108, 108, 111, 33}
Dim Encoding As New System.Text.UTF8Encoding()
Dim MyString As String

MyString = Encoding.GetString(Bytes)
' MyString is now "Hello!"
```

For more information about different character encodings, see recipe 1.15.

1.17 Use Common Regular Expressions

Problem

You need to create a regular expression to use with validation, text searching, or text replacement (see recipes 1.18 to 1.20).

Solution

Use the regular expression engine provided in .NET through the types in the *System.Text.RegularExpressions* namespace.

Discussion

Regular expressions are a platform-independent syntax for describing patterns in text. What makes regular expressions particularly useful are their rich set of wildcards. For example, you can use ordinary *String* methods to find a series of specific characters (such as the word "hello") in a string. Using a regular expression, however, you can find any word in a string that is five letters long and begins with an "h".

All regular expressions are made up of two kinds of characters: literals and metacharacters. *Literals* represent a specific defined character. *Metacharacters* are wildcards that can represent a range of values. For example, \s represents any whitespace character (such as a space or tab). \w represents any "word" (alphanumeric) character. \d represents any digit. Thus, the regular expression below represents four groups of digits, separated by dashes (as in 412-333-9026).

```
\d\d\d-\d\d\d-\d\d\d\d
```

You can simplify this expression using a multiplier. With a multiplier, you specify a fixed number of repetitions of character using curly braces. \d{3} means three repetitions of a digit, and \d{3,1} means one to three repetitions of the digit. You'll notice that the multiplier always works on the character that immediately precedes it. Here's how you can simplify the phone number expression shown above:

```
\d{3}-\d{3}-\d{4}
```

Other multipliers can represent a variable number of characters, like + (one or more matches) and * (zero or more matches). Like the curly braces, these metacharacters always apply to the character that immediately precedes them. For example 0+2 means "any number of 0 characters, followed by a single 2." The number 02 would match, as would 0000002. You can also use parentheses to group together a subexpression. For example, (01)+2 would find match any string that starts with one or more sequences of 01 and ends with 2. Matches includes 012, 01012, 0101012, and so on.

Finally, you can delimit your own range of characters using square brackets. [a-c] would match any single character from *a* to *c* (lowercase only). The expression shown below would match any word that starts with a letter from *a* to *c*, continues with one or more characters from *a* to *z*, and ends with *ing*. Possible matches to the expression below include acting and counting.

```
[a-c][a-z]+ing
```

Range expressions are quite flexible. You can combine multiple allowed ranges, as in [A-Za-z] or you can even specify all allowed values, in which case you won't use a dash, as in [ABCD]. Table 1-1 presents a comprehensive list of regular expression metacharacters.

> **Note**   Regular expressions also support using named groups as placeholders. This is primarily useful if you want to retrieve a piece of variable data in between two patterns. Two named group examples are shown in this chapter, one in recipe 1.19 and one in recipe 1.20.

Keeping in mind these rules, you can construct regular expressions for validating simple types of data. However, more complex strings might require daunting regular expressions that are difficult to code properly. In fact, there are entire books written about regular expression processing, including the excellent *Mastering Regular Expressions* (O'Reilly, 2002) by Jeffrey and Friedl. As a shortcut, instead of writing your own regular expressions you can consider using or modifying a prebuilt regular expression. Many sources are available on the Internet, including *http://regexlib.com*, which includes regular expression you might use for specific regional types of data (postal codes, and so on). In addition, Table 1-2 presents some common regular expression examples.

Table 1-1   Regular expression metacharacters

Character	Rule
{m}	Requires m repetitions of the preceding character. For example, 7{3} matches 777.
{m, n}	Requires m to n repetitions of the preceding character. For example, 7{2,3} matches 77 and 777 but not 7777.
*	Zero or more occurrences of the previous character or subexpression. For example, 7*8 matches 7778 or just 8.
+	One or more occurrences of the previous character or subexpression. For example, 7+8 matches 7778 or 78 but not just 8.
?	One or zero occurrences of the previous character or subexpression. For example, 7?8 matches 78 and 8 but not 778.
( )	Groups a subexpression that will be treated as a single element. For example, (78)+ matches 78 and 787878.
|	Either of two matches. For example 8|6 matches 8 or 6.
[ ]	Matches one character in a range of valid characters. For example, [A-C] matches A, B, or C.
[^]	Matches a character that isn't in the given range. For example, [^A-B] matches any character except A and B.
.	Any character except newline.
\s	Any whitespace character (such as a tab or space).
\S	Any non-whitespace character.
\d	Any digit character.
\D	Any non-digit character.
\w	Any "word" character (letter, number, or underscore).
\W	Any non-word character.
\	Use to search for a special character. For example, use \\ for the literal \ and use \+ for the literal +.
^	Represents the start of the string. For example, ^777 can only find a match if the string begins with 777.
$	Represents the end of the string. For example, 777$ can only find a match if the string ends with 777.

Table 1-2 Some useful regular expressions

Type of Data	Expression	Rules Imposed
Host name	`([\w\-]+\.)+` `([\w\-]{2,3})`	Must consist of only word characters (alphanumeric characters and the underscore), and must end with a period and an extension of two or three characters (such as www.contoso.com).
Internet URL	`((http)|(https)|` `(ftp)):\/\/([\-\w]+` `\.)+\w{2,3}(\/[%\-\w]` `+(\.\w{2,})?)*`	Similar to host name, but must begin with the prefix http:// or https:// or ftp:// and allows a full path portion (such as http://www.contoso.com /page.htm).
E-mail address	`([\w\-]+\.)*[\w\-]+` `@([\w\-]+\.)+([\w\-]` `{2,3})`	Must consist only of word characters, must include an at sign (@), and must end with a period and an extension of two or three characters (such as someone@somewhere.com).
IP address	`[1-2]?\d{1,2}\.[1-2]` `?\d{1,2}\.[1-2]?\d` `{1,2}\.[1-2]?\d{1,2}`	There are four sets of digits separated by periods. If any of these digit sets is three characters long, it must start with a 1 or 2 (such as 128.0.0.1).
Time (in 24-hour format)	`([0|1|2]{1}\d):` `([0|1|2|3|4|5]{1}\d)`	Must begin with a 0, 1, or 2 followed by a second digit and a colon. The minute portion must begin with a 1, 2, 3, 4, 5 (e.g. 14:34).
Date (mm/dd/yy)	`[012]?\d\/[0123]` `?\d\/[0]\d`	Month values can begin with a 0, 1, or 2 if they're two digits long. Day values can begin with a 0, 1, 2, or 3 if they're two digits long (such as 12/24/02).
Date (dd-MMM-yyyy)	`[0-3]\d-(JAN|FEB|` `MAR|APR|MAY|JUN|JUL|` `AUG|SEP|OCT|NOV|DEC)` `-\d{4}`	Matches dates that use one of the proscribed month short forms (such as 29-JAN-2002)
Phone number	`\d{3}-\d{3}-\d{4}`	Digits must be separated by hyphens (e.g., 416-777-9344). You can use a similar approach for Social Security numbers.
Specific length password	`\w{4,10}`	A password that must be at least four characters long, but no longer than ten characters (such as "hello").
Advanced password	`[a-zA-Z]\w{3,9}`	A password that will allow four to ten total characters, but must start with a letter.
Another advanced password	`[a-zA-Z]\w*\d+\w*`	A password that starts with a letter character, followed by zero or more word characters, a digit, and then zero or more word characters. In short, it forces a password to contain a number somewhere inside it (such as hell4o).

Keep in mind that different regular expressions impose different degrees of rules. For example, an e-mail regular expression might require an at sign and restrict all non-word characters. Another e-mail address expression might require an at sign and a period, restrict all non-word characters, and force the final extension to be exactly two or three characters long. Both expressions can be used to validate e-mail addresses, but the second one is more restrictive (and therefore preferable). In Table 1-2, several Internet-related regular expressions limit domain name extensions to three characters (as in .com or .org). They need to be tweaked if you want to support longer domain name extensions such as .info, which are being introduced gradually.

Similarly, some of the date expressions in Table 1-2 reject obvious invalid values (a date on the thirteenth month), but are unable to reject trickier nonexistent dates such as February 30th. To improve upon this situation, you might want to leverage additional .NET Framework classes or custom code.

> **Note**   Sometimes, you can avoid writing a complex regular expression by using validation provided by .NET Framework classes. For example, you can validate URLs and file paths using .NET classes (see recipes 1.21 and 1.22). You can also verify dates and times with the *DateTime* type (as described in recipe 2.16).

1.18 Validate Input with a Regular Expression

Problem

You want to validate a common user-submitted value contained in a string, such as an e-mail address, date, or user name.

Solution

Create the *System.Text.RegularExpressions.Regex* class with the appropriate regular expression, and call the *IsMatch* method with the value you want to test. Make sure to include the $ and ^ characters in your expression so that you match the entire string.

Discussion

Although creating a regular expression can be difficult, applying one is not. You simply need to create a *Regex* instance, supply the regular expression in the constructor, and then test for a match. The following code example verifies an e-mail address using a regular expression from Table 1-2. In order for it work, you must have imported the *System.Text.RegularExpressions* namespace.

```
Dim Expression _
    As New Regex("^([\w\-]+\.)*[\w\-]+@([\w\-]+\.)+([\w\-]{2,3})$")

' Test for a single match.
If Expression.IsMatch("me@somewhere.com")
    ' This succeeds.
End If

' Test for a single match.
If Expression.IsMatch("@somewhere.com")
    ' This fails.
End If
```

Notice that the regular expression in the previous code has two slight modifications from the version in Table 1-2. It starts with the ^ character (indicating the beginning of the string) and ends with the $ character (indicating the end of the string). Thus, there will only be a match if the full string matches the full regular expression. Without the addition of these two characters, a match could be found inside the string you supply (in other words, "my address is me@somewhere.com" would match because it contains a valid e-mail address).

> **Note**   ASP.NET includes a special Web control called the *Regular-ExpressionValidator* that can be used to validate text input. When using this control, you don't need to specify the ^ and $ positional metacharacters.

1.19 Find All Occurrences of a Pattern in a String

Problem

You want to find every time a certain pattern occurs in a string and retrieve the corresponding text.

Solution

Use the *Regex.Matches* method to retrieve a collection with all the matches in a string.

Discussion

The *System.Text.RegularExpressions* namespace defines two classes that are used with matches. The *Match* class represents a single match and contains information such as the position in the string where the match was found, the length, and the text of the match. The *MatchCollection* class is a collection of *Match* instances. You can retrieve a *MatchCollection* that contains all the matches for a specific regular expression by calling *Regex.Matches* and supplying the search text.

The following example puts these classes into practice with a phone number regular expression. It finds all the phone numbers in a given string and stores them in a *MatchCollection*. Then, the code iterates through the *MatchCollection*, displaying information about each match. In order for this code to work, you must have imported the *System.Text.RegularExpressions* namespace.

```
Dim Expression As New Regex("\d{3}-\d{3}-\d{4}")

Dim Text As String
Text = "Marcy (416-777-2222) phoned John at 010-999-2222 yesterday."

' Retrieve all matches.
Dim Matches As MatchCollection
Matches = Expression.Matches(Text)

Console.WriteLine("Found " & Matches.Count.ToString() & " matches.")

' Display all the matches.
Dim Match As Match
For Each Match In Matches
    Console.WriteLine("Found: " & Match.Value & " at " _
                    & Match.Index.ToString())
Next
```

The output for this example displays both phone numbers:

```
Found 2 matches.
Found: 416-777-2222 at 7
Found: 010-999-2222 at 36
```

Sometimes you want to extract a subset of data from a larger pattern. In this case, you can use a named group, which will act as a placeholder for the subset of data. You can then retrieve matches by group name. A named group takes this form:

```
(?<match>exp)
```

where `match` is the name you have assigned to the group, and `exp` specifies the type of characters that can match. For example, consider this regular expression, which creates a named group for the area code part of a telephone number:

```
(?<AreaCode>\d{3})-\d{3}-\d{4}
```

The example below shows how to use this regular expression to match all phone numbers, but only retrieve the area code:

```
Dim Expression As New Regex("(?<AreaCode>\d{3})-\d{3}-\d{4}")

Dim Text As String
Text = "Marcy (416-777-2222) phoned John at 010-999-2222 yesterday."

' Retrieve all matches.
Dim Matches As MatchCollection
Matches = Expression.Matches(Text)

' Display all the matches.
Dim Match As Match
For Each Match In Matches
    Console.WriteLine("Full match: " & Match.Value)
    Console.WriteLine("Area code:  " & Match.Groups("AreaCode").Value)
Next
```

The output is as follows:

```
Full match: 416-777-2222
Area code:  416
Full match: 010-999-2222
Area code:  010
```

1.20 Replace All Occurrences of a Pattern in a String

Problem

You want to find every time a certain pattern occurs in a string and alter the corresponding text.

Solution

Use the *Regex.Replace* method. You can supply either a string literal or a replacement expression for the new text.

Discussion

The *Regex.Replace* method has several overloads and allows a great deal of flexibility. The simplest technique is to simply replace values with a fixed string literal. For example, imagine you have a string that could contain a credit card number in a specific format. You could replace all occurrences of any credit card number, without needing to know the specific number itself, by using a regular expression.

Here's an example that obscures phone numbers:

```
Dim Expression As New Regex("\d{3}-\d{3}-\d{4}")

Dim Text As String
Text = "Marcy (555-777-2222) phoned John at 555-999-2222 yesterday."

' Replace all phone numbers with "XXX-XXX-XXXX"
Text = Expression.Replace(Text, "XXX-XXX-XXXX")
Console.WriteLine(Text)
```

This produces the following output:

```
Marcy (XXX-XXX-XXXX) phoned John at XXX-XXX-XXXX yesterday.
```

Notice that the *Replace* method doesn't change the string you supply. Instead, it returns a new string with the modified values.

You can also perform regular expression replacements that transform the text in a match using a replacement pattern. In this case, you need to use named groups as placeholders. A description of named groups is provided in recipe 1.19. As a basic example, the regular expression below matches a phone number and places the first three digits into a named group called *AreaCode*:

```
(?<AreaCode>\d{3})-\d{3}-\d{4}
```

The trick is that with the *Regex.Replace* method, you can use the named group in your replacement expression. In the replacement expression, the same group is entered using curly braces and the **$** operator, as in:

```
${AreaCode}
```

A full discussion of this topic is beyond the scope of this book, but the following example provides a quick demonstration. It replaces all dates in a block of text, changing mm/dd/yy formatting to dd-mm-yy form.

```
Dim Expression As New Regex( _
  "(?<month>\d{1,2})/(?<day>\d{1,2})/(?<year>\d{2,4})")

Dim Text As String
Text = "Today's date is 12/30/03 and yesterday's was 12/29/03."
```

```
Console.WriteLine("Before: " & Text)
Text = Expression.Replace(Text, "${day}-${month}-${year}")
Console.WriteLine("After:  " & Text)
```

The program generates this output:

```
Before: Today's date is 12/30/03 and yesterday's was 12/29/03.
After:  Today's date is 30-12-03 and yesterday's was 29-12-03.
```

1.21 Manipulate a Filename

Problem

You want to retrieve a portion of a path or verify that a file path is in a normal (standardized) form.

Solution

Process the path using the *System.IO.Path* class.

Discussion

File paths are often difficult to work with in code because there are an unlimited number of ways to represent the same directory. For example, you might use an absolute path (c:\temp), a UNC path (\\myserver\\myshare\temp), or one of many possible relative paths (c:\temp\myfiles\..\ or c:\temp\myfiles\..\..\temp). This is especially the case if you want the user to supply a file or path value. In this case, the user could specify a relative path that points to an operating system file. If your code doesn't detect the problem, sensitive information could be returned or damaged, because all of the .NET file I/O classes support relative paths.

The solution is to use the shared methods of the *Path* class to make sure you have the information you expect. For example, here's how you take a filename that might include a qualified path and extract just the filename:

```
Filename = System.IO.Path.GetFileName(Filename)
```

And here's how you might append the filename to a directory path using the *Path.Combine* method:

```
Dim Filename As String = "..\..\myfile.txt"
Dim Path As String = "c:\temp"

Filename = System.IO.Path.GetFileName(Filename)
Path = System.IO.Path.Combine(Path, Filename)
' Path is now "c:\temp\myfile.txt"
```

The advantage of this approach is that a trailing backslash (\) is automatically added to the path name if required. The *Path* class also provides the following useful methods for manipulating path information:

- *ChangeExtension* modifies the current extension of the file in a string. If no extension is specified, the current extension will be removed.

- *GetDirectoryName* returns all the directory information, which is the text between the first and last directory separators (\).

- *GetFileNameWithoutExtension* is similar to *GetFileName*, but it omits the extension.

- *GetFullPath* has no effect on an absolute path, and it changes a relative path into an absolute path using the current directory. For example, if c:\temp\ is the current directory, calling *GetFullPath* on a file name such as test.txt returns c:\temp\ test.txt.

- *GetPathRoot* retrieves a string with the root (for example, "c:\"), provided that information is in the string. For a relative path, it returns a null reference (*Nothing*).

- *HasExtension* returns *True* if the path ends with an extension.

- *IsPathRooted* returns *True* if the path is an absolute path, and *False* if it's a relative path.

> **Note**   In most cases, an exception will be thrown if you try to supply an invalid path to one of these methods (for example, paths that include spaces or other illegal characters).

1.22 Manipulate a URI

Problem

You want to retrieve a portion of a URI (such as the prefix, directory, page, or query string arguments).

Solution

Process the URI using the *System.Uri* class.

Discussion

As with file path information, URIs can be written in several different forms, and represent several types of information, including Web requests (http:// and https://), FTP requests (ftp://), files (file://), news (news://), e-mail (mailto://), and so on. The *Uri* class provides a generic way to represent and manipulate URIs. You create a *Uri* instance by supplying a string that contains an absolute URI.

```
Dim MyUri As New Uri("http://search.yahoo.com/bin/search?p=dog")
```

The *Uri* class converts the supplied string into a standard form by taking the following steps, if needed:

- Converting the URI scheme to lower case (for example, HTTP to http).

- Converts the host name to lower case.

- Removes default and empty port numbers.

The *Uri* class can only store absolute URIs. If you want to use a relative URI string, you must also supply the base URI in the constructor:

```
Dim BaseUri As New Uri("http://search.yahoo.com")
Dim MyUri As New Uri(BaseUri, "bin/search?p=dog")
```

You can then use the *Uri* properties to retrieve various separate pieces of information about the URI, such as the scheme, host name, and so on. In the case of HTTP request, a URI might also include a bookmark and query string arguments.

```
Dim MyUri As New Uri("http://search.yahoo.com/bin/search?p=dog")
Console.WriteLine("Scheme: " & MyUri.Scheme)
Console.WriteLine("Host:   " & MyUri.Host)
Console.WriteLine("Path:   " & MyUri.AbsolutePath)
Console.WriteLine("Query:  " & MyUri.Query)
Console.WriteLine("Type:   " & MyUri.HostNameType.ToString())
Console.WriteLine("Port:   " & MyUri.Port)
```

The output for this example is:

```
Scheme: http
Host:   search.yahoo.com
Path:   /bin/search
Query:  ?p=dog
Type:   Dns
Port:   80
```

Incidentally, you can retrieve the final portion of the path or Web page by using the *System.Uri* and *System.IO.Path* class in conjunction. This works because the *Path* class recognizes the slash (/) in addition to the backslash (\) as an alternate path separator.

```
Dim MyUri As New Uri("http://search.yahoo.com/bin/search?p=dog")
Dim Page As String
Page = System.IO.Path.GetFileName(MyUri.AbsolutePath)
' Page is now "search"
```

You can also call *ToString* to retrieve the full URI in string format, and use *CheckHostName* and *CheckSchemeName* to verify that the URI is well-formed (although this won't indicate whether the URI points to a valid resource).

1.23 Validate a Credit Card with Luhn's Algorithm

Problem

You want to verify that a supplied credit card number is valid.

Solution

Manually compute and verify the checksum using Luhn's algorithm, which all credit card numbers must satisfy.

Discussion

Luhn's algorithm is a formula that combines the digits of a credit card (doubling alternate digits) and verifies that the final sum is divisible by 10. If it is, the credit card number is valid and could be used for an account.

Here's a helper function that you can use to test Luhn's algorithm:

```
Private Function ValidateLuhn(ByVal value As String) As Boolean

    Dim CheckSum As Integer = 0
    Dim DoubleFlag As Boolean = (value.Length Mod 2 = 0)

    Dim Digit As Char
    Dim DigitValue As Integer
    For Each Digit In value
        DigitValue = Integer.Parse(Digit)
        If DoubleFlag Then
            DigitValue *= 2
            If DigitValue > 9 Then
                DigitValue -= 9
```

```
                End If
            End If
            CheckSum += DigitValue
            DoubleFlag = Not DoubleFlag
        Next

        Return (CheckSum Mod 10 = 0)

    End Function
```

You can test the function as follows:

```
If ValidateLuhn("5191701142626689") Then
    ' This is a valid credit card number.
End If
```

Be aware that this method assumes any dashes and special characters have been stripped out of the string. If you can't be certain that this step has been taken, you might want to add code to verify that each character is a digit by iterating through the characters in the string and calling the *Char.IsDigit* method on each character. Recipe 1.6 demonstrates this technique.

You can also use additional checks to determine the credit card issuer by examining the credit card number prefix. (See the article "Checking Credit Card Numbers" at *http://perl.about.com/library/weekly/aa073000b.htm.*) Determining that a credit card is valid doesn't determine that it's connected to an actual account. For this task, you need to run the number through a credit card server. However, Luhn's algorithm provides a quick way to identify and refuse invalid input.

1.24 Validate an ISBN

Problem

You want to verify that a supplied ISBN number is valid.

Solution

Manually compute and verify the check digit using Mod 11 arithmetic.

Discussion

Verifying an ISBN number is similar to validating a credit card. In this case, you multiply each digit by its position (except for the last number), add together the numbers, and verify that the remainder of the sum divided by 11 matches the final check digit.

Here's a helper function that you can use to test an ISBN:

```
Private Function ValidateISBN(ByVal value As String) As Boolean

    Dim CheckSum As Integer = 0

    Dim i As Integer
    For i = 0 To value.Length - 2
        CheckSum += Integer.Parse(value.Chars(i)) * (i + 1)
    Next

    Dim CheckDigit As Integer
    CheckDigit = Integer.Parse(value.Chars(value.Length - 1))

    Return (CheckSum Mod 11 = CheckDigit)

End Function
```

You can test the function as follows:

```
If ValidateISBN("1861007353") Then
    ' This is a valid ISBN.
End If
```

Remember that this method assumes all dashes have been stripped out of the string. If you can't be certain that this step has been taken, you might want to add code to remove or ignore the dash character.

1.25 Perform a SoundEx String Comparison

Problem

You want to compare two strings based on their sound.

Solution

Implement a text-matching algorithm such as SoundEx.

Discussion

The SoundEx algorithm is one of the best-known algorithms for "fuzzy" text matching. It's designed to convert a word into a code based on one possible phonetic representation. Similar sounding words map to the same codes, enabling you to identify which words sound the same.

There are several SoundEx variants, all of which provide slightly different implementations of the same core rules:

- **Simplified** The original SoundEx from late 1800s.

- **Miracode** The modified SoundEx from 1910.

- **KnuthEd2** The SoundEx algorithm from *The Art of Computer Programming, Volume 3: Sorting and Searching, Second Edition* (Addison-Wesley, 1998).

- **SQLServer** SQL Server's variant of SoundEx.

SoundEx codes are four characters long. They begin with the first letter of the word and have three numeric digits to indicate the following phonetic sounds. For example, the SoundEx code for the name Jackson is J250.

The following class encodes words using SoundEx.

```
Public Class SoundexComparison

    Public Shared Function GetSoundexCode(ByVal word As String) As String
        word = word.ToUpper()

        ' Keep the first character of the word.
        Dim SoundexCode As String = word.Substring(0, 1)

        Dim i As Integer
        For i = 1 To word.Length - 1

            ' Transform a single character.
            Dim Character As String = Transform(word.Substring(i, 1))

            ' Decide whether to append this character code,
            ' depending on the previous sound.
            Select Case word.Substring(i - 1, 1)
                Case "H", "W"
                    ' Ignore
                Case "A", "E", "I", "O", "U"
                    ' Characters separated by a vowel represent distinct
                    ' sounds, and should be encoded.
                    SoundexCode &= Character
                Case Else
                    If SoundexCode.Length = 1 Then
                        ' We only have the first character, which is never
                        ' encoded. However, we need to check whether it is
                        ' the same phonetically as the next character.
```

```
                If Transform(word.Substring(0, 1)) <> Character Then
                    SoundexCode &= Character
                End If
            Else
                ' Only add if it does not represent a duplicated
                ' sound.
                If Transform(word.Substring(i - 1, 1)) <> _
                  Character Then
                    SoundexCode &= Character
                End If
            End If
        End Select

    Next

    ' A SoundEx code must be exactly 4 characters long.
    ' Pad it with zeroes in case the code is too short.
    SoundexCode = SoundexCode.PadRight(4, "0"c)

    ' Truncate the code if it is too long.
    Return SoundexCode.Substring(0, 4)
End Function

Private Shared Function Transform(ByVal character As String) As String
    ' Map the character to a SoundEx code.
    Select Case character
        Case "B", "F", "P", "V"
            Return "1"
        Case "C", "G", "J", "K", "Q", "S", "X", "Z"
            Return "2"
        Case "D", "T"
            Return "3"
        Case "L"
            Return "4"
        Case "M", "N"
            Return "5"
        Case "R"
            Return "6"
        Case Else
            ' All other characters are ignored.
            Return String.Empty
    End Select
End Function

End Class
```

The following Console application creates a SoundEx code for two different strings and compares them.

```
Public Module SoundexTest

    Public Sub Main()
        Console.Write("Enter first word: ")
        Dim WordA As String = Console.ReadLine()
        Console.Write("Enter second word: ")
        Dim WordB As String = Console.ReadLine()

        Dim CodeA, CodeB As String
        CodeA = SoundexComparison.GetSoundexCode(WordA)
        CodeB = SoundexComparison.GetSoundexCode(WordB)

        Console.WriteLine(WordA & " = " & CodeA)
        Console.WriteLine(WordB & " = " & CodeB)

        If CodeA = CodeB Then
            Console.WriteLine("These words match a SoundEx comparison.")
        End If

        Console.ReadLine()
    End Sub

End Module
```

Here's a sample output:

```
Enter first word: police
Enter second word: poeleeze
police = P420
poeleeze = P420
These words match a SoundEx comparison.
```

A SoundEx comparison is only one way to compare strings based on sounds. It was originally developed to match surnames in census surveys, and it has several well-known limitations. More advanced algorithms will treat groups of characters or entire phonetic syllables as single units (allowing "tion" and "shun" to match, for example). For more information about SoundEx, you can refer to the U.S. NARA (National Archives and Records Administration) Web site at *http://www.archives.gov/research_room/genealogy/census/soundex.html*.

2

Numbers, Dates, and Other Data Types

Programming is, to a large extent, the science of dealing with data. In the previous chapter, you saw how to use .NET strings and regular expressions to manipulate text. In this chapter, we consider the rest of the core types in the Microsoft .NET Framework, including numbers, dates, and specialty types such as GUIDs and enumerations.

Some of the recipes in this chapter focus on fundamentals for dealing with data types. For example, you'll learn how to validate dates, format numeric values, access trigonometric functions, and convert binary and hexadecimal values. Other recipes present more advanced techniques that might require custom classes. Recipes 2.5, 2.6, 2.7 show you how to deal with complex numbers, vectors, and matrixes—all of which are types of data that have no core support in the .NET Framework. Fortunately, .NET makes it easy to write a custom class that encapsulates all the functionality you need.

> **Note**   This chapter includes lengthy examples that work with *Fraction*, *ComplexNumber*, and *Vector* classes. To simplify the code, these classes use public member variables for their constituent values rather than full property procedures. Of course, full property procedures represent the best style for object-oriented programming, and you'll find that the online examples for this chapter use them instead of public variables.

This chapter also presents recipes that demonstrate how to convert basic data types to binary and back, and how to pull off a few more enigmatic tricks, such as evaluating a mathematical expression contained in a string (recipe 2.9), determining the day of a week for a specific date (recipe 2.12), and converting the name of an enumeration into the corresponding enumerated value (recipe 2.20).

2.1 Perform Mathematical and Trigonometric Operations

Problem

You need to perform a mathematical operation such as taking the sine, logarithm, absolute value, and so on.

Solution

Use the *System.Math* class, which provides a collection of helper utilities for this task.

Discussion

Microsoft Visual Basic .NET provides operators for common tasks such as addition and subtraction (+, -), multiplication and division (*, /), exponentiation (^), integer division (\), and finding the remainder (*Mod*). For all other operations, you can use the methods exposed by the *Math* class. Here are three examples:

```
' Get a sin of an angle measured in radians.
x = Math.Sin(y)

' Round a number to two decimal places.
x = Math.Round(y, 2)

' Get the absolute value of a number.
x = Math.Abs(y)
```

Useful *Math* class members include:

■ Constants *PI* and *E* (the natural logarithmic base).

■ Trigonometric functions *Sin*, *Cos*, *Tan*, *Asin*, *Acos*, *Atan*, and hyperbolic *Sinh*, *Cosh*, and *Tanh*.

■ Logarithmic function *Log* and *Log10*.

■ Power functions *Exp* (returns e raised to a specified power), *Pow* (which raises a number to an indicated power), and *Sqrt*.

- Comparative functions *Max* and *Min*, which return the higher or lower of two numbers, respectively.

- Boundary functions *Floor* (returns the largest whole number less than or equal to the supplied number, effectively truncating it), and *Ceiling* (returns the smallest whole number greater than or equal to the specified number).

- Sign-related functions *Abs* (which removes the sign).

- *Round*, which rounds a number to a specified number of decimal places.

2.2 Convert a Number into a Formatted String

Problem

You want to convert a numeric type (*Decimal, Int32, Double,* and so on) into a formatted string.

Solution

Use the overloaded version of the *ToString* method that accepts a format string.

Discussion

There are two types of numeric format strings: standard and custom. *Standard format strings* use a preset format according to the current culture and are identified by a single letter. You use that letter, in conjunction with a number that indicates the precision, when converting a number to a string. Here are a few common examples:

```
Dim Number As Decimal = 12345.6D

' The format specifier for currency is "C"
Dim MoneyString As String = Number.ToString("C")
' MoneyString is now "12,345.60"

' The format specifier for scientific notation is "E"
' The code also specifies 2 decimal places.
Dim ScientificString As String = Number.ToString("E2")
' ScientificString is now "1.23E+004"

' The format specifier for ordinary numbers is "N"
Dim NormalString As String = Number.ToString("N")
' NormalString is now "12,345.60"
```

Table 2-1 presents a full list of standard numeric format specifiers.

Table 2-1   Standard Numeric Format Specifiers

String	Name	Description
C or c	Currency	The number is converted to a string that represents a currency amount (such as "$12,345.68").
D or d	Decimal	The number is padded with zeros on the left side according the precision. For example, D8 would format the number 12345 to "00012345". This is only supported for integer types.
E or e	Scientific (exponential)	The number is converted to a string in exponential form with one digit preceding the decimal point. The precision specifier indicates the desired number of digits after the decimal point (the default is six). For example, 12345.6789 will be formatted as "1.234568E+004" with the default precision.
F or f	Fixed-point	The number is converted to a string with a number of decimal places equal to the precision specifier (the default is two). Rounding is performed as needed. For example, the number 12345.6789 would format to "12345.68".
G or g	General	The number is converted to the most compact decimal form, using fixed or scientific notation. The precision specifier determines the number of significant digits in the resulting string. If the precision specifier is omitted, the number of significant digits is determined by the type of number being converted (5 for an *Int16*, 10 for an *Int32*, 19 for an *Int64*, 7 for a *Single*, 15 for a *Double*, and 29 for a *Decimal*).
N or n	Number	The number is converted to a string with comma separators between each group of three digits to the left of the decimal point. The precision specifier indicates the desired number of decimal places (the default is two). Rounding is performed as needed. For example, 12345.6789 formats to "12,345.68".
P or p	Percent	The number is converted to a string that represents a percent. The converted number is multiplied by 100, and a percent sign (%) is appended. For example, 0.126 formats to "12.60 %".
R or r	Round-trip	The round-trip format guarantees that a floating-point number can be converted to a string and back to the number (using the *Double.Parse* or *Single.Parse* method) without losing any information. This specifier uses the general format, with 15 spaces of precision for a *Double* and 7 spaces of precision for a *Single*. If this is insufficient, a full 17 digits of precision will be used for a *Double*, and 9 digits of precision for a *Single*.
X or x	Hexadecimal	The number is converted to a string of hexadecimal digits, so 123456789 formats to "75bcd15". The case of the format specifier indicates whether to use uppercase or lowercase characters for alphabetic digits. The precision specifier indicates the minimum number of digits desired in the resulting string, and the number will be padded with zeros accordingly. This is only supported for integer types.

You can also create your own *custom format strings* and pass them to the *ToString* method. This is rarely necessary, but you can consult the MSDN help for more information.

2.3 Generate a Random Number

Problem

You want to create a statistically random number quickly.

Solution

Create an instance of the *System.Random* class, and call the *Next* or *NextDouble* method.

Discussion

The *Random* class uses a pseudorandom number generator, which means that it uses an algorithm to generate numbers that are statistically random when viewed in sequence.

To use the *Random* class, you simply create an instance and call either *Next* or *NextDouble*. *NextDouble* returns a double-precision floating-point number greater than or equal to 0.0, and less than 1.0. *Next* generates an integer within the maximum and minimum range you specify.

```
Dim RandomGenerator As New Random()

' Retrieve a random fraction number from 0.0 to 1.0.
Dim RandomDouble As Double = RandomGenerator.NextDouble()

' Retrieve a random integer number from 1 to 6.
Dim RandomInt As Integer = RandomGenerator.Next(1, 7)

' Retrieve another random integer from 1 to 6.
RandomInt = RandomGenerator.Next(1, 7)
```

Notice that the maximum bound for the *Next* method is always one higher than the maximum integer in your range.

The *Random* class is ideal when you need to generate a quick random value for a game, simulation, or test. However, it's not suitable for use with cryptography, because an attacker can guess the "random" number you will generate by examining previous random values and determining how you are seeding the random generator. If you need cryptographically secure random numbers, you can use the *System.Security.Cryptography.RNGCryptoServiceProvider* class, which is described in Chapter 18 (see recipe 18.15). However, this class is much slower than *Random*, which will become noticeable if you need to generate thousands of random numbers rapidly.

> **Note** By default, the *Random* class is seeded using the current date and time when you create it. After that, it continues down a "list" of random values. However, if you create two instances of the *Random* class at exactly the same millisecond (which is quite possible on fast computers), they will be both positioned at the same location in the list, and they will generate the same sequence of "random" numbers! To avoid this problem, only use one *Random* number generator and retain it for the life of your application. Always avoid code that creates more than one *Random* object in close succession, like this:
>
> ```
> ' Because this loop executes so quickly, it's easy to create two
> ' Random objects with the same seed and end up with
> ' short sequences of identical numbers (like 8888333322).
> Dim i As Integer
> For i = 0 To 10
>     Dim RandomGenerator As New Random()
>     Console.WriteLine(RandomGenerator.Next(1, 7))
> Next
> ```

2.4 Work with Non–Base 10 Number Systems

Problem

You want to convert a base 10 number to a hexadecimal, octal, or binary number (or vice versa).

Solution

Use the overloaded *Convert.ToString* and *Convert.ToInt32* shared methods that accept a number indicating the base.

Discussion

Although you can't work directly with non–base 10 numbers in Visual Basic .NET, you can easily convert base 10 values into a string representation that uses a base 2 (binary), base 8 (octal), base 10, or base 16 (hexadecimal). To do so, you use the overloaded *Convert.ToString* method that accepts two parameters: the base 10 number and the base that should be used for the converted number (which must be 2, 8, 10, or 16).

```
Dim Number As Integer = 3023
Console.WriteLine("Binary: " & Convert.ToString(Number, 2))
Console.WriteLine("Octal: " & Convert.ToString(Number, 8))
Console.WriteLine("Hexadecimal: " & Convert.ToString(Number, 16))
```

The output for this code is:

```
Binary: 101111001111
Octal: 5717
Hexadecimal: bcf
```

You can also use the shared *Convert.ToInt32*, *Convert.ToInt16*, or *Convert.ToInt64* methods to convert a non–base 10 number from a string into an integer type:

```
Dim Binary As String = "01"
Dim Number As Integer = Convert.ToInt32(Binary, 2)

' Double the number.
Number *= 2

' Convert it back to binary.
Binary = Convert.ToString(Number, 2)
' Binary is now "10".
```

If you need to perform calculations with non–base 10 numbers, you have two choices. You could use the *ToInt32* number to convert your numbers to decimal, perform the calculation, and then use *ToString* to convert the number back into its native representation, as shown above. Alternatively, you could create a custom class that represents the number and provides dedicated methods such as *Add*, *Subtract*, *Multiply*, and so on, which perform native calculations. Recipes 2.5 and 2.6 show similar techniques with classes that represent complex numbers and vectors.

2.5 Work with Complex Numbers

Problem

You need to perform calculations with complex numbers (numbers that involve i, the square root of –1).

Solution

Create your own complex number class.

Discussion

The .NET Framework does not include any built-in support for complex number calculations. However, it's quite easy to create a class to represent complex numbers. This class will include methods such as *Add*, *Subtract*, *Multiply*, and *DivideBy*, and a few complex-number helper functions such as *GetModulus* and *GetConjugate*. In addition, the class will support cloning and comparing (useful for sorting arrays of complex numbers), and it will override the *Equals* method to perform value equality testing and *ToString* to provide an appropriate string representation. Chapter 4 provides recipes that allow you to implement these refinements in your own custom classes.

The full code for the *ComplexNumber* class is shown here:

```
Public Class ComplexNumber
    Implements ICloneable, IComparable

    ' The real and imaginary component.
    Public Real As Double
    Public Imaginary As Double

    ' Create a new complex number.
    Public Sub New(ByVal real As Double, ByVal imaginary As Double)
        Me.Real = real
        Me.Imaginary = imaginary
    End Sub

    ' Add a complex number to the current one.
    Public Function Add(ByVal complexNumber As ComplexNumber) As ComplexNumber
        Return New ComplexNumber(Me.Real + complexNumber.Real, _
                                 Me.Imaginary + complexNumber.Imaginary)
    End Function

    ' Add a real number to the current complex number.
    Public Function Add(ByVal real As Double) As ComplexNumber
        Return New ComplexNumber(Me.Real + real, Me.Imaginary)
    End Function

    ' Subtract a complex number from the current one.
    Public Function Subtract(ByVal complexNumber As ComplexNumber) _
      As ComplexNumber
        Return New ComplexNumber(Me.Real - complexNumber.Real, _
                                 Me.Imaginary - complexNumber.Imaginary)
    End Function
```

```
' Subtract a real number from the current complex number.
Public Function Subtract(ByVal real As Double) As ComplexNumber
    Return New ComplexNumber(Me.Real - real, Me.Imaginary)
End Function

' Multiply a complex number by the current one.
Public Function Multiply(ByVal complexNumber As ComplexNumber) _
  As ComplexNumber
    Dim x, y, u, v As Double
    x = Me.Real : y = Me.Imaginary
    u = complexNumber.Real : v = complexNumber.Imaginary
    Return New ComplexNumber(x * u - y * v, x * v + y * u)
End Function

' Multiply the current number by a real number.
Public Function Multiply(ByVal real As Double) As ComplexNumber
    Return New ComplexNumber(Me.Real * real, Me.Imaginary * real)
End Function

' Divide the current number by another complex number.
Public Function DivideBy(ByVal complexNumber As ComplexNumber) _
  As ComplexNumber
    Dim x, y, u, v As Double
    x = Me.Real : y = Me.Imaginary
    u = complexNumber.Real : v = complexNumber.Imaginary
    Dim Sum As Double = u * u + v * v
    Return New ComplexNumber((x * u + y * v) / Sum, (y * u - x * v) / Sum)
End Function

' Divide the current number by a real number.
Public Function DivideBy(ByVal real As Double) As ComplexNumber
    Return New ComplexNumber(Me.Real / real, Me.Imaginary / real)
End Function

' Test for value equality between the number and another complex number.
Public Overloads Overrides Function Equals(ByVal obj As Object) As Boolean
    If Not TypeOf obj Is ComplexNumber Then Return False

    Dim Compare As ComplexNumber = CType(obj, ComplexNumber)
    Return (Me.Real = Compare.Real And Me.Imaginary = Compare.Imaginary)
End Function

' Test for value equality between two complex numbers.
Public Overloads Shared Function Equals(ByVal objA As Object, _
  ByVal objB As Object) As Boolean
    If Not (TypeOf objA Is ComplexNumber) Or _
      Not (TypeOf objB Is ComplexNumber) Then Return False
```

```
        Dim ComplexA As ComplexNumber = CType(objA, ComplexNumber)
        Dim ComplexB As ComplexNumber = CType(objB, ComplexNumber)
        Return (ComplexA.Real = ComplexB.Real _
          And ComplexA.Imaginary = ComplexB.Imaginary)
    End Function


    ' Define some helper methods.
    Public Function GetModulus() As Double
        Return Math.Sqrt(Me.Real ^ 2 + Me.Imaginary ^ 2)
    End Function


    Public Function GetModulusSquared() As Double
        Return Me.Real ^ 2 + Me.Imaginary ^ 2
    End Function


    Public Function GetArgument() As Double
        Return Math.Atan2(Me.Imaginary, Me.Real)
    End Function


    Public Function GetConjugate() As ComplexNumber
        Return New ComplexNumber(Me.Real, -Me.Imaginary)
    End Function


    ' Return a string representation of a complex number
    Public Overrides Function ToString() As String
        Return Me.Real.ToString() & ", " & Me.Imaginary.ToString() & "i"
    End Function


    ' Copy a complex number.
    Public Function Clone() As Object Implements System.ICloneable.Clone
        Return New ComplexNumber(Me.Real, Me.Imaginary)
    End Function


    ' Compare two complex numbers (allows array sorting).
    Public Function CompareTo(ByVal obj As Object) As Integer _
      Implements System.IComparable.CompareTo
        If Not (TypeOf obj Is ComplexNumber) Then Return 0

        Dim Compare As ComplexNumber = CType(obj, ComplexNumber)
        Return Me.GetModulus().CompareTo(Compare.GetModulus())
    End Function

End Class
```

Notice that Visual Basic .NET does not support operator overloading, so you must use methods to perform operations on complex numbers (*Add*, *Subtract*, and so on) rather than predefined operators (such as + and -). This is only a minor inconvenience.

A simple complex number test is shown below.

```
Dim c1 As New ComplexNumber(3, 3)
Dim c2 As New ComplexNumber(1, -4)
Dim c3 As New ComplexNumber(3, 3)

If c1.Equals(c3)
    ' This will succeed, as c1 = c3.
    Console.WriteLine("Passed value equality test.")
End If

c1 = c1.Multiply(c2)
c1 = c1.Add(c3)

' This displays "18, -6i"
Console.WriteLine(c1.ToString())
```

2.6 Work with Vectors

Problem

You need to perform calculations with three-dimensional vectors.

Solution

Create your own simple vector class.

Discussion

The .NET Framework does not include any built-in support for vector calculations. However, it's quite easy to create a class to represent vectors. This class will include methods such as *Add*, *Subtract*, *Multiply*, and *DivideBy*, and well as a few vector-specific functions such as *GetCrossProduct* and *GetDotProduct*. In addition, the class will support cloning and comparing (useful for sorting arrays of vectors), and it will override the *Equals* method to perform value equality testing and *ToString* to provide an appropriate string representation. Chapter 4 provides recipes that allow you to implement these refinements in your own custom classes.

The full code for the *Vector* class is shown here:

```
Public Class Vector
    Implements ICloneable, IComparable

    ' The coordinates.
    Public x, y, z As Double
```

```vbnet
' Create a new vector.
Public Sub New(ByVal x As Double, ByVal y As Double, ByVal z As Double)
    Me.x = x
    Me.y = y
    Me.z = z
End Sub

' Add a vector to the current vector.
Public Function Add(ByVal vector As Vector) As Vector
    Return New Vector(Me.x + vector.x, Me.y + vector.y, Me.z + vector.z)
End Function

' Subtract a vector from the current vector.
Public Function Subtract(ByVal vector As Vector) As Vector
    Return New Vector(Me.x - vector.x, Me.y - vector.y, Me.z - vector.z)
End Function

' Multiply the current vector by a scalar.
Public Function Multiply(ByVal n As Double) As Vector
    Return New Vector(Me.x * n, Me.y * n, Me.z * n)
End Function

' Divide the current vector by a scalar.
Public Function DivideBy(ByVal n As Double) As Vector
    Return New Vector(Me.x / n, Me.y / n, Me.z / n)
End Function

' Define some helper methods.
Public Function GetCrossProduct(ByVal vector As Vector) As Vector
    Return New Vector(Me.y * vector.z - Me.z * vector.y, _
      -Me.x * vector.z + Me.z * vector.x, _
      Me.x * vector.y - Me.y * vector.x)
End Function

Public Function GetDotProduct(ByVal vector As Vector) As Double
    Return (Me.x * vector.x + Me.y * vector.y + Me.z * vector.z)
End Function

Public Function Length() As Double
    Return Math.Sqrt(Me.x * Me.x + Me.y * Me.y + Me.z * Me.z)
End Function

Public Function Normalize() As Vector
    Dim nLength As Double
    nLength = Length()
    If nLength = 0 Then Throw New DivideByZeroException()
    Return New Vector(Me.x / nLength, Me.y / nLength, Me.z / nLength)
End Function
```

```
' Test for value equality between the current vector and another.
Public Overloads Function Equals(ByVal obj As Object) As Boolean
    If Not (TypeOf obj Is Vector) Then Return False

    Dim Compare As Vector = CType(obj, Vector)
    Return (Me.x = Compare.x And Me.y = Compare.y And Me.z = Compare.z)
End Function

' Test for value equality between two vectors.
Public Overloads Shared Function Equals(ByVal objA As Object, _
  ByVal objB As Object) As Boolean
    If Not (TypeOf objA Is Vector) Or _
      Not (TypeOf objB Is Vector) Then Return False

    Dim VectorA As Vector = CType(objA, Vector)
    Dim VectorB As Vector = CType(objB, Vector)

    Return (VectorA.x = VectorB.x And VectorA.y = VectorB.y _
      And VectorA.z = VectorB.z)
End Function

Public Overrides Function ToString() As String
    Return "(" & Me.x.ToString() & ", " & _
      Me.y.ToString() & ", " & Me.z.ToString() & ")"
End Function

' Copy a vector.
Public Function Clone() As Object Implements System.ICloneable.Clone
    Return New Vector(Me.x, Me.y, Me.z)
End Function

' Compare two vectors (allows array sorting).
Public Function CompareTo(ByVal obj As Object) As Integer _
  Implements System.IComparable.CompareTo
    If Not (TypeOf obj Is Vector) Then Return 0

    Dim Compare As Vector = CType(obj, Vector)
    Return Me.Length().CompareTo(Compare.Length())
End Function

End Class
```

Remember that Visual Basic .NET does not support operator overloading, so you must use methods to perform operations on vectors (*Add*, *Subtract*, and so on) rather than predefined operators (such as + and -). This is only a minor inconvenience.

The following code shows a simple vector test:

```
Dim v1 As New Vector(10, 2, -3)
Dim v2 As New Vector(1, -2, -4)
Dim v3 As New Vector(10, 2, -3)

If v1.Equals(v3) Then
    ' This will succeed, as c1 = c3.
    Console.WriteLine("Passed value equality test.")
End If

v1 = v1.GetCrossProduct(v2)

' This displays "(-14, 37, -22)"
Console.WriteLine(v1.ToString())
```

2.7 Work with Matrixes

Problem

You want to use matrix calculations (matrix multiplications, additions, normalizations, and so on).

Solution

Download a free component, such as Lutz Roeder's Mapack.

Discussion

The .NET Framework does not include any built-in support for matrix manipulation, aside from a *Matrix* class in the *System.Drawing.Drawing2D* namespace, which is intended for graphical operations and only supports a 3-by-3 matrix. Writing your own matrix code from scratch would be quite a chore, but fortunately there are prebuilt matrix components available for free, like Mapack. (See *http://www.aisto.com/roeder* or the Web site for this book.) Mapack is a fully featured library for matrix manipulation, with complete C# source code. You can use it to inspire your own matrix classes, or you can use it as is in any application (in which case it is provided without any warranty or support).

Once you add a reference to the Mapack.dll library, you can create matrixes of any size, set their values individually, and call methods to perform tasks such as multiplying, transposing, and inverting. Here's an example:

```
' Create a 1x2 matrix and set values.
Dim MatrixA As New Mapack.Matrix(1, 2)
MatrixA(0, 0) = 5 : MatrixA(0, 1) = 2
```

```
' Create a 2x1 matrix and set values.
Dim MatrixB As New Mapack.Matrix(2, 1)
MatrixB(0, 0) = 5 : MatrixB(1, 0) = 2

' Multiply the matrixes and display the result.
Dim Result As Mapack.Matrix = _
  CType(MatrixA.Multiply(MatrixB), Mapack.Matrix)
Console.WriteLine(Result.ToString())
' Displays 29.
```

2.8 Work with Fractions Without Using Decimals

Problem

You want to perform mathematical operations with fractions without converting to decimal notation (and possibly introducing rounding errors).

Solution

Create your own simple fraction class.

Discussion

The .NET Framework does not include any built-in support for fraction calculations. However, it's quite easy to create a class to represent vectors. This class will include methods such as *Add*, *Subtract*, *Multiply*, and *DivideBy*. It will also include a *Normalize* function that will reduce a fraction to lowest terms using Euclid's algorithm and adjust its sign. In addition, the class will support cloning and comparing (useful for sorting arrays of fractions), and it will override the *Equals* method to perform value equality testing and *ToString* to provide an appropriate string representation. Chapter 4 provides recipes that allow you to implement these refinements in your own custom classes.

The full code for the *Fraction* class is shown here:

```
Public Class Fraction
    Implements ICloneable, IComparable

    ' The two components of any fraction.
    Public Denominator As Integer
    Public Numerator As Integer

    ' Create a new fraction.
    Public Sub New(ByVal numerator As Integer, ByVal denominator As Integer)
        Me.Numerator = numerator
        Me.Denominator = denominator
    End Sub
```

```vb
' Add fraction to current fraction.
Public Function Add(ByVal fraction As Fraction) As Fraction
    Return New Fraction(Me.Numerator * fraction.Denominator + _
        fraction.Numerator * Me.Denominator, _
        Me.Denominator * fraction.Denominator).Normalize()
End Function

' Subtract a fraction from current fraction.
Public Function Subtract(ByVal fraction As Fraction) As Fraction
    Return New Fraction(Me.Numerator * fraction.Denominator - _
        fraction.Numerator * Me.Denominator, _
        Me.Denominator * fraction.Denominator).Normalize()
End Function

' Multiply a fraction by the indicated fraction.
Public Function Multiply(ByVal fraction As Fraction) As Fraction
    Return New Fraction(Me.Numerator * fraction.Numerator, _
        Me.Denominator * fraction.Denominator).Normalize()
End Function

' Divide a fraction by the indicated fraction.
Public Function DivideBy(ByVal fraction As Fraction) As Fraction
    Return New Fraction(Me.Numerator * fraction.Denominator, _
        Me.Denominator * fraction.Numerator).Normalize()
End Function

' Reduces a fraction and adjusts its sign
Public Function Normalize() As Fraction
    Dim NormalizedFraction As Fraction = CType(Me.Clone(), Fraction)

    If (NormalizedFraction.Numerator <> 0) And _
      (NormalizedFraction.Denominator <> 0) Then
        ' Fix signs
        If NormalizedFraction.Denominator < 0 Then
            NormalizedFraction.Denominator *= -1
            NormalizedFraction.Numerator *= -1
        End If

        Dim divisor As Integer = GCD(NormalizedFraction.Numerator, _
          NormalizedFraction.Denominator)

        NormalizedFraction.Numerator \= divisor
        NormalizedFraction.Denominator \= divisor
    End If

    Return NormalizedFraction
End Function
```

```vb
' Returns the greatest common divisor using Euclid's algorithm
Private Function GCD(ByVal x As Integer, ByVal y As Integer) As Integer
    Dim temp As Integer

    x = Math.Abs(x)
    y = Math.Abs(y)

    Do While (y <> 0)
        temp = x Mod y
        x = y
        y = temp
    Loop

    Return x
End Function

' Convert the fraction to decimal notation.
Public Function GetDouble() As Double
    Dim Reduced As Fraction = CType(Me.Clone(), Fraction).Normalize()
    Return CType(Reduced.Numerator, Double) / _
      CType(Reduced.Denominator, Double)
End Function

' Test for value equality between the current fraction and another.
Public Overloads Function Equals(ByVal obj As Object) As Boolean
    If Not (TypeOf obj Is Fraction) Then Return False

    Dim Compare As Fraction = CType(obj, Fraction)
    Return (Me.GetDouble() = Compare.GetDouble())
End Function

' Test for value equality between two fractions.
Public Overloads Shared Function Equals(ByVal objA As Object, _
  ByVal objB As Object) As Boolean
    If Not (TypeOf objA Is Fraction) Or _
      Not (TypeOf objB Is Fraction) Then Return False

    Dim FractionA As Fraction = CType(objA, Fraction)
    Dim FractionB As Fraction = CType(objB, Fraction)

    Return (FractionA.GetDouble() = FractionB.GetDouble())
End Function

' Get a string representation of the fraction.
Public Overrides Function ToString() As String
    Return Me.Numerator.ToString & "/" & Me.Denominator.ToString
End Function
```

```
' Copy a fraction.
Public Function Clone() As Object Implements System.ICloneable.Clone
    Return New Fraction(Me.Numerator, Me.Denominator)
End Function

' Compare two fractions (allows array sorting).
Public Function CompareTo(ByVal obj As Object) As Integer _
  Implements System.IComparable.CompareTo
    If Not (TypeOf obj Is Fraction) Then Return 0

    Dim Compare As Fraction = CType(obj, Fraction)
    Return Me.GetDouble().CompareTo(Compare.GetDouble())
End Function

End Class
```

Currently, the methods such as *Add*, *Multiply*, and so on only support other fractions. If you want to be able to multiply using an integer data type without converting it to a fraction, you could add overloads of these methods. Because Visual Basic .NET does not support operator overloading, you must use the methods (*Add*, *Subtract*, and so on) rather than the predefined operators (such as + and -).

A simple fraction test is shown here:

```
Dim f1 As New Fraction(2, 3)
Dim f2 As New Fraction(1, 2)
Dim f3 As New Fraction(2, 3)

If f1.Equals(f3) Then
    ' This will succeed, as f1 = f3.
    Console.WriteLine("Passed value equality test.")
End If

f1 = f1.Add(f2)      'Fraction is now 7/6
f1 = f1.DivideBy(f2) 'Fraction is now 7/3

' This displays "7/3"
Console.WriteLine(f1.ToString())
```

2.9 Evaluate a String Expression

Problem

You want to evaluate a mathematical expression that is specified as a string (as in "2 + 3").

Solution

Create a component that wraps the expression evaluator provided with Microsoft JScript, and consume this component from any application that needs this functionality. Or, use the Microsoft Script Control COM component.

Discussion

The JScript .NET engine provides an expression evaluator that can evaluate a mathematical expression or any JScript code (including functions) in a string. Multiple lines can be separated with line-break characters. However, you can't access this functionality directly from another language. Instead, you need to make a simple JScript wrapper to expose this functionality:

```
package JScriptUtil
{
    class ExpressionEvaluator
    {
        public function Evaluate(expr : String) : String
        {
            return eval(expr);
        }
    }
}
```

Save this in a .js text file, and compile it using the JScript compiler (jsc.exe) using the following command line:

```
jsc.exe /t:library JScriptUtil.js
```

Finally, add a reference to the compiled assembly to your Visual Basic .NET application, and a reference to the *Microsoft.JScript* assembly. You can then create instances of your custom *ExpressionEvaluator* class and call the *Evaluate* method with a string. You might need to refer to the MSDN reference to determine what operators are used in the JScript language, although the standard mathematical ones are obvious.

The following example shows a Console application that puts the JScript expression evaluator to work with a mathematical calculation:

```
Imports JScriptUtil

Public Module ExpressionTest

    Public Sub Main()
        Dim Expression As String = "2 * (5 + 1) / 3"
```

```
        Dim Eval As New JScriptUtil.ExpressionEvaluator()
        Dim Result As String = Eval.Evaluate(expression)

        Console.WriteLine(Expression & " = " & Result)
        ' Displays "2 * (5 + 1) / 3 = 4"

        Console.ReadLine()
    End Sub

End Module
```

Although extremely powerful, the dynamic expression evaluation provided by JScript .NET is unsuitable for some situations. Because it has the ability to execute any JScript code in the context of the caller, it could create a security risk for applications. For that reason, you might want to consider creating a custom expression evaluator written in C# or Visual Basic .NET code. One example, written using regular expressions, is provided in *Programming Microsoft Visual Basic .NET (Core Reference),* by Francesco Balena, and is included with the samples for this chapter. It can be used as a starting point to developing your own expression evaluator.

Note   There is yet another option—use the Microsoft Script Control. You can add a reference to this COM component from any .NET application (which creates a new reference named *Interop.MSScriptControl*), and use code like this:

```
Dim sc As New MSScriptControl.ScriptControl()

' Specify the language.
sc.Language = "VBScript"

Dim Result As String = CType(sc.Eval("2 * (5 + 1) / 3"), String)
```

However, you will need to ensure that this component is installed on registered on any computer that will run your application. This limitation won't apply with the JScript expression evaluator, because it is a core part of the .NET Framework.

2.10 Get the System Date and Time

Problem

You need to retrieve the current date and time.

Solution

Use the *DateTime.Now* shared property.

Discussion

DateTime.Now retrieves the current date and time as a *DateTime* structure. You can then retrieve specific date information from its properties, such as *Month*, *Day*, *Date*, *Hour*, *Millisecond*, and even *DayOfWeek*.

```
Dim Now As DateTime = DateTime.Now

Console.WriteLine("The current date is: " & Now.ToString())
Console.WriteLine("It's a " & Now.DayOfWeek.ToString())
```

The output for this code is as follows:

```
The current date is: 2002-10-31 5:24:14 PM
It's a Thursday
```

If you want to retrieve only the date portion of the current day, you can use the *DateTime.Today* shared method. The time portion will be set to 12:00 AM (00:00:00).

2.11 Add and Subtract Dates and Times

Problem

You need to perform calculations with dates and times.

Solution

Use the *TimeSpan* and *DateTime* structures, both of which provide *Add* and *Subtract* methods.

Discussion

The .NET Framework provides two structures for manipulating date and time information. The *DateTime* structure stores a reference to a single date and time (such as January 20, 2004 at 12:00 AM). The *TimeSpan* structure stores an interval of time (such as three hours). *TimeSpan* is ultimately measured in ticks (a unit of time equal to 100 nanoseconds), and *DateTime* is stored as the number of ticks since 12:00:00 midnight, January 1, 0001 C.E. The greater a *DateTime* is, the later the date. The greater a *TimeSpan* is, the larger the interval of time.

There are several ways to use *DateTime* and *TimeSpan* to perform calculations. All of the following are valid options:

■ Use the *DateTime.Add* or *DateTime.Subtract* method with a *TimeSpan* value (which returns a new *DateTime*).

■ Use *DateTime.Subtract* with a *DateTime* value (which returns a *TimeSpan* representing the difference).

■ Combine two *TimeSpan* values using the *TimeSpan.Add* or *TimeSpan.Subtract* method (both of which return a new *TimeSpan*).

■ Use a higher-level *DateTime* method such as *AddDays*, *AddHours*, *AddMinutes*, and so on. These methods return a new *DateTime* and can accept negative numbers.

For example, here is how you might check the current time against a fixed expiration date:

```
If DateTime.Now > (ExpirationDate.AddDays(30))
    ' More than thirty days have elapsed since expiration date.
End If
```

Here's how you can benchmark code:

```
Dim InitialTime As Date = DateTime.Now
' (Insert the code to benchmark here, or make the appropriate function calls.)

Dim ElapsedTime As TimeSpan = DateTime.Now.Subtract(InitialTime)
Console.WriteLine("Total time: " & ElapsedTime.TotalSeconds.ToString())
```

Here's one way you could delay code in a loop for a specified interval of time (although using *Thread.Sleep* is a more efficient approach).

```
Dim InitialTime As DateTime = DateTime.Now
Dim WaitSpan As TimeSpan = TimeSpan.FromSeconds(10)
Dim LoopTime As TimeSpan
```

```
' Wait for 10 seconds.
Do
    LoopTime = DateTime.Now.Subtract(InitialTime)
Loop Until TimeSpan.Compare(LoopTime, WaitSpan) = 1
```

Note that you can't use the comparison operators (< and >) with dates. However, you can retrieve a number that represents the *TimeSpan* interval, using properties such as *TotalHours*, *TotalMinutes*, *TotalMilliseconds*, or *Ticks*. The code below rewrites the time delay loop with a more readable equivalent using the *TimeSpan.Ticks* property.

```
' Wait for 10 seconds.
Do
    LoopTime = DateTime.Now.Subtract(InitialTime)
Loop Until LoopTime.Ticks > WaitSpan.Ticks
```

2.12 Determine Days of the Week, Leap Years, and More

Problem

You want to determine date information, such as what day of the week a given date falls on, whether a year is a leap year, and how many days are in a month.

Solution

Use a *Calendar*-derived class from the *System.Globalization* namespace, such as *GregorianCalendar*, or use the properties of a *DateTime* object.

Discussion

The *System.Globalization* namespace includes classes that contain culture-related calendar information. These classes derive from the base class *Calendar* and include *GregorianCalendar* (the Western standard), *HebrewCalendar*, *JulianCalendar*, *JapaneseCalendar*, and so on.

The *Calendar* classes define a number of basic methods, including:

■ *GetDaysInMonth* returns the number of days in a given month.

■ *GetDaysInYear* returns the number of days in a given year.

■ *IsLeapYear* returns *True* if the specified year is a leap year.

■ Methods that require you to supply a *DateTime* instance, such as *GetDayOfWeek*, *GetDayOfYear*, and so on. This functionality is also available through *DateTime* properties.

```
Dim Calendar As New System.Globalization.GregorianCalendar()

Console.WriteLine("Days in December 2000: " & _
  Calendar.GetDaysInMonth(2000, 12, _
  Calendar.CurrentEra).ToString())
Console.WriteLine("Is 2004 a leap year? " & _
  Calendar.IsLeapYear(2004))
Console.WriteLine("Days in 2004: " & _
  Calendar.GetDaysInYear(2004))
Console.WriteLine("Today is a " & _
  Calendar.GetDayOfWeek(DateTime.Now).ToString())
```

The output is as follows:

```
Days in December 2000: 31
Is 2004 a leap year? True
Days in 2004: 366
Today is a Friday
```

2.13 Get Day and Month Names in Other Languages

Problem

You want to retrieve the name of a day or month in another language.

Solution

Create a *CultureInfo* object for the appropriate culture, and use the *GetDayName* or *GetMonthName* methods.

Discussion

The *System.Globalization* namespace defines a *DateTimeFormatInfo* type that contains culture-specific date information. You can retrieve the *DateTimeFormatInfo* object for a culture from the *CultureInfo.DateTimeFormat* property. However, you need to create the *CultureInfo* object yourself, using a valid culture name, such as "en-US". (The full list of culture names is provided in the MSDN reference.)

```
' Create a CultureInfo object representing French - France.
Dim Culture As New System.Globalization.CultureInfo("fr-FR")
```

```
' Get the corresponding DateTimeFormatInfo object.
Dim FormatInfo As System.Globalization.DateTimeFormatInfo
FormatInfo = Culture.DateTimeFormat

Console.WriteLine(FormatInfo.GetDayName(DayOfWeek.Monday))
' Displays "lundi"

Console.WriteLine(FormatInfo.GetMonthName(1))
' Displays "janvier"
```

2.14 Format a Date

Problem

You want to convert a date or time into a formatted string.

Solution

Create a *DateTime* instance to represent the date, and then use the overloaded *ToString* method that accepts a format specifier.

Discussion

There are two types of date format strings: standard and custom. *Standard format strings* use a preset format according to the current culture and are identified by a single letter. They might retrieve part of the *DateTime* information (just a time, or just a date), and they might format it in a different order or using a different short form. Here are a few common examples:

```
Dim Now As DateTime = DateTime.Now

' Get just the long time, using the specifier "T"
Dim LongTime As String = Now.ToString("T")
' LongTime is now "3:51:24 PM"

' Get just the short date, using the specifier "d"
Dim ShortDate As String = Now.ToString("d")
' ShortDate is now "4/10/2003"

' Get just the long date, using the specifier "D"
Dim LongDate As String = Now.ToString("D")
' LongDate is now "Tuesday, April 10, 2003"
```

Table 2-2 lists the standard date format specifiers and their results (assuming the computer is running under the en-US culture).

Table 2-2 Standard Date Format Specifiers

String	Name	Description
d	Short date pattern	4/10/2003
D	Long date pattern	Tuesday, April 10, 2003
t	Short time pattern	3:51 PM
T	Long time pattern	3:51:24 PM
f	Full date/time pattern (short time)	Tuesday, April 10, 2003 3:51 PM
F	Full date/time pattern (long time)	Tuesday, April 10, 2003 3:51:24 PM
g	General date/time pattern (short time)	4/10/2003 3:51 PM
G	General date/time pattern (long time)	4/10/2003 3:51:24 PM
M or m	Month day pattern	April 10
R or r	RFC1123 pattern	Tue, 10 Apr 2003 15:51:24 GMT
s	Sortable date/time pattern; conforms to ISO 8601	2003-04-10T15:51:24
u	Universal sortable date/time pattern	2003-04-10 15:51:24Z
U	Full date/time pattern (long time). This is the same as F, except that it uses universal (GMT) time.	Tuesday, April 10, 2003 3:51:24 PM
Y or y	Year month pattern	April, 2003

If you need to precisely control the format of a date, you must use a *custom format string*. The custom format string is made up of characters that represent the position for various date and time characters, along with any literal values you need. Table 2-3 shows the full list of custom date format specifiers. Notice that where you have the choice of a single or double character ("d" or "dd"), the only difference is how the number will be padded if it's one digit. For example, "d" represents the date number. A date on the ninth day of a month will be converted to "9" with the "d" specifier, or "09" with the "dd" specifier.

```
Dim Now As DateTime = DateTime.Now

' Get a custom formatted string.
Dim Custom As String = Now.ToString("hh:mm, G\MT zzz")
' Custom is now "05:13 GMT -09:00"

Custom = Now.ToString("dddd MMMM yy gg")
' Custom is now "Thursday April 03 A.D."
```

Table 2-3   Custom Date Format Specifiers

Character	Description
d or dd	Displays the current day of the month as a number between 1 and 31.
ddd	Displays the abbreviated name of the day.
dddd	Displays the full name of the day.
f, ff, fff, ffff, fffff, ffffff, or fffffff	Displays seconds fractions represented in 1, 2, 3, 4, 5, 6, or 7 digits, respectively.
g or gg	Displays the era (A.D., for example)
h or hh	Displays the hour in the range 1–12.
H or HH	Displays the hour in the range 0–23.
m or mm	Displays the minute in the range 0–59.
M or MM	Displays the current month as a number between 1 and 12.
MMM	Displays the abbreviated name of the month.
MMMM	Displays the full name of the month.
s or ss	Displays the seconds in the range 0–59.
t	Displays the first character of the AM/PM designator.
tt	Displays the AM/PM designator.
y or yy	Displays the year as a maximum two-digit number. The first two digits of the year are omitted.
yyyy	Displays the four-digit year. If the year is less than four digits in length, preceding zeros are appended as necessary to make the displayed year four digits long.
z or zz	Displays the time zone offset for the system's current time zone relative to Greenwich mean time, in whole hours only.
zzz	Displays the time zone offset for the system's current time zone relative to Greenwich mean time, in hours and minutes.
:	Time separator.
/	Date separator.
'	Displays the literal value of any string between two single quotation marks ('). This is only required for special characters, such as the slash (/); other literals can be inserted directly.

2.15 Generate a Culture-Invariant Date String

Problem

You want to convert a date or time into a formatted string that has the same representation, regardless of the globalization settings of the current computer.

Solution

Use the overloaded *DateTime.ToString* method that accepts an *IFormatProvider* instance, and supply the *DateTimeFormatInfo.InvariantInfo* object.

Discussion

In some cases, you want dates to be formatted identically regardless of the settings on the computer running the code. This might be the case if the string value of the date is being inserted into a legacy database. Using a custom format string will offer some protection (if you are careful to only use numeric date information), but to be completely reassured you should specify the culture settings when you create the string.

In order to do this, you must use an overloaded version of the *DateTime.ToString* method that accepts an *IFormatProvider* instance. Rather than construct your own *IFormatProvider*, you can retrieve one that is guaranteed to be invariant over all computers from the *System.Globalization.DateTimeFormatInfo* object. You should still specify a format provider to indicate the format you want, as described in recipe 2.14.

```
Dim Now As DateTime = DateTime.Now

Dim DateString As String
DateString = Now.ToString("G", _
   System.Globalization.DateTimeFormatInfo.InvariantInfo)
' This string will always be in the form "10/31/2002 18:17:14",
' on any computer.
```

You'll notice that the defaults applied by the invariant *IFormatProvider* match the default U.S. culture settings, as described in Table 2-2.

2.16 Validate a User-Supplied Date

Problem

You want to convert a user-supplied string containing date information into a *DateTime* instance without introducing the possibility for error.

Solution

Use the *DateTime.ParseExact* method with a custom format string.

Discussion

The *DateTime* structure includes a *Parse* method that creates a *DateTime* instance from a string. However, this method is aggressive and prone to error. It tries everything possible to avoid throwing a *FormatException*, even ignoring unrecognized characters or filling in assumed dates. If this isn't acceptable in your application, you can use the *ParseExact* method, which allows you to define the format you expect for the string. If the format does not match exactly, or there is any discrepancy in the string, an exception is thrown.

ParseExact requires three parameters: the string with the date, a standard or custom format specifier describing the format of the string (see recipe 2.13), and a *CultureInfo* object. You can omit the *CultureInfo* parameter to use the machine-specific default, or use the technique shown in recipe 2.14 to use an invariant *CultureInfo*.

```
Dim DateString As String = "03/17/1977"

' Note that you must use apostrophes to escape the /,
' which is a special character.
Dim d2 As DateTime = DateTime.ParseExact(DateString, "MM'/'dd'/'yyyy", _
    Nothing)

Console.WriteLine("The date parsed as: " & d2.ToString())
' Displays "The date parsed as: 1977-03-17 12:00:00 AM"
' Note that all DateTime instances have an associated time,
' which defaults to 12:00:00 AM.
```

When accepting dates from users, it's far better to prevent invalid input rather than deal with it after the fact. Controls such as *DateTimePicker* (for Microsoft Windows applications) and *Calendar* (for Microsoft ASP.NET Web applications) can remove the possibility for error by removing the necessity for a string conversion step.

2.17 Generate a GUID

Problem

You want to create a new Globally Unique Identifier (GUID).

Solution

Use the shared *System.Guid.NewGuid* method.

Discussion

A GUID is a 128-bit integer. GUID values are tremendously useful in programming because they're statistically unique. In other words, you can create GUID values continuously with little chance of every creating a duplicate. For that reason, GUIDs are commonly used to uniquely identify queued tasks, user sessions, and other dynamic information. They also have the advantage over random numbers or sequence numbers in the fact that they can't easily be guessed. For example, if you write an XML Web service that assigns a new GUID to each user session, a malicious user won't be able to determine what GUID a user will receive based on what GUIDs other users received earlier.

The .NET Framework provides a *Guid* structure that represents a single GUID value. To create a new GUID, simply call the static *Guid.NewGuid* method, which creates a new GUID with a random value. You can then convert this value to a string by calling the *ToString* method.

```
Dim NewGuid As Guid = Guid.NewGuid()

Console.WriteLine(NewGuid.ToString)
' This writes a value like ""382c74c3-721d-4f34-80e5-57657b6cbc27"
```

GUID strings are by convention represented in string form as series of lower-case hexadecimal digits in groups of 8, 4, 4, 4, and 12 digits and separated by hyphens (xxxxxxxx-xxxx-xxxx-xxxx-xxxxxxxxxxxx). This is the representation you will receive when you call the *ToString* method, although you can use the "N" format specifier and call *ToString("N")* to retrieve a formatted string with the dashes omitted.

> **Note** The random GUID values that the *Guid* class creates are not guaranteed to be cryptographically secure. That means that an attacker who understands the pseudo-random algorithm used to create GUID values might be able to predict a "random" GUID your application generates. If this is a concern, you can create a cryptographically secure GUID using the recipe for secure randomness in Chapter 18 (see recipe 18.16).

2.18 Convert Basic Types to Binary

Problem

You need to convert basic data types to a binary representation, possibly before encrypting them or writing them to a stream.

Solution

Use the *BitConverter.GetBytes* method to convert integers, individual characters, and floating point numbers to binary. Use the *System.IO.BinaryWriter* class to convert decimals and strings, or if you need to combine the binary output of multiple values.

Discussion

The .NET Framework includes the built-in intelligence to convert most basic types into binary representation. If you need to convert an individual value into a byte array, you can use the overloaded *GetBytes* method of the *BitConverter* class. Here's an example:

```
Dim MyInt As Integer = 100
Dim Bytes() As Byte
Bytes = BitConverter.GetBytes(MyInt)

Console.WriteLine("An integer requires: " & _
    Bytes.Length.ToString() & " bytes.")
```

If you want to combine the binary output for multiple values into one array, it's easiest to use the *MemoryStream* class in concert with the *Binary-Writer* class (both of which are found in the *System.IO* namespace). You'll also use the *BinaryWriter* class to convert a single decimal value or string into binary representation, because the *BitConverter* class doesn't support these types.

To use the *BinaryWriter* class, call the overloaded *BinaryWriter.Write* method with any simple data type. Then, when all values are written, you can convert the entire stream into a single byte array by calling *Memory-Stream.ToArray*. The code below demonstrates this technique. It assumes you have imported the *System.IO* namespace.

```
' Create a buffer in memory.
Dim ms As New MemoryStream

' Create a BinaryWriter that allows you to place binary data in that buffer.
Dim w As New BinaryWriter(ms)
```

```
' Write the values.
Dim MyInt As Integer = 100
Dim MyString As String = "Sample Text"
w.Write(MyInt)
w.Write(MyString)

' Convert the stream to a byte array.
Dim Bytes() As Byte
Bytes = ms.ToArray()
```

To retrieve the information, you can use the *BinaryReader* class. First, you'll have to re-create the *MemoryStream* by using one of the overloaded constructors that accepts a byte array:

```
' Recreate the memory stream.
Dim ms As New MemoryStream(Bytes)
Dim r As New BinaryReader(ms)

' Read the values.
Dim MyInt As Integer
Dim MyString As String
MyInt = r.ReadInt32()
MyString = r.ReadString()
```

Reading information with *BinaryReader* is easy. It also saves a good deal of painstaking array copying and offset counting that would be needed if you were using the *BitConverter* class without streams. However, you must read values in the same order that you wrote them, and you must use the method that corresponds to the appropriate type of data.

Of course, if you are writing binary data directly to a file, you won't need to use methods such as *ToArray*. Instead, you would simply substitute a *FileStream* object in place of the *MemoryStream*.

```
' Create a new file.
Dim fs As New FileStream("C:\test.bin", FileMode.Create)
' Create a BinaryWriter that allows you to place binary data in that file.
Dim w As New BinaryWriter(fs)

' Write the values.
Dim MyInt As Integer = 100
Dim MyString As String = "Sample Text"
w.Write(MyInt)
w.Write(MyString)

' Close the file.
w.Close()
fs.Close()
```

> **Note**   You can also convert complex objects into a stream of bytes or byte array, provided they're serializable. For more information on this technique, refer to recipes 4.8 and 4.9 in Chapter 4.

2.19 Test Byte Arrays for Equality

Problem

You want to compare the bytes in two byte arrays to see if they have the same information.

Solution

Iterate over the array and compare each byte, or use the *BitConverter.ToString* method to create a string representation of the entire array.

Discussion

There is no way to directly test to arrays for equal content. You can use the *Is* operator, but this will only return *True* if both variables point to the *same* array. It will fail if the arrays are duplicate copies of identical data.

```
If Array1 Is Array2 Then
    ' This is a reference comparison, which only tests whether
    ' the variables reference the same array object.
End If
```

A shortcut is to use the *BitConverter.ToString* method to put both byte arrays into a standard string format. You can then compare the two strings:

```
If BitConverter.ToString(Array1) = BitConverter.ToString(Array2) Then
    ' Compare the string representations.
End If
```

This approach is not recommended for extremely large byte arrays, because memory will be wasted creating the strings. A better (and faster) approach is simply to create a helper function that iterates through bytes arrays and verifies their equality.

```
Private Function CompareByteArrays(arrayA() As Byte, arrayB() As Byte) _
  As Boolean
```

```
        If Not (arrayA.Length = arrayB.Length) Then
            Throw New ArgumentException("Arrays must be same length")
        End If

        Dim i As Integer
        For i = 0 To arrayA.Length - 1
            If Not (arrayA(i) = arrayB(i)) Then
                Return False
            End If
        Next

        Return True

    End Function
```

Now you can use this helper function to compare binary arrays:

```
Dim BytesA() As Byte = {32, 22, 10}
Dim BytesB() As Byte = {32, 12, 10}

Console.WriteLine("Math: " & CompareByteArrays(BytesA, BytesB).ToString())
```

2.20 Convert the Name of an Enumerated Value into the Value

Problem

You want to set an enumeration using the string name of a value, not the integer value, or you want to retrieve all the names used for constants in an enumeration.

Solution

Use the *Enum.GetNames* method to get an array of all enumeration names and the *Enum.Parse* method to convert a string into the corresponding value from an enumeration.

Discussion

An enumeration is a group of integer constants with descriptive names. Usually, you'll use enumeration values by name. Sometimes, however, it's necessary to convert enumeration values into strings, and vice versa. One reason might be to provide a user with a list of enumerated values and give them the chance to choose one.

As an example, consider the *System.Drawing.KnownColor* enumeration, which lists known system colors. You could use the *Enum.GetNames* method to retrieve a string array with all the color names, and add them to a listbox.

```
' Get the names of all enumerated values.
Dim ColorNames() As String
ColorNames = System.Enum.GetNames(GetType(KnownColor))

' Add the contents of the entire array to the list box.
lstColors.Items.AddRange(ColorNames)
```

To demonstrate the reverse task, you can handle the *ListBox.Selection-Changed* event, so that every time an entry is clicked in the list, a new color is set in a label. To perform this task, the listbox text must be converted to a *KnownColor* value and then used with the *Color.FromKnownColor* helper method, which creates a *Color* object based on the value.

```
Private Sub lstColors_SelectedIndexChanged(ByVal sender As System.Object, _
  ByVal e As System.EventArgs) Handles lstColors.SelectedIndexChanged

    ' Find the enumerated value that corresponds to the selected text.
    Dim ColorEnum As Object
    ColorEnum = System.Enum.Parse(GetType(KnownColor), lstColors.Text)

    Dim SelectedColor As KnownColor
    SelectedColor = CType(ColorEnum, KnownColor)

    ' Use the enumerated value to set the background color of the label.
    lbl.BackColor = System.Drawing.Color.FromKnownColor(SelectedColor)

End Sub
```

Figure 2-1 shows this sample program in action. Accomplishing the same result without using the enumeration would involve quite a bit of code—you would have to add each color value manually.

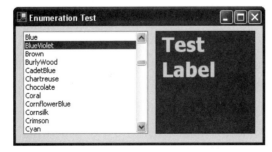

Figure 2-1   Converting enumerated values to strings and back.

3

Arrays and Collections

Arrays and collections are a key part of any programmer's toolkit. They allow you to aggregate large amounts of information into a structured pattern and often allow you to perform searches, sorting, and key-based lookup. In this chapter, we'll consider all of these basics, beginning with the canonical *System.Array* class, where you'll learn how to quickly populate and resize an array (recipes 3.1 and 3.2) and create nonrectangular arrays or irregular arrays with non-zero lower bounds (recipes 3.3 and 3.4). Next, we'll consider specialized collection types such as the *Hashtable*, *ArrayList*, *SortedList*, *Queue*, and *Stack*, all of which provide higher-level functionality that's indispensable for some tasks.

Before reading the recipes in this chapter, it helps to understand two fundamentals that apply to arrays and all other collection types.

- Arrays and collections are *reference types*. That means that if you pass an array or collection to a method, the array and all its items can be modified. Marking the parameter with *ByVal* will prevent the function code from replacing the array with a different array, but it won't stop the code from modifying the items that are in the array.

- If you are storing a reference type inside an array or collection, you are storing an object *reference*, not the object *content*. This has implications when considering array size, and it also means that a single object can be a part of multiple collections or arrays at the same time. Recipe 3.16 examines this possibility.

> **Note** Several of the recipes in this chapter assume you have imported the *System.Collections* namespace, where most collection types are defined. This namespace is imported by default in Microsoft Visual Studio .NET

3.1 Create and Populate an Array in One Step

Problem

You want to create an array and fill it with initial values in one step.

Solution

Use an initializer, and specify the values in curly braces.

Discussion

Microsoft Visual Basic .NET introduces a new initializer syntax that allows you to create a variable and set it in one step. This syntax can be used with arrays. You simply need to specify a comma-delimited list of all values, in order, inside curly braces. You can't specify the bounds of the array, because it will be inferred by the number of items you specify.

Here are two simple examples with one-dimensional arrays:

```
' Creates an array from index 0 to 9, with ten elements.
Dim MyIntegers() As Integer = {1, 2, 3, 4, 5, 6, 7, 8, 9, 10}

' Creates an array from index 0 to 3, with four elements.
Dim MyColors() As String = {"blue", "green", "pink", "yellow"}
```

You can use the same approach with complex objects that need to be instantiated using a constructor. Just specify the *New* keyword inside the curly braces each time you want to create an object.

```
' Create and initialize an array with three point objects.
Dim Points() As Point = _
  {New Point(0, 0), New Point(10, -3), New Point(3, 0)}
```

Finally, it's also possible to use this approach to fill multidimensional arrays. In this case, when defining the array you must add a comma for every additional dimension. You use multiple sets of braces to group the subdimensions, as shown here:

```
' Create a two-dimensional (2x3) integer array.
' Same as Dim Integers2(1, 2) As Integer
Dim Integers2(,) As Integer = {{3, 2, 6}, {9, 4, 6}}

' This displays "2"
Console.WriteLine(Integers2(0, 1).ToString())

' Create a three-dimensional (2x2x2) integer array.
' Same as Dim Integers3(1, 1, 1) As Integer
Dim Integers3(,,) As Integer = {{{3, 5}, {2, 7}}, {{0, 1}, {9, 8}}}

' This displays "7"
Console.WriteLine(Integers3(0, 1, 1).ToString())
```

3.2 Resize an Array

Problem

You need to expand the dimensions of an array.

Solution

The Visual Basic .NET *ReDim* statement with the *Preserve* keyword.

Discussion

The *ReDim* keyword allows you to specify new dimensions for an array after defining it. However, the existing items will be lost, unless you specify the *Preserve* keyword. When using *Preserve*, you can only resize the last dimension of the array. Thus, if you are resizing a two-dimensional array, you can only expand the second dimension. If you are resizing a one-dimensional array, you can resize the first (and only) dimension.

```
Dim IntArray(10, 10) As Integer

' (Configure the array here.)

' Add ten more columns to every row
ReDim Preserve IntArray(10, 20)

' The following statement will generate an exception.
' You cannot add more rows with the Preserve keyword.
ReDim Preserve IntArray(20, 20)
```

Technically, the *ReDim* statement releases the current array and creates a new one. If *Preserve* is specified, it copies the data to the new array. This process imposes some overhead, so it's always best to resize an array infrequently. One technique is to double the capacity of an array each time it must be resized. (Although in this case, your code must be aware of empty array elements and ignore them.) A more efficient approach is usually to use an *Array-List* when you need a resizable array, as shown in recipe 3.5.

3.3 Create an Array That Is Not Bounded at Zero

Problem

You need to create an array that follows idiosyncratic dimension numbering (for example, has a lower bound of –2 or 5 instead of 0).

Solution

Don't attempt this unless required for compatibility reasons—it makes your code less usable and much more obscure. If required, use the *Array.Create-Instance* method.

Discussion

The *Array.CreateInstance* method allows you to create a nonstandard array. As parameters, you specify the type of object that will be contained in the array, the length of the array, and the lower bounds. The latter two parameters must be submitted as arrays, with one entry for each dimension. (This means you can use the *CreateInstance* method to create a jagged array that has different bounds for each row, as described in recipe 3.4.)

The following example creates a one dimensional array that has bounds from –5 to –1, sets a test value, and then iterates over all values, using the same approach that you would use with a standard array.

```
Dim Lengths() As Integer = {5}
Dim LowerBounds() As Integer = {-5}

' Create a 1-dimensional Array of type String,
' with bounds from -5 to -1.
Dim OddArray As Array = Array.CreateInstance(GetType(String), _
    Lengths, LowerBounds)

Console.WriteLine("Lower bound: " & OddArray.GetLowerBound(0).ToString())
Console.WriteLine("Upper bound: " & OddArray.GetUpperBound(0).ToString())
```

```
' Set an array value.
OddArray(-3) = "This is a test."

Dim i As Integer
For i = OddArray.GetLowerBound(0) To OddArray.GetUpperBound(0)
    Console.WriteLine(i.ToString() & ": " & OddArray(i))
Next i
```

This code requires late binding. If you have disabled late binding (by enabling *Option Strict*, as is often recommended), you'll have to use the more awkward *Array.SetValue* and *Array.GetValue* syntax. Here's how you would set a value:

```
OddArray.SetValue("This is a test.", -3)
```

And here's how you would retrieve it:

```
Console.WriteLine(i.ToString() & ": " & OddArray.GetValue(i).ToString())
```

Remember that values are always retrieved as generic object types and must be cast to the correct type, further complicating code. You must also check for null references for noninitialized array elements. For these reasons, creating nonstandard arrays should only be undertaken if required for legacy reasons.

> **Note**   If you want to use an array with nonstandard lower bounds because the index number of the dimension corresponds to something in the real world, you are better off creating a custom class or collection with the desired behavior.

3.4 Create a Jagged Array

Problem

You need to create a nonrectangular array. For example, you might want to create a two-dimensional array in which different rows have different numbers of column elements.

Solution

Don't attempt this unless required for compatibility reasons—it makes your code less usable and much more obscure. If required, use the *Array.Create-Instance* method.

Discussion

Jagged arrays (sometimes described as *arrays of arrays*) introduce complexity, and should be used sparingly. However, they do have legitimate uses and are supported by Visual Basic .NET.

One way to create a multidimensional array is by including multiple sets of closed brackets when you define the array. As an example, the following code creates an array with 12 rows (one for each month), and a variable number of columns in each row (matching the number of days in the month).

```
' This array has 12 rows (representing months).
' Each row has a variable number of columns.
Dim Sales(11)() As Double


' Fill the array
Dim Days, Month As Integer
Dim Calendar As New System.Globalization.GregorianCalendar()
For Month = 1 To 12
    ' Size each row to the number of days in the corresponding month.
    Days = Calendar.GetDaysInMonth(2002, Month, Calendar.CurrentEra)
    Sales(Month - 1) = New Double(Days - 1) {}
Next


' Walk through the array and print all values.
Dim MonthRow() As Double
For Each MonthRow In Sales
    Console.Write("Month: ")

    Dim Column As Double
    For Each Column In MonthRow
        Console.Write(Column.ToString())
    Next
    Console.WriteLine()
Next
```

When you run this program, it will display a series of zeros (because no values were set). These values show the jagged structure of the array:

```
Month: 000000000000000000000000000000000
Month: 0000000000000000000000000000
Month: 000000000000000000000000000000000
Month: 00000000000000000000000000000000
Month: 000000000000000000000000000000000
Month: 00000000000000000000000000000000
Month: 000000000000000000000000000000000
Month: 000000000000000000000000000000000
Month: 00000000000000000000000000000000
Month: 000000000000000000000000000000000
Month: 00000000000000000000000000000000
Month: 000000000000000000000000000000000
```

The only limitation of this example is that every row must have the same data type. It's also possible to explicitly create an array of *Array* objects, where each *Array* object uses a different data type.

```
Dim StringArray() As String = {"blue", "green"}
Dim IntArray() As Integer = {1, 2, 3, 4, 5, 6}

Dim JaggedArray() As Array = {StringArray, IntArray}


Dim i, j As Integer
For i = 0 To JaggedArray.GetUpperBound(0)
    Console.Write("Row " & i.ToString & ": ")
    For j = 0 To JaggedArray(i).GetUpperBound(0)
        Console.Write(JaggedArray(i).GetValue(j).ToString() & " ")
    Next
    Console.WriteLine()
Next
```

This code displays two lines:

```
Row 0: blue green
Row 1: 1 2 3 4 5 6
```

Keep in mind that an overuse of jagged arrays usually indicates a problem that could be solved more elegantly using custom classes and collections.

3.5 Use a Dynamic *ArrayList*

Problem

You want to use a one-dimensional array that allows items to be inserted and removed dynamically and resizes itself automatically.

Solution

Use the *System.Collections.ArrayList* class.

Discussion

The *ArrayList* class is quite straightforward. Items are added using the *Add* method. Items can be removed using the *Remove, RemoveRange,* or *RemoveAt* methods. The latter two methods remove items based on their index numbers, while *Remove* searches the collection for the indicated item and then removes it. Instead of using the *GetLength* method, as you would with an array, you use the equivalent property *Count*.

```
Dim List As New ArrayList()
List.Add("blue")
List.Add("green")
List.Add("yellow")
List.Add("red")

' Remove "blue" by index number.
List.RemoveAt(0)

' Remove "green" using a search.
List.Remove("green")

Console.WriteLine("Items: " & List.Count.ToString())

' Display ArrayList contents ("yellow" and "red").
Dim Item As String
For Each Item In List
    Console.WriteLine(Item)
Next
```

The *ArrayList* class uses a capacity system similar to the *StringBuilder* class described in recipe 1.14. When an *ArrayList* is first created, it allocates an internal buffer for 16 items. If more items are needed, it expands the count by doubling it (to 32, then 64, and so on). If you know how many items an *Array-List* will contain, you can reserve the required space in advance by specifying it in the *ArrayList* constructor. This can improve performance slightly.

```
' Reserve space for 50 elements.
Dim List As New ArrayList(50)
```

The *ArrayList* is weakly typed, which means that it stores everything as a base *Object* type. When retrieving an item, you need to cast it accordingly.

```
Dim Item As String = CType(List(0), String)
```

This behavior can introduce problems in an application because there's no way to ensure that the wrong type of object isn't added to an array. To solve this problem, you might want to create a custom strongly typed collection, as described in recipe 3.16.

> **Note** Microsoft .NET does provide one strongly typed list, although it's easy to overlook: the *StringCollection* class, which is provided in the *System.Collections.Specialized* namespace. This class only accepts strings (although duplicate string entries are completely acceptable).

3.6 Fill an *ArrayList* from an Array

Problem

You need to copy items from an array into an *ArrayList*.

Solution

You can add an entire range of items into an *ArrayList* quickly using the *AddRange* method.

Discussion

The *ArrayList.AddRange* method accepts any object that implements the *ICollection* interface (including an array or another *ArrayList*), and copies all the items it contains into the *ArrayList*.

```
Dim Colors() As String = {"blue", "green", "pink", "yellow"}

' Copy the strings in the Colors array into the List ArrayList.
Dim List As New ArrayList()
List.AddRange(Colors)

' Display the contents of the ArrayList.
Dim Item As String
For Each Item In List
    Console.WriteLine(Item)
Next
```

Keep in mind that if you are using a reference type, when you copy it into the *ArrayList* you are copying the reference, not the content of the object. Thus, both the *ArrayList* and the original array will be referencing the same object in memory.

3.7 Convert an *ArrayList* to an Array

Problem

You need to convert an *ArrayList* into a strongly typed array.

Solution

Use the *ArrayList.ToArray* method.

Discussion

Converting an *ArrayList* to an ordinary array is a useful task. For example, you might create a utility function that uses an *ArrayList* internally to quickly create a collection and dynamically add items. Using an *ArrayList* is intrinsically easier than using an array, because you don't need to worry about array dimensions. However, when you return the information from the function, you should use a generic array, which is more common and has the advantage of type safety.

In theory, you could inspect the *Count* property of the *ArrayList*, create a corresponding array, and iterate through the *ArrayList*, copying elements one by one. However, the *ArrayList* provides a simpler approach through its *ToArray* method. When using *ToArray*, you simply specify the type of array. The *ToArray* method will inspect every item in the *ArrayList,* attempt to convert it to the specified type, and then copy the reference to the array. If any item can't be converted, an exception will be thrown.

The following example shows a trivial function that searches a sentence for certain words, adding them to an *ArrayList* as they are found. When the operation is complete, the *ArrayList* is converted to an array of strings. The *ToArray* method returns an *Array* object, which must be cast to a strongly typed array using the *CType* function.

```
Private Function FindAnimalWords(ByVal sentence As String) As String()

    ' Fill the collection.
    Dim Words As New ArrayList()
    Dim Word As String
    For Each Word In sentence.Split()
        Select Case Word
            Case "dog", "cat", "fox", "mouse"
                Words.Add(Word)
        End Select
    Next

    ' Convert the ArrayList to an array, and then cast
    ' the generic array to a strongly typed array using CType().
    Return CType(Words.ToArray(GetType(String)), String())

End Function
```

Here's a simple code snipped to test this word search function:

```
Dim Sentence As String = "The quick brown fox jumps over the lazy dog"
Dim Animals() As String = FindAnimalWords(Sentence)
```

> **Note**   The specialized *Queue* and *Stack* collections (described in rec-
> ipes 3.12 and 3.13) also provide a *ToArray* method that allows you to
> copy elements into a strongly typed array, much as with the *ArrayList*.

3.8 Sort Items in an Array or *ArrayList*

Problem

You need to sort the items in an array or *ArrayList*. The items in the array or
ArrayList implement *IComparable* (as do all basic .NET data types).

Solution

Use the *Array.Sort* or *ArrayList.Sort* methods.

Discussion

Both the *Array* and *ArrayList* types expose a *Sort* method. This method uses an
optimized sort algorithm and compares objects using the *IComparable* interface. If the objects in the array don't support this interface, you'll need to use a
custom comparer (as explained in recipe 3.9). If there's more than one type of
object in the same collection, you won't be able to sort it.

The following example sorts strings in an *ArrayList*. In this case, the type
of sort is culture specific and will order items alphabetically (with lowercase letters positioned before the same uppercase letter).

```
' Create and populate an ArrayList.
Dim Sentence As String = "The quick brown fox jumped over the lazy dog"
Dim List As New ArrayList()

' Split the sentence into an array of words,
' and add each word to the ArrayList.
List.AddRange(Sentence.Split())

Console.WriteLine("--- Unsorted ---")
Dim Value As String
For Each Value In List
    Console.WriteLine(Value)
Next
```

```
' Sorts the values of the ArrayList.
List.Sort()
Console.WriteLine(vbNewLine & "---- Sorted ----")

For Each Value In List
    Console.WriteLine(Value)
Next
```

The output of this test is shown here:

```
--- Unsorted ---
The
quick
brown
fox
jumped
over
the
lazy
dog

---- Sorted ----
brown
dog
fox
jumped
lazy
over
quick
the
The
```

The *Sort* method is overloaded in both the *Array* and *ArrayList* classes to accept index numbers specifying just a subset of the array that should be sorted, and a custom *IComparer* object that can perform a custom sort.

```
' Sort 5 items, starting at position 3 (the fourth item).
List.Sort(3, 5, Nothing)
```

If you wish to use a dictionary collection that sorts itself automatically, you might be interested in the *SortedList* class described in recipe 3.14. The *SortedList* class allows two ways to access items: by index number (in which case items are always accessed in their sorted order) or through the associated key value.

3.9 Sort Non-Comparable Items in an *Array* or *ArrayList*

Problem

You want to sort an *Array* or *ArrayList*, but the items it contains do not implement *IComparable*.

Solution

Create a custom *IComparer* that can sort the type of object contained in the *Array* or *ArrayList*. Pass an instance of this *IComparer* object to the *Sort* method of the *Array* or *ArrayList* object.

Discussion

Some objects define a native sort order by implementing the *IComparable* interface. Others do not, either because there's no obvious criteria to use for sorting, or because there are several equally valid sort criteria. In these cases, you can create a custom *IComparer*, which is an object with a single purpose in life—to sort a specific type of object.

There are two reasons that you might use a custom *IComparer* rather than implement *IComparable*:

■ You need to sort an object in multiple different ways. However, an *IComparable* object will only sort itself in one way.

■ You didn't create the object, and therefore you can't modify the class code to implement *IComparable*.

For example, consider the *System.IO.FileInfo* object, which encapsulates information about a file. There are several ways that it might make sense to sort files, including by name, size, or creation date. However, the *FileInfo* class does not implement *IComparable*, so it has no intrinsic support for sorting.

To create an *IComparer*, you must implement a single method, *Compare*. Below is a custom *FileInfoComparer* that compares two *FileInfo* objects. It allows three different types of sorts, depending on the *FileInfoCompareType* value specified as a constructor argument. An equally valid approach would be to create three separate *IComparer* objects, one for each type of sort, but that approach would require more code.

```
' Define three ways a FileInfo object can be sorted.
Public Enum FileInfoCompareType
    Name
    CreateDate
    Size
End Enum

Public Class FileInfoComparer
    Implements IComparer

    Private _CompareType As FileInfoCompareType

    Public ReadOnly Property CompareType() As FileInfoCompareType
        Get
            Return _CompareType
        End Get
    End Property

    Public Sub New(ByVal compareType As FileInfoCompareType)
        Me._CompareType = compareType
    End Sub

    Public Function Compare(ByVal objA As Object, ByVal objB As Object) _
      As Integer Implements System.Collections.IComparer.Compare

        Dim FileA, FileB As FileInfo
        FileA = CType(objA, FileInfo)
        FileB = CType(objB, FileInfo)

        ' Determine the comparison type.
        Select Case CompareType
            Case FileInfoCompareType.CreateDate
                Return Date.Compare(FileA.CreationTime, FileB.CreationTime)
            Case FileInfoCompareType.Name
                Return String.Compare(FileA.Name, FileB.Name)
            Case FileInfoCompareType.Size
                Return Decimal.Compare(FileA.Length, FileB.Length)
        End Select

    End Function

End Class
```

To test this *IComparer*, you can retrieve an array of *FileInfo* objects for a directory using the *DirectoryInfo.GetFiles* method. You can sort this array by calling *Array.Sort* and supplying the *IComparer* instance. Below is a complete Console application that demonstrates this technique. In order to use this code as written, you must import the *System.IO* namespace where the *DirectoryInfo* and *FileInfo* types are defined.

```
Public Module CustomArraySort

    Public Sub Main()
        Dim Dir As New DirectoryInfo("C:\")

        ' Retrieve an array of FileInfo objects.
        Dim Files() As FileInfo = Dir.GetFiles()

        ' Sort the array by filename.
        Array.Sort(Files, New FileInfoComparer(FileInfoCompareType.Name))

        ' Display the list of files to confirm its order.
        Console.WriteLine("An alphabetic file list:")
        Dim File As FileInfo
        For Each File In Files
            Console.WriteLine(File.Name)
        Next

        Console.ReadLine()
    End Sub

End Module
```

3.10 Use a *Hashtable* Instead of a Generic Collection

Problem

You need a dictionary (key-based) collection, or you want to replace the Visual Basic generic collection with a more powerful alternative.

Solution

Use the *System.Collections.Hashtable* type.

Discussion

The *Hashtable* class is a dictionary collection, where every item is indexed with a unique value. *Hashtable* collections are ideal for situations where you need to quickly retrieve individual items, because you can look up items using the corresponding key values, rather than by iterating through the contents of the entire collection. However, unlike arrays or the *ArrayList* class, you can't access items using an index number.

When using a *Hashtable*, you must decide what information to use for indexing items. This data must be unique. It might be derived from the object itself, or you might generate it on demand using a GUID or a sequence number. For example, consider the simple *Customer* class defined here:

```
Public Class Customer

    Private _ID As Integer
    Private _FirstName As String
    Private _LastName As String

    Public Sub New(ByVal id As Integer, ByVal firstName As String, _
      ByVal lastName As String)
        Me.ID = id
        Me.FirstName = firstName
        Me.LastName = lastName
    End Sub

    Public Property ID() As Integer
        Get
            Return Me._ID
        End Get
        Set(ByVal Value As Integer)
            Me._ID = Value
        End Set
    End Property

    Public Property FirstName() As String
        Get
            Return Me._FirstName
        End Get
        Set(ByVal Value As String)
            Me._FirstName = Value
        End Set
    End Property

    Public Property LastName() As String
        Get
            Return Me._LastName
        End Get
        Set(ByVal Value As String)
            Me._LastName = Value
        End Set
    End Property

End Class
```

When storing this information in a *Hashtable*, you might want to use the unique customer ID to index each *Customer* object.

```
' Create three customers.
Dim CustomerA As New Customer(1001, "Henry", "Bloge")
Dim CustomerB As New Customer(1020, "Janice", "Newport")
Dim CustomerC As New Customer(4420, "Heide", "Kraus")

' Add the customers to the collection, indexed by ID.
Dim Items As New Hashtable()
Items.Add(CustomerA.ID, CustomerA)
Items.Add(CustomerB.ID, CustomerB)
Items.Add(CustomerC.ID, CustomerC)

' Retrieve an item.
Dim Cust As Customer = CType(Items(1020), Customer)
Console.WriteLine("Retrieved: " & Cust.FirstName & " " & Cust.LastName)
' Displays "Retrieved: Janice Newport"

' Now create a new Customer object that duplicates CustomerA.
Dim CustomerACopy As New Customer(1001, "Henry", "Bloge")

' Check for this customer in the collection.
If Not Items.Contains(CustomerACopy) Then
    ' This code always runs, because the object has not been added.
    Console.WriteLine("Object is not in the collection.")
End If

' Check for this customer key in the collection.
If Items.ContainsKey(CustomerACopy.ID) Then
    ' This code always runs, because the key exists in the collection.
    Console.WriteLine("An object with this ID is in the collection.")
End If
```

Note that like the *ArrayList*, the *Hashtable* stores items as the generic object type, and you must use casting code when retrieving an item.

Some other useful *Hashtable* members include:

■ *Remove* deletes an item from the collection. You specify the key of the item you want removed.

■ *Contains* and *ContainsKey* return *True* or *False*, depending on whether a specified key is in the *Hashtable*. This provides a quick way to perform a simple search.

■ *ContainsValue* returns *True* or *False*, depending on whether a specified object is in the *Hashtable*. For example, in the previous code example where the *Hashtable* was used to store *Customer* objects, you could call *ContainsValue* with a *Customer* object. It would return *True* only if this object is already in the collection.

- The *Keys* property provides a read-only collection of all the keys used in the *Hashtable*.

- The *Values* property provides a read-only collection of all the objects in the *Hashtable*.

Note   The *Hashtable* class works more or less the same way as the standard Visual Basic 6 *Collection* type, which is still included in Visual Basic .NET for backward compatibility. However, for most programming tasks, a *Hashtable* is preferable to a generic collection, because a *Hashtable* ensures that every item has a key that can be used to locate or remove the item. Without a key, the only way to find an item is by iterating through the entire collection and examining each object. Furthermore, only the *Hashtable* supports any type of object as a key. The generic collection is limited to string values.

   If you don't have a suitable value to use as a key, you can always use the reference of the object you are adding:

```
' Use the object reference as a key.
Dim Col As New Hashtable()
Col.Add(ItemA, ItemA)
```

   This allows you to quickly remove an object using the following syntax:

```
Col.Remove(ItemA)
```

3.11 Enumerate Items in a *Hashtable*

Problem

You need to enumerate over the contents of a *Hashtable*.

Solution

Use the *DictionaryEntry* type with a *For/Each* block.

Discussion

With a generic collection, you perform enumeration using the type in the collection (or one of its base types). The *Hashtable* does not support this convention. Instead, you must iterate over a collection of *DictionaryEntry* objects.

There is one *DictionaryEntry* object for each item stored in the collection. You can retrieve the key for the item from the *DictionaryEntry.Key* property, and you can retrieve the item in the collection from the *DictionaryEntry.Value* property.

The following code demonstrates this technique on a collection that contains strings:

```
' Create the collection and add two items.
Dim Col As New Hashtable()
Dim ItemA As String = "ItemA"
Dim ItemB As String = "ItemB"
Col.Add("First Item", ItemA)
Col.Add("Second Item", ItemB)

' Enumerate over the collection contents.
Dim Item As DictionaryEntry
For Each Item In Col
    Console.WriteLine("Key: " & Item.Key.ToString())
    Console.WriteLine("Object: " & Item.Value.ToString())
    Console.WriteLine()
Next
```

Looking at the output for this code, you'll notice that the enumeration actually takes place backward, starting with the most recently added item:

```
Key: Second Item
Object: ItemB

Key: First Item
Object: ItemA
```

This approach has the advantage that you can easily determine the keys of all items in a collection.

3.12 Use a *Queue* (FIFO Collection)

Problem

You need a collection where items will be retrieved in the same order they are added.

Solution

Use the *System.Collections.Queue* type, which provides a first-in, first-out collection.

Discussion

Queues are used for a variety of sequential programming tasks. For example, you might use a queue to store a list of tasks that needs to be performed with a server-side component. Because the queue is a first-in, first-out collection, the oldest items are always dealt with first.

Conceptually, the *Queue* is a dynamically sized array that stores objects, much as the *ArrayList* does. The *Queue* starts with an initial capacity of 32 items (unless you supply a different capacity in the constructor) and doubles the capacity as needed. You can retrieve the number of items from the *Count* property, add an item with the *Enqueue* method, or retrieve an item with the *Dequeue* method, which simultaneously removes the item from the *Queue*. It's also possible to use *Peek* to retrieve the next item in the *Queue* without removing it. However, you can't retrieve queued objects out of order or by index number.

Here's the code needed to create a simple queue and read all items:

```
Dim Queue As New Queue()

Queue.Enqueue("Item A")
Queue.Enqueue("Item B")
Queue.Enqueue("Item C")

' Retrieve all items and clear the queue.
Dim Item As String
Do While Queue.Count > 0
    Item = CType(Queue.Dequeue, String)
    Console.WriteLine("Retrieved: " & Item)
    Console.WriteLine(Queue.Count.ToString() & " items remaining.")
Loop
```

Here's the output for this test:

```
Retrieved: Item A
2 items remaining.
Retrieved: Item B
1 items remaining.
Retrieved: Item C
0 items remaining.
```

3.13 Use a *Stack* (LIFO Collection)

Problem

You need a collection where items will be retrieved in the reverse order (so that the most recently added item is always accessed first).

Solution

Use the *System.Collections.Stack* type, which provides a last-in, first-out collection.

Discussion

Stacks are used for programming tasks where you always need to access the most recent items first. Like the *ArrayList* and *Queue, Stack* is a dynamically sized array that stores objects. It starts with an initial capacity of 32 items (unless you supply a different capacity in the constructor) and doubles the capacity as needed. You can retrieve the number of items from the *Count* property, add an item at the top of a *Stack* with the *Push* method, or retrieve an item with the *Pop* method, which simultaneously removes the item from the *Stack* array. It's also possible to use *Peek* to retrieve the next item in the *Stack* without removing it. However, you can't retrieve objects out of order or by index number.

Here's the code needed to create a simple stack and read all items:

```
Dim Stack As New Stack()

Stack.Push("Item A")
Stack.Push("Item B")
Stack.Push("Item C")

' Retrieve all items and clear the queue.
Dim Item As String
Do While Stack.Count > 0
    Item = CType(Stack.Pop, String)
    Console.WriteLine("Retrieved: " & Item)
    Console.WriteLine(Stack.Count.ToString() & " items remaining.")
Loop
```

Here's the output for this test:

```
Retrieved: Item C
2 items remaining.
Retrieved: Item B
1 items remaining.
Retrieved: Item A
0 items remaining.
```

3.14 Use a Sorted List

Problem

You want to use a collection that is automatically sorted every time an item is added or removed.

Solution

Use the *System.Collections.SortedList* type, which sorts items based on the key.

Discussion

The *SortedList* class is a key-based dictionary collection that stores items in a perpetually ordered state. That makes it slower when adding or removing items. However, using a *SortedList* collection is usually faster than continuously resorting an *Array* or *ArrayList*. Behind the scenes, a sorted list uses two arrays: one to store key values, and one to store the data itself (or the object reference).

The most important aspect to understand about the *SortedList* class is that it orders items based on the key value, not the object itself. This means that the key must be a type that supports *IComparable* (such as an integer or a string). Alternatively, you can specify a custom *IComparer* as an argument to the *SortedList* constructor. This *IComparer* will then be used to sort all items, much as in recipe 3.9.

The following code retrieves a set of *FileInfo* objects from the current directory, adds them to a sorted list collection, and uses the filename as the key value. In order to run this code, you must import the *System.IO* namespace.

```
Dim Dir As New DirectoryInfo("C:\")

' Retrieve an array of FileInfo.
Dim Files() As FileInfo
Files = Dir.GetFiles()

' Add them to a sorted list, indexed by filename.
Dim List As New SortedList()
Dim File As FileInfo
For Each File In Files
    List.Add(File.Name, File)
Next

' Verify the order.
Dim Item As DictionaryEntry
For Each Item In List
    Console.WriteLine(CType(Item.Value, FileInfo).Name)
Next
```

Because the *SortedList* uses the key value, not the object, this approach is unsuitable if the filename might change. In this case, the *FileInfo* object will remain sorted under the original filename. There's no way to modify the key value for an object—you can only remove the item and add it again.

3.15 Create Shallow and Deep Copies of a Collection or Array

Problem

You need to copy a collection.

Solution

To create a shallow copy, use the *Clone* method. To create a deep copy, iterate over the collection, and copy each item.

Discussion

All collection types provide a *Clone* method that makes it easy to quickly copy the entire collection.

```
' Create an ArrayList and add some items.
Dim ListA As New ArrayList()
ListA.Add("blue")
ListA.Add("green")
ListA.Add("yellow")

' Create a duplicate ArrayList.
Dim ListB As ArrayList()
ListB = CType(ListA.Clone(), ArrayList)
```

This is known as a *shallow copy,* and it works fine for value types (or reference types that behave like value types, such as *String*). However, this method isn't always appropriate when used with ordinary classes. As an example, consider what happens if you create an *ArrayList,* populate it with the basic *Customer* class (shown in recipe 3.10), and then clone it.

```
' Create an ArrayList with three customers.
Dim ListA As New ArrayList()
ListA.Add(New Customer(1001, "Henry", "Bloge"))
ListA.Add(New Customer(1020, "Janice", "Newport"))
ListA.Add(New Customer(4420, "Heide", "Kraus"))

' Create a duplicate ArrayList.
Dim ListB As New ArrayList()
ListB = CType(ListA.Clone(), ArrayList)
```

The *Customer* class is, like every class, a reference type. This means that the *ArrayList* doesn't actually store *Customer* objects. Instead, it stores a list of object references that point to *Customer* objects, which are floating about in a different portion of memory (known as the managed heap). When you call *Clone*, you duplicate the references, but you don't actually duplicate the objects. Thus, you have two collections that reference the same objects.

In some cases, this might be the behavior you want (as it reduces the overall memory overhead). However, if you intend to continue using both collections, this probably isn't the behavior you want, because if you retrieve a reference and change an object using one collection, the changes will automatically affect the other.

In this situation, the only approach is to use manual code to create a *deep copy*. You need to enumerate through the collection and duplicate each individual item.

```
Dim ListB As New ArrayList()

' Clone the objects.
Dim Item As Customer
For Each Item In ListA
    ' Clone the object in ListA into the corresponding row in ListB.
    ListB.Add(New Customer(Item.ID, Item.FirstName, Item.LastName))
Next
```

The actual method you use to clone the object depends. In our simple example, you would need to instantiate a new *Customer* object manually. However, if the object implements the *ICloneable* interface, you can call the object's *Clone* method to create a new copy.

```
For Each Item In ListA
    ListB.Add(CType(Item.Clone(), Customer))
Next
```

If the object is serializable, you can also use another approach that involves serializing the object to memory, duplicating it, and then deserializing the copy. This process, and the *ICloneable* interface, are discussed in Chapter 4.

3.16 Create a Strongly Typed Collection

Problem

You need to create a collection that can only contain one type of object and rejects attempts to add other data types.

Solution

Create a custom collection class by deriving from *System.Collections.Collection-Base*, and implement type-safe *Add*, *Remove*, and *Item* methods.

Discussion

You could create a custom collection by implementing the *IList*, *ICollection*, and *IEnumerable* interfaces. However, .NET provides an easier option with the abstract *CollectionBase* class. Internally, the *CollectionBase* uses an *ArrayList*, which is exposed through the protected property *List*.

As an example, consider the simple *Customer* object shown here:

```
Public Class Customer

    Private _ID As Integer
    Private _FirstName As String
    Private _LastName As String

    Public Sub New(ByVal id As Integer, ByVal firstName As String, _
      ByVal lastName As String)
        Me.ID = id
        Me.FirstName = firstName
        Me.LastName = lastName
    End Sub

    Public Property ID() As Integer
        Get
            Return Me._ID
        End Get
        Set(ByVal Value As Integer)
            Me._ID = Value
        End Set
    End Property

    Public Property FirstName() As String
        Get
            Return Me._FirstName
        End Get
        Set(ByVal Value As String)
            Me._FirstName = Value
        End Set
    End Property
```

```
    Public Property LastName() As String
        Get
            Return Me._LastName
        End Get
        Set(ByVal Value As String)
            Me._LastName = Value
        End Set
    End Property

End Class
```

You can derive a type-safe *CustomerCollection* from *CollectionBase*. Then you add a strongly typed *Add* method and a default property named *Item*, which automatically casts the retrieved object to the correct type.

```
Public Class CustomerCollection
    Inherits System.Collections.CollectionBase

    Public Sub Add(ByVal item As Customer)
        Me.List.Add(item)
    End Sub

    Public Sub Remove(ByVal index As Integer)
        If index > Count - 1 Or index < 0 Then
            Throw New ArgumentOutOfRangeException( _
              "No item at the specified index.")
        Else
            List.RemoveAt(index)
        End If
    End Sub

    Default Public Property Item(ByVal index As Integer) As Customer
        Get
            Return CType(Me.List.Item(index), Customer)
        End Get
        Set(ByVal Value As Customer)
            Me.List.Item(index) = Value
        End Set
    End Property

End Class
```

Here's a simple test of the type-safe *CustomerCollection*:

```
Dim Customers As New CustomerCollection()

' This succeeds.
Customers.Add(New Customer(1001, "Henry", "Bloge"))

' This fails at compile time.
Customers.Add("This is a string")
```

One limitation of the *CollectionBase* approach is that you can only create nonkeyed collections (such as the *ArrayList*). If you need to create a strongly typed dictionary collection, see recipe 3.17.

Incidentally, the .NET Framework includes one strongly typed collection class: the *StringCollection* class in the *System.Collections.Specialized* namespace, which only allows *String* objects.

3.17 Create a Strongly Typed Dictionary Collection

Problem

You need to create a key-based collection that can only contain one type of object and rejects attempts to add other data types.

Solution

Create a custom dictionary collection class by deriving from *System.Collections.DictionaryBase*, and implement type-safe *Add*, *Remove*, and *Item* methods.

Discussion

With a custom dictionary collection, you can place restrictions on the type of objects stored in the collection and on the type of object used to index items in the collection. Internally, the *DictionaryBase* object uses an ordinary weakly typed *Hashtable*, which is exposed through the protected property *Dictionary*. However, external code can't directly access this collection. Instead, it must use one of the type-safe methods you add to your custom class.

As an example, consider the simple *Customer* object shown in recipe 3.16. Using *DictionaryBase*, you can derive a type-safe *CustomerDictionary* that has a strongly typed *Add* method, which requires an integer key and only accepts *Customer* objects for insertion in a collection. You'll also implement a *Remove* method and a default property named *Item*, which automatically casts the retrieved object to the correct type.

```
Public Class CustomerDictionary
    Inherits System.Collections.DictionaryBase

    Public Sub Add(ByVal key As Integer, ByVal item As Customer)
        Me.Dictionary.Add(key, item)
    End Sub

    Public Sub Remove(ByVal key As Integer)
        Me.Dictionary.Remove(key)
    End Sub
```

```
        Default Public Property Item(ByVal key As Integer) As Customer
            Get
                Return CType(Me.Dictionary.Item(key), Customer)
            End Get
            Set(ByVal value As Customer)
                Me.Dictionary.Item(key) = value
            End Set
        End Property
End Class
```

Here's a simple test of the type-safe *CustomerDictionary*:

```
Dim Customers As New CustomerDictionary()
Dim CustomerA As New Customer(1001, "Henry", "Bloge")

' This succeeds.
Customers.Add(CustomerA.ID, CustomerA)

' This fails because the object is not a Customer.
Customers.Add(9024, "This is a string")

' This fails because the ID is not an integer.
Customers.Add(CustomerA.FirstName, CustomerA)
```

Incidentally, the .NET Framework includes one strongly typed dictionary class: the *StringDictionary* class in the *System.Collections.Specialized* namespace, which only allows *String* objects.

3.18 Remove Items While Iterating Through a Collection

Problem

You need to search for items and delete them. However, you can't delete items while iterating through a collection.

Solution

Add the items that you want to delete to another collection. Then iterate through this collection and remove all items from the original collection.

Discussion

Enumerating through a collection is strictly a read-only operation. However, you can enumerate through a collection to find the items you need to remove, and then delete them in a second step, as shown below.

```
Dim List As New ArrayList()
List.Add("This")
List.Add("is")
List.Add("a")
List.Add("simple")
List.Add("test")

' Mark words that start with "t" for deletion.
Dim ItemsToDelete As New ArrayList()
Dim Item As String
For Each Item In List
    If Item.Substring(0, 1).ToUpper() = "T" Then
        ItemsToDelete.Add(Item)
    End If
Next

' Delete the words that are marked for deletion.
For Each Item In ItemsToDelete
    List.Remove(Item)
Next

' Display remaining (3) items.
For Each Item In List
    Console.WriteLine(Item)
Next
```

This two-step approach requires very little additional memory. Even if you are storing large items in a collection, you'll simply copy the reference, not the object content, to the new collection.

Some collection types, such as the *ArrayList*, allow you to remove items by index number. In this case, you can use the slightly more efficient code below that does not require a search when looking up the items for deletion:

```
Dim ItemsToDelete As New ArrayList()
Dim Item As String

' Move through the list by index number, and store the index number
' of every item that needs to be deleted.
Dim i As Integer
For i = 0 To List.Count - 1
    Item = CType(List.Item(i), String)
    If Item.Substring(0, 1).ToUpper() = "T" Then
        ItemsToDelete.Add(i)
    End If
Next
```

```
' Count backward to prevent index renumbering problems.
Dim Index As Integer
For i = (ItemsToDelete.Count - 1) To 0 Step -1
    Index = CType(ItemsToDelete(i), Integer)
    List.RemoveAt(Index)
Next
```

3.19 Iterate Through Collection Items in Random Order

Problem

You need to enumerate through all the items in a collection, but you don't want to visit items in order.

Solution

Create the *RandomIterator* class shown below, and use it to store an *ArrayList* of randomly ordered items.

Discussion

By default, enumeration moves through the items of a collection in order from first to last. And while it's easy to randomly select a single item in a collection using the *Random* class, it's more difficult to randomly walk through all items in a collection and ensure that each one is visited only once.

The solution is the *RandomIterator* class shown below. It stores a private collection and inserts all items into that collection in a random order. You can then walk through this collection of randomly ordered items.

```
Public Class RandomIterator
    Implements IEnumerable

    Private Items As New ArrayList()

    Public Sub New(ByVal collection As IEnumerable, _
      Optional ByVal seed As Integer = 0)
        Dim Rand As Random
        If seed = 0 Then
            Rand = New Random()
        Else
            Rand = New Random(seed)
        End If
```

```
        Dim obj As Object
        For Each obj In collection
            Items.Insert(Rand.Next(0, Items.Count + 1), obj)
        Next
    End Sub

    Public Function GetEnumerator() As System.Collections.IEnumerator _
        Implements System.Collections.IEnumerable.GetEnumerator

        ' Return the enumerator for the internal collection.
        Return Items.GetEnumerator()
    End Function

End Class
```

The constructor performs most of the work for the *RandomIterator* class. It accepts a collection object and duplicates all the items into the internal collection, inserting them at random positions. Remember, if your collection stores reference types, this operation doesn't actually clone the object; it simply copies the reference. (Thus, it doesn't matter which collection you use to access the object, you are still working with the same object.) Once the internal *ArrayList* is filled, you can call *GetEnumerator* to enumerate through the collection of randomly ordered objects.

> **Note**   You'll notice that the constructor optionally accepts a seed for the random number generator. You should set this value if you need to create several *RandomIterator* objects at the same time. Otherwise, on a fast computer the items could conceivably be created at the same millisecond, given the same seed value, and then ordered in the same "random" order.

The following example shows a Console application that puts the *RandomIterator* class at work:

```
Public Module RandomIterationTest

    Public Sub Main()
        Dim Colors() As String = {"blue", "green", "pink", "yellow"}
        Dim Color As String
```

```
        For Each Color In New RandomIterator(Colors)
            Console.WriteLine(Color)
        Next
        Console.WriteLine()

        For Each Color In New RandomIterator(Colors)
            Console.WriteLine(Color)
        Next

        Console.ReadLine()
    End Sub

End Module
```

Both of these lists are randomly sorted. Here's an example of the output you might see:

```
yellow
blue
pink
green

blue
pink
yellow
green
```

This example is adapted from a sample first provided by VB-2-The-Max (http://www.vb2themax.com).

4

Objects, Interfaces, and Patterns

In Microsoft .NET, everything is an object. To truly master Visual Basic .NET programming, you need to understand these object internals. You also need to understand the patterns used in .NET code to copy, compare, dispose, and convert object types so that you can implement them in your own classes.

The first batch of recipes in this chapter (4.1 to 4.8) covers the ingredients you need to build complete, well-rounded objects. The later recipes in this chapter consider common techniques for building and using objects, with an emphasis on different approaches to serialization (recipes 4.9 to 4.12) and object-oriented programming (OOP) patterns that can help you solve common problems without reinventing the wheel (recipes 4.15 to 4.18).

The recipes in this chapter place the emphasis on doing OOP the *right* way, which means adopting the conventions of the .NET Framework. For example, when we create a custom *Exception* object (recipe 4.13), we'll implement the standard conventions needed to support serialization and inner exceptions. When we create a custom *EventArgs* object (recipe 4.14), we'll make it serializable so that it can be fired across application boundaries. And when we deal with objects that need support for cloning, comparing, conversion, and more, we'll use the canonical interfaces provided by the .NET Framework. Understanding these unwritten rules is the key to writing extensible, reusable .NET objects.

> **Note**   Property procedures are an indispensable part of object-oriented programming, but they do lead to much lengthier code. For that reason, some of the examples in this chapter omit the property procedure code, especially if it duplicates an earlier example. In this case, a descriptive one-line comment is inserted in its place. This indicates that the property procedure code is quite straightforward and requires no special attention. If you would like to browse the full class code with all property procedures, refer to downloadable sample code for this chapter.

4.1 Create a Value Type

Problem

You need to create an object that supports value type semantics.

Solution

Define the type as a structure. If you absolutely must use a class (for example, to use inheritance), override the *Equals* and the *GetHashCode* methods so that your class *acts* like a structure.

Discussion

In .NET, value types (such as *DateTime*, *Int32*, and so on) inherit from the *System.ValueType* class. Comparisons performed with value types act on the full contents of the object, not the object reference. Similarly, assignments performed with value types copy the entire contents of the object, not just the object reference. This behavior is best suited to simple classes that require only a small amount of memory to store their information. Because the memory for value types is allocated on the stack, not the managed heap, value types often perform better than reference types (although this won't be the case if you create large value types and use frequent assignment statements to copy the data).

The *ValueType* class is noninheritable, so you can't use it to create your own value types. However, you can use the *Structure* keyword in Visual Basic .NET. Here is a sample *Person* type implemented both as a structure and a class:

```
Public Structure PersonStructure

    Private _FirstName As String
    Private _LastName As String
```

```vbnet
    Public Property FirstName() As String
        Get
            Return _FirstName
        End Get
        Set(ByVal Value As String)
            _FirstName = Value
        End Set
    End Property

    Public Property LastName() As String
        Get
            Return _LastName
        End Get
        Set(ByVal Value As String)
            _LastName = Value
        End Set
    End Property

    Public Sub New(ByVal firstName As String, ByVal lastName As String)
        ' Note that the syntax is slightly different than in a class.
        ' You cannot assign directly to a property procedure
        ' in the structure code itself.
        Me._FirstName = firstName
        Me._LastName = lastName
    End Sub

End Structure

Public Class PersonClass

    Private _FirstName As String
    Private _LastName As String

    Public Property FirstName() As String
        Get
            Return _FirstName
        End Get
        Set(ByVal Value As String)
            _FirstName = Value
        End Set
    End Property

    Public Property LastName() As String
        Get
            Return _LastName
        End Get
        Set(ByVal Value As String)
            _LastName = Value
        End Set
    End Property
```

```
Public Sub New(ByVal firstName As String, ByVal lastName As String)
    Me.FirstName = firstName
    Me.LastName = lastName
End Sub

End Class
```

The following code tests the difference between a value type and reference type operation.

```
Dim StructureA As New PersonStructure("John", "Davenport")
Dim StructureB As New PersonStructure("John", "Davenport")

Dim ClassA As New PersonClass("John", "Davenport")
Dim ClassB As New PersonClass("John", "Davenport")

If StructureA.Equals(StructureB) Then
    ' This always happens.
    Console.WriteLine("Structures contain the same content.")
End If

If ClassA.Equals(ClassB) Then
    ' This never happens.
    Console.WriteLine("Classes point to the same instance.")
End If

Console.WriteLine("Assigning classes and structures...")
StructureA = StructureB
ClassA = ClassB

If CType(StructureA, Object) Is CType(StructureB, Object) Then
    ' This never happens.
    Console.WriteLine("Both variables point to the same structure.")
End If

If ClassA Is ClassB Then
    ' This always happens.
    Console.WriteLine("Both variables point to the same class.")
End If
```

It's important to understand how structures work if they contain objects. When you call *Equals* on a structure, the *Equals* method is called on every contained variable. If a structure contains a reference type, .NET will perform a reference comparison for that variable. Similarly, when you assign one structure to another, .NET will copy the contents of all contained value types, but only the reference of any contained reference types.

Structures don't support all the features of classes. For example, structures always include a default no-argument constructor. Structures also don't support inheritance. If you need to create a class that has value type behavior, you can override the *Equals* method, as shown here:

```
Public Overloads Overrides Function Equals(ByVal obj As Object) As Boolean
    If Not TypeOf obj Is PersonClass Then Return False

    Dim Compare As PersonClass = CType(obj, PersonClass)
    Return (Me.FirstName = Compare.FirstName And _
            Me.LastName = Compare.LastName)
End Function

Public Overloads Shared Function Equals(ByVal objA As Object, _
  ByVal objB As Object) As Boolean
    If Not (TypeOf objA Is PersonClass) Or _
        Not (TypeOf objB Is PersonClass) Then Return False

    Dim PersonA As PersonClass = CType(objA, PersonClass)
    Dim PersonB As PersonClass = CType(objB, PersonClass)
    Return (PersonA.FirstName = PersonB.FirstName And _
            PersonA.LastName = PersonB.LastName)
End Function
```

When creating a class that acts like a value type, you should also override the *GetHashCode* method so that identical objects return identical hash codes. By convention, .NET hash codes are always numeric and often use an *XOR* to combine multiple values, as shown in the following code:

```
Public Overloads Function GetHashCode() As Integer
    Return Me.FirstName.GetHashCode() Xor Me.LastName.GetHashCode()
End Function
```

Even after taking this step, you won't be able to easily copy the contents of a class—for that, you'll need to implement the *ICloneable* interface, as discussed in recipe 4.2.

> **Note** No matter what approach you take to create a value type (overriding the *Equals* method or using a structure), you won't be able to use your custom type in a comparison statement with the equal sign (=). This is because Visual Basic .NET does not support operator overloading, and there is thus no way for you to define the meaning of the equal sign. Instead, you must use the *Equals* method to test value type equality.

4.2 Create a Cloneable Object

Problem

You want to create a straightforward way for developers to create copies of an object you create.

Solution

Implement the *ICloneable* interface, and use the *MemberwiseClone* method.

Discussion

Many .NET objects provide a *Clone* method that allows the contents of an object to be duplicated in a new object. The correct way to use this pattern with your own objects is by implementing the *ICloneable* interface.

The *ICloneable* interface defines a single *Clone* method. This method can make use of a protected method that all classes inherit from the base *System.Object* type: *MemberwiseClone*. This method performs a shallow copy of all the data in the object. Here's a simple implementation with the *Person* class introduced in recipe 4.1.

```
Public Class Person
    Implements ICloneable

    Private _FirstName As String
    Private _LastName As String

    ' (Property procedure and constructor code omitted.)

    Public Function Clone() As Object Implements System.ICloneable.Clone
        Return Me.MemberwiseClone()
    End Function

End Class
```

Here's how you clone the *Person* object:

```
Dim OriginalPerson As New Person("Lisa", "Xi")
Dim ClonedPerson As Person = CType(OriginalPerson.Clone(), Person)
```

This approach works perfectly well if your object contains only value types. However, if your class contains a reference type, its contents won't be copied. Instead, only the object reference will be duplicated. For example, in the *MarriedCouple* class that follows, the *Clone* method simply creates a new

MarriedCouple that references the same *Person* objects (*PartnerA* and *PartnerB*).

```
Public Class MarriedCouple
    Implements ICloneable

    Private _PartnerA As Person
    Private _PartnerB As Person

    ' (Property procedure and constructor code omitted.)

    Public Function Clone() As Object Implements System.ICloneable.Clone
        Return Me.MemberwiseClone()
    End Function

End Class
```

The solution is to explicitly duplicate all reference types in your cloning code. If these types expose a *Clone* method, this step is easy:

```
Public Class MarriedCouple
    Implements ICloneable

    Private _PartnerA As Person
    Private _PartnerB As Person

    ' (Property procedure and constructor code omitted.)

    Public Function Clone() As Object Implements System.ICloneable.Clone
        Dim NewCouple As MarriedCouple
        NewCouple = CType(Me.MemberwiseClone(), MarriedCouple)
        NewCouple.PartnerA = CType(NewCouple.PartnerA.Clone(), Person)
        NewCouple.PartnerB = CType(NewCouple.PartnerB.Clone(), Person)
        Return NewCouple
    End Function

End Class
```

Here's the code you'll need to test the deep cloning approach with the *MarriedCouple* object:

```
Dim PersonA As New Person("Lisa", "Xi")
Dim PersonB As New Person("Andrew", "Sempf")
Dim Couple As New MarriedCouple(PersonA, PersonB)

Dim ClonedCouple As MarriedCouple = CType(Couple.Clone(), MarriedCouple)

If Couple Is ClonedCouple Then
    ' This never happens.
```

```
        Console.WriteLine("The references are the same. The cloning failed.")
    Else
        Console.WriteLine("There are two distinct MarriedCouple objects.")
    End If

    If (Couple.PartnerA Is ClonedCouple.PartnerA) Or _
      (Couple.PartnerB Is ClonedCouple.PartnerB) Then
        ' This never happens.
        Console.WriteLine("A shallow clone was performed. " & _
          Part of the data is shared.")
    Else
        Console.WriteLine("Each MarriedCouple has a distinct pair " & _
          "of Person objects.")
    End If
```

4.3 Create a Type-Safe *Clone* Method

Problem

You want to create a *Clone* method that returns an object of the correct type. However, the *ICloneable.Clone* method always returns a generic object.

Solution

Make the method that implements *ICloneable.Clone* private, and add another, strongly typed *Clone* method.

Discussion

The *ICloneable* interface always returns a generic *System.Object* reference, which means that the client must use casting code to convert the object to the appropriate type. However, you can remove this extra step by adding a strongly typed *Clone* method, as shown here.

```
Public Class Person
    Implements ICloneable

    Private _FirstName As String
    Private _LastName As String

    ' (Property procedure and constructor code omitted.)

    Private Function CloneMe() As Object Implements System.ICloneable.Clone
        Return Me.MemberwiseClone()
    End Function
```

```
Public Function Clone() As Person
    Return CType(Me.CloneMe(), Person)
End Function
```

```
End Class
```

Now, if the client clones the object using the *ICloneable* interface, the *Person.CloneMe* method will be used and a weakly typed object will be returned. However, if the client uses the method named *Clone* from the *Person* class, a strongly typed *Person* object will be returned.

4.4 Create a Comparable Object

Problem

You need to provide a mechanism that allows two custom objects to be compared.

Solution

Determine what data you want to use for the basis of your comparison, and implement the *IComparable* interface.

Discussion

The *IComparable* interface defines a single *CompareTo* method that accepts an object for comparison and returns an integer. The integer can take one of the following three values:

■   Zero, which means the objects are equal.

■   Less than zero (typically - 1), which means that the current object is less than the object that was supplied as a parameter.

■   Greater than zero (typically 1), which means that the current object is greater than the object that was supplied as a parameter.

You can evaluate the object contents on your own and decide which value to return. However, you can often use the *CompareTo* method of one of the contained data types to make the comparison. For example, in the code that follows, the *Person* object performs an alphabetical comparison (based on the last name, then the first name) on two *Person* instances using the *String.CompareTo* implementation.

```
Public Class Person
    Implements IComparable

    Private _FirstName As String
    Private _LastName As String

    ' (Property procedure and constructor code omitted.)

    Public Function CompareTo(ByVal obj As Object) As Integer _
      Implements System.IComparable.CompareTo

        If Not TypeOf obj Is Person Then
            Throw New ArgumentException("Object is not a Person")
        End If

        Dim Compare As Person = CType(obj, Person)

        ' Compare last names
        Dim result As Integer = Me.LastName.CompareTo(Compare.LastName)

        ' If last names are equal, compare first names
        If result = 0 Then
            result = Me.FirstName.CompareTo(Compare.FirstName)
        End If

        Return result
    End Function

End Class
```

Here's a simple test of a comparable object:

```
Dim PersonA As New Person("Andrew", "Sempf")
Dim PersonB As New Person("Andrew", "Sempf")

If PersonA Is PersonB Then
    ' This never happens.
    Console.WriteLine("These Person objects point to the same data " & _
      "in memory.")
End If

If PersonA.CompareTo(PersonB) = 0 Then
    ' This always happens.
    Console.WriteLine("These Person objects represent the same person.")
End If
```

Once you implement *CompareTo*, you can sort arrays or *ArrayList* objects that contain your object, as described in recipe 3.8. If you need to create an object that can be sorted in several different ways, you will need to create separate *IComparer* instances, as described in recipe 3.9.

> **Note**   Implementing *IComparable* does not give you the ability to use the greater than (>) and less than (<) operators to compare your objects because Visual Basic .NET does not support operator overloading. Instead, you must call *CompareTo* explicitly.

4.5 Create a Disposable Object

Problem

You need to create an object that frees unmanaged resources deterministically.

Solution

Implement the *IDisposable* pattern. Clients will call the *Dispose* method to release the object's resources.

Discussion

The *IDisposable* interface defines a single method, called *Dispose*. In this method, the class will release all its unmanaged resources. For best performance, when implementing *IDisposable* you should follow these best practices:

- Suppress garbage collector finalization for the object, provided it has no managed resources to release.

- Implement a finalizer that calls your *Dispose* method when the object is garbage collected. That way, if your object is released without *Dispose* being called (a common error), the resources will still be freed eventually.

- Call *Dispose* on any contained objects, provided the *Dispose* method is triggered directly and not called by the garbage collector (in which case a contained object could still be in use).

Be aware that it's of no use to implement *Dispose* with managed resources, because even if you set the variables to *Nothing*, the garbage collector still needs to run to reclaim the memory.

Here's how you would apply the disposable pattern in a custom class:

```
Public Class MyDisposableClass
    Implements IDisposable

    ' Implement IDisposable.
    ' This is the method the client calls to dispose the object.
    Public Overloads Sub Dispose() Implements System.IDisposable.Dispose
        Dispose(True)
        GC.SuppressFinalize(Me)
    End Sub

    ' This method is only called if the object is garbage
    ' collected without being properly disposed.
    Protected Overrides Sub Finalize()
        Dispose(False)
    End Sub

    ' The custom code for releasing resources goes here.
    Protected Overridable Overloads Sub Dispose(ByVal disposing As Boolean)
        If disposing Then
            ' Disposal was triggered manually by the client.
            ' Call Dispose() on any contained classes.
        End If

        ' Release unmanaged resources.
        ' Set large member variables to Nothing (null).
    End Sub

End Class
```

Notice that there's no way to force a client to call *Dispose*. Using a finalizer instead of a *Dispose* method won't help because the unmanaged resources won't be released until the garbage collector is activated or the application ends. On a system where memory is plentiful, this can take a long time!

You can also implement *IDisposable* indirectly by implementing *System.ComponentModel.IComponent*, which extends *IDisposable*, or inheriting from *System.ComponentModel.Component*, as described in recipe 4.6.

> **Note** To see a disposable object in action, run the sample code for this recipe. It uses a disposable object that displays Console messages to indicate its state. You'll be able to contrast a properly disposed object (which releases its resources immediately) with one that is just abandoned by setting the object reference to *Nothing* (which typically won't release its resources until the application ends).

4.6 Create an Object That Can Appear in the Component Tray

Problem

You want to create a class that has basic design-time support and can be added to a form's component at design-time.

Solution

Derive your class from *System.ComponentModel.Component*.

Discussion

The .NET class library includes many classes that can be added to a form, Web page, or another type of component at design time. For example, as shown in Figure 4-1, you can add the *System.Windows.Forms.Timer* object class directly to the component tray of a form, even though it has no visual representation. This allows the programmer to configure properties and connect event handlers at design time.

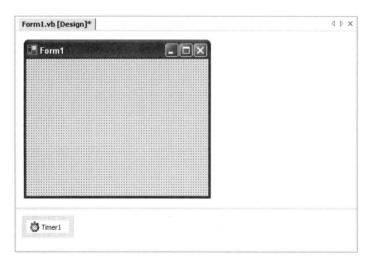

Figure 4-1   A component object in the component tray.

To create a class that supports design-time creation, you must implement the *IComponent* interface. You can do this directly, or indirectly by deriving from *System.ComponentModel.Component* or *System.ComponentModel.MarshalByValueComponent*. The former is used for classes that may be *remoted* (accessed from another application domain through a proxy), whereas the latter is for objects that may be copied into new application domains. Typically, classes that provide a service derive from *Component*, while classes that primarily contain data (such as the *DataSet*) derive from *MarshalByValueComponent*.

Once you derive from the component class, you need to add a small amount of boilerplate code to support the disposable pattern because the *IComponent* interface extends the *IDisposable* interface. For more information about the *IDisposable* interface, see recipe 4.5.

Here's a bare-bones example of a component class:

```
Public Class MyComponent
    Inherits System.ComponentModel.Component

    Protected Overloads Overrides Sub Dispose(disposing As Boolean)
        If disposing Then
            ' Disposal was triggered manually by the client.
            ' Call Dispose() on any contained classes.
        End If

        ' Release unmanaged resources.
        ' Set large member variables to Nothing (null).

        ' Call Dispose on the base class.
        MyBase.Dispose(disposing)
    End Sub

End Class
```

You should create component classes in a dedicated class library assembly. Once you have compiled the assembly, you can add the component classes to the Toolbox. Simply right-click the Toolbox, choose Add/Remove Items, and select the appropriate assembly. All component classes in the assembly will appear in the Toolbox and can now be dragged and dropped into the component tray (at which point a reference will be added to the assembly in your project). Figure 4-2 shows an example that includes two new components from an assembly.

> **Note** The *System.ComponentModel* namespace includes many attributes you can use to decorate the properties of a component class and influence how they will appear in the Properties window. For example, you can use *DescriptionAttribute* to add a text description that will appear in the window, *DefaultValueAttribute* to specify the initial value, *DefaultPropertyAttribute* to configure which property will be initially selected when the control receives focus at design-time, and so on.

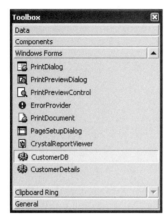

Figure 4-2   Component objects in the Toolbox.

4.7 Create a Convertible Object

Problem

You want to create a class that can be converted to common data types such as *Int32* and *String*.

Solution

Implement the *IConvertible* interface. Add conversion code for the supported data types, and throw an *InvalidCastException* for all unsupported data types.

Discussion

The *IConvertible* interface defines 17 methods for converting an object into basic .NET types. The first method, *GetTypeCode*, simply returns a value from the *System.TypeCode* enumeration identifying the type, which will always be *TypeCode.Object* for your custom classes, as shown here:

```
Public Function GetTypeCode() As TypeCode _
  Implements IConvertible.GetTypeCode
    Return TypeCode.Object
End Function
```

The other 16 methods perform the actual conversions and begin with the word *To*, as in *ToBoolean*, *ToByte*, *ToString*, and so on. If a method doesn't apply to your object, simply throw an *InvalidCastException* in the method.

Here's a partial example with a complex number class:

```vb
Public Class ComplexNumber
    Implements IConvertible

    Private _Real As Double
    Private _Imaginary As Double

    Public Property Real() As Double
        Get
            Return _Real
        End Get
        Set(ByVal Value As Double)
            _Real = Value
        End Set
    End Property

    Public Property Imaginary() As Double
        Get
            Return _Imaginary
        End Get
        Set(ByVal Value As Double)
            _Imaginary = Value
        End Set
    End Property

    Public Function GetModulus() As Double
        Return Math.Sqrt(Me.Real ^ 2 + Me.Imaginary ^ 2)
    End Function

    Public Function ToBoolean(ByVal provider As System.IFormatProvider) _
      As Boolean Implements System.IConvertible.ToBoolean
        Throw New InvalidCastException
    End Function

    Public Function ToDateTime(ByVal provider As System.IFormatProvider) _
      As Date Implements System.IConvertible.ToDateTime
        Throw New InvalidCastException
    End Function

    Public Function ToDecimal(ByVal provider As System.IFormatProvider) _
      As Decimal Implements System.IConvertible.ToDecimal
        Return CType(GetModulus(), Decimal)
    End Function

    Public Function ToDouble(ByVal provider As System.IFormatProvider) _
      As Double Implements System.IConvertible.ToDouble
```

```
        Return GetModulus()
    End Function

    ' (Other conversion methods omitted.)

End Class
```

To perform a conversion, a client can call a conversion method directly or use the *System.Convert* class, which works with any *IConvertible* object.

```
Dim MyDouble As Double = Convert.ToDouble(MyComplexNumber)
```

In addition, *IConvertible* allows your object to work with some batch conversions. For example, you can use the *ArrayList.ToArray* method to create a strongly typed array if your *ArrayList* contains the same type of object, and this type of object implements *IConvertible*. Recipe 3.7 demonstrates this technique.

4.8 Create a Serializable Object

Problem

You need to create an object that can be serialized (converted to a stream of bytes).

Solution

Add the *Serializable* attribute to your class.

Discussion

Serializable objects can be converted into a stream of bytes and recreated at a later point in time. You can use serialization to save an object to disk (as explained in recipe 4.9) or to send an object between application domains with .NET Remoting (in which case, the .NET runtime manages the serialization and deserialization transparently).

In order for serialization to work, your object must meet all the following criteria:

- The object must have a *Serializable* attribute preceding the class declaration.

- All the public and private variables of the class must be serializable.

- If the class derives from another class, all parent classes must also be serializable.

Here's a serializable *Person* class:

```
<Serializable()> _
Public Class Person

    Private _FirstName As String
    Private _LastName As String

    Public Property FirstName() As String
        Get
            Return _FirstName
        End Get
        Set(ByVal Value As String)
            _FirstName = Value
        End Set
    End Property

    Public Property LastName() As String
        Get
            Return _LastName
        End Get
        Set(ByVal Value As String)
            _LastName = Value
        End Set
    End Property

    ' (Constructor code omitted.)

End Class
```

In addition, a class might contain data that shouldn't be serialized; perhaps because it's large and can easily be recreated, it won't have the same meaning when the object is deserialized (like an unmanaged file handle), or it could compromise security. In these cases, you can add a *NonSerialized* attribute before the appropriate variables, as in the following code:

```
<Serializable()> _
Public Class Person

    Private _FirstName As String
    Private _LastName As String
    <NonSerialized()> Private _Password As String

    ' (Property procedure and constructor code omitted.)

End Class
```

4.9 Serialize an Object to Disk

Problem

You need to persist a serializable object to a file and recreate it later.

Solution

Use .NET serialization with the help of *BinaryFormatter* or *SoapFormatter*.

Discussion

All serializable objects can be converted into a stream of bytes, and vice versa. To serialize an object manually, you need to use a class that supports *IFormatter*. The .NET Framework includes two: *BinaryFormatter*, which serializes an object to a compact binary representation, and *SoapFormatter*, which uses the SOAP XML format, and results in a longer text-based message. The *BinaryFormatter* class is found in the *System.Runtime.Serialization.Formatters.Binary* namespace, while *SoapFormatter* is found in the *System.Runtime.Serialization.Formatters.Soap* namespace. In order to use *SoapFormatter*, you must add a reference to the assembly *System.Runtime.Serialization.Formatters.Soap*. Both methods serialize all the private and public data in a class, along with the assembly and type information needed to ensure the object can be deserialized exactly.

The following example shows a Console application that serializes an object to a binary file, displays the information the file contains, and then restores it. In this case, we use *SoapFormatter* in conjunction with the serializable *Person* class shown in recipe 4.8. In order to use the code as written, you must import the *System.IO* namespace and the *System.Runtime.Serialization.Formatters.Soap* namespace.

```
Public Module SerializationTest

    Public Sub Main()
        Dim Person As New Person("John", "Davenport")

        ' Construct a formatter.
        Dim Formatter As New SoapFormatter

        ' Serialize the object to a file.
        Dim fs As New FileStream("person.dat", FileMode.Create)
        Formatter.Serialize(fs, Person)
        fs.Close()
```

```
        ' Open the file and display its contents.
        fs = New FileStream("person.dat", FileMode.Open)
        Dim r As New StreamReader(fs)
        Console.WriteLine(r.ReadToEnd())

        ' Deserialize the object.
        fs.Position = 0
        Person = CType(Formatter.Deserialize(fs), Person)
        Console.WriteLine(Person.FirstName & " " & Person.LastName)

        Console.ReadLine()
    End Sub

End Module
```

Here is the output for this program, which shows the serialized data and assembly information:

```
<SOAP-ENV:Envelope xmlns:xsi="http://www.w3.org/2001/XMLSchema-instance"
 xmlns:xsd="http://www.w3.org/2001/XMLSchema"
 xmlns:SOAP-ENC="http://schemas.xmlsoap.org/soap/encoding/"
 xmlns:SOAP-ENV="http://schemas.xmlsoap.org/soap/envelope/"
 xmlns:clr="http://schemas.microsoft.com/soap/encoding/clr/1.0"
 SOAP-ENV:encodingStyle="http://schemas.xmlsoap.org/soap/encoding/">
<SOAP-ENV:Body>
  <a1:Person id="ref-1"
   xmlns:a1="http://schemas.microsoft.com/clr/ConsoleApplication1%2C%20
   Version%3D1.0.1052.2014%2C%20Culture%3Dneutral%2C%20PublicKeyToken%3Dnull">
    <_FirstName id="ref-3">John</_FirstName>
    <_LastName id="ref-4">Davenport</_LastName>
  </a1:Person>
</SOAP-ENV:Body>
</SOAP-ENV:Envelope>


John Davenport
```

Note that the serialization process works on all the private member variables. Thus, the XML uses the names _FirstName and LastName for its elements, not the property names *FirstName* and *LastName*.

The serialization process serializes every referenced object and fails if it finds any unserializable type (unless it is preceded by the *NonSerialized* attribute). This means that if your object references other objects, which reference yet more objects, all these objects will be serialized into the same stream, which will have implications for the size of the file.

Both *BinaryFormatter* and *SoapFormatter* also implement *IRemotingFormatter*, which means they can be used to serialize objects that are being transmitted to another application domain. This process takes place transparently when you use .NET Remoting.

> **Note**   Not all objects are serializable. You will know if an object is serializable by examining its class declaration, which is shown in the MSDN reference. If the class declaration is preceded by the *Serializable* attribute, the class can be serialized. If an object isn't serializable, you will need to use another technique to store the information, such as manually retrieving values and storing them, or using the *XmlSerializer* class, as described in recipe 4.11.

4.10 Clone a Serializable Object

Problem

You want to create an exact copy of a serializable object. This is useful if the object doesn't expose a dedicate *Clone* method.

Solution

Serialize the object to a memory stream, and then deserialize the memory stream.

Discussion

Serialization provides a quick and convenient way to clone an object, provided it's serializable. You can use any formatter to perform this magic, but *Binary-Formatter* makes the most sense (because it requires the least amount of memory). You use the *MemoryStream* class as an intermediary.

The following example clones the serializable *Person* object from recipe 4.8. In order to use it as written, you'll need to import the *System.Runtime.Serialization.Formatters.Binary* namespace.

```
Public Module CloningWithSerialization

    Public Sub Main()
        Dim OriginalPerson As New Person("John", "Davenport")

        ' Construct a formatter.
        Dim Formatter As New BinaryFormatter

        ' Serialize the object to memory.
        Dim ms As New System.IO.MemoryStream()
        Formatter.Serialize(ms, OriginalPerson)
```

```
                ' Deserialize the object.
                ms.Position = 0
                Dim ClonedPerson As Person = CType(Formatter.Deserialize(ms), Person)

                Console.ReadLine()
            End Sub

End Module
```

Formatters serialize an entire object graph. Thus, if you serialize an object that references another object, when you deserialize the memory stream you will actually create two new objects. This means that the serialization approach to cloning always creates a deep copy. For that reason, it's sometimes useful to use this type of logic in your own objects when implementing *ICloneable*. For example, the following code rewrites the cloneable *MarriedCouple* class from recipe 4.2 with a version that uses serialization instead of the protected *MemberwiseClone* method. Remember that in order for this to work, both *MarriedCouple* and *Person* must be serializable.

```
<Serializable()> _
Public Class MarriedCouple
    Implements ICloneable

    Private _PartnerA As Person
    Private _PartnerB As Person

    ' (Property procedure and constructor code omitted.)

    Public Function Clone() As Object Implements System.ICloneable.Clone
        Dim Formatter As New BinaryFormatter

        ' Serialize the object to memory.
        Dim ms As New System.IO.MemoryStream()
        Formatter.Serialize(ms, Me)

        ' Deserialize the cloned object.
        ms.Position = 0
        Return Formatter.Deserialize(ms)
    End Function

End Class
```

4.11 Serialize Public Members of a Nonserializable Object

Problem

You want to serialize an object that isn't marked with the *Serializable* attribute.

Solution

Use the *System.Xml.Serialization.XmlSerializer* class, which provides a more limited form of serialization.

Discussion

The *XmlSerializer* class allows you to serialize an object that isn't explicitly marked as serializable. This is especially convenient if you need to store state for an object and you aren't able to modify the class code to make it serializable (perhaps because you don't have access to the source code).

The *XmlSerializer* class works much like the binary and SOAP formatters described in recipe 4.9, but with several limitations. First of all, it doesn't store any type information about the object, which could lead to unexpected errors if you try to deserialize information that was serialized by an earlier version of the same class. More important, *XmlSerializer* can only store information from public fields and property procedures. Any private variables will be reset to their default values when the object is recreated.

The *XmlSerializer* class also has two other requirements due to the way that it works:

- The class you want to serialize must include a default zero-argument constructor. The *XmlSerializer* class uses this constructor when creating the new object during deserialization.

- All class properties must be readable *and* writable. This is because *XmlSerializer* uses property get procedures to retrieve information and property set procedures to restore the data after deserialization. As a result, you won't be able to deserialize an object successfully if properties must be set in a specific order because you have no control over the order *XmlSerializer* uses.

Finally, *XmlSerializer* always serializes data to XML, which means a serialized object will never be as small as it would be with *BinaryFormatter*.

Following is a code sample that duplicates a nonserializable *Person* object using *XmlSerializer*. In order to use this example as written, you'll need to import the *Sysetm.IO* namespace. Remember, when you create *XmlSerializer* you must supply a *Type* object that indicates the class you want to serialize or deserialize. This is because no type information is stored in the serialization format itself.

```
Public Module SerializationTest

    Public Sub Main()
        Dim Person As New Person("John", "Davenport")
```

```
' Construct the serializer.
Dim Serializer As New _
    System.Xml.Serialization.XmlSerializer(GetType(Person))

' Serialize the object to a file.
Dim fs As New FileStream("person.dat", FileMode.Create)
Serializer.Serialize(fs, Person)
fs.Close()

' Open the file and display its contents.
fs = New FileStream("person.dat", FileMode.Open)
Dim r As New StreamReader(fs)
Console.WriteLine(r.ReadToEnd())

' Deserialize the object.
fs.Position = 0
Person = CType(Serializer.Deserialize(fs), Person)
Console.WriteLine(Person.FirstName & " " & Person.LastName)

Console.ReadLine()
    End Sub

End Module
```

The output for this test shows the serialization data:

```
<?xml version="1.0"?>
<Person xmlns:xsd="http://www.w3.org/2001/XMLSchema"
 xmlns:xsi="http://www.w3.org/2001/XMLSchema-instance">
  <FirstName>John</FirstName>
  <LastName>Davenport</LastName>
</Person>

John Davenport
```

> **Note**   The *XmlSerializer* class is used transparently to transmit data to and from a Web service. The *System.Xml.Serialization* namespace also includes attributes you can use to configure the serialization of a class. For example, you can apply attributes to configure the name used for the element in an XML file (*XmlElementAttribute*) or to instruct the serializer to ignore a property or public variable (*XmlIgnoreAttribute*).

4.12 Perform Selective Serialization with the Memento Pattern

Problem

You want to serialize only part of an object or an object that inherits from another nonserializable object.

Solution

Create a dedicated, serializable object to hold the information that must be persisted.

Discussion

The memento pattern allows you to handle object serialization in a more flexible manner. Some of the reasons you might use the memento pattern include the following:

- You want to serialize an object that wouldn't otherwise be serializable (perhaps because it derives from a nonserializable object).

- You want to serialize a portion of an object. The *NonSerialized* attribute can also help in this case, but you can't use it to prevent the serialization of the information in a class that your code derives from.

- You want to allow an object to be serialized in different ways. For example, sometimes you might want to only persist a subset of the total available data, while other times you might need to serialize more information.

With the memento pattern, the basic technique is to create a dedicated serializable object that holds the data you want to persist. This object is called a *memento*.

For example, consider the custom *ColoredMenuItem* class shown in the following code, which stores information about the text and colors of a custom menu entry. It inherits from *MenuItem* and adds two properties. For a full description of the *ColoredMenuItem* and how you can create custom menus, refer to recipe 12.20.

```
Public Class ColoredMenuItem
    Inherits MenuItem

    Private _ForeColor As Color
    Private _BackColor As Color

    Public Property ForeColor() As Color
        Get
            Return _ForeColor
        End Get
        Set(ByVal Value As Color)
            _ForeColor = Value
        End Set
    End Property

    Public Property BackColor() As Color
        Get
            Return _BackColor
        End Get
        Set(ByVal Value As Color)
            _BackColor = Value
        End Set
    End Property

    ' (Painting code omitted.)

End Class
```

You can't serialize the *ColoredMenuItem* class even if you apply the *Serializable* attribute because the base *MenuItem* class isn't serializable. Thus, the best approach is to create a memento that holds the data you want to persist:

```
<Serializable()> _
Public MustInherit Class Memento
End Class

<Serializable()> _
Public Class ColoredMenuItemMemento
    Inherits Memento

    Private _ForeColor As Color
    Private _BackColor As Color
    Private _Text As String

    Public Property ForeColor() As Color
        Get
            Return _ForeColor
        End Get
```

```
        Set(ByVal Value As Color)
            _ForeColor = Value
        End Set
    End Property

    Public Property BackColor() As Color
        Get
            Return _BackColor
        End Get
        Set(ByVal Value As Color)
            _BackColor = Value
        End Set
    End Property

    Public Property Text() As String
        Get
            Return _Text
        End Get
        Set(ByVal Value As String)
            _Text = Value
        End Set
    End Property

    Public Sub New(ByVal text As String, ByVal foreColor As Color, _
        ByVal backColor As Color)
        Me.Text = text
        Me.ForeColor = foreColor
        Me.BackColor = backColor
    End Sub

End Class
```

The next step is to add methods to the *ColoredMenuItem* that allow data to be transferred to and from the memento. In this case, it helps to define a generic interface:

```
Public Interface IMemento

    Function GetMemento() As Memento
    Sub SetMemento(memento As Memento)

End Interface
```

Now the *ColoredMenuItem* must implement the *IMemento* interface and add the following code:

```
Public Function GetMemento() As Memento Implements IMemento.GetMemento
    Return New ColoredMenuItemMemento(Text, ForeColor, BackColor)
End Function
```

```
Public Sub SetMemento(ByVal memento As Memento) Implements IMemento.SetMemento
    Dim ColoredMemento As ColoredMenuItemMemento
    ColoredMemento = CType(memento, ColoredMenuItemMemento)
    ForeColor = ColoredMemento.ForeColor
    BackColor = ColoredMemento.BackColor
    Text = ColoredMemento.Text
End Sub
```

In addition, you can add a constructor that creates a new *ColoredMenu-Item* based on the information in the memento:

```
Public Sub New(ByVal memento As ColoredMenuItemMemento)
    Me.New(memento.Text, memento.ForeColor, memento.BackColor)
End Sub
```

The sample code for this recipe provides a simple Windows test application. It creates a menu with several *ColoredMenuItem* instances (see Figure 4-3) and allows you to serialize this collection to a file and then restore it. The serialization code shows another trick: serializing multiple objects into a single stream.

Figure 4-3　Testing memento serialization

Below is the code that reads the menu and serializes all the contained items. It then clears the menu.

```
Private Sub cmdSerialize_Click(ByVal sender As System.Object, _
    ByVal e As System.EventArgs) Handles cmdSerialize.Click

    ' Construct a formatter.
    Dim Formatter As New BinaryFormatter()
```

```vbnet
    ' Serialize the menu mementos to a file.
    Dim fs As New FileStream("MyMenuItem.dat", FileMode.Create)

    ' Start by writing the number of objects that will be serialized.
    fs.WriteByte(CType(mnuColors.MenuItems.Count, Byte))

    ' Serialize all the menu items to the same file.
    Dim Item As ColoredMenuItem
    For Each Item In mnuColors.MenuItems
        Dim Memento As ColoredMenuItemMemento
        Memento = CType(Item.GetMemento(), ColoredMenuItemMemento)
        Formatter.Serialize(fs, Memento)
    Next
    fs.Close()

    ' Clear the menu.
    mnuColors.MenuItems.Clear()

End Sub
```

And here's the code that reads the file and restores the menu items:

```vbnet
Private Sub cmdDeserialize_Click(ByVal sender As System.Object, _
  ByVal e As System.EventArgs) Handles cmdDeserialize.Click

    mnuColors.MenuItems.Clear()

    ' Construct a formatter.
    Dim Formatter As New BinaryFormatter()

    ' Read the number of menu items in the file.
    Dim fs As New FileStream("MyMenuItem.dat", FileMode.Open)
    Dim ItemCount As Integer = fs.ReadByte()

    ' Deserialize each memento and apply it.
    Dim i As Integer
    For i = 1 To ItemCount
        Dim Memento As ColoredMenuItemMemento
        Memento = CType(Formatter.Deserialize(fs), ColoredMenuItemMemento)
        mnuColors.MenuItems.Add(New ColoredMenuItem(Memento))
    Next
    fs.Close()

End Sub
```

4.13 Throw a Custom Exception

Problem

You need to indicate an application-specific error condition to the caller of your code.

Solution

Derive a custom exception object from the *System.ApplicationException* class, and add the recommended constructors. Use the *Throw* statement to throw the exception.

Discussion

.NET Framework guidelines suggest that you always use exception objects to indicate error conditions (not return values or another mechanism). If you need to indicate a generic error condition, use one of the existing framework exceptions (such as *InvalidCastException*, *SecurityException*, *DivideByZeroException*, or *ArgumentException*) with a custom description. If, however, you need to indicate an application-specific error, you should create a custom exception object. This custom exception object should derive from *ApplicationException*, not the base *Exception* class, and end with the word *Exception*.

Every exception should have the three basic constructors shown here:

```
Public Sub New()
    ' (Creates an uninitialized exception.)
    MyBase.New()
End Sub

Public Sub New(ByVal message As String)
    ' Creates an exception with a text message.
    MyBase.New(message)
End Sub

Public Sub New(ByVal message As String, ByVal inner As Exception)
    ' Creates an exception with a text message and a nested (inner)
    ' exception object.
    MyBase.New(message, inner)
End Sub
```

Notice that these constructors simply call the base class implementation, which performs the work.

In addition, you need to add a deserialization constructor to the *Exception* object if you want to make it serializable, along with the *Serializable* attribute.

The *Serializable* attribute is not enough on its own because the base *Exception* class implements *ISerializable* to perform custom serialization. If your exception does not include any data, this constructor can simply call the base class implementation:

```
Public Sub New(ByVal info As SerializationInfo, _
  ByVal context As StreamingContext)
    MyBase.New(info, context)
End Sub
```

Life becomes slightly more complicated if your exception adds its own properties. In this case, you must implement additional constructors to accept information for these properties. You must also implement *GetObjectData* to store the new information on serialization and configure the deserialization constructor so that it reads the new information. As an example, consider the custom exception shown here.

```
<Serializable()> _
Public Class CustomException
    Inherits ApplicationException

    ' The custom data.
    Private _CustomValue As Integer

    Public ReadOnly Property CustomValue() As Integer
        Get
            Return _CustomValue
        End Get
    End Property

    Public Sub New()
        MyBase.New()
    End Sub

    Public Sub New(ByVal message As String)
        MyBase.New(message)
    End Sub

    Public Sub New(ByVal message As String, ByVal inner As Exception)
        MyBase.New(message, inner)
    End Sub

    ' This constructor takes the added value.
    Public Sub New(ByVal message As String, ByVal value As Integer)
        MyBase.New(message)
        Me._CustomValue = value
    End Sub
```

```
' Store data during serialization.
Public Overrides Sub GetObjectData(ByVal info As SerializationInfo, _
  ByVal context As StreamingContext)
    MyBase.GetObjectData(info, context)
    info.AddValue("Value", Me._CustomValue)
End Sub

' Retrieve data during deserialization.
Public Sub New(ByVal info As SerializationInfo, _
  ByVal context As StreamingContext)
    MyBase.New(info, context)
    Me._CustomValue = info.GetInt32("Value")
End Sub
```

```
End Class
```

You can also override the *Message* property to give a better textual representation of your exception by incorporating the custom data with the message.

As with any other type of exception, you can throw the custom exception using the *Throw* keyword:

```
Throw New CustomException("Error", 100)
```

4.14 Raise a Custom Event

Problem

You need to send data with a custom event.

Solution

Derive a custom event argument object from the *System.EventArgs* class, add the information you need, and declare the event. Use *RaiseEvent* to fire the event.

Discussion

.NET events follow a common syntax. The first argument is the sender of the event (as a weakly typed *System.Object* instance). The second argument is an object derived from *System.EventArgs* that contains any additional information. The custom *EventArgs* class should always be named in the form *EventName-EventArgs*.

Here's an event declaration that follows these conventions and can be added to the declaration of any class:

```
Public Event TaskCompleted(sender As Object, e As TaskCompletedEventArgs)
```

The custom *EventArgs* object simply needs to add informational properties and constructors as needed. You should also make it serializable if there's a possibility that the event might need to cross application domain boundaries. For example, if your custom object is a remotable class, all its events should use serializable event arguments.

```
Public Class TaskCompletedEventArgs
    Inherits EventArgs

    ' The custom data.
    Private _CustomValue As Integer

    Public ReadOnly Property CustomValue() As Integer
        Get
            Return _CustomValue
        End Get
    End Property

    Public Sub New(customValue As Integer)
        MyBase.New()
        Me._CustomValue = customValue
    End Sub

End Class
```

You raise events using the *RaiseEvent* statement, indicating the name of the event and passing the defined event arguments:

```
RaiseEvent TaskComplete(Me, New TaskCompletedEventArgs(100))
```

It's recommended that you use a dedicated protected method (named *OnEventName*) that raises the event, particularly if your class is inheritable. This allows inheritors to override the event and provide extended functionality. In the following code, the *TaskProcess* class shows this pattern.

```
Public Class TaskProcess

    Public Event TaskCompleted(sender As Object, e As TaskCompletedEventArgs)

    Public Sub DoTask()
        ' (Task processing code goes here.)
        OnTaskComplete(New TaskCompletedEventArgs(100))
    End Sub

    Public Sub OnTaskComplete(e As TaskCompletedEventArgs)
        RaiseEvent TaskCompleted(Me, e)
    End Sub

End Class
```

4.15 Use the Singleton Pattern

Problem

You want to ensure that only one copy of a class can be instantiated at once and provide global access to this instance.

Solution

Add a private constructor to the class and a shared variable that holds the singleton instance.

Discussion

The syntax for creating a singleton in languages that target .NET is quite a bit simpler than in many other languages, due to the way the common language runtime operates. The basic pattern is to add a shared variable that returns an instance of the singleton class, as shown here:

```
Public Class MySingleton

    Private Sub New()
        ' A private constructor ensures this class can't be created directly,
        ' except by code in this class.
    End Sub

    ' This shared member is available even without an instance of the class.
    Public ReadOnly Shared Instance As New MySingleton()

    ' This is a sample instance member.
    Public Sub DoSomething()
    End Sub

End Class
```

The code accesses the global instance of the singleton through the *Instance* property, like this:

```
' Call the Singleton's DoSomething method.
MySingleton.Instance.DoSomething()
```

It's important to realize that .NET uses lazy loading to minimize memory consumption. That means that an instance of *MySingleton* isn't created when the application first starts. Instead, an instance is created the first time your code accesses the *Instance* variable (or any other shared member of the class). After this point, your code will always receive the same singleton instance from the *Instance* variable.

It's not necessary to use locking code with this example because the CLR automatically guarantees thread-safety for all shared members. That means there's no possibility for two instances of the singleton to be created if two threads try to access the *Instance* property at the same time. However, if you use any global instance data and your program uses multithreading, you will need to add locks to ensure that this data is updated properly, as described in Chapter 7.

> **Note**   The Microsoft Visual Studio .NET migration wizard uses a variant of the singleton pattern when migrating Visual Basic 6 forms. This ensures that a single instance of a form can be accessed globally, without needing to create it explicitly (which matches the behavior of Visual Basic 6 code).

4.16 Use the Factory Pattern

Problem

You want the ability to create classes generically, without knowing their specific types.

Solution

Create a dedicated factory class that can construct the type of class you need.

Discussion

The factory pattern is one of the best-known creational patterns. It provides an abstracted mechanism for creating classes.

In the factory pattern, as shown in Figure 4-4, every class has its own corresponding factory class. In order for the factory pattern to work, all of these classes must derive from two abstract base classes.

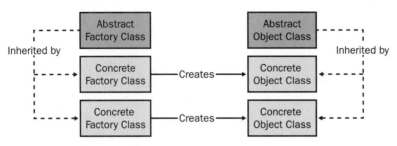

Figure 4-4 The abstract factory pattern

For example, imagine you want to create a generic component that queries a database. This component might need to use different classes to connect to the database, depending on the database type. However, you want to create this class without needing to know all the classes it might support in the future. In this case, the abstract factory pattern suits perfectly.

The first step is to define the base classes:

```
Public MustInherit Class DatabaseConnection
    Public MustOverride Function ExecuteQuery(ByVal SQL As String) _
      As DataSet
End Class

Public MustInherit Class DatabaseConnectionFactory
    Public MustOverride Function GetConnection( _
      ByVal connectionString As String) As DatabaseConnection
End Class
```

In this case, the abstract classes are as simple as possible. The *Database-Connection* class provides only one method, and *DatabaseConnectionFactory* only requires one piece of information (which it will pass to the *DatabaseConnection* constructor).

Next, you can define multiple sets of concrete classes for individual databases. Here is an example for an Oracle database:

```
Public Class OracleConnection
    Inherits DatabaseConnection

    Public Overrides Function ExecuteQuery(ByVal SQL As String) _
      As System.Data.DataSet
        ' (Code to perform an Oracle query goes here.)
    End Function

    Public Sub New(ByVal connectionString As String)
        ' (Initialize the connection here.)
    End Sub

End Class
```

```
Public Class OracleConnectionFactory
    Inherits DatabaseConnectionFactory

    Public Overrides Function GetConnection( _
      ByVal connectionString As String) As DatabaseConnection
        Return New OracleConnection(connectionString)
    End Function

End Class
```

It's now possible to create a generic object that can create a connection and perform a query, but only needs to use the abstract classes:

```
Public Class Query

    Public Function GetUserRecords( _
      ByVal factory As DatabaseConnectionFactory, _
      ByVal connectionString As String) As DataSet
        ' Use the appropriate concrete object to get the records.
        ' You could even perform multiple tasks here, like aggregating
        ' the results from several queries.
        Dim Con As DatabaseConnection
        Con = factory.GetConnection(connectionString)

        Dim SQL As String = "SELECT * FROM Users"
        Return Con.ExecuteQuery(SQL)
    End Function

End Class
```

Thus, you can add new concrete classes for different databases, and use them with the *GetUserRecords* method without needing to change any of the code in the *GetUserRecords* method itself.

These sample classes show the complete underpinnings of the abstract factory pattern. However, it's unlikely that you would use the abstract factory pattern in exactly the way shown because the .NET Framework already includes various database connection classes and a generic interface as a part of Microsoft ADO.NET. However, ADO.NET doesn't include a database connection factory. The downloadable code for this chapter shows a practical example of how you might combine ADO.NET and your own abstract factory class to help make database code more generic.

> **Note**   You can use a variation of the abstract factory pattern that uses interfaces instead of abstract classes. This is often called the *builder pattern*.

4.17 Use the Registry Pattern

Problem

You need a convenient way to track objects and retrieve them by name from multiple places in your code.

Solution

Use the registry pattern, which centralizes access to a set of objects through one registry object.

Discussion

A registry object acts as a repository for a collection of items that you need to identify and retrieve later. For example, you might use a registry to track all the currently loaded forms in a Microsoft Windows application. The .NET Framework does not provide any built-in method to offer this functionality.

First of all, you need to create your registry object. Clients register and unregister elements in the registry, giving them convenient names for later retrieval. The registry object shown here tracks form instances by name:

```
Public Class OpenFormsRegistry
    Private Shared Forms As New Hashtable

    Public Shared Sub RegisterForm(ByVal form As Form, _
      ByVal name As String)
        Forms(name) = form
    End Sub

    Public Shared Sub UnregisterForm(ByVal name As String)
        Forms.Remove(name)
    End Sub

    Public Shared Function GetForm(ByVal name As String) As Form
        Return CType(Forms(name), Form)
    End Function

    Public Shared Function GetForms() As ICollection
        Return Forms.Values
    End Function

End Class
```

Depending on your needs, you might want to add additional methods such as *GetAllForms*, which might be useful if you need to perform some sort of check across all windows in an application before exiting. In this example, the registry is a class that consists of shared members. Alternatively, you could use a module (which compiles to the same intermediate language (IL) code as a class with shared members), or a singleton as described in recipe 4.15.

The name you use to register form instances also depends on your application. For example, if you only allow one instance of a form to be loaded at once, you could use the class name of the form. Here's an example that uses this approach to register a form on startup:

```
Private Sub Form1_Load(ByVal sender As System.Object, _
   ByVal e As System.EventArgs) Handles MyBase.Load
      OpenFormsRegistry.RegisterForm(Me, Me.Name)
End Sub
```

4.18 Use the Lazy Initialization Pattern

Problem

You have an object that contains data that's expensive to create and might not be required.

Solution

Use the lazy initialization pattern to create or to retrieve the information "just in time."

Discussion

The lazy initialization pattern is often used with stateful objects that need to retrieve data from a database, but it can be applied to any object that's expensive to create. The basic approach is to use a Boolean private member variable *IsInitialized* to track whether the object data has been retrieved yet. Here's a basic skeleton that illustrates the concept by setting a string variable:

```
Public Class MyObject

    Private IsInitialized As Boolean = False
    Private _Data As String

    Public ReadOnly Property Data() As String
        Get
            If Not IsInitialized Then Initialize()
            Return _Data
        End Get
    End Property
```

```
Private Sub Initialize()
    ' Fetch data from data source.
    Me._Data = "Data Value"
    Me.IsInitialized = True
End Sub

End Class
```

> **Note** The Visual Studio .NET debugger can exhibit some unusual behavior with lazy initialization. If you display a lazy-initialized property in the debugger (using a watch window or the Command window, or even just moving the mouse over the property name to use IntelliSense), Visual Studio .NET will run the initialization code automatically. However, if the initialization code is triggered this way while in break mode, any breakpoints in the initialization code will be ignored.

A related model is the "IsDirty" pattern, which uses a Boolean *IsDirty* variable that tracks whether any changes have been made to the object. Then, when the object is asked to persist changes (perhaps by calling a dedicated *Save* method), it only performs the time consuming update if the *IsDirty* flag is *True*, meaning that at least one value has been changed.

```
Public Class MyObject

    Private _Data As String
    Private IsDirty As Boolean

    Public ReadOnly Property Data() As String
        Get
            Return _Data
        End Get
        Set(ByVal Value As String)
            IsDirty = True
            _Data = Value
        End Set
    End Property

    Public Sub Save()
        If IsDirty
            ' (Add code to persist change.)
        End If
    End Sub

End Class
```

5

Files and Directories

Previous versions of Microsoft Visual Basic have always been underweight when it came to file management. Most Visual Basic 6.0 programmers used legacy functions such as *Open* and *Input* that were built into the language and identified files using numbers. More adventurous developers could use the File Scripting Objects (FSO) model, which provided an object-oriented way to manipulate files, but lacked important features such as the ability to read and write binary files. In Microsoft .NET, the story is completely different—for the first time, Visual Basic developers have a rich set of objects that allow them to retrieve file system information, move and rename files and directories, create text and binary files, and even monitor a specific path for changes.

The first batch of recipes in this chapter describes the basics for manipulating files and directories. Later recipes include advanced techniques, such as 'ecting files with wildcards (recipe 5.6), performing recursive searches (reci-7 and 5.8), reading just-in-time file information (recipe 5.9), and using iso-es to allow file creation in low-security contexts (recipe 5.15). You'll he starting points for dealing with some more specialized formats, files (recipe 5.18) and ZIP files (recipe 5.19).

, the example applications require command-line argu-
are using Visual Studio .NET, you can enter these argu-
.ıe project properties (under the Configuration Properties |
,ıng node). Keep in mind that if you need to enter directory or
ames that incorporate spaces, you will need to place the full
.ne in quotation marks. Also, most of the code examples in this
chapter assume that you have imported the *System.IO* namespace.

5.1 Manipulate a File

Problem

You want to delete, rename, or check if a file exists. Or, you want to retrieve information about a file such as its attribute or creation date.

Solution

Create a *FileInfo* instance for the file, and use its properties and methods.

Discussion

To create a *FileInfo* object, you simply supply a relative or fully qualified path to the *FileInfo* constructor. This file doesn't necessarily need to exist. You can then use the *FileInfo* properties and methods to retrieve file information or manipulate the file.

Table 5-1 lists some useful *FileInfo* members that are also exposed, in more or less the same form, by the *DirectoryInfo* object described in recipe 5.2. Table 5-2 lists members that are exclusive to the *FileInfo* class.

Table 5-1 Common *FileInfo* and *DirectoryInfo* Members

Member	Description
Exists	*Exists* returns *True* or *False*, depending on whether a file or directory exists at the specified location. Some other *FileInfo* or *DirectoryInfo* properties might return an error if the file or directory doesn't exist.
Attributes	Returns one or more values from the *FileAttributes* enumeration, which represents the attributes of the file or directory.
CreationTime, *LastAccessTime*, and *LastWriteTime*	Return *DateTime* instances that describe when a file or directory was created, last accessed, and last updated, respectively.
FullName, *Name*, and *Extension*	Returns a string that represents the fully qualified name, the directory or file name (with extension), and the extension on its own.
Delete	Removes the file or directory, if it exists. If you want to delete a directory that contains other directories, you must use the overloaded *Delete* method that accepts a parameter named *recursive* and set it to *True*.

Table 5-1   Common *FileInfo* and *DirectoryInfo* Members

Member	Description
Refresh	Updates the object so that it's synchronized with any file system changes that have taken place since the *FileInfo* or *DirectoryInfo* object was created (for example, if an attribute was changed manually using Windows Explorer).
MoveTo	Copies the directory and its contents or copies the file. For a *DirectoryInfo* object, you need to specify the new path. For a *FileInfo* object you specify a path and filename. *MoveTo* can also be used to rename a file or directory without changing its location.

Table 5-2   *FileInfo* Members

Member	Description
Length	*Length* returns the file size as a number of bytes.
DirectoryName and *Directory*	*DirectoryName* returns the name of the parent directory, whereas *Directory* returns a full *DirectoryInfo* object (see recipe 5.2) that represents the parent directory and allows you to retrieve more information about it.
CopyTo	Copies a file to the new path and filename specified as a parameter. It also returns a new *FileInfo* object that represents the new (copied) file. You can supply an optional additional parameter of *True* to allow overwriting.
Create and *CreateText*	*Create* creates the specified file and returns a *FileStream* object that you can use to write to it. *CreateText* performs the same task, but returns a *StreamWriter* object that wraps the stream.
Open, OpenRead, OpenText, and *OpenWrite*	Open a file (provided it exists). *OpenRead* and *OpenText* open a file in read-only mode, returning a *FileStream* or *StreamReader*. *OpenWrite* opens a file in write-only mode, returning a *FileStream*.

The following Console application takes a filename from a supplied parameter argument and displays information about that file.

```
Public Module FileInformation

    Public Sub Main(ByVal args() As String)
        If args.Length = 0 Then
            Console.WriteLine("Please supply a filename.")
        Else
            Dim FileName As String = args(0)
            Dim CheckFile As New FileInfo(FileName)
```

```
            ' Display file information.
            Console.WriteLine("Checking file: " & CheckFile.Name)
            Console.WriteLine("In directory: " & CheckFile.DirectoryName)
            Console.WriteLine("File exists: " & CheckFile.Exists.ToString())
            If CheckFile.Exists Then
                Console.Write("File created: ")
                Console.WriteLine(CheckFile.CreationTime.ToString())
                Console.Write("File last updated: ")
                Console.WriteLine(CheckFile.LastWriteTime.ToString())
                Console.Write("File last accessed: ")
                Console.WriteLine(CheckFile.LastAccessTime.ToString())
                Console.Write("File size (bytes): ")
                Console.WriteLine(CheckFile.Length.ToString())
                Console.Write("File attribute list: ")
                Console.WriteLine(CheckFile.Attributes.ToString())

                ' Uncomment these lines to display the full file content.
                'Dim r As StreamReader = CheckFile.OpenText()
                'Console.WriteLine(r.ReadToEnd())
                'r.Close()

                Console.ReadLine()
            End If
        End If
    End Sub

End Module
```

Here is the output you might expect:

```
Checking file: ConsoleApplication1.exe
In directory: E:\Temp\ConsoleApplication1\bin
File exists: True
File created: 29/05/2002 1:53:28 PM
File last updated: 25/11/2002 9:10:29 AM
File last accessed: 25/11/2002 9:50:56 AM
File size (bytes): 7680
File attribute list: Archive
```

> **Note**   Most of the functionality provided by the *FileInfo* object can be accessed using shared methods of the *File* class. Generally, you should use *FileInfo* if you want to retrieve more than one piece of information at a time because it performs security checks once (when you create the *FileInfo* instance) rather than every time you call a method. The *File* object also lacks a *Length* property.

5.2 Manipulate a Directory

Problem

You want to delete, rename, or check if a directory exists. Or, you want to retrieve information about a directory such as its attributes or creation date.

Solution

Create a *DirectoryInfo* instance for the directory, and use its properties and methods.

Discussion

The *DirectoryInfo* object works almost the same as the *FileInfo* object. You can use the same properties for retrieving attributes, names, and file system timestamps. You can also use the same methods for moving, deleting, and renaming directories as you would with files. These members are described in Table 5-1. In addition, the *DirectoryInfo* object provides some directory-specific members, which are shown in Table 5-3.

Table 5-3   *DirectoryInfo* Members

Member	Description
Create	Creates the specified directory. If the path specifies multiple directories that don't exist, they will all be created at once.
Parent and *Root*	Returns a *DirectoryInfo* object that represents the parent or root directory.
CreateSubdirectory	Creates a directory with the specified name in the directory represented by the *DirectoryInfo* object. It also returns a new *DirectoryInfo* object that represents the subdirectory.
GetDirectories	Returns an array of *DirectoryInfo* objects, with one for each subdirectory contained in this directory.
GetFiles	Returns an array of *FileInfo* objects, with one for each file contained in this directory.

The following Console application takes a directory path from a supplied parameter argument and displays information about that directory.

```
Public Module DirectoryInformation

    Public Sub Main(ByVal args() As String)
```

```
        If args.Length = 0 Then
            Console.WriteLine("Please supply a directory name.")
        Else
            Dim DirectoryName As String = args(0)

            ' Display directory information.
            Dim CheckDir As New DirectoryInfo(DirectoryName)
            Console.WriteLine("Checking Directory: " & CheckDir.Name)
            Console.WriteLine("In directory: " & CheckDir.Parent.Name)
            Console.Write("Directory exists: ")
            Console.WriteLine(CheckDir.Exists.ToString())
            If CheckDir.Exists Then
                Console.Write("Directory created: ")
                Console.WriteLine(CheckDir.CreationTime.ToString())
                Console.Write("Directory last updated: ")
                Console.WriteLine(CheckDir.LastWriteTime.ToString())
                Console.Write("Directory last accessed: ")
                Console.WriteLine(CheckDir.LastAccessTime.ToString())
                Console.Write("Directory attribute list: ")
                Console.WriteLine(CheckDir.Attributes.ToString())

                Console.WriteLine("Directory contains: " & _
                    CheckDir.GetFiles.Length.ToString() & " files")
            End If
        End If

        Console.ReadLine()
    End Sub

End Module
```

Here is the output you might expect:

```
Checking directory: bin
In directory: ConsoleApplication1
Directory exists: True
Directory created: 2002-05-29 1:53:14 PM
Directory last updated: 2002-11-21 10:48:47 AM
Directory last accessed: 2002-11-25 9:55:06 AM
Directory attribute list: Directory
Directory contains: 13 files
```

5.3 Retrieve File Version Information

Problem

You want to retrieve file version information (such as the publisher of a file, its revision number, associated comments, and so on).

Solution

Use the *GetVersionInfo* method of the *System.Diagnostics.FileVersionInfo* class.

Discussion

In previous versions of Visual Basic, you needed to call Windows API functions to retrieve file version information. With the .NET Framework, you simply need to use the *FileVersionInfo* class and call the *GetVersionInfo* method with the filename as a parameter. You can then retrieve extensive information through the *FileVersionInfo* properties.

The *FileVersionInfo* properties are too numerous to list here, but the following code snippet shows an example of what you might retrieve:

```
Public Module FileVersionInformation

    Public Sub Main(ByVal args() As String)
        If args.Length = 0 Then
            Console.WriteLine("Please supply a filename.")
        Else
            Dim FileName As String = args(0)
            Dim Info As FileVersionInfo
            Info = FileVersionInfo.GetVersionInfo(FileName)

            ' Display version information.
            Console.WriteLine("Checking File: " & Info.FileName)
            Console.WriteLine("Product Name: " & Info.ProductName)
            Console.WriteLine("Product Version: " & Info.ProductVersion)
            Console.WriteLine("Company Name: " & Info.CompanyName)
            Console.WriteLine("File Version: " & Info.FileVersion)
            Console.WriteLine("File Description: " & Info.FileDescription)
            Console.WriteLine("Original Filename: " & Info.OriginalFilename)
            Console.WriteLine("Legal Copyright: " & Info.LegalCopyright)
            Console.WriteLine("InternalName: " & Info.InternalName)
            Console.WriteLine("IsDebug: " & Info.IsDebug)
            Console.WriteLine("IsPatched: " & Info.IsPatched)
            Console.WriteLine("IsPreRelease: " & Info.IsPreRelease)
            Console.WriteLine("IsPrivateBuild: " & Info.IsPrivateBuild)
            Console.WriteLine("IsSpecialBuild: " & Info.IsSpecialBuild)
        End If

        Console.ReadLine()
    End Sub

End Module
```

Here's the output this code produces with the sample file c:\windows\explorer.exe (supplied as a command-line argument):

```
Checking File: c:\windows\explorer.exe
Product Name: Microsoftr Windowsr Operating System
Product Version: 6.00.2600.0000
Company Name: Microsoft Corporation
File Version: 6.00.2600.0000 (xpclient.010817-1148)
File Description: Windows Explorer
Original Filename: EXPLORER.EXE
Legal Copyright: c Microsoft Corporation. All rights reserved.
InternalName: explorer
IsDebug: False
IsPatched: False
IsPreRelease: False
IsPrivateBuild: False
IsSpecialBuild: False
```

5.4 Use Bitwise Arithmetic with File Attributes

Problem

You want to correct examine or modify file attribute information.

Solution

Use bitwise arithmetic with the *And* and *Or* keywords.

Discussion

The *FileInfo.Attributes* and *DirectoryInfo.Attributes* properties represent file attributes such as archive, system, hidden, read-only, compressed, and encrypted. (Refer to the MSDN reference for the full list.) Because a file can possess any combination of attributes, the *Attributes* property accepts a combination of enumerated values. To individually test for a single attribute, or change a single attribute, you need to use bitwise arithmetic.

For example, consider the following code:

```
' This file has the archive, read-only, and encrypted attributes.
Dim MyFile As New FileInfo("data.txt")

' This displays the string "ReadOnly, Archive, Encrypted"
Console.WriteLine(MyFile.Attributes.ToString())

' This test fails, because other attributes are set.
```

```
If MyFile.Attributes = FileAttributes.ReadOnly Then
    Console.WriteLine("File is read-only.")
End If

' This test succeeds, because it filters out just the read-only attribute.
' The parentheses are required.
If (MyFile.Attributes And FileAttributes.ReadOnly) = _
  FileAttributes.ReadOnly Then
    Console.WriteLine("File is read-only.")
End If
```

Essentially, the *Attributes* setting is made up (in binary) of a series of ones and zeros, such as 00010011. Each *1* represents an attribute that is present, while each *0* represents an attribute that is not. When you use the *And* operation with an enumerated value, it automatically performs a *bitwise And*, which compares each individual digit against each digit in the enumerated value. For example, if you combine a value of 00100001 (representing an individual file's archive and read-only attributes) with the enumerated value 00000001 (which represents the read-only flag), the resulting value will be 00000001—it will only have a 1 where it can be matched in both values. You can then test this resulting value against the *FileAttributes.ReadOnly* enumerated value using the equals sign.

Similar logic allows you to verify that a file does *not* have a specific attribute:

```
If Not (MyFile.Attributes And FileAttributes.Compressed) = _
  FileAttributes.Compressed Then
    Console.WriteLine("File is not compressed.")
End If
```

When setting an attribute, you must also use bitwise arithmetic. In this case, it's needed to ensure that you don't inadvertently wipe out the other attributes.

```
' This adds just the read-only attribute.
MyFile.Attributes = MyFile.Attributes Or FileAttributes.ReadOnly

' This removes just the read-only attribute.
MyFile.Attributes = MyFile.Attributes And Not FileAttributes.ReadOnly
```

5.5 Read to and Write from a Binary File

Problem

You want to read or write data from a binary file.

Solution

Use the *BinaryReader* or *BinaryWriter* to wrap the underlying *FileStream*.

Discussion

The *BinaryReader* and *BinaryWriter* classes provide an easy way to work with binary data. The *BinaryWriter* class provides an overloaded *Write* method that takes any basic string or number data type, converts it to a set of bytes, and writes it to a file stream. The *BinaryReader* performs the same task in reverse— you call methods such as *ReadString* or *ReadInt32*, and it retrieves the data from the current position in the file stream and converts it to the desired type.

Here's a simple code snippet that writes data to a binary file, and reads it back.

```
' Define the sample data.
Dim MyString As String = "Sample Value"
Dim MySingle As Single = 88.21

' Write the data to a new file using a BinaryWriter.
Dim fs As New FileStream("data.bin", FileMode.Create)
Dim w As New BinaryWriter(fs)

w.Write(MyString)
w.Write(MySingle)
w.Close()

' Read the data with a BinaryReader.
fs = New FileStream("data.bin", FileMode.Open)
Dim r As New BinaryReader(fs)
Console.WriteLine(r.ReadString())
Console.WriteLine(r.ReadSingle)
r.Close()
```

Remember when writing data using *BinaryWriter* to store the data in an intermediate variable rather than write the data directly. This way, you can know if numeric types are being written as integers, decimals, singles, and so on. Otherwise, you won't know whether to call a method such as *ReadInt32* or *ReadSingle* when retrieving the information, and the wrong choice will generate an error!

> **Note** To convert more complex objects into binary representation, you'll need to use object serialization, as discussed in recipe 4.9.

5.6 Filter Files with Wildcards

Problem

You need to process multiple files based on a filter expression (such as *.txt or rec03??.bin).

Solution

Use the overloaded version of the *DirectoryInfo.GetFiles* method that accepts a filter expression.

Discussion

The *DirectoryInfo* and *Directory* objects both provide a way to search the current directories for files that match a specific filter expression. These search expressions can use the standard ? and * wildcards.

For example, the following code snippet retrieves the names of all the files in the c:\temp directory that have the extension *.txt*. The code then iterates through the retrieved *FileInfo* collection of matching files and displays the name and size of each one.

```
Dim File, Files() As FileInfo

' Check all the text files in temporary directory.
Dim Dir As New DirectoryInfo("c:\temp")
Files = Dir.GetFiles("*.txt")

' Display the name of all the files.
For Each File In Files
    Console.Write("Name: " & File.Name & "   ")
    Console.WriteLine("Size: " & File.Length.ToString)
Next
```

If you want to search subdirectories, you will need to add your own recursion, as described in recipe 5.7.

> **Note**   You can use a similar technique to retrieve directories that match a specified search pattern by using the overloaded *Directory-Info.GetDirectories* method.

5.7 Process Files Recursively

Problem

You need to perform a task with all the files in the current directory and any subdirectories.

Solution

Use the *DirectoryInfo.GetFiles* method to retrieve a list of files in a directory, and use recursion to walk through all subdirectories.

Discussion

Both the *Directory* and *DirectoryInfo* classes provide a *GetFiles* method, which retrieves files in the current directory. They also expose a *GetDirectories* method, which retrieves a list of subdirectories. To process a tree of directories, you can call the *GetDirectories* method recursively, working your way down the directory structure.

The *FileSearcher* class that follows shows how you can use this technique to perform a recursive search. The *SearchDirectory* routine adds all the files that match a specific pattern to an *ArrayList* and then calls *SearchDirectory* individually on each subdirectory.

```
Public Class FileSearcher

    Private _Matches As New ArrayList
    Private _FileFilter As String
    Private Recursive As Boolean

    Public ReadOnly Property Matches() As ArrayList
        Get
            Return _Matches
        End Get
    End Property

    Public Property FileFilter() As String
        Get
            Return _FileFilter
        End Get
        Set(ByVal Value As String)
            _FileFilter = Value
        End Set
    End Property
```

```
Public Sub New(ByVal fileFilter As String)
    Me.FileFilter = fileFilter
End Sub

Public Sub Search(ByVal startingPath As String, _
  ByVal recursive As Boolean)
    Matches.Clear()
    Recursive = recursive
    SearchDirectory(New DirectoryInfo(startingPath))
End Sub

Private Sub SearchDirectory(ByVal dir As DirectoryInfo)

    ' Get the files in this directory.
    Dim FileItem As FileInfo
    For Each FileItem In dir.GetFiles(FileFilter)
        ' If the file matches, add it to the collection.
        Matches.Add(FileItem)
    Next

    ' Process the subdirectories.
    If Recursive Then
        Dim DirItem As DirectoryInfo

        For Each DirItem In dir.GetDirectories()
            Try
                ' This is the recursive call.
                SearchDirectory(DirItem)
            Catch Err As UnauthorizedAccessException
                ' Error thrown if you don't have security permissions
                ' to access directory - ignore it.
            End Try
        Next
    End If

End Sub

End Class
```

Here's an example that demonstrates searching with the *FileSearcher* class:

```
Dim Searcher As New FileSearcher("*.txt")

' Perform a single-directory search.
Searcher.Search("c:\temp", False)
```

```
' Display results.
Console.WriteLine("Search results:")
Dim File As FileInfo
For Each File In Searcher.Matches
    Console.WriteLine(File.FullName)
Next

' Perform a recursive directory search.
Searcher.Search("c:\temp", True)

' Display results.
Console.WriteLine("Recursive search results:")
For Each File In Searcher.Matches
    Console.WriteLine(File.FullName)
Next
```

It would be easy to enhance the *FileSearcher* class to support other types of search criteria, such as file size or attributes. In addition, the code would become more failsafe if *ArrayList* were replaced with a type-safe collection that could only accept *FileInfo* objects, as described in recipe 3.16.

5.8 Search for a File with Specific Text

Problem

You need to perform a search for a file that contains specific text.

Solution

Search through a file character-by-character using the *FileStream.ReadByte* method, and try to build up a matching string.

Discussion

Full-text searching is fairly easy to implement, although it can be time consuming, and it typically works best with text files. All you need to do is scan through a file, attempting to read each byte and convert it to a character. If you read a character that matches the requested text, you can then check to see if the next character matches, and so on.

The following *FileTextSearcher* class encapsulates the functionality required to perform a full-text search that works with any type of file.

```
Public Class FileTextSearcher

    Private _Matches As New ArrayList
    Private _FileFilter As String
    Private _SearchText As String
    Private _CaseSensitive As Boolean = True

    Public ReadOnly Property Matches() As ArrayList
        Get
            Return _Matches
        End Get
    End Property

    Public Property FileFilter() As String
        Get
            Return _FileFilter
        End Get
        Set(ByVal Value As String)
            _FileFilter = Value
        End Set
    End Property

    Public Property SearchText() As String
        Get
            Return _SearchText
        End Get
        Set(ByVal Value As String)
            _SearchText = Value
        End Set
    End Property

    Public Property CaseSensitive() As Boolean
        Get
            Return _CaseSensitive
        End Get
        Set(ByVal Value As Boolean)
            _CaseSensitive = Value
        End Set
    End Property

    Public Sub New(ByVal fileFilter As String, ByVal searchText As String)
        Me.FileFilter = fileFilter
        Me.SearchText = searchText
    End Sub
```

```vbnet
Public Sub Search(ByVal startingPath As String)
    Matches.Clear()
    SearchDirectory(New DirectoryInfo(startingPath))
End Sub

Private Sub SearchDirectory(ByVal dir As DirectoryInfo)
    ' Get the files in this direcory.
    Dim FileItem As FileInfo
    For Each FileItem In dir.GetFiles(FileFilter)
        ' Test if file matches.
        If TestFileForMatch(FileItem) Then
            Matches.Add(FileItem)
        End If
    Next

    ' You could add recursive logic here by calling SearchDirectory
    ' on all subdirectories (see recipe 5.7).
End Sub

Private Function TestFileForMatch(ByVal file As FileInfo) As Boolean
    ' Open the file.
    Dim fs As FileStream = file.OpenRead()
    Dim Match As Boolean = False

    ' Search for the text.
    Dim MatchCount, MatchPosition As Integer
    Dim Character, MatchCharacter As String

    ' Read through the entire file.
    Do Until fs.Position = fs.Length
        ' Get a character from the file.
        Character = Convert.ToChar(fs.ReadByte())

        ' Retrieve the next character to be matched from the search text.
        MatchCharacter = SearchText.Substring(MatchPosition, 1)

        If String.Compare(Character, MatchCharacter, _
          Not Me.CaseSensitive) = 0 Then
            ' They match. Now try to match the next character.
            MatchPosition += 1
        Else
            ' They don't match. Start again from the beginning.
            MatchPosition = 0
        End If

        ' Check if the entire string has been matched.
        If MatchPosition = SearchText.Length - 1 Then
            Return True
```

```
            End If
        Loop

        fs.Close()
        Return False
    End Function

End Class
```

Here's how you can use this class to search a set of Visual Basic code files for a specific variable named *MyVariable*:

```
Dim Searcher As New FileTextSearcher("*.vb", "MyVariable")
Searcher.Search("c:\temp")

' Display results.
Dim File As FileInfo
For Each File In Searcher.Matches
    Console.WriteLine(File.FullName)
Next
```

5.9 Fill a *TreeView* with a Just-In-Time Directory Tree

Problem

You need to show a directory tree with the *TreeView* control, but filling the directory tree structure at startup is too time consuming.

Solution

React to the *BeforeExpand* event to fill in subdirectories just before they are displayed.

Discussion

You can use the recursion technique shown in recipe 5.7 to build an entire directory tree. However, scanning the file system in this way can be slow, particularly for large drives. For this reason, professional file management software (and Windows Explorer) use a different technique—they query the necessary directory information when the user requests it.

The *TreeView* control, shown in Figure 5-1, is particularly well suited to this approach because it provides a *BeforeExpand* event that fires before a new level of nodes is displayed. You can use a placeholder (such as an asterisk or empty *TreeNode*) in all the directory branches that are not filled in. This allows you to fill-in parts of the directory tree as they are displayed.

Figure 5-1 A directory tree with the *TreeView*

To support this technique, you should first create a procedure that adds a single directory node. The first level of subdirectories is entered using subnodes with an asterisk placeholder.

```
Private Sub Fill(ByVal dirNode As TreeNode)

    Dim Dir As New DirectoryInfo(DirNode.FullPath)
    Dim DirItem As DirectoryInfo

    Try
        For Each DirItem In Dir.GetDirectories
            ' Add node for the directory.
            Dim NewNode As New TreeNode(DirItem.Name)
            DirNode.Nodes.Add(NewNode)
            NewNode.Nodes.Add("*")
        Next
    Catch Err As UnauthorizedAccessException
        ' Error thrown if you don't have security permissions
        ' to access directory - ignore it.
    End Try

End Sub
```

When the form first loads, you can call this function to fill the root level of directories:

```
Private Sub Form1_Load(ByVal sender As System.Object, _
  ByVal e As System.EventArgs) Handles MyBase.Load

    ' Set the first node.
    Dim RootNode As New TreeNode("c:\")
    treeFiles.Nodes.Add(RootNode)
```

```
' Fill the first level and expand it.
Fill(RootNode)
treeFiles.Nodes(0).Expand()

End Sub
```

Finally, each time the user expands a node, you can react by using the *Fill* procedure to fill in the requested directory:

```
Private Sub treeFiles_BeforeExpand(ByVal sender As Object, _
  ByVal e As TreeViewCancelEventArgs) Handles treeFiles.BeforeExpand

    ' Check for the dummy node.
    If e.Node.Nodes(0).Text = "*" Then
        ' Disable redraw.
        treeFiles.BeginUpdate()

        e.Node.Nodes.Clear()
        Fill(e.Node)

        ' Enable redraw.
        treeFiles.EndUpdate()
    End If

End Sub
```

5.10 Test Two Files for Equality

Problem

You need to quickly compare the content of two files.

Solution

Calculate the hash code of each file using the *HashAlgorithm* class, and compare the hash codes.

Discussion

There are a number of ways you might want to compare more than one file. For example, you could examine a portion of the file for similar data, or you could read through each file byte-by-byte, comparing each byte as you go. Both of these approaches are valid, but in some cases it's more convenient to use a *hash code* algorithm.

A hash code algorithm generates a small (typically about 20 bytes) binary fingerprint for a file. While it's *possible* for different files to generate the same hash codes, it's statistically unlikely. In fact, even a minor change (for example, modifying a single bit in the source file) has a 50% chance of independently changing each bit in the hash code. For this reason, hash codes are often used in security code to detect data tampering.

To create a hash code, you must first create a *HashAlgorithm* object, typically by calling the shared *HashAlgorithm.Create* method. The *HashAlgorithm* class is defined in the *System.Security.Cryptography* namespace. You can then call *HashAlgorithm.ComputeHash*, which returns a byte array with the hash data.

The following code demonstrates a simple Console application that reads two file names that are supplied as arguments and tests them for equality.

```
Public Module FileCompare

    Public Sub Main(ByVal args() As String)
        If args.Length <> 2 Then
            Console.WriteLine("Wrong number of arguments.")
            Console.WriteLine("Specify two files.")

        Else
            Console.WriteLine("Comparing " & args(0) & " and " & args(1))

            ' Create the hashing object.
            Dim Hash As System.Security.Cryptography.HashAlgorithm
            Hash = System.Security.Cryptography.HashAlgorithm.Create()

            ' Calculate the hash for the first file.
            Dim fsA As New FileStream(args(0), FileMode.Open)
            Dim HashA() As Byte = Hash.ComputeHash(fsA)
            fsA.Close()

            ' Calculate the hash for the second file.
            Dim fsB As New FileStream(args(1), FileMode.Open)
            Dim HashB() As Byte = Hash.ComputeHash(fsB)
            fsB.Close()

            ' Compare the hashes.
            If BitConverter.ToString(HashA) = _
              BitConverter.ToString(HashB) Then
                Console.WriteLine("Files match.")
            Else
                Console.WriteLine("No match.")
            End If
        End If
```

```
        Console.ReadLine()
    End Sub

End Module
```

The hashes are compared by converting them first into strings. Alternatively, you could compare them by iterating over the byte array and comparing each value.

5.11 Monitor the File System for Changes

Problem

You need to react when a file system change is detected in a specific path (such as a file modification or creation).

Solution

Use the *FileSystemWatcher* component, which monitors a path and raises events when files or directories are modified.

Discussion

When linking together multiple applications and business processes, it's often necessary to create a program that waits idly and only springs into action when a new file is received or changed. You can create this type of program by scanning a directory periodically, but you face a key tradeoff. The more often you scan, the more system resources you waste. The less often you scan, the longer it might take to detect the appropriate event. The solution is to use the *FileSystemWatcher* class to react directly to Windows file events.

To use *FileSystemWatcher*, you must create an instance and set the following properties:

■   ***Path***   indicates the directory you want to monitor.

■   ***Filter***   indicates the types of files you are monitoring.

■   ***NotifyFilter***   indicates the type of changes you are monitoring.

The *FileSystemWatcher* raises four events: *Created*, *Deleted*, *Renamed*, and *Changed*. All of these events provide information through their *FileSystemEventArgs* parameter, including the name of the file (*Name*), the full path (*FullPath*), and the type of change (*ChangeType*). If you need, you can disable these events by setting the *FileSystemWatcher.EnableRaisingEvents* property to *False*.

Figure 5-2 shows an example Windows form that monitors a directory for new files (until the form is closed). The directory being monitored can be changed by typing in a new path and clicking the Start Monitoring button.

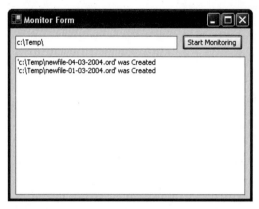

Figure 5-2   A file monitoring form

In this example, the *FileSystemWatcher* class has been created and connected manually. However, you can perform all of these steps at design time by adding *FileSystemWatcher* to the component tray, configuring it with the Properties window, and adding event handlers, in which case the code would be generated automatically as part of the form designer code.

```
Public Class MonitorForm
    Inherits System.Windows.Forms.Form

    ' (Designer code omitted.)

    ' This is tracked as a form-level variable, because it must live as long
    ' as the form exists.
    Private Watch As New FileSystemWatcher()

    ' Configure the FileSystemWatcher when the form is loaded.
    Private Sub MonitorForm_Load(ByVal sender As System.Object, _
        ByVal e As System.EventArgs) Handles MyBase.Load

        ' Attach the event handler.
        AddHandler Watch.Created, AddressOf Watch_Created

    End Sub

    Private Sub cmdMonitor_Click(ByVal sender As System.Object, _
        ByVal e As System.EventArgs) Handles cmdMonitor.Click
```

```
    Try
        Watch.Path = txtMonitorPath.Text
        Watch.Filter = "*.*"
        Watch.IncludeSubdirectories = True
        Watch.EnableRaisingEvents = True
    Catch Err As Exception
        MessageBox.Show(Err.Message)
    End Try

End Sub

' Fires when a new file is created in the directory being monitored.
Private Sub Watch_Created(sender As Object, _
  e As System.IO.FileSystemEventArgs)

    ' Add the new file name to a list.
    lstFilesCreated.Items.Add("'" & e.FullPath & _
      "' was " & e.ChangeType.ToString())

End Sub

End Class
```

The *Created*, *Deleted*, and *Renamed* events are easy to handle. However, if you want to use the *Changed* event, you need to use the *NotifyFilter* property to indicate the types of changes you are looking for. Otherwise, your program might be swamped by an unceasing series of events as files are modified.

The *NotifyFilter* property can be set using any combination of the following values from the *NotifyFilters* enumeration:

- *Attributes*
- *CreationTime*
- *DirectoryName*
- *FileName*
- *LastAccess*
- *LastWrite*
- *Security*
- *Size*

You can combine any of these values using bitwise arithmetic through the *Or* keyword. In other words, to monitor for *CreationTime* and *DirectoryName* changes, you would use this code:

```
Watch.NotifyFilter = NotifyFilters.CreationTime Or NotifyFilters.DirectoryName
```

5.12 Create a Temporary File

Problem

You want to get a file name that you can use for a temporary file.

Solution

Use the shared *Path.GetTempFileName* method.

Discussion

There are a number of approaches to generating temporary files. In simple cases, you might just create a file in the application directory, possibly using a GUID filename or a timestamp in conjunction with a random value. However, the *System.IO.Path* class provides a helper method that can save you some work. It returns a unique filename (in the current user's temporary directory) that you can use to create a file for storing temporary information. This might be a path like c:\documents and settings\username\local settings\temp\tmpac9.tmp.

```
Dim TempFile As String = Path.GetTempFileName()
Console.WriteLine("Using " & TempFile)
Dim fs As New FileStream(TempFile, FileMode.Create)

' (Write some data.)

fs.Close()

' Now delete the file.
File.Delete(TempFile)
```

If you call *GetTempFileName* multiple times, you will receive a different filename each time, even if you don't create a file with that name. This system is designed to avoid name collision between multiple applications.

5.13 Get the Executable Path

Problem

You want to retrieve the path where the current executable is stored.

Solution

Read the shared *StartupPath* property of the *System.Windows.Forms.Application* class.

Discussion

The *System.Windows.Forms.Application* class allows you to retrieve the directory where the executable is stored, even if it isn't a Windows application.

```
Console.Write("Executable is: ")
Console.WriteLine(System.Windows.Forms.Application.ExecutablePath)
Console.Write("Executable is executing in: ")
Console.WriteLine(System.Windows.Forms.Application.StartupPath)
```

In order to use this technique, you must reference the *System.Windows.Forms* namespace. Alternatively, you can simply find the current working path (using recipe 5.14) or use reflection to find the codebase location of the currently executing assembly (as described in recipe 9.1).

5.14 Set the Current Working Path

Problem

You want to set the current working directory so you can use relative paths in your code.

Solution

Use the shared *Directory.GetCurrentDirectory* and *Directory.SetCurrentDirectory* methods.

Discussion

Relative paths are automatically interpreted in relation to the current working directory. You can retrieve the current working directory by calling *Directory.GetCurrentDirectory*, or change it using *Directory.SetCurrentDirectory*. In addition, you can use the shared *Path.GetFullPath* method to convert a relative path into an absolute path using the current working directory.

Here's a simple test that demonstrates these concepts:

```
Console.WriteLine("Using: " & Directory.GetCurrentDirectory())
Console.Write("The relative path myfile.txt will automatically become ")
Console.WriteLine(Path.GetFullPath("myfile.txt"))

Console.WriteLine("Changing current directory to c:\")
Directory.SetCurrentDirectory("c:\")
Console.Write("The relative path myfile.txt will automatically become ")
Console.WriteLine(Path.GetFullPath("myfile.txt"))
```

The output for this example might be the following:

```
Using: D:\Temp\ConsoleApplication1\bin
The relative path myfile.txt will automatically become
D:\Temp\ConsoleApplication1\bin\myfile.txt
Changing current directory to c:\
The relative path myfile.txt will automatically become c:\myfile.txt
```

> **Note**   If you use relative paths, it's recommended that you set the working path at the start of each file interaction. Otherwise, you could introduce unnoticed security vulnerabilities that could allow a malicious user to force your application into accessing or overwriting system files by tricking it into using a different working directory.

5.15 Use an Isolated Store

Problem

You need to store data in a file, but your application doesn't run with the required *FileIOPermission*.

Solution

Use a user-specific isolated store.

Discussion

The .NET Framework includes support for isolated storage, which allows you to read and write to a user-specific virtual file system that the common language runtime manages. When you create isolated storage files, the data is automatically serialized to a unique location in the user profile path (typically a path like c:\document and settings\[username]\local settings\application data\isolated storage\[guid_identifier]).

One reason you might use isolated storage is to give an untrusted application limited ability to store data. For example, the default common language runtime security policy gives local code *FileIOPermission*, which allows it to open or write to any file. Code that you run from a remote server on the local Intranet is automatically assigned less permission—it lacks the *FileIOPermission*, but has the *IsolatedStoragePermission*, giving it the ability to use isolated stores. (The security policy also limits the maximum amount of space that can be used in an isolated store.) Another reason you might use an isolated store is to better secure data. For example, data in one user's isolated store will be restricted from another nonadministrative user. Also, because isolated stores are sorted in directories using GUID identifiers, it might not be as easy for an attacker to find the data that corresponds to a specific application.

The following example shows how you can access isolated storage. It assumes you have imported the *System.IO.IsolatedStorage* namespace.

```
' Create the store for the current user.
Dim Store As IsolatedStorageFile
Store = IsolatedStorageFile.GetUserStoreForAssembly()

' Create a folder in the root of the isolated store.
Store.CreateDirectory("MyFolder")

' Create a file in the isolated store.
Dim Stream As New IsolatedStorageFileStream( _
    "MyFolder\MyFile.txt", FileMode.Create, Store)

Dim w As New StreamWriter(Stream)

' (You can now write to the file as normal.)

w.Close()
```

Note   You can also use methods such as *IsolatedStorageFile.GetFileNames* and *IsolatedStorageFile.GetDirectoryNames* to enumerate the contents of an isolated store.

By default, each isolated store is segregated by user and assembly. That means that when the same user runs the same application, the application will access the data in the same isolated store. However, you can choose to segregate it further by application domain, so that multiple instances of the same application receive different isolated stores.

```
' Access isolated storage for the current user and assembly
' (which is equivalent to the first example).
Store = New IsolatedStorageFile.GetStore(IsolatedStorageScope.User Or _
    IsolatedStorageScope.Assembly, Nothing, Nothing)


' Access isolated storage for the current user, assembly,
' and application domain. In other words, this data is only
' accessible by the current application instance.
Store = New IsolatedStorageFile.GetStore(IsolatedStorageScope.User Or _
    IsolatedStorageScope.Assembly Or IsolatedStorageScope.Domain, _
    Nothing, Nothing)
```

The files are stored as part of a user's profile, so users can access their isolated storage files on any workstation they log on to if roaming profiles are configured on your LAN. By letting the .NET Framework and the common language runtime provide these levels of isolation, you can relinquish responsibility for maintaining separation between files, and you don't have to worry that programming oversights or misunderstandings will cause loss of critical data.

5.16 Read Application Configuration Settings

Problem

You need to store application-specific settings that can be modified easily without recompiling code.

Solution

Read settings from an application configuration file.

Discussion

Configuration files are ideal repositories for information such as directory paths and database connection strings. One useful feature about configuration files is the fact that they are tied to a particular directory, not a particular computer (as a registry setting would be). Thus, if several clients load the same application from the same directory, they will share the same custom settings. However, you might need to add additional security to prevent users from reading or modifying a configuration file that is shared in this way.

To create a configuration file for your application, give the file the same name as your application, plus the extension .config. For example, the application MyApp.exe would have a configuration file MyApp.exe.config. The only exception is Web applications including Web pages and Web services, which are loaded by Microsoft ASP.NET and Internet Information Services (IIS). In this case, ASP.NET always uses a file with the name *web.config* from the corresponding virtual directory.

> **Note**   Visual Studio .NET provides a shortcut for creating configuration files. Simply right-click the project in the Solution Explorer, and select Add | New Item. Then choose Application Configuration File under the Local Project Items node.
>
>   The application configuration file is automatically assigned the name *app.config*. You should not change this name. When Visual Studio .NET compiles your project, it will create the configuration file in the appropriate directory, with the correct name. This allows you to rename your application's assembly name at design-time without needing to alter the name of the corresponding configuration file.

You can add an unlimited number of name-value pairs to a configuration file. You add these settings to the *<appSettings>* portion of the file using *<add>* elements. Every custom setting has a string value and a unique string key that identifies it. Here is a configuration file with one custom setting (named *CustomPath*):

```
<?xml version="1.0"?>
<configuration>

  <appSettings>
    <add key="CustomPath"
        value="c:\Temp\MyFiles" />
  </appSettings>

  <!-- Other configuration sections can go here,
      but aren't necessary. -->

</configuration>
```

You can retrieve custom settings through the *System.Configuration.ConfigurationSettings* class using the key name. Settings are always retrieved as strings. The following code snippet assumes you have imported the *System.Configuration* namespace.

```
' Retrieve the custom path setting.
Dim MyPath As String
MyPath = ConfigurationSettings.AppSettings("CustomPath")
' MyPath is now set to "c:\Temp\MyFiles"
```

If you want to store more than one related setting in a configuration file, you might want to create a custom configuration section, along with a custom section reader. This technique is described in recipe 5.17.

> **Note**   If a class library uses the *AppSettings* class, it will access the configuration file that was loaded by the executable application. Thus, if the application MyApp.exe loads the assembly MyLib.dll, all configuration file access in MyLib.dll will be directed to the file MyApp.exe.config.

5.17 Create Custom Configuration Sections

Problem

You want to use a custom configuration setting to organize related custom settings.

Solution

Register your custom setting with the *System.Configuration.NameValueSection-Handler* class. You can then use the shared *ConfigurationSettings.GetConfig* method to retrieve a collection of settings from the section.

Discussion

.NET uses an extensible system of configuration file settings. You have multiple options for reading custom settings from a configuration file:

■ Place your custom settings in the *<appSettings>* group, and access them through the *ConfigurationSettings.AppSettings* collection. This approach was used in recipe 5.16.

■ Create your own custom section handler by implementing *IConfigurationSectionHandler* and registering it in the configuration file. This provides unlimited flexibility, but is rarely required.

- Place your configuration settings in a custom group, and register a prebuilt configuration section reader such as *NameValueSectionHandler* or *SingleTagSectionHandler*. This is the approach we'll use in this section.

To use *NameValueSectionHandler*, you should first create the group with the custom settings and add it to your configuration file. The example that follows contains a custom section called *<mySection>* in a group named *<mySectionGroup>*. This section has a single setting, named *key1*.

```
<mySectionGroup>
    <mySection>
        <add key="key1" value="value1" />
    </mySection>
</mySectionGroup>
```

Next you must register the section for processing with *NameValueSectionHandler*, which you identify using its strong name. Notice that the type information shown in the following code must all be entered on a single line. It's broken into multiple lines in this listing to fit the bounds of the page.

```
<configuration>
    <configSections>
        <sectionGroup name="mySectionGroup">
            <section name="mySection"
             type="System.Configuration.NameValueSectionHandler,system,
             Version=1.0.3300.0, Culture=neutral,
             PublicKeyToken=b77a5c561934e089, Custom=null" />
        </sectionGroup>
    </configSections>

    <mySectionGroup>
        <mySection>
            <add key="key1" value="value1" />
        </mySection>
    </mySectionGroup>

</configuration>
```

Depending on the version of .NET that you have installed, you might need to modify the version information in the type section of the *<sectionGroup>* tag. You can check the version information for the System.dll assembly using the Windows Explorer global assembly cache (GAC) extension.

Once you have made this change, retrieving the custom information is easy. First you need to import two namespaces into your application:

```
Imports System.Configuration
Imports System.Collections.Specialized
```

Then you simply need to use the *ConfigurationSettings.GetConfig* method, which retrieves the settings in a collection from a single section. You specify the section in the *GetConfig* method using a path-like syntax.

```
Dim Settings As NameValueCollection
Settings = CType( _
  ConfigurationSettings.GetConfig("mySectionGroup/mySection"), _
  NameValueCollection)

' Displays "value1"
Console.WriteLine(Settings("key1"))
```

5.18 Read Header Information from MP3 Files

Problem

You need to read information about the song, artist, and album from an MP3 file.

Solution

Read the ID3v2 tag from the end of the MP3 file.

Discussion

Most MP3 files store information in a 128-byte ID3v2 tag at the end of the file. This tag starts with the word *TAG* and contains information about the artist, album, and song title in ASCII encoding. You can convert this data from bytes into a string using the *Encoding* object returned by the *System.Text.Encoding.ASCII* property.

The *MP3TagData* class shown here provides access to MP3 data, and it provides a *ReadFromFile* method that retrieves the information from a valid MP3 file.

```
Public Class MP3TagData

    Private _Artist As String
    Private _SongTitle As String
    Private _Album As String
    Private _Year As String

    Public ReadOnly Property Artist() As String
        Get
            Return _Artist
        End Get
    End Property
```

```
Public ReadOnly Property SongTitle() As String
    Get
        Return _SongTitle
    End Get
End Property

Public ReadOnly Property Album() As String
    Get
        Return _Album
    End Get
End Property

Public ReadOnly Property Year() As String
    Get
        Return _Year
    End Get
End Property

Public Sub ReadFromFile(ByVal filename As String)
    ' Clear existing values.
    _SongTitle = ""
    _Artist = ""
    _Album = ""
    _Year = ""

    Dim fs As New FileStream(filename, FileMode.Open)

    ' Read the MP3 tag.
    fs.Seek(0 - 128, SeekOrigin.End)
    Dim Tag(2) As Byte
    fs.Read(Tag, 0, 3)

    ' Verify that a tag exists.
    If System.Text.Encoding.ASCII.GetString(Tag).Trim() = "TAG" Then
        _SongTitle = GetTagData(fs, 30)
        _Artist = GetTagData(fs, 30)
        _Album = GetTagData(fs, 30)
        _Year = GetTagData(fs, 4)
    End If

    fs.Close()
End Sub

Private Function GetTagData(ByVal stream As Stream, _
  ByVal length As Integer) As String

    ' Read the data.
    Dim Bytes(length - 1) As Byte
    stream.Read(Bytes, 0, length)
```

```
        Dim TagData As String = System.Text.Encoding.ASCII.GetString(Bytes)

        ' Trim nulls.
        Dim TrimChars() As Char = {Char.Parse(" "), Char.Parse(vbNullChar)}
        TagData = TagData.Trim(TrimChars)
        Return TagData

    End Function

End Class
```

> **Note** Data in the MP3 tag is given a fixed width and is padded with nulls. You must trim these null characters from the string manually. Otherwise, they can cause problems depending on how you use the string in your application.

The following code shows how you can use the *MP3TagData* class to retrieve and display MP3 information:

```
Dim MP3Tag As New MP3TagData()
MP3Tag.ReadFromFile("c:\mp3\mysong.mp3")

Console.WriteLine("Album: " & MP3Tag.Album)
Console.WriteLine("Artist: " & MP3Tag.Artist)
Console.WriteLine("Song: " & MP3Tag.SongTitle)
Console.WriteLine("Year: " & MP3Tag.Year)
```

5.19 Get Started with ZIP Files

Problem

You need to manipulate compressed ZIP archives, either to retrieve file information from a zip or to compress and uncompress individual files.

Solution

Use a dedicated .NET component, such as the freely reusable #ziplib.

Discussion

There are several commercial components that allow you to work with ZIP files. However, there's also at least one fully featured and freely redistributable

ZIP component: #ziplib (also known as *SharpZipLib*), developed by Mike Krueger using a similar open-source Java component. You can download #ziplib with the code samples for this book, or from the Web site *http://www.icsharpcode.net/opensource/sharpziplib*. This site includes samples in Visual Basic and C# and limited documentation.

To use #ziplib in a project, simply add a reference to the SharpZipLib.dll assembly and import the following namespace:

```
Imports ICSharpCode.SharpZipLib.Zip
```

To retrieve information about the files in a ZIP archive, you could use code similar to this:

```
Dim ZipStream As New ZipInputStream(File.OpenRead("test.zip"))
Dim Entry As ZipEntry = ZipStream.GetNextEntry()

Do Until Entry Is Nothing
    Console.WriteLine("Name: " & Entry.Name)
    Console.WriteLine("Date: " & Entry.DateTime.ToString())
    Console.WriteLine("Uncompressed Size: " & Entry.Size.ToString())
    Console.WriteLine("Compressed Size: " + Entry.CompressedSize.ToString())
    Console.WriteLine()
    Entry = ZipStream.GetNextEntry()
Loop

ZipStream.Close()
```

Here's an example of the output this code can generate for a ZIP archive containing three files:

```
Name: COPYING.txt
Date: 12/07/2001 4:49:48 PM
Uncompressed Size: 18349
Compressed Size: 6956

Name: Documentation.chm
Date: 15/07/2002 10:21:12 AM
Uncompressed Size: 321684
Compressed Size: 266795

Name: Readme.pdf
Date: 25/07/2002 11:05:08 AM
Uncompressed: 82763
Compressed Size: 79186
```

You can also use #ziplib to compress and decompress files. Refer to the code samples included with the component for more information.

5.20 Get Started with PDF Files

Problem

You want to read data from a PDF file or programmatically generate a PDF file.

Solution

Evaluate a third-party component, or a free open-source component from *http://www.sourceforge.net*.

Discussion

The PDF file format using a complex multipart format that includes embedded data such as images and fonts. In order to successfully retrieve information from a PDF file, you will need to use a third-party component. Some retail components are available, along with two freely downloadable components on SourceForge. These include the Report.NET library (*http://sourceforge.net/projects/report*) and the PDF.NET library (*http://sourceforge.net/projects/pdflibrary*).

Exporting data to a PDF file is conceptually similar to printing it, and you need to explicitly control the coordinates of outputted text and images. The following code snippet shows an extremely simple sample showing how Report.NET can be used to create a basic PDF file using the current 0.06.01 release. In order to use this example, you must add a reference to the Reports.dll assembly and import the *Root.Reports* namespace.

```
' Create the PDF File.
Dim Doc As New Report(New PdfFormatter())

' Define the font information.
Dim FontDef As New FontDef(Doc, "Helvetica")
Dim FontProp As New FontPropMM(FontDef, 25)

' Create a new page.
Dim PDFPage As New Page(Doc)

' Add a line of text.
PDFPage.AddCenteredMM(80, New RepString(FontProp, "Hello World!"))

' Save the document.
Doc.Save("SimpleText.pdf")
```

6

XML

XML is the *lingua franca* of application development—a common syntax that underlies Web services, Microsoft ADO.NET, and a slew of cross-platform programming initiatives. At times, the sheer number of XML extensions and grammars can be overwhelming. Common XML tasks don't just include parsing an XML file, but also validating it against a schema, applying an XSL transform to create a new document or HTML page, and searching intelligently with XPath. All of these topics are covered in this chapter.

The Microsoft .NET Framework includes a rich complement of classes for manipulating XML documents in the *System.Xml* group of namespaces. These namespaces, outlined in the following list, contain the classes we concentrate on in this chapter.

- **System.Xml** contains the core classes for manipulating XML documents, including *XmlDocument*, which provides an in-memory representation of XML (see recipes 6.1 to 6.3), and the *XmlTextReader* and *XmlTextWriter* classes, which transfer XML information to and from a file (see recipe 6.6).

- **System.Xml.Schema** contains the classes for manipulating XSD schema files and applying schema validation (see recipe 6.9).

- **System.Xml.Serialization** contains classes that allow you to convert objects into XML, without using the formatters described in Chapter 4. See recipe 6.7 for more information.

- **System.Xml.XPath** contains a .NET implementation of an *XPath* parser for searching XML documents. You'll use this functionality indirectly with XSL transformations (see recipe 6.8) and the *XmlNode.SelectNodes* method (see recipe 6.5).

■ ***System.Xml.Xsl***   contains classes that allow you to transform an XML document into another document using an XSLT stylesheet (see recipe 6.8).

Many of the examples in this chapter require a sample XML document. The sample we will use is called *orders.xml*. It contains a simple list of ordered items along with information about the ordering client, and it's shown here:

```
<?xml version="1.0"?>
<Order id="2003-04-12-4996">
    <Client id="CMPSO33UL">
        <Name>CompuStation</Name>
    </Client>
    <Items>
        <Item id="2003">
            <Name>Calculator</Name>
            <Price>24.99</Price>
        </Item>
        <Item id="4311">
            <Name>Laser Printer</Name>
            <Price>400.75</Price>
        </Item>
    </Items>
</Order>
```

> **Note**   Before using the examples in this chapter, you should import the *System.Xml* namespace.

6.1 Load an XML Document into Memory

Problem

You need to load an XML document into memory, perhaps so you can browse its nodes, change its structure, or perform other operations.

Solution

Use the *XmlDocument* class, which provides a *Load* method for retrieving XML information and a *Save* method for storing it.

Discussion

.NET provides a slew of XML objects. The ones you use depend in part upon your programming task. The *XmlDocument* class provides an in-memory representation of XML. It allows you to deal with XML data in your application *as* XML. The *XmlDocument* class also allows you to browse through the nodes in any direction, insert and remove nodes, and change the structure on the fly. These tasks are not as easy with the simpler *XmlTextWriter* and *XmlTextReader* classes, which are explained in recipe 6.6.

To use the *XmlDocument* class, simply create a new instance of the class, and call the *Load* method with a filename, *Stream*, *TextReader*, or *XmlReader* object. You can even supply a URL that points to an XML document. The *Xml-Document* instance will be populated with the tree of elements, or *nodes*. The jumping-off point for accessing these nodes is the root element, which is provided through the *XmlDocument.DocumentElement* property. *DocumentElement* is an *XmlElement* object that can contain one or more nested *XmlNode* objects, which in turn can contain more *XmlNode* objects, and so on. An *XmlNode* is the basic ingredient of an XML file and can be an element, an attribute, a comment, or contained text. Figure 6-1 shows part of the hierarchy created by *XmlDocument* for the orders.xml file.

When dealing with an *XmlNode* or a class that derives from it (such as *XmlElement* or *XmlAttribute*), you can use the following basic properties:

- **ChildNodes** is an *XmlNodeList* collection that contains the first level of nested nodes.

- **Name** is the name of the node.

- **NodeType** returns an enumerated value that indicates the type of the node (element, attribute, text, and so on).

- **Value** is the content of the node, if it's a text or CDATA node.

- **Attributes** provides a collection of node objects representing the attributes applied to the element.

- **InnerText** retrieves a string with the concatenated value of the node and all nested nodes.

- **InnerXml** retrieves a string with the concatenated XML markup for the current node and all nested nodes.

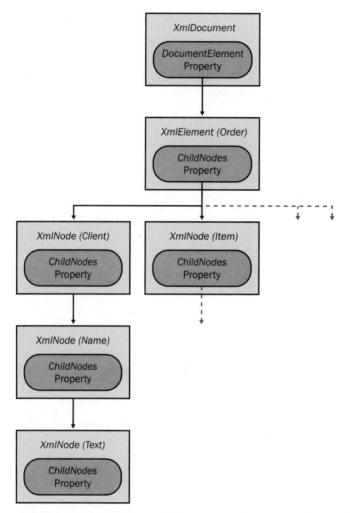

Figure 6-1 A partial tree of the orders.xml document loaded into an *XmlDocument*.

The following code loads the orders.xml document into memory and displays some information from the node tree.

```
Public Module XmlDocumentTest

    Public Sub Main()
        ' Load the document.
        Dim Doc As New XmlDocument
        Doc.Load("orders.xml")

        ' Display some information from the document.
        Dim Node As XmlNode
        Node = Doc.DocumentElement
```

```
        Console.WriteLine("This is order " & Node.Attributes(0).Value)

        For Each Node In Doc.DocumentElement.ChildNodes
            Select Case Node.Name
                Case "Client"
                    Console.WriteLine("Prepared for " & _
                        Node.ChildNodes(0).ChildNodes(0).Value)
                Case "Items"
                    Console.WriteLine("Contains " & _
                        Node.ChildNodes.Count.ToString() & " items")
            End Select
        Next

        Console.ReadLine()
    End Sub

End Module
```

The output is shown here:

```
This is order 2003-04-12-4996
Prepared for CompuStation
Contains 2 items
```

6.2 Process All Nodes in a Document

Problem

You want to iterate through all nodes in an XML tree and display or modify the related information.

Solution

Create a generic procedure for processing the node, and call it recursively.

Discussion

The *XmlDocument* stores a tree of *XmlNode* objects. You can walk through this tree structure recursively to process every node.

For example, consider the following code, which displays information about every node in a document. A depth parameter tracks how many layers deep the nesting is and uses it to format the output with a variable-sized indent.

```
Public Module XmlOuputTest

    Public Sub Main()
        ' Load the document.
        Dim Doc As New XmlDocument
        Doc.Load("orders.xml")
```

```
        ' Start the node walk at the root node (depth = 0).
        DisplayNode(Doc.DocumentElement, 0)

        Console.ReadLine()
    End Sub

    Private Sub DisplayNode(ByVal node As XmlNode, ByVal depth As Integer)
        ' Define the indent level.
        Dim Indent As New String(" "c, depth * 4)

        ' Display the node type.
        Console.WriteLine(Indent & node.NodeType.ToString() & _
                        ": <" & node.Name & ">")

        ' Display the node content, if applicable.
        If node.Value <> String.Empty Then
            Console.WriteLine(Indent & "Value: " & node.Value)
        End If

        ' Display all nested nodes.
        Dim Child As XmlNode
        For Each Child In node.ChildNodes
            DisplayNode(Child, depth + 1)
        Next
    End Sub

End Module
```

When using the orders.xml document, the output is as follows:

```
Element: <Order>
    Element: <Client>
        Element: <Name>
            Text: <#text>
            Value: CompuStation
    Elements: <Items>
        Element: <Item>
            Element: <Name>
                Text: <#text>
                Value: Calculator
            Element: <Price>
                Text: <#text>
                Value: 24.99
        Element: <Item>
            Element: <Name>
                Text: <#text>
                Value: Laser Printer
            Element: <Price>
                Text: <#text>
                Value: 400.75
```

An alternative solution to this problem is to use the *XmlTextReader*, which always steps through nodes one at a time, in order.

6.3 Insert Nodes in an XML Document

Problem

You need to modify an XML document by inserting new data.

Solution

Create the node using the appropriate *XmlDocument* method (such as *CreateElement*, *CreateAttribute*, *CreateNode*, and so on). Then insert it using the appropriate *XmlNode* method (such as *InsertAfter*, *InsertBefore*, or *AppendChild*).

Discussion

Inserting a node is a two-step process. You must first create the node, and then you insert it in the appropriate location. Optionally, you can then call *XmlDocument.Save* to persist changes to a file.

To create a node, you use one of the *XmlDocument* methods that starts with the word *Create*, depending on the type of node. This ensures that the node will have the same namespace as the rest of the document. Next you must find a suitable related node and use one of its insertion methods to add the new node to the tree. The following example demonstrates this technique to add a new item:

```
Public Module XmlInsertTest

    Public Sub Main()
        ' Load the document.
        Dim Doc As New XmlDocument
        Doc.Load("orders.xml")

        ' Create a new element.
        Dim ItemNode As XmlNode
        ItemNode = Doc.CreateElement("Item")

        ' Add the attribute.
        Dim Attribute As XmlAttribute
        Attribute = Doc.CreateAttribute("id")
        Attribute.Value = "4312"
        ItemNode.Attributes.Append(Attribute)
```

```
        ' Create and add the sub-elements for this node.
        Dim NameNode, PriceNode As XmlNode
        NameNode = Doc.CreateElement("Name")
        PriceNode = Doc.CreateElement("Price")
        ItemNode.AppendChild(NameNode)
        ItemNode.AppendChild(PriceNode)

        ' Add the text data.
        NameNode.AppendChild(Doc.CreateTextNode("Stapler"))
        PriceNode.AppendChild(Doc.CreateTextNode("12.20"))

        ' Add the new element.
        ' In this case, we add it as a child at the end of the item list.
        Doc.DocumentElement.ChildNodes(1).AppendChild(ItemNode)

        ' Save the document.
        Doc.Save("orders.xml")

        Console.WriteLine("Changes saved.")
        Console.ReadLine()
    End Sub

End Module
```

The new document looks like this:

```
<?xml version="1.0"?>
<Order id="2003-04-12-4996">
  <Client id="CMPSO33UL">
    <Name>CompuStation</Name>
  </Client>
  <Item id="2003">
    <Name>Calculator</Name>
    <Price>24.99</Price>
  </Item>
  <Item id="4311">
    <Name>Laser Printer</Name>
    <Price>400.75</Price>
  </Item>
  <Item id="4312">
    <Name>Stapler</Name>
    <Price>12.20</Price>
  </Item>
</Order>
```

Alternatively, you might be able to use *CloneNode*, which creates an exact copy of a node, to simplify the task of adding similar data. *CloneNode* accepts a Boolean depth parameter. If you supply *True*, *CloneNode* will duplicate the entire branch, with all nested nodes. Here's the equivalent code using *CloneNode*:

```
' Load the document.
Dim Doc As New XmlDocument
Doc.Load("orders.xml")

' Create a new element based on an existing product.
Dim ItemNode As XmlNode
ItemNode = Doc.DocumentElement.ChildNodes(1).LastChild.CloneNode(True)

' Modify the node data.
ItemNode.Attributes(0).Value = "4312"
ItemNode.ChildNodes(0).ChildNodes(0).Value = "Stapler"
ItemNode.ChildNodes(1).ChildNodes(0).Value = "12.20"

' Add the new element.
Doc.DocumentElement.ChildNodes(1).AppendChild(ItemNode)

' Save the document.
Doc.Save("orders.xml")
```

Notice that in this case, certain assumptions are being made about the existing nodes (for example, that the first child in the item node is always the name, and the second child is always the price). If this assumption isn't guaranteed to be true, you might need to examine the node name programmatically.

6.4 Find Specific Elements by Name

Problem

You need to retrieve a specific node from an *XmlDocument*, and you know its name but not its position.

Solution

Use the *XmlDocument.GetElementsByTagName* method.

Discussion

The *XmlDocument* class provides a convenient *GetElementsByTagName* method that searches an entire document for nodes that have the indicated element name. It returns the results as a collection of *XmlNode* objects.

This code demonstrates how you could use *GetElementsByTagName* to calculate the total price of an order:

```
Public Module XmlSearchTest

    Public Sub Main()
        ' Load the document.
        Dim Doc As New XmlDocument
        Doc.Load("orders.xml")

        ' Retrieve all prices.
        Dim PriceNodes As XmlNodeList
        PriceNodes = Doc.GetElementsByTagName("Price")

        Dim PriceNode As XmlNode
        Dim Price As Decimal
        For Each PriceNode In PriceNodes
            Price += Decimal.Parse(PriceNode.ChildNodes(0).Value)
        Next

        Console.WriteLine("Total order costs: " & Price.ToString())
        Console.ReadLine()
    End Sub

End Module
```

If your elements include an attribute of type ID, you can also use a method called *GetElementById* to retrieve an element that has a matching ID value. However, neither method allows you the flexibility to search portions of an XML document—for that flexibility, you need XPath, as described in recipe 6.5.

6.5 Find Elements with an XPath Search

Problem

You need to search an XML document or a portion of an XML document for nodes that match certain criteria.

Solution

Use an XPath expression with the *SelectNodes* or *SelectSingleNode* method.

Discussion

The *XmlNode* class defines two methods that perform XPath searches: *Select-Nodes* and *SelectSingleNode*. These methods operate on all contained child nodes. Because the *XmlDocument* inherits from *XmlNode*, you can call *Xml-Document.SelectNodes* to search an entire document.

Basic XPath syntax uses a pathlike notation. For example, the path /Order/Items/Item indicates an *Item* element that is nested inside an *Items* element, which, in turn, in nested in a root *Order* element. This is an absolute path. The following example uses an XPath absolute path to find the name of every item in an order.

```
Public Module XPathSearchTest

    Public Sub Main()
        ' Load the document.
        Dim Doc As New XmlDocument
        Doc.Load("orders.xml")

        ' Retrieve the name of every item.
        ' This could not be accomplished as easily with the
        ' GetElementsByTagName() method, because Name elements are
        ' used in Item elements and Client elements.
        Dim Nodes As XmlNodeList
        Nodes = Doc.SelectNodes("/Order/Items/Item/Name")

        Dim Node As XmlNode
        For Each Node In Nodes
            Console.WriteLine(Node.InnerText)
        Next

        Console.ReadLine()
    End Sub

End Module
```

XPath provides a rich and powerful search syntax, and it's impossible to explain all of the variations you can use in a short recipe. However, Table 6-1 outlines some of the key ingredients in more advanced XPath expressions and includes examples that show how they would work with the orders.xml document.

Table 6-1 XPath Expression Syntax

Expression	Meaning
/	Starts an absolute path that selects from the root node.
	/Order/Items/Item selects all *Item* elements that are children of an *Items* element, which is itself a child of the root *Order* element.
//	Starts a relative path that selects nodes anywhere.
	//Item/Name selects all of the *Name* elements that are children of an *Item* element, regardless of where they appear in the document.
@	Selects an attribute of a node.
	/Order/@id selects the attribute named *id* from the root *Order* element.
*	Selects any element in the path.
	/Order/* selects both *Items* and *Client* nodes because both are contained by a root *Order* element.
|	Combines multiple paths.
	/Order/Items/Item/Name|Order/Client/Name selects the *Name* nodes used to describe a *Client* and the *Name* nodes used to describe an *Item*.
.	Indicates the current (default) node.
..	Indicates the parent node.
	//Name/.. selects any element that is parent to a *Name*, which includes the *Client* and *Item* elements.
[ ]	Define selection criteria that can test a contained node or attribute value.
	/Order[@id="2003-04-12-4996"] selects the *Order* elements with the indicated attribute value.
	/Order/Items/Item[Price > 50] selects products above $50 in price.
	/Order/Items/Item[Price > 50 and Name="Laser Printer"] selects products that match two criteria.
starts-with	This function retrieves elements based on what text a contained element starts with.
	/Order/Items/Item[starts-with(Name, "C")] finds all *Item* elements that have a name element that starts with the letter *C*.
position	This function retrieves elements based on position.
	/Order/Items/Item[position()=2] selects the second *Item* element.
count	This function counts elements. You specify the name of the child element to count, or an asterisk (*) for all children.
	/Order/Items/Item[count(Price) = 1] retrieves *Item* elements that have exactly one nested *Price* element.

> **Note**   XPath expressions and all element and attribute names that you use inside them are always case sensitive.

6.6 Load an XML Document into a Class

Problem

You want to use an XML document to persist information, but interact with the data using a custom object in your code.

Solution

Use the *XmlDocument* or *XmlTextReader* class to read XML data, and transfer it into an object. Use *XmlDocument* or *XmlTextWriter* class to persist the XML data.

Discussion

It's common to want to work with full-fledged objects in your code and use XML only as a file format for persisting data. To support this design, you can create a class with *Save* and *Load* methods. The *Save* method commits the current data in the object to an XML format, whereas the *Load* method reads the XML document and uses its data to populate the object.

For example, the data in the orders.xml would require three classes to represent the *Order*, *Item*, and *Client* entities. You might create the *Item* and *Client* classes as follows:

```
Public Class Item
    Private _ID As String
    Private _Name As String
    Private _Price As Decimal

    Public Property ID() As String
        Get
            Return _ID
        End Get
        Set(ByVal Value As String)
            _ID = Value
        End Set
    End Property
End Property
```

```vb
    Public Property Name As String
        Get
            Return _Name
        End Get
        Set(ByVal Value As String)
            _Name = Value
        End Set
    End Property

    Public Property Price As Decimal
        Get
            Return _Price
        End Get
        Set(ByVal Value As Decimal)
            _Price = Value
        End Set
    End Property

    Public Sub New(ByVal id As String, ByVal name As String, _
      ByVal price As Decimal)
        Me.ID = id
        Me.Name = name
        Me.Price = price
    End Sub

End Class

Public Class Client
    Private _ID As String
    Private _Name As String

    Public Property ID() As String
        Get
            Return _ID
        End Get
        Set(ByVal Value As String)
            _ID = Value
        End Set
    End Property

    Public Property Name As String
        Get
            Return _Name
        End Get
        Set(ByVal Value As String)
            _Name = Value
        End Set
    End Property
```

```
Public Sub New(ByVal id As String, ByVal name As String)
    Me.ID = id
    Me.Name = name
End Sub
```

```
End Class
```

The *Order* class would then contain a single *Client,* and a collection of *Item* objects. It would also add the *Save* and *Load* methods that transfer the data to and from the XML file. Here's an example that supports loading only:

```
Public Class Order
    Private _ID As String
    Private _Client As Client
    Private _Items() As Item

    Public Property ID() As String
        Get
            Return _ID
        End Get
        Set(ByVal Value As String)
            _ID = Value
        End Set
    End Property

    Public Property Client As Client
        Get
            Return _Client
        End Get
        Set(ByVal Value As Client)
            _Client = Value
        End Set
    End Property

    Public Property Items() As Item()
        Get
            Return _Items
        End Get
        Set(ByVal Value As Item())
            _Items = Value
        End Set
    End Property

    Public Sub New(ByVal id As String, ByVal client As Client, _
      ByVal items As Item())
        Me.ID = id
        Me.Client = client
        Me.Items = items
    End Sub
```

```
Public Sub New(ByVal xmlFilePath As String)
    Me.Load(xmlFilePath)
End Sub

Public Sub Load(ByVal xmlFilePath As String)
    Dim Doc As New XmlDocument
    Doc.Load(xmlFilePath)

    ' Find the Order node.
    Dim Node As XmlNode
    Node = Doc.GetElementsByTagName("Order")(0)
    Me.ID = Node.Attributes(0).Value

    ' Find the Client node.
    Node = Doc.GetElementsByTagName("Client")(0)
    Me.Client = New Client(Node.Attributes(0).Value, Node.InnerText)

    ' Find the Item nodes.
    Dim Nodes As XmlNodeList
    Nodes = Doc.GetElementsByTagName("Item")
    Dim Items As New ArrayList
    For Each Node In Nodes
        Items.Add(New Item(Node.Attributes(0).Value, _
                Node.ChildNodes(0).InnerText, _
                Decimal.Parse(Node.ChildNodes(1).InnerText)))
    Next

    ' Convert the collection of items into a strongly typed array.
    Me.Items = CType(Items.ToArray(GetType(Item)), Item())
End Sub

Public Sub Save(ByVal xmlFilePath As String)
    ' (Save code omitted.)
End Sub

End Class
```

> **Note**   To improve this design, you might want to substitute the array of
> *Item* objects with a strongly typed collection, as described in recipe 3.16.

The client can then use the following code to inspect products, without
having to interact with the underlying XML format at all:

```
Dim XmlOrder As New Order("orders.xml")

' Display the prices of all items.
Dim Item As Item
For Each Item In XmlOrder.Items
    Console.WriteLine(Item.Name & ": " & Item.Price.ToString())
Next
```

There are countless variations of this design. For example, you might create a class that writes a file directly to disk. Or, you might add another layer of abstraction using streams, so that the client could save the serialization data to disk, transmit it to another component, or even add encryption with a *Crypto-Stream* wrapper. Alternatively, you could use the *XmlSerializer* class to automate the work for you, as described in recipe 6.7.

6.7 Use XML Serialization with Custom Objects

Problem

You want to use an XML document as a serialization format and load the data into an object for manipulation in your code, preferably with as little code as possible.

Solution

Use *XmlSerializer* to transfer data from your object to XML, and vice versa.

Discussion

The *XmlSerializer* class allows you to convert objects to XML data, and vice versa. This process is used natively by Web services and provides a customizable serialization mechanism that won't require a single line of custom code. The *XmlSerializer* class is even intelligent enough to correctly create arrays when it finds nested elements.

The only requirements for using *XmlSerializer* are as follows:

- The *XmlSerializer* only serializes properties and public variables.

- The classes you want to serialize must include a default zero-argument constructor. The *XmlSerializer* uses this constructor when creating the new object during deserialization.

- All class properties must be readable *and* writable. This is because *XmlSerializer* uses property get procedures to retrieve information, and property set procedures to restore the data after deserialization.

To use serialization, you must first mark up your data objects with attributes that indicate the desired XML mapping. These attributes are found in the *System.Xml.Serialization* namespace and include the following:

- ■ ***XmlRoot***   specifies the name of the root element of the XML file. By default, *XmlSerializer* will use the name of the class. This attribute can be applied to the class declaration.

- ■ ***XmlElement***   indicates the element name to use for a property or public variable. By default, *XmlSerializer* will use the name of the property or public variable.

- ■ ***XmlAttribute***   indicates that a property or public variable should be serialized as an attribute, not an element, and specifies the attribute name.

- ■ ***XmlEnum***   configures the text that should be used when serializing enumerated values. By default, the name of the enumerated constant is used.

- ■ ***XmlIgnore***   indicates that a property or public variable should not be serialized.

For example, the following code shows the classes needed to represent the orders.xml items. In this case, the only attribute that was needed was *XmlAttribute*, which maps the ID property to an attribute named *id*. To use the code as written, you must import the *System.Xml.Serialization* namespace.

```
Public Class Order
    Private _ID As String
    Private _Client As Client
    Private _Items() As Item

    <XmlAttributeAttribute("id")> _
    Public Property ID() As String
        Get
            Return _ID
        End Get
        Set(ByVal Value As String)
            _ID = Value
        End Set
    End Property

    Public Property Client() As Client
        Get
            Return _Client
        End Get
        Set(ByVal Value As Client)
```

```vb
                _Client = Value
            End Set
        End Property


        Public Property Items() As Item()
            Get
                Return _Items
            End Get
            Set(ByVal Value As Item())
                _Items = Value
            End Set
        End Property

        Public Sub New(ByVal id As String, ByVal client As Client, _
           ByVal items As Item())
            Me.ID = id
            Me.Client = client
            Me.Items = items
        End Sub

        Public Sub New()
            ' (XML serialization requires the default constructor.)
        End Sub

    End Class

    Public Class Item
        Private _ID As String
        Private _Name As String
        Private _Price As Decimal

        <XmlAttributeAttribute("id")> _
        Public Property ID() As String
            Get
                Return _ID
            End Get
            Set(ByVal Value As String)
                _ID = Value
            End Set
        End Property

        Public Property Name() As String
            Get
                Return _Name
            End Get
            Set(ByVal Value As String)
                _Name = Value
            End Set
        End Property
```

```vb
        Public Property Price() As Decimal
            Get
                Return _Price
            End Get
            Set(ByVal Value As Decimal)
                _Price = Value
            End Set
        End Property

        Public Sub New(ByVal id As String, ByVal name As String, _
          ByVal price As Decimal)
            Me.ID = id
            Me.Name = name
            Me.Price = price
        End Sub

        Public Sub New()
            ' (XML serialization requires the default constructor.)
        End Sub

    End Class

    Public Class Client
        Private _ID As String
        Private _Name As String

        <XmlAttributeAttribute("id")> _
        Public Property ID() As String
            Get
                Return _ID
            End Get
            Set(ByVal Value As String)
                _ID = Value
            End Set
        End Property

        Public Property Name() As String
            Get
                Return _Name
            End Get
            Set(ByVal Value As String)
                _Name = Value
            End Set
        End Property

        Public Sub New(ByVal id As String, ByVal name As String)
            Me.ID = id
            Me.Name = name
        End Sub
```

```
Public Sub New()
    ' (XML serialization requires the default constructor.)
End Sub
```

```
End Class
```

Here's the code needed to create a new *Order* object, serialize the results to an XML document, deserialize the document back to an object, and display some basic order information.

```
' Create the order.
Dim Client As New Client("CMPSO33UL", "CompuStation")

Dim Item1 As New Item("2003", "Calculator", Convert.ToDecimal(24.99))
Dim Item2 As New Item("4311", "Laser Printer", Convert.ToDecimal(400.75))
Dim Items() As Item = {Item1, Item2}

Dim Order As New Order("2003-04-12-4996", Client, Items)

' Serialize the order to a file.
Dim Serializer As New System.Xml.Serialization.XmlSerializer(GetType(Order))
Dim fs As New FileStream("orders.xml", FileMode.Create)
Serializer.Serialize(fs, Order)
fs.Close()

' Deserialize the order from the file.
fs = New FileStream("orders.xml", FileMode.Open)
Order = CType(Serializer.Deserialize(fs), Order)
fs.Close()

' Display the prices of all items.
Dim Item As Item
For Each Item In Order.Items
    Console.WriteLine(Item.Name & ": " & Item.Price.ToString())
Next
```

> **Note** This approach isn't necessarily better than that presented in recipe 6.6. It does require less code and can prevent some types of error. However, it also forces you to give up a layer of abstraction (the custom reading and writing code) that can be used to perform validation, manage multiple versions of the same XML document, or map XML documents to .NET objects that don't match exactly. The approach you use depends on the needs of your application.

6.8 Perform an XSL Transform

Problem

You want to transform an XML document into another document using an XSLT stylesheet.

Solution

Use the *Transform* method of the *System.Xml.Xsl.XslTransform* class.

Discussion

XSLT (or XSL transforms) is an XML-based language designed to transform one XML document into another document. XSLT can be used to create a new XML document with the same data but arranged in a different structure, or to select a subset of the data in a document. It can also be used to create a different type of structured document. XSLT is commonly used in this manner to format an XML document into an HTML page.

XSLT is a rich language, and creating XSL transforms is beyond the scope of this book. However, you can learn how to create simple XSLT documents by looking at a basic example. Here's a stylesheet that could be used to transform orders.xml into an HTML summary page:

```
<?xml version="1.0" encoding="UTF-8" ?>
<xsl:stylesheet xmlns:xsl="http://www.w3.org/1999/XSL/Transform"
    version="1.0" >

  <xsl:template match="Order">
    <html><body><p>
    Order <b><xsl:value-of select="Client/@id"/></b>
    for <xsl:value-of select="Client/Name"/></p>
    <table border="1">
    <td>ID</td><td>Name</td><td>Price</td>
    <xsl:apply-templates select="Items/Item"/>
    </table></body></html>
  </xsl:template>

  <xsl:template match="Items/Item">
    <tr>
    <td><xsl:value-of select="@id"/></td>
    <td><xsl:value-of select="Name"/></td>
    <td><xsl:value-of select="Price"/></td>
    </tr>
  </xsl:template>

</xsl:stylesheet>
```

Essentially, every XSL stylesheet consists of a set of templates. Each template matches some set of elements in the source document and then describes the contribution that the matched element will make to the resulting document. In order to match the template, the XSLT document uses *XPath* expressions, as described in recipe 6.5.

The orders.xslt stylesheet contains two *template* elements (as children of the root *stylesheet* element). The first template matches the root *Order* element. When it finds it, it output the tags necessary to start an HTML table with appropriate column headings and inserts some data about the client using the *value-of* command, which outputs the text result of an *XPath* expression. In this case, the *XPath* expressions (Client/@id and Client/Name) match the *id* attribute and the *Name* element.

Next, the *apply-templates* command is used to branch off and perform processing of any contained *Item* elements. This is required because there might be multiple *Item* elements. Each *Item* element is matched using the *XPath* expression Items/Item. The root *Order* node isn't specified because *Order* is the current node. Finally, the initial template writes the tags necessary to end the HTML document.

To apply this XSLT stylesheet in .NET, use the *XslTransform* class, as shown in the following code. In this case, the code uses the overloaded version of the *Transform* method that saves the result document directly to disk, although you could receive it as a stream and process it inside your application instead.

```
Public Module TransformTest

    Public Sub Main()
        Dim Transform As New System.Xml.Xsl.XslTransform

        ' Load the XSL stylesheet.
        Transform.Load("orders.xslt")

        ' Transform orders.xml into orders.html using orders.xslt.
        Transform.Transform("orders.xml", "orders.html")

        Console.WriteLine("File 'orders.html' written successfully.")
        Console.ReadLine()
    End Sub

End Module
```

The final result of this process is the HTML file shown in the following listing. Figure 6-2 shows how this HTML is displayed in a browser.

```
<html>
  <body>
    <p>
    Order <b>CMPSO33UL</b>
    for CompuStation</p>
    <table border="1">
      <td>ID</td>
      <td>Name</td>
      <td>Price</td>
      <tr>
        <td>2003</td>
        <td>Calculator</td>
        <td>24.99</td>
      </tr>
      <tr>
        <td>4311</td>
        <td>Laser Printer</td>
        <td>400.75</td>
      </tr>
    </table>
  </body>
</html>
```

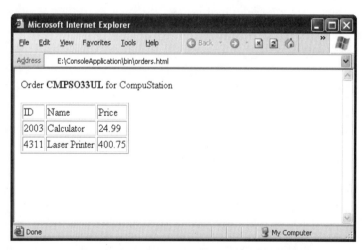

Figure 6-2   Figure 6-2   The stylesheet output for orders.xml

6.9 Validate an XML Document Against a Schema

Problem

You want to ensure that an XML document conforms to an XML schema.

Solution

Use *XmlValidatingReader* and handle the *ValidationEventHandler* event.

Discussion

An XML schema defines the rules that a given type of XML document must follow. The schema includes rules that define

■   The elements and attributes that can appear in a document.

■   The data types for elements and attributes.

■   The structure of a document, including what elements are children of other elements.

■   The order and number of child elements that appear in a document.

■   Whether elements are empty, can include text, or require fixed values.

XML schema documents are beyond the scope of this chapter, but much can be learned from a simple example. Essentially, an XSD document lists the elements that can occur using element tags. The type attribute indicates the data type. Here's an example for the product name:

```
<xs:element name="Name" type="xs:string" />
```

The basic schema data types are defined at *http://www.w3.org/TR/xmlschema-2*. They map closely to .NET data types and include *string*, *int*, *long*, *decimal*, *float*, *dateTime*, *boolean*, and *base64Binary*, to name a few of the most frequently used types.

Elements that consist of more than one subelement are called *complex types*. You can nest them together using a *sequence* tag, if order is important, or a *choice* tag if it's not. Here's how you might model the *Client* element:

```
<xs:element name="Client">
    <xs:complexType>
        <xs:sequence>
            <xs:element name="Name" type="xs:string" />
        </xs:sequence>
    </xs:complexType>
</xs:element>
```

By default, a listed element can occur exactly one time in a document. You can configure this behavior by specifying the *maxOccurs* and *minOccurs* attributes:

```
<xs:element name="Item" minOccurs="0" maxOccurs="unbounded">
```

Here's the complete schema for the orders.xml file:

```xml
<?xml version="1.0" encoding="utf-8"?>
<xs:schema id="Orders" xmlns=""
  xmlns:xs="http://www.w3.org/2001/XMLSchema"

  xmlns:msdata="urn:schemas-microsoft-com:xml-msdata">
  <xs:element name="Order">
    <xs:complexType>
      <xs:sequence>
        <xs:element name="Client">
          <xs:complexType>
            <xs:sequence>
              <xs:element name="Name" type="xs:string" />
            </xs:sequence>
            <xs:attribute name="id" type="xs:string" />
          </xs:complexType>
        </xs:element>
        <xs:element name="Items">
          <xs:complexType>
            <xs:sequence>
              <xs:element name="Item" minOccurs="0" maxOccurs="unbounded">
                <xs:complexType>
                  <xs:sequence>
                    <xs:element name="Name" type="xs:string" />
                    <xs:element name="Price" type="xs:decimal" />
                  </xs:sequence>
                  <xs:attribute name="id" type="xs:string" />
                </xs:complexType>
              </xs:element>
            </xs:sequence>
          </xs:complexType>
        </xs:element>
      </xs:sequence>
      <xs:attribute name="id" type="xs:string" />
    </xs:complexType>
  </xs:element>
</xs:schema>
```

The *XmlValidatingReader* class enforces all of these schema rules, and it also checks that the XML document is *well formed* (which means there are no illegal characters, all opening tags have a corresponding closing tag, and so on). To check a document, you read through it one node at a time by calling the *XmlValidatingReader.Read* method. If an error is found, *XmlValidatingReader* raises a *ValidationEventHandler* event with information about the error. If you wish, you can handle this event and continue processing the document to find more errors. If you don't handle this event, an *XmlException* will be raised when the first error is encountered, and processing will be aborted. To test only if a document is well-formed, you can use the *XmlValidatingReader* without a schema.

The next example shows a utility class that displays all errors in an XML document when the *ValidateXml* method is called. Errors are displayed in a Console window, and a final Boolean variable is returned to indicate the success or failure of the entire validation operation. Remember that you'll need to import the *System.Xml.Schema* namespace in order to use this class.

```
Public Class ConsoleValidator

    ' Set to True if at least one error exist.
    Private Failed As Boolean

    Public Function ValidateXml(ByVal XmlFilename As String, _
      ByVal schemaFilename As String) As Boolean

        ' Create the validator.
        Dim r As New XmlTextReader(XmlFilename)
        Dim Validator As New XmlValidatingReader(r)
        Validator.ValidationType = ValidationType.Schema
        Dim Schema As New System.Xml.Schema.XmlSchema

        ' Load the schema file into the validator.
        Dim Schemas As New XmlSchemaCollection
        Schemas.Add(Nothing, schemaFilename)
        Validator.Schemas.Add(Schemas)

        ' Set the validation event handler.
        AddHandler Validator.ValidationEventHandler, _
          AddressOf Me.ValidationEventHandler

        Failed = False

        Try
            ' Read all XML data.
            While Validator.Read()
            End While
        Catch Err As XmlException
            ' This happens if the XML document includes illegal characters
            ' or tags that aren't properly nested or closed.
            Console.WriteLine("A critical XML error has occured.")
            Failed = True
        End Try

        Validator.Close()

        Return Not Failed

    End Function
```

```
    Private Sub ValidationEventHandler(ByVal sender As Object, _
      ByVal args As System.Xml.Schema.ValidationEventArgs)
        Failed = True

        ' Display the validation error.
        Console.WriteLine("Validation error: " & args.Message)
    End Sub

End Class
```

Here's how you would use the class:

```
Dim ConsoleValidator As New ConsoleValidator
Console.WriteLine("Validating XML file orders.xml with orders.xsd.")

Dim Success As Boolean
Success = ConsoleValidator.ValidateXml("orders.xml", "orders.xsd")
```

If the document is valid, no messages will appear, and the *Success* variable will be set to *True*. But consider what happens if you use a document that breaks schema rules, like the orders_wrong.xml file shown here:

```
<?xml version="1.0"?>
<Order id="2003-04-12-4996">
    <Client id="CMPSO33UL">
        <Namely>CompuStation</Namely>
    </Client>
    <Items>
        <Item id="2003">
            <Name>Calculator</Name>
            <Price>twenty-four</Price>
        </Item>
        <Item id="4311">
            <Price>400.75</Price>
            <Name>Laser Printer</Name>
        </Item>
    </Items>
</Order>
```

If you attempt to validate this document, the output will indicate each error, and the *Success* variable will be set to *False*:

```
Validation error: Element 'Client' has invalid child element 'Namely'.
Expected 'Name'.
Validation error: The 'Namely' element is not declared.
Validation error: The 'Price' element has an invalid value according to its
data type.
Validation error: Element 'Item' has invalid child element 'Price'.
Expected 'Name'.
```

If you want to validate an XML document and then process it, you can use *XmlValidatingReader* to scan a document as it's read into an in-memory *Xml-Document*. Here's how it works:

```
Dim Doc As New XmlDocument()
Dim r As New XmlTextReader("orders.xml")
Dim Validator As New XmlValidatingReader(r)

' Load the schema into the validator.
Validator.ValidationType = ValidationType.Schema
Dim Schema As New System.Xml.Schema.XmlSchema()
Dim Schemas As New XmlSchemaCollection()
Schemas.Add(Nothing, "..\..\..\orders.xsd")
Validator.Schemas.Add(Schemas)

' Load the document and validate it at the same time.
' Don't handle the ValidationEventHandler event. Instead, allow any errors
' to be thrown as an XmlSchemaException.
Try
    Doc.Load(Validator)
    ' (Validation succeeded if you reach here.)
Catch Err As XmlSchemaException
    ' (Validation failed if you reach here.)
End Try
```

> **Note** Microsoft Visual Studio .NET includes a visual schema designer that allows you to create schema files at design-time using graphical elements. You can also use the command-line utility xsd.exe to quickly create a schema from an XML document, which you can use as a starting point.

6.10 Store Binary Data with a Base64 Transform

Problem

You need to store binary data in an XML file.

Solution

Use *Convert.ToBase64String* to create a string representation of the data that will not contain any illegal characters.

Discussion

XML documents can't contain extended characters, or special characters such as the greater than (>) or less than (<) symbols, which are used to denote elements. However, you can convert binary data into a string representation that is XML-legal by using a Base64 transform.

In Base64 encoding, each sequence of three bytes is converted to a sequence of four bytes. Each Base64 encoded character has one of the 64 possible values in the range {A-Z, a-z, 0-9, +, /, =}.

Here's an example that creates a new node in the orders.xml for Base64-encoded image data. In order to use this code as written, you must import the *System.IO* namespace.

```
Public Module StoreBase64Data

    Public Sub Main()
        ' Load the document.
        Dim Doc As New XmlDocument
        Doc.Load("orders.xml")

        ' Create a new element.
        Dim LogoNode As XmlNode
        LogoNode = Doc.CreateElement("Logo")

        ' Retrieve the picture data.
        Dim fs As New FileStream("logo.bmp", FileMode.Open)
        Dim LogoBytes(Convert.ToInt32(fs.Length)) As Byte
        fs.Read(LogoBytes, 0, LogoBytes.Length)

        ' Encode the picture data and add it as text.
        Dim EncodedText As String = Convert.ToBase64String(LogoBytes)
        LogoNode.AppendChild(Doc.CreateTextNode(EncodedText))

        ' Add the new element.
        Doc.DocumentElement.ChildNodes(0).AppendChild(LogoNode)

        ' Save the document.
        Doc.Save("orders_pic.xml")

        Console.WriteLine("File successfully 'orders_pic.xml' written.")
        Console.ReadLine()
    End Sub

End Module
```

Here's the resulting (slightly abbreviated) XML document:

```
<?xml version="1.0"?>
<Order id="2003-04-12-4996">
  <Client id="CMPS033UL">
    <Name>CompuStation</Name>
    <Logo>R0lGOD1h0wAfALMPAAAAAIAAAACAAICAAAAAgIAAgACAgICAgMDAwP8AAD...</Logo>
  </Client>

  <!-- Items omitted. -->

</Order>
```

You can use *Convert.FromBase64String* to retrieve the image data from the XML document.

> **Note**   Visual Studio .NET uses a Base64 transform to store binary information that's added to a form at design time in the corresponding XML resources file.

7

Multithreading

In the pre–Microsoft .NET world, Visual Basic developers had to jump through extraordinary hurdles to use threads and often wound up with corrupted data or a crashed integrated development environment (IDE) for their trouble. In Microsoft Visual Basic .NET, working with threads is as easy as creating an object and calling a method. However, multithreading safely and efficiently isn't as straightforward.

This chapter presents a few basic patterns that can help you design a robust multithreading framework. You'll see basic recipes for calling a method asynchronously through a delegate (recipes 7.1 to 7.4) and with the *Thread* class (recipes 7.5 to 7.8), and learn how to update a Windows user interface from a background thread (7.9). You'll also see how to create the popular thread wrapper class (7.11) and build a continuous task processor (7.12).

> **Note** The recipes in this chapter aren't a replacement for a dedicated tutorial about multithreading. If you haven't written multithreaded code before, you should start with a more general introduction. Both *Programming Microsoft Visual Basic .NET Core Reference* (Microsoft Press, 2002) and my own *The Book of VB .NET* (No Starch Press, 2002) can provide an excellent introduction.

Developers usually add multithreading to an application in order to handle multiple tasks at the same time (for example, a server that might need to interact with several clients simultaneously), add responsiveness, or reduce wait times for short tasks that might otherwise be held up by other, more intensive work. In order to simulate long tasks, many of the recipes in this chapter use the *Delay* method shown here:

```
Private Function Delay(ByVal seconds As Integer) As Integer

    Dim StartTime As DateTime = DateTime.Now
    Do
        ' Do nothing.
    Loop While DateTime.Now.Subtract(StartTime).TotalSeconds < seconds
    Return seconds

End Function
```

This function simply waits the indicated amount of time and then returns the number of seconds it waited. The shared *Thread.Sleep* method could also be used with the same effect, but I've used this approach because it simulates code executing (rather than simply pausing the thread temporarily). The method returns the wait time because this allows the recipes to demonstrate another important concept—retrieving data from a separate thread. This task isn't as straightforward as it is when calling a function synchronously.

> **Note** The .NET Framework includes types for multithreading programming in the *System.Threading* namespace. The recipes in this chapter assume you have imported this namespace.

7.1 Call Any Method Asynchronously with a Delegate

Problem

You want a method to execute on another thread, so your program can continue with other tasks.

Solution

Create a delegate for the method. You can then use the *BeginInvoke* and *EndInvoke* methods.

Discussion

The .NET Framework includes support for delegates, which act like type-safe function pointers. Using a delegate, you can store a reference to a procedure and then invoke it through the delegate. This process is similar to the way you might invoke a class method through an interface.

Behind the scenes, delegates are actually dynamically generated classes. As part of their functionality, they contain the ability to call the referenced method synchronously or asynchronously, so that it won't block your code. To invoke a delegate asynchronously, you use the *BeginInvoke* method. You can retrieve the result later using the *EndInvoke* method.

For example, imagine you have the following function definition:

```
Private Function TimeConsumingTaskA(ByVal seconds As Integer) As Integer
    ' (Code omitted.)
End Function
```

A delegate for this function would define the exact same signature. That means that parameters and return value must be the same in number and data type, although the names are not important.

```
Private Delegate Function TimeConsumingTask(ByVal sec As Integer) As Integer
```

Now you can invoke *TimeConsumingTaskA* through the *TimeConsuming-Task* delegate synchronously

```
' Create an instance of the delegate.
Dim Invoker As New TimeConsumingTask(AddressOf TimeConsumingTaskA)

' Invoke the delegate synchronously.
' This is equivalent to: TimeConsumingTaskA(30)
Invoker(30)
```

or asynchronously

```
' Create an instance of the delegate.
Dim Invoker As New TimeConsumingTask(AddressOf TimeConsumingTaskA)

' Invoke the delegate asynchronously.
Dim AsyncResult As IAsyncResult
AsyncResult = Invoker.BeginInvoke(30, Nothing, Nothing)

' (Do something else here.)

' Retrieve the results from the asynchronous call.
' If it is not complete, this call effectively makes it synchronous,
' and waits for it to complete.
Dim Result As Integer = Invoker.EndInvoke(AsyncResult)
```

Notice that when using *BeginInvoke*, the ordinary function parameters come first, followed by two additional parameters, which allow you to specify a callback and state information (see recipe 7.4). You can create a delegate to asynchronously call any method, whether it's shared, public, private, or even belongs to a Web service or .NET Remoting proxy. You can also check if a delegate call has completed using the returned *IAsyncResult* object, which provides a Boolean *IsCompleted* property.

> **Note** If you make an asynchronous call to a procedure that does not return any information, you won't need to call *EndInvoke*. However, it's still recommended for error handling. If an unhandled exception occurs while the asynchronous method is executing, you won't be notified until you call *EndInvoke*. Thus, if you need to add any exception-handling logic, you should add it to the *EndInvoke* call, not *BeginInvoke*.

Following is a full example that demonstrates two tasks that execute at the same time using an asynchronous call through a delegate. Each task delays 30 seconds, but the total delay is dramatically reduced.

```
Public Module AsynchronousInvoke

    Private Delegate Function TimeConsumingTask(ByVal seconds As Integer) _
      As Integer

    Public Sub Main()
        Dim StartTime As DateTime = DateTime.Now
        Dim ResultA, ResultB As Integer

        ' Start the first task on a new thread.
        ' Specify a delay of 30 seconds.
        Dim AsyncInvoker As New TimeConsumingTask( _
          AddressOf TimeConsumingTaskA)
        Dim AsyncResult As IAsyncResult
        AsyncResult = AsyncInvoker.BeginInvoke(30, Nothing, Nothing)

        ' Start the second task on the main thread.
        ' Specify a delay of 30 seconds.
        ' This blocks until complete.
        ResultB = TimeConsumingTaskB(30)
```

```
    ' Retrieve the result of the asynchronous tasks.
    ' If it is not already complete, this blocks until complete.
    ResultA = AsyncInvoker.EndInvoke(AsyncResult)

    Console.WriteLine("Method A delayed for: " & ResultA.ToString())
    Console.WriteLine("Method B delayed for: " & ResultB.ToString())
    Console.WriteLine("Total seconds taken to execute: " & _
        DateTime.Now.Subtract(StartTime).TotalSeconds.ToString())

    Console.ReadLine()
End Sub

Private Function TimeConsumingTaskA(ByVal seconds As Integer) As Integer
    Return Delay(seconds)
End Function

Private Function TimeConsumingTaskB(ByVal seconds As Integer) As Integer
    Return Delay(seconds)
End Function

' (Delay function omitted.)

End Module
```

Here's the output you should see:

```
Method A delayed for: 30
Method B delayed for: 30
Total seconds taken to execute: 30.894424
```

The delegate approach masks much of the complexity of threading because you don't need to worry about marshalling data. However, if you call more than one delegate that interact with the same piece of data (like a form-level variable), you will need to add locking code, or a conflict could occur.

> **Note**   Although simple, delegates also have certain limitations that the *Thread* class does not. For example, you can't control the priority of an asynchronous delegate thread, and you are limited in the number of asynchronous calls that will actually execute asynchronously (depending on how many threads the common language runtime makes available in its pool).

7.2 Wait for Several Asynchronous Calls to Complete

Problem

You want to call multiple procedures asynchronously and suspend further processing until they are all complete.

Solution

Retrieve the *WaitHandle* for each call, and use the shared *WaitHandle.WaitAll* method.

Discussion

When you call the *BeginInvoke* method, you receive an *IAsyncResult* object that allows you to check the status of the thread and complete the request. In addition, the *IAsyncResult* interface defines an *AsyncWaitHandle* property that allows you to retrieve a *WaitHandle* for the asynchronous request.

The *WaitHandle* class defines three methods: *WaitAll*, *WaitAny*, and *WaitOne*. You can use the shared *WaitAll* method with an array of *WaitHandle* objects to wait for a group of asynchronous tasks to complete.

The following code shows an example that starts three tasks (taking 10, 30, and 15 seconds, respectively). The *WaitAll* method will return after all tasks have completed, in approximately 30 seconds.

```
Public Module AsynchronousInvoke

    Private Delegate Function TimeConsumingTask(ByVal seconds As Integer) _
      As Integer

    ' The WaitAll() method must execute on a MTA thread.
    <MTAThread()> _
    Public Sub Main()
        Dim ResultA, ResultB, ResultC As Integer

        ' Define and start three tasks.
        Dim AsyncInvoker As New TimeConsumingTask(AddressOf Delay)
        Dim AsyncResultA, AsyncResultB, AsyncResultC As IAsyncResult
        AsyncResultA = AsyncInvoker.BeginInvoke(10, Nothing, Nothing)
        AsyncResultB = AsyncInvoker.BeginInvoke(30, Nothing, Nothing)
        AsyncResultC = AsyncInvoker.BeginInvoke(15, Nothing, Nothing)

        Console.WriteLine("Call A is: " & AsyncResultA.IsCompleted.ToString())
        Console.WriteLine("Call B is: " & AsyncResultB.IsCompleted.ToString())
        Console.WriteLine("Call C is: " & AsyncResultC.IsCompleted.ToString())
```

```
      ' Block until all tasks are complete.
      Console.WriteLine("Waiting...")
      Dim WaitHandles() As WaitHandle = {AsyncResultA.AsyncWaitHandle, _
        AsyncResultB.AsyncWaitHandle, AsyncResultC.AsyncWaitHandle}
      WaitHandle.WaitAll(WaitHandles)

      Console.WriteLine("Call A is: " & AsyncResultA.IsCompleted.ToString())
      Console.WriteLine("Call B is: " & AsyncResultB.IsCompleted.ToString())
      Console.WriteLine("Call C is: " & AsyncResultC.IsCompleted.ToString())

      Console.ReadLine()
   End Sub

   ' (Delay function omitted.)

End Module
```

7.3 Wait for One of Many Asynchronous Calls to Complete

Problem

You want to call multiple procedures asynchronously and suspend processing until any one call completes.

Solution

Retrieve the *WaitHandle* for each call, and use the shared *WaitHandle.WaitAny* method.

Discussion

The *System.Threading.WaitHandle* class provides a *WaitAny* method that accepts an array of *WaitHandle* objects and blocks until at least one *WaitHandle* is completed. When *WaitAny* returns, it provides an index number that indicates the position of the completed *WaitHandle* in the array.

The following example launches three calls at once. It then waits until at least one call finishes, displays the results, and then resumes waiting for one of the next two calls to complete. It uses an *ArrayList* to manage the *WaitHandle* objects, removing them as they are completed. The *ArrayList* is copied to a strongly typed array just before the *WaitAny* call is made.

```
Public Module AsynchronousInvoke

   Private Delegate Function TimeConsumingTask(ByVal seconds As Integer) _
      As Integer
```

```vb
' The WaitAny() method must execute on a MTA thread.
<MTAThread()> _
Public Sub Main()
    Dim ResultA, ResultB, ResultC As Integer

    ' Define and start three tasks.
    Dim AsyncInvoker As New TimeConsumingTask(AddressOf Delay)
    Dim AsyncResultA, AsyncResultB, AsyncResultC As IAsyncResult
    AsyncResultA = AsyncInvoker.BeginInvoke(10, Nothing, Nothing)
    AsyncResultB = AsyncInvoker.BeginInvoke(30, Nothing, Nothing)
    AsyncResultC = AsyncInvoker.BeginInvoke(15, Nothing, Nothing)

    Dim WaitHandles() As WaitHandle
    Dim WaitHandleList As New ArrayList()
    WaitHandleList.Add(AsyncResultA.AsyncWaitHandle)
    WaitHandleList.Add(AsyncResultB.AsyncWaitHandle)
    WaitHandleList.Add(AsyncResultC.AsyncWaitHandle)

    Dim StartTime As DateTime = DateTime.Now
    Do
        WaitHandles = CType( _
          WaitHandleList.ToArray(GetType(WaitHandle)), WaitHandle())

        ' Block until at least one request is complete.
        Console.WriteLine("Waiting...")
        Dim CompletedIndex As Integer = WaitHandle.WaitAny(WaitHandles)
        WaitHandleList.RemoveAt(CompletedIndex)

        ' Display the current status.
        Console.WriteLine( _
          DateTime.Now.Subtract(StartTime).TotalSeconds.ToString() & _
          " seconds elapsed.")
        Console.WriteLine("Call A is: " & _
          AsyncResultA.IsCompleted.ToString())
        Console.WriteLine("Call B is: " & _
          AsyncResultB.IsCompleted.ToString())
        Console.WriteLine("Call C is: " & _
          AsyncResultC.IsCompleted.ToString())
    Loop Until WaitHandleList.Count = 0

    Console.WriteLine("Completed.")
    Console.ReadLine()
End Sub

' (Delay function omitted.)

End Module
```

The results will appear as follows:

```
Waiting...
10.1445872 seconds elapsed.
Call A is: True
Call B is: False
Call C is: False

Waiting...
18.6868704 seconds elapsed.
Call A is: True
Call B is: False
Call C is: True

Waiting...
31.0746832 seconds elapsed.
Call A is: True
Call B is: True
Call C is: True

Completed.
```

7.4 Use a Callback with an Asynchronous Call

Problem

You want to be notified as soon as an asynchronous call completes, without needing to poll the *IAsyncResult* object.

Solution

Use a callback, which will be triggered automatically when the call completes.

Discussion

Often, when you start a multithreaded task in an application, you don't want the additional complexity and overhead of monitoring that task. The solution is to use a callback. With a callback, your code executes a function or subroutine asynchronously and carries on with other work. Your callback procedure is automatically invoked when the asynchronous call is finished.

The callback approach allows you to separate the code that processes asynchronous tasks from the code that performs work on the main thread. However, it also works best if the work performed by the main thread is independent from the work you are performing asynchronously. One example might be a desktop application that downloads new status information from a Web service and updates the display periodically.

To use a callback, you simply pass the address of the callback procedure you want to use to the *BeginInvoke* method.

```
AsyncInvoker As New TimeConsumingTask(AddressOf Delay)

' Invoke the method and supply a callback.
' Note that the code does not retain the IAsyncResult object that is returned
' from BeginInvoke() because it is not needed.
AsyncInvoker.BeginInvoke(10, AddressOf Callback, Nothing)
```

The callback procedure must have the signature defined by the *System.AsyncCallback* delegate. This includes a single parameter: the *IAsyncResult* object for the asynchronous call. Typically, you'll use this to call *EndInvoke* to retrieve the result from the delegate.

```
Private Sub Callback(ByVal ar As IAsyncResult)
    ' Retrieve the result for the call that just ended.
    Dim Result As Integer = AsyncInvoker.EndInvoke(ar)

    ' Display the result.
    Console.WriteLine(Result.ToString())
End Sub
```

In this example, *AsyncInvoker* is retained as a class member variable. That means that it can be conveniently accessed in the callback procedure. However, this design won't work if you want to make multiple asynchronous calls at once and handle them all using the same callback. In this case, you need to use the second optional *BeginInvoke* parameter to supply a custom state object.

For example, consider a time-consuming method that looks up weather readings from a database based on the city name. You might choose to use asynchronous calls so that the user can submit multiple city name queries at once. When a query completes, the callback runs. At this point, you need to be able to retrieve the original delegate to complete the call, and you need to retrieve information so you can match the answer (the temperature reading) with the original question (the city name). The easiest solution is to create a custom class that encapsulates these two pieces of information:

```
Public Class GetWeatherAsyncCallInfo

    Private _AsyncInvoker As GetWeatherDelegate
    Private _CityName As String

    Public Property AsyncInvoker() As GetWeatherDelegate
        Get
```

```
            Return _AsyncInvoker
        End Get
        Set(ByVal Value As GetWeatherDelegate)
            _AsyncInvoker = Value
        End Set
    End Property

    Public Property CityName() As String
        Get
            Return _CityName
        End Get
        Set(ByVal Value As String)
            _CityName = Value
        End Set
    End Property

    Public Sub New(ByVal [delegate] As GetWeatherDelegate, _
      ByVal cityQuery As String)
        Me.AsyncInvoker = [delegate]
        Me.CityName = cityQuery
    End Sub

End Class
```

Now, you can create a *GetWeatherAsyncCallInfo* object and pass it to the *BeginInvoke* method. It will then be returned in the callback procedure. Here is a complete Console application that demonstrates how this works.

```
Public Module AsynchronousInvoke

    Public Delegate Function GetWeatherDelegate(ByVal cityName As String) _
      As Single

    Public Sub Main()
        ' Define and start three tasks.
        Dim AsyncInvokerA As New GetWeatherDelegate(AddressOf GetWeather)
        Dim QueryA As New GetWeatherAsyncCallInfo(AsyncInvokerA, "New York")
        AsyncInvokerA.BeginInvoke("New York", AddressOf Callback, QueryA)

        Dim AsyncInvokerB As New GetWeatherDelegate(AddressOf GetWeather)
        Dim QueryB As New GetWeatherAsyncCallInfo(AsyncInvokerB, "Tokyo")
        AsyncInvokerB.BeginInvoke("Tokyo", AddressOf Callback, QueryB)

        Dim AsyncInvokerC As New GetWeatherDelegate(AddressOf GetWeather)
        Dim QueryC As New GetWeatherAsyncCallInfo(AsyncInvokerC, "Montreal")
        AsyncInvokerC.BeginInvoke("Montreal", AddressOf Callback, QueryC)
```

```
            Console.WriteLine("Waiting... press Enter to exit.")
            Console.ReadLine()
    End Sub

    Private Function GetWeather(ByVal cityName As String) As Single
        ' This code would query the database for the requested info.
        ' Instead, we pause and return a random "temperature reading."
        Dim Rand As New Random()
        Delay(Rand.Next(5, 10))
        Return Rand.Next(30, 100)
    End Function

    Private Sub Callback(ByVal ar As IAsyncResult)
        ' Retrieve the state object.
        Dim QueryInfo As GetWeatherAsyncCallInfo = CType(ar.AsyncState, _
            GetWeatherAsyncCallInfo)

        ' Complete the call and retrieve the result.
        Dim Result As Single = QueryInfo.AsyncInvoker.EndInvoke(ar)

        Console.WriteLine("Result for: " & QueryInfo.CityName & _
            " is: " & Result.ToString())
    End Sub

    ' (Delay function omitted.)

End Module
```

The output for a test run is as follows:

```
Waiting... press any key to exit.
Result for: Tokyo is: 47
Result for: New York is: 75
Result for: Montreal is: 51
```

Notice that the callback will execute on the same thread as the asynchronous task, which is not the main thread of the application. This means that if the callback accesses a class member variable, it needs to use locking code (as shown in recipe 7.6). Similarly, if the callback accesses a portion of a Windows user interface, it needs to marshal the call to the correct thread (see recipe 7.9). In this case, the callback accesses the *Console* object, which is known to be thread-safe, and so no locking code is required.

7.5 Perform an Asynchronous Task with the *Thread* Class

Problem

You want to execute a task on another thread and be able to control that thread's priority, state, and so on.

Solution

Create a new *System.Threading.Thread* object that references the code you want to execute asynchronously, and use the *Start* method.

Discussion

The *Thread* object allows you to write multithreaded code with a finer degree of control than that provided by asynchronous delegates. As with delegates, the *Thread* class can only point to a single method. However, unlike delegates, the *Thread* class can only execute a method that takes no parameters and has no return value. (In other words, it must match the signature of the *System.Threading.ThreadStart* delegate.) If you need to send data or instructions to a thread, or retrieve data from a thread, you will have to use a custom-threaded object, as shown in recipes 7.7 and 7.8.

The following example starts two threads, both of which iterate through a loop and write to the *Console* object. Because *Console* is thread-safe, no locking is required. If the user presses a key before the threads have finished processing, the threads are automatically aborted.

```
Public Module ThreadTest

    Public Sub Main()
        ' Define threads and point to code.
        Dim ThreadA As New Thread(AddressOf Task)
        Dim ThreadB As New Thread(AddressOf Task)

        ' Name the threads (aids debugging).
        ThreadA.Name = "Thread A"
        ThreadB.Name = "Thread B"

        ' Start threads.
        ThreadA.Start()
        ThreadB.Start()

        Console.WriteLine("Press Enter to exit...")
        Console.ReadLine()
```

```
                    ' If the threads aren't yet finished, abort them.
                    If (ThreadA.ThreadState And ThreadState.Running) = _
                      ThreadState.Running Then
                        ThreadA.Abort()
                    End If
                    If (ThreadB.ThreadState And ThreadState.Running) = _
                      ThreadState.Running Then
                        ThreadB.Abort()
                    End If
                End Sub

                Private Sub Task()
                    Dim i As Integer
                    For i = 1 To 5
                        Console.WriteLine(Thread.CurrentThread.Name & _
                          " at: " & i.ToString)
                        Delay(1)
                    Next
                    Console.WriteLine(Thread.CurrentThread.Name & " completed")
                End Sub

                ' (Delay function omitted.)

        End Module
```

Notice that this code tests the state of the threads using a bitwise *And* operation. That's because the *ThreadState* property can include multiple *ThreadState* values, and the code needs to filter out the one it wants to test for.

The output for this example looks like this:

```
Press any key to exit...
Thread A at: 1
Thread B at: 1
Thread A at: 2
Thread B at: 2
Thread A at: 3
Thread B at: 3
Thread A at: 4
Thread B at: 4
Thread A at: 5
Thread B at: 5
Thread A completed
Thread B completed
```

Threads support a variety of properties, including the following:

■ *IsAlive* returns *True* unless the thread is stopped, aborted, or has not yet been started.

- *IsBackground* is *False* by default. If you set this to *True*, you create a background thread. Background threads are identical to foreground threads, except they can't prevent a process from ending. Once all the foreground threads in your application have terminated, the common language runtime automatically aborts all background threads that are still alive.

- *Name* allows you to set a string name identifying the thread.

- *Priority* indicates the scheduling priority of the thread as compared to other threads, using a value from the *ThreadPriority* enumeration. For example, if you heighten the *Priority* of *ThreadA* in the preceding example, you will notice that *ThreadA* completes its task faster than *ThreadB*.

- *ThreadState* provides a combination of *ThreadState* values, which indicate whether the thread is started, running, or waiting, is a background thread, and so on.

Threads also support a few basic methods:

- *Start* starts a thread executing for the first time.

- *Abort* aggressively kills a thread using the *ThreadAbortException*.

- *Sleep* pauses a thread for a specified amount of time.

- *Join* waits until the thread terminates (or a specified timeout elapses).

- *Suspend* pauses a thread for an indefinite amount of time, while *Resume* returns it to life.

- *Interrupt* resumes execution on a thread if it's currently waiting, blocked, or sleeping.

Note   Threads cannot be reused. Once a thread finishes its task, its state changes permanently to *ThreadState.Stopped*. You cannot call *Start* on the thread again. If you want to create a continuously executing, reusable thread, you need to add a loop, as described in recipe 7.12.

7.6 Use Synchronization Code with Multiple Threads

Problem

You need to access the same object from multiple threads, without causing a concurrency problem.

Solution

Use the *SyncLock* statement to gain exclusive access to the object.

Discussion

Trying to access an object on more than one thread at once is inherently dangerous, because a single command in a high-level language like Visual Basic .NET might actually compile to dozens of low-level machine language instructions. If two threads try to modify data at the same time, there's a very real possibility that the changes made by one thread will be overwritten—and this is only one of many possible threading errors, all of which occur sporadically and are extremely difficult to diagnose.

To overcome these limitations, you can use locking, which allows you to obtain exclusive access to an object. You can then safely modify the object without worrying that another thread might try to read or change it while your operation is in progress. Locking is built into Visual Basic .NET through the *SyncLock* statement. *SyncLock* works with any reference object (value types such as integers are not supported, so they must be wrapped in a class).

For example, consider the thread-safe counter object shown in the following code. It automatically locks itself before a change is made. Thus, multiple threads can call *Increment* at the same time without any danger that their changes will collide.

```
Public Class Counter

    Private _Value As Integer

    Public ReadOnly Property Value() As Integer
        Get
            Return _Value
        End Get
    End Property

    Public Sub Increment()
        SyncLock Me
            _Value += 1
```

```
            End SyncLock
        End Sub

End Class
```

Here's a Console application that demonstrates how multiple threads can use the same counter:

```
Public Module ThreadTest

    Private Counter As New Counter()

    Public Sub Main()
        ' Define threads and point to code.
        Dim ThreadA As New Thread(AddressOf Task)
        Dim ThreadB As New Thread(AddressOf Task)

        ' Name the threads (aids debugging).
        ThreadA.Name = "Thread A"
        ThreadB.Name = "Thread B"

        ' Start threads.
        ThreadA.Start()
        ThreadB.Start()

        Console.WriteLine("Press Enter to exit...")
        Console.ReadLine()

        ' If the threads aren't yet finished, abort them.
        If (ThreadA.ThreadState And ThreadState.Running) = _
          ThreadState.Running Then
            ThreadA.Abort()
        End If
        If (ThreadB.ThreadState And ThreadState.Running) = _
          ThreadState.Running Then
            ThreadB.Abort()
        End If
    End Sub

    Private Sub Task()
        Dim i As Integer
        For i = 1 To 5
            Delay(1)
            Counter.Increment()
            Console.WriteLine(Thread.CurrentThread.Name & _
              " set Counter.Value = " & Counter.Value.ToString())
        Next
    End Sub
```

```
' (Delay function omitted.)
```

```
End Module
```

The output for this example is as follows:

```
Press any key to exit...
Thread A set Counter.Value = 1
Thread B set Counter.Value = 2
Thread A set Counter.Value = 3
Thread B set Counter.Value = 4
Thread B set Counter.Value = 5
Thread A set Counter.Value = 6
Thread A set Counter.Value = 7
Thread B set Counter.Value = 8
Thread A set Counter.Value = 9
Thread B set Counter.Value = 10
```

Be Careful with Locks

When you lock an object, all other threads that attempt to access it are put into a waiting queue. Thus, you should always hold locks for as short a time as possible, to prevent long delays and possible timeout errors.

In addition, using the *SyncLock* statement indiscriminately can lead to problems if you attempt to acquire multiple locks at once. For example, consider the following two methods:

```
Public Sub MethodA()
    SyncLock ObjectA
        SyncLock ObjectB
            ' (Do something with A and B).
        End SyncLock
    End SyncLock
End Sub

Public Sub MethodB()
    SyncLock ObjectB
        SyncLock ObjectA
            ' (Do something with A and B).
        End SyncLock
    End SyncLock
End Sub
```

Assume *MethodA* gets a hold of *ObjectA* and then tries to obtain a lock of *ObjectB*. In the meantime, *MethodB* obtains exclusive access to *ObjectB* and tries for *ObjectA*. Both methods will wait for each other to release an object, with neither method giving in. This conflict is known as a *deadlock*, and it's a good reason to make your threading code as simple as possible. In addition, you might want to consider more advanced locking through the *Monitor* class, which allows you to test if an exclusive lock can be made and specify a timeout period for attempting to acquire a lock.

7.7 Use the *Thread* Object with a Task That Requires Data

Problem

You want to execute a task on a separate thread, and you need to supply certain input parameters.

Solution

Create a custom threaded class that incorporates a parameterless method, along with the additional information as member variables.

Discussion

When you create a *Thread* object, you must supply a delegate that points to a method without parameters. This causes a problem if you need to pass information to the thread. The easiest solution is to wrap the threaded code and the required information into a single class.

Consider the example where you want to write a large amount of information to a file in the background. You can encapsulate this logic in the task class shown here:

```
Public Class FileSaver

    Private _FilePath As String
    Private _FileData() As Byte

    Public ReadOnly Property FilePath() As String
        Get
            Return _FilePath
        End Get
```

```
        End Property

        Public ReadOnly Property FileData() As Byte()
            Get
                Return _FileData
            End Get
        End Property

        Public Sub New(ByVal path As String, ByVal dataToWrite() As Byte)
            Me._FilePath = path
            Me._FileData = dataToWrite
        End Sub

        Public Sub Save()
            Dim fs As System.IO.FileStream
            Dim w As System.IO.BinaryWriter
            Try
                fs = New System.IO.FileStream(FilePath, IO.FileMode.OpenOrCreate)
                w = New System.IO.BinaryWriter(fs)
                w.Write(FileData)
            Finally
                ' This ensures that the file is closed,
                ' even if the thread is aborted.
                w.Close()
            End Try
        End Sub

End Class
```

Now, to use this task class you create a *FileSaver*, set its properties accordingly, and then start the *Save* method using a new thread.

```
Public Module ThreadTest

    Public Sub Main()
        ' Create the task object.
        Dim Data() As Byte = {}
        Dim Saver As New FileSaver("myfile.bin", Data)

        ' Create the thread.
        Dim FileSaverThread As New Thread(AddressOf Saver.Save)

        FileSaverThread.Start()

        Console.WriteLine("Press Enter to exit...")
        Console.ReadLine()
```

```
      ' If the threads aren't yet finished, abort them.
      If (FileSaverThread.ThreadState And ThreadState.Running) = _
        ThreadState.Running Then
          FileSaverThread.Abort()
      End If
  End Sub

End Module
```

7.8 Use the *Thread* Object with a Task That Returns Data

Problem

You want to execute a task on a separate thread, and you want to retrieve the data it produces.

Solution

Create a custom threaded class that incorporates a parameterless method, along with a method or property to retrieve the information. In addition, you might want to use an event to notify the caller.

Discussion

When you create a *Thread* object, you must supply a delegate that points to a method without a return value. This limits your ability to retrieve information from the thread once its work is complete. The easiest solution is to wrap the threaded code and the return value into a single class. You can then add methods that allow the main application thread to retrieve the return value and progress information. You can also add a custom event that allows the threaded object to notify the main thread as soon as its task is finished.

For example, consider the weather lookup function provided in recipe 7.4. You could wrap this function into a threaded object that looks like this:

```
Public Class WeatherLookup

    ' The input information.
    Private _CityName As String

    ' The output information.
    Private _Temperature As Single

    ' The task progress informaton.
    Private _IsCompleted As Boolean = False
```

```vb
' An event used to notify when the task is complete.
Public Event WeatherLookupCompleted(ByVal sender As Object, _
  ByVal e As WeatherLookupCompletedEventArgs)

Public ReadOnly Property CityName() As String
    Get
        Return _CityName
    End Get
End Property

Public Sub New(ByVal cityQuery As String)
    Me._CityName = cityQuery
End Sub

' This method is executed on the new thread.
Public Sub Lookup()
    ' This code would query the database for the requested info.
    ' Instead, we pause and return a random "temperature reading."
    Dim Rand As New Random()
    Delay(Rand.Next(5, 10))
    _Temperature = Rand.Next(30, 100)
    _IsCompleted = True
    RaiseEvent WeatherLookupCompleted(Me, _
      New WeatherLookupCompletedEventArgs(_CityName, _Temperature))
End Sub

' This method is called by the main thread to check the task status.
Public ReadOnly Property IsCompleted() As Boolean
    Get
        Return _IsCompleted
    End Get
End Property

' This method is called by the main thread to retrieve the task result.
Public Function GetResult() As Single
    If _IsCompleted Then
        Return _Temperature
    Else
        Throw New InvalidOperationException("Not completed.")
    End If
End Function

' (Delay function omitted.)

End Class
```

> **Note**   In this example, the task object provides a simple *IsCompleted* flag that allows the main thread to check if the task is complete. Optionally, you could add finer-grained progress information, like a numeric *PercentCompleted* value that would indicate the amount of the task that has been completed.

The *WeatherLookupCompleted* event uses a custom *EventArgs* object that contains information about the city name and retrieved temperature:

```
Public Class WeatherLookupCompletedEventArgs
    Inherits EventArgs

    Private _CityName As String
    Private _Temperature As Single

    Public ReadOnly Property CityName() As String
        Get
            Return _CityName
        End Get
    End Property

    Public ReadOnly Property Temperature() As Single
        Get
            Return _Temperature
        End Get
    End Property

    Public Sub New(ByVal cityName As String, ByVal temperature As Single)
        Me._CityName = cityName
        Me._Temperature = temperature
    End Sub

End Class
```

This Console application creates a single task object, attaches an event handler, and starts the task on a separate thread:

```
Public Module ThreadTest

    Public Sub Main()
        ' Create the task object.
        Dim Lookup As New WeatherLookup("London")
        AddHandler Lookup.WeatherLookupCompleted, AddressOf LookupCompleted
```

```
' Create the thread.
Dim LookupThread As New Thread(AddressOf Lookup.Lookup)
LookupThread.Start()

Console.WriteLine("Press Enter to exit...")
Console.ReadLine()

' If the threads aren't yet finished, abort them.
If (LookupThread.ThreadState And ThreadState.Running) = _
  ThreadState.Running Then
    LookupThread.Abort()
End If
End Sub

Private Sub LookupCompleted(ByVal sender As Object, _
  ByVal e As WeatherLookupCompletedEventArgs)
    Console.WriteLine(e.CityName & " is: " & e.Temperature)
End Sub

End Module
```

Notice that the *LookupCompleted* event handler will actually execute on the lookup thread, not the main application thread. Thus, if you need to access a shared resource in this procedure, you need to use locking code.

With this approach, the main thread is still responsible for creating, tracking, and otherwise managing any threads it creates. It's possible, and often useful, to move this responsibility to the task class. One popular design pattern is to create a task class that acts as a thread wrapper, as shown in recipe 7.11.

7.9 Marshal User Interface Code to the Correct Thread

Problem

You need to update a user interface element on a window from another thread.

Solution

Place your update logic in a separate subroutine, and use the *Control.Invoke* method to marshal this code to the user interface thread.

Discussion

Windows controls are not thread-safe. That means that it isn't safe to update a user interface control from any thread other than the thread that created it. In fact, you might test code that ignores this restriction without experiencing any trouble, only to have the same code cause maddeningly elusive problems in a production environment.

This problem isn't restricted to code that executes in a custom-threaded object. It also applies to code that responds to a callback or event from a threaded object. That's because the callback or event-handling code will take place on the worker thread that raises the callback or event. Fortunately, you can solve this problem using the *Invoke* method, which is provided by all .NET controls. The *Invoke* method takes a *MethodInvoker* delegate that points to a method with no parameters or return value. The code in that method will be executed on the user interface thread.

```
' UpdateMethod() contains the code that modifies a Windows control.
Dim UpdateDelegate As New MethodInvoker(AddressOf UpdateMethod)

' UpdateMethod() will now be invoked on the user interface thread.
ControlToUpdate.Invoke(UpdateDelegate)
```

Of course, life often isn't this simple. The preceding approach works well if the update logic is hard-coded, but what if you need to update a control based on the contents of a variable? There's no way to use the *MethodInvoker* delegate to point to a procedure that accepts arguments, so you need to create a custom wrapper object.

One possibility is the custom *ControlTextUpdater* class shown in the following code. It references a single control and provides methods like *AddText* and *ReplaceText*. When called, these methods store the new text in a class member variable and marshal the call to the user interface thread using the *Invoke* method.

```
Public Class ControlTextUpdater

    ' The reference is retained as a generic control,
    ' allowing this helper class to be reused in other scenarios.
    Private _ControlToUpdate As Control

    Public ReadOnly Property ControlToUpdate() As Control
        Get
            Return _ControlToUpdate
        End Get
    End Property

    Public Sub New(ByVal controlToUpdate As Control)
        Me._ControlToUpdate = controlToUpdate
    End Sub
```

```
' Stores the text to add.
Private _NewText As String

Public Sub AddText(ByVal newText As String)
    SyncLock Me
        Me._NewText = newText
        ControlToUpdate.Invoke(New MethodInvoker( _
          AddressOf ThreadSafeAddText))
    End SyncLock
End Sub

Private Sub ThreadSafeAddText()
    Me.ControlToUpdate.Text &= _NewText
End Sub

Public Sub ReplaceText(ByVal newText As String)
    SyncLock Me
        Me._NewText = newText
        ControlToUpdate.Invoke(New MethodInvoker( _
          AddressOf ThreadSafeReplaceText))
    End SyncLock
End Sub

Private Sub ThreadSafeReplaceText()
    Me.ControlToUpdate.Text = _NewText
End Sub


End Class
```

As a precaution, the class locks itself just before updating the text. Otherwise, an update could be corrupted if a caller submits new text before the previous text has been applied.

To demonstrate how you would use a class like this in a Windows application, it helps to consider a more sophisticated example. In this case, we'll build on the weather lookup example described in recipe 7.8.

The application (shown in Figure 7-1) provides a single form that allows a user to submit multiple task requests at a time. The requests are processed on separate threads, and the results are written to a textbox in a thread-safe manner.

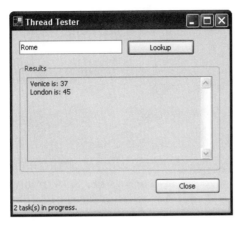

Figure 7-1   A front-end to a multithreaded task processor

The full code is available with the download for this chapter, although we'll examine the key elements here. First of all, the weather lookup code is modified slightly so that every weather lookup task has an automatically associated GUID. This ensures that the task can be uniquely identified.

```
Public Class WeatherLookup

    ' A unique identifier for this task.
    Private _Guid = Guid.NewGuid()

    Public ReadOnly Property Guid() As Guid
        Get
            Return _Guid
        End Get
    End Property

    ' (Other properties and methods omitted.)

End Class
```

This GUID is also added to the *WeatherLookupCompletedEventArgs*, so the client knows what task has been completed when the event fires.

The form stores a hashtable collection that contains all the threads that are currently in progress.

```
Private TaskThreads As New Hashtable()
```

This collection allows the application to determine how many tasks are in progress at all times. A timer runs continuously, updating a panel in the status bar with this information:

```
Private Sub tmrRefreshStatus_Tick(ByVal sender As System.Object, _
  ByVal e As System.EventArgs) Handles tmrRefreshStatus.Tick

    pnlStatus.Text = TaskThreads.Count.ToString() & _
      " task(s) in progress."

End Sub
```

The use of a hashtable collection also allows the application to abort all tasks when it exits:

```
Private Sub Form1_Closing(ByVal sender As Object, _
  ByVal e As System.ComponentModel.CancelEventArgs) Handles MyBase.Closing

    ' Abort any in-progress threads.
    Dim Item As DictionaryEntry
    For Each Item In TaskThreads
        Dim TaskThread As Thread = Item.Value
        If (TaskThread.ThreadState And ThreadState.Running) = _
          ThreadState.Running Then
            TaskThread.Abort()
        End If
    Next

End Sub
```

When the Lookup button is clicked, a new task object and thread are created. The thread is stored in the *TaskThreads* collection, indexed by its GUID. The task object is not, although it could be.

```
Private Sub cmdLookup_Click(ByVal sender As System.Object, _
  ByVal e As System.EventArgs) Handles cmdLookup.Click

    ' Create the task object.
    Dim Lookup As New WeatherLookup(txtCity.Text)
    AddHandler Lookup.WeatherLookupCompleted, AddressOf LookupCompleted

    ' Create the thread.
    Dim LookupThread As New Thread(AddressOf Lookup.Lookup)
    LookupThread.Start()

    TaskThreads.Add(Lookup.Guid.ToString(), LookupThread)

End Sub
```

When the lookup is completed, a *WeatherLookupCompleted* event fires. At this point, a new *Updater* is created to safely add the retrieved text to the textbox. Also, the corresponding thread is removed from the *TaskThreads* collection. Notice that synchronization code is required for this step because the *TaskThreads* collection might be accessed by another thread (for example, by the main thread if the timer fires or the user starts a new lookup).

```
Private Sub LookupCompleted(ByVal sender As Object, _
    ByVal e As WeatherLookupCompletedEventArgs)

    ' Create the update object.
    Dim Updater As New ControlTextUpdater(txtResults)

    ' Perform a thread-safe update.
    Updater.AddText(e.CityName & " is: " & e.Temperature.ToString() & _
        vbNewLine)

    ' Remove the task object.
    SyncLock TaskThreads
        TaskThreads.Remove(e.TaskGuid.ToString())
    End SyncLock

End Sub
```

> **Caution** Allowing the user to create threads without any limit is a recipe for disaster. If the user makes use of this ability to generate dozens of threads, the entire system will run slower. The solution is to check the number of queued tasks and disable the Lookup button when it reaches a certain threshold.

7.10 Stop a Thread Politely

Problem

You want to stop a thread, but allow it to clean up the current task and end on its own terms.

Solution

Create a Boolean *StopRequested* flag that the threaded code can poll periodically.

Discussion

When you use the *Abort* method to stop a thread, a *ThreadAbortException* is raised to the code that is currently running. The thread can handle this exception with code in a *Catch* or *Finally* block, but the exception cannot be suppressed. In other words, even if the exception is handled, it will be rethrown when the code in the *Catch* and *Finally* blocks finishes, until the thread finally terminates.

The *Abort* method isn't always appropriate. A less disruptive choice is to create a more considerate thread that checks for stop requests. For example, shown here is a custom-threaded object that loops for ten minutes, or until a stop request is received.

```
Public Class Worker

    Private _StopRequested As Boolean = False

    Public Sub RequestStop()
        _StopRequested = True
    End Sub

    Public Sub DoWork()
        Dim StartTime As DateTime = DateTime.Now
        Do
            If _StopRequested Then
                Exit Do
            End If
        Loop Until DateTime.Now.Subtract(StartTime).TotalMinutes > 9
    End Sub

End Class
```

Here is a Console application you can use to test the *Worker* class. Notice that three steps are taken:

- The stop is requested.

- The code waits for the thread to stop for a maximum of 30 seconds.

- If the thread still hasn't stopped, the code uses the *Abort* method.

```
Public Module ThreadTest

    Public Sub Main()
        ' Create the task object.
        Dim Worker As New Worker()

        ' Create the thread.
        Dim WorkerThread As New Thread(AddressOf Worker.DoWork)
        WorkerThread.Start()

        Console.WriteLine("Press Enter to request a stop...")
        Console.ReadLine()

        Worker.RequestStop()

        ' Wait for the thread to stop (or timeout after 30 seconds).
        WorkerThread.Join(TimeSpan.FromSeconds(30))

        If WorkerThread.ThreadState = ThreadState.Running Then
            Console.WriteLine("An abort was required.")
            WorkerThread.Abort()
        End If

        Console.WriteLine("Thread is stopped.")
    End Sub

End Module
```

Starting and stopping a thread is the most common type of interaction required between the main thread and worker thread of your application. However, you could add additional methods to allow you to send other instructions to your threaded code.

7.11 Create a Thread Wrapper Class

Problem

You want to remove the thread management code from your main thread and allow the task objects to manage their threads transparently.

Solution

Create a thread wrapper class that stores a reference to the thread *and* encapsulates the task-specific logic.

Discussion

One common design pattern with multithreading is to create a *thread wrapper*. This wrapper provides the typical methods you would expect in a *Thread*, like *Start* and *Stop*, along with all the task-specific code, and provides properties for required input values and calculated values.

Here's an abstract base class that defines the basic structure of a well-behaved thread wrapper:

```
Public MustInherit Class ThreadWrapperBase

    ' This is the thread where the task is carried out.
    Public ReadOnly Thread As System.Threading.Thread

    Public Sub New()
        ' Create the thread.
        Me.Thread = New System.Threading.Thread(AddressOf Me.StartTask)
    End Sub

    ' Start the task on the worker thread.
    Public Overridable Sub Start()
        Me.Thread.Start()
    End Sub

    ' Stop the task by aborting the thread.
    ' You can override this method to use polite stop requests instead.
    Public Overridable Sub [Stop]()
        Me.Thread.Abort()
    End Sub

    ' Tracks the status of the task.
    Private _IsCompleted As Boolean

    Public ReadOnly Property IsCompleted() As Boolean
        Get
            Return _IsCompleted
        End Get
    End Property

    Private Sub StartTask()
        _IsCompleted = False
        DoTask()
        _IsCompleted = True
    End Sub

    ' This method contains the code that actually performs the task.
```

```
    Protected MustOverride Sub DoTask()

End Class
```

And here's a very basic task class that derives from it:

```
Public Class Worker
    Inherits ThreadWrapperBase

    ' (You can add properties here for input values and output values.)
    ' (You can also define a WorkerCompleted event.)

    Protected Overrides Sub DoTask()
        Dim StartTime As DateTime = DateTime.Now
        Do
            ' Do nothing.
        Loop Until DateTime.Now.Subtract(StartTime).TotalMinutes > 4
    End Sub

End Class
```

The thread wrapper improves encapsulation and simplifies programming from the application's point of view, because it only has to track the *Worker* object (rather than the *Worker* object and the *Thread* object). Here's the code you would use to test the classes we've created:

```
Public Module ThreadTest

    Public Sub Main()
        ' Create the task object.
        Dim Worker As New Worker()

        ' Start the task on its internal thread.
        Worker.Start()

        Console.WriteLine("Press Enter to exit...")
        Console.ReadLine()

        ' Abort the task if needed.
        If Not Worker.IsCompleted Then
            Console.WriteLine("Thread is still running.")
            Worker.Stop()
            Console.WriteLine("Thread is aborted.")
        End If
    End Sub

End Module
```

7.12 Create a Reusable Task Processor

Problem

You need a dedicated thread that will process queue tasks and process them continuously.

Solution

Create a threaded class that stores tasks in a queue and monitors the queue continuously.

Discussion

A common pattern in distributed application design is a *task processor*: a dedicated thread that performs requested tasks on a first-in-first-out basis. This thread lives for the life of the application and uses an internal collection (typically a queue) to store requested tasks until it has a chance to process them.

Creating a task processor is fairly easy. However, to do it properly, you need to leverage the stop request pattern and thread wrapper pattern shown in recipes 7.10 and 7.11, respectively.

The first step is to define a class that encapsulates task data. For this example, we allow any task to contain a block of binary data (perhaps containing an image that needs to be processed or a document that needs to be encrypted), and a GUID to uniquely identify the task.

```
Public Class Task

    Private _SomeData() As Byte
    Private _Guid As Guid = Guid.NewGuid()

    Public Property SomeData() As Byte()
        Get
            Return _SomeData
        End Get
        Set(ByVal Value() As Byte)
            _SomeData = Value
        End Set
    End Property

    Public ReadOnly Property Guid() As Guid
        Get
            Return _Guid
        End Get
```

```
    End Property

End Class
```

The *TaskProcessor* class derives from *ThreadWrapperBase* (shown in recipe 7.11). It adds a *SubmitTask* method that allows new tasks to be entered into the queue and a *GetIncompleteTaskCount* method that allows you check the number of outstanding tasks. *TaskProcessor* also overrides the *DoTask* method with the worker code. *DoTask* runs continuously in a loop (provided a stop has not been requested), dequeuing items one at a time and then processing them. If no items are found, the thread is paused for 5 seconds. In addition, the *Stop* method is overridden so that it attempts to stop the thread cleanly with the *_StopRequested* flag before using an *Abort*.

```
Public Class TaskProcessor
    Inherits ThreadWrapperBase

    Private _Tasks As New Queue()
    Private _StopRequested As Boolean

    Public Sub SubmitTask(ByVal task As Task)
        SyncLock _Tasks
            _Tasks.Enqueue(task)
        End SyncLock
    End Sub

    Public Function GetIncompleteTaskCount() As Integer
        Return _Tasks.Count
    End Function

    Protected Overrides Sub DoTask()
        Do
            If _Tasks.Count > 0 Then
                SyncLock _Tasks
                    ' Retrieve the next task (in FIFO order).
                    Dim Task As Task = CType(_Tasks.Dequeue(), Task)
                End SyncLock

                ' (Process the task here.)
                Delay(10)
            Else
                ' No tasks are here. Suspend processing for 5 seconds.
                Thread.Sleep(TimeSpan.FromSeconds(5))
            End If
        Loop Until _StopRequested
    End Sub
```

```
    Public Overrides Sub [Stop]()
        ' Request a polite stop for up to 10 seconds.
        _StopRequested = True
        Me.Thread.Join(TimeSpan.FromSeconds(10))

        ' Call the base class implementation,
        ' which aborts the thread if necessary.
        MyBase.Stop()
    End Sub

    ' (Delay function omitted.)

End Class
```

The following Console application demonstrates the task processor in action. It creates and submits three tasks, and it aborts the processor when the user presses the Enter key.

```
Public Module ThreadTest

    Public Sub Main()

        ' Create the task processor.
        Dim TaskProcessor As New TaskProcessor()

        ' Start the processor.
        TaskProcessor.Start()

        ' Assign three tasks.
        TaskProcessor.SubmitTask(New Task())
        TaskProcessor.SubmitTask(New Task())
        TaskProcessor.SubmitTask(New Task())

        Console.WriteLine(TaskProcessor.GetIncompleteTaskCount().ToString & _
            " tasks underway.")

        Console.WriteLine("Press Enter to stop...")
        Console.ReadLine()

        Console.WriteLine(TaskProcessor.GetIncompleteTaskCount().ToString & _
            " tasks still underway.")
        TaskProcessor.Stop()
    End Sub

End Module
```

7.13 Use a Pool of Threads

Problem

You need to create an unbounded number of threads without degrading performance.

Solution

Use the *ThreadPool* class to map a large number of tasks to a fixed number of reusable threads.

Discussion

The *System.Threading.ThreadPool* class allows you to execute code using a pool of threads provided by the common language runtime. Using this pool simplifies your code, and it can improve performance, particularly if you use a large number of short-lived threads. The *ThreadPool* class avoids the overhead of continually creating and destroying threads by using a pool of reusable threads. You use the *ThreadPool* class to queue a task, and the task is processed on the first available thread. The *ThreadPool* class is capped at 25 threads per CPU, which prevents the type of performance degradation that can occur when you create more threads than the operating system can efficiently schedule at one time.

Scheduling a task with *ThreadPool* is easy. You must simply meet two requirements. First of all, the method that you want to queue must match the signature of the *WaitCallback* delegate, which means they must accept a single state object:

```
Public Sub WaitCallback(ByVal state As Object)
    ' Code omitted.
End Sub
```

The state object allows you to submit information about the task to the asynchronous method. However, if you are wrapping your task into a custom task object, you won't need to use this information, because all the state details will be provided in the task class itself.

Once you have a method that matches the required signature, you can pass it to the shared *ThreadPool.QueueUserWorkItem* method. (You can also supply the optional state object.) The *QueueUserWorkItem* method schedules the task for asynchronous execution. Assuming a thread is available, it will start processing in a matter of seconds.

```
ThreadPool.QueueUserWorkItem(New WaitCallback(AddressOf WaitCallback), _
  Nothing)
```

Here's a simple *Worker* class that can be used with *ThreadPool*:

```
Public Class Worker

    Private _IsCompleted As Boolean

    Public ReadOnly Property IsCompleted() As Boolean
        Get
            Return _IsCompleted
        End Get
    End Property

    Public Sub DoWork(ByVal state As Object)
        _IsCompleted = False
        Delay(10)
        _IsCompleted = True
    End Sub

    ' (Delay function omitted.)

End Class
```

And here's a Console application that queues two *Worker* items for asynchronous execution and then waits for them to complete:

```
Public Module ThreadTest

    Public Sub Main()
        Dim WorkerThreads, CompletionPortThreads As Integer
        ThreadPool.GetMaxThreads(WorkerThreads, CompletionPortThreads)
        Console.WriteLine("This thread pool provides " & _
          WorkerThreads.ToString() & " threads.")
        ThreadPool.GetAvailableThreads(WorkerThreads, CompletionPortThreads)
        Console.WriteLine(WorkerThreads.ToString() & _
          " threads are currently available.")

        ' Create and queue two task objects.
        Dim WorkerA As New Worker()
        ThreadPool.QueueUserWorkItem( _
          New WaitCallback(AddressOf WorkerA.DoWork), Nothing)
        Dim WorkerB As New Worker()
        ThreadPool.QueueUserWorkItem( _
          New WaitCallback(AddressOf WorkerB.DoWork), Nothing)

        ThreadPool.GetAvailableThreads(WorkerThreads, CompletionPortThreads)
        Console.WriteLine(WorkerThreads.ToString() & _
          " threads are currently available.")
```

```
      Do
      Loop Until WorkerA.IsCompleted And WorkerB.IsCompleted

      Console.WriteLine("All queued items completed.")
      ThreadPool.GetAvailableThreads(WorkerThreads, CompletionPortThreads)
      Console.WriteLine(WorkerThreads.ToString() & _
        " threads are currently available.")

      Console.ReadLine()
    End Sub

End Module
```

The display output for this application is as follows:

```
This thread pool provides 25 threads.
25 threads are currently available.
23 threads are currently available.
All queued items completed.
25 threads are currently available.
```

Unfortunately, using .NET *ThreadPool* class isn't quite as powerful as designing your own thread pool. Notably, there is no way to cancel tasks once they are submitted or specify a priority so that some tasks are performed in a different order than they are received. It's also impossible to retrieve any information about ongoing tasks from *ThreadPool*—you can only inspect the number of available threads.

> **Note** The *ThreadPool* class is an application-wide resource. That means that if you use the *ThreadPool* class to perform multiple different tasks, all your worker items will be competing for the same set of 25 threads.

8

Network Programming

The need for computers and devices to communicate across a network is one of the key *ingredients* of enterprise programming. In its relentless goal to simplify programming, the .NET Framework includes a slew of new networking classes that are logical, efficient, and consistent.

The only drawback to networking with .NET is that no single dominant model exists. In this chapter, you'll learn how to manage network interaction using sockets (recipes 8.8 to 8.11), but you won't learn about two higher-level distributed programming frameworks—Web Services and .NET Remoting—which have their own dedicated chapters later in this book. Typically, socket-based network programming is ideal for closed systems that don't require interoperability, where developers want to have complete flexibility to tailor communication and control the data before it hits the wire.

Of course, this chapter doesn't concentrate exclusively on socket programming. You'll also learn about Web interaction, such as downloading a Web page from the Internet (recipe 8.5) or a single piece of information (recipe 8.6). You'll also learn how to retrieve Web connectivity information for the current computer, look up Internet Protocol (IP) addresses and domain names, and ping another computer to gauge its response time. At the end of this chapter, two recipes (8.13 and 8.14) show how you can build on the Transmission Control Protocol (TCP) classes included with .NET to work with higher-level protocols such as Post Office Protocol 3 (POP3) for e-mail and File Transfer Protocol (FTP) for transferring files.

8.1 Get Web Connectivity Information for the Current Computer

Problem

You need to determine programmatically if the current computer can connect to the Internet.

Solution

Use the Microsoft Windows API function *InternetGetConnectedState*.

Discussion

The *InternetGetConnectedState* function returns *True* if the current computer is configured to access the Internet. It also returns a *dwFlags* parameter that specifies the type of connection using one (or more) of a series of constants.

The following Console application defines the *InternetGetConnectedState* function and uses it to test the current computer's connectivity:

```
Public Module GetInternetState

    ' Declare the API function.
    Private Declare Function InternetGetConnectedState Lib "wininet" _
      (ByRef dwFlags As Long, ByVal dwReserved As Long) As Long

    ' Define the possible types of connections.
    Private Enum ConnectStates
        LAN = &H2
        Modem = &H1
        Proxy = &H4
        Offline = &H20
        Configured = &H40
        RasInstalled = &H10
    End Enum

    Public Sub Main()
        ' Get the connected status.
        Dim dwFlags As Long
        Dim Connected As Boolean = _
          (InternetGetConnectedState(dwFlags, 0&) <> 0)

        If Connected Then
            Console.WriteLine("This computer is connected to the Internet.")
```

```
      ' Display all connection flags.
      Console.Write("Connection flags:")
      Dim ConnectionType As ConnectStates
      For Each ConnectionType In _
        System.Enum.GetValues(GetType(ConnectStates))
          If (ConnectionType And dwFlags) = ConnectionType Then
              Console.Write(" " & ConnectionType.ToString())
          End If
      Next
   End If

   Console.ReadLine()
End Sub

End Module
```

A sample output is shown here:

```
This computer is connected to the Internet.
Connection flags: LAN
```

Notice that the *InternetGetConnectedState* reflects how the computer is configured. It doesn't reflect whether the computer is configured correctly (in other words, whether the Internet connection is actually working).

8.2 Get the IP Address of the Current Computer

Problem

You want to retrieve the IP address of the current computer, perhaps to use later in networking code.

Solution

Use the *System.Net.Dns* class, which provides shared *GetHostName* and *GetHostByName* methods.

Discussion

The *Dns* class provides domain name resolution services. You can invoke its *GetHostName* to retrieve the host name for the current computer. You can then translate the host name into an IP address using *GetHostByName*.

```
Dim HostName As String
Dim IPAddress As String
```

```
' Look up the host name and IP address.
HostName = System.Net.Dns.GetHostName()
IPAddress = System.Net.Dns.GetHostByName(HostName).AddressList(0).ToString()

Console.WriteLine("Host name:" & HostName)
Console.WriteLine("IP address:" & IPAddress)
```

Be aware that the *GetHostByName* method returns a list of usable IP addresses. In most cases, this address list will contain only one entry.

If you run this code, you'll see something like this:

```
Host name: fariamat
IP address: 24.114.131.70
```

8.3 Look Up a Host Name for an IP Address

Problem

You want to determine the IP address for a computer based on its domain name by performing a Domain Name System (DNS) query.

Solution

Use the *System.Net.Dns* class, which wraps this functionality in the *GetHostByName* method.

Discussion

On the Web, publicly accessible IP addresses are often mapped to host names that are easier to remember using a network of DNS servers, which are a fundamental part of the Internet backbone. To perform a DNS lookup, the computer might contact its cache or a DNS sever (which might in turn forward the request to a DNS root server).

This entire process is transparent if you use the *System.Net.Dns* class, which allows you to retrieve the IP address for a host name by calling *GetHostByName*. Here's how you might retrieve the list of IP addresses mapped to *http://www.yahoo.com*:

```
Dim IP As System.Net.IPAddress

For Each IP In System.Net.Dns.GetHostByName("www.yahoo.com").AddressList
    Console.WriteLine(IP.AddressFamily.ToString())
    Console.WriteLine(IP.ToString())
Next
```

8.4 Ping an IP Address

Problem

You want to check if a computer is online and gauge its response time.

Solution

Send a ping message.

Discussion

A *ping message* contacts a device at a specific IP address, sends a test message, and requests that the remote device respond by echoing back the packet. You can measure the time taken for a ping response to be received to gauge the connection latency between two computers.

Despite the simplicity of ping messages compared to other types of network communication, implementing a ping utility in .NET requires a significant amount of complex low-level networking code. The .NET class library doesn't have a prebuilt solution—instead, you must use raw sockets.

However, at least one developer has solved the ping problem. Lance Olson, a developer at Microsoft, has provided C# code that allows you to ping a host by name or IP address and measure the milliseconds taken for a response. This code has been adapted into a *PingUtility* component, which is available with the code in this book's sample files.

To use the ping utility, you must first add a reference to the PingUtility.dll assembly. You can then use the shared *Pinger.GetPingTime* method with an IP address or domain name. The *GetPingTime* method returns the number of milliseconds that elapse before a response is received.

```
Console.WriteLine("Milliseconds to contact www.yahoo.com: " & _
  PingUtility.Pinger.GetPingTime("www.yahoo.com"))
Console.WriteLine("Milliseconds to contact www.seti.org: " & _
  PingUtility.Pinger.GetPingTime("www.seti.org"))
Console.WriteLine("Milliseconds to contact the local computer: " & _
  PingUtility.Pinger.GetPingTime("127.0.0.1"))
```

The ping test allows you to verify that other computers are online. It can also be useful if your application needs to evaluate several different remote computers that provide the same content and to determine which one will offer the lowest network latency for communication.

> **Note** A ping attempt might not succeed if a firewall forbids it. For example, many heavily trafficked sites ignore ping requests because they're wary of being swamped by a flood of simultaneous pings that will tie up the server (in essence, a denial of service attack).

8.5 Download a File Using HTTP

Problem

You want to retrieve a file from the Web.

Solution

Use the *HttpWebRequest* class to create your request, the *WebResponse* class to retrieve the response from the Web server, and some form of reader (typically a *StreamReader* for HTML or text data or a *BinaryReader* for a binary file) to parse the response data.

Discussion

Downloading a file from the Web takes the following four basic steps:

1. Use the shared *Create* method of the *System.Net.WebRequest* class to specify the page you want. This method returns a *WebRequest*-derived object, depending on the type of Uniform Resource Identifier (URI) you use. For example, if you use an HTTP URI (with the scheme http://), it will create an *HttpWebRequest* instance. If you use a file system URI (with the scheme file://), it will create a *FileWebRequest* instance.

2. Use the *GetResponse* method of the *HttpWebRequest* object to return a *WebResponse* object for the page.

3. Create a *StreamReader* or *BinaryReader* for the *WebResponse* stream.

4. Perform any steps you need to with the stream, such as writing it to a file.

The following code is a test application that retrieves and displays the HTML of a Web page. For it to work, you must import both the *System.Net* and the *System.IO* namespaces.

```
Public Module DownloadTest

    Public Sub Main()
        Dim Url As String = "http://www.prosetech.com/index.html"

        ' Create the request.
        Dim PageRequest As HttpWebRequest = _
          CType(WebRequest.Create(Url), HttpWebRequest)

        ' Get the response.
        ' This takes the most significant amount of time, particularly
        ' if the file is large, because the whole response is retrieved.
        Dim PageResponse As WebResponse = PageRequest.GetResponse()
        Console.WriteLine("Response received.")

        ' Read the response stream.
        Dim r As New StreamReader(PageResponse.GetResponseStream())
        Dim Page As String = r.ReadToEnd()
        r.Close()

        ' Display the retrieved data.
        Console.Write(Page)

        Console.ReadLine()
    End Sub

End Module
```

To deal efficiently with large files that need to be downloaded from the Web, you might want to use asynchronous techniques, as described in Chapter 7. You can also use the *WebRequest.BeginGetResponse*, which doesn't block your code and calls a callback procedure when the response has been retrieved.

8.6 Retrieve a Single Piece of Information from a Web Page

Problem

You want to extract a single piece of information from a Web page.

Solution

Use the *WebResponse* class to retrieve the stream, copy it to a string, and use a regular expression.

Discussion

You can extract information from a Web stream in several ways. You could read through the stream, use methods of the *String* class such as *IndexOf*, or apply a regular expression. The latter of these—using a regular expression—is the most flexible and powerful.

The first step is to create a regular expression that filters out the information you need. Recipe 1.17 provides several examples and a reference to basic regular expression syntax. For example, most Web pages include a text title that is stored in a *<title></title>* tag. To retrieve this piece of information, you use the following regular expression:

```
<title>(?<match>.*?)</title>
```

This expression retrieves all the text between the opening and closing *<title>* tag and places it in a named group called *match*. The following sample code uses this regular expression to retrieve the title from a URL the user enters. It requires three namespace imports: *System.Net*, *System.IO*, and *System.Text. RegularExpressions*.

```
Public Module ExtractTitleTest

    Public Sub Main()
        Console.WriteLine("Enter a URL, and press Enter.")
        Console.Write(">")
        Dim Url As String = Console.ReadLine()

        Dim Page As String
        Try
            ' Create the request.
            Dim PageRequest As HttpWebRequest = _
                CType(WebRequest.Create(Url), HttpWebRequest)

            ' Get the response.
            ' This takes the most significant amount of time, particularly
            ' if the file is large, because the whole response is retrieved.
            Dim PageResponse As WebResponse = PageRequest.GetResponse()
            Console.WriteLine("Response received.")
```

```
    ' Read the response stream.
    Dim r As New StreamReader(PageResponse.GetResponseStream())
    Page = r.ReadToEnd()
    r.Close()

Catch Err As Exception
    Console.WriteLine(Err.ToString())
    Return
End Try

' Define the regular expression.
Dim TitlePattern As String = "<title>(?<match>.*?)</title>"
Dim TitleRegex As New Regex(TitlePattern, _
  RegexOptions.IgnoreCase Or RegexOptions.Singleline)

' Find the title.
Dim TitleMatch As Match = TitleRegex.Match(Page)

' Display the title.
If TitleMatch.Success Then
    Console.WriteLine("Found title: " & _
      TitleMatch.Groups("match").Value)
End If

Console.ReadLine()
    End Sub

End Module
```

Here's the output for a test run that retrieves the title from the Yahoo! search engine:

```
Enter a URL, and press Enter.
>http://yahoo.com
Response received.
Found title: Yahoo!
```

If the Web page is extremely large, this approach might not be efficient because the entire stream is copied to a string in memory. Another option is to read through the stream character-by-character and try to build up a match to a search pattern. This approach requires more custom code and is demonstrated in detail with text searching in a file in recipe 5.8.

> **Note**   Screen scraping solutions such as this one can be quite brittle. If the user interface for the Web site changes and the expected pattern is altered, you'll no longer be able to extract the information you need. If you have control over the Web site, you can implement a much more robust approach using a Web service to return the desired information. Web services also support the full set of basic data types, which prevents another possible source of errors.

8.7 Find All Links in a Web Page

Problem

You want to retrieve all the hyperlinks in a Web page (perhaps because you want to download those pages also).

Solution

Retrieve the page using *WebResponse*, and use a regular expression to search for URIs.

Discussion

Retrieving links in a Web page is conceptually quite easy but often more difficult in practice. The problem is that Web pages follow a semi-standardized format and tolerate a great deal of variance. For example, a hyperlink can be added in the *href* attribute of an anchor, the *onclick* attribute of a JavaScript element such as a button, and so on. The URI itself could be relative (in which case it needs to be interpreted relative to the current page), fully qualified (in which case it can have one of countless schemes, including http:// or file:// or mailto://), or it might just be a *bookmark* (an anchor tag with an *href* that starts with the # character). Dealing with these myriad possibilities isn't easy.

The first step is to craft a suitable regular expression. In this case, we'll consider only the links that are provided in the *href* attribute of an anchor tag. Here's one regular expression that retrieves all *href* values from a Web page:

```
href\s*=\s*(?:"(?<match>[^"]*)"|(?<match>\S+))
```

Another option is to retrieve absolute paths only. The following line of code is a slightly less complicated regular expression that matches *href* values that start with *http://*.

```
href\s*=\s*"(?<match>http://.*?)"
```

The following sample application uses the first option. It then manually checks the retrieved URIs to see if they are bookmarks (in which case they are discarded) and to determine if they're relative or absolute. If the bookmarks are relative paths, the *System.Uri* class is used with the current page *Uri* to transform them into fully qualified paths.

```
Public Module ExtractURITest

    Public Sub Main()
        Console.WriteLine("Enter a URL, and press Enter.")
        Console.Write(">")
        Dim Url As String = Console.ReadLine()

        Dim BaseUri As Uri
        Dim Page As String
        Try
            BaseUri = New Uri(Url)

            ' Create the request.
            Dim PageRequest As HttpWebRequest = _
                CType(WebRequest.Create(Url), HttpWebRequest)

            ' Get the response.
            ' This takes the most significant amount of time, particularly
            ' if the file is large, because the whole response is retrieved.
            Dim PageResponse As WebResponse = PageRequest.GetResponse()
            Console.WriteLine("Response received.")

            ' Read the response stream.
            Dim r As New StreamReader(PageResponse.GetResponseStream())
            Page = r.ReadToEnd()
            r.Close()

        Catch Err As Exception
            Console.WriteLine(Err.ToString())
            Console.ReadLine()
            Return
        End Try

        ' Define the regular expression.
        Dim HrefPattern As String
        HrefPattern = "href\s*=\s*(?:""(?<match>[^""]*)""|(?<match>\S+))"
```

```vb
        Dim HrefRegex As New Regex(HrefPattern, _
          RegexOptions.IgnoreCase Or RegexOptions.Compiled)

        ' Find and display all the href matches.
        Dim HrefMatch As Match = HrefRegex.Match(Page)
        Do While HrefMatch.Success
            Dim Link As String = HrefMatch.Groups(1).Value

            If Link.Substring(0, 1) = "#" Then
                ' Ignore this match, it was just a bookmark.
            Else
                ' Attempt to determine if this is a fully-qualified link
                ' by comparing it against some known schemes.
                Dim Absolute As Boolean = False
                If Link.Length > 8 Then
                    Dim Scheme As String
                    Scheme = Uri.UriSchemeHttp & "://"
                    If Link.Substring(0, Scheme.Length) = Scheme Then _
                      Absolute = True
                    Scheme = Uri.UriSchemeHttps & "://"
                    If Link.Substring(0, Scheme.Length) = Scheme Then _
                      Absolute = True
                    Scheme = Uri.UriSchemeFile & "://"
                    If Link.Substring(0, Scheme.Length) = Scheme Then _
                      Absolute = True
                End If

                ' (You could compare it against additional schemes here.)

                If Absolute Then
                    Console.WriteLine(Link)
                Else
                    Console.WriteLine(New Uri(BaseUri, Link).ToString())
                End If
            End If
            HrefMatch = HrefMatch.NextMatch()
        Loop

        Console.ReadLine()
    End Sub

End Module
```

This code investigates each URI by comparing it against a few common schemes. Another approach would be to try to instantiate a new *System.Uri* instance using the retrieved URI string. If the string is not an absolute path, an error would occur. You could catch the resulting exception and respond accordingly.

Here's the partial output for a sample test:

```
Enter a URL, and press Enter.
>http://www.nytimes.com
Response received.
http://www.nytimes.com/pages/jobs/index.html
http://www.nytimes.com/pages/realestate/index.html
http://www.nytimes.com/pages/automobiles/index.html
http://www.nytimes.com/pages/world/index.html
http://www.nytimes.com/pages/national/index.html
http://www.nytimes.com/pages/politics/index.html
http://www.nytimes.com/pages/business/index.html
http://www.nytimes.com/pages/technology/index.html
http://www.nytimes.com/pages/science/index.html
...
```

8.8 Communicate Using TCP

Problem

You need to send data between two computers on a network using a TCP/IP connection.

Solution

Use the *TcpClient* and *TcpListener* classes.

Discussion

TCP is a reliable, connection-based protocol that allows two computers to communicate over a network. It provides built-in flow-control, sequencing, and error handling, which makes it very reliable and easy to program with.

To create a TCP connection, one computer must act as the server and start listening on a specific *endpoint*. (An endpoint is defined as an IP address, which identifies the computer and port number.) The other computer must act as a client and send a connection request to the endpoint where the first computer is listening. Once the connection is established, the two computers can take turns exchanging messages. .NET makes this process easy through its stream abstraction. Both computers simply write to and read from a *Network-Stream* to transmit data.

> **Note**   Even though a TCP connection always requires a server and a client, there's no reason an individual application can't be both. For example, in a peer-to-peer application, one thread is dedicated to listening for incoming requests (acting as a server) while another thread is dedicated to initiate outgoing connections (acting as a client).

Once a TCP connection is established, the two computers can send any type of data by writing it to the *NetworkStream*. However, it's a good idea to begin designing a networked application by defining constants that represent the allowable commands. Doing so ensures that your application code doesn't need to hardcode communication strings.

```
Public Class ServerMessages

    Public Const AcknowledgeOK As String = "OK"
    Public Const AcknowledgeCancel As String = "Cancel"
    Public Const Disconnect As String = "Bye"

End Class

Public Class ClientMessages

    Public Const RequestConnect As String = "Hello"
    Public Const Disconnect As String = "Bye"

End Class
```

In this example, the defined vocabulary is very basic. You would add more constants depending on the type of application. For example, in a file transfer application, you might include a client message for requesting a file. The server might then respond with an acknowledgment and return file details such as the file size. These constants must be compiled into a separate class library assembly, which must be referenced by both the client and server. Both the client and the server will also need to import the *System.Net*, *System.Net.Sockets*, and *System.IO* namespaces.

The following code is a template for a basic TCP server. It listens at a fixed port, accepts the first incoming connection, and then waits for the client to request a disconnect. At this point, the server could call the *AcceptTcpClient* method again to wait for the next client, but instead, it simply shuts down.

```
Public Module TcpServerTest

    Public Sub Main()
        ' Create a new listener on port 8000.
        Dim Listener As New TcpListener(8000)

        Console.WriteLine("About to initialize port.")
        Listener.Start()

        Console.WriteLine("Listening for a connection...")

        Try
            ' Wait for a connection request,
            ' and return a TcpClient initialized for communication.
            Dim Client As TcpClient = Listener.AcceptTcpClient()
            Console.WriteLine("Connection accepted.")

            ' Retrieve the network stream.
            Dim Stream As NetworkStream = Client.GetStream()

            ' Create a BinaryWriter for writing to the stream.
            Dim w As New BinaryWriter(Stream)

            ' Create a BinaryReader for reading from the stream.
            Dim r As New BinaryReader(Stream)

            If r.ReadString() = ClientMessages.RequestConnect Then
                w.Write(ServerMessages.AcknowledgeOK)
                Console.WriteLine("Connection completed.")
                Do
                Loop Until r.ReadString() = ClientMessages.Disconnect
                Console.WriteLine()
                Console.WriteLine("Disconnect request received.")
                w.Write(ServerMessages.Disconnect)
            Else
                Console.WriteLine("Could not complete connection.")
            End If

            ' Close the connection socket.
            Client.Close()
            Console.WriteLine("Connection closed.")

            ' Close the underlying socket (stop listening for new requests).
            Listener.Stop()
            Console.WriteLine("Listener stopped.")

        Catch Err As Exception
```

```
                Console.WriteLine(Err.ToString())
            End Try

            Console.ReadLine()
        End Sub

    End Module
```

The following code is a template for a basic TCP client. It contacts the server at the specified IP address and port. In this example, the loopback address (127.0.0.1) is used, which always points to the current computer. Keep in mind that a TCP connection requires two ports: one at the server end, and one at the client end. However, only the server port needs to be specified. The client port can be chosen dynamically at runtime from the available ports, which is what the *TcpClient* class will do by default.

```
Public Module TcpClientTest

    Public Sub Main()
        Dim Client As New TcpClient()
        Try
            Console.WriteLine("Attempting to connect to the server " & _
              "on port 8000.")
            Client.Connect(IPAddress.Parse("127.0.0.1"), 8000)
            Console.WriteLine("Connection established.")

            ' Retrieve the network stream.
            Dim Stream As NetworkStream = Client.GetStream()

            ' Create a BinaryWriter for writing to the stream.
            Dim w As New BinaryWriter(Stream)

            ' Create a BinaryReader for reading from the stream.
            Dim r As New BinaryReader(Stream)

            ' Start a dialogue.
            w.Write(ClientMessages.RequestConnect)
            If r.ReadString() = ServerMessages.AcknowledgeOK Then
                Console.WriteLine("Connected.")
                Console.WriteLine("Press Enter to disconnect.")
                Console.ReadLine()
                Console.WriteLine("Disconnecting...")
                w.Write(ClientMessages.Disconnect)
            Else
                Console.WriteLine("Connection not completed.")
            End If
```

```
                    ' Close the connection socket.
                    Client.Close()
                    Console.WriteLine("Port closed.")

                Catch Err As Exception
                    Console.WriteLine(Err.ToString())
                End Try

                Console.ReadLine()
            End Sub

        End Module
```

Here's a sample connection transcript on the server side:

```
About to initialize port.
Listening for a connection...
Connection accepted.
Connection completed.

Disconnect request received.
Connection closed.
Listener stopped.
```

And here's a sample connection transcript on the client side:

```
Attempting to connect to the server on port 8000.
Connection established.
Connected.
Press Enter to disconnect.

Disconnecting...
Port closed.
```

8.9 Create a Multithreaded TCP Network Server

Problem

You want to create a TCP server that can simultaneously handle multiple TCP clients.

Solution

Every time a new client connects, start a new thread to handle the request.

Discussion

A single TCP endpoint (IP address and port) can serve multiple connections. In fact, the operating system takes care of most of the work for you. All you need to do is launch a worker object on the server that will handle the connection on a new thread.

For example, consider the basic TCP client and server classes shown in recipe 8.8. You can convert the server into a multithreaded server that supports multiple simultaneous connections quite easily. First create a class that will interact with an individual client:

```vb
Public Class ClientHandler

    Private Client As TcpClient
    Private ID As String

    Public Sub New(ByVal client As TcpClient, ByVal ID As String)
        Me.Client = client
        Me.ID = ID
    End Sub

    Public Sub Start()
        ' Retrieve the network stream.
        Dim Stream As NetworkStream = Client.GetStream()

        ' Create a BinaryWriter for writing to the stream.
        Dim w As New BinaryWriter(Stream)

        ' Create a BinaryReader for reading from the stream.
        Dim r As New BinaryReader(Stream)

        If r.ReadString() = ClientMessages.RequestConnect Then
            w.Write(ServerMessages.AcknowledgeOK)
            Console.WriteLine(ID & ": Connection completed.")
            Do
            Loop Until r.ReadString() = ClientMessages.Disconnect
            Console.WriteLine(ID & ": Disconnect request received.")
            w.Write(ServerMessages.Disconnect)
        Else
            Console.WriteLine(ID & ": Could not complete connection.")
        End If

        ' Close the connection socket.
        Client.Close()
        Console.WriteLine(ID & ": Client connection closed.")
```

```
        Console.ReadLine()
    End Sub

End Class
```

Next modify the server code so that it loops continuously, creating new *ClientHandler* instances as required and launching them on new threads. Here's the revised code:

```
Dim ClientNum As Integer
Do
    Try
        ' Wait for a connection request,
        ' and return a TcpClient initialized for communication.
        Dim Client As TcpClient = Listener.AcceptTcpClient()
        Console.WriteLine("Server: Connection accepted.")

        ' Create a new object to handle this connection.
        ClientNum += 1
        Dim Handler As New ClientHandler(Client, "Client " & _
            ClientNum.ToString())

        ' Start this object working on another thread.
        Dim HandlerThread As New System.Threading.Thread( _
            AddressOf Handler.Start)
        HandlerThread.IsBackground = True
        HandlerThread.Start()

        ' (You could also add the Handler and HandlerThread to
        ' a collection to track client sessions.)

    Catch Err As Exception
        Console.WriteLine(Err.ToString())
    End Try
Loop
```

The following code shows the server-side transcript of a session with two clients:

```
Server: About to initialize port.
Server: Listening for a connection...
Server: Connection accepted.
Client 1: Connection completed.
Server: Connection accepted.
Client 2: Connection completed.
Client 2: Disconnect request received.
Client 2: Client connection closed.
Client 1: Disconnect request received.
Client 1: Client connection closed.
```

You might want to add additional code to the network server so that it tracks the current worker objects in a collection. Doing so would allow the server to abort these tasks if it needs to shut down and enforce a maximum number of simultaneous clients. For more information, see the multithreading recipes in Chapter 7.

8.10 Communicate Using UDP

Problem

You need to send data between two computers on a network using a User Datagram Protocol (UDP) stream.

Solution

Use the *UdpClient* class, and use two threads: one to send data, and the other to receive it.

Discussion

UDP is a connectionless protocol that doesn't include any flow control or error checking. Unlike TCP, UDP shouldn't be used where communication is critical. However, because of its lower overhead, UDP is often used for "chatty" applications where it's acceptable to lose some messages. For example, imagine you want to create a network where individual clients send information about the current temperature at their location to a server every few minutes. You might use UDP in this case because the communication frequency is high and the damage caused by losing a packet is trivial (because the server can just continue to use the last received temperature reading).

The UDP template application shown in the following code uses two threads: one to receive messages, and one to send them. To test this application, load two instances at the same time. On computer A, specify the IP address for computer B. On computer B, specify the address for computer A. You can then send text messages back and forth at will. (You can simulate a test on a single computer by using two different ports and the loopback IP address 127.0.0.1.)

```
Public Module UdpTest

    Private LocalPort As Integer

    Public Sub Main()
```

```vb
    ' Define endpoint where messages are sent.
    Console.WriteLine("Connect to IP: ")
    Dim IP As String = Console.ReadLine()
    Dim Port As Integer = 8800
    Dim RemoteEndPoint As New IPEndPoint(IPAddress.Parse(IP), _
      Port)

    ' Define local endpoint (where messages are received).
    LocalPort = 8800

    ' Create a new thread for receiving incoming messages.
    Dim ReceiveThread As New System.Threading.Thread( _
      AddressOf ReceiveData)
    ReceiveThread.IsBackground = True
    ReceiveThread.Start()

    Dim Client As New UdpClient()

    Try
        Dim Text As String
        Do
            Text = Console.ReadLine()

            ' Send the text to the remote client.
            If Text <> "" Then
                ' Encode the data to binary using UTF8 encoding.
                Dim Data() As Byte = _
                  System.Text.Encoding.UTF8.GetBytes(Text)

                ' Send the text to the remote client.
                Client.Send(Data, Data.Length, RemoteEndPoint)
            End If
        Loop Until Text = ""

    Catch Err As Exception
        Console.WriteLine(Err.ToString())
    End Try

    Console.ReadLine()
End Sub

Private Sub ReceiveData()
    Dim Client As New UdpClient(LocalPort)
    Do
        Try
            ' Receive bytes.
            Dim Data() As Byte = Client.Receive(Nothing)
```

```
                    ' Convert bytes to text using UTF8 encoding.
                    Dim Text As String = System.Text.Encoding.UTF8.GetString(Data)

                    ' Display the retrieved text.
                    Console.WriteLine(">> " & Text)

                Catch Err As Exception
                    Console.WriteLine(Err.ToString())
                End Try
            Loop
        End Sub

    End Module
```

Note that UDP applications cannot use the *NetworkStream* abstraction that TCP applications can. Instead, they must convert all data to a stream of bytes using an encoding class, as described in recipe 1.15 and recipe 2.18.

8.11 Send a Broadcast Message

Problem

You want to send a message to every user on the local subnet.

Solution

Use the *UdpClient* class with the appropriate broadcast address.

Discussion

Broadcasts are network messages that are forwarded to all the devices on a local subnet. When a broadcast message is received, the client decides whether to discard (depending on whether any application is monitoring the appropriate port). Broadcasts can't travel beyond a subnet because routers block all broadcast messages. Otherwise, the network could be swamped in traffic.

To send a broadcast message, you use a broadcast IP address, which is the IP address that identifies the network and has all the host bits set to 1. For example, if the network is identified by the first three bytes (140.80.0), the broadcast address would be 140.80.0.255. Alternatively, you can set all bits to 1 (the address 255.255.255.255), which specifies the entire network. In this case, the broadcast message will still travel only inside the local subnet because routers won't allow it to pass.

```
Dim IP As String = "255.255.255.255"
Dim Port As Integer = 8800

Dim RemoteEndPoint As New IPEndPoint(IPAddress.Parse(IP), _
  Port)

Dim Client As New UdpClient()
Dim Data() As Byte = System.Text.Encoding.UTF8.GetBytes("Broadcast Message")

' Send the broadcast message.
Client.Send(Data, Data.Length, RemoteEndPoint)
```

8.12 Send E-Mail Through SMTP

Problem

You want to send an e-mail address using a Simple Mail Transfer Protocol (SMTP) server.

Solution

Use the *SmtpMail* and *MailMessage* classes in the *System.Web.Mail* namespace.

Discussion

The classes in the *System.Web.Mail* namespace provide a bare-bones wrapper for the Collaboration Data Objects for Windows 2000 (CDOSYS) component. They allow you to compose and send formatted e-mail messages using SMTP.

Using these types is easy. You simply create a *MailMessage* object, specify the sender and recipient e-mail address, and place the message content in the *Body* property:

```
Dim MyMessage As New MailMessage()
MyMessage.To = "someone@somewhere.com"
MyMessage.From = "me@somewhere.com"
MyMessage.Subject = "Hello"
MyMessage.Priority = MailPriority.High
MyMessage.Body = "This is the message!"
```

If you want, you can send an HTML message by changing the message format and using HTML tags:

```
MyMessage.BodyFormat = MailFormat.Html
MyMessage.Body = "<HTML><HEAD></HEAD>" & _
  "<BODY>This is the message!</BODY></HTML>"
```

You can even add file attachments using the *MailMessage.Attachments* collection and the *MailAttachment* class.

```
Dim MyAttachment As New MailAttachment("c:\mypic.gif")
MyMessage.Attachments.Add(MyAttachment)
```

To send the message, you simply specify the SMTP server name and call the *SmtpMail.Send* method.

```
SmtpMail.SmtpServer = "test.mailserver.com"
SmtpMail.Send(MyMessage)
```

However, there is a significant catch to using the *SmtpMail* class to send an e-mail message. This class requires a local SMTP server or relay server on your network. In addition, the *SmtpMail* class doesn't support authentication, so if your SMTP server requires a username and password, you won't be able to send any mail. To overcome these problems, you can use the CDOSYS component directly through COM Interop (assuming you have a server version of Windows or Microsoft Exchange). Alternatively, you might want to access Microsoft Outlook using COM Automation, as described in Chapter 19 (see recipe 19.6).

Here's an example that uses the CDOSYS component to deliver SMTP using a server that requires authentication:

```
Dim MyMessage As New CDO.Message()
Dim Config As New CDO.Configuration()

' Specify the configuration.
Config.Fields(cdoSendUsingMethod).Value = cdoSendUsingPort
Config.Fields(cdoSMTPServer).Value = "test.mailserver.com"
Config.Fields(cdoSMTPServerPort).Value = 25
Config.Fields(cdoSMTPAuthenticate).Value = cdoBasic
Config.Fields(cdoSendUserName).Value = "username"
Config.Fields(cdoSendPassword).Value = "password"

' Update the configuration.
Config.Fields.Update()
MyMessage.Configuration = Config

' Create the message.
MyMessage.To = "someone@somewhere.com"
MyMessage.From = "me@somewhere.com"
MyMessage.Subject = "Hello"
MyMessage.TextBody = "This is the message!"

' Send the CDOSYS Message
MyMessage.Send()
```

> **Note**   Note that the SMTP protocol can't be used to retrieve e-mail. For this task, you need the POP3 (as described in recipe 8.13) or IMAP protocol.

For more information about using and configuring your own SMTP server, you can refer to the Microsoft introduction to Internet e-mail and mail servers at *http://www.microsoft.com/TechNet/prodtechnol/iis/deploy/config/mail.asp*.

8.13 Retrieve E-Mail Through POP3

Problem

You want to retrieve messages from a POP3 mail server.

Solution

Create a dedicated class that sends POP3 commands over a TCP connection.

Discussion

POP3 is a common e-mail protocol used to download messages from a mail server. POP3, like many Internet protocols, defines a small set of commands that are sent as simple ASCII-encoded messages over a TCP connection (typically on port 110).

Here's a listing of a typical POP3 dialogue, starting immediately after the client makes a TCP connection:

```
Server sends:+OK <22689.1039100760@mail.prosetech.com>
Client sends:USER <UserName>
Server sends:+OK
Client sends:PASS <Password>
Server sends:+OK
Client sends:LIST
Server sends:+OK
Server sends:<Message list terminated by a period>
Clients sends:RETR <MessageNumber>
Server sends:+OK
Server sends:<Message body terminated by a period>
Client sends:QUIT
Server sends:+OK
```

To add this functionality to your .NET applications, you can create a *Pop3Client* class that encapsulates all the logic for communicating with a POP3 server. Your application can then retrieve information about messages using the *Pop3Client* class. We'll explore this class piece by piece in this recipe. To see the complete code, download the recipes for this chapter in this book's sample files.

The first step is to define a basic skeleton for the *Pop3Client* class. It should store a *TcpClient* instance as a member variable, which will be used to send all network messages. You can also add generic *Send* and *ReceiveResponse* messages, which translate data from binary form into the ASCII encoding used for POP3 communication.

```vb
Public Class Pop3Client
    Inherits System.ComponentModel.Component

    ' The internal TCP connection.
    Private Client As New TcpClient()
    Private Stream As NetworkStream

    ' The connection state.
    Private _Connected As Boolean = False
    Public ReadOnly Property Connected() As Boolean
        Get
            Return _Connected
        End Get
    End Property

    Private Sub Send(ByVal message As String)
        ' Send the command in ASCII format.
        Dim MessageBytes() As Byte = Encoding.ASCII.GetBytes(message)
        Stream.Write(MessageBytes, 0, MessageBytes.Length)

        Debug.WriteLine(message)
    End Sub

    Private Function GetResponse() As String
        ' Build up the response string until the line termination
        ' character is found.
        Dim Character, Response As String
        Do
            Character = Chr(Stream.ReadByte()).ToString()
            Response &= Character
        Loop Until Character = Chr(13)

        Response = Response.Trim(New Char() {Chr(13), Chr(10)})
        Debug.WriteLine(Response)
```

```
        Return Response
    End Function


    ' (Other code omitted.)

End Class
```

You'll notice that the *Pop3Client* is derived from the *Component* class. This nicety allows you to add and configure an instance of the *Pop3Client* class at design time using Microsoft Visual Studio .NET.

You can also add constants for common POP3 commands. One easy way to add constants is to group them in a private class nested inside *Pop3Client*, as shown here:

```
' Some command constants.
Private Class Commands
    ' These constants represent client commands.
    Public Const List As String = "LIST" & vbNewLine
    Public Const User As String = "USER "
    Public Const Password As String = "PASS "
    Public Const Delete As String = "DELE "
    Public Const GetMessage As String = "RETR "
    Public Const Quit As String = "QUIT" & vbNewLine

    ' These two constants represent server responses.
    Public Const ServerConfirm As String = "+OK"
    Public Const ServerNoMoreData As String = "."
End Class
```

The next step is to create a basic method for connecting to the POP3 server and disconnecting from it. Because *Pop3Client* derives from *Component*, it indirectly implements *IDisposable*. Therefore, you can also override the *Dispose* method to ensure that connections are properly cleaned up when the class is disposed.

```
Public Sub Connect(ByVal serverName As String, ByVal userName As String, _
  ByVal password As String)
    If Connected Then Me.Disconnect()

    ' Connect to the POP3 server
    ' (which is almost always at port 110).
    Client.Connect(serverName, 110)
    Stream = Client.GetStream()

    ' Check if connection worked.
    CheckResponse(GetResponse())

    ' Send user name.
```

```
        Send(Commands.User & userName & vbNewLine)

        ' Check response.
        CheckResponse(GetResponse())

        ' Send password.
        Send(Commands.Password & password & vbNewLine)

        ' Check response.
        CheckResponse(GetResponse())

        _Connected = True
    End Sub

    Public Sub Disconnect()
        If Connected Then
            Send(Commands.Quit)
            CheckResponse(GetResponse())
            _Connected = False
        End If
    End Sub

    Protected Overloads Overrides Sub Dispose(ByVal disposing As Boolean)
        If disposing Then Disconnect()
        MyBase.Dispose(disposing)
    End Sub
```

> **Note**   Some mail servers will not allow the password to be transmit-
> ted in clear text. In this case, you will need to manually encrypt the
> password information first using the appropriate algorithm before you
> submit it to the *Pop3Client* class.

The *Pop3Client* class uses a private *CheckResponse* procedure, which verifies that the server's message is the excepted confirmation and throws an
exception if it isn't.

```
Private Sub CheckResponse(ByVal response As String)
    If Not (response.Substring(0, 3) = Commands.ServerConfirm) Then
        Client.Close()
        _Connected = False
        Throw New ApplicationException("Response " & response & _
          " not expected.")
    End If
End Sub
```

The only remaining step is to implement three higher-level methods: *Get-MessageList*, which the client calls to retrieve a list of message headers, *GetMessageContent*, which the client calls to retrieve the body of a single message, and *DeleteMessage*, which is typically used to remove a message after its content is downloaded.

To support the *GetMessageList* method, you need to create a simple class for storing message header information, which includes a message number and size in bytes.

```
Public Class MessageHeader

    Private _Number As Integer
    Private _Size As Integer

    Public ReadOnly Property Number() As Integer
        Get
            Return _Number
        End Get
    End Property

    Public ReadOnly Property Size() As Integer
        Get
            Return _Size
        End Get
    End Property

    Public Sub New(ByVal number As Integer, ByVal size As Integer)
        Me._Number = number
        Me._Size = size
    End Sub

End Class
```

The *GetMessageList* method returns an array of *MessageHeader* objects. When the server returns a period (.) on a separate line, the list is complete.

```
Public Function GetMessageList() As MessageHeader()
    If Not Connected Then Throw New _
      InvalidOperationException("Not connected.")

    Send(Commands.List)
    CheckResponse(GetResponse())

    Dim Messages As New ArrayList()
    Do
        Dim Response As String = GetResponse()
```

```
            If Response = Commands.ServerNoMoreData Then
                ' No more messages.
                Return CType(Messages.ToArray(GetType(MessageHeader)), _
                    MessageHeader())
            Else
                ' Create an EmailMessage object for this message.
                ' Include the header information.
                Dim Values() As String = Response.Split()
                Dim Message As New MessageHeader(Val(Values(0)), Val(Values(1)))

                Messages.Add(Message)
            End If
        Loop
    End Function
```

To retrieve the information for a single message, the client calls *Get-MessageContent* with the appropriate message number. The message content includes headers that indicate the sender, recipient, and path taken, along with the message subject, priority, and body. A more sophisticated version of the *Pop3Client* might parse this information into a class that provides separate properties for these details.

```
Public Function GetMessageContent(ByVal messageNumber As Integer) As String
    If Not Connected Then Throw New _
        InvalidOperationException("Not connected.")

    Send(Commands.GetMessage & messageNumber.ToString() & vbNewLine)
    CheckResponse(GetResponse)
    Dim Line, Content As String

    ' Retrieve all message text until the end point.
    Do
        Line = GetResponse()
        If Line = Commands.ServerNoMoreData Then
            Return Content
        Else
            Content &= Line & vbNewLine
        End If
    Loop
End Function
```

Finally *DeleteMessage* removes a message from the server based on its message number.

```
Public Sub DeleteMessage(ByVal messageNumber As Integer)
    If Not Connected Then Throw New _
        InvalidOperationException("Not connected.")
```

```
        Send(Commands.Delete & messageNumber.ToString() & vbNewLine)
        CheckResponse(GetResponse())
End Sub
```

You can test the *Pop3Client* class with a simple program such as the following one, which retrieves all the messages for a given account:

```
Public Module Pop3Test

    Public Sub Main()
        ' Get the connection information.
        Dim Server, Name, Password As String
        Console.Write("POP3 Server: ")
        Server = Console.ReadLine()
        Console.Write("Name: ")
        Name = Console.ReadLine()
        Console.Write("Password: ")
        Password = Console.ReadLine()
        Console.WriteLine()

        ' Connect.
        Dim POP3 As New Pop3Client()
        POP3.Connect(Server, Name, Password)

        ' Retrieve a list of message, and display the corresponding content.
        Dim Messages() As MessageHeader = POP3.GetMessageList()
        Console.WriteLine(Messages.Length().ToString() & " messages.")

        Dim Message As MessageHeader
        For Each Message In Messages
            Console.WriteLine(New String("-"c, 60))
            Console.WriteLine("Message Number: " & Message.Number.ToString())
            Console.WriteLine("Size: " & Message.Size.ToString())
            Console.WriteLine()
            Console.WriteLine(POP3.GetMessageContent(Message.Number))
            Console.WriteLine(New String("-"c, 60))
            Console.WriteLine()
        Next

        Console.WriteLine("Press Enter to disconnect.")
        Console.ReadLine()
        POP3.Disconnect()
    End Sub

End Module
```

The output for a typical session is as follows:

```
POP3 Server: mail.server.com
Name: matthew
Password: opensesame


1 messages.
------------------------------------------------------------------------
Message Number: 1
Size: 1380


Return-Path: <someone@somewhere.com>
Delivered-To: somewhere.com%someone@somewhere.com
Received: (cpmta 15300 invoked from network); 5 Dec 2002 06:57:13 -0800
Received: from 66.185.86.71 (HELO fep01-mail.bloor.is.net.cable.rogers.com)
  by smtp.c000.snv.cp.net (209.228.32.87) with SMTP; 5 Dec 2002 06:57:13 -0800
X-Received: 5 Dec 2002 14:57:13 GMT
Received: from fariamat ([24.114.131.60])
        by fep01-mail.bloor.is.net.cable.rogers.com
        (InterMail vM.5.01.05.06 201-253-122-126-106-20020509) with ESMTP
        id <20021205145711.SJDZ4718.fep01-mail.bloor.is.net.cable.rog-
ers.com@fariamat>
        for <someone@somewhere.com>; Thu, 5 Dec 2002 09:57:11 -0500
Message-ID: <004c01c29c6f$186c5150$3c837218@fariamat>
From: <someone@somewhere.com>
To: <someone@somewhere.com>
Subject: Test Message
Date: Thu, 5 Dec 2002 10:00:48 -0500
MIME-Version: 1.0
Content-Type: text/plain;
        charset="iso-8859-1"
Content-Transfer-Encoding: 7bit
X-Priority: 3
X-MSMail-Priority: Normal
X-Mailer: Microsoft Outlook Express 6.00.2600.0000
X-MIMEOLE: Produced By Microsoft MimeOLE V6.00.2600.0000
X-Authentication-Info: Submitted using SMTP AUTH LOGIN at fep01--
mail.bloor.is.net.cable.rogers.com from [24.114.131.60] at
Thu, 5 Dec 2002 09:57:11 -0500
Status: RO
X-UIDL: Pe9pStHkIFc7yAE


Hi! This is a test message!
------------------------------------------------------------------------


Press Enter to disconnect.
```

You can see the transcript of commands sent and received in the Debug output window in Visual Studio .NET.

8.14 Access an FTP Site

Problem

You want to retrieve or upload files from an FTP server.

Solution

Use a third-party component, or create a dedicated class that sends FTP commands over a TCP connection.

Discussion

FTP (File Transfer Protocol) is a common protocol used to upload and download files from a server. FTP, like many Internet protocols, defines a small set of commands that are sent as simple ASCII-encoded messages over a TCP connection (typically on port 21).

The following is a listing of a typical FTP dialogue, starting immediately after the client makes a TCP connection. Notice that every line sent from the server begins with an FTP response code.

```
Server sends: 220-FTP server ready.
Server sends: 220-<<
Server sends: 220-
Server sends: 220->>
Server sends: 220 This is a private system - No anonymous login
Client sends: USER <UserName>
Server sends: 331 User <UserName> OK. Password required
Client sends: PASS <Password>
Server sends: 230-User authenticated.
Client sends: PASV
Server sends: 227 Entering Passive Mode (66,185,95,103,166,76)
Client sends: TYPE I
Server sends: 200 TYPE is now 8-bit binary
Client sends: RETR <FileName>
Server sends: 150 Accepted data connection
< file transferred on separate connection >
Server sends: 226-File successfully transferred
Server sends: 226 0.001 seconds (measured here), 2.09 Mbytes per second
Client sends: QUIT
Server sends: 221-Goodbye. You uploaded 0 and downloaded 3 kbytes.
```

FTP is a fairly detailed protocol, and implementing a successful FTP client is not a trivial task. One challenge is that FTP works in two modes: active and passive. In *active mode*, the FTP server attempts to transfer files to a client by treating the client as a server. In other words, the client must open a new connection and wait for an incoming server request. This configuration won't work with most firewalls, which is why most FTP use is over passive connections. In *passive mode*, the server provides a new server connection that the client can connect to for downloading data. To switch to passive mode, you use the *PASV* command.

The remainder of this recipe presents a bare-bones FTP client that can log on and download files. If you want more sophisticated FTP functionality, such as the ability to browse the directory structure and upload files, you can use a commercial component or you can extend this code. For a reference of valid FTP commands and return codes, refer to *http://www.vbip.com/winsock /winsock_ftp_ref_01.asp*.

The *FtpClient* class works on a similar principle to the *Pop3Client* class in recipe 8.13. The basic outline defines recognized command constants and an internal TCP connection.

```
Public Class FtpClient
    Inherits System.ComponentModel.Component

    ' The internal TCP connection.
    Private Client As New TcpClient()
    Private Stream As NetworkStream

    ' The connection state.
    Private _Connected As Boolean = False
    Public ReadOnly Property Connected() As Boolean
        Get
            Return _Connected
        End Get
    End Property

    ' Some command constants.
    Private Class Commands
        Public Const User As String = "USER "
        Public Const Password As String = "PASS "
        Public Const Quit As String = "QUIT" & vbNewLine
        Public Const GetFile As String = "RETR "
        Public Const UsePassiveMode As String = "PASV" & vbNewLine
        Public Const UseBinary As String = "TYPE I" & vbNewLine
        Public Const UseAscii As String = "TYPE A" & vbNewLine
    End Class
```

```
Private Enum ReturnCodes
    ServiceReady = 220
    Accepted = 200
    PasswordRequired = 331
    UserLoggedIn = 230
    EnteringPassiveMode = 227
    StartingTransferAlreadyOpen = 125
    StartingTransferOpening = 150
    TransferComplete = 226
End Enum

' (Other code omitted.)

End Class
```

Next we add private functions for sending and receiving data, as well as a helper function that verifies that a given response begins with an expected return code.

```
Private Function Send(ByVal message As String) As String
    ' Send the command in ASCII format.
    Dim MessageBytes() As Byte = Encoding.ASCII.GetBytes(message)
    Stream.Write(MessageBytes, 0, MessageBytes.Length)

    Debug.WriteLine(message)

    ' Return the response code.
    Return GetResponse()
End Function

Private Function GetResponse() As String
    ' Retrieve all the available lines.
    Dim Character As String
    Dim Response As String = ""

    Do
        Do
            Character = Chr(Stream.ReadByte()).ToString()
            Response &= Character
        Loop Until Character = Chr(10)
    Loop While Stream.DataAvailable

    Response = Response.Trim(New Char() {Chr(13), Chr(10)})
    Debug.WriteLine(Response)
    Return Response
End Function
```

```
Private Function CheckCode(ByVal response As String, _
  ByVal expectedCode As ReturnCodes) As Boolean
    Return Val(response.Substring(0, 3)) = expectedCode
End Function
```

The next step is to add the basic methods for connecting and disconnecting to an FTP server:

```
Public Sub Connect(ByVal serverName As String, ByVal userName As String, _
  ByVal password As String)
    If Connected Then Me.Disconnect()

    ' Connect to the POP3 server
    ' (which is almost always at port 21).
    Client.Connect(serverName, 21)
    Stream = Client.GetStream()

    ' Send user name.
    Dim Response As String
    Response = GetResponse()
    Response = Send(Commands.User & userName & vbNewLine)

    If CheckCode(Response, ReturnCodes.PasswordRequired) Then
        ' Send password.
        Response = Send(Commands.Password & password & vbNewLine)
    End If

    If Not (CheckCode(Response, ReturnCodes.UserLoggedIn)) _
      And Not (CheckCode(Response, ReturnCodes.ServiceReady)) Then
        Throw New ApplicationException("Could not log in.")
    End If

    _Connected = True
End Sub


Public Sub Disconnect()
    If Connected Then
        If Not TransferClient Is Nothing Then
            TransferClient.Close()
        End If
        Send(Commands.Quit)
        _Connected = False
    End If
End Sub
```

The most complicated part of *FtpClient* is the code needed for downloading files. *FtpClient* uses passive mode, which means it must use a separate *TcpClient* instance to download files.

```
' Second connection for retrieving a file.
Private TransferClient As TcpClient
Private TransferEndpoint As IPEndPoint
```

The private *CreateTransferClient* procedure instructs the FTP server to use passive mode, retrieves the new IP address and port that it should use, and initializes the *TcpClient* object accordingly:

```
Private Sub CreateTransferClient()
    Dim Response As String = Send(Commands.UsePassiveMode)

    If Not CheckCode(Response, ReturnCodes.EnteringPassiveMode) Then
        Throw New ApplicationException("Error entering passive mode.")
    End If

    ' The IP address and port number is appended to the response.
    ' Retrieve these details.
    Dim StartPos As Integer = Response.IndexOf("(")
    Dim EndPos As Integer = Response.IndexOf(")")
    Dim IPAndPort As String = Response.Substring(StartPos + 1, _
        EndPos - StartPos - 1)
    Dim IPParts() As String = IPAndPort.Split(","c)

    Dim IP As String = IPParts(0) + "." + IPParts(1) + "." + _
        IPParts(2) + "." + IPParts(3)
    Dim Port As Integer = Convert.ToInt32(IPParts(4)) * 256 + _
        Convert.ToInt32(IPParts(5))

    ' Create the data transfer connection.
    TransferClient = New TcpClient()

    TransferEndpoint = New IPEndPoint(IPAddress.Parse(IP), Port)
End Sub
```

In addition, the private *SetMode* procedure sends a message to the server indicating whether the file is binary or ASCII-based.

```
Private Sub SetMode(ByVal binaryMode As Boolean)
    Dim Response As String
    If binaryMode Then
        Response = Send(Commands.UseBinary)
    Else
        Response = Send(Commands.UseAscii)
    End If

    If Not CheckCode(Response, ReturnCodes.Accepted) Then
        Throw New ApplicationException("Could not change mode.")
    End If
End Sub
```

To download a file, your application calls the *DownloadFile* method with the filename and a Boolean variable indicating whether binary or ASCII mode should be used. The *DownloadFile* method uses *SetMode* and *CreateTransferClient* accordingly. Once the connection is made, the *NetworkStream* is returned to the client, who can read from it and close it when complete. Using a stream avoids the overhead of storing the retrieved data in memory (for example, in a byte array), which can be quite enormous if a file several megabytes large is being downloaded.

```
Public Function DownloadFile(ByVal filename As String, _
  ByVal binaryMode As Boolean) As NetworkStream
    ' Create a connection to the second port in passive mode.
    CreateTransferClient()
    TransferClient.Connect(TransferEndpoint)

    SetMode(binaryMode)

    Dim Response As String = Send(Commands.GetFile & filename & vbNewLine)

    If Not CheckCode(Response, ReturnCodes.StartingTransferAlreadyOpen) _
      And Not (CheckCode(Response, ReturnCodes.StartingTransferOpening)) Then
        Throw New ApplicationException("Could not open connection.")
    End If

    ' Let the client read data from the network stream.
    ' This is more efficient that creating and returning an
    ' intermediate byte array, but it also relies on the client
    ' to close the stream.
    Return TransferClient.GetStream()
End Function
```

The filename can be a complete relative path, as long as you use the forward slash (/) character to separate directories. For example, images/mypic.gif is valid, but images\mypic.gif is not.

When the transfer is complete, the client must call *ConfirmDownloadComplete*, which reads the confirmation message from the server and frees it up to serve new requests.

```
Public Sub ConfirmDownloadComplete()
    Dim Response As String = GetResponse()
    CheckCode(Response, ReturnCodes.TransferComplete)
End Sub
```

Putting it all together is easy. The following Console application connects to an FTP server and attempts to download a file. You can watch a transcript of all sent and received messages in the Debug window.

```vb
Public Module FtpTest

    Public Sub Main()
        ' Connect to an FTP server.
        Dim FTP As New FtpClient()
        FTP.Connect("ftp.adobe.com", "anonymous", "me@somewhere.com")

        ' Request a file.
        Dim Stream As NetworkStream = FTP.DownloadFile("license.txt", True)

        ' Copy the data into file 1K at a time.
        Dim fs As New FileStream("c:\license.txt", IO.FileMode.Create)
        Dim BytesRead As Integer
        Do
            Dim Bytes(1024) As Byte
            BytesRead = Stream.Read(Bytes, 0, Bytes.Length)
            fs.Write(Bytes, 0, BytesRead)
        Loop While BytesRead > 0

        ' Close the network stream and the file.
        Stream.Close()
        fs.Close()

        ' Retrieve the server confirmation message.
        FTP.ConfirmDownloadComplete()

        Console.WriteLine("File transfer complete.")
        Console.WriteLine("Press Enter to disconnect.")
        Console.ReadLine()

        FTP.Disconnect()
    End Sub

End Module
```

9

Reflection

Reflection is used to retrieve the internal details of assemblies and types at runtime. Reflection is commonly used to discover which classes exist in an assembly, and which properties, methods, and events exist in a class. Collectively, this information is known as *metadata*. You can also use reflection to dynamically generate code, instantiate types or call methods by name, and interact with unknown objects. Simply put, reflection is the slightly mind-bending technique of exploring code structures programmatically.

Reflection is a key ingredient in many Microsoft .NET Framework features. For example, reflection is required to support Microsoft ASP.NET data binding, to pre-compile regular expression classes, and to allow some types of Web Service extensibility. In most cases, you'll use reflection indirectly without even realizing it. However, there are some tasks that do require your code to use reflection directly. One example is if you want to create a highly modular, extensible application, in which case you'll use reflection to load types at runtime (see recipe 9.6). Other examples of reflection include loading an assembly from the Internet (recipe 9.7), using custom attributes (recipe 9.9), and compiling code programmatically (recipe 9.12). We'll examine all these techniques in this chapter, along with the basics of exploring assemblies, types, and members (recipes 9.1 to 9.5).

9.1 Generate a Dynamic About Box

Problem

You want to retrieve version information at runtime for display in an About box.

Solution

Retrieve a reference to the current assembly using *Assembly.GetExecutingAssembly*, and retrieve its *AssemblyName*, which includes version information.

Discussion

It's important for an application to correctly report its version (and sometimes additional information such as its filename and culture) without needing to hardcode this data. Reflection provides the ideal solution because it allows you to retrieve these details directly from the assembly's metadata.

The following code snippet displays several pieces of information about the current assembly using reflection. It also shows how you can retrieve some of the same information indirectly from the *System.Windows.Forms.Application* class (regardless of the application type).

```
Public Module TestReflection

    Public Sub Main()
        Dim ExecutingApp As System.Reflection.Assembly
        ExecutingApp = System.Reflection.Assembly.GetExecutingAssembly()

        Dim Name As System.Reflection.AssemblyName
        Name = ExecutingApp.GetName()

        ' Display metadata information.
        Console.WriteLine("Application: " & Name.Name)
        Console.WriteLine("Version: " & Name.Version.ToString())
        Console.WriteLine("Code Base: " & Name.CodeBase)
        Console.WriteLine("Culture: " & Name.CultureInfo.DisplayName)
        Console.WriteLine("Culture Code: " & Name.CultureInfo.ToString())
        ' (If the assembly is signed, you can also use Name.KeyPair to
        ' retrieve the public key.)

        ' Some additional can be retrieved from the Application class.
        ' The version information is identical.
        Console.WriteLine("Assembly File: " & _
           System.Windows.Forms.Application.ExecutablePath)
        Console.WriteLine("Version: " & _
           System.Windows.Forms.Application.ProductVersion)

        ' The Company and Product information is set through the
        ' AssemblyCompany and AssemblyProduct attributes, which are
        ' usually coded in the AssemblyInfo.vb file.
        Console.WriteLine("Company: " & _
           System.Windows.Forms.Application.CompanyName)
```

```
      Console.WriteLine("Product: " & _
        System.Windows.Forms.Application.ProductName)

      ' The culture information retrieves the current culture
      ' (in this case, en-US), while the reflection code
      ' retrieves the culture specified in the assembly
      ' (in this case, none).
      Console.WriteLine("Culture: " & _
        System.Windows.Forms.Application.CurrentCulture.ToString())
      Console.WriteLine("Culture Code: " & _
        System.Windows.Forms.Application.CurrentCulture.DisplayName)

      Console.ReadLine()
   End Sub

End Module
```

Note that *GetExecutingAssembly* always returns a reference to the assembly where the code is executing. In other words, if you launch a Microsoft Windows application (assembly *A*) that uses a separate component (assembly *B*), and the component invokes *GetExecutingAssembly*, it will receive a reference to assembly *B*. You can also use *GetCallingAssembly*, which retrieves the assembly where the calling code is located, or *GetEntryAssembly*, which always returns the executable assembly for the current application domain.

Note   *Assembly* is a reserved keyword in Microsoft Visual Basic .NET. Thus, if you want to reference the *System.Reflection.Assembly* type, you must use a fully qualified reference or you must enclose the word *Assembly* in square brackets.

```
' This works.
Dim Asm As System.Reflection.Assembly

' This also works, assuming you have imported the
' System.Reflection namespace.
Dim Asm As [Assembly]

' This generates a compile-
time error because the word Assembly is reserved.
Dim Asm As Assembly
```

9.2 List Assembly Dependencies

Problem

You want to list all the assemblies that are required by another assembly.

Solution

Use the *Assembly.GetReferencedAssemblies* method.

Discussion

All .NET assemblies include a header that lists assembly references. If the referenced assembly has a strong name, the header includes the required version and public key for the referenced assembly.

Once you retrieve a reference to an assembly, it's easy to find its dependencies using the *GetReferencedAssemblies* method. Consider this code, which iterates through the assembly references of the current executing assembly:

```
Public Module TestReflection

    Public Sub Main()
        Dim ExecutingAssembly As System.Reflection.Assembly
        ExecutingAssembly = System.Reflection.Assembly.GetExecutingAssembly()

        Dim ReferencedAssemblies() As System.Reflection.AssemblyName
        ReferencedAssemblies = ExecutingAssembly.GetReferencedAssemblies()

        Dim ReferencedAssembly As System.Reflection.AssemblyName
        For Each ReferencedAssembly In ReferencedAssemblies
            Console.Write(ReferencedAssembly.Name & " (")
            Console.WriteLine(ReferencedAssembly.Version.ToString() & ")")
        Next

        Console.ReadLine()
    End Sub

End Module
```

This code produces output such as the following:

```
mscorlib (1.0.3300.0)
Microsoft.VisualBasic (7.0.3300.0)
System (1.0.3300.0)
System.Data (1.0.3300.0)
System.Xml (1.0.3300.0)
```

You can also find the assembly references for any assembly on the computer hard drive. Use the *Assembly.LoadFrom* method, as shown here:

```
Asm = Assembly.LoadFrom("c:\temp\myassembly.dll")
```

If the assembly is found in the global assembly cache (GAC), you can use the *Assembly.Load* or *Assembly.LoadWithPartialName* methods instead, which retrieve the assembly using all or part of its strong name. For example, you can find out what assemblies are required to support the core *System.Web.dll* assembly using this code:

```
Asm = Assembly.LoadWithPartialName("System.Web")
```

9.3 Get Type Information from a Class or an Object

Problem

You want to retrieve information about any .NET type (class, interface, structure, enumeration, and so on).

Solution

Use the Visual Basic .NET command *GetType* with the class name. Or use the *Object.GetType* instance method with any object.

Discussion

The *System.Type* class is one of the core ingredients in reflection. It allows you to retrieve information about any .NET type and drill down to examine type members such as methods, properties, events, and fields. To retrieve a *Type* object for a given class, you use the Visual Basic *GetType* command, as shown here:

```
' Retrieve information about the System.Xml.XmlDocument class.
Dim TypeInfo As Type
TypeInfo = GetType(System.Xml.XmlDocument)
```

Alternatively, you can retrieve type information from an object by calling the *GetType* method.

```
' Create a "mystery" object.
Dim MyObject As Object = New System.Xml.XmlDocument()

' Retrieve information about the object.
Dim TypeInfo As Type = MyObject.GetType()
```

Both of these approaches have equivalent results. The only difference is that one works with uninstantiated class names, and the other technique requires a live object.

Finally, you can also create a *Type* object using a string with a fully qualified class name and the shared *Type.GetType* method.

```
Dim TypeName As String = "System.Xml.XmlDocument"
Dim TypeInfo As Type = Type.GetType(TypeName)
```

Note   The shared *Type.GetType* method will only consider the types in the current (executing) assembly and any of its referenced assemblies. In other words, if you try to retrieve the type *XmlDocument*, you must have a reference to the System.Xml.dll assembly, or the call will fail. To get around this limitation, you can retrieve a type from a specific assembly using the *Assembly.GetType* instance method, as described in recipe 9.5.

The *Type* class provides a large complement of methods and properties. The following code snippet shows a simple test for retrieving basic type information:

```
Public Module TestReflection
    Public Sub Main()
        Dim TypeInfo As Type
        TypeInfo = GetType(System.Xml.XmlDocument)

        Console.WriteLine("Type Name: " & TypeInfo.Name)
        Console.WriteLine("Namespace: " & TypeInfo.Namespace)
        Console.WriteLine("Assembly: " & TypeInfo.Assembly.FullName)

        If TypeInfo.IsClass Then
            Console.WriteLine("It's a Class")
        ElseIf TypeInfo.IsValueType Then
            Console.WriteLine("It's a Structure")
        ElseIf TypeInfo.IsInterface Then
            Console.WriteLine("It's an Interface")
        ElseIf TypeInfo.IsEnum Then
            Console.WriteLine("It's an Enumeration")
        End If

        Console.ReadLine()
    End Sub

End Module
```

The output of this code is as follows:

```
Type Name: XmlDocument
Namespace: System.Xml
Assembly: System.Xml, Version=1.0.3300.0, Culture=neutral, PublicKeyToken=b77a5
c
561934e089
It's a Class
```

One of the most interesting operations you can perform with a type is to examine its members. This technique is demonstrated in recipe 9.4.

9.4 Examine a Type for Members

Problem

You want to retrieve information about the properties, events, methods, and other members exposed by a type.

Solution

Use methods such as *Type.GetMethods*, *Type.GetProperties*, *Type.GetEvents*, and so on.

Discussion

The *Type* class is a starting point for a detailed examination of any .NET type. You can use the following methods to delve into the structure of a type:

- **GetConstructors**   retrieves an array of *ConstructorInfo* objects, which detail the constructors for a type.

- **GetMethods**   retrieves an array of *MethodInfo* objects, which describe the functions and subroutines provided by a type.

- **GetProperties**   retrieves an array of *PropertyInfo* objects, which describe the properties for a type.

- **GetEvents**   retrieves an array of *EventInfo* objects, which describe the constructors for a type.

- **GetFields**   retrieves an array of *FieldInfo* objects, which represent the member variables of a type.

- **GetInterfaces**   retrieves an array of *Type* objects, which represent the interfaces implemented by this type.

All the *xxxInfo* classes are contained in the *System.Reflection* namespace and derive from *MemberInfo*. They add additional informational properties. For example, using *MethodInfo*, you can determine the data type of all method arguments and return values. In addition, you can retrieve a single *MemberInfo* array for a type by using the *GetMembers* method. This array will contain all the events, properties, constructors, and so on for the type.

As a rule of thumb, the *xxxInfo* methods return all the members of type, whether they are public, private, shared, or instance members. You can filter which members are returned by passing in values from the *System.Reflection.BindingFlags* enumeration when you call the method. For example, use *BindingFlags.Instance* in conjunction with *BindingFlags.Public* to retrieve public instance members only.

The following example demonstrates a test program that asks for the name of a class and then provides information about all its members. To shorten the amount of code required, all members are printed using the generic *DisplayMembers* subroutine shown here:

```
Private Sub DisplayMembers(ByVal members() As MemberInfo)

    Dim Member As MemberInfo
    For Each Member In members
        Console.WriteLine(Member.ToString())
    Next
    Console.WriteLine()

End Sub
```

The disadvantage of this approach is that every type of member is dealt with as a generic *MemberInfo* and displayed using the *ToString* method. *ToString* lists all the important information about a method, but it uses C# syntax, which means that data types precede variable names and function definitions, subroutines are distinguished from functions using the *void* keyword, and so on. A more detailed reflector would create a Visual Basic–specific display by examining the properties of the specialized *MemberInfo* classes.

Below is a partial listing of the code. For the full example, consult the book's sample code for this chapter.

```
Public Module TestReflection

    Public Sub Main()
        Console.Write("Enter the name of a type to reflect on: ")
        Dim TypeName As String = Console.ReadLine()
        Dim TypeInfo As Type
        If TypeName <> "" Then TypeInfo = Type.GetType(TypeName)
        Console.WriteLine()
```

```
        If TypeInfo Is Nothing Then
            Console.WriteLine("Invalid type name.")
            Return
        End If

        ' List shared fields.
        Dim Fields As FieldInfo() = TypeInfo.GetFields((BindingFlags.Static _
          Or BindingFlags.NonPublic Or BindingFlags.Public))
        Console.WriteLine(New String("-"c, 79))
        Console.WriteLine("**** Shared Fields ****")
        Console.WriteLine(New String("-"c, 79))
        DisplayMembers(Fields)

        ' List shared properties.
        Dim Properties As PropertyInfo()
        Properties = TypeInfo.GetProperties((BindingFlags.Static _
          Or BindingFlags.NonPublic Or BindingFlags.Public))
        Console.WriteLine(New String("-"c, 79))
        Console.WriteLine("**** Shared Properties ****")
        Console.WriteLine(New String("-"c, 79))
        DisplayMembers(Properties)

        ' (Remainder of code omitted.)
    End Sub

  ' (DisplayMembers function omitted.)

End Module
```

A typical test run produces the following (abbreviated) output:

```
Enter the name of a type to reflect on: System.String


-------------------------------------------------------------------------------
**** Shared Fields ****
-------------------------------------------------------------------------------
System.String Empty
Char[] WhitespaceChars
Int32 TrimHead
Int32 TrimTail
Int32 TrimBoth


-------------------------------------------------------------------------------
**** Shared Methods ****
-------------------------------------------------------------------------------
System.String Join(System.String, System.String[])
System.String Join(System.String, System.String[], Int32, Int32)
...
```

9.5 Examine an Assembly for Types

Problem

You want to display all the types in an assembly.

Solution

Use the *Assembly.GetTypes* method.

Discussion

The *Assembly.GetTypes* method returns an array of *Type* objects that represent all the classes, interfaces, enumerations, and other types defined in an assembly. You can use this method in conjunction with the methods of the *Type* class (shown in recipe 9.4) to "walk" the structure of an assembly.

The following example demonstrates a simple knock-off of the IL disassembler (ILDASM) included with the .NET Framework SDK. It's a Windows application that allows the user to choose an assembly file and then displays a hierarchical tree that shows all the types it contains. Figure 9-1 shows the test application at work on a thread test created for Chapter 7.

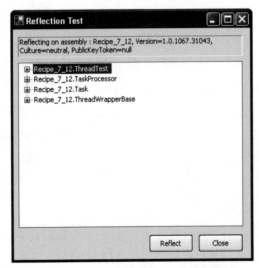

Figure 9-1   A reflection browser that uses the *TreeView* control.

Using the reflector, you can drill down to find more information about members, including the data types for properties and method parameters, and the signature for event handlers, as shown in Figure 9-2.

Figure 9-2   Viewing members in the reflection browser.

The bulk of the code in this example is in the *Click* event handler for the Reflect button. The event handler prompts the user to choose an assembly, loads it, and iterates through all the types and members.

```
Private Sub cmdReflect_Click(ByVal sender As System.Object, _
  ByVal e As System.EventArgs) Handles cmdReflect.Click

    ' Show a dialog box that allows the user to choose an assembly.
    Dim dlgOpen As New OpenFileDialog()
    dlgOpen.Filter = "Assemblies (*.dll;*.exe) | *.dll;*.exe"

    If dlgOpen.ShowDialog() <> DialogResult.OK Then Return

    ' Load the selected assembly.
    Dim Asm As System.Reflection.Assembly
    Try
        Asm = System.Reflection.Assembly.LoadFrom(dlgOpen.FileName)
    Catch Err As Exception
        MessageBox.Show(Err.ToString, "Invalid Assembly", _
          MessageBoxButtons.OK, MessageBoxIcon.Exclamation)
        Return
    End Try
```

```vbnet
lblAssembly.Text = "Reflecting on assembly : " & Asm.FullName

' Define some variables used to "walk" the program structure.
Dim Types(), TypeInfo As Type
Dim Events(), EventInfo As System.Reflection.EventInfo
Dim Methods(), MethodInfo As System.Reflection.MethodInfo
Dim Parameters(), ParameterInfo As System.Reflection.ParameterInfo
Dim Properties(), PropertyInfo As System.Reflection.PropertyInfo
Dim nodeParent, node, subNode As TreeNode

' Build up the TreeView.
' Begin by iterating over all the types.
treeTypes.Nodes.Clear()
Types = Asm.GetTypes()
For Each TypeInfo In Types
    nodeParent = treeTypes.Nodes.Add(TypeInfo.FullName)

    ' Add nodes for all the properties.
    node = nodeParent.Nodes.Add("Properties")
    Properties = TypeInfo.GetProperties()
    For Each PropertyInfo In Properties
        subNode = node.Nodes.Add(PropertyInfo.Name)

        ' Add information about the property.
        subNode.Nodes.Add("Type: " & PropertyInfo.PropertyType.ToString())
        subNode.Nodes.Add("Readable: " & PropertyInfo.CanRead)
        subNode.Nodes.Add("Writeable: " & PropertyInfo.CanWrite)
    Next

    ' Add nodes for all the Methods.
    node = nodeParent.Nodes.Add("Methods")
    Methods = TypeInfo.GetMethods()
    For Each MethodInfo In Methods
        subNode = node.Nodes.Add(MethodInfo.Name & "()")

        ' Add information about the method parameters.
        Parameters = MethodInfo.GetParameters()
        For Each ParameterInfo In Parameters
            subNode.Nodes.Add("Parameter '" & ParameterInfo.Name & _
              "': " & ParameterInfo.ParameterType.ToString())
        Next
        If MethodInfo.ReturnType.ToString() <> "System.Void" Then _
          subNode.Nodes.Add("Return: " & MethodInfo.ReturnType.ToString())
    Next

    ' Add nodes for all the events.
    node = nodeParent.Nodes.Add("Events")
    Events = TypeInfo.GetEvents()
```

```
    For Each EventInfo In Events
        subNode = node.Nodes.Add(EventInfo.Name)
        subNode.Nodes.Add(EventInfo.EventHandlerType.Name)
    Next
Next

End Sub
```

9.6 Instantiate a Type by Name

Problem

You want to create an instance of an object that's named in a string.

Solution

Use the *Assembly.CreateInstance* method or the *Activator.CreateInstance* method.

Discussion

Both the *System.Reflection.Assembly* and the *System.Activator* classes provide a *CreateInstance* method. This recipe uses the *Assembly* class, and recipe 9.8 features an example with the *Activator* class.

To use *CreateInstance*, you supply a fully qualified type name. The *CreateInstance* method searches the assembly for the corresponding type, and then it creates and returns a new instance of the object (or a null reference if the object can't be found). You can also use overloaded versions of *CreateInstance* to supply constructor arguments or specify options that control how the search will be performed.

Here's an example that instantiates the *MyClass* type found in the *MyNamespace* namespace:

```
Dim MyObject As Object = Asm.CreateInstance("MyNamespace.MyClass")
```

The most common reason for loading a type by name is to support extremely configurable applications. For example, you might create an application that can be used with a variety of different logging components. To allow you to seamlessly replace the logging component without recompiling the code, you might load the logging component through reflection and interact with it through a generic interface. The assembly name and class name for the logging component would be read at startup from a configuration file.

To implement such a system, you would begin by defining a generic interface. In this case, we'll create an *ILogger* interface with one method, called *Log*.

```
Public Interface ILogger
    Sub Log(ByVal message As String)
End Interface
```

This interface is compiled into a separate assembly. You can then develop multiple logger classes, each of which will typically reside in its own assembly. Different logger classes might record messages in an event log, database, and so on. The following code shows a *ConsoleEventLogger class*, which simply displays the log message in a Console window:

```
Public Class ConsoleLogger
    Implements LogInterfaces.ILogger

    Public Sub Log(ByVal message As String) _
      Implements LogInterfaces.ILogger.Log
        Console.WriteLine(message)
    End Sub

End Class
```

To decide which logger to use, the main application uses a configuration file with two settings. *LogAssemblyFilename* indicates the name of the log assembly, and *LogClassName* indicates the name of the logging class in that assembly.

```
<?xml version="1.0" encoding="utf-8" ?>
<configuration>

  <appSettings>
    <add key="LogAssemblyFilename" value="ConsoleLogger.dll" />
    <add key="LogClassName" value="ConsoleLogger.ConsoleLogger" />
  </appSettings>

</configuration>
```

The main application reads these configuration files and uses reflection to load the corresponding assembly and instantiate the logging class. It then interacts with the object through the *ILogger* interface.

```
Public Module DynamicLoadTest

    Public Logger As LogInterfaces.ILogger

    Public Sub Main()
        Dim AssemblyName As String
```

```
      AssemblyName = ConfigurationSettings.AppSettings( _
        "LogAssemblyFilename")
      Console.WriteLine("Loading logger: " & AssemblyName)

      ' Load the assembly.
      Dim LogAsm As System.Reflection.Assembly
      LogAsm = System.Reflection.Assembly.LoadFrom(AssemblyName)

      Dim ClassName As String
      ClassName = ConfigurationSettings.AppSettings("LogClassName")

      ' Create the class.
      Console.WriteLine("Creating type: " & ClassName)
      Logger = CType(LogAsm.CreateInstance(ClassName), _
        LogInterfaces.ILogger)

      ' Use the class.
      Logger.Log("*** This is a test log message. ***")

      Console.ReadLine()
    End Sub

End Module
```

When you run this sample, you'll see the log message in the Console window, as shown here:

```
Loading logger: ConsoleLogger.dll
Creating type: ConsoleLogger.ConsoleLogger
*** This is a test log message. ***
```

9.7 Load an Assembly from a Remote Location

Problem

You want to run an assembly from a server on your local network or the Internet.

Solution

Use the *Assembly.LoadFrom* method with a Uniform Resource Identifier (URI) that points to the remote assembly.

Discussion

The *Assembly.LoadFrom* method accepts an ordinary file path, a network universal naming convention (UNC) path, or a URL Web path. *LoadFrom* is sometimes used with highly dynamic applications that load components from the Web.

Here's a basic example that loads an assembly using a URI:

```
Dim Asm As System.Reflection.Assembly
Dim AsmPath As String = "http://myserver/mydir/myassembly.dll"
Asm = System.Reflection.Assembly.LoadFrom(AsmPath)
```

If you call *LoadFrom* and supply a path to a remote assembly, that assembly will be automatically downloaded to the GAC and then executed. The next time you use *LoadFrom* with the same path, the existing copy in the GAC will be used, unless a newer version is available at the indicated path. This approach ensures optimum performance.

Remember, the source of your code will influence the security context that is assigned. If you download code and then execute it from your hard drive, it will have full permissions. However, if you use *LoadFrom* and supply an intranet or Internet URL, the code will be assigned much lower permissions. (Typically, it will be given permission to execute but nothing more.) To circumvent this limitation, you can customize the security policy to grant additional permissions based on how the assembly is signed or the location from which it is downloaded. For more information, refer to a dedicated book about code access security, such as *Visual Basic .NET Code Security Handbook*, by Eric Lippert (Wrox Press, 2002).

9.8 Invoke a Method by Name

Problem

You want to invoke a method or set a property that's named in a string.

Solution

Use the *Type.InvokeMember* method.

Discussion

The *Type* class provides an *InvokeMember* method that's similar to the *CallByName* function in Visual Basic 6. It requires the object; the name of the field, property, or method (as a string); a flag that indicates whether the string corresponds to a field, property, or method; and an array of objects for any required parameters. For example, you can call a method with no arguments using this syntax:

```
Dim MyObject As New MyClass()
Dim TypeInfo As Type = MyObject.GetType()

' Call Refresh() on MyObject.
Dim Args() As Object = {}
TypeInfo.InvokeMember("Refresh", BindingFlags.Public Or _
    BindingFlags.InvokeMethod, Nothing, MyObject, Args)
```

Here's an example that calls a method that requires two arguments:

```
Dim Args() As Object = {42, "New Name"}
TypeInfo.InvokeMember("UpdateProduct", BindingFlags.Public Or _
    BindingFlags.InvokeMethod, Nothing, MyObject, Args)
```

You can even invoke shared members, such as the *Math.Sin* method, as shown here:

```
Dim TypeInfo As Type = GetType(Math)
Dim Args() As Object = {45}
Dim Result As Object
Result = TypeInfo.InvokeMember("Sin", BindingFlags.Public Or _
    BindingFlags.InvokeMethod Or BindingFlags.Static, Nothing, Nothing, _
    Args)
Console.WriteLine(Result.ToString())     ' Displays 0.85...
```

The following example allows a user to invoke any instance member for a class, provided that it doesn't require any parameters. The code creates the required type from the supplied string name using the *System.Activator* class. Figure 9-3 shows the results of a dynamic call to *System.Guid.NewGuid*.

```
Private Sub cmdInvoke_Click(ByVal sender As System.Object, _
    ByVal e As System.EventArgs) Handles cmdInvoke.Click
    If txtClassName.Text = "" Then
        MessageBox.Show("Enter a class name.")
        Return
    End If

    ' Get the type.
    Dim TypeInfo As Type
    TypeInfo = Type.GetType(txtClassName.Text)
    If TypeInfo Is Nothing Then
        MessageBox.Show("Class name not recognized.")
        Return
    End If
```

```
Try
    ' Try to create the object.
    ' The CreateInstance() method uses the constructor that
    ' matches the supplied parameters. (In this case, none.)
    Dim Target As Object = Activator.CreateInstance(TypeInfo)

    ' Invoke the method with no parameters.
    Dim Result As Object = TypeInfo.InvokeMember(txtMethodName.Text, _
      Reflection.BindingFlags.InvokeMethod, Nothing, Target, _
      New Object() {})

    ' Check if a result is retrieved, and display its string
    ' representation.
    If Not Result Is Nothing Then
        txtResult.Text = Result.ToString()
    End If
Catch Err As Exception
    MessageBox.Show(Err.ToString)
End Try

End Sub
```

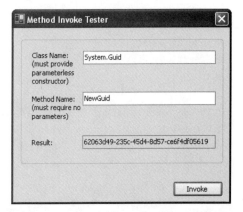

Figure 9-3 Dynamically invoking the *Guid.NewGuid* method.

> **Note** You can also access methods, properties, and fields using the appropriate *MemberInfo*-derived class. For example, you can use the *GetValue* and *SetValue* methods of the *PropertyInfo* class and the *Invoke* method of the *MethodInfo* class.

9.9 Create, Apply, and Identify a Custom Attribute

Problem

You want to use custom attributes to decorate members and classes.

Solution

Create a class that derives from *System.Attribute*, apply it to a class or a member, and use the *Type.GetCustomAttributes* method to retrieve it during reflection.

Discussion

Attributes are a cornerstone of .NET extensibility. Using attributes, you can specify additional information about a type or a member that doesn't relate directly to the code. For example, .NET uses attributes to tell the debugger how to treat code, to tell Microsoft Visual Studio .NET how to display components and controls in the Properties windows, to implement COM+ services such as object pooling, and to support Web Services and Web Service–related extensibility mechanisms such as SOAP headers and SOAP extensions. You can also define and use your own custom attributes and then check for them during reflection. Most likely, you'll use custom attributes if you need to support your own specialized extensibility mechanism or if you want to configure how a hosting application works with the objects it hosts (for example, in a .NET Remoting scenario).

The first step is to create a custom attribute class by deriving from the *System.Attribute* class and adding the required properties. By convention, the name of this class should end with *Attribute*. For example, the custom *LegacyAttribute* class shown in the following code might be used to support an internal software tracking and auditing system by identifying code that is migrated over from a non-.NET platform:

```
Public Enum PlatformType
    VisualBasic6
    CPlus
    C
    VBScript
End Enum

<AttributeUsage(AttributeTargets.All)> _
Public Class LegacyAttribute
    Inherits Attribute
```

```
Private _PreviousPlatform As PlatformType
Private _MigratedBy As String
Private _MigratedDate As DateTime

Public Property PreviousPlatform() As PlatformType
    Get
        Return _PreviousPlatform
    End Get
    Set(ByVal Value As PlatformType)
        _PreviousPlatform = Value
    End Set
End Property

Public Property MigratedBy() As String
    Get
        Return _MigratedBy
    End Get
    Set(ByVal Value As String)
        _MigratedBy = Value
    End Set
End Property

Public Property MigratedDate() As DateTime
    Get
        Return _MigratedDate
    End Get
    Set(ByVal Value As DateTime)
        _MigratedDate = Value
    End Set
End Property

Public Sub New(ByVal previousPlatform As PlatformType, _
  ByVal migratedBy As String, ByVal migratedDate As String)
    Me.PreviousPlatform = previousPlatform
    Me.MigratedBy = migratedBy
    Me.MigratedDate = DateTime.Parse(migratedDate)
End Sub

End Class
```

Notice that the date is passed to the constructor as a string. A string is used because of the type restrictions placed on attribute declarations. You can use any integral data type (*Byte, Short, Integer, Long*) or floating-point data type (*Single* and *Double*), as well as *Char, String, Boolean*, any enumerated type, or *System.Type*. However, you can't use any other type, including more complex objects and the *DateTime* structure.

Every custom attribute class requires the *AttributeUsage* attribute, which defines the language elements you can use with the attribute. You can use any combination of values from the *AttributeTargets* enumeration, including *All*, *Assembly*, *Class*, *Constructor*, *Delegate*, *Enum*, *Event*, *Field*, *Interface*, *Method*, *Module*, *Parameter*, *Property*, *ReturnValue*, and *Struct*. The custom *LegacyAttribute* can be used on all language elements that support attributes.

```
<AttributeUsage(AttributeTargets.All)> _
Public Class LegacyAttribute
```

The next step is to put the custom attribute to use. The following code shows the contents of an extremely simple assembly that defines two empty classes, one with the custom attribute and one without:

```
egacy(PlatformType.VBScript, "Matthew", "2003-12-01")> _
ublic Class ClassWithAttribute
    ' (Code omitted.)
End Class

Public Class ClassWithoutAttribute
    ' (Code omitted.)
End Class
```

The following Console application searches for *LegacyAttribute* using reflection, and reports its findings to the user:

```
Public Module CustomAttributeTest

    Public Sub Main()
        Console.WriteLine("Reporting legacy code in SampleAssembly.dll")

        ' Get the assembly.
        Dim Asm As System.Reflection.Assembly
        Asm = System.Reflection.Assembly.LoadFrom("SampleAssembly.dll")

        ' Examine all types.
        Dim Types(), TypeInfo As Type
        Types = Asm.GetTypes()

        For Each TypeInfo In Types
            Dim Attributes() As Object
            ExamineAttributes(TypeInfo.GetCustomAttributes(False), _
              TypeInfo.Name)

            ' Search members as well.
            Dim Members(), MemberInfo As System.Reflection.MemberInfo
            Members = TypeInfo.GetMembers()
            For Each MemberInfo In Members
```

```
                    ExamineAttributes(MemberInfo.GetCustomAttributes(False), _
                        MemberInfo.Name)
                Next
            Next

            Console.ReadLine()
        End Sub

        ' Check the collection of custom attributes for a LegacyAttribute.
        Private Sub ExamineAttributes(ByVal attributes() As Object, _
            ByVal searchElement As String)
            Dim CustomAttribute As LegacyAttribute
            For Each CustomAttribute In attributes
                Console.WriteLine()
                Console.WriteLine("Found a legacy component in " & searchElement)
                Console.WriteLine("Previous Platform: " & _
                    CustomAttribute.PreviousPlatform.ToString())
                Console.WriteLine("Migrated By: " & CustomAttribute.MigratedBy)
                Console.WriteLine("Migrated On: " & _
                    CustomAttribute.MigratedDate.ToShortDateString())
            Next
        End Sub

End Module
```

The results are as follows:

```
Reporting legacy code in SampleAssembly.dll

Found a legacy component in ClassWithAttribute
Previous Platform: VBScript
Migrated By: Matthew
Migrated On: 12/01/2003
```

9.10 Identify the Caller of a Procedure

Problem

You want your class to determine some information about the calling code, probably for diagnostic purposes.

Solution

Use the *System.Diagnostics.StackTrace* class.

Discussion

You can't retrieve information about the caller of a procedure through reflection. Reflection can only act on metadata stored in the assembly, whereas the caller of a procedure is determined at runtime. However, .NET includes two useful diagnostic classes that fill this role: *StackTrace* and *StackFrame*.

The stack holds a record of every call that is open and not yet completed. As new calls are made, new methods are added to the top of the stack. For example, if method *A* calls method *B*, both method *A* and *B* will be on the stack (with method *B* occupying the top position because it is the most recent).

The *StackTrace* object holds a picture of the entire stack. Each method call on the stack is represented by an individual *StackFrame* object. You can retrieve a *StackFrame* by calling *StackTrace.GetFrame* and supplying the index number for the frame. The stack is numbered from bottom to top, with the *StackFrame* at position 0 representing the root method. Figure 9-4 shows the *StackTrace* in a sample case where method *A* calls method *B*.

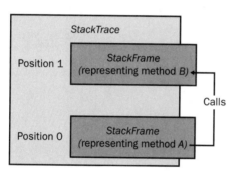

Figure 9-4   A simple *StackTrace*.

The *StackFrame* class includes methods such as *GetFileName* and *GetFileLineNumber*, which can help you track down the source of the call. The *StackFrame* class is also a jumping-off point for a more detailed exploration using reflection. Namely, you can use the *StackFrame.GetMethod* method to retrieve a *MethodBase* object for the corresponding method, and then you can examine details such as the data type of the method, the data types of the method parameters, and so on.

If you create a *StackTrace* object using the default parameterless constructor, it will contain a picture of the current stack. You can also create a *StackTrace* object using an exception, in which case it will contain a picture of the stack at the time the exception was thrown. The Console application on the following page demonstrates both techniques.

```vbnet
Public Module StackFrameTest

    Public Sub Main()
        Try
            ' Launch the series of method calls that
            ' will ultimately end with an error.
            A()
        Catch Err As Exception
            ' Show the current stack.
            Dim TraceNow As New StackTrace()
            Console.WriteLine("Here are the methods currently on the stack:")
            DisplayStack(TraceNow)

            ' Show the stack at the time the error occurred.
            Dim TraceError As New StackTrace(Err, True)
            Console.WriteLine("Here are the methods that were on the " & _
              "stack when the error occurred:")
            DisplayStack(TraceError)
        End Try

        Console.ReadLine()
    End Sub

    Private Sub DisplayStack(ByVal stackTrace As StackTrace)
        Dim Frame As StackFrame
        Dim i As Integer
        For i = 0 To stackTrace.FrameCount - 1
            Frame = stackTrace.GetFrame(i)
            Console.Write((i + 1).ToString() & ": ")
            Console.Write(Frame.GetMethod().DeclaringType.Name & ".")
            Console.WriteLine(Frame.GetMethod().Name & "()")
            Console.Write("    in: " & Frame.GetFileName())
            Console.WriteLine(" at line: " & Frame.GetFileLineNumber())
        Next
        Console.WriteLine()
    End Sub

    Private Sub A()
        B()
    End Sub

    Private Sub B()
        C()
    End Sub

    Private Sub C()
        D()
    End Sub
```

```
    Private Sub D()
        Throw New Exception()
    End Sub

End Module
```

The output is as follows:

```
Here are the methods currently on the stack:
1: StackFrameTest.Main()
     in:   at line: 0

Here are the methods that were on the stack when the error occurred:
1: StackFrameTest.D()
     in: C:\VBCookbook\Chapter 09\Recipe 9-10\Module1.vb at line: 46
2: StackFrameTest.C()
     in: C:\VBCookbook\Chapter 09\Recipe 9-10\Module1.vb at line: 42
3: StackFrameTest.B()
     in: C:\VBCookbook\Chapter 09\Recipe 9-10\Module1.vb at line: 38
4: StackFrameTest.A()
     in: C:\VBCookbook\Chapter 09\Recipe 9-10\Module1.vb at line: 34
5: StackFrameTest.Main()
     in: C:\VBCookbook\Chapter 09\Recipe 9-10\Module1.vb at line: 7
```

9.11 Reflect on a WMI Class

Problem

You want to use reflection to retrieve information about a Windows Management Instrumentation (WMI) class.

Solution

Create a *ManagementClass* object for the WMI class, and then explore it using properties such as *ManagementClass.Methods*, *ManagementClass.Properties*, *MethodData.InParameters*, and *MethodData.OutParameters*.

Discussion

Windows Management Instrumentation is a core component of the Windows operating system that allows your code to retrieve a vast amount of system and hardware information using a query-like syntax. The basic unit of WMI is the WMI class, which is similar to a .NET class, exposing properties and methods. However, you can't use a WMI class directly from .NET code; instead, you access a WMI class by using the generic wrapper objects in the *System.Management* namespace, such as *ManagementClass* (which represents any WMI class) and *MethodData* (which represents the collection of data associated with a WMI method).

Because the WMI classes are not a part of the .NET Framework, you can't analyze them at runtime using .NET reflection. However, you can inspect the properties of the .NET WMI types (such as *ManagementClass.Methods* and *ManagementClass.Properties*) to retrieve similar information about the supported functionality in a WMI class. The .NET WMI types also allow you to check whether specific WMI functionality is available on the current computer (because some WMI methods are not available on all versions of Windows).

The following Console application displays the list of methods provided by the *Win32_Printer* WMI class (which is used to retrieve information about or interact with the currently installed printers). In order to use this code, you need to add a reference to the System.Management.dll assembly and import the *System.Management* namespace.

```
Public Module WMIReflectionTest

    Public Sub Main()
        Dim PrintClass As New ManagementClass("Win32_Printer")

        ' Find all the methods provided by this class.
        Dim Method As MethodData
        For Each Method In PrintClass.Methods

            ' Display basic method information.
            Console.WriteLine(New String("-"c, 79))
            Console.WriteLine("**** " & Method.Name & " ****")
            Console.WriteLine(New String("-"c, 79))
            Console.WriteLine("Origin: " & Method.Origin)

            ' Display the arguments required for this method.
            Dim InParams As ManagementBaseObject
            InParams = Method.InParameters
            Dim PropData As PropertyData
            If Not InParams Is Nothing Then
                For Each PropData In InParams.Properties
                    Console.WriteLine()
                    Console.WriteLine("InParam_Name: " & PropData.Name)
                    Console.WriteLine("InParam_Type: " & _
                        PropData.Type.ToString())
                Next PropData
            End If
```

```
                    ' Display the output parameters (return value).
                    Dim OutParams As ManagementBaseObject
                    OutParams = Method.OutParameters
                    If Not OutParams Is Nothing Then
                        For Each PropData In OutParams.Properties
                            Console.WriteLine()
                            Console.WriteLine("OutParam_Name: " & PropData.Name)
                            Console.WriteLine("OutParam_Type: " & _
                                PropData.Type.ToString())
                        Next PropData
                    End If
                    Console.WriteLine()
                Next

            Console.ReadLine()
        End Sub

End Module
```

Here's part of the output generated by this example:

```
-----------------------------------------------------------------------------
**** Reset ****
-----------------------------------------------------------------------------
Origin: CIM_LogicalDevice

OutParam_Name: ReturnValue
OutParam_Type: UInt32


-----------------------------------------------------------------------------
**** Pause ****
-----------------------------------------------------------------------------
Origin: Win32_Printer

OutParam_Name: ReturnValue
OutParam_Type: UInt32


-----------------------------------------------------------------------------
**** Resume ****
-----------------------------------------------------------------------------
Origin: Win32_Printer

OutParam_Name: ReturnValue
OutParam_Type: UInt32
  . . .
```

> **Note**   You can find reference information about WMI classes online at *http://msdn.microsoft.com/library/en-us/wmisdk/wmi /wmi_start_page.asp*. You can also download a Visual Studio .NET component that allows you to browse WMI classes on the current computer via the Server Explorer window at *http: //msdn.microsoft.com/library/default.asp?url=/downloads/list/wmi.asp*.

9.12 Compile Source Code Programmatically

Problem

You want to compile code from a string or a source file using a custom .NET program.

Solution

Use the *Microsoft.VisualBasic.VBCodeProvider* to create an *ICodeCompiler* object.

Discussion

The .NET Framework allows you to access the Microsoft Visual Basic, Visual C#, Visual J#, and JScript language compilers. To compile code using one of these engines, you call the *CreateCompiler* method of the appropriate code provider class. (In the case of Visual Basic .NET, this class is *Microsoft.VisualBasic.VBCodeProvider*.) The *CreateCompiler* method returns an *ICodeCompiler* object that allows you to create assemblies in memory or on disk.

Compiling code can be a painstaking task. You need to ensure that you supply all the required assemblies, include all the appropriate import statements, specify additional parameters that determine whether debug information will be generated, and so on. To test dynamic code compilation, you can use an application such as the one shown in Figure 9-5, which reads code from a text box, attempts to compile it into an executable file, and then launches it.

Figure 9-5   A program for dynamic assembly creation.

When the user clicks Compile, several steps happen. An *ICodeCompiler* object is created, a number of basic assembly references are added, and the code is compiled to an executable assembly. Then, provided that no errors are discovered, the application is launched, as shown in Figure 9-6.

Figure 9-6   A dynamically generated assembly.

To run this code, you must import two namespaces: *Microsoft.VisualBasic* (where the code provider is defined), and *System.CodeDom.Compiler*. This code uses the *CompileAssemblyFromSource* method, which parses the code in a string. You could also use *CompileAssemblyFromFile* to compile the code found in any text file (such as a .vb file).

```
Private Sub cmdCompile_Click(ByVal sender As System.Object, _
    ByVal e As System.EventArgs) Handles cmdCompile.Click

    ' Create the compiler.
    Dim VB As New VBCodeProvider()
```

```
    Dim Compiler As ICodeCompiler = VB.CreateCompiler()

    ' Define some parameters.
    ' In this case, we choose to save the assembly file to a file.
    Dim Param As New CompilerParameters()
    Param.GenerateExecutable = True
    Param.OutputAssembly = "TestApp.exe"
    Param.IncludeDebugInformation = False

    ' Add some common assembly references (based on the currently
    ' running application).
    Dim Asm As System.Reflection.Assembly
    For Each Asm In AppDomain.CurrentDomain.GetAssemblies()
        Param.ReferencedAssemblies.Add(Asm.Location)
    Next

    ' Compile the code.
    Dim Results As CompilerResults
    Results = Compiler.CompileAssemblyFromSource(Param, txtCode.text)

    ' Check for errors.
    If Results.Errors.Count > 0 Then
        Dim Err As CompilerError
        Dim ErrorString As String
        For Each Err In Results.Errors
            ErrorString &= Err.ToString()
        Next
        MessageBox.Show(ErrorString)
    Else
        ' Launch the new application.
        Dim ProcessInfo As New ProcessStartInfo("TestApp.exe")
        Process.Start(ProcessInfo)
    End If

End Sub
```

> **Note** It's also possible to dynamically create code using the types in the *System.CodeDom* namespace or emit IL instructions using the *System.Reflection.Emit* namespace. These types are fascinating, and they underlie some advanced features in .NET (such as regular expression compilation). However, they also require extremely lengthy code, are difficult to implement, and are of limited usefulness to most application developers.

10

Windows Programming

For most programmers, development centers on the features (and quirks) of the Microsoft Windows operating system. In this chapter, we'll consider some of the most frequently asked questions about development with Microsoft Visual Basic .NET. You'll learn how to use Windows-specific resources such as environment variables, the registry, the Start menu, the clipboard, and Windows help. You'll also learn how to interact with other currently running Windows processes, handle operating system events, and deploy your application with a Windows Installer setup utility.

It's important to understand that the Microsoft .NET Framework does not attempt to replicate the entire Win32 API, only its core features. To create managed interfaces for every available API function would be a monumental (and counterproductive) undertaking. Most developers will find that .NET provides 99 percent of the most commonly required Windows functionality and makes it easier to use than ever before. However, in order to use some features you will need to delve back into the unmanaged world.

To create the recipes for this chapter, we'll need several different types of solutions, including:

- **The *Microsoft.Win32* namespace** In an effort to make .NET more generic (and portable to other platforms), a significant amount of Windows-specific functionality is held in this namespace, including classes for accessing the registry (recipe 10.1) and handling operating system events (recipe 10.3).

- **The *System.Diagnostics* namespace** This namespace contains some of the lower-level functionality needed to launch (recipe 10.8), examine (recipe 10.9), and terminate (recipe 10.10) Windows processes.

- **The Win32 API**   You'll need to use unmanaged API calls for some tasks, such as playing a WAV file (recipe 10.14), and programmatically shutting down Windows (recipe 10.13).

- **The Windows Script Host**   Using COM Interop, you can access the Windows Script Host component, which allows you to create shortcuts (recipe 10.5), send keystrokes to other applications (recipe 10.12), and more.

10.1 Access the Registry

Problem

You want to store and retrieve values in the Windows registry.

Solution

Use the *Registry* and *RegistryKey* classes from the *Microsoft.Win32* namespace.

Discussion

Unlike previous versions of Visual Basic, Visual Basic .NET provides unrestricted access to the Windows registry through the *Registry* and *RegistryKey* classes. *Registry* is the starting point for accessing the Windows registry: it provides shared fields that return *RegistryKey* objects for first-level registry paths (or registry base keys). The two most important fields are

- *CurrentUser*, which contains user-specific preferences. This is the most common location for storing registry information in an application, and it corresponds to the registry base key HKEY_CURRENT_USER.

- *LocalMachine*, which contains configuration data that applies to all users on the current computer. You might use this path to store application-specific information like an installation path. This field corresponds to the registry base key HKEY_LOCAL_MACHINE.

Once you have a *RegistryKey* object, you can navigate down to deeper nested levels using a path-like syntax and then set and retrieve individual values. Commonly, an application will store settings in the subpath \Software\ *CompanyName**ProductName* or \Software*CompanyName**ProductName*\ *Category* under a registry base key. To retrieve a *RegistryKey* object for a nested key, you use the *RegistryKey.OpenSubKey* method. If you want to open a key in writable mode, you must supply an optional *True* parameter to the *OpenSub-Key* method.

```
Dim Key As RegistryKey
Key = Registry.LocalMachine.OpenSubKey("Software\MyCompany\MyApp", True)
```

To write a value, you use *SetValue*, and to retrieve a value, you use *GetValue*. Values are usually retrieved as strings.

```
Dim Value As String

' Retrieve the MyValueName value.
Value = CType(Key.GetValue("MyValueName"), String)

' Save the value MyValueName.
Key.SetValue("MyValueName", Value)
```

You can implement registry access in your application in several ways. You can retrieve all the values when the application starts and save them when it closes, or you can retrieve and save them just-in-time. The *RegistryData* class shown in the following example follows the latter approach. A reference to the appropriate *RegistryKey* is retrieved when the class is instantiated (and the key is created if needed). From that point on, property *Get* procedures wrap the code needed to retrieve registry values, and property *Set* procedures wrap the code needed to write to the registry.

```
Imports Microsoft.Win32

Public Class RegistryData

    Private Key As RegistryKey
    Private Const RegistryPath As String = "Software\TestCompany\TestApp\"

    Public Property DefaultDocumentPath() As String
        Get
            ' If the key is not found, the application
            ' startup path is used as a default.
            Return CType(Key.GetValue("DefaultDocumentPath", _
                Application.StartupPath), String)
        End Get
        Set(ByVal Value As String)
            Key.SetValue("DefaultDocumentPath", Value)
        End Set
    End Property

    Public Sub New()
        Key = Registry.CurrentUser.OpenSubKey(RegistryPath, True)
```

```
            If Key Is Nothing Then
                ' Key does not exist. Create it.
                Key = Registry.CurrentUser.CreateSubKey(RegistryPath)
            End If
        End Sub

End Class
```

The following code demonstrates how you would use the *RegistryData* class to retrieve information for an Open dialog box in a Windows application:

```
Public Class RegistryTestForm
    Inherits System.Windows.Forms.Form

    ' This creates the key if needed.
    Public RegistryData As New RegistryData()

    Private Sub cmdTest_Click(ByVal sender As System.Object, _
      ByVal e As System.EventArgs) Handles cmdTest.Click
        Dim dlgOpen As New OpenFileDialog()

        ' Returns the registry value or default.
        dlgOpen.InitialDirectory = RegistryData.DefaultDocumentPath

        ' Show the Open dialog box with the default initial directory.
        dlgOpen.ShowDialog()

        ' Check if a filename was selected.
        If dlgOpen.FileName = "" Then
            ' Cancel was clicked. Do nothing.
        Else
            ' Store the directory where this file exists.
            RegistryData.DefaultDocumentPath = _
              System.IO.Path.GetDirectoryName(dlgOpen.FileName)

            ' (You can now perform an application-specific task
            '  with the file.)
        End If

    End Sub

End Class
```

10.2 Retrieve Environment Variables

Problem

You want to retrieve information from a Windows environment variable (for example, to find out the computer name, username, logon server, and so on).

Solution

Use the *GetEnvironmentVariable* or *GetEnvironmentVariables* methods of the *System.Environment* class.

Discussion

The Windows operating system stores some commonly used information in environment variables. You can access this information by using the *Environment.GetEnvironmentVariable* method and supplying the name of the variable. The following code snippet uses this technique to retrieve the name of the current computer:

```
Dim ComputerName As String
ComputerName = Environment.GetEnvironmentVariable("COMPUTERNAME")
```

Applications can define and set their own environment variables. (Typically, this step is performed by the installation program.) You can retrieve any environment variable in .NET code, provided that you know its name, using the *GetEnvironmentVariable* method. However, the *Environment* class doesn't provide any methods for setting environment variables. If you need to perform this task, you should use the Windows Script Host, which is described in recipe 10.5.

In addition, you can retrieve all the environment variables on the current computer using the *GetEnvironmentVariables* method. This technique is used in the following code to fill a *ListView* control (as shown in Figure 10-1).

```
Dim Variables As IDictionary
Variables = Environment.GetEnvironmentVariables()

Dim Variable As System.Collections.DictionaryEntry
For Each Variable In Variables
    Dim listItem As New ListViewItem(Variable.Key.ToString())
    listItem.SubItems.Add(Variable.Value.ToString())
    listSettings.Items.Add(listItem)
Next
```

Figure 10-1 A list of environment variables.

10.3 Handle Operating System Events

Problem

You want your code to react to a Windows system event, such as a modification of system or desktop settings.

Solution

Add an event handler to one of the shared events provided by the *Microsoft.Win32.SystemEvents* class.

Discussion

The *SystemEvents* class provides references to several global system events, including:

■ ***DisplaySettingsChanged*** occurs when the display settings (for example, screen resolution) are changed.

■ ***InstalledFontsChanged*** occurs when the user adds fonts to or removes fonts from the system.

■ ***LowMemory*** occurs if the system is running out of available RAM.

■ *PaletteChanged*   occurs when the user switches to an application that uses a different 256-color palette. This event occurs only in 256-color mode.

■ *PowerModeChanged*   occurs when the user suspends or resumes the system.

■ *SessionEnding*   occurs when the user is trying to log off or shut down the system. At this point, other applications (including your .NET application that is handling the event) can attempt to cancel the shutdown. You can also retrieve a value that indicates whether the current user is logging off or the entire operating system is shutting down.

■ *SessionEnded*   occurs when the user is logging off or shutting down the system. At this point, you can no longer stop the computer from shutting down. However, you can retrieve a value that indicates whether the current user is logging off or the entire operating system is shutting down.

■ *TimeChanged*   occurs if the user changes the time on the system clock.

■ *UserPreferenceChanging*   occurs when a user preference is about to change (in other words, a change has been requested).

■ *UserPreferenceChanged*   occurs when a user preference has changed.

These events are all shared events, which means that you can add an event handler without needing to create an instance of the *SystemEvents* class. Here's an example that attaches as event handler for the *SessionEnding* event:

```
AddHandler SystemEvents.SessionEnding, AddressOf SessionEnding
```

You should note that the event callbacks take place on a system thread, not on your application thread. Therefore, if you want to update the user interface or modify a shared variable in an event handler for a system event, you'll need to use the synchronization steps explained in Chapter 7 (for example, recipes 7.6 and 7.9). In addition, you shouldn't perform any time-consuming processing in the event handler so that you don't slow down other applications waiting for an event.

The following example handles the *SessionEnding* event and attempts to cancel the shutdown if it corresponds to a user logoff operation. To test this example properly, you must compile the program and run it outside of the Microsoft Visual Studio .NET development environment.

```
Public Class ShutdownTestForm
    Inherits System.Windows.Forms.Form

    Private Sub ShutdownTestForm_Load(ByVal sender As System.Object, _
      ByVal e As System.EventArgs) Handles MyBase.Load

        AddHandler Microsoft.Win32.SystemEvents.SessionEnding, _
          AddressOf SessionEnding

    End Sub

    Private Sub SessionEnding(ByVal sender As Object, _
      ByVal e As Microsoft.Win32.SessionEndingEventArgs)

        If e.Reason = Microsoft.Win32.SessionEndReasons.Logoff Then
            ' It was a user initiated shutdown. Try to cancel it.
            ' (There is no guarantee that this request will be honored,
            '  so you may want to respond to the SessionEnded event to
            '  perform last minute cleanup.)
            e.Cancel = True

            MessageBox.Show("Attempting to cancel the logoff operation.")
        Else
            MessageBox.Show("System is shutting down.")
        End If

    End Sub

End Class
```

Note that if the system is shutting down, your application has a limited amount of time to end. If you don't click the OK button on the message box quickly enough, the application might be terminated forcibly.

10.4 Access the Desktop and the Start Menu

Problem

You want to access shortcuts or other files on the desktop or the Start menu.

Solution

You can access the underlying Start menu and desktop directories directly by retrieving the corresponding environment variables.

Discussion

.NET does not provide any classes for interacting with the desktop or Start menu. However, you can find the corresponding directories using Windows environment variables.

For example, you can retrieve the current user's profile directory from the environment variable *USERPROFILE*. This directory contains two important subdirectories: \Desktop (which holds the files that are displayed on the current user's desktop) and \Start Menu (which holds the user-specific shortcuts on the Start menu). You can also use the environment variable *ALLUSERSPROFILE* to retrieve the \All Users profile directory, which has settings that apply to all users. The \All Users directory includes a \Start Menu directory with global shortcuts, where most applications are installed.

The following example uses both of these approaches to show the files on the desktop and some of the programs installed on the computer:

```
Public Module DesktopShortcutTest

    Public Sub Main()
        ' Get the desktop directory for the current user.
        Dim DesktopDir, StartMenuDir As String
        DesktopDir = Environment.GetEnvironmentVariable("USERPROFILE") & _
            "\Desktop"
        StartMenuDir = Environment.GetEnvironmentVariable("ALLUSERSPROFILE") _
            & "\Start Menu"

        ' Display the names of the files on the desktop.
        Console.WriteLine("These are the files on your desktop:")
        Dim Dir As New System.IO.DirectoryInfo(DesktopDir)
        Dim File As System.IO.FileInfo
        For Each File In Dir.GetFiles()
            Console.WriteLine(File.Name)
        Next

        ' Display the shortcuts groups in the first level of the
        ' all users Start menu (under the Programs group).
        Console.WriteLine("These are shortcut groups in your Programs menu:")
        Dir = New System.IO.DirectoryInfo(StartMenuDir & "\Programs")
        Dim ShortcutGroup As System.IO.DirectoryInfo
        For Each ShortcutGroup In Dir.GetDirectories()
            Console.WriteLine(ShortcutGroup.Name)
        Next

        Console.ReadLine()
    End Sub

End Module
```

This environment variable technique is useful for retrieving information from these special paths, but it won't help you create shortcuts because shortcuts are special file types that use a proprietary format. However, you can create shortcuts programmatically using the Windows Script Host (WSH) object, as described in recipe 10.5.

> **Note** The user profile directory is typically a path such as C:\Documents and Settings*username*, while the All Users profile is usually stored in a path such as C:\Documents and Settings\All Users.

10.5 Create Desktop or Start Menu Shortcuts

Problem

You want to add a new shortcut to the desktop or the Start menu.

Solution

Use COM Interop to access the Windows Script Host component, which provides a *WshShell.CreateShortcut* method.

Discussion

There are several approaches that you can take if you want to programmatically create a shortcut file. You can use an unmanaged call to a legacy API (such as the Visual Basic 6 setup toolkit DLL), create the file by hand (in which case you need an in-depth understanding of its proprietary format), or create a dedicated Windows Installer setup program. The easiest approach is to use the Windows Script Host component, which is included with the Windows operating system. You can interact with this COM component through COM Interop. All you need to do is add a reference, as shown in Figure 10-2.

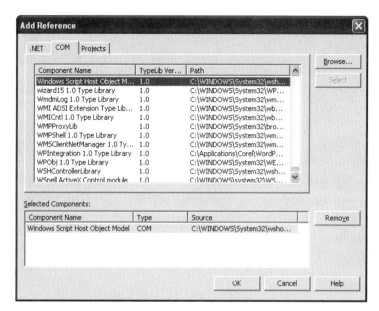

Figure 10-2   Adding a reference to the Windows Script Host.

Note   The Windows Script Host is built into Microsoft Windows 98, Windows Me, Windows 2000, Windows XP, and Windows Server 2003 through the file wshom.ocx (in the Windows System32 directory). You can also download the most recent version of the Windows Script Host (version 5.6) from *http://msdn.microsoft.com/scripting*. The Windows Script Host can also be used to map network drives, connect to printers, retrieve and modify environment variables, and modify registry keys. See *http://msdn.microsoft.com/library/en-us/script56/html /wsconwhatiswsh.asp* for the complete documentation.

Creating a new shortcut with the Windows Script Host is quite easy. First, you create an instance of the *WshShell* object. You can then use the *WshShell.SpecialFolders* collection to retrieve a path to any one of the following folders:

- AllUsersDesktop
- AllUsersStartMenu
- AllUsersPrograms
- AllUsersStartup

- Desktop

- Favorites

- Fonts

- MyDocuments

- NetHood

- PrintHood

- Programs

- Recent

- SendTo

- StartMenu

- Startup

- Templates

Once you have the appropriate path, you can use the *WshShell.Create-Shortcut* method to create an *IWshShortcut* object. You can then configure the shortcut by modifying the properties of the *IWshShortcut* object and invoke its *Save* method to store the final result.

Here's a full example that creates a shortcut to the Windows Notepad application:

```
Public Module CreateShortcutTest

    Public Sub Main()
        ' Create the Windows Script Host shell object.
        Dim WshShell As New IWshRuntimeLibrary.WshShell()
        Dim DesktopDir As String = _
          CType(WshShell.SpecialFolders.Item("Desktop"), String)
        Dim Shortcut As IWshRuntimeLibrary.IWshShortcut

        ' Shortcut files have the (hidden) extension .lnk
        Shortcut = CType( _
          WshShell.CreateShortcut(DesktopDir & "\NotepadShortcut.lnk"), _
          IWshRuntimeLibrary.IWshShortcut)

        ' Specify some basic shortcut properties.
        Shortcut.TargetPath = "C:\Windows\notepad.exe"
        Shortcut.WindowStyle = 1
        Shortcut.Hotkey = "CTRL+SHIFT+N"
        Shortcut.Description = "Run Notepad"
        Shortcut.WorkingDirectory = DesktopDir
```

```
        ' Specify the first icon in the notepad.exe file.
        Shortcut.IconLocation = "notepad.exe, 0"

        ' Save the shortcut file.
        Shortcut.Save()

        Console.WriteLine("Shortcut created.")
        Console.ReadLine()
    End Sub

End Module
```

You can also create shortcuts that reference Web sites (and even insert them in the favorites menu, if desired). Simply alter the *TargetPath* property, as shown here:

```
Shortcut = _
  CType(WshShell.CreateShortcut(DesktopDir & "\Prosetech.lnk"), _
    IWshRuntimeLibrary.IWshShortcut)
Shortcut.TargetPath = "http://www.prosetech.com"

' (Other configuration omitted.)

Shortcut.Save()
```

10.6 Start a Windows Application with a *Main* Subroutine

Problem

You want to start a Windows application without a startup form.

Solution

Create a module with a public *Main* method. Show all forms modally, or use the *Application.Run* method.

Discussion

There are several reasons that you might want to start a Windows application without using a startup form, including:

■ You want to show several forms at once.

■ You need to process command-line parameters (as described in recipe 10.7).

- You need to programmatically decide which form to show initially.

- You want to run your program in the background and provide a system tray icon that allows the user to access the full interface.

In these cases, you can start your application using a startup method. This startup method is a public method named *Main* that you will place in any module in your project. Here's one example:

```
Public Module StartModule

    Public Sub Main()
        ' (Code omitted.)
    End Sub


End Module
```

You can then configure your project to start using this code. Right-click the project, select Properties, and then browse to the Common Properties | General node. Under Startup Object, choose Sub Main, as shown in Figure 10-3.

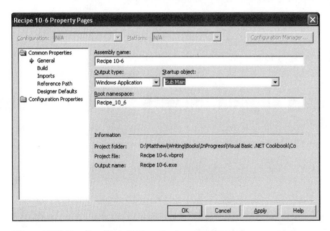

Figure 10-3   Configuring a startup method.

There's one important fact to note about startup methods: as soon as the *Main* method finishes executing, the application terminates and any open windows are automatically closed. This behavior is different from that of Visual Basic 6, which keeps the application running until all windows are closed. As a consequence, in your startup method, you should show windows modally, as in the example below.

```
Public Module StartModule

    Public Sub Main()
        Dim frm As New Form1()
```

```
    ' ShowDialog() shows a modal window, which interrupts the code.
    ' The Main() method does not continue until the window is closed.
    frm.ShowDialog()

    ' Show() shows a modeless window, which does not interrupt the code.
    ' The Main() method code continues, the application terminates
    ' prematurely, and the window is closed automatically.
    frm.Show()
  End Sub

End Module
```

Another option is to use the *Application.Run* method to create a message loop. For example, if you want to show several windows at once, you can display them all modelessly and then use *Application.Run* to set up a message loop on the main window. When it's closed, the application will end.

```
Public Module StartModule

  Public Sub Main()
    Dim frmMain As New MainForm()
    Dim frmSecondary As New Form1()

    ' Show both windows modelessly.
    frmMain.Show()
    frmSecondary.Show()

    ' Keep the application running until frmMain is closed.
    Application.Run(frmMain)
  End Sub

End Module
```

You can also use *Application.Run* without supplying a window name to start a message loop that continues until you explicitly terminate it.

```
Application.Run()
```

This approach is useful if you want to decide programmatically when to end the application. It also allows you to show several windows and end the application when *any one* of these windows is closed. All you need to do is use the *Application.Exit* method anywhere in your program. The following code snippet ends the message loop when a window is closed:

```
Private Sub Form1_Closed(ByVal sender As Object, ByVal e As EventArgs) _
  Handles MyBase.Closed

    Application.Exit()

End Sub
```

10.7 Retrieve Command-Line Parameters

Problem

You need to retrieve the command-line parameters that are used to execute your application.

Solution

Create a *Main* subroutine that accepts an array of strings. This array will be automatically populated with all command-line arguments.

Discussion

Command-line arguments are most commonly used in Console applications. In fact, many Console utilities require command-line parameters to supply a minimum amount of information. Command-line arguments are often used in document-based Windows-based applications to quickly open specific files. For example, the command *winword.exe mydoc.doc* could be used to launch Microsoft Word and open the mydoc.doc file in one operation.

To retrieve command-line arguments in a Windows or Console application, your program must start with a *Main* subroutine. You should modify the *Main* subroutine so that it accepts an array of strings, as shown here:

```
Public Module StartModule

    Public Sub Main(args() As String)
        ' (Code omitted.)
    End Sub

End Module
```

The *args* array will be populated with all the command-line arguments, in order. For example, if you execute the command *myapp.exe /a /b /c*, there will be three strings in the array, one for each parameter. Depending on the application, order might or might not be important for your parameters. The following example prints out all the supplied parameters:

```
Public Module CommandLineArgumentTest

    Public Sub Main(ByVal args() As String)
        Console.WriteLine("You supplied " & args.Length().ToString() & _
            " parameters.")
        Dim Argument As String
        For Each Argument In args
```

```
                Console.WriteLine(Argument)
          Next
     End Sub

End Module
```

You can test this example without resorting to the command line. Simply right-click the project in Solution Explorer and select Properties. Then browse to the Configuration Properties | Debugging node (shown in Figure 10-4) and supply the parameter list.

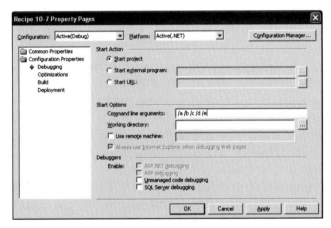

Figure 10-4   Using command-line parameters in Visual Studio .NET.

> **Note**   Parameters are separated based on spaces. For example, the command *myapp.exe /a/b/c* will return a single */a/b/c* parameter. If you need to supply a parameter that includes a space, you can use quotation marks. This approach is necessary if you want to specify a filename parameter and the filename includes spaces. Here's an example:
>
> ```
> myapp.exe "my file with spaces.txt" /d /e
> ```
>
> This command provides three parameters:
>
> ```
> my file with spaces.txt
> /d
> /e
> ```

Note that the quotation marks are stripped out transparently before your program receives the argument list.

10.8 Run the Application That Owns a File Extension

Problem

You want to launch the application that is registered to handle a specific file type.

Solution

Use the *Start* method of the *System.Diagnostics.Process* class.

Discussion

In Visual Basic 6, the only way to execute a program is to directly invoke the executable or use the Win32 API. In Visual Basic .NET, the situation is greatly improved with a specialized *Process* class that can launch an application based on the file types that are registered with Windows.

The *Process* class allows you to launch an application such as Microsoft Word (to display .doc files) or Adobe Acrobat Reader (to display .pdf files) without needing to know the exact location of the application on the computer's hard disk. You simply pass the name of the document file to the shared *Start* method of the *System.Diagnostics.Process* class.

As an example, consider the following code, which displays a file selection dialog box and then automatically opens the file using the registered application. For this example to work, you must import the *System.Diagnostics* namespace (which is true by default in Visual Studio .NET).

```
Dim dlgOpen As New OpenFileDialog()

If dlgOpen.ShowDialog() = DialogResult.OK Then
    Process.Start(dlgOpen.FileName)
End If
```

> **Note**   If you try to launch a file and there's no application registered to handle the corresponding file type, you'll receive a *System.ComponentModel.Win32Exception* exception. You can catch this exception and inform the user of the problem.

In some cases, you might want to configure the startup settings in more detail. You can do so by first creating a *System.Diagnostics.ProcessStartInfo* object, which encapsulates the information that will be used to launch the application. You can then pass the *ProcessStartInfo* instance to the shared *Process.Start* method.

```
Dim dlgOpen As New OpenFileDialog()

If dlgOpen.ShowDialog() = DialogResult.OK Then
    Dim ProcessStart As New ProcessStartInfo(dlgOpen.FileName)
    Process.Start(ProcessStart)
End If
```

You can change how the application will be executed by modifying the properties of the *ProcessStartInfo* object. For example, you can change the startup parameters or working directory. More interestingly, you can choose to use a different *verb*. By default, when you use *Process.Start*, the "open" verb will be used and the document will be loaded in the corresponding application. However, many applications register verbs for other actions, such as printing. The following example checks if a print verb is available for a file type and then uses it. For example, if you use this approach with a .doc file and you have Microsoft Word installed, Word will print the document in the background and then shut down.

```
Dim dlgOpen As New OpenFileDialog()
If dlgOpen.ShowDialog() = DialogResult.OK Then
    Dim ProcessStart As New ProcessStartInfo(dlgOpen.FileName)

    Dim CanPrint As Boolean = False
    Dim Verb As String
    For Each Verb In ProcessStart.Verbs
        If Verb.ToLower() = "print" Then
            ' This is a print-able document.
            CanPrint = True

            ' Configure ProcessStart to use the print action.
            ProcessStart.Verb = Verb
            Exit For
        End If
    Next

    If CanPrint Then
        Process.Start(ProcessStart)
    Else
        MessageBox.Show("Can't print this type of document.")
    End If
End If
```

10.9 Find Other Running Processes

Problem

You want to retrieve information about processes that are currently running.

Solution

Use the *GetProcesses* or *GetProcessesByName* methods of the *System.Diagnostics.Process* class.

Discussion

The *System.Diagnostics.Process* class represents a Windows process. It provides an exhaustive list of properties, which are detailed on MSDN. Using this information, you can

- Examine an application's memory, thread, and CPU usage.

- Determine when an application started and how long it has been executing.

- Retrieve information from the executable file that was used to launch the application.

You can also use the *Process* class methods to end a process (as described in recipe 10.10), and you can handle the *Process.Exited* event to react when another process terminates for any reason.

You can retrieve an array of *Process* objects that represent all the currently executing processes on a computer using the *Process.GetProcesses* method. You can retrieve information about a single process using the *Process.GetProcessesByName* method and supplying the process name. The process name is usually the same as the executable name, without the file extension.

Note Both *GetProcesses* and *GetProcessesByName* include an overloaded version that allows you to specify a computer name. You can use this method to retrieve information about a process running on another computer.

The following example shows a simple Console application that reports a few statistics about its own process. The information it displays is only a small subset of the total information that the *Process* class makes available.

```
Public Module ProcessInfoTest

    Public Sub Main()
        Dim Proc As Process

        ' This gets the current process by name.
        ' Alternatively, you could use the GetCurrentProcess() method instead.
        Proc = Process.GetProcessesByName("ConsoleApplication1")(0)

        Console.WriteLine("Start time: " & Proc.StartTime.ToString())
        Console.WriteLine("Memory use: " & Proc.PagedMemorySize.ToString())
        Console.WriteLine("Number of threads: " & Proc.Threads.Count)
        Console.WriteLine("Executable file: " & Proc.MainModule.FileName)
        Console.WriteLine("Responding: " & Proc.Responding.ToString())

        ' Display modules this process has loaded.
        Console.WriteLine("Loaded modules:")
        Dim ProcModule As ProcessModule
        For Each ProcModule In Proc.Modules
            Console.WriteLine(" " & ProcModule.FileName)
        Next

        Console.ReadLine()
    End Sub

End Module
```

The output for this application is shown in the following code listing. Only part of the list of loaded modules is shown. You'll notice that even though only one thread is in use in the application itself, .NET is using a total of seven threads to manage it.

```
Start time: 2003-01-13 10:47:35 AM
Memory use: 8216576
Number of threads: 7
Executable file: C:\Temp\ConsoleApplication1\bin\ConsoleApplication1.exe
Responding: True
Loaded modules:
 C:\Temp\ConsoleApplication1\bin\ConsoleApplication1.exe
 C:\WINDOWS\System32\ntdll.dll
 C:\WINDOWS\System32\mscoree.dll
 C:\WINDOWS\system32\KERNEL32.dll
 C:\WINDOWS\Microsoft.NET\Framework\v1.0.3705\MSVCR70.dll
 C:\WINDOWS\Microsoft.NET\Framework\v1.0.3705\fusion.dll
 . . .
```

The first time you access a property of a *Process* object, all the information will be retrieved and cached. If you want to update the information stored in the *Process* object with the current values, invoke the *Process.Refresh* method.

Here's another application that retrieves the full list of processes and displays them in a *DataGrid* control using data binding:

```
Public Class ProcessViewForm
    Inherits System.Windows.Forms.Form

    ' (Windows designer code omitted.)

    Private Sub ProcessViewForm_Load(ByVal sender As System.Object, _
       ByVal e As System.EventArgs) Handles MyBase.Load
         gridProcesses.DataSource = System.Diagnostics.Process.GetProcesses()
    End Sub

End Class
```

A partial view of the result is shown in Figure 10-5.

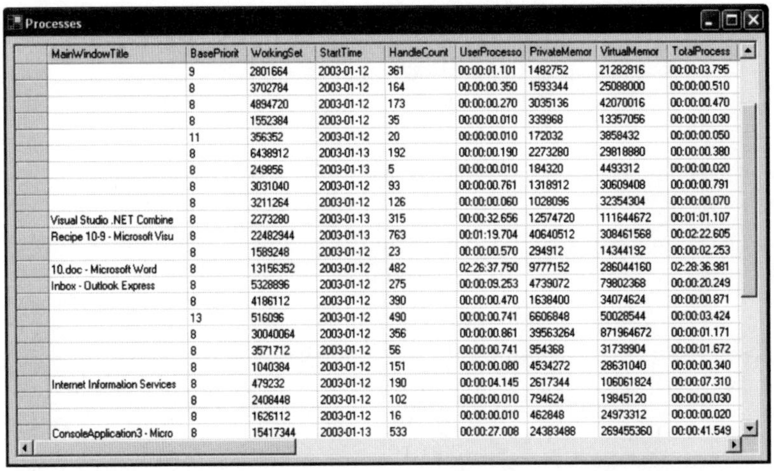

MainWindowTitle	BasePriorit	WorkingSet	StartTime	HandleCount	UserProcesso	PrivateMemor	VirtualMemor	TotalProcess
	9	2801664	2003-01-12	361	00:00:01.101	1482752	21282816	00:00:03.795
	8	3702784	2003-01-12	164	00:00:00.350	1593344	25088000	00:00:00.510
	8	4894720	2003-01-12	173	00:00:00.270	3035136	42070016	00:00:00.470
	8	1552384	2003-01-12	35	00:00:00.010	339968	13357056	00:00:00.030
	11	356352	2003-01-12	20	00:00:00.010	172032	3858432	00:00:00.050
	8	6438912	2003-01-13	192	00:00:00.190	2273280	29818880	00:00:00.380
	8	249856	2003-01-13	5	00:00:00.010	184320	4493312	00:00:00.020
	8	3031040	2003-01-12	93	00:00:00.761	1318912	30609408	00:00:00.791
	8	3211264	2003-01-12	126	00:00:00.060	1028096	32354304	00:00:00.070
Visual Studio .NET Combine	8	2273280	2003-01-13	315	00:00:32.656	12574720	111644672	00:01:01.107
Recipe 10-9 - Microsoft Visu	8	22482944	2003-01-13	763	00:01:19.704	40640512	308461568	00:02:22.605
	8	1589248	2003-01-12	23	00:00:00.570	294912	14344192	00:00:02.253
10.doc - Microsoft Word	8	13156352	2003-01-12	482	02:26:37.750	9777152	286044160	02:28:36.981
Inbox - Outlook Express	8	5328896	2003-01-12	275	00:00:09.253	4739072	79802368	00:00:20.249
	8	4186112	2003-01-12	390	00:00:00.470	1638400	34074624	00:00:00.871
	13	516096	2003-01-12	490	00:00:00.741	6606848	50028544	00:00:03.424
	8	30040064	2003-01-12	356	00:00:00.861	39563264	871964672	00:00:01.171
	8	3571712	2003-01-12	56	00:00:00.741	954368	31739904	00:00:01.672
	8	1040384	2003-01-12	151	00:00:00.080	4534272	28631040	00:00:00.340
Internet Information Services	8	479232	2003-01-12	190	00:00:04.145	2617344	106061824	00:00:07.310
	8	2408448	2003-01-12	102	00:00:00.010	794624	19845120	00:00:00.030
	9	1626112	2003-01-12	16	00:00:00.010	462848	24973312	00:00:00.020
ConsoleApplication3 - Micro	8	15417344	2003-01-13	533	00:00:27.008	24383488	269455360	00:00:41.549

Figure 10-5 Partial information for currently running processes.

> **Note** You might experience a security error if you attempt to retrieve information about a process that's privileged. You can catch this error in your code when attempting to access the *Process* property. However, if you perform data binding with a restricted process, an untrappable error will occur when you navigate to the corresponding row and the *DataGrid* control attempts to retrieve the information for that process.

10.10 Terminate Another Process

Problem

You want to end a process that's currently running.

Solution

Find the process using *Process.GetProcessesByName*, and then terminate it using *Process.CloseMainWindow* or *Process.Kill*.

Discussion

The *Process* class provides two methods for ending a process: *CloseMainWindow* and *Kill*. *CloseMainWindow* sends a close message to the main window of an application and is the equivalent of the user closing the window. *CloseMainWindow* is preferable to *Kill* because it allows an orderly shutdown. For example, an application such as Microsoft Word will prompt the user to save any open documents. However, *CloseMainWindow* might not end an application. Most applications will ask for user verification before exiting.

Kill, on the other hand, immediately terminates the process, which might result in lost data. *Kill* is the equivalent of terminating the process with the Windows Task Manager. *Kill* should be used only as a last resort. For example, when shutting down the Windows operating system, Windows attempts to close any open applications and then kills them if the process is still running after a short period of time (approximately 30 seconds). *Kill* is also the only way to terminate a process that doesn't have a visual interface.

Before you use *CloseMainWindow* or *Kill*, you must find the appropriate *Process*. If you know the process friendly name (which is usually the executable name without the .exe extension), you can use the *GetProcessesByName* method. Alternatively, you can retrieve all processes with the *GetProcesses* method and then examine other *Process* properties to find the correct instance (as described in recipe 10.9).

The following example shows a Console application that attempts to close Microsoft Excel. If the program is still running 30 seconds after the *CloseMainWindow* request, the application is terminated with the *Kill* method.

```
Public Module ProcessKillTest

    Public Sub Main()
        ' Use an array, as there may be multiple instances of Excel running.
        Dim Proc, Processes() As Process
```

```
        Processes = Process.GetProcessesByName("excel")
        For Each Proc In Processes
            ' Attempt to close the window.
            ' If there is an unsaved Excel document, this will bring
            ' up the save changes prompt.
            Proc.CloseMainWindow()

            ' Wait up to 30 seconds.
            Proc.WaitForExit(30000)

            ' Kill the process if it is still runnning.
            If Not Proc.HasExited Then
                Proc.Kill()
                Console.WriteLine("Application was terminated forcibly.")
            Else
                Console.WriteLine("Application ended peacefully.")
            End If
        Next

        Console.ReadLine()
    End Sub

End Module
```

> **Note** You can't use *CloseMainWindow* or *Kill* to end processes that are running on remote computers.

10.11 Allow Only One Instance of Your Application to Run

Problem

You want to ensure that only one instance of your application can be running at once.

Solution

In the startup code for your application, check the currently running processes to see if your application is already loaded.

Discussion

Limiting your application to a single instance is simply a matter of refusing to start if your application detects that another instance is already present. You can examine currently running processes using the *System.Diagnostics.Process* class, as described in recipe 10.9.

The following Console application provides a simple demonstration. Typically, if you detect more than one running instance, you will simply end the application quietly on startup. However, the example displays a message to facilitate testing.

```
Public Module OneInstanceTest

    Public Sub Main()
        Dim Proc() As Process

        ' Determine the full name of the current process.
        Dim ModuleName, ProcName As String
        ModuleName = Process.GetCurrentProcess.MainModule.ModuleName
        ProcName = System.IO.Path.GetFileNameWithoutExtension(ModuleName)

        ' Find all processes with this name.
        Proc = Process.GetProcessesByName(ProcName)
        If Proc.Length > 1 Then
            ' There is more than one process with this name.
            ' Therefore, this instance should end.
            Console.WriteLine("This instance should end.")
        Else
            Console.WriteLine("This instance can continue.")
        End If

        Console.ReadLine()
    End Sub

End Module
```

Remember that it's only necessary to perform this test once at startup.

If you think that there might be more than one application with your friendly name, you can retrieve the full list of processes using the *Process.Get-Processes* method. You can then investigate each one in more detail. For example, you might want to examine the *Process.MainModule* property to determine the executable filename.

10.12 Send Keystrokes to an Application

Problem

You want to interact with an application programmatically by sending keystrokes.

Solution

Use the *WshShell.SendKeys* method from the Windows Script Host. Alternatively, use the *SendKeys* class in the *System.Windows.Forms* namespace, in conjunction with the *FindWindow* and *SetForegroundWindow* methods from the Win32 API.

Discussion

Ideally, application interaction should work through known interfaces. For example, you can "drive" Microsoft Office using dedicated Office COM components, as described in Chapter 19. However, many applications don't expose any programmatic interface, in which case, the only way you can interact with the application is by sending keystrokes to the user interface.

There is more than one way to send keys to a running application. The approach in this recipe uses the Windows Script Host COM component, which was introduced in recipe 10.5. Another option is to use the *System.Windows.Forms.SendKeys* class, which works almost identically. However, the .NET Framework does not provide any classes for activating other windows. Thus, if you want to send keys to another application using the managed *SendKeys* class, you will also have to use unmanaged functions from the Win32 API such as *FindWindow* and *SetForegroundWindow* first.

To use the Windows Script Host, you must add a reference to the Windows Script Host Object Model (as shown in Figure 10-2). You can then create a *WshShell* instance and use the *SendKeys* method, which allows you to send any combination of keystrokes. There are three types of keystrokes that you can send:

- **Literals.** For example, the parameter *abc* sends the *a* keystroke, followed by the *b* keystroke, followed by the *c* keystroke.

- **Special characters enclosed in curly braces.** Examples include *{F1}* through *{F16}*, *{UP}*, *{DOWN}*, *{LEFT}*, and *{RIGHT}*, *{DEL}*, *{INSERT}*, *{BACKSPACE}*, *{HOME}*, *{END}*, *{ENTER}*, *{ESC}*, *{CAPSLOCK}*, *{NUMLOCK}*, *{TAB}*, *{PGDN}* (page down), and *{PGUP}* (page up). You can also use the tilde (~) instead of *{ENTER}*.

- **Key combinations.**   In this case, + represents the Shift key, ^ represents the Ctrl key, and % represents the Alt key. Thus, +*a* is a capital *A*. You can also group multiple keys by using parentheses. Thus, *%(ec)* is the key combination of *Alt+e+c*, and *%ec* is a combination of *Alt+e*, followed by the *c* key.

> **Note**   Both the Windows Script Host and the managed *SendKeys* class use the same syntax for specifying keystrokes.

Be aware that when using the *SendKeys* method, it's entirely possible to send messages faster than they can be processed. For that reason, you should be careful to insert short pauses between key presses.

The following example shows a Console application that runs the calculator and uses it to perform a simple calculation. It then copies the result to the clipboard and then displays the result in the Console window (using the clipboard technique from recipe 10.16).

```
Public Module SendKeyTest

    Private Shell As IWshRuntimeLibrary.WshShell

    Public Sub Main()
        Shell = New IWshRuntimeLibrary.WshShell()

        ' Start the calculator.
        Shell.Run("calc")
        Threading.Thread.Sleep(100)

        ' Give focus to the calculator, so it will receive keystrokes.
        Shell.AppActivate("Calculator")

        ' Send a series of keys (representing a calculation of 101 * 2.
        SendKeys("101")
        SendKeys("*")
        SendKeys("2~")

        ' Use the calculator's ability to copy results to the clipboard.
        SendKeys("^c")

        ' Retrieve the data from the clipboard.
        Console.Write("The calculator result is: ")
        Console.WriteLine(Clipboard.GetDataObject().GetData(DataFormats.Text))
```

```
        Console.ReadLine()
    End Sub

    ' Send the key and pause 500 milliseconds.
    Private Sub SendKeys(ByVal key As String)
        Shell.SendKeys(key)
        Threading.Thread.Sleep(500)
    End Sub

End Module
```

10.13 Force a Windows Shutdown or Logoff

Problem

You want to log off or shut down Windows programmatically.

Solution

Use the unmanaged *ExitWindowsEx* API function.

Discussion

The .NET Framework doesn't include the functionality needed to shut down or restart Windows. However, you can easily do so using the *ExitWindowsEx* function from the user32.dll library. This function accepts a parameter that indicates whether you want a logoff (value 0), a restart (value 2), or a shutdown (value 1). In addition, you can add a force constant (value 4) to force the system to take the indicated action even if the user attempts to cancel it. This drastic step is usually resented by users and should be used with caution.

The following Console application imports the *ExitWindowsEx* function, defines the related constants, and uses it to request a system logoff:

```
Public Module ShutdownTest

    ' This is the API function for exiting Windows.
    Private Declare Function ExitWindowsEx Lib "user32" _
        (ByVal uFlags As Long, ByVal dwReserved As Long) As Long

    ' This enumeration holds related constants.
    Private Enum ExitWindowsFlags
        ' Use this constant to log the user off without a reboot.
        Logoff = 0
```

```
        ' Use this constant to cause a system reboot.
        Reboot = 2

        ' Use this constant to cause a system shutdown
        ' (and turn of the computer, if the hardware supports it).
        Shutdown = 1

        ' Add this constant to any of the other three
        ' to force the shutdown or reboot even if the user tries to cancel it.
        Force = 4
    End Enum

    Public Sub Main()
        ExitWindowsEx(ExitWindowsFlags.Logoff, 0&)
    End Sub

End Module
```

10.14 Play a WAV File

Problem

You need to play a .wav audio file.

Solution

Use the unmanaged *sndPlaySoundA* API function.

Discussion

The .NET Framework doesn't include any managed classes for playing audio files. However, the winmm.dll library included with Windows includes a function named *sndPlaySoundA* that accepts the name of a WAV file and a parameter indicating how to play it. You can choose to play a sound synchronously, asynchronously, or in a continuous background loop. When you play a sound synchronously, the function interrupts the execution of the program until the sound is complete. If you play a sound asynchronously, the function will return immediately, and the sound will play in the background.

The following example form allows a sound to be played in several different ways. The form code is shown here, and the form itself is shown in Figure 10-6 on the following page.

```vbnet
Public Class SoundTestForm
    Inherits System.Windows.Forms.Form

    ' (Windows designer code omitted.)

    ' This function plays a WAV file.
    Private Declare Function PlaySound Lib "WINMM.DLL" Alias _
        "sndPlaySoundA" (ByVal lpszSoundName As String, ByVal uFlags As _
        Long) As Long

    ' This enumeration holds related constants.
    Private Enum PlaySoundFlags
        ' This flag pauses the application until the sound finishes playing.
        Sync = &H0

        ' This flag indicates that the sound should be played asynchronously
        ' in the background while your application continues to execute.

        Async = &H1

        ' Plays the sound continuously in a loop. This flag must be used
        ' with SND_ASYNC. To stop the play, call sndPlaySound
        ' again with a 0& as the first argument.
        [Loop] = &H8

        ' By default, if you play a new sound while another sound is still
        ' playing, the first sound is interrupted. This flag instructs
        ' the application to wait instead.
        NoStop = &H10

        ' By default, if you attempt to play a file the does not exist,
        ' Windows plays the default system sound. This flag
        ' stops the default sound from being playing in this circumstance.
        NoDefault = &H2
    End Enum

    Private Sub cmdPlaySync_Click(ByVal sender As System.Object, _
      ByVal e As System.EventArgs) Handles cmdPlaySync.Click
        Me.Cursor = Cursors.WaitCursor
        PlaySound("testsound.wav", PlaySoundFlags.Sync)
        Me.Cursor = Cursors.Default
    End Sub

    Private Sub cmdPlayAsync_Click(ByVal sender As System.Object, _
      ByVal e As System.EventArgs) Handles cmdPlayAsync.Click
        Me.Cursor = Cursors.WaitCursor
        PlaySound("testsound.wav", PlaySoundFlags.Async)
        Me.Cursor = Cursors.Default
    End Sub
```

```
Private Sub cmdPlayLoop_Click(ByVal sender As System.Object, _
   ByVal e As System.EventArgs) Handles cmdPlayLoop.Click
      PlaySound("testsound.wav", _
        PlaySoundFlags.Async Or PlaySoundFlags.Loop)
End Sub

Private Sub cmdEndLoop_Click(ByVal sender As System.Object, _
   ByVal e As System.EventArgs) Handles cmdEndLoop.Click
      PlaySound(Nothing, PlaySoundFlags.Async)
End Sub

End Class
```

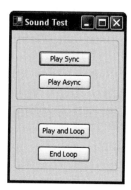

Figure 10-6   A sound test application.

> **Note**   For more powerful control over sound and graphics, you can use Microsoft DirectX 9. Microsoft provides a full set of managed interfaces for DirectX 9. You can download both DirectX and the DirectX SDK at *http://msdn.microsoft.com/downloads/list/directx.asp*.

10.15 Display the Standard Directory Selection Dialog Box

Problem

You want to display a standard dialog box for directory selection.

Solution

In .NET 1.1, use the *FolderBrowserDialog* class in the *System.Windows.Forms* namespace. In .NET 1.0, you must derive a class from *System.Windows.Forms.Design.FolderNameEditor* so that you can use the protected *FolderBrowser* class it contains.

Discussion

The .NET Framework includes several classes that wrap standard dialog boxes, such as the *OpenFileDialog* and *SaveFileDialog* classes. However, .NET 1.0 does not include any class for selecting a directory. .NET 1.1 (included with Visual Studio .NET 2003) resolves this problem by adding the *FolderBrowserDialog* class. This recipe demonstrates how to use this class, and how to create a very similar solution for .NET 1.0 applications.

To use the *FolderBrowserDialog*, you simply need to create an instance, set the descriptive text and initial path, and then call the *ShowDialog* method to display the selection window. The code snippet below demonstrates this technique, and the resulting window is shown in Figure 10-7.

```
Dim dlgDirectory As New FolderBrowserDialog()

' Set the initial path and descriptive text.
dlgDirectory.SelectedPath = "C:\"
dlgDirectory.Description = "Select a folder."

' Show the directory selection window.
If dlgDirectory.ShowDialog() = DialogResult.OK Then
    MessageBox.Show("You chose: " & dlgDirectory.SelectedPath)
End If
```

Figure 10-7   The standard directory selection dialog box.

If you are using .NET 1.0, you don't have the benefit of the *FolderBrowserDialog* class. You could create your own control, but it isn't easy to create one that closely resembles the Windows default and provides all its functionality. Several solutions are possible, including using the *SHBrowseForFolder* API function from shell32.dll. However, calling *SHBrowseForFolder* is complicated by several interoperability issues (the function uses structures and pointers), so it isn't much easier than creating the functionality from scratch.

There is one shortcut, however. The *FolderNameEditor* class in the *System.Windows.Forms.Design* namespace provides a managed implementation that wraps the Win32 API in a *FolderBrowser* class. Unfortunately, *FolderBrowser* is a protected class, which means that it's available only to the *FolderNameEditor* code and to any class that derives from *FolderNameEditor*. One way to access *FolderBrowser* is to create a class that derives from *FolderNameEditor* and exposes the *FolderBrowser* functionality.

The custom class *CustomFolderBrowserDialog* demonstrates this technique. Be aware that before you can derive a class from *FolderNameEditor*, you must add a reference to the *System.Design.dll* assembly where the class is defined.

```
Public Class CustomFolderBrowserDialog
    Inherits System.Windows.Forms.Design.FolderNameEditor

    ' An instance of the protected FolderBrowser class.
    Private Browser As FolderBrowser

    Public Sub New()
        Browser = New FolderBrowser()

        ' Configure the FolderBrowser properties as needed.
        ' You could wrap this logic in custom property procedures,
        ' but you would need to create new enumerations, as the
        ' FolderBrowserFolder and FolderBrowserStyles enumerations
        ' are not accessible outside of this class.
        Browser.StartLocation = FolderBrowserFolder.Desktop
        Browser.Style = FolderBrowserStyles.RestrictToFilesystem
    End Sub

    ' Display the directory selection dialog box.
    Public Function ShowDialog() As DialogResult
        Return Browser.ShowDialog()
    End Function

    ' The descriptive text that appears in the window.
    Public Property Description() As String
        Get
```

```
            Return Browser.Description
        End Get
        Set(ByVal Value As String)
            Browser.Description = Value
        End Set
    End Property


    ' The path the user selected.
    Public ReadOnly Property SelectedPath() As String
        Get
            Return Browser.DirectoryPath
        End Get
    End Property

End Class
```

You can now use the custom class to show a directory selection window. The process is almost identical to using the *FolderBrowserDialog* included with .NET 1.1. The only missing feature is the ability to set the initially selected path.

```
Dim dlgDirectory As New CustomFolderBrowserDialog()

' Set the initial path and descriptive text.
dlgDirectory.Description = "Select a folder."

' Show the directory selection window.
If dlgDirectory.ShowDialog() = DialogResult.OK Then
    MessageBox.Show("You chose: " & dlgDirectory.SelectedPath)
End If
```

The directory selection window is shown in Figure 10-7.

10.16 Use the Clipboard

Problem

You want to paste data to or retrieve data from the Windows clipboard.

Solution

Use the *SetDataObject* and *GetDataObject* methods of the *System.Windows.Forms.Clipboard* class.

Discussion

The *System.Windows.Forms.Clipboard* class allows you to place data on the Windows clipboard and retrieve it. You can use the *Clipboard* class in any type of application, from Windows programs to Console utilities (although you'll need to add a reference to the *System.Windows.Forms.dll* assembly). Valid clipboard data includes core .NET types (strings, numbers, and so on) and any serializable type, including your own custom classes if they include the *Serializable* attribute. As an example, consider the *PersonData* class shown here:

```
<Serializable()> _
Public Class PersonData

    Private _FirstName As String
    Private _LastName As String

    Public Property FirstName() As String
        Get
            Return _FirstName
        End Get
        Set(ByVal Value As String)
            _FirstName = Value
        End Set
    End Property

    Public Property LastName() As String
        Get
            Return _LastName
        End Get
        Set(ByVal Value As String)
            _LastName = Value
        End Set
    End Property

    Public Sub New(ByVal firstName As String, ByVal lastName As String)
        Me.FirstName = firstName
        Me.LastName = lastName
    End Sub
End Class
```

To place data on the clipboard, you use the shared *Clipboard.SetDataObject* method:

```
Dim Person As New PersonData("Bob", "Jones")
Clipboard.SetDataObject(Person)
```

To retrieve data, you use the shared *Clipboard.GetDataObject* method, which returns an *IDataObject* object that wraps the data. You can then query the *IDataObject* to determine if it contains a specific type of data. *IDataObject.GetDataPresent* checks for a specific type of data and returns *True* if it exists, *IDataObject.GetData* retrieves the data itself, and *IDataObject.GetFormats* retrieves all the data formats currently on the clipboard.

Here's the code you could use to retrieve the *PersonData* object from the clipboard:

```
' Retrieve the clipboard data.
Dim Data As IDataObject = Clipboard.GetDataObject()

' Check if the clipboard contains a PersonData instance.
If Data.GetDataPresent(GetType(PersonData)) Then
    Dim Person As PersonData
    Person = CType(Data.GetData(GetType(PersonData)), PersonData)
    MessageBox.Show("Retrieved: " & Person.FirstName & " " & Person.LastName)
Else
    MessageBox.Show("No PersonData found.")
End If
```

Here's a code snippet that displays all the data formats that are currently on the clipboard:

```
Dim Data As IDataObject = Clipboard.GetDataObject()
Dim Format As String

For Each Format In Data.GetFormats()
    MessageBox.Show(Format)
Next
```

10.17 Display Context-Sensitive Help

Problem

You want to display a specific help file topic depending on the currently selected control.

Solution

Use the *HelpProvider* component, and set the *HelpKeyword* and *HelpNavigator* extender properties for each control.

Discussion

.NET provides support for context-sensitive help through the *System.Windows.Forms.HelpProvider* class. The *HelpProvider* class is a special *extender* control. You add it to the component tray of a form, and it extends all the controls on the form with a few additional properties, including *HelpNavigator* and *HelpKeyword*. For example, Figure 10-8 shows a form that has two controls and a *HelpProvider* named *HelpProvider1*. The *ListBox1* control, which is currently selected, has several help-specific properties that are provided through *Help-Provider*.

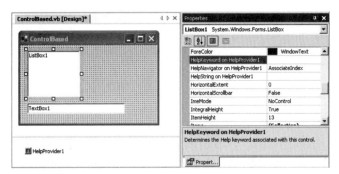

Figure 10-8   The *HelpProvider* extender properties.

To use context-sensitive help with *HelpProvider*, you simply need to follow these three steps:

1. Set the *HelpProvider.HelpNamespace* property with the name of the help file. (For example, an HTML Help file might be named myhelp.chm.)

2. For every control that requires context-sensitive help, set the *HelpNavigator* extender property to *HelpNavigator.Topic*.

3. For every control that requires context-sensitive help, set the *HelpKeyword* extender property with the name of the topic that should be linked to this control. (The topic names are help-file specific and can be configured in your help authoring tools.)

If the user presses the F1 key while a control has focus, the help file will be launched automatically and the linked topic will be displayed in the help window. If the user presses F1 while positioned on a control that doesn't have a linked help topic, the help settings for the containing control will be used (for example, a group box or a panel). If there are no containing controls or the containing control doesn't have any help settings, the form's help settings will be used. If the form's help settings are also lacking, *HelpProvider* will attempt to launch whatever help file is defined at the project level.

You can also use the *HelpProvider* methods to set or modify context-sensitive help mapping at run time. The book's sample files include a program that uses context-sensitive help in this way to provide control-specific, frame-specific, and form-specific help.

10.18 Catch Unhandled Errors

Problem

You want to be notified if your application is about to exit because of an unhandled error, possibly so that you can log the problem or perform some final cleanup.

Solution

Create an event handler for the *AppDomain.UnhandledException* event.

Discussion

The *AppDomain.UnhandledException* event fires when an unhandled error occurs, just before the application is terminated. This event doesn't give you the chance to rectify the problem, but it does provide the exception object, which allows you to log the error and perform last-minute cleanup.

The following Console application uses this technique. Before it exits, it displays information about the offending error.

```
Public Module ErrorHandlerTest

    Public Sub Main()
        ' Connect a default unhandled exception handler.
        AddHandler AppDomain.CurrentDomain.UnhandledException, _
          AddressOf UnhandledException

        ' End the program with an unhandled exception.
        Dim x As Integer
        x = x \ x
    End Sub

    Private Sub UnhandledException(ByVal sender As Object, _
      ByVal e As UnhandledExceptionEventArgs)
        Console.WriteLine("*** An error was encountered. ***")
        Console.WriteLine(e.ExceptionObject.ToString())
        Console.WriteLine("*** Press any key to exit. ***")
        Console.ReadLine()
    End Sub

End Module
```

The easiest way to test this application is to run it outside of the development environment. The *UnhandledException* event won't occur while you debug the application in Visual Studio .NET, unless you configure the debugging settings (under Debug | Exceptions in the main menu) to continue on unhandled exceptions.

10.19 Create a Windows Installer Setup Project

Problem

You want to deploy your application using a setup program that can copy files, create shortcuts, and add registry entries.

Solution

Create a Windows Installer setup project using Visual Studio .NET.

Discussion

Thanks to the .NET *zero-touch deployment model*, you can copy your compiled application to any other computer without registering components or modifying the registry. However, most professional applications require an automated setup program that can copy files to the appropriate locations and add program shortcuts to the Start menu. Visual Studio .NET allows you to build this type of setup program by creating a *setup project*.

The setup project is a special type of Visual Studio .NET project. Unlike other project types, it is not language-specific. Instead of writing code or installation scripts, you configure setup options through designers and property windows. The project compiles to a Windows Installer setup application (an .msi file).

To create a setup project, you should begin by opening the project you want to deploy. Then right-click the solution item in Solution Explorer, and choose Add | New Project. Choose Setup Project from the Setup And Deployment Projects group, as shown in Figure 10-9.

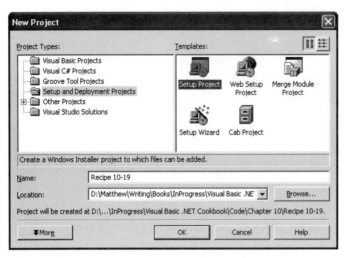

Figure 10-9 A Visual Studio .NET setup project.

To create a basic setup, you need to complete at least these steps:

1. Enter basic setup information (such as *Author*, *Manufacturer*, *ManufacturerUrl*, *Title*, *ProductName*, and *Version*) in the Properties window. Most of these settings are descriptive strings that are used in the Setup Wizard or in the Add/Remove Programs window.

2. Right-click your setup project in the Solution Explorer, and select View | File System to display the File System Designer, which is where you specify the files that should be installed during the setup procedure. (See Figure 10-10.)

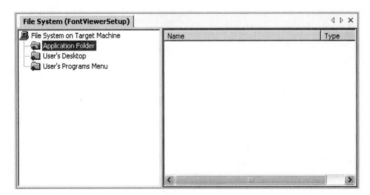

Figure 10-10 The File System Designer.

> **Note**   Initially, the File System Designer displays a short list of commonly used destination folders. You can add links to additional folders by right-clicking in the directory pane and choosing Add Special Folder. There are options that map to the computer's Fonts folder, Favorites folder, Startup folder, and many more, allowing you to install files and shortcuts in a variety of places.

3.   Click the Application Folder item. Using the Properties window, configure the default directory as needed (which will be Program Files\ *[Manufacturer]\[ProductName]* by default).

4.   To add your application, click the Application Folder item. Then on the right side of the window, right-click and choose Add | Project Output. (See Figure 10-11.) Select the primary output of your application project, and click OK. You might also want to add other files (by selecting Add | File), such as the icon you want to use for your application shortcut.

Figure 10-11   Adding a project output (assembly file).

5.   To add a shortcut, select the User's Programs Menu item, right-click the right side of the window, and choose Create New Shortcut. A special window will appear that allows you to choose the linked file from one of the other folders. (See Figure 10-12.) For example, you could browse to the application folder and choose the application's .exe file for the shortcut target.

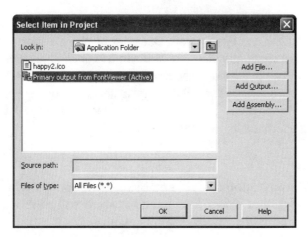

Figure 10-12   Adding a shortcut.

At this point, you have a fully functional setup project that you can compile and deploy. To create the .msi setup file at any time, right-click the setup project and choose Build. An .msi file for your setup project will be created in the bin directory, with the name of your project. You can use other setup designers to configure the setup user interface, add registry settings, install additional files, and more. The book's sample files include a sample application and Windows Installer setup project.

> **Note**   A Visual Studio .NET setup project can't install the .NET Framework. If you need the .NET Framework, you must install it using one of the techniques described in recipe 10.20 before you install your application on a new client.

10.20 Install the .NET Framework on a Client

Problem

You want to install the .NET Framework on another computer so that it can run custom .NET applications.

Solution

Use the redistributable Dotnetfx.exe executable.

Discussion

Visual Studio .NET setup projects can't be used to install the .NET Framework. Microsoft recommends that you install the .NET Framework on clients that don't already have it using the Dotnetfx.exe redistributable file before you attempt to install a .NET application. You can obtain Dotnetfx.exe in several ways:

■ You can download Dotnetfx.exe from the Microsoft download center at *http://msdn.microsoft.com/library/default.asp?url=/downloads/list /netdevframework.asp.*

■ A client can download Dotnetfx.exe using the Microsoft Windows Update feature.

■ You can find Dotnetfx.exe on the .NET Framework SDK CD in the dotNETRedist directory. It's available on the Microsoft Visual Studio .NET Windows Component Update CD in the dotNetFramework directory and on the Microsoft Visual Studio .NET DVD in the \wcu\ dotNetFramework directory.

> **Note** It's possible to create a bootstrapper setup that installs the .NET framework and then launches your setup application automatically. This approach complicates deployment and doesn't add a compelling benefit in most scenarios. However, if you would like to pursue this approach, refer to the MSDN white paper at *http://msdn.microsoft.com/library /en-us/dnnetdep/html/dotnetframedepguid.asp*, which describes in detail the process you must follow.

10.21 Associate a File Extension with Your Application

Problem

You want to register your application to open automatically when the user selects certain file types in Windows Explorer.

Solution

Use the File Types Designer to configure a setup project accordingly.

Discussion

You can register file types by modifying the registry manually using the techniques explained in recipe 10.1. However, a much better approach is to make these configurations once—at installation time—using the features built in to the Visual Studio .NET setup project.

To use this approach, begin by creating a setup project as described in recipe 10.19. Then follow these steps:

1. Right-click your setup project in Solution Explorer, and select View | File Types to display the File Types Designer. (See Figure 10-13.) The File Types Designer is where you specify file types that should be registered to your application during the setup procedure.

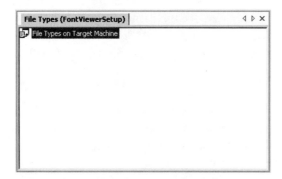

Figure 10-13   The File Types Designer.

2. Right-click in the File Types Designer window, and choose Add File Type. For each file type, you must specify the following information:

    ❑ **Name**   The name of the document type

    ❑ **Extensions**   The associated file extensions

    ❑ **Command**   The program that is registered to handle this file type

    In addition, you can specify an icon (using the *Icon* property) and a two- or three-word description of the format (using the *Description* property). A completed entry is shown in Figure 10-14.

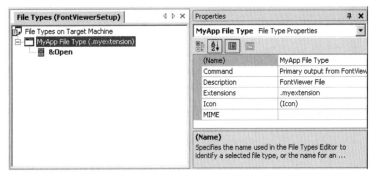

Figure 10-14   Adding a file type.

3. Add supported actions for the file type. Each action has three pieces
    of information:

    ❑ **Name**   This describes the action (for example, in a Windows
        Explorer context menu).

    ❑ **Arguments**   These are the command-line arguments that will
        be passed to the application. The symbol *%1* passes the file-
        name. Usually, an open operation will pass only the filename,
        while other actions might pass additional parameters. (For
        example, a print command might pass the filename and the
        parameter */p.*) Your program must check the command-line
        arguments and take the appropriate action (in this case, open-
        ing the file), as described in recipe 10.7.

    ❑ **Verb**   This indicates the type of action, such as open or print.

Figure 10-15 shows a completed file type action for opening an application.

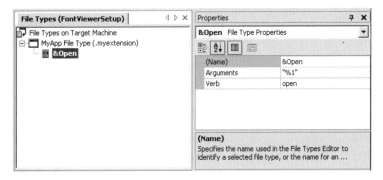

Figure 10-15   Adding a file type action.

> **Note** Don't use the File Types Designer to take over basic file types such as .bmp, .html, or .mp3. Almost all computer users have preferred applications for accessing these file types, and trying to override these preferences will only anger your users.

11

Windows Controls

The Microsoft .NET Framework includes a rich object model for creating and configuring Windows Forms. These types, which are found in the *System.Windows.Forms* namespace, abstract away most of the headaches of the Win32 API and also make it possible to perform tasks that would otherwise be extremely complex. They also mean that most of the solutions you might have used in the Microsoft Visual Basic 6 world no longer apply. In fact, some (such as *control arrays*, which are replaced in recipe 11.3) might even be counterproductive.

In this chapter you'll learn how to take charge of the .NET control classes. For example, you'll learn a few fundamentals such as adding controls programmatically (recipe 11.1), using drag-and-drop operations (recipe 11.11), and saving window positions and sizes (recipe 11.18). You'll also see how to enhance text boxes and combo boxes (recipes 11.8 and 11.9), use form inheritance (recipe 11.15) and context menus (recipes 11.12 and 11.13), work in multiple languages (recipe 11.14), and apply the Windows XP styles (recipe 11.21).

11.1 Add a Control at Runtime

Problem

You need to add a new control programmatically.

Solution

Create an instance of the appropriate control class, and then add the control object to a form or a container control.

Discussion

In the world of .NET, there really isn't any difference between creating a control at design time and creating one at runtime. When you add a design-time control, Microsoft Visual Studio .NET adds the required .NET code to the form's *InitializeComponent* subroutine. Alternatively, you can create the control with the same .NET code later, after the form has been displayed.

To do so, you simply instantiate a control class, configure the properties accordingly (particularly the size and position coordinates), and then add the control to the form or another container. Every control provides a *Controls* property that references a *ControlCollection* that contains all the child controls. To add a child control, you invoke the *ControlCollection.Add* method. In addition, if you need to handle the events for the new control, you can connect them to existing subroutines using the *AddHandler* statement.

The following application generates buttons dynamically and attaches their *Click* event handlers. Buttons are placed in a random position on the window, are numbered using a form-level counter variable, and are tracked in an *ArrayList*. A Clear button allows the user to remove all the dynamically generated buttons from the form using the *ControlCollection.Remove* method.

```
Public Class ButtonGenerator
    Inherits System.Windows.Forms.Form

    ' (Designer code omitted.)

    Private ButtonCounter As Integer = 0
    Private DynamicButtons As New ArrayList()

    Private Sub cmdCreateNew_Click(ByVal sender As System.Object, _
      ByVal e As System.EventArgs) Handles cmdCreateNew.Click
        ' Generate the new button.
        Dim NewButton As New Button()

        ' Configure the properties of the button.
        Dim Rand As New Random()
        NewButton.Size = New System.Drawing.Size(88, 28)
        NewButton.Left = Rand.Next(150, Me.Width - NewButton.Width)
        NewButton.Top = Rand.Next(100, Me.Height - NewButton.Height)
        ButtonCounter += 1
        NewButton.Text = "New Button " & ButtonCounter.ToString()

        ' Add the button to the form.
        Me.Controls.Add(NewButton)
```

```
        ' Attach an event handler to the Click event.
        AddHandler NewButton.Click, AddressOf NewButton_Click

        ' Store the button in a collection.
        DynamicButtons.Add(NewButton)
    End Sub

    Private Sub NewButton_Click(ByVal sender As System.Object, _
      ByVal e As System.EventArgs)
        ' Retrieve a reference to the button that was clicked.
        Dim Button As Button = CType(sender, Button)
        MessageBox.Show("You clicked: " & Button.Text)
    End Sub

    Private Sub cmdClear_Click(ByVal sender As System.Object, _
      ByVal e As System.EventArgs) Handles cmdClear.Click
        Dim Button As Button
        For Each Button In DynamicButtons
            ' Remove the button.
            Me.Controls.Remove(Button)
        Next

        ' Empty the collection.
        DynamicButtons.Clear()
        ButtonCounter = 0
    End Sub
End Class
```

The result of clicking the button several times is shown in Figure 11-1.

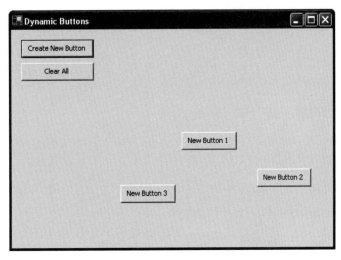

Figure 11-1   Generating buttons programmatically.

11.2 Store Arbitrary Data in a Control

Problem

You want to link a piece of data to a control.

Solution

Use the *Control.Tag* property.

Discussion

Every class that derives from *System.Windows.Forms.Control* provides a *Tag* property that can be used to store an instance of any type of object. The *Tag* property isn't used by the control or the .NET Framework. Instead, it's reserved as a convenient storage place for application-specific information. When retrieving data from the *Tag* property, you'll need to use the *CType* function to cast the object from the generic *System.Object* type to its original type.

Many other classes that are used with .NET controls also provide a *Tag* property. Notable examples include the *ListViewItem* and *TreeNode* classes (which represent items in a *ListView* or *TreeView* control). One class that does *not* provide a *Tag* property is *MenuItem*.

As an example, consider the custom *Person* class, which stores information about a single individual:

```
Public Class Person

    Private _FirstName As String
    Private _LastName As String
    Private _BirthDate As Date

    Public Property FirstName() As String
        Get
            Return _FirstName
        End Get
        Set(ByVal Value As String)
            _FirstName = Value
        End Set
    End Property

    Public Property LastName() As String
        Get
            Return _LastName
        End Get
```

```
        Set(ByVal Value As String)
            _LastName = Value
        End Set
    End Property

    Public Property BirthDate() As Date
        Get
            Return _BirthDate
        End Get
        Set(ByVal Value As Date)
            _BirthDate = Value
        End Set
    End Property

    Public Sub New(ByVal firstName As String, ByVal lastName As String, _
      ByVal birthDate As Date)
        Me.FirstName = firstName
        Me.LastName = lastName
        Me.BirthDate = birthDate
    End Sub

End Class
```

To test the *Tag* property, you can create a form with a *TreeView* and add several nodes. Each node will represent a separate person. Some information will be shown in the node text, but the full *Person* instance will be stored in the *Tag* property.

```
Private Sub TagTestForm_Load(ByVal sender As System.Object, _
  ByVal e As System.EventArgs) Handles MyBase.Load

    ' Fill the TreeView with three items.
    Dim NewPerson As New Person("John", "Smith", DateTime.Now)
    Dim NewNode As New TreeNode(NewPerson.LastName)
    NewNode.Tag = NewPerson
    treePersons.Nodes.Add(NewNode)

    NewPerson = New Person("Gustavo", "Camargo", DateTime.Now)
    NewNode = New TreeNode(NewPerson.LastName)
    NewNode.Tag = NewPerson
    treePersons.Nodes.Add(NewNode)

    NewPerson = New Person("Douglas", "Groncki", DateTime.Now)
    NewNode = New TreeNode(NewPerson.LastName)
    NewNode.Tag = NewPerson
    treePersons.Nodes.Add(NewNode)

End Sub
```

When a node is selected, the corresponding *Person* instance is retrieved, and the information is used to refresh a label control. Figure 11-2 shows this program in action.

```
Private Sub treePersons_AfterSelect(ByVal sender As System.Object, _
  ByVal e As System.Windows.Forms.TreeViewEventArgs) _
  Handles treePersons.AfterSelect

    Dim SelectedPerson As Person = CType(e.Node.Tag, Person)
    lblSelected.Text = "You selected " & SelectedPerson.FirstName & _
      " " & SelectedPerson.LastName & " (born " & _
      SelectedPerson.BirthDate.ToString() & ")"

End Sub
```

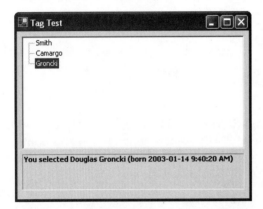

Figure 11-2 Storing data in the *Tag* property.

You could use a similar approach to store much more complex data (such as a reference to a *DataRow* representing the node) or much simpler information (such as a unique ID number that allows you to fetch additional information if needed).

11.3 Replace a Control Array

Problem

You want to provide the same functionality as a Visual Basic 6 control array in Visual Basic .NET.

Solution

Create an event handler that handles multiple controls, and examine the *sender* parameter to identify which control fired the event.

Discussion

It's possible to create a control array in a Visual Basic .NET project by making heavy use of the *VisualBasic.Compatibility* namespace. However, there are other solutions using only native .NET features that are better performing, more elegant, and easier to manage than using these legacy features.

One of the easiest approaches is simply to handle multiple events with a single event handler. You can then determine which control fired the event by examining the *sender* event parameter. The only limitation to this approach is that all the events handled by a single event handler must have the same signature.

The following example shows a single event handler that handles the *CheckedChanged* event from three radio button controls. Depending on which radio button is clicked, a different text box is enabled. The program is shown in action in Figure 11-3.

```
Public Class MultipleControlHandlerTest
    Inherits System.Windows.Forms.Form

    ' (Designer code omitted.)

    Private Sub RadioButton_CheckedChanged( _
      ByVal sender As System.Object, ByVal e As System.EventArgs) _
      Handles RadioButton1.CheckedChanged, RadioButton2.CheckedChanged, _
      RadioButton3.CheckedChanged
        ' Determine which control fired the event.
        Dim RadioButton As RadioButton = CType(sender, RadioButton)

        ' Disable all textboxes.
        TextBox1.Enabled = False
        TextBox2.Enabled = False
        TextBox3.Enabled = False

        ' Enable the associated textbox.
        If RadioButton Is RadioButton1 Then
            TextBox1.Enabled = True
        ElseIf RadioButton Is RadioButton2 Then
            TextBox2.Enabled = True
        ElseIf RadioButton Is RadioButton3 Then
            TextBox3.Enabled = True
        End If
    End Sub

End Class
```

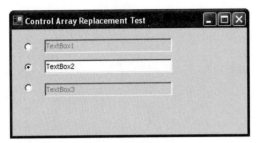

Figure 11-3   Handling multiple events with the same event handler.

In some cases, you might not need to examine the control sender. Instead, you might simply be able to cast the sender parameter to a *Control* object and then retrieve the information you need. For example, consider a case where you want to display help text in another control when a user moves the mouse over a button. You can store the help text for each button in the button's *Tag* property. In the *MouseMove* event, you simply need to retrieve this text and display it accordingly:

```
Private Sub Button_MouseMove(ByVal sender As Object, _
    ByVal e As System.Windows.Forms.MouseEventArgs) _
    Handles Button1.MouseMove, Button2.MouseMove, _
    Button3.MouseMove, Button4.MouseMove

    Dim ctrl As Control = CType(sender, Control)
    lblHelpText.Text = CType(ctrl.Tag, String)

End Sub
```

11.4 Clear All Controls on a Form

Problem

You want to clear all the input controls on a form.

Solution

Iterate recursively through the collection of controls, and clear the *Text* property whenever you find an input control.

Discussion

You can iterate through the controls on a form using the *Form.Controls* collection, which includes all the controls that are placed directly on the form surface. However, if any of these controls are container controls (such as a group box, a panel, or a tab page), they might contain more controls. Thus, it's necessary to use recursive logic that searches the *Controls* collection of every control on the form.

The following example shows a form that calls a *ClearControls* function recursively to clear all text boxes. Figure 11-4 shows the form.

```
Public Class TestClearForm
    Inherits System.Windows.Forms.Form

    ' (Designer code omitted.)

    Private Sub cmdClear_Click(ByVal sender As System.Object, _
      ByVal e As System.EventArgs) Handles cmdClear.Click
        ClearControls(Me)
    End Sub

    Private Sub ClearControls(ByVal ctrl As Control)
        ' Check if the current control should be cleared.
        ' Currently, the control is only cleared if it is a textbox.
        If TypeOf ctrl Is TextBox Then
            ctrl.Text = ""
        End If

        ' Process controls recursively.
        ' This is required if controls contain other controls
        ' (for example, if you use panels, group boxes, or other
        ' container controls).
        Dim ctrlChild As Control
        For Each ctrlChild In ctrl.Controls
            ClearControls(ctrlChild)
        Next
    End Sub
End Class
```

Figure 11-4   A self-clearing form.

11.5 Store Objects in a List

Problem

You want to store custom objects in a list, and customize their display.

Solution

You can add custom objects directly to the *ListBox.Items* collection. However, you must override the *ToString* method in your custom class to set the text that will appear in the *ListBox*, or set the *ListBox.DisplayMember* property.

Discussion

The .NET list controls (the *ListBox*, *ComboBox*, and *CheckedListBox*) can hold any type of object, whether it's an ordinary string or a custom class or structure that contains several pieces of information. However, if you attempt to store custom classes in a list box, you might discover that the text does not appear correctly. Instead, the fully qualified class name will be shown for each item in the list. The reason for this behavior is that the list box calls the contained object's *ToString* method to retrieve the text it should display. If you haven't added your own *ToString* method, your class uses the default *ToString* implementation it inherits from the *System.Object* class, which simply returns the fully qualified class name.

Here's an example of a custom class that can be used in a list control without problem:

```
Public Class Person

    Private _FirstName As String
    Private _LastName As String
    Private _BirthDate As Date

    Public Property FirstName() As String
        Get
            Return _FirstName
        End Get
        Set(ByVal Value As String)
            _FirstName = Value
        End Set
    End Property
```

```
    Public Property LastName() As String
        Get
            Return _LastName
        End Get
        Set(ByVal Value As String)
            _LastName = Value
        End Set
    End Property

    Public Property BirthDate() As Date
        Get
            Return _BirthDate
        End Get
        Set(ByVal Value As Date)
            _BirthDate = Value
        End Set
    End Property

    Public Sub New(ByVal firstName As String, ByVal lastName As String, _
      ByVal birthDate As Date)
        Me.FirstName = firstName
        Me.LastName = lastName
        Me.BirthDate = birthDate
    End Sub

    Public Overrides Function ToString() As String
        Return LastName & ", " & FirstName
    End Function

End Class
```

You can add *Person* objects to a list box in much the same way that you would add string information:

```
Dim NewPerson As New Person("John", "Smith", DateTime.Now)
lstPersons.Items.Add(NewPerson)

NewPerson = New Person("Gustavo", "Camargo", DateTime.Now)
lstPersons.Items.Add(NewPerson)

NewPerson = New Person("Douglas", "Groncki", DateTime.Now)
lstPersons.Items.Add(NewPerson)
```

You can also retrieve the *Person* instance for the selected item just as easily:

```
Dim SelectedPerson As Person
SelectedPerson = CType(lstpersons.SelectedItem, Person)
```

In the list box, the items will appear as shown in Figure 11-5.

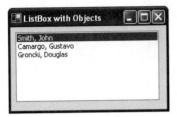

Figure 11-5   Custom objects in a list box.

This technique works best if you are able to tweak the code for the custom class as needed. However, there might be a case where you want to use an object whose code you cannot modify—it might even be a class from the .NET class library. In this case, you can use the *DisplayMember* property. This takes the string name of a property in the bound object. For example, you could set *DisplayMember* to "LastName" and the list box would show the last name for each item. In order for this to work, *LastName* must be implemented as a full property, not just a public variable.

11.6 Force a *ListBox* to Scroll

Problem

You want to scroll a list box programmatically so that certain items in the list are visible.

Solution

Set the *ListBox.TopIndex* property, which sets the first visible list item.

Discussion

In some cases, you might have a list box that stores a significant amount of information or one that you add information to periodically. It's often the case that the most recent information, which is added at the end of the list, is more important than the information at the top of the list. One solution is to scroll the list box so that recently added items are visible.

The following code example is for a form with two buttons (shown in Figure 11-6). One button adds a batch of 10 items to the form, while the other button adds 10 items and then scrolls the list box to the last full page, using the *TopIndex* property.

```
Public Class ListScrollTest
    Inherits System.Windows.Forms.Form

    ' (Designer code omitted.)

    Private Sub cmdAdd_Click(ByVal sender As System.Object, _
      ByVal e As System.EventArgs) Handles cmdAdd.Click
        AddTenItems()
    End Sub

    Private Sub cmdAddScroll_Click(ByVal sender As System.Object, _
      ByVal e As System.EventArgs) Handles cmdAddScroll.Click
        AddTenItems()
        ListBox1.TopIndex = ListBox1.Items.Count - 1
    End Sub

    Private Counter As Integer

    Private Sub AddTenItems()
        Dim i As Integer
        For i = 0 To 9
            Counter += 1
            ListBox1.Items.Add("Item " & Counter.ToString())
        Next
    End Sub

End Class
```

Figure 11-6   Programmatically scrolling a list box.

11.7 Use a Hyperlink

Problem

You want to add a hyperlink to a form that, when clicked, performs an action (such as launching Microsoft Internet Explorer and opening your company Web site).

Solution

Use the *LinkLabel* control.

Discussion

The *LinkLabel* control is a special type of label that can include hyperlinks. You define where the hyperlinks are and then handle the *LinkClicked* event to determine what action should be taken.

To create a hyperlink, add a *LinkLabel* control to the form, and then enter the full text. By default, all the text will be included in the link. To change the link text, find the *LinkArea* property in the Properties window and click the ellipsis (...) to launch a special editor that allows you to mark the hyperlink text by selecting it (see Figure 11-7).

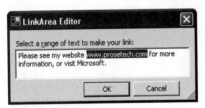

Figure 11-7 Setting the link text for a *LinkLabel* control.

However, a more flexible option is to simply add links programmatically using the *LinkLabel.Links.Add* method. This allows you to specify multiple links for the same *LinkLabel*. You simply have to identify the zero-based position of the first letter in the link text, and the length of the link text. You can even associate additional data with each link by submitting an optional *Object* parameter. For example, the following code adds two links and associates each one with a distinct string that identifies the related Web site.

```
Private Sub LinkTest_Load(ByVal sender As System.Object, _
    ByVal e As System.EventArgs) Handles MyBase.Load

    ' Add the link on the word "www.prosetech.com"
    lnkSite.Links.Add(22, 17, "http://www.prosetech.com")
```

```
' Add the link on the word "Microsoft"
lnkSite.Links.Add(71, 9, "http://www.microsoft.com")

End Sub
```

When the *LinkClicked* event occurs, you can execute any .NET code. If your label has multiple links defined, you might want to examine the *LinkLabelLinkClickedEventArgs* object to retrieve the link data and determine the appropriate action. The code shown here launches Internet Explorer with the text that is associated with the link.

```
Private Sub lnkSite_LinkClicked(ByVal sender As System.Object, _
  ByVal e As System.Windows.Forms.LinkLabelLinkClickedEventArgs) _
  Handles lnkSite.LinkClicked

    ' Mark the link as visited.
    e.Link.Visited = True

    ' Retrieve the related URL.
    Dim Url As String = CType(e.Link.LinkData, String)

    ' Launch the default web browser using this link.
    Process.Start(Url)

End Sub
```

If you would like a clicked link to change color (as in an Internet browser), you can set the *LinkLabelLinkClickedEventArgs.Visited* property to *True* when the link is clicked. Figure 11-8 shows a form with two links.

Figure 11-8   A *LinkLabel* control with two hyperlinks.

11.8 Restrict a Text Box to Numeric Input

Problem

You need to create a text box that will reject only all non-numeric keystrokes.

Solution

Add an event handler for the *TextBox.KeyPress* event, and set the *KeyPressEventArgs.Handled* property to *True* to reject an invalid keystroke.

Discussion

The best way to correct invalid input is to prevent it from being entered in the first place. This approach is easy to implement with the .NET text box because it provides a *KeyPress* event that occurs after the keystroke has been received but before it has been displayed. You can use the *KeyPressEventArgs* event parameter to effectively "cancel" an invalid keystroke by setting the *Handled* property to *True*.

To allow only numeric input, you must allow a keystroke only if it corresponds to a number (0 through 9) or a special control key (such as delete or the arrow keys). The keystroke character is provided to the *KeyPress* event through the *KeyPressEventArgs.KeyChar* property. You can use two shared methods of the *Char* class—*IsDigit* and *IsControl*—to quickly test the character.

Here's the complete code you would use to prevent non-numeric input:

```
Private Sub TextBox1_KeyPress(ByVal sender As Object, _
    ByVal e As System.Windows.Forms.KeyPressEventArgs) _
    Handles TextBox1.KeyPress

    If Not Char.IsDigit(e.KeyChar) And Not Char.IsControl(e.KeyChar) Then
        e.Handled = True
    End If

End Sub
```

Notice that this code rejects the decimal separator. If you need to allow this character (for example, to permit the user to enter a fractional currency amount), you'll have to modify the code slightly, as shown here:

```
If Char.IsDigit(e.KeyChar) Or Char.IsControl(e.KeyChar) Then
    ElseIf e.KeyChar = "." And TextBox1.Text.IndexOf(".") = -1 Then
    Else
    e.Handled = True
End If
```

This code allows only a single decimal point, but it makes no restriction about how many significant digits can be used.

11.9 Use an Auto-Complete Combo Box

Problem

You want to create a combo box that automatically completes what the user is typing based on the item list.

Solution

You can implement a basic auto-complete combo box by handling the *KeyPress* event.

Discussion

Many professional applications include some type of auto-complete control. This control might fill in values based on a list of recent selections (as Microsoft Excel does when entering cell values) or might display a drop-down list of near matches (as Internet Explorer does when typing a URL). You can create a basic auto-complete combo box by handling the *KeyPress* and *TextChanged* events, searching for matching items in the appropriate list, and then filling in the appropriate item. The important step is that after you fill in a matching item, you must programmatically select the characters between the current insertion point and the end of the text. This allows the user to continue typing and replace the auto-complete text as needed.

```
' Track if a special key is pressed
' (in which case the text replacement operation will be skipped).
Private ControlKey As Boolean = False

' Determine whether a special key was pressed.
Private Sub TestCombo_KeyPress(ByVal sender As Object, _
  ByVal e As System.Windows.Forms.KeyPressEventArgs) _
  Handles TestCombo.KeyPress
    ' Retrieve a reference to the ComboBox that sent this event.
    Dim Combo As ComboBox = CType(sender, ComboBox)

    If Asc(e.KeyChar) = Keys.Escape Then
        ' Clear the text.
        Combo.SelectedIndex = -1
        Combo.Text = ""
```

```
            ControlKey = True
        ElseIf Char.IsControl(e.KeyChar) Then
            ControlKey = True
        Else
            ControlKey = False
        End If
End Sub

' Perform the text substituion.
Private Sub TestCombo_TextChanged(ByVal sender As Object, _
    ByVal e As System.EventArgs) Handles TestCombo.TextChanged
        ' Retrieve a reference to the ComboBox that sent this event.
        Dim Combo As ComboBox = CType(sender, ComboBox)

        If Combo.Text <> "" And Not ControlKey Then
            ' Search for a matching entry.
            Dim MatchText As String = Combo.Text
            Dim Match As Integer = Combo.FindString(MatchText)

            ' If a matching entry is found, insert it now.
            If Match <> -1 Then
                Combo.SelectedIndex = Match

                ' Select the added text so it can be replaced
                ' if the user keeps typing.
                Combo.SelectionStart = MatchText.Length
                Combo.SelectionLength = Combo.Text.Length - Combo.SelectionStart
            End If

        End If
End Sub
```

Figure 11-9 shows the auto-complete combo box.

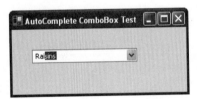

Figure 11-9 An auto-complete combo box.

11.10 Sort a *ListView* Based on Any Column

Problem

You want to sort a *ListView*, but the *Sort* method sorts only based on the first column.

Solution

Create a custom *IComparer* that can sort *ListViewItem* objects, and pass it to the *ListView.Sort* method.

Discussion

The *ListView* control provides a *Sort* method that orders items alphabetically based on the text in the first column. If you want to sort based on other column values, perform a descending sort, or order items in any other way, you need to create a custom *IComparer* class that can perform the work.

The *IComparer* interface was first introduced in recipe 3.9. It defines a single method named *Compare*, which takes two objects and determines which one should be ordered first. The following example shows a custom *ListView-ItemComparer* class that implements *IComparer*. It provides two additional properties: *Column* and *Numeric*. *Column* indicates the column that should be used for sorting, and *Numeric* is a Boolean flag that can be set to *True* if you want to perform number-based comparisons instead of alphabetic comparisons.

```
Public Class ListViewItemComparer
    Implements IComparer

    Private _Column As Integer
    Private _Numeric As Boolean = False

    Public Property Column() As Integer
        Get
            Return _Column
        End Get
        Set(ByVal Value As Integer)
            _Column = Value
        End Set
    End Property
```

```vb
    Public Property Numeric() As Boolean
        Get
            Return _Numeric
        End Get
        Set(ByVal Value As Boolean)
            _Numeric = Value
        End Set
    End Property

    Public Sub New(ByVal columnIndex As Integer)
        Column = columnIndex
    End Sub

    Public Function Compare(ByVal x As Object, ByVal y As Object) As Integer _
        Implements System.Collections.IComparer.Compare
        Dim ListX As ListViewItem = CType(x, ListViewItem)
        Dim ListY As ListViewItem = CType(y, ListViewItem)

        If Numeric Then
            ' Convert column text to numbers before comparing.
            ' If the conversion fails, just use the value 0.
            Dim ListXVal, ListYVal As Decimal
            Try
                ListXVal = Decimal.Parse(ListX.SubItems(Column).Text)
            Catch
                ListXVal = 0
            End Try

            Try
                ListYVal = Decimal.Parse(ListY.SubItems(Column).Text)
            Catch
                ListYVal = 0
            End Try

            Return Decimal.Compare(ListXVal, ListYVal)
        Else
            ' Keep the column text in its native string format
            ' and perform an alphabetic comparison.
            Dim ListXText As String = ListX.SubItems(Column).Text
            Dim ListYText As String = ListY.SubItems(Column).Text

            Return String.Compare(ListXText, ListYText)
        End If
    End Function

End Class
```

Now, to sort the *ListView* you simply need to create a *ListViewItemComparer* instance, configure it appropriately, and then set it in the *ListView.ListViewItem-Sorter* property before you call the *ListView.Sort* method.

Here's the code you might add to the *ColumnClick* event handler to automatically order items when a column header is clicked.

```
Private Sub ListView1_ColumnClick(ByVal sender As Object, _
  ByVal e As System.Windows.Forms.ColumnClickEventArgs) _
  Handles ListView1.ColumnClick

    Dim Sorter As New ListViewItemComparer(e.Column)
    ListView1.ListViewItemSorter = Sorter
    ListView1.Sort()

End Sub
```

11.11 Use the Drag-and-Drop Feature

Problem

You want to use the drag-and-drop feature to exchange information between two controls (possibly in separate windows or in separate applications).

Solution

Start a drag-and-drop operation using *DoDragDrop*, and then respond to the *DragEnter* and *DragDrop* events.

Discussion

A *drag-and-drop* operation allows the user to transfer information from one place to another by clicking an item and "dragging" it to another location. A drag-and-drop operation consists of three basics steps:

1.   The user clicks a control, holds the mouse button down, and begins dragging. If the control supports the drag-and-drop feature, it sets aside some information.

2.   The user drags the mouse over another control. If this control accepts the dragged type of content, the mouse cursor changes to the special drag-and-drop icon (arrow and page). Otherwise, the mouse cursor becomes a circle with a line drawn through it.

3.   When the user releases the mouse button, the data is sent to the control, which can then process it appropriately.

To start a drag-and-drop operation, you call the source control's *DoDrag-Drop* method. At this point you submit the data and specify the type of operations that will be supported (copying, moving, and so on). This example initiates a drag-and-drop operation when the user clicks a text box:

```
Private Sub TextBox_MouseDown(ByVal sender As Object, _
   ByVal e As System.Windows.Forms.MouseEventArgs) _
   Handles TextBox1.MouseDown, TextBox2.MouseDown

    Dim txt As TextBox = CType(sender, TextBox)

    ' Select the text (so the user knows what data is being dragged.)
    txt.SelectAll()

    ' Start the drag-and-drop operation.
    txt.DoDragDrop(txt.Text, DragDropEffects.Copy)

End Sub
```

Controls that can receive dragged data must have their *AllowDrop* property set to *True*. These controls will receive a *DragEnter* event when the mouse drags the data over them. At this point, you can examine the data that is being dragged, decide whether the control can accept the drop, and set the *DragEventArgs.Effect* property accordingly:

```
Private Sub TextBox_DragEnter(ByVal sender As Object, _
   ByVal e As System.Windows.Forms.DragEventArgs) _
   Handles TextBox1.DragEnter, TextBox2.DragEnter

    ' Allow any text data to be dropped.
    If (e.Data.GetDataPresent(DataFormats.Text)) Then
        e.Effect = DragDropEffects.Copy
    Else
        e.Effect = DragDropEffects.None
    End If

End Sub
```

The final step is to respond to the *DragDrop* event, which occurs when the user releases the mouse button:

```
Private Sub TextBox_DragDrop(ByVal sender As Object, _
   ByVal e As System.Windows.Forms.DragEventArgs) _
   Handles TextBox1.DragDrop, TextBox2.DragDrop

    ' Enter the dropped data into the textbox.
    Dim txt As TextBox = CType(sender, TextBox)
    txt.Text = CType(e.Data.GetData(DataFormats.Text), String)

End Sub
```

Using the code we've presented so far, you can create a simple drag-and-drop test application (shown in Figure 11-10) that allows text to be dragged from one text box to the other. You can also drag text from another application and drop it into either text box.

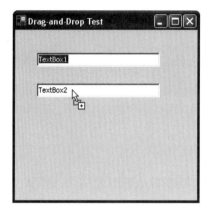

Figure 11-10   A drag-and-drop test application with two text boxes.

11.12 Show a Linked Context Menu Generically

Problem

You want to show context menus for multiple controls with a minimum amount of code.

Solution

Write a generic event handler that retrieves the context menu that is associated with a control.

Discussion

You can associate a control with a context menu by settings the control's *ContextMenu* property. However, this is only a convenience—in order to display the context menu, you must retrieve the menu and call its *Show* method, supplying both a parent control and a pair of coordinates. Usually, you implement this logic in an event handler for the *MouseDown* event.

The good news is that the logic for showing context menus is completely generic, no matter what the control is. Every control supports the *ContextMenu* property (which is inherited from the base *Control* class), which means you can easily write a generic event handler that will display context menus for all controls.

The event handler shown here handles the *MouseDown* event for a label, picture box, and text box, and it shows the associated context menu.

```
Private Sub Control_MouseDown(ByVal sender As System.Object, _
  ByVal e As System.Windows.Forms.MouseEventArgs) _
  Handles PictureBox1.MouseDown, Label1.MouseDown, TextBox1.MouseDown

    If e.Button = MouseButtons.Right Then
        Dim ctrl As Control = CType(sender, Control)
        If Not ctrl.ContextMenu Is Nothing Then
            ctrl.ContextMenu.Show(ctrl, New Point(e.X, e.Y))
        End If
    End If

End Sub
```

11.13 Use Part of the Main Menu for a Context Menu

Problem

You want to create a context menu that shows the same entries as part of an application main menu.

Solution

Use the *CloneMenu* method to duplicate a portion of the main menu.

Discussion

In many applications, a control's context-sensitive menu duplicates a portion of the main menu. Unlike Visual Basic 6, .NET differentiates between context menus and main menus, and a menu item can only belong to one menu at a time.

The solution is to make a duplicate copy of a portion of the menu using the *CloneMenu* method. The *CloneMenu* method not only copies the appropriate *MenuItem* items (and any contained submenus), it also registers the *MenuItem* with the same event handlers. Thus, when a user clicks a cloned menu item in a context menu, the same event handler will be triggered as if the user clicked the duplicate menu item in the main menu.

Here's the code that duplicates all the menu items in a top-level File menu:

```
Dim mnuContext As New ContextMenu()
Dim mnuItem As MenuItem
```

```
' Copy the menu items from the File menu into a context menu.
For Each mnuItem In mnuFile.MenuItems
    mnuContext.MenuItems.Add(mnuItem.CloneMenu())
Next

' Attach the context menu to the textbox.
TextBox1.ContextMenu = mnuContext
```

You can now display this context menu as normal:

```
Private Sub TextBox1_MouseDown(ByVal sender As Object, _
  ByVal e As System.Windows.Forms.MouseEventArgs) Handles TextBox1.MouseDown

    If e.Button = MouseButtons.Right Then
        TextBox1.ContextMenu.Show(TextBox1, New Point(e.X, e.Y))
    End If

End Sub
```

A simple test application is shown in Figure 11-11.

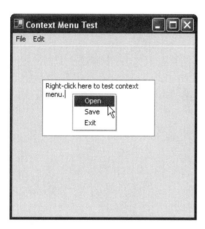

Figure 11-11   Copying part of a main menu to a context menu.

11.14 Make a Multilingual Form

Problem

You need to create a localizable form that can be deployed in more than one language.

Solution

Store all locale-specific information in resource files, which are compiled into satellite assemblies.

Discussion

The .NET Framework includes built-in support for localization through its use of resource files. The basic idea is to store information that is locale-specific (for example, button text), in a resource file. You can then create multiple resource files for multiple different cultures and compile them into satellite assemblies. When you run the application, .NET will automatically use the correct satellite assembly based on the locale settings of the current computer.

You can read to and write from resource files manually. However, Visual Studio .NET also includes extensive design-time support for localized forms. It works like this:

1.   First set the *Localizable* property of the Form to *True* using the Properties window.

2.   Set the *Language* property of the Form to the locale for which you would like to enter information (see Figure 11-12). Then configure the localizable properties of all the controls on the form. Instead of storing your changes in the form designer code, Visual Studio .NET will actually create a new resource file to hold your data.

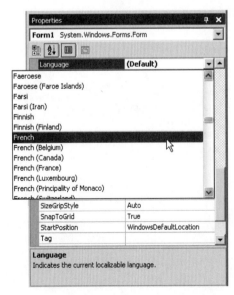

Figure 11-12   Selecting a language for localizing a form.

3. Repeat step 2 for each language that you want to support. Each time, a new resource file will be used. If you change the *Language* property to a locale you have already configured, your previous settings will reappear, and you'll be able to modify them.

You can now compile and test your application on differently localized systems. Visual Studio .NET will create a separate directory and satellite assembly for each resource file in the project. You can select Project | Show All Files from the Visual Studio .NET menu to see how these files are arranged, as shown in Figure 11-13.

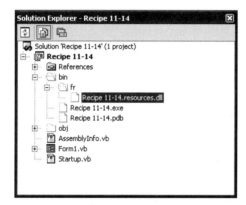

Figure 11-13 A French-locale satellite assembly.

As a testing shortcut, you can also force your application to adopt a specific culture by modifying the *Thread.CurrentUICulture* property of the application thread.

```
Thread.CurrentThread.CurrentUICulture = New CultureInfo("fr")
```

However, you must modify this property before the form has loaded. You might need to use a *Main* startup method for this task, as demonstrated in the downloadable code sample for this recipe.

> **Note** You can also use a utility called Winres.exe (included with Visual Studio .NET) to edit resource information. It provides a scaled-down form editor that does not include the capability to modify code, which is ideal for translators and other nonprogramming professionals who might need to enter locale-specific information.

11.15 Use Form Inheritance

Problem

You want to create and apply a consistent template to multiple forms.

Solution

Create a base form class, and derive all other forms from this class.

Discussion

Using inheritance with form classes is just as straightforward as using it with any other type of control class. You can use it to standardize visual appearance for multiple similar windows (for example, in a wizard) or in similar windows in multiple applications.

To use form inheritance, follow these three steps:

1. Create a base form, and configure as you would any other form.

2. Compile the project.

3. Create a derived form.

There are two approaches to create your derived form. You can create it automatically with Visual Studio .NET by right-clicking the project item in Solution Explorer and choosing Add | Inherited Form. You'll be prompted to enter the name for the new form and to select the form it should derive from (see Figure 11-14). Alternatively, you can simply add an *Inherits* statement to an existing form. Just make sure to specify the fully-qualified class name, as shown here:

```
Public Class DerivedForm
    Inherits MyNamespace.BaseForm
```

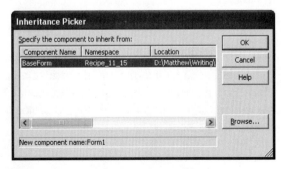

Figure 11-14 Adding a derived form.

> **Note** The easiest way to manage base forms is to place them in a separate class library assembly. You can then reference this assembly DLL in any projects that need to create derived forms. However, you can put base and derived forms in the same project, as long as you remember that you'll need to recompile the project before base form changes will appear in any derived forms.

When you use form inheritance, you'll discover that the controls on the base form cannot be modified. You'll also be prevented from attaching event handlers through the form editor, although you can write the code manually and it'll work perfectly well.

To fine-tune this behavior, you have several options:

- By default, all controls in the base form are marked with the *Friend* accessibility keyword, which makes them inaccessible. However, if you change the control declarations to use the *Protected* keyword, you'll be able to access them—and modify their properties—in the derived form.

- If you want to allow a limited ability to customize a control (for example, to change the text of a button but not its position), you can add a dedicated property procedure to the base form that wraps the appropriate property of the control. That way, the derived form can use this property to make changes—in fact, it will even appear in the Properties window for the form!

- Occasionally, you might want to define control event handlers in the base form. In this case, you can mark the event handler with the *Overridable* accessibility keyword if you want the derived form to be able to replace this event handler with its own logic.

- As with ordinary class inheritance, you can include *MustOverride* methods that the base form must implement.

11.16 Create a Form That Can't Be Moved

Problem

You want to create a form that occupies a fixed location on the screen and cannot be moved.

Solution

Make a borderless form by setting *FormBorderStyle* to *None*.

Discussion

You can create a borderless form by setting the *FormBorderStyle* property to *None*. Borderless forms cannot be moved. However, they also lack any kind of border—if you want the customary blue border, you'll need to add it yourself either with manual drawing code or by using a background image.

There is one other approach to creating an immovable form that provides a basic control-style border. First, set the *ControlBox*, *MinimizeBox*, and *MaximizeBox* properties to *False*. Then, set the *Text* property to an empty string. The form will have a raised gray border or black line (depending on the *FormBorderStyle* option you use), similar to a button. Figure 11-15 shows both types of immovable forms.

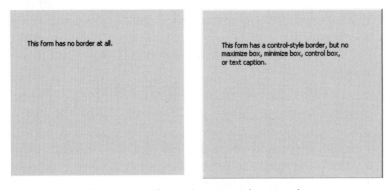

Figure 11-15   Two types of forms that cannot be moved.

11.17 Make a Borderless Form Movable

Problem

You want to create a borderless form that can be moved. This might be the case if you are creating a custom window that has a unique look (for example, for a visually rich application such as a game or a media player).

Solution

Create another control that responds to the *MouseDown*, *MouseUp*, and *MouseMove* events and programmatically moves the form.

Discussion

Borderless forms omit the title bar portion, which makes it impossible for them to be moved by the user. You can compensate for this shortcoming by adding a control to the form that serves the same purpose.

For example, Figure 11-16 shows a form that includes a label for dragging. When the label is clicked, the code sets a form-level flag to indicate it's in drag mode, and the current mouse position is recorded.

```
' Tracks whether the form is in drag mode. If it is, mouse movements
' over the label will be translated into form movements.
Dim Dragging As Boolean

' Stores the offset where the label is clicked.
Dim PointClicked As Point

Private Sub lblDrag_MouseDown(ByVal sender As Object, _
   ByVal e As System.Windows.Forms.MouseEventArgs) Handles lblDrag.MouseDown

    If e.Button = MouseButtons.Left Then
        Dragging = True
        PointClicked = New Point(e.X, e.Y)
    Else
        Dragging = False
    End If

End Sub
```

Figure 11-16   A movable borderless form.

Next, as the user moves the mouse over the label, the form is automatically moved correspondingly. The result is that the form appears to be "attached" to the mouse pointer, which the user can move at will.

```
Private Sub lblDrag_MouseMove(ByVal sender As Object, _
  ByVal e As System.Windows.Forms.MouseEventArgs) Handles lblDrag.MouseMove

    If Dragging Then
        Dim PointMoveTo As Point

        ' Find the current mouse position in screen coordinates.
        PointMoveTo = Me.PointToScreen(New Point(e.X, e.Y))

        ' Compensate for the position the control was clicked.
        PointMoveTo.Offset(-PointClicked.X, -PointClicked.Y)

        ' Move the form.
        Me.Location = PointMoveTo
    End If

End Sub
```

Finally, when the user releases the mouse button, dragging mode is switched off.

```
Private Sub lblDrag_MouseUp(ByVal sender As Object, _
  ByVal e As System.Windows.Forms.MouseEventArgs) Handles lblDrag.MouseUp

    Dragging = False

End Sub
```

You might want to combine this approach with recipe 12.19, which demonstrates how to create an irregularly shaped (nonrectangular) window.

11.18 Save the Size and Location of a Form

Problem

You want to store the size and position of a resizable form and restore it the next time the form is shown.

Solution

Store the *Left*, *Top*, *Width*, and *Height* form properties in the registry.

Discussion

The registry is an ideal place for storing position and size information for a form. Typically, you'll store each form in a separate key, perhaps using the class name of the form. These keys will be stored under an application-specific key.

To automate this process, it helps to create a dedicated class that saves and retrieves form settings. The *FormSettingStore* class shown in the following example fills this role. It provides a *SaveSettings* method that accepts a form and writes its size and position information to the registry, and an *ApplySettings* method that accepts a form, and applies the settings from the registry. The registry key path and the name of the form subkey are stored as class member variables.

```
Public Class FormSettingStore

    Private _RegPath As String
    Private _FormName As String
    Private Key As RegistryKey

    Public ReadOnly Property RegistryPath() As String
        Get
            Return _RegPath
        End Get
    End Property

    Public ReadOnly Property FormName() As String
        Get
            Return _FormName
        End Get
    End Property

    Public Sub New(ByVal registryPath As String, ByVal formName As String)
        Me._RegPath = registryPath
        Me._FormName = formName

        ' Create the key if it doesn't exist.
        Key = Registry.LocalMachine.CreateSubKey(registryPath & Me.FormName)
    End Sub

    Public Sub SaveSettings(ByVal form As System.Windows.Forms.Form)
        Key.SetValue("Height", form.Height)
        Key.SetValue("Width", form.Width)
        Key.SetValue("Left", form.Left)
        Key.SetValue("Top", form.Top)
    End Sub
```

```
Public Sub ApplySettings(ByVal form As System.Windows.Forms.Form)
    ' If form settings are not available, the current form settings
    ' are used instead.
    form.Height = CType(Key.GetValue("Height", form.Height), Integer)
    form.Width = CType(Key.GetValue("Width", form.Width), Integer)
    form.Left = CType(Key.GetValue("Left", form.Left), Integer)
    form.Top = CType(Key.GetValue("Top", form.Top), Integer)
End Sub

End Class
```

To use the *FormSettingStore* class, simply add the event handling code shown here to any form. This code saves the form properties when the form closes and restores them when the form is loaded.

```
Private FormSettings As New FormSettingStore("Software\MyApp\", Me.Name)

Private Sub Form1_Load(ByVal sender As System.Object, _
  ByVal e As System.EventArgs) Handles MyBase.Load
      FormSettings.ApplySettings(Me)
End Sub

Private Sub Form1_Closed(ByVal sender As Object, _
  ByVal e As System.EventArgs) Handles MyBase.Closed
    FormSettings.SaveSettings(Me)
End Sub
```

11.19 Synchronize Controls on a Form

Problem

You want to create a record-browser where all control values are updated automatically for the current record.

Solution

Use a custom class to encapsulate the data, add instances of it to an *ArrayList* collection, and use .NET data binding.

Discussion

.NET data binding is most commonly used in ADO.NET applications, where you need to display one or more records in a *DataTable*. However, it can be used just as easily in other types of applications by replacing the *DataTable* or *DataSet* with a collection of custom objects.

For example, consider an example where you want to use multiple controls to show different pieces of information about a person. The person information is wrapped into a dedicated class, which is shown here.

```
Public Class Person

    Public _FirstName As String
    Public _LastName As String
    Public _BirthDate As Date

    Public Property FirstName() As String
        Get
            Return _FirstName
        End Get
        Set(ByVal Value As String)
            _FirstName = Value
        End Set
    End Property

    Public Property LastName() As String
        Get
            Return _LastName
        End Get
        Set(ByVal Value As String)
            _LastName = Value
        End Set
    End Property

    Public Property BirthDate() As Date
        Get
            Return _BirthDate
        End Get
        Set(ByVal Value As Date)
            _BirthDate = Value
        End Set
    End Property

    Public Sub New(ByVal firstName As String, ByVal lastName As String, _
      ByVal birthDate As Date)
        Me.FirstName = firstName
        Me.LastName = lastName
        Me.BirthDate = birthDate
    End Sub

End Class
```

To store multiple *Person* instances, you can use an *ArrayList*, as shown here:

```
Dim Persons As New ArrayList()

Dim NewPerson As New Person("John", "Smith", New DateTime(1976, 6, 6))
Persons.Add(NewPerson)

NewPerson = New Person("Gustavo", "Camargo", New DateTime(1926, 2, 6))
Persons.Add(NewPerson)

NewPerson = New Person("Douglas", "Groncki", New DateTime(1980, 3, 30))
Persons.Add(NewPerson)
```

Finally, you can connect multiple controls to the same *ArrayList*. To connect a list control, you simply need to set its *DataSource* property to reference the *ArrayList*. You should also set the *DisplayMember* property with the name of the property in the bound object that you want to display. (Instead of using *DisplayMember*, you can override the *Person.ToString* method so that it returns a custom text representation for your object, as demonstrated in recipe 11.5.)

```
lstPersons.DataSource = Persons
lstPersons.DisplayMember = "LastName"
```

Many other .NET controls, like buttons, text boxes, and labels, don't provide any specialized data binding features. Instead, they support data binding through the *DataBindings* collection, which is inherited from the *Control* class. The *DataBindings* collection allows you to link any control property to a property in a custom class. For example, you can bind the *Text* property of a text box to the *Person.FirstName* property. Values from the *Person* object will automatically be inserted into the text box, and changes to the text box will be automatically applied to the *Person* object.

Here's the data-binding code that connects two text boxes and a *DateTimePicker* control:

```
txtFirstName.DataBindings.Add("Text", Persons, "FirstName")
txtLastName.DataBindings.Add("Text", Persons, "LastName")
dtBirth.DataBindings.Add("Value", Persons, "BirthDate")
```

Figure 11-17 shows the resulting form. Note that you can change the *Person* values using the text boxes or *DateTimePicker* control. However, if you change the last name, the list box information won't be refreshed automatically. For that reason, you should use a piece of read-only information as the list box *DisplayMember*, or you should detect changes and rebind the list box as needed.

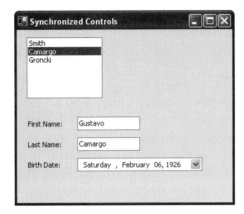

Figure 11-17   Synchronized controls.

11.20 Create a System Tray Application

Problem

You want to create an application that displays an icon in the system tray and runs in the background.

Solution

Start your application with a component class that includes the *NotifyIcon* control. Show other forms if needed when the user clicks on the *NotifyIcon* control or selects a context menu option.

Discussion

System tray applications are usually long-running applications that run quietly in the background, possibly performing some periodic task or waiting for an event (such as the creation of a file or a notification from the operating system). System tray applications might provide a user interface, but they don't present it on startup. Instead, they create an icon in the system tray and then wait for user interaction.

To create a system tray application, you need to start your application with a *Main* subroutine, not a form. To make life easy, you should code this *Main* subroutine in a component class, not an ordinary module. This is because component classes automatically have design-time support, which means you can configure the system tray icon and add a context menu in Visual Studio .NET at design time instead of writing tedious code.

To add a component class, right-click on the project item in Solution Explorer and select Add | Add Component. Then, add a *NotifyIcon* control to the form, and configure it. As a bare minimum, you must supply an icon for the *Icon* property. In addition, you might want to add a context menu and link it to the *NotifyIcon* using the *ContextMenu* property. The *NotifyIcon* control automatically displays its context menu when it's right-clicked, unlike other controls.

The design-time component surface that you might have is shown in Figure 11-18.

Figure 11-18   The design-time surface for a system tray application.

Note   You cannot edit a context menu at design time on a component surface. Instead, you can add the context menu to a form, configure it using the designer, and then copy the context menu to the design-time surface of the component class.

Next, create a startup method in the component class that creates an instance of the component and starts a message loop. You can also start a thread or timer to perform a periodic task, or attach additional event handlers. To handle menu events, you simply need to attach event handlers to the *Click* event of each menu item. The full component code for a basic system tray application framework is shown here. It can be started and stopped (by clicking the Exit menu item).

```
Public Class App
    Inherits System.ComponentModel.Component

    ' (Component designer code omitted.)
```

```
Public Shared Sub Main()
    ' Create the component.
    ' It's at this point that the system tray icon will appear.
    Dim App As New App()

    ' Keep the application running even when this subroutine ends.
    ' Use Application.Exit() to end the application.
    Application.Run()
End Sub

Private Sub mnuExit_Click(ByVal sender As Object, _
  ByVal e As System.EventArgs) Handles mnuExit.Click
    Application.Exit()
End Sub

End Class
```

11.21 Apply Windows XP Control Styles

Problem

You want your controls to have the updated Windows XP appearance on Windows XP systems.

Solution

In .NET 1.0, you must create a manifest file. In .NET 1.1, you simply need to call the *Application.EnableVisualStyles* method.

Discussion

Windows XP styles are automatically applied to the non-client area of a form (such as the border and the minimize and maximize buttons). However, they won't be applied to controls such as buttons and group boxes unless you take additional steps.

First of all, you must configure all your form's button-style controls (such as buttons, check boxes, and radio buttons). These controls provide a *FlatStyle* property, which must be set to *System*.

The next step depends on the version of .NET that you are using. If you are using .NET 1.1 (provided with Visual Studio .NET 2003), you simply need to call the *Application.EnableVisualStyles* method before you show any forms. For example, you can start your application with the startup routine shown on the following page.

```
Public Module Startup

    Public Sub Main()
        ' Enable visual styles.
        Application.EnableVisualStyles()

        ' Show the main form for your application.
        Application.Run(New StartForm)
    End Sub

End Module
```

If you are using .NET 1.0, you don't have the convenience of the *Application.EnableVisualStyles* method. However, you can still use visual styles—you simply need to create a *manifest file* for your application. This manifest file (an ordinary text file with XML content) tells Windows XP that your application requires the new version of the Comctl32.dll file. This file, which defines the new control styles, is included on all Windows XP computers. Windows XP will read and apply the settings from the manifest file automatically, provided you deploy it in the application directory and give it the correct name. The manifest file should have the same name as the executable used for your application, plus the extension .manifest (so TheApp.exe would have the manifest file TheApp.exe.manifest—even though this looks like two extensions).

Following is a sample manifest file. You can copy this file for your own applications—just rename it accordingly. It's also recommended that you modify the name value to use your application name, although this step isn't necessary.

```xml
<?xml version="1.0" encoding="UTF-8" standalone="yes"?>
<assembly xmlns="urn:schemas-microsoft-com:asm.v1" manifestVersion="1.0">
<assemblyIdentity
    version="1.0.0.0"
    processorArchitecture="X86"
    name="TheApp"
    type="win32" />

<dependency>
<dependentAssembly>
<assemblyIdentity
    type="win32"
    name="Microsoft.Windows.Common-Controls"
    version="6.0.0.0"
    processorArchitecture="X86"
    publicKeyToken="6595b64144ccf1df"
    language="*" />

</dependentAssembly>
</dependency>
</assembly>
```

To test that this technique is working, run the application. The Windows XP styles won't appear in the Visual Studio .NET design-time environment. Figure 11-19 shows the difference between the Windows XP and non–Windows XP control styles.

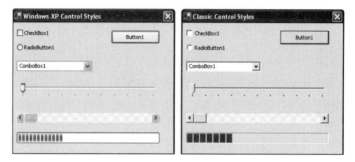

Figure 11-19   Control styles with and without Windows XP.

Note   If you supply a manifest file for an application running on a pre–Windows XP version of Windows, it will simply be ignored, and the classic control styles will be used. For this reason, you might want to test your application both with and without a manifest file.

12

Printing and Drawing with GDI+

The Microsoft .NET Framework includes a new model for two-dimensional drawing and printing. It's called GDI+, and it's represented by the types in the *System.Drawing* namespace. GDI+ isn't an entirely new drawing system—in fact, it's really just a .NET wrapper on top of the classic GDI (Graphics Device Interface) functions in the Microsoft Windows API. However, the GDI+ classes make it much easier to draw complex shapes, work with coordinates and transforms, and control image processing and rendering quality. GDI+ is also used for printing.

In this chapter, the recipes deal with two uses of GDI+. First you'll learn about printing, using GDI+ to print simple and complex documents (recipes 12.2 and 12.3). You'll also learn the techniques needed to center and wrap text (recipes 12.4 and 12.5), create a print preview (recipe 12.7), and retrieve information about print queues (recipes 12.8 and 12.9).

The second portion of this chapter deals with custom on-screen drawing and image manipulation, using shapes, fonts, bitmaps, and more. You'll learn how to convert images (12.11), how to use painting techniques (recipes 12.12 and 12.13), and how to remove flicker with double buffering (recipe 12.18). We'll also consider examples that show irregularly shaped windows (recipe 12.19) and owner-drawn controls (recipes 12.20 and 12.21).

12.1 Find All Installed Printers

Problem

You need to retrieve a list of available printers.

Solution

Read the names in the *PrinterSettings.InstalledPrinters* collection.

Discussion

The *System.Drawing.Printing.PrinterSettings* class encapsulates the settings for a printer and information about the printer. For example, you can use the *PrinterSettings* class to determine supported paper sizes, paper sources, and resolutions and check for the ability to print color or double-sided (or *duplexed*) pages. In addition, you can retrieve default page settings for margins, page orientation, and so on.

The *PrinterSettings* class provides a shared *InstalledPrinters* collection, which includes the name of every printer that's installed on the computer. If you want to find out more information about the settings for a specific printer, you simply need to create a *PrinterSettings* instance and set the *PrinterName* property accordingly.

The following code shows a Console application that finds all the printers that are installed on a computer and displays information about the paper sizes and the resolutions supported by each one. In order to use the example as written, you must import the *System.Drawing.Printing* namespace.

```
Public Module PrinterListTest

    Public Sub Main()
        Dim Printer As New PrinterSettings()
        Dim PrinterName As String

        For Each PrinterName In PrinterSettings.InstalledPrinters
            ' Display the printer name.
            Console.WriteLine("Printer: " & PrinterName)

            ' Retrieve the printer settings.
            Printer.PrinterName = PrinterName

            ' Check that this is a valid printer.
            ' (This step might be required if you read the printer name
            ' from a user-supplied value or a registry or configuration file
            ' setting.)
```

```
        If Printer.IsValid Then
            ' Display the list of valid resolutions.
            Console.WriteLine("Supported Resolutions:")
            Dim Resolution As PrinterResolution
            For Each Resolution In Printer.PrinterResolutions
                Console.WriteLine("   " & Resolution.ToString())
            Next
            Console.WriteLine()

            ' Display the list of valid paper sizes.
            Console.WriteLine("Supported Paper Sizes:")
            Dim Size As PaperSize
            For Each Size In Printer.PaperSizes
                If System.Enum.IsDefined(Size.Kind.GetType, Size.Kind) Then
                    Console.WriteLine("   " & Size.ToString())
                End If
            Next
            Console.WriteLine()
        End If
    Next

    Console.ReadLine()
End Sub

End Module
```

Here's the type of output this utility displays:

```
Printer: HP LaserJet 5L
Supported Resolutions:
  [PrinterResolution High]
  [PrinterResolution Medium]
  [PrinterResolution Low]
  [PrinterResolution Draft]
  [PrinterResolution X=600 Y=600]
  [PrinterResolution X=300 Y=300]

Supported Paper Sizes:
  [PaperSize Letter Kind=Letter Height=1100 Width=850]
  [PaperSize Legal Kind=Legal Height=1400 Width=850]
  [PaperSize Executive Kind=Executive Height=1050 Width=725]
  [PaperSize A4 Kind=A4 Height=1169 Width=827]
  [PaperSize Envelope #10 Kind=Number10Envelope Height=950 Width=412]
  [PaperSize Envelope DL Kind=DLEnvelope Height=866 Width=433]
  [PaperSize Envelope C5 Kind=C5Envelope Height=902 Width=638]
  [PaperSize Envelope B5 Kind=B5Envelope Height=984 Width=693]
  [PaperSize Envelope Monarch Kind=MonarchEnvelope Height=750 Width=387]

Printer: Generic PostScript Printer
. . .
```

You don't necessarily need to take this approach when creating an application that provides printing features. As you'll see in recipe 12.2, you can use the *PrintDialog* to prompt the user to choose a printer and its settings. The *PrintDialog* class can automatically apply its settings to the appropriate *PrintDocument* without any additional code.

> **Note** You can print a document in almost any type of application. However, your application must include a reference to the System.Drawing.dll assembly. If you are using a project type in Microsoft Visual Studio .NET that wouldn't normally have this reference (such as a Console application), you must add it.

12.2 Print a Simple Document

Problem

You need to print text or images.

Solution

Handle the *PrintDocument.PrintPage* event, and use the *DrawString* and *DrawImage* methods of the *Graphics* class to print data to the page.

Discussion

.NET uses an asynchronous event-based printing model. To print a document, you create a *System.Drawing.Printing.PrintDocument* instance, configure its properties, and then call its *Print* method, which schedules the print job. The common language runtime will then fire the *BeginPrint*, *PrintPage*, and *EndPrint* events of the *PrintDocument* class on a new thread. You handle these events and use the provided *System.Drawing.Graphics* object to output data to the page.

Printer settings are configured through the *PrintDocument.PrinterSettings* and *PrintDocument.DefaultPageSettings* properties. The *PrinterSettings* property returns a full *PrinterSettings* object (as described in recipe 12.1), which identifies the printer that will be used. The *DefaultPageSettings* property provides a full *PageSettings* object that specifies printer resolution, margins, orientation, and so on. You can configure these properties in code, or you can use the *System.Windows.Forms.PrintDialog* class to let the user make the changes using the standard Windows print dialog (shown in Figure 12-1).

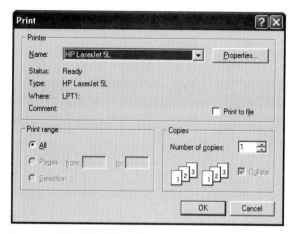

Figure 12-1   The *PrintDialog*.

In the print dialog box, the user can select a printer and choose a number of copies. The user can also click the Properties button to configure advanced settings like page layout and printer resolution. Finally, the user can either accept or cancel the print operation by clicking OK or Cancel.

Before showing the *PrintDialog*, you must explicitly attach it to a *Print-Document* object by setting the *PrintDialog.Document* property. Then, any changes the user makes in the print dialog will be automatically applied to the *PrintDocument* object. The next example creates a new document, allows the user to configure print settings, and then starts an asynchronous print operation. It all starts when the user clicks a button.

```
Private Sub cmdPrint_Click(ByVal sender As System.Object, _
  ByVal e As System.EventArgs) Handles cmdPrint.Click

    ' Create the document and attach an event handler.
    Dim MyDoc As New PrintDocument()
    AddHandler MyDoc.PrintPage, AddressOf MyDoc_PrintPage

    ' Allow the user to choose a printer and specify other settings.
    Dim dlgSettings As New PrintDialog()
    dlgSettings.Document = MyDoc
    Dim Result As DialogResult = dlgSettings.ShowDialog()

    ' If the user clicked OK, print the document.
    If Result = DialogResult.OK Then
        ' This method returns immediately, before the print job starts.
```

```
        ' The PrintPage event will fire asynchronously.
        MyDoc.Print()
    End If

End Sub
```

> **Note** In some cases, you might show the *PrintDialog* simply to allow the user to configure settings, not to start a print job. In this case, your code would not call the *Print* method when the user clicks the OK button.

The actual printing logic is shown in the following code. In .NET, printing to a page is exactly the same as drawing to a window using GDI+. You use the same *Graphics* class, with its methods for drawing shapes, texts, and images. You must also track your position, because every *Graphics* class method requires explicit coordinates that indicate where to draw on the page. You can retrieve the page margins from the passed-in *PrintPageEventArgs* object.

```
Private Sub MyDoc_PrintPage(ByVal sender As Object, _
    ByVal e As PrintPageEventArgs)

    ' Define the font.
    Dim MyFont As New Font("Arial", 30)

    ' Determine the position on the page.
    ' In this case, we read the margin settings
    ' (although there is nothing that prevents your code
    '  from going outside the margin bounds.)
    Dim x As Single = e.MarginBounds.Left
    Dim y As Single = e.MarginBounds.Top

    ' Determine the height of a line (based on the font used).
    Dim LineHeight As Single = MyFont.GetHeight(e.Graphics)

    ' Print five lines of text.
    Dim i As Integer
    For i = 0 To 4
        ' Draw the text with a black brush,
        ' using the font and coordinates we have determined.
        e.Graphics.DrawString("This is line " & i.ToString(), _
            MyFont, Brushes.Black, x, y)
```

```
      ' Move down the equivalent spacing of one line.
      y += LineHeight
   Next
   y += LineHeight

   ' Draw an image.
   e.Graphics.DrawImage(Image.FromFile(Application.StartupPath & _
      "\test.bmp"), x, y)

End Sub
```

The printed document is shown, in Adobe Acrobat, in Figure 12-2.

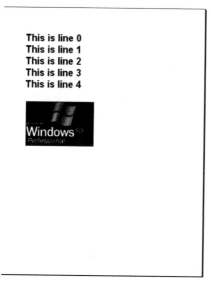

Figure 12-2 The printed document.

This example has one limitation: it can only print a single page. To print more complex documents and span multiple pages, you will probably want to create a specialized class that encapsulates the document information, the current page, and so on. This technique is demonstrated in recipe 12.3.

12.3 Print a Document That Has Multiple Pages

Problem

You want to print complex documents with multiple pages and possibly print several different documents at once.

Solution

Place the information you want to print into a custom class that derives from *PrintDocument*, and set the *PrintPageEventArgs.HasMorePages* property to *True* as long as there are pages remaining.

Discussion

The *PrintDocument.PrintPage* event allows you to print only a single page. If you need to print more pages, you need to set the *PrintPageEventArgs.Has-MorePages* property to *True* in the *PrintPage* event handler. As long as *Has-MorePages* is *True*, the *PrintDocument* class will continue firing *PrintPage* events, one for each page. However, it's up to you to track what page you are on, what data should be placed on each page, and so on. To facilitate this tracking, it's a good idea to create a custom class.

The following example shows a class called *TextDocument*. This class inherits from *PrintDocument* and adds three properties. *Text* stores an array of text lines, *PageNumber* reflects the last printed page, and *Offset* indicates the last line that was printed from the *Text* array.

```
Public Class TextDocument
    Inherits PrintDocument

    Private _Text() As String
    Private _PageNumber As Integer
    Private _Offset As Integer

    Public Property Text() As String()
        Get
            Return _Text
        End Get
        Set(ByVal Value As String())
            _Text = Value
        End Set
    End Property

    Public Property PageNumber() As Integer
        Get
            Return _PageNumber
        End Get
        Set(ByVal Value As Integer)
            _PageNumber = Value
        End Set
    End Property
```

```
Public Property Offset() As Integer
    Get
        Return _Offset
    End Get
    Set(ByVal Value As Integer)
        _Offset = Value
    End Set
End Property


Public Sub New(ByVal text() As String)
    Me.Text = text
End Sub
```

```
End Class
```

Depending on the type of material you are printing, you might want to modify this class. For example, you could store an array of image data, some content that should be used as a header or footer on each page, font information, or even the name of a file from which you want to read the information. Encapsulating the information in a single class makes it easier to print more than one document at the same time.

The code that initiates printing is the same as in recipe 12.2, only now it creates a *TextDocument* instance instead of a *PrintDocument* instance:

```
' Generate some text.
Dim PrintText(100) As String
Dim i As Integer
For i = 0 To 100
    PrintText(i) = i.ToString()
    PrintText(i) &= " - lorum ipso facto lorum ipso facto lorum ipso"
Next


' Create the custom document.
Dim MyDoc As New TextDocument(PrintText)
AddHandler MyDoc.PrintPage, AddressOf MyDoc_PrintPage


' Allow the user to choose the printer and settings.
Dim dlgSettings As New PrintDialog()
dlgSettings.Document = MyDoc
Dim Result As DialogResult = dlgSettings.ShowDialog()


If Result = DialogResult.OK Then
    MyDoc.Print()
End If
```

The *PrintPage* event handler keeps track of the current line and checks if there is space on the page before attempting to print the next line. If a new page is needed, the *HasMorePages* property is set to *True* and the *PrintPage* event fires again for the next page. If not, the print operation is completed.

```vbnet
Private Sub MyDoc_PrintPage(ByVal sender As Object, _
  ByVal e As PrintPageEventArgs)

    ' Retrieve the document that sent this event.
    ' You could store the document in a class member variable,
    ' but this approach allows you to use the same event handler
    ' to handle multiple print documents at once.
    Dim Doc As TextDocument = CType(sender, TextDocument)

    ' Define the font and determine the line height.
    Dim MyFont As New Font("Arial", 10)
    Dim LineHeight As Single = MyFont.GetHeight(e.Graphics)

    ' Create variables to hold position on page.
    Dim x As Single = e.MarginBounds.Left
    Dim y As Single = e.MarginBounds.Top

    ' Increment the page counter (to reflect the page that is about to be
    ' printed).
    Doc.PageNumber += 1

    ' Print all the information that can fit on the page.
    ' This loop ends when the next line would go over the margin bounds,
    ' or there are no more lines to print.
    Do
        e.Graphics.DrawString(Doc.Text(Doc.Offset), MyFont, _
          Brushes.Black, x, y)

        ' Move to the next line of data.
        Doc.Offset += 1

        ' Move the equivalent of one line down the page.
        y += LineHeight
    Loop Until (y + LineHeight) > e.MarginBounds.Bottom Or _
      Doc.Offset > Doc.Text.GetUpperBound(0)

    If Doc.Offset < Doc.Text.GetUpperBound(0) Then
        ' There is still at least one more page.
        ' Signal this event to fire again.
        e.HasMorePages = True
    Else
        ' Printing is complete.
        Doc.Offset = 0
    End If

End Sub
```

12.4 Print Centered Text

Problem

You want to center text vertically or horizontally on a page.

Solution

Calculate the available space between the margins, subtract the width or height of the text you want to print (using the *Graphics.MeasureString* and *Font.Get-Height* methods), and divide by two to find the appropriate coordinate.

Discussion

Printing centered text is easy. The only caveat is that you need to perform the coordinate calculations, as with all print operations.

Here is a code snippet that prints a block of three lines of text that are centered horizontally and vertically:

```
Private Sub MyDoc_PrintPage(ByVal sender As Object, _
  ByVal e As PrintPageEventArgs)

    ' Define the font and text.
    Dim Font As New Font("Arial", 35)
    Dim Text As String = "This is a centered line of text."
    Dim LineHeight As Single = Font.GetHeight(e.Graphics)
    Dim LineWidth As Single = e.Graphics.MeasureString(Text, Font).Width

    ' Calculate the starting left and top coordinates.
    Dim x, y As Single
    x = (e.PageBounds.Width - LineWidth) / 2
    y = (e.PageBounds.Height - LineHeight * 3) / 2

    ' Print three lines of text.
    Dim i As Integer
    For i = 0 To 2
        ' Draw the text with a black brush,
        ' using the font and coordinates we have determined.
        e.Graphics.DrawString(Text, Font, Brushes.Black, x, y)

        ' Move down the equivalent spacing of one line.
        y += LineHeight
    Next

End Sub
```

There are actually two approaches to measure the height of a given line of text. You can use the height component returned from the *Graphics.Measure-String* method or the value returned from *Font.GetHeight*. These values are not necessarily the same—in fact, for most fonts the *Font.GetHeight* value will be slightly smaller.

For the purposes of line spacing, it's recommended that you always use *Font.GetHeight*. You should be aware, however, that there is more than one version of the *GetHeight* method. You must use the overloaded version that allows you to specify a *Graphics* object. Otherwise, the height you receive will be calculated for display purposes, not for the printer.

> **Note**   You can also print centered text by using an overloaded version of the *DrawString* method that takes a bounding rectangle, inside which you can center text. This approach surrenders some flexibility (for example, it won't help if you need to center mixed content that includes different fonts or graphics), but it requires less code. See recipe 12.5 for an example.

12.5 Print Wrapped Text

Problem

You want to parse a large block of text into distinct lines that fit on a page.

Solution

Use the *Graphics.DrawString* method overload that accepts a bounding rectangle. Or, if you need custom wrapping ability, write code that moves through the text word by word and measures it using the *Graphics.MeasureString* method until the line exceeds a set threshold.

Discussion

Often, you'll need to break a large block of text into separate lines that can be printed individually on a page. In .NET, you can take two approaches: one that performs the wrapping for you, and one by which your code controls the wrapping process.

To use automatic wrapping, you simply need to use the version of the *Graphics.DrawString* method that accepts a bounding rectangle. You specify a rectangle that represents where you want the text to be displayed. The text is then wrapped automatically to fit within those confines.

The following code demonstrates this approach using the bounding rectangle that represents the printable portion of the page. It prints a large block of text from a text box on the form. Notice that the shared *RectangleF.op_Implicit* method is used to convert the *Rectangle* structure that represents page margins to a *RectangleF*, which is required for the *DrawString* method.

```
Private Sub MyDoc_PrintPage(ByVal sender As Object, _
   ByVal e As PrintPageEventArgs)

   ' Define the font and text.
   Dim Font As New Font("Arial", 15)

   e.Graphics.DrawString(txtData.Text, Font, Brushes.Black, _
      RectangleF.op_Implicit(e.MarginBounds), StringFormat.GenericDefault)

End Sub
```

The wrapped text is shown in Figure 12-3.

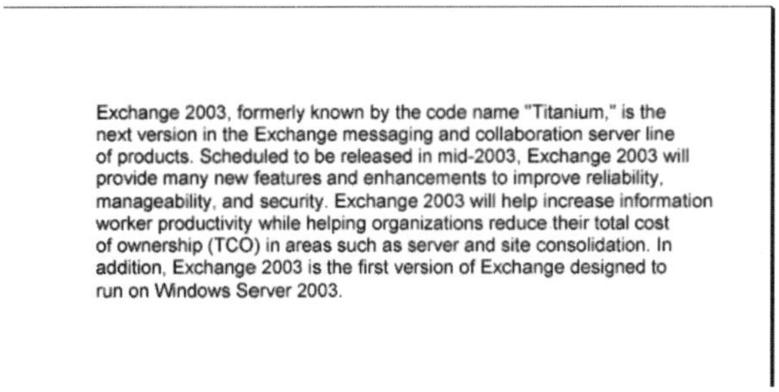

Exchange 2003, formerly known by the code name "Titanium," is the next version in the Exchange messaging and collaboration server line of products. Scheduled to be released in mid-2003, Exchange 2003 will provide many new features and enhancements to improve reliability, manageability, and security. Exchange 2003 will help increase information worker productivity while helping organizations reduce their total cost of ownership (TCO) in areas such as server and site consolidation. In addition, Exchange 2003 is the first version of Exchange designed to run on Windows Server 2003.

Figure 12-3   The printed document with wrapping.

You can also modify the *StringFormat* parameter to specify different options for the text alignment. For example, the next code snippet centers the block of text vertically on the page, and then centers each line of wrapped text.

```
Private Sub MyDoc_PrintPage(ByVal sender As Object, _
   ByVal e As PrintPageEventArgs)

   ' Define the font and text.
   Dim Font As New Font("Arial", 15)
```

```
Dim Format As StringFormat = StringFormat.GenericDefault
' Center the block of text on the page (vertically).
Format.LineAlignment = StringAlignment.Center
' Center the individual lines of text (horizontally).
Format.Alignment = StringAlignment.Center

e.Graphics.DrawString(txtData.Text, Font, Brushes.Black, _
    RectangleF.op_Implicit(e.MarginBounds), StringFormat.GenericDefault)

End Sub
```

> **Note**   Although you can configure the *StringFormat* object to right-align text (using an *Alignment* value of *StringAlignment.Far*), the results will be far from ideal. This right-alignment does not take into account the precise size of the text based on font hinting and kerning, so the right margin of the text will not line up perfectly.

Complex document-oriented applications often require fine-grained control over the wrapping process. In this case, you can use an alternate approach and perform the text wrapping manually. Because most fonts are nonproportional (meaning each character has a different width), you can't use the number of characters to decide where to divide a sentence. Instead, you need to manually walk through the sentence character by character, looking for spaces. Every time a space is found, you add the current word to the line text, and decide whether or not to start printing the next line (based on its length).

The following code wraps a block of text manually. Notice that the string manipulation code uses the *StringBuilder* class whenever possible, which is faster when appending characters.

```
Private Sub MyDoc_PrintPage(ByVal sender As Object, _
    ByVal e As PrintPageEventArgs)

    ' Define the font and text.
    Dim Font As New Font("Arial", 15)
    Dim LineHeight As Single = Font.GetHeight(e.Graphics)

    ' Create variables to hold position on page.
    Dim x As Single = e.MarginBounds.Left
    Dim y As Single = e.MarginBounds.Top

    ' Once the amount of border at the end of the line
    ' drops below the threshold, the line is wrapped
```

```
' (provided you are at the end of the word.)
' Depending on the font size, you will need to tweak the threshold.
' Generally, the larger the font, the larger the threshold
' will need to be to prevent a long word that will run off the page.
Dim Threshold As Integer = 200

' Retrieve data from a text box.
Dim TextToPrint As New System.Text.StringBuilder(txtData.Text)

' Contains a single printed line.
Dim Line As New System.Text.StringBuilder()

Do
    ' Take one character from the text, and
    ' add it to the current line.
    Line.Append(TextToPrint.Chars(0))
    TextToPrint = TextToPrint.Remove(0, 1)

    ' Check if you have reached a word break.
    If Line.Chars(Line.Length - 1) = " " Then

        ' It's time to decide whether to
        ' print the line or add another word.
        Dim LineString As String = Line.ToString()
        If e.Graphics.MeasureString(LineString, Font).Width > _
          (e.PageBounds.Width - Threshold) Then
            e.Graphics.DrawString(LineString, Font, Brushes.Black, x, y)
            y += LineHeight
            Line = New System.Text.StringBuilder()
        End If

    End If
Loop While TextToPrint.Length > 0

' Print the last line.
e.Graphics.DrawString(Line.ToString(), Font, Brushes.Black, x, y)

End Sub
```

You can make this algorithm quite a bit more intelligent. Currently, it's possible (although unlikely) that an extremely large word could occur, taking the line from an accepted width to an unacceptable width (and simultaneously crossing both the threshold and the page boundary). You'll see that this becomes a problem for extremely large fonts.

To prevent this problem, you can check for this condition and then remove the added word if a problem occurs. In this case, you'd also need to check that no single word exceeds the width of the page, in which case the word can't be printed (without hyphenation, anyway). A really intelligent wrapping algorithm would compare the possible line lengths with or without a word and choose the option that deviates the least from the threshold. Finally, you could also add support for multipage printing by checking for the end of the page (as in recipe 12.3).

12.6 Print from a File

Problem

You want to print data from a file without loading it into memory first.

Solution

Use the *PrintDocument.BeginPrint* event to open a stream to the file and the *PrintDocument.EndPrint* event to close the stream.

Discussion

When printing a large document, you might want to save the memory overhead by printing the data as it's read from a stream. This way, the entire document doesn't need to be held in memory at the same time.

The easiest way to use this approach is to adopt the design from recipe 12.3 and derive a custom *PrintDocument* class. This class would track the filename of the document and hold a reference to the underlying file stream. This class would also encapsulate the logic for opening and closing the file stream by overriding the *OnBeginPrint* and *OnEndPrint* methods, which saves you from needing to handle the corresponding events.

The *TextFileDocument* class, shown in the following code, provides an example. *TextFileDocument* abstracts access to the underlying file stream by providing a *ReadWord* method that allows the printing code to retrieve the next word. This approach allows you to easily wrap the text as you print it.

```
Public Class TextFileDocument
    Inherits PrintDocument

    ' The filename that will be opened when the print job starts.
    Private _Filename As String

    ' Indicates if data is available in the stream.
    Private _DataAvailable As Boolean = False
```

```
' These private variables track the open file.
' The client using this class cannot access these details directly.
Private Stream As System.IO.FileStream
Private Reader As System.IO.StreamReader

Public ReadOnly Property Filename() As String
    Get
        Return _Filename
    End Get
End Property

Public ReadOnly Property DataAvailable() As Boolean
    Get
        Return _DataAvailable
    End Get
End Property

Public Sub New(ByVal filename As String)
    ' Make sure we are using a fully-qualified path
    ' (in case the working directory changes before the print job starts).
    _Filename = System.IO.Path.GetFullPath(filename)
    If Not System.IO.File.Exists(_Filename) Then
        Throw New System.IO.FileNotFoundException(_Filename)
    End If
End Sub

Protected Overrides Sub OnBeginPrint( _
  ByVal e As System.Drawing.Printing.PrintEventArgs)
    ' Open the file.
    Stream = New System.IO.FileStream(Filename, IO.FileMode.Open)
    Reader = New System.IO.StreamReader(Stream)
    _DataAvailable = True
End Sub

Protected Overrides Sub OnEndPrint( _
  ByVal e As System.Drawing.Printing.PrintEventArgs)
    ' Close the file.
    Reader.Close()
    Stream.Close()
    Stream = Nothing
    Reader = Nothing
    _DataAvailable = False
End Sub
```

```
Public Function ReadWord() As String
    If Reader Is Nothing Then
        Throw New ApplicationException("File not open.")
    End If

    Dim Character As Char
    Dim CharNumber As Integer
    Dim Word As New System.Text.StringBuilder()

    ' This loop adds letters until a whole word is finished.
    ' The word is deemed complete when the file ends
    ' or a space is encountered.
    Do
        ' Read a single character out of the file.
        ' A -1 signals the end of the file.
        CharNumber = Reader.Read()
        If CharNumber <> -1 Then
            Character = Chr(CharNumber)
            Word.Append(Character)
        End If
    Loop Until Character = " " Or CharNumber = -1

    ' Set a property to indicate when the file is out of data.
    If CharNumber = -1 Then
        _DataAvailable = False
    End If

    Return Word.ToString()
End Function

End Class
```

The client application creates a *TextFileDocument* instance (supplying the filename to read), attaches an event handler, and starts printing:

```
' Create the document and attach an event handler.
Dim MyDoc As TextFileDocument
Try
    MyDoc = New TextFileDocument(Application.StartupPath & "\text.txt")
Catch Err As System.IO.FileNotFoundException
    MessageBox.Show("File not found.")
    Return
End Try

AddHandler MyDoc.PrintPage, AddressOf MyDoc_PrintPage

' Allow the user to choose a printer and specify other settings.
Dim dlgSettings As New PrintDialog()
```

```
dlgSettings.Document = MyDoc
Dim Result As DialogResult = dlgSettings.ShowDialog()

' If the user clicked OK, print the document.
If Result = DialogResult.OK Then
    ' This method returns immediately, before the print job starts.
    ' The PrintPage event will fire asynchronously.
    MyDoc.Print()
End If
```

Finally, the printing code reads the words one by one and wraps the text manually.

```
Private Sub MyDoc_PrintPage(ByVal sender As Object, _
  ByVal e As PrintPageEventArgs)

    ' Retrieve the TextFileDocument that is being printed.
    Dim Doc As TextFileDocument = CType(sender, TextFileDocument)

    ' Define the font and text.
    Dim Font As New Font("Arial", 15)
    Dim LineHeight As Single = Font.GetHeight(e.Graphics)

    ' Create variables to hold position on page.
    Dim x As Single = e.MarginBounds.Left
    Dim y As Single = e.MarginBounds.Top
    Dim Threshold As Integer = 200

    ' Contains a single printed line.
    Dim Line As New System.Text.StringBuilder()

    Do
        ' Add one word to the current line.
        Line.Append(Doc.ReadWord())

        ' It's time to decide whether to print the line or add another word.
        Dim LineString As String = Line.ToString()
        If e.Graphics.MeasureString(LineString, Font).Width > _
          (e.PageBounds.Width - Threshold) Then
            e.Graphics.DrawString(LineString, Font, Brushes.Black, x, y)
            y += LineHeight
            Line = New System.Text.StringBuilder()
        End If
    Loop While Doc.DataAvailable

    ' Print the last line.
    e.Graphics.DrawString(Line.ToString(), Font, Brushes.Black, x, y)

End Sub
```

12.7 Display a Dynamic Print Preview

Problem

You want to use an on-screen preview that shows how a printed document will look.

Solution

Use the *PrintPreviewControl* or *PrintPreviewDialog*.

Discussion

As described earlier, the code used to print a document to a page is almost identical to the code used to draw graphics on a window. This makes it possible for you to create code that can print or draw a print preview with equal ease. However, you don't need to go to this extra step because .NET already provides a control that can take a print document, run your printing code, and use it to generate a graphical on-screen preview. In fact, .NET provides two such controls: *PrintPreviewDialog*, which shows a preview in a standalone window, and *PrintPreviewControl*, which shows a preview in one of your own custom forms.

To use a standalone print preview, you simply create a *PrintPrevewDialog* object, assign the document, and call the *PrintPreviewDialog.Show* method.

```
Dim dlgPreview As New PrintPreviewDialog()
dlgPreview.Document = MyDoc
dlgPreview.Show()
```

The print preview window (shown in Figure 12-4) provides all the controls the user needs to move from page to page, zoom in, and so on. The window even provides a print button that allows the user to send the document directly to the printer. You can tailor the window to some extent by modifying the *PrintPreviewDialog* properties.

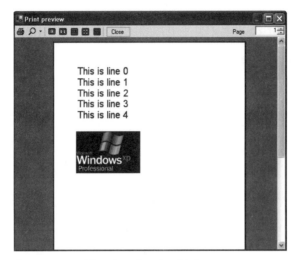

Figure 12-4   The *PrintPreviewDialog*.

You can also add the *PrintPreviewControl* to any of your forms to show a preview alongside other information. Visual Studio .NET will then add the following control declaration to the designer code:

```
Friend WithEvents Preview As System.Windows.Forms.PrintPreviewControl
```

In this case, you don't need to call the *Show* method. As soon as you set the *PrintPreviewControl.Document* property, the preview is generated. To clear the preview, set the *Document* property to *Nothing*, and to refresh the preview, simply reassign the *Document* property.

```
Preview.Document = MyDoc
```

PrintPreviewControl only shows the preview pages, not any additional controls. However, you can add your own controls for zooming, tiling multiple pages, and so on. You simply need to adjust the *PrintPreviewControl* properties accordingly.

For example, the following code changes the zoom to 20 percent.

```
Preview.Zoom = 0.2
```

This code shows a two-by-three grid of pages (allowing up to six pages to be shown at the same time):

```
Preview.Columns = 2
Preview.Rows = 3
```

Figure 12-5 shows the *PrintPreviewControl* in a custom window with some added controls for zooming.

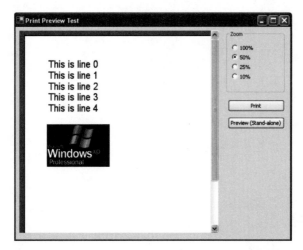

Figure 12-5   The *PrintPreviewControl* in a custom window.

12.8 Retrieve Print Queue Information

Problem

You want to determine the status of all jobs in the print queue.

Solution

Use Windows Management Instrumentation to perform a query with the *Win32_PrintJob* class.

Discussion

Windows Management Instrumentation, or *WMI*, allows you to retrieve a vast amount of system information using a query-like syntax. One of the tasks you can perform with WMI is to retrieve a list of outstanding print jobs, along with information about each one.

In order to use WMI, you need to add a reference to the System.Management.dll assembly. You should then import the *System.Management* namespace. The following code assumes you have added a reference to the System.Management.dll assembly. It retrieves a list of all the print jobs in the queue and displays information about each one in the Console window.

```vb
Public Module PrintQueueTest

    Public Sub Main()
        ' Select all the outstanding print jobs.
        ' You could customize this expression to get jobs from a
        ' specific printer or user.
        Dim Query As String = "SELECT * FROM Win32_PrintJob"
        Dim JobQuery As New ManagementObjectSearcher(query)
        Dim Jobs As ManagementObjectCollection = JobQuery.Get()

        ' Display information for all jobs in the queue.
        Dim Job As ManagementObject
        For Each Job In Jobs
            Console.WriteLine("Caption: " & Job("Caption"))
            Console.WriteLine("DataType: " & Job("DataType"))
            Console.WriteLine("Description: " & Job("Description"))
            Console.WriteLine("Document: " & Job("Document"))
            Console.WriteLine("DriverName: " & Job("DriverName"))
            Console.WriteLine("ElapsedTime: " & Job("ElapsedTime"))
            Console.WriteLine("HostPrintQueue: " & Job("HostPrintQueue"))
            Console.WriteLine("InstallDate: " & Job("InstallDate"))
            Console.WriteLine("JobId: " & Job("JobId").ToString())
            Console.WriteLine("JobStatus: " & Job("JobStatus"))
            Console.WriteLine("Name: " & Job("Name"))
            Console.WriteLine("Notify: " & Job("Notify"))
            Console.WriteLine("Owner: " & Job("Owner"))
            Console.WriteLine("PagesPrinted: " & _
              Job("PagesPrinted").ToString())
            Console.WriteLine("Parameters: " & Job("Parameters"))
            Console.WriteLine("PrintProcessor: " & Job("PrintProcessor"))
            Console.WriteLine("Priority: " & Job("Priority").ToString())
            Console.WriteLine("Size: " & Job("Size").ToString())
            Console.WriteLine("StartTime: " & Job("StartTime"))
            Console.WriteLine("Status: " & Job("Status"))
            Console.WriteLine("StatusMask: " & Job("StatusMask").ToString())
            Console.WriteLine("TimeSubmitted: " & Job("TimeSubmitted"))
            Console.WriteLine("TotalPages: " & Job("TotalPages").ToString())
            Console.WriteLine("UntilTime: " & Job("UntilTime"))
        Next

        Console.ReadLine()
    End Sub

End Module
```

Here's the sample output you might see if the queue holds a single job:

```
Caption: Acrobat Distiller, 58
DataType: RAW
Description: Acrobat Distiller, 58
Document: http://www.google.ca/
DriverName: AdobePS Acrobat Distiller
ElapsedTime:
HostPrintQueue: \\FARIAMAT
InstallDate:
JobId: 58
JobStatus: Paused | Printing
Name: Acrobat Distiller, 58
Notify: Matthew
Owner: Matthew
PagesPrinted: 0
Parameters:
PrintProcessor: WinPrint
Priority: 1
Size: 2293760
StartTime:
Status: Degraded
StatusMask: 17
TimeSubmitted: 20030117095826.632000-300
TotalPages: 1
UntilTime:
```

Note To test this code, you might want to pause a printer (using the Printers and Faxes window) and then print a document. As long as the printer is paused, the document will remain in the queue.

This example assumes that you don't have *Option Explicit* enabled. If you do, you will need to check for a null reference before you can retrieve the *Job* properties, and then call the *ToString* method to convert each piece of the job information to a string. For example, the *InstallDate* field is not always available. In order to display this information if it exists without causing an error if it doesn't, you must use the following lengthier code:

```
Console.WriteLine("InstallDate: ")
If Not Job("InstallDate") Is Nothing
    Console.WriteLine(Job("InstallDate").ToString())
End If
```

12.9 Manage Print Jobs

Problem

You want to pause or resume a print job or print queue.

Solution

Use the *Pause* and *Resume* methods of the WMI *Win32_PrintJob* and *Win32_Printer* classes.

Discussion

WMI isn't limited to information retrieval tasks (such as those shown in recipe 12.8). You can also execute certain WMI class methods to interact with the Windows operating system. One example is the *Pause* and *Resume* methods that allow you to manage printers and print jobs.

The following Console application provides a straightforward example. Every time the application finds a print job in the queue, it checks to see if the job or the printer is paused. If so, it tries to resume the job or the printer. Note that Windows permissions might prevent you from pausing or removing a print job created by another user. In fact, depending on the permissions of the current user account, a *System.Management.ManagementException* exception may be thrown when you attempt to retrieve status information for a print job.

```
Public Module PrintQueueTest

    Public Sub Main()
        ' Select all the outstanding print jobs.
        Dim Query As String = "SELECT * FROM Win32_PrintJob"
        Dim JobQuery As New ManagementObjectSearcher(Query)
        Dim Jobs As ManagementObjectCollection = JobQuery.Get()

        ' Examine all jobs in the queue.
        Dim Job As ManagementObject
        For Each Job In Jobs
            ' Check if the job is paused (has Status 1).
            If (CType(Job("StatusMask").ToString(), Integer) And 1) = 1 Then
                Console.WriteLine("Job is paused. Attempting to resume.")

                ' Attempt to resume the job.
                Dim ReturnValue As Integer
                ReturnValue = CType( _
                  Job.InvokeMethod("Resume", Nothing).ToString(), Integer)
```

```
            ' Display information about the return value.
            If ReturnValue = 0 Then
                Console.WriteLine("Successfully resumed job.")
            ElseIf ReturnValue = 5 Then
                Console.WriteLine("Access denied.")
            Else
                Console.WriteLine( _
                    "Unrecognized return value when resuming job.")
            End If
        End If


        ' Find the corresponding printer for this job.
        Query = "SELECT * FROM Win32_Printer WHERE DriverName='" & _
          Job("DriverName") & "'"

        Dim PrinterQuery As New ManagementObjectSearcher(Query)
        Dim Printers As ManagementObjectCollection = PrinterQuery.Get()

        ' Examine each matching printer (should be exactly one match).
        Dim Printer As ManagementObject
        For Each Printer In Printers
            ' Check if the printer is paused
            ' (has ExtendedPrinterStatus 8).
            If (CType(Printer("ExtendedPrinterStatus").ToString(), _
              Integer) And 8) = 8 Then
                Console.WriteLine("Printer is paused. " & _
                  "Attempting to resume.")

                ' Attempt to resume the printer.
                Dim ReturnValue As Integer
                ReturnValue = Val(Printer.InvokeMethod( _
                  "Resume", Nothing).ToString())

                ' Display information about the return value.
                If ReturnValue = 0 Then
                    Console.WriteLine( _
                      "Successfully resumed printing.")
                ElseIf ReturnValue = 5 Then
                    Console.WriteLine("Access denied.")
                Else
                    Console.WriteLine( _
                        "Unrecognized return value when resuming printer.")
                End If
            End If
        Next
    Next
```

```
        Console.ReadLine()
    End Sub

End Module
```

Other WMI methods that you might use in a printing scenario include *AddPrinterConnection*, *SetDefaultPrinter*, *CancelAllJobs*, and *PrintTestPage*, all of which work with the *Win32_Printer* class. For more information about using WMI to retrieve information about Windows hardware, refer to the MSDN documentation at *http://msdn.microsoft.com/library/en-us/wmisdk/wmi/computer_system_hardware_classes.asp*.

> **Note**   The *Pause* and *Resume* methods might not be supported in versions of Windows earlier than Windows XP. In that case, you might need to use Windows API functions such as the *SetPrinter* function from winspool.drv.

12.10 Find All Installed Fonts

Problem

You want to retrieve a list of all the fonts on the current computer.

Solution

Create a new instance of the *System.Drawing.Text.InstalledFontCollection* class, which contains a collection of *FontFamily* objects representing all the installed fonts.

Discussion

The *InstalledFontCollection* class allows you to retrieve information about currently installed fonts. The following code uses this technique to fill a list box named *lstFonts* with a list of valid font names:

```
Dim FontFamilies As New System.Drawing.Text.InstalledFontCollection()

Dim Family As FontFamily
For Each Family In FontFamilies.Families
    lstFonts.Items.Add(Family.Name)
Next
```

When an entry is chosen in the list box, the font of a label control is updated:

```
Private Sub lstFonts_SelectedIndexChanged(ByVal sender As System.Object, _
    ByVal e As System.EventArgs) Handles lstFonts.SelectedIndexChanged

    lblSample.Font = New Font(lstFonts.Text, 30)

End Sub
```

Figure 12-6 shows a screen shot of this simple test application.

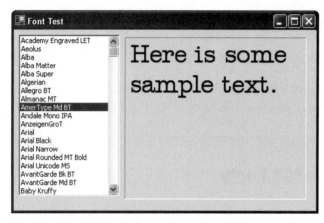

Figure 12-6   Testing fonts.

12.11 Convert the Format of an Image

Problem

You want to batch convert the format of one or more image files.

Solution

Use the *Image.FromFile* method to load the image, and use the *Image.Save* method overload that allows you to specify a new *ImageFormat*.

Discussion

.NET includes an impressive set of image-processing features. The core class is *System.Drawing.Image*, which allows you to open and save multiple types of images. The *Image* class supports the following formats:

- Bitmap (BMP)

- Enhanced Windows metafile image (EMF)

- Exchangeable Image File (EXIF)

- Graphics Interchange Format (GIF)

- Windows icon (ICO)

- Joint Photographic Experts Group (JPEG)

- Memory bitmap (BMP)

- W3C Portable Network Graphics (PNG)

- Tag Image File Format (TIFF)

- Windows metafile (WMF)

These formats are defined by the *ImageFormat* class in the *System.Drawing.Imaging* namespace. Using the *Image* class and the *ImageFormat* class, you can specify a new format to use when saving a file. The Console application shown here uses this technique—it reads all the BMP files in a directory and saves JPEG versions of each one. In order to use this code as written, you must import the *System.Drawing*, *System.Drawing.Imaging* and *System.IO* namespaces.

```
Public Module ImageConverter

    Public Sub Main()
        Dim Dir As New DirectoryInfo(Directory.GetCurrentDirectory())
        Console.WriteLine("Processing images in " & Dir.FullName)

        ' Retrieve all the bitmap files in this directory.
        Dim File As FileInfo
        For Each File In Dir.GetFiles("*.bmp")
            Console.WriteLine("Converting: " & File.Name)

            ' Load the image into memory.
            Dim Image As Image = Image.FromFile(File.FullName)

            ' Create a new filename.
            Dim JpgName As String
            JpgName = Path.GetFileNameWithoutExtension(File.FullName) & ".jpg"

            ' Save the filename as a JPEG.
            Image.Save(JpgName, ImageFormat.Jpeg)
            Console.WriteLine("Saved: " & JpgName)

            Console.WriteLine()
        Next
```

```
        Console.ReadLine()
    End Sub

End Module
```

Not only can you convert between any image file types, but you can also specify additional parameters that influence how the image data is processed. For example, you might change the compression of a TIFF file to the quality of a JPEG file. You can do this using *Encoder* objects, which you supply to an overloaded version of the *Image.Save* method. Many useful *Encoder* objects can be retrieved from the shared properties of the *System.Drawing.Imaging.Encoder* class. These properties include *ChrominanceTable*, *ColorDepth*, *Compression*, *LuminanceTable*, *Quality*, *RenderMethod*, *SaveFlag*, *ScanMethod*, *Transformation*, and *Version*.

More information is available in the MSDN reference. In addition, the next example shows how you can use an *Encoder* object to save JPEG files with different quality parameters.

```
Public Module ImageConverter

    Public Sub Main()

        ' Get an ImageCodecInfo object that represents the JPEG codec.
        ' This is accomplished by searching for the corresponding MIME type.
        Dim CodecInfo As ImageCodecInfo = GetEncoderInfo("image/jpeg")

        ' Create an Encoder object based for the Quality parameter.
        Dim Enc As Encoder = Encoder.Quality

        ' Create the array that will hold all encoding parameters.
        ' In this case, it will only hold the quality parameter.
        Dim EncParams As New EncoderParameters(1)

        Dim Dir As New DirectoryInfo(Directory.GetCurrentDirectory())
        Console.WriteLine("Processing images in " & Dir.FullName)

        ' Retrieve all the bitmap files in the current directory.
        Dim File As FileInfo
        For Each File In Dir.GetFiles("*.bmp")
            Console.WriteLine("Converting: " & File.Name)

            ' Load the image into memory.
            Dim Image As Image = Image.FromFile(File.FullName)

            ' Create a new filename.
            Dim JpgName As String
```

```
                        ' Save the bitmap as a JPEG file with quality level 25.
                        EncParams.Param(0) = New EncoderParameter(Enc, 25L)
                        JpgName = Path.GetFileNameWithoutExtension(File.FullName) & _
                            "25" & ".jpg"
                        Image.Save(JpgName, CodecInfo, EncParams)
                        Console.WriteLine("Saved: " & JpgName)

                        ' Save the bitmap as a JPEG file with quality level 50.
                        EncParams.Param(0) = New EncoderParameter(Enc, 50L)
                        JpgName = Path.GetFileNameWithoutExtension(File.FullName) & _
                            "50" & ".jpg"
                        Image.Save(JpgName, CodecInfo, EncParams)
                        Console.WriteLine("Saved: " & JpgName)

                        ' Save the bitmap as a JPEG file with quality level 75.
                        EncParams.Param(0) = New EncoderParameter(Enc, 75L)
                        JpgName = Path.GetFileNameWithoutExtension(File.FullName) & _
                            "75" & ".jpg"
                        Image.Save(JpgName, CodecInfo, EncParams)
                        Console.WriteLine("Saved: " & JpgName)

                        Console.WriteLine()
                Next

                Console.ReadLine()
        End Sub

        Private Function GetEncoderInfo(ByVal mimeType As String) _
            As ImageCodecInfo
                Dim i As Integer
                Dim Encoders() As ImageCodecInfo = ImageCodecInfo.GetImageEncoders()
                For i = 0 To Encoders.Length - 1
                        If Encoders(i).MimeType = mimeType Then
                                Return Encoders(i)
                        End If
                Next
                Return Nothing
        End Function

End Module
```

The output for this console application will look like this:

```
Processing images in C:\Temp\Recipe 12-11\bin
Converting: test.bmp
Saved: test25.jpg
Saved: test50.jpg
Saved: test75.jpg
```

12.12 Paint Static Content

Problem

You want to draw custom elements on a form and make sure they are not erased when the form is minimized or obscured.

Solution

Place all your drawing code in an event handler for the *Control.Paint* or *Form.Paint* events.

Discussion

When any part of a form disappears from view, Windows automatically discards all of its graphical information. When the form reappears, Windows fires the *Paint* event to instruct the form to redraw itself. Thus, any custom painting logic should always be coded in a *Paint* event handler so that the window is refreshed accurately. To make matters even easier, the *Paint* event always provides a *PaintEventArgs* parameter. This *PaintEventArgs* references a *Graphics* object that represents the drawing surface for the control or the form. You use the *Graphics* object's methods to draw text, shapes, or images.

Here's an example that draws a gradient rectangle on the background of the form (as shown in Figure 12-7):

```
Private Sub TestForm_Paint(ByVal sender As Object, _
  ByVal e As System.Windows.Forms.PaintEventArgs) Handles MyBase.Paint

    Dim Rectangle As New Rectangle(5, 5, Me.ClientRectangle.Width - 10, _
      Me.ClientRectangle.Height - 10)

    ' Draw the rectangle border.
    Dim DrawingPen As New Pen(Color.Blue, 2)
    e.Graphics.DrawRectangle(DrawingPen, Rectangle)

    ' Fill the rectangle with a gradient.
    Dim DrawingBrush As New _
      System.Drawing.Drawing2D.LinearGradientBrush( _
      Rectangle, Color.Blue, Color.Gold, 45)
    e.Graphics.FillRectangle(DrawingBrush, Rectangle)

End Sub
```

Figure 12-7   A form with a gradient rectangle.

In this example, the drawing code uses the size of the form. Thus, it's a good idea to add an additional bit of logic to invalidate the form if the size changes, ensuring that the form will be redrawn with a gradient background that fills the form:

```
Private Sub Form1_Resize(ByVal sender As Object, _
  ByVal e As System.EventArgs) Handles MyBase.Resize

    ' Indicate that the form is no longer valid,
    ' and Windows should trigger a repaint.
    Me.Invalidate()

End Sub
```

This approach is easy to implement for static forms in which the graphical content is always the same. In this case, you can hardcode the drawing logic in the *Paint* event handler. It's not as easy if you are using a dynamic form, in which the graphical content changes. In that case, you will need to use form-level variables to track the drawn content so that it can be refreshed in the *Paint* event handler. This approach is shown in recipe 12.13.

12.13 Paint Dynamic Content

Problem

You want to draw a combination of elements on a form and track them so that they can be redrawn later.

Solution

Place all your drawing code in an event handler for the *Form.Paint* event. When you need to update the form, call the *Form.Invalidate* method.

Discussion

In many applications, drawing takes place in response to another action, such as a user clicking a button or clicking directly on the form surface. Consider the example shown in Figure 12-8, in which the user can draw a small square object anywhere on a form simply by clicking with the mouse.

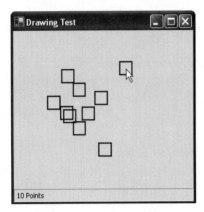

Figure 12-8   Custom drawing.

In this case, you have two choices:

■ **Use drawing *and* refreshing logic.**   When the user clicks on the form, draw the square and store some information about it. When the *Paint* event fires, redraw all the squares that have been drawn so far.

■ **Use invalidation.**   When the user clicks on the form, store some information about the square and invalidate the portion of the form where the user clicked. Then Windows will fire the *Paint* event and refresh that portion of the screen.

In most cases, the second option is the most elegant because it concentrates all your drawing logic into a single function. The following code shows how you would implement this approach.

```
Public Class DrawTest
    Inherits System.Windows.Forms.Form

    ' (Designer code omitted.)
```

```
' This ArrayList tracks the user-drawn shapes.
Private Points As New ArrayList()

Private Sub DrawTest_Paint(ByVal sender As Object, _
  ByVal e As System.Windows.Forms.PaintEventArgs) Handles MyBase.Paint
    Dim DrawingPen As New Pen(Color.Blue, 2)

    ' Draw all the shapes that have been drawn so far.
    Dim Point As Rectangle
    For Each Point In Points
        e.Graphics.DrawRectangle(DrawingPen, Point)
    Next
    pnlPoints.Text = " " & Points.Count.ToString() & " Points"
End Sub

Private Sub DrawTest_MouseDown(ByVal sender As Object, _
  ByVal e As System.Windows.Forms.MouseEventArgs) Handles MyBase.MouseDown
    If e.Button = MouseButtons.Left Then
        ' Define the new shape.
        Dim Point As New Rectangle(e.X, e.Y, 20, 20)

        ' Store the shape for later refreshes.
        Points.Add(Point)

        ' Invalidate the portion of the form where the new shape will be.
        ' Windows will call your Paint event, and update only this region.
        Me.Invalidate(Rectangle.Inflate(Point, 3, 3))
    End If
End Sub

End Class
```

When you invalidate a portion of the form, all your drawing code will execute. However, Windows will only refresh the portion of the form that you specified when calling the *Invalidate* method. That means that screen flicker will be kept to a minimum, but the drawing speed might decrease if the logic in your *Paint* event handler is very complex or time-consuming. In that case, it would be better to use separate drawing and refreshing logic, as shown here:

```
Public Class DrawTest
    Inherits System.Windows.Forms.Form

    ' (Designer code omitted.)

    ' This ArrayList tracks the user-drawn shapes.
    Private Points As New ArrayList()
```

```
            Private Sub DrawTest_Paint(ByVal sender As Object, _
              ByVal e As System.Windows.Forms.PaintEventArgs) Handles MyBase.Paint
                ' Draw all the shapes that have been drawn so far.
                Dim Point As Rectangle
                For Each Point In Points
                    DrawShape(e.Graphics, Point)
                Next
                pnlPoints.Text = " " & Points.Count.ToString() & " Points"
            End Sub

            Private Sub DrawTest_MouseDown(ByVal sender As Object, _
              ByVal e As System.Windows.Forms.MouseEventArgs) Handles MyBase.MouseDown
                If e.Button = MouseButtons.Left Then
                    ' Define the new shape.
                    Dim Point As New Rectangle(e.X, e.Y, 20, 20)

                    ' Store the shape for later refreshes.
                    Points.Add(Point)

                    ' Draw the shape.
                    ' Note that you need to explicitly create the
                    ' GDI+ drawing surface for the form.
                    Dim g As Graphics = Me.CreateGraphics()
                    DrawShape(g, Point)
                    g.Dispose()
                    pnlPoints.Text = " " & Points.Count.ToString() & " Points"
                End If
            End Sub

            Private Sub DrawShape(ByVal g As Graphics, ByVal shape As Rectangle)
                ' Draw the actual shape using the supplied Graphics object.
                Dim DrawingPen As New Pen(Color.Blue, 2)
                g.DrawRectangle(DrawingPen, shape)
            End Sub

        End Class
```

12.14 Use System Colors

Problem

You want to use system-defined colors when drawing.

Solution

Use the properties of the *System.Drawing.SystemColors* class.

Discussion

When mixing standard Windows interface elements with your own drawing code, you need to take special care that you follow the system color scheme. Otherwise, you might end up with illegible text—or just garishly ugly windows.

Retrieving system color information is easy. You can simply use the shared properties of the *System.Drawing.SystemColors* class. In addition, you can use the *System.Drawing.KnownColors* enumeration to retrieve a list of friendly (human-readable) color names and system color names.

Here's an example that draws text on a form using the background and foreground colors of the form title bar:

```
Private Sub Form_Paint(ByVal sender As Object, _
  ByVal e As System.Windows.Forms.PaintEventArgs) Handles MyBase.Paint

    Dim BrushText As New SolidBrush(SystemColors.ActiveCaptionText)
    Dim BrushBackground As New SolidBrush(SystemColors.ActiveCaption)

    e.Graphics.FillRectangle(BrushBackground, 5, 5, _
      Me.ClientRectangle.Width - 10, Me.ClientRectangle.Height - 10)
    e.Graphics.DrawString("Test", New Font("Arial", 14), BrushText, 10, 10)

End Sub
```

12.15 Improve the Rendering Quality

Problem

You want to ensure that drawn shapes are rendered in the best possible detail.

Solution

Set the *SmoothingMode* and *TextRenderingHint* properties of the *Graphics* object before drawing.

Discussion

The *Graphics* object provides two stateful properties that configure the rendering quality. *SmoothingMode* allows you to use automatic antialiasing, which improves the look of curves with shading. For example, if you draw a black circle on a white background, antialiasing might add a small amount of gray shading to take away the jaggedness. *TextRenderingHint* performs analogous control that affects text you draw using the *Graphics.DrawString* method.

The following code snippet draws two ellipses with two captions, using the default quality first and then a higher-quality version. Figure 12-9 shows the results.

```
Private Sub Form_Paint(ByVal sender As Object, _
    ByVal e As System.Windows.Forms.PaintEventArgs) Handles MyBase.Paint

    Dim Pen As New Pen(Color.Green, 3)
    Dim Font As New Font("Arial", 12, FontStyle.Bold)

    ' Draw using the default quality.
    e.Graphics.DrawEllipse(Pen, 10, 10, 200, 200)
    e.Graphics.DrawString("Low Quality", Font, Brushes.Black, 50, 220)

    ' Specify higher-quality antialiasing.
    e.Graphics.SmoothingMode = Drawing.Drawing2D.SmoothingMode.AntiAlias
    e.Graphics.TextRenderingHint = _
        Drawing.Text.TextRenderingHint.ClearTypeGridFit
    e.Graphics.DrawEllipse(Pen, 250, 10, 200, 200)
    e.Graphics.DrawString("High Quality", Font, Brushes.Black, 300, 220)

End Sub
```

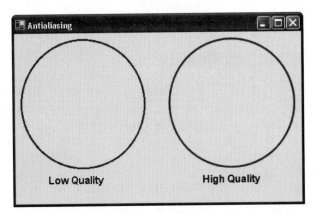

Figure 12-9 Customizing rendering quality.

> **Note** By default, no aliasing is used for drawing shapes. Thus, it's often advantageous to modify the *SmoothingMode* property if drawing speed isn't a concern. On the other hand, the default text quality depends on system settings. The text quality setting is usually configured to use antialiasing already (or advanced optimizations for LCD screens), and thus doesn't need to be modified in your code.

12.16 Perform Hit Testing with Shapes

Problem

You want to detect if a user clicks inside a shape.

Solution

Test the point where the user clicked with the *Rectangle.Contains* or *Graphics-Path.IsVisible* method.

Discussion

If you are creating a program that has custom graphical elements the user can interact with, you need to be able to determine when the user's mouse is inside or outside a given shape. The .NET Framework provides two methods that can help with this task. The first is the *Rectangle.Contains* method, which takes a point and returns *True* if the point is inside the rectangle.

For example, you might add the following code to the drawing program demonstrated in recipe 12.13 to check if the point where the user right-clicked lies inside any of the squares on the form.

```
Private Sub DrawTest_MouseDown(ByVal sender As Object, _
  ByVal e As System.Windows.Forms.MouseEventArgs) Handles MyBase.MouseDown

    If e.Button = MouseButtons.Left Then
        ' (Drawing code omitted.)

    ElseIf e.Button = MouseButtons.Right Then
        ' Check if a square was clicked.
        Dim Point As Rectangle
        Dim Inside As Boolean = False
        For Each Point in Points
            If Point.Contains(e.X, e.Y) Then
                Inside = True
            End If
        Next

        If Inside Then
            MessageBox.Show("Point lies in a square.")
        Else
            MessageBox.Show("Point does not lie in a square.")
        End If
    End If

End Sub
```

In many cases, you can retrieve a rectangle for another type of shape. For example, you can use *Image.GetBounds* to retrieve the invisible rectangle that represents the image boundaries.

The second approach is to use the *GraphicsPath* class in the *System.Drawing.Drawing2D* namespace. This approach is useful if you want to test if a point is contained inside a non-rectangular shape. The first step is to create a new *GraphicsPath* and add the shape (or add multiple shapes) to the *GraphicsPath*. Then, you can use the *IsVisible* method with the clicked point. For example, you can create a *GraphicsPath* that contains an ellipse and a square with this code:

```
Dim Path As New System.Drawing.Drawing2D.GraphicsPath()

Private Sub Form_Load(ByVal sender As System.Object, _
   ByVal e As System.EventArgs) Handles MyBase.Load

    Path.AddEllipse(60, 60, 100, 100)
    Path.AddRectangle(New Rectangle(10, 10, 50, 50))

End Sub
```

The painting code draws and fills the *GraphicsPath*:

```
Private Sub Form_Paint(ByVal sender As Object, _
   ByVal e As System.Windows.Forms.PaintEventArgs) Handles MyBase.Paint

    e.Graphics.SmoothingMode = Drawing.Drawing2D.SmoothingMode.AntiAlias

    Dim Pen As New Pen(Color.Green, 4)
    e.Graphics.DrawPath(Pen, Path)
    e.Graphics.FillPath(Brushes.Yellow, Path)

End Sub
```

Now you can see if the user clicks inside the ellipse using *IsVisible*:

```
Private Sub Form_MouseDown(ByVal sender As Object, _
   ByVal e As System.Windows.Forms.MouseEventArgs) Handles MyBase.MouseDown

    If Path.IsVisible(e.X, e.Y) Then
        MessageBox.Show("You clicked inside the GraphicsPath.")
    End If

End Sub
```

Figure 12-10 shows the application in action.

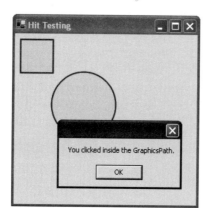

Figure 12-10 Hit testing with a *GraphicsPath* object.

12.17 Draw Picture Thumbnails

Problem

You want to draw a scaled-down version of a larger image.

Solution

Use the *Image.GetThumbnailImage* method, and specify the size of thumbnail that you want.

Discussion

The *Image* class provides the built-in smarts for generating thumbnails through the *GetThumbnailImage* method. You simply need to pass the width and height of the thumbnail you want, and the *Image* class will create a new *Image* object that fits these criteria. Antialiasing is used when reducing the image to ensure the best possible image quality, although some blurriness and loss of detail is inevitable. In addition, you can supply a notification callback, allowing you to create thumbnails asynchronously.

The following code generates a 50-by-50-pixel thumbnail:

```
Dim Img As Image = Image.FromFile("test.jpg")
Dim Thumbnail As Image = Img.GetThumbnailImage(50, 50, Nothing, Nothing)
```

When generating a thumbnail, it's important to ensure that the aspect ratio remains constant. For example, if you reduce a 200-by-100 picture to a 50-by-50 thumbnail, the width will be compressed to one quarter and the height will be compressed to one half, distorting the image. To ensure that the aspect ratio remains constant, you can change *either* the width or height to a fixed size, and then adjust the other dimension proportionately.

The following code reads a graphic from a file, creates a proportional thumbnail, and then displays it on a form:

```
Private Sub Form_Paint(ByVal sender As Object, _
    ByVal e As System.Windows.Forms.PaintEventArgs) Handles MyBase.Paint

    ' Read the image from a file.
    Dim Img As Image = Image.FromFile("test.jpg")

    Dim ThumbnailWidth, ThumbnailHeight As Integer

    ' Adjust the largest dimension to a set 50 pixels.
    ' This ensures that a thumbnail will not be larger than 50x50 pixels.
    ' If you are showing multiple thumbnails, you would reserve a
    ' 50x50 pixel square for each one.
    If ThumbnailWidth > ThumbnailHeight Then
        ThumbnailWidth = 50

        ' Scale the height proportionately.
        ThumbnailHeight = CInt((50 / Img.Width) * Img.Height)
    Else
        ThumbnailHeight = 50

        ' Scale the width proportionately.
        ThumbnailWidth = CInt((50 / Img.Height) * Img.Width)
    End If

    ' Create the thumbnail.
    Img = Img.GetThumbnailImage(ThumbnailWidth, ThumbnailHeight, _
        Nothing, Nothing)

    ' Display the thumbnail.
    e.Graphics.DrawImage(Img, 10, 10)

End Sub
```

12.18 Use Double Buffering to Increase Redraw Speed

Problem

You want to optimize drawing for a form that is frequently refreshed and want to reduce flicker.

Solution

Render the graphics to an in-memory bitmap, and then copy the finalized bitmap to the form.

Discussion

In some applications you need to repaint a form or control frequently. This is commonly the case when performing animation. For example, you might use a timer to invalidate your form every second. Your painting code could then redraw an image at a new location, creating the illusion of motion. The problem with this approach is that every time you invalidate the form, Windows repaints the window background (clearing the form), and then runs your painting code, which draws the graphic element by element. This can cause substantial on-screen flicker.

Double buffering is a technique you can implement to reduce this flicker. With double buffering, your drawing logic writes to an in-memory bitmap, which is copied to the form at the end of the drawing operation in a single, seamless repaint operation. Flickering is reduced dramatically.

The first step when implementing double buffering is to ensure that the form background isn't repainted automatically when the form is invalidated. This automatic clearing is the most significant cause of flicker, because it replaces your image with a blank frame (if only for a fraction of a second). To prevent background painting, override the form's *OnPaintBackground* method so that it takes no action.

```
Protected Overrides Sub OnPaintBackground( _
   ByVal pevent As System.Windows.Forms.PaintEventArgs)

   ' Do nothing.

End Sub
```

The next step is to create the painting code. Here is an example that animates a rising and falling ball as it traces an ellipse across a form:

```vb
' Indicates whether the animation is currently being shown.
Private Animating As Boolean = False

' Track the speed and position of the ball (in the Y-axis).
Private BallInitialVelocity As Double
Private BallPosition As Double

' Track how long the ball has been in motion.
Private StartTime As DateTime

Private Sub Form_Paint(ByVal sender As Object, _
  ByVal e As System.Windows.Forms.PaintEventArgs) Handles MyBase.Paint

    ' Check if the animation is in progress.
    If Animating Then

        ' Create an in-memory bitmap with the same size as the form.
        Dim Drawing As New Bitmap(Me.ClientRectangle.Width, _
          Me.ClientRectangle.Height, e.Graphics)

        ' Get the GDI+ drawing surface for the in-memory bitmap.
        Dim g As Graphics = Graphics.FromImage(Drawing)

        g.SmoothingMode = System.Drawing.Drawing2D.SmoothingMode.HighQuality

        ' Paint the background.
        g.FillRectangle(Brushes.Yellow, New Rectangle(New Point(0, 0), _
          Me.ClientSize))

        ' Calculate the new velocity and position of the ball.
        Dim Elapsed As Double = DateTime.Now.Subtract(StartTime).TotalSeconds
        Dim BallVelocity As Double = BallInitialVelocity + 50 * Elapsed
        BallPosition += (BallVelocity * Elapsed) / 10

        ' Draw the ball.
        Dim Pen As New Pen(Color.Blue, 10)
        g.DrawEllipse(Pen, CInt(Elapsed * 100), CInt(BallPosition), 10, 10)

        ' Copy the final image to the form.
        e.Graphics.DrawImageUnscaled(Drawing, 0, 0)

        ' Release the GDI+ resources for the in-memory image.
        g.Dispose()

        If BallPosition > Me.ClientRectangle.Height Then
```

```
        ' Stop the animation.
        tmrInvalidate.Stop()
        Animating = False
    End If

Else
    ' There is no animation underway. Paint the background.
    MyBase.OnPaintBackground(e)
End If

End Sub
```

To start the animation, the user clicks a button. The event-handling code sets the initial properties of the ball and starts a timer.

```
Private Sub cmdStart_Click(ByVal sender As System.Object, _
  ByVal e As System.EventArgs) Handles cmdStart.Click

    Animating = True
    BallInitialVelocity = -100
    BallPosition = Me.ClientRectangle.Height - 10
    StartTime = DateTime.Now

    tmrInvalidate.Start()

End Sub
```

The timer simply invalidates the form (in this case, every 20 milliseconds). The result is smooth, flicker-free animation.

```
Private Sub tmrInvalidate_Tick(ByVal sender As System.Object, _
  ByVal e As System.EventArgs) Handles tmrInvalidate.Tick

    Me.Invalidate()

End Sub
```

12.19 Display an Irregularly Shaped Window

Problem

You want to create a non-rectangular form.

Solution

Create a new *Region* object that has the shape you want for the form, and assign it to the *Form.Region* property.

Discussion

To create a non-rectangular form, you first need to define the shape you want. The easiest approach is to use the *System.Drawing.Drawing2D.GraphicsPath* object, which can accommodate any combination of ellipses, rectangles, and closed curves. You can add shapes to a *GraphicsPath* instance using methods such as *AddEllipse*, *AddRectangle*, and *AddClosedCurve*. Once you are finished defining the shape you want, you can create a *Region* object from this *GraphicsPath*—just submit the *GraphicsPath* in the *Region* class constructor. Finally, you can assign the *Region* to the form.

In the example that follows, an irregularly shaped form (shown in Figure 12-11) is created using two curves made of multiple points, which are converted into a closed figure using the *GraphicsPath.CloseAllFigures* method.

```
Private Sub Form1_Load(ByVal sender As System.Object, _
  ByVal e As System.EventArgs) Handles MyBase.Load

   Dim Path As New System.Drawing.Drawing2D.GraphicsPath()
   Dim PointsA() As Point = {New Point(0, 0), New Point(40, 60), _
     New Point(Me.Width - 100, 10)}
   Path.AddCurve(PointsA)

   Dim PointsB() As Point = {New Point(Me.Width - 40, Me.Height - 60), _
     New Point(Me.Width, Me.Height), New Point(10, Me.Height)}
   Path.AddCurve(PointsB)

   Path.CloseAllFigures()

   Me.Region = New Region(Path)

End Sub
```

Figure 12-11   A non-rectangular form.

> **Note**   When creating a non-rectangular form, you may omit the title
> bar portion, which will make it impossible for the user to move the
> form. If you want to add this ability using custom code, refer to rec-
> ipe 11.17.

12.20 Create an Owner-Drawn Menu

Problem

You want to create a menu that includes pictures, formatted text, or colored
item backgrounds.

Solution

Set the *OwnerDraw* property to *True* for each *MenuItem* control you want to
draw, and handle the *MeasureItem* and *DrawItem* events.

Discussion

The *MenuItem* class that is included with the .NET Framework is fairly limited.
It doesn't provide any ability to change menu font, colors, or even add the common thumbnail icon. To add any of these enhancements, you'll need to combine your menu with custom drawing logic.

Fortunately, .NET makes it easy to replace the standard drawing logic with
your own custom code. All you need to do is set the *OwnerDraw* property for
a *MenuItem* to *True*. A context menu or main menu can contain a mix of
owner-drawn and ordinary menu items, but typically you will perform the
drawing work for all items except the top-level headings. Regardless of whether
a menu item is owner-drawn or not, it will have its standard appearance in the
Visual Studio .NET design-time environment.

Once you set the *OwnerDraw* property to *True*, you must handle two
MenuItem events. First you must respond to the *MeasureItem* event to indicate
the size the menu item should have. Second you must respond to the *DrawItem*
event to actually draw the shapes, the text, and the images on the provided
GDI+ surface, which represents the menu item.

The following example shows a basic implementation of an owner-drawn
menu that uses the default menu font and colors. These event handlers are used

to draw three different menu items. The appearance of these menu items is very similar to the normal menu control.

```
Private Sub mnu_MeasureItem(ByVal sender As System.Object, _
  ByVal e As System.Windows.Forms.MeasureItemEventArgs) _
  Handles mnuNew.MeasureItem, mnuOpen.MeasureItem, mnuSave.MeasureItem

    ' Retrieve current item.
    Dim mnuItem As MenuItem = CType(sender, MenuItem)

    Dim MenuFont As New Font("Tahoma", 8)

    ' Measure size needed to display text.
    e.ItemHeight = CInt(e.Graphics.MeasureString( _
      mnuItem.Text, MenuFont).Height + 5)
    e.ItemWidth = CInt(e.Graphics.MeasureString( _
      mnuItem.Text, MenuFont).Width + 5)

End Sub

Private Sub mnu_DrawItem(ByVal sender As Object, _
  ByVal e As System.Windows.Forms.DrawItemEventArgs) _
  Handles mnuNew.DrawItem, mnuOpen.DrawItem, mnuSave.DrawItem

    ' Retrieve current item.
    Dim mnuItem As MenuItem = CType(sender, MenuItem)

    e.DrawBackground()

    ' Draw the text with the supplied colors and in the set region.
    e.Graphics.DrawString(mnuItem.Text, e.Font, _
      New SolidBrush(e.ForeColor), e.Bounds.Left + 7, e.Bounds.Top + 3)

End Sub
```

You can now modify this menu to add shapes, formatting, or images. The challenge when creating a custom menu is deciding how to associate the formatting-related information for the menu (such as the font size, background color, associated image, and so on) with the menu item. A good approach is to derive a custom class that includes this information by deriving from *MenuItem*. This class can also override the *OnMeasureItem* and *OnDrawItem* methods to perform the custom drawing logic in the class, so your form code won't need to handle these events.

The *ColoredMenuItem* class shown here adds three menu enhancements: support for a custom background color, support for a custom foreground color, and support for a custom font. The drawing code simply reads these values directly from the class instance.

```
Public Class ColoredMenuItem
    Inherits MenuItem

    Private _ForeColor As Color
    Private _BackColor As Color
    Private _Font As Font

    Public Property ForeColor() As Color
        Get
            Return _ForeColor
        End Get
        Set(ByVal Value As Color)
            _ForeColor = Value
        End Set
    End Property

    Public Property BackColor() As Color
        Get
            Return _BackColor
        End Get
        Set(ByVal Value As Color)
            _BackColor = Value
        End Set
    End Property

    Public Property Font() As Font
        Get
            Return _Font
        End Get
        Set(ByVal Value As Font)
            _Font = Value
        End Set
    End Property

    ' To enhance this class, you can add additional constructors that don't
    ' need all this information. In your drawing logic, you can then use
    ' default values for menu colors and the menu font if you find this
    ' information has not been supplied by the user.
    Public Sub New(ByVal text As String, ByVal foreColor As Color, _
      ByVal backColor As Color, ByVal font As Font)
        Me.Text = text
        Me.ForeColor = foreColor
        Me.BackColor = backColor
        Me.Font = font
```

```
                ' This menu item will always be owner drawn.
                Me.OwnerDraw = True
         End Sub

         Protected Overrides Sub OnMeasureItem( _
            ByVal e As System.Windows.Forms.MeasureItemEventArgs)
                ' Measure size needed to display text.
                e.ItemHeight = CInt(e.Graphics.MeasureString(Text, Font).Height + 5)
                e.ItemWidth = CInt(e.Graphics.MeasureString(Text, Font).Width + 5)
         End Sub

         Protected Overrides Sub OnDrawItem( _
            ByVal e As System.Windows.Forms.DrawItemEventArgs)
                ' Reverse the background and foreground colors
                ' if the item is selected.
                Dim ForeBrush, BackBrush As Brush
                If (e.State And DrawItemState.Selected) = DrawItemState.Selected Then
                    ForeBrush = New SolidBrush(BackColor)
                    BackBrush = New SolidBrush(ForeColor)
                Else
                    ForeBrush = New SolidBrush(ForeColor)
                    BackBrush = New SolidBrush(BackColor)
                End If

                ' Draw the menu item background.
                e.Graphics.FillRectangle(BackBrush, e.Bounds)

                ' Draw the menu item text.
                e.Graphics.DrawString(Text, Font, ForeBrush, e.Bounds.Left + 7, _
                    e.Bounds.Top + 3)
         End Sub

End Class
```

Using the *ColoredMenuItem* class is slightly more work than using the basic *MenuItem* class. The problem is that you can't design menus that use the *ColoredMenuItem* class with the Visual Studio .NET menu editor. Instead, you'll need to create and configure the menu programmatically through code.

```
Private Sub Form_Load(ByVal sender As System.Object, _
   ByVal e As System.EventArgs) Handles MyBase.Load

    ' Define the font for all menu items.
    Dim Font As New Font("Tahoma", 8, FontStyle.Bold)

    ' Create the menu items.
    Dim Blue As New ColoredMenuItem("Blue", Color.White, Color.Blue, Font)
    Dim Green As New ColoredMenuItem("Green", Color.White, Color.Green, Font)
```

```
Dim Lavender As New ColoredMenuItem("Lavender", Color.White, _
    Color.Lavender, Font)
Dim Crimson As New ColoredMenuItem("Crimson", Color.White, _
    Color.Crimson, Font)

' Add the items to the main menu.
mnuColors.MenuItems.AddRange( _
    New MenuItem() {Blue, Green, Lavender, Crimson})

End Sub
```

The custom-colored menu is shown in Figure 12-12.

Figure 12-12   An owner-drawn menu.

Using the approach shown in this recipe, you can create your own rich menus that mimic the new look of the menus in Office XP and Visual Studio .NET. However, this task requires a significant amount of carefully tweaked painting logic. An easier approach might be to adapt a menu component that has been developed by a third party. The online downloads for this book and the companion site at *http://www.prosetech.com* provide links to free sample menu controls that are available on the Internet.

12.21 Create an Owner-Drawn List Box

Problem

You want to create a list box that includes pictures, formatted text, or colored item backgrounds.

Solution

Set the list box *DrawMode* to *OwnerDrawVariable*, and handle the *Measure-Item* and *DrawItem* events.

Discussion

By implementing an owner-drawn list box, you can draw custom content in a list box item in the same way that you would draw graphics in a *Paint* event handler. The only challenge is deciding where to store item-specific graphics or formatting information.

To create a basic owner-drawn list box, set the *ListBox.DrawMode* property to *OwnerDrawVariable* (or you can use *OwnerDrawFixed* if you know that every list item will have the same height). This signals that you want to write the drawing logic for the control. Next you need to handle two events: *MeasureItem*, in which you specify the size of an item row, and *DrawItem*, in which you use the GDI+ *Graphics* class to output images, shapes, or text.

The following code shows the simplest possible owner-drawn list box. It uses a fixed item height (15 pixels), calls *ToString* on the list object and outputs the text using the current list box font. The cell is given white text if it's selected (in which case it will have a blue background). The operation of this control matches the ordinary list box behavior fairly closely.

```
Private Sub lstFonts_MeasureItem(ByVal sender As Object, _
  ByVal e As System.Windows.Forms.MeasureItemEventArgs) _
  Handles lstFonts.MeasureItem

      ' Set a fixed height.
      e.ItemHeight = 15

End Sub

Private Sub lstFonts_DrawItem(ByVal sender As Object, _
  ByVal e As System.Windows.Forms.DrawItemEventArgs) Handles lstFonts.DrawItem

    ' Draw the background.
    e.DrawBackground()

    ' Determine the color based on whether or not the item is selected.
    Dim Brush As Brush
    If (e.State And DrawItemState.Selected) = DrawItemState.Selected Then

        e.DrawFocusRectangle()
        Brush = Brushes.White
    Else
```

```
        Brush = Brushes.Black
    End If

    ' Draw the item text.
    e.Graphics.DrawString(lstFonts.Items.Item(e.Index).ToString(), _
        lstFonts.Font, Brush, e.Bounds.X, e.Bounds.Y)

End Sub
```

To create a more interesting list box, you can customize these event handlers to use different colors, formatting, or images. (This approach is shown in the QuickStart samples included with Visual Studio .NET.) However, a much better approach is to let the items themselves determine their own formatting using a custom class. This class should encapsulate all the information you need to draw the object, possibly including display text, a font, an image, a foreground and background color, and so on.

The *CustomListItem* class shown here allows each list item to specify its own font:

```
Public Class CustomListItem
    Private _Text As String
    Private _Font As Font

    Public Property Text() As String
        Get
            Return _Text
        End Get
        Set(ByVal Value As String)
            _Text = Value
        End Set
    End Property

    Public Property Font() As Font
        Get
            Return _Font
        End Get
        Set(ByVal Value As Font)
            _Font = Value
        End Set
    End Property

    Public Sub New(ByVal text As String, ByVal font As Font)
        Me.Text = text
        Me.Font = font
    End Sub
```

```
        Public Overrides Function ToString() As String
            Return Text
        End Function

    End Class
```

Now the *DrawItem* event handler retrieves the custom *CustomListItem* instance for the row and draws the text using the specified font:

```
Private Sub lstFonts_DrawItem(ByVal sender As Object, _
  ByVal e As System.Windows.Forms.DrawItemEventArgs) Handles lstFonts.DrawItem

    ' Draw the background.
    e.DrawBackground()

    ' Determine the color based on whether or not the item is selected.
    Dim Brush As Brush
    If (e.State And DrawItemState.Selected) = DrawItemState.Selected Then
        e.DrawFocusRectangle()
        Brush = Brushes.White
    Else
        Brush = Brushes.Black
    End If

    ' Get the font from the current item.
    Dim Font As Font
    Font = CType(lstFonts.Items(e.Index), CustomListItem).Font

    ' Draw the item text.
    e.Graphics.DrawString(lstFonts.Items.Item(e.Index).ToString(), _
        Font, Brush, e.Bounds.X, e.Bounds.Y)

End Sub
```

The *MeasureItem* event handler also needs to take the size of the font into consideration:

```
Private Sub lstFonts_MeasureItem(ByVal sender As Object, _
  ByVal e As System.Windows.Forms.MeasureItemEventArgs) _
  Handles lstFonts.MeasureItem

    ' Get the height from the current item's font.
    Dim Font As Font
    Font = CType(lstFonts.Items(e.Index), CustomListItem).Font
    e.ItemHeight = Font.Height

End Sub
```

To test this application, you can use the technique from recipe 12.10 to create a *CustomListItemFont* instance for every installed font. Remember, the custom-drawn content won't appear in the Visual Studio .NET design-time environment.

```
Private Sub Form_Load(ByVal sender As System.Object, _
  ByVal e As System.EventArgs) Handles MyBase.Load

    Dim FontFamilies As New System.Drawing.Text.InstalledFontCollection()

    Dim Family As FontFamily
    For Each Family In FontFamilies.Families
        Try
            Dim Font As New Font(Family.Name, 12)
            Dim Item As New CustomListItem(Family.Name, Font)
            lstFonts.Items.Add(Item)
        Catch
            ' Ignore fonts that don't support the default size.
        End Try
    Next

End Sub
```

The resulting list box is shown in Figure 12-13.

Figure 12-13   An owner-drawn list box.

Remember, you can extend this control by creating a new list item object. For example, you could create list boxes that accommodate thumbnail images by adding a property of type *Image* to the *CustomListItem* class.

13

Windows Services

Windows services are long-running applications that have no visual interface and run quietly in the background. Windows services are used to support essential services such as Internet Information Services (IIS), Microsoft SQL Server, COM+, and Message Queuing, and they typically run under a local system account and load when your computer is first started. The Windows Service Control Manager (SCM) mediates Windows services, and you can start, stop, and configure services through the Computer Management administrative console.

Unlike Microsoft Visual Basic 6, which had no intrinsic support for Windows services, .NET includes types in the *System.ServiceProcess* namespace for creating, controlling, and installing Windows services. Visual Studio .NET even provides a dedicated Windows service project type. If you create a Windows service application, Visual Studio .NET will generate a basic class that extends *System.ServiceProcess.ServiceBase*, includes the basic initialization logic required to run the service, and provides an *OnStart* and *OnStop* method where you will add your code. The *OnStart* method is triggered when the service is started by the SCM (either automatically at startup or manually), and the *OnStop* method is triggered when the service is stopped. Remember, all Windows services must perform their work asynchronously. Thus, you must use the *OnStart* code to configure a new timer, a thread, or an event handler where the actual work will take place. The *OnStop* method will detach these resources and stop any in-progress work.

> **Note** To learn more about the basics of asynchronous programming, refer to the recipes in Chapter 7.

The first two recipes in this chapter show the basic design patterns for creating a Windows service. Recipe 13.3 shows you how to install a Windows service (a necessity before you can test or use it), while recipes 13.5, 13.6, and 13.7 show how you can interact with installed Windows services, either to retrieve information or control their execution. Finally, recipe 13.8 considers how you can use a system tray to provide status information from a Windows service.

13.1 Use a Windows Service with a Timer

Problem

You want to create a Windows service that periodically "wakes up" and performs a task.

Solution

Initialize a timer when the service is started, and react to the timer events to perform your task.

Discussion

When a Windows service is launched, the SCM calls the *OnStart* method. The *OnStart* method should perform as little work as possible—in fact, if the *OnStart* method hasn't completed after 30 seconds, the SCM will abort the service completely. One possible design is to use the *OnStart* method to create a timer. The timer event-handling code will then perform the actual work.

The following example creates a Windows service that performs a task every 10 seconds. This task consists of writing a debug message and writing a single piece of information in a text file. To use this example as written, you must import the *System.ServiceProcess* and *System.Timers* namespaces.

```
Public Class TimerService
    Inherits System.ServiceProcess.ServiceBase

    Public Sub New()
        MyBase.New()
        InitializeComponent()
    End Sub

    <MTAThread()> _
    Public Shared Sub Main()
        Dim ServicesToRun() As ServiceBase
        ServicesToRun = New ServiceBase() {New TimerService}
```

```
        System.ServiceProcess.ServiceBase.Run(ServicesToRun)
End Sub

Private Sub InitializeComponent()
    Me.ServiceName = "TimerService"
End Sub

' This fires every 10 seconds.
Private WithEvents ServiceTimer As New Timer(10000)

' Track the number of timer events.
Private Counter As Integer

Protected Overrides Sub OnStart(ByVal args() As String)
    ' Start the timer.
    ServiceTimer.Start()
End Sub

Protected Overrides Sub OnStop()
    ' Stop the timer.
    ServiceTimer.Stop()
End Sub

Private Sub DoWork(ByVal sender As Object, _
  ByVal e As ElapsedEventArgs) Handles ServiceTimer.Elapsed

    Counter += 1
    Debug.WriteLine("Repetition #" & Counter.ToString())

    Try
        Dim fs As New System.IO.FileStream( _
          "c:\ServiceTest.txt", IO.FileMode.Create)
        Dim w As New System.IO.StreamWriter(fs)
        w.Write("Test #" & Counter.ToString())
        w.Flush()
        fs.Close()

    Catch Err As Exception
        Debug.WriteLine(Err.ToString())
    End Try

End Sub

End Class
```

To enhance this example, you might want to add a Boolean member variable that the *OnStop* method can set to instruct the *Timer* event handler to stop processing. This technique is shown in recipe 13.2.

> **Note** *System.Timers.Timer* is known as a *server timer*, and it differs from the *System.Windows.Forms.Timer* class you might be familiar with. A server timer, unlike a user interface timer, uses multiple threads. In other words, if you schedule a server timer to fire every 10 seconds and the task takes more than 10 seconds, more than one thread might run at once. This could cause synchronization problems. For example, if two threads run the *DoWork* method shown earlier, an error could be generated because the file cannot be accessed by two threads at once.

13.2 Use a Windows Service with a Thread

Problem

You want to create a Windows service that performs some type of long-running task continuously.

Solution

Create a new thread when the service is started, and perform all your work on that thread.

Discussion

As explained earlier, the *OnStart* method is used to set your Windows service processing in motion, but it can't perform the work directly itself. One of the most common design patterns is to use the *OnStart* method to create and start a new thread. The *OnStop* method can then terminate this thread.

This thread can process continuously, using a loop if it needs to repeat the same work. In addition, you might want to use a Boolean member variable to allow the *OnStop* method to signal a polite stop (a technique first described in recipe 7.10).

The following example shows a Windows service that loops continuously, writing debug messages. To test that it is working, you should use recipe 13.4 to attach a debugger so that you can see these messages. To use this example as written, you must import the *System.ServiceProcess* and *System.Threading* namespaces.

```vb
Public Class ThreadService
    Inherits System.ServiceProcess.ServiceBase

    Public Sub New()
        MyBase.New()
        InitializeComponent()
    End Sub

    <MTAThread()> _
    Public Shared Sub Main()
        Dim ServicesToRun() As ServiceBase
        ServicesToRun = New ServiceBase() {New ThreadService}

        System.ServiceProcess.ServiceBase.Run(ServicesToRun)
    End Sub

    Private Sub InitializeComponent()
        Me.ServiceName = "ThreadService"
    End Sub

    ' This is the thread where the actual work takes place.
    Private ServiceThread As Thread

    ' This signals the thread to stop processing.
    Private StopThread As Boolean = False

    Protected Overrides Sub OnStart(ByVal args() As String)
        ' Create and start the thread.
        ServiceThread = New Thread(AddressOf DoWork)
        ServiceThread.Start()
    End Sub

    Protected Overrides Sub OnStop()
        ' Try to signal the thread to end nicely,
        ' and wait up to 20 seconds.
        StopThread = True
        ServiceThread.Join(TimeSpan.FromSeconds(20))

        ' If the thread is still running, abort it.
        If (ServiceThread.ThreadState And _
          ThreadState.Running) = ThreadState.Running Then
            ServiceThread.Abort()
        End If
    End Sub

    Private Sub DoWork()
        Dim Counter As Integer
        Do Until StopThread
            Counter += 1
```

```
            Debug.WriteLine("Now Starting Iteration #" & _
               Counter.ToString())
            Thread.Sleep(TimeSpan.FromSeconds(10))
         Loop
      End Sub

End Class
```

13.3 Create a Windows Service Installer

Problem

You need to install your Windows service so that you can run or test it.

Solution

Create an installer class, and use the InstallUtil command-line utility.

Discussion

Because Windows services are controlled by the SCM, you must install them before you can run or debug them. To install a Windows service, you must create an installer class. Microsoft Visual Studio .NET can generate this installer class automatically. In the Solution Explorer, simply right-click your service code file, choose View Designer, and select the Add Installer link that displays in the Properties window (as shown in Figure 13-1).

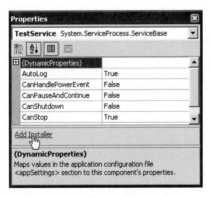

Figure 13-1   The Add Installer link.

A new ProjectInstaller.vb file will be added to your project. This file contains all the code required to install the service. This installer uses two installer components that are automatically added to the design-time view: *ServiceProcessInstaller1* and *ServiceInstaller1* (as shown in Figure 13-2).

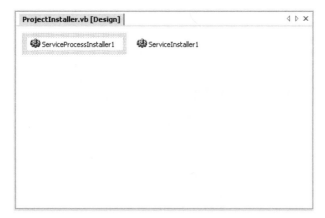

Figure 13-2   The installer components.

You can modify the *ServiceProcessInstaller.Account* property to configure the user account that will be used to run the service when it is first installed. You can set this to *LocalSystem* so that the service runs under a system account with broad privileges. You can also modify the *ServiceInstaller.StartType* property to determine whether the service will be launched automatically at startup. Both of these details can also be configured later using the Computer Management console. The name of the service is set by the *ServiceInstaller.Service-Name* property.

Following is a sample project installer class. To use this example as written, you must import the *System.ServiceProcess*, *System.Configuration.Install*, and *System.ComponentModel* namespaces.

```
<RunInstaller(True)> Public Class ProjectInstaller
    Inherits System.Configuration.Install.Installer

    Public Sub New()
        MyBase.New()
        InitializeComponent()
    End Sub

    Friend ServiceProcessInstaller1 As ServiceProcessInstaller
    Friend ServiceInstaller1 As ServiceInstaller

    Private Sub InitializeComponent()
        Me.ServiceProcessInstaller1 = New ServiceProcessInstaller()
        Me.ServiceInstaller1 = New ServiceInstaller()
```

```
      Me.ServiceProcessInstaller1.Account = _
        ServiceAccount.LocalSystem
      Me.ServiceInstaller1.ServiceName = "TestService"

      ' Add the two installers.
      Me.Installers.AddRange(New Installer() _
        {Me.ServiceProcessInstaller1, Me.ServiceInstaller1})
   End Sub

End Class
```

There are two ways to install a Windows service using an installer. You can create a dedicated setup project using Visual Studio .NET, or you can use the InstallUtil command-line utility. The second option is more convenient for simple testing or single-machine deployment.

To use InstallUtil, build your project, browse to the Bin directory using a command-line window, and type in the following instruction (where WindowsService1 is the name of your application):

```
InstallUtil WindowsService1.exe
```

If there are any embedded spaces in the name of the service file, you'll need to use quotation marks.

```
InstallUtil "Recipe 13-1.exe"
```

To uninstall a service, add the /u parameter. If the service is currently running, it will be stopped first and then uninstalled.

```
InstallUtil WindowsService1.exe /u
```

You can now find and start the service using the Computer Management administrative console (shown in Figure 13-3).

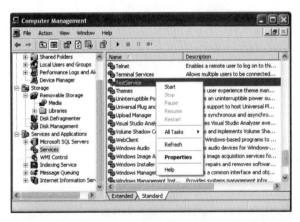

Figure 13-3 Starting the service with the Computer Management console.

> **Note**   Both recipe 13.1 and recipe 13.2 include a sample installer that you can use to install the Windows service, as described in this recipe.

13.4 Debug a Windows Service

Problem

You want to debug a Windows service in Visual Studio .NET (watch debug messages, use variable watches and breakpoints, and so on).

Solution

Start the Windows service through the SCM as you would ordinarily, and attach the Visual Studio .NET debugger manually.

Discussion

You can't run a Windows service from the Visual Studio .NET integrated development environment (IDE) because Windows services can be executed only by the SCM. However, you can start the Windows service through the SCM, and *then* attach the debugger.

To debug a Windows service, follow these steps:

1.   Load the source code for the project into Visual Studio .NET.

2.   Install the service if necessary, and then start it using the Computer Management console. (See recipe 13.3 for more information.)

3.   In Visual Studio .NET, choose Tools | Debug Processes. The Processes window will appear, as shown in Figure 13-4.

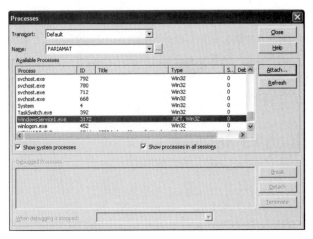

Figure 13-4   Attaching the debugger to a running process.

4. If you are running your service under a system account, enable the Show System Processes check box.

5. When you find the matching service, select it by clicking the Attach button. (The process will have the same name as the executable file for your service.)

6. In the Attach To Process window, choose to debug the code as a common language runtime application (as shown in Figure 13-5). Then click OK.

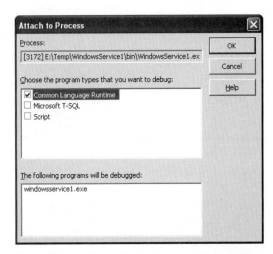

Figure 13-5   Choosing the program type to debug.

You can now set breakpoints, pause execution, and create variable watches as you would with any other application in Visual Studio .NET. If you test the application in recipe 13.2, you'll see debug output like that shown in Figure 13-6.

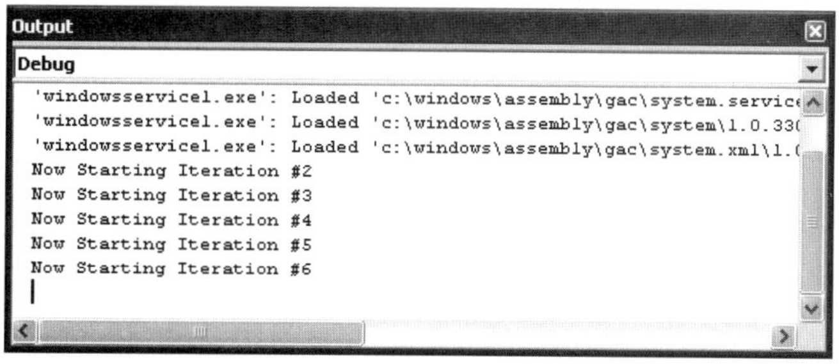

Figure 13-6   The debug output for a Windows service.

13.5 Retrieve Information About Installed Windows Services

Problem

You want to retrieve information about all the services on your computer.

Solution

Use the shared *ServiceController.GetServices* method.

Discussion

.NET allows you to interact with any installed Windows service using the *ServiceContoller* class. The *ServiceController* class includes information such as

- The service name and description.

- The status of the service (running, stopped, paused, and so on).

- Whether or not the service supports pause and continue and shutdown.

- What other services this service depends on.

You can create a *ServiceController* object bound to a specific service by specifying the service name in the constructor, as shown here:

```
Dim TestService As New ServiceController("TestService")
```

You can also use the *GetServices* method to retrieve all the services on the computer. For example, this code iterates over all the services on the computer and prints the name and status of each on the following page.

```
Dim Service, Services() As System.ServiceProcess.ServiceController
Services = System.ServiceProcess.ServiceController.GetServices()

For Each Service In Services
    Console.WriteLine(Service.ServiceName & " is " & _
      Service.Status.ToString())
Next
```

> **Note** To create this application, you need to import a reference to the System.Services.dll assembly, which is included in Windows service projects automatically.

You can also use data binding to display all the public information exposed in a *ServiceController*. For example, if you add the following code to a form, you can fill a *DataGrid* with comprehensive information about all the services on your computer:

```
Private Sub Form1_Load(ByVal sender As System.Object, _
  ByVal e As System.EventArgs) Handles MyBase.Load

    gridServices.DataSource = _
      System.ServiceProcess.ServiceController.GetServices()

End Sub
```

Some of the information in this form is shown in Figure 13-7.

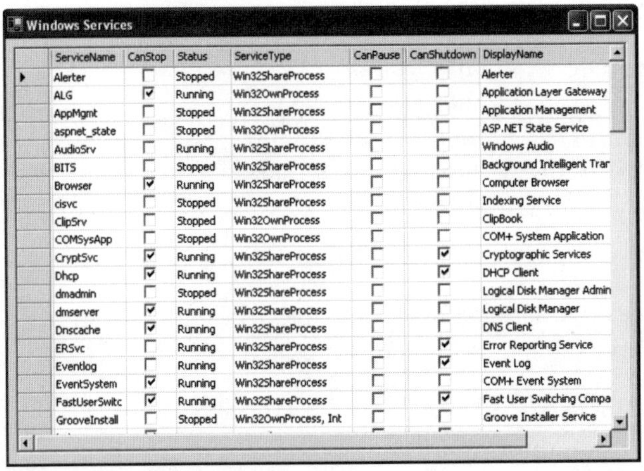

ServiceName	CanStop	Status	ServiceType	CanPause	CanShutdown	DisplayName
Alerter	[ ]	Stopped	Win32ShareProcess	[ ]	[ ]	Alerter
ALG	[x]	Running	Win32OwnProcess	[ ]	[ ]	Application Layer Gateway
AppMgmt	[ ]	Stopped	Win32ShareProcess	[ ]	[ ]	Application Management
aspnet_state	[ ]	Stopped	Win32OwnProcess	[ ]	[ ]	ASP.NET State Service
AudioSrv	[ ]	Running	Win32ShareProcess	[ ]	[ ]	Windows Audio
BITS	[ ]	Stopped	Win32ShareProcess	[ ]	[ ]	Background Intelligent Trar
Browser	[x]	Running	Win32ShareProcess	[ ]	[ ]	Computer Browser
cisvc	[ ]	Stopped	Win32ShareProcess	[ ]	[ ]	Indexing Service
ClipSrv	[ ]	Stopped	Win32OwnProcess	[ ]	[ ]	ClipBook
COMSysApp	[ ]	Stopped	Win32OwnProcess	[ ]	[ ]	COM+ System Application
CryptSvc	[x]	Running	Win32ShareProcess	[ ]	[x]	Cryptographic Services
Dhcp	[x]	Running	Win32ShareProcess	[ ]	[x]	DHCP Client
dmadmin	[ ]	Stopped	Win32ShareProcess	[ ]	[ ]	Logical Disk Manager Admin
dmserver	[x]	Running	Win32ShareProcess	[ ]	[ ]	Logical Disk Manager
Dnscache	[x]	Running	Win32ShareProcess	[ ]	[ ]	DNS Client
ERSvc	[ ]	Running	Win32ShareProcess	[ ]	[x]	Error Reporting Service
Eventlog	[ ]	Running	Win32ShareProcess	[ ]	[x]	Event Log
EventSystem	[x]	Running	Win32ShareProcess	[ ]	[ ]	COM+ Event System
FastUserSwitc	[x]	Running	Win32ShareProcess	[ ]	[x]	Fast User Switching Compa
GrooveInstall	[ ]	Stopped	Win32OwnProcess, Int	[ ]	[ ]	Groove Installer Service

Figure 13-7 The Windows services on the current computer.

> **Note**   The *ServiceController* class also provides a shared *GetDevices* method that returns an array of *ServiceController* instances representing all the device driver services on the current computer.

13.6 Start and Stop a Windows Service Programmatically

Problem

You want to start or stop a Windows service that is installed on the current computer.

Solution

Use the *Stop* and *Start* methods of the *ServiceController* class.

Discussion

Recipe 13.5 shows the properties of the *ServiceController* class. The *ServiceController* class also provides methods such as *Start*, *Stop*, *Pause*, and *Continue*.

As an example, here's how you might start a service programmatically:

```
Dim TestService As New ServiceController("TestService")
TestService.Start()
```

The *ServiceController* class methods allow you to start and stop services and monitor their status, but they won't allow you to interact in an application-specific way. In other words, you can't send a message or call a method in your Windows service code. To do that, you'd need to create a Windows service that hosts a remotable object. Another application that wants to communicate with this service must then call a method of the remotable object. This approach requires .NET Remoting, as described in Chapter 17.

13.7 Interact with Windows Services on Another Computer

Problem

You need to start or stop a service that is running on another computer.

Solution

Create a *ServiceController* instance using the constructor that accepts a machine name. You can then use the *Stop* and *Start* methods of the *ServiceController* class.

Discussion

You can create a *ServiceController* instance that represents a service running on another computer, provided that you have the required network rights, by specifying the computer name in the *ServiceController* constructor. Here's one example:

```
Dim TestService As New ServiceController("TestService", " ComputerName")
```

You can also use *GetServices* or *GetDevices* to retrieve service information from another computer by supplying a machine name.

```
Dim Services() As ServiceController
Services = ServiceController.GetServices("ComputerName")
```

13.8 Create a Windows Service That Uses a System Tray Icon

Problem

You want to create a Windows service that uses some type of user interface, such as a system tray icon.

Solution

If possible, do not implement any user interface in a Windows service. As a last resort, enable desktop interaction using the Computer Management console.

Discussion

Microsoft guidelines discourage user interfaces with any Windows service application. Adding a user interface can lead to security risks and can prevent the service from running at all if the required permission isn't granted. In fact, Windows services should be able to run with absolutely no user intervention—there might not even be a user logged on to the computer.

In cases where you do need a user interface to configure some aspects of the Windows service operation (or to view some data that it has processed), it's recommended that you create a separate application. For example, your Windows service can be configured to write data to a database or an event log, and you can create a separate program that can read this information and present it to the user. A more advanced design is to use .NET Remoting to allow a user interface tool to talk to a Windows service. In this way, you can use a program that can configure a Windows service in real time if required. (This design is similar to the way the SQL Server works with its system tray utility.) For more information on this approach, refer to the .NET Remoting recipes in Chapter 17.

However, if you decide to provide some basic interface through a Windows service, it is possible. For example, you might want to add a system tray icon that indicates the status of the current operation. You can easily add a *NotifyIcon* control to your Windows service project and configure it in your service code. Following is a rudimentary example that modifies the icon text to show the processing state. To use this example as written, you must import the *System.ServiceProcess* and *System.Threading* namespaces.

```
Public Class IconService
    Inherits System.ServiceProcess.ServiceBase

    <MTAThread()> _
    Shared Sub Main()
        Dim ServicesToRun() As ServiceBase
        ServicesToRun = New ServiceBase(){New IconService()}
        System.ServiceProcess.ServiceBase.Run(ServicesToRun)
    End Sub


    Private Components As System.ComponentModel.IContainer
    Friend ServiceIcon As System.Windows.Forms.NotifyIcon


    Private Sub InitializeComponent ()
        Me.Components = New System.ComponentModel.Container()
        Dim resources As New System.Resources.ResourceManager( _
          GetType(IconService))

        ' Configure the system tray icon.
        ' The bitmap is retrieved from a resource file.
        ' This code is generated automatically by Visual Studio .NET.
        Me.ServiceIcon = New System.Windows.Forms.NotifyIcon(Me.Components)
```

```vbnet
        Me.ServiceIcon.Icon = CType( _
          resources.GetObject("ServiceIcon.Icon"), System.Drawing.Icon)
        Me.ServiceIcon.Text = ""
        Me.ServiceIcon.Visible = True

        Me.ServiceName = "IconService"

        ' (Some of the automatically generated designer code is omitted.)
    End Sub

    Private ServiceThread As Thread
    Private StopThread As Boolean = False

    Protected Overrides Sub OnStart(ByVal args() As String)
        ServiceIcon.Text = "Starting ..."
        ServiceThread = New Thread(AddressOf DoWork)
        ServiceThread.Start()
    End Sub

    Protected Overrides Sub OnStop()
        ServiceIcon.Text = "Stopping ..."

        ' Try to signal the thread to end nicely,
        ' (and wait up to 20 seconds).
        StopThread = True
        ServiceThread.Join(TimeSpan.FromSeconds(20))

        ' If the thread is still running, abort it.
        If (ServiceThread.ThreadState And _
          ThreadState.Running) = ThreadState.Running Then
            ServiceThread.Abort()
        End If
    End Sub

    Private Sub DoWork()
        Do Until StopThread
            ServiceIcon.Text = "Processing"
            Thread.Sleep(TimeSpan.FromSeconds(10))
        Loop
        ServiceIcon.Text = "Not Processing"
    End Sub

End Class
```

You could extend this design by adding a context menu with event handlers for menu items. Remember, though, that this design isn't recommended because it will limit the scenarios in which you can use this service.

If you install this example Windows service, by default it will not work. When you attempt to start the service, an exception may be thrown or it may start but not display the system tray icon. The solution is to manually enable desktop interaction privileges using the Computer Management console. Find the service in the list, right-click it, and select Properties. Then, in the Log On tab, select the Allow Service To Interact With Desktop check box, as shown in Figure 13-8.

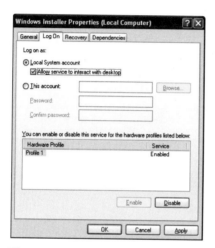

Figure 13-8   Allowing a service to interact with the desktop.

14

ADO.NET

The Microsoft .NET Framework includes an entirely new data access framework that allows you to query data sources, fill disconnected *DataSet* containers, and continue to work with relational data long after the original connection has been closed. In this chapter, we tackle some of the most commonly asked ADO.NET questions and provide tips for improving performance, creating robust applications, and simplifying user interface code when using ADO.NET.

It goes without saying that you shouldn't use this chapter to learn basic ADO.NET programming. Straightforward tasks such as executing commands, using a *DataReader*, and iterating through a *DataSet* aren't covered (nor are the basics of SQL). If you need a comprehensive introduction to ADO.NET, consider David Sceppa's excellent book *Microsoft ADO.NET Core Reference* (Microsoft Press, 2002). You can then turn to the recipes in this chapter to resolve some common points of confusion or enhance your knowledge with some commonly requested tips and techniques.

The recipes at the beginning of this chapter discuss ADO.NET essentials such as connection pooling (recipe 14.1), using unique IDs (recipes 14.2 and 14.3), preventing SQL injection attacks (recipe 14.4), and executing batch queries (recipe 14.5). Later recipes show various ways to customize *DataAdapter* logic (recipes 14.7 and 14.8), handle concurrency problems (recipe 14.9), and deal with large binary fields (recipe 14.11). Finally, the recipes toward the end of the chapter dive into data binding with Microsoft Windows Forms and ADO.NET, showing you how to synchronize controls (recipe 14.13), filter and sort records (recipe 14.14), handle table relations (recipe 14.15), and deal with different types of data (recipes 14.16, 14.17, and 14.18).

Almost all the examples in this chapter use the Microsoft SQL Server provider and require that you import the *System.Data.SqlClient* namespace. The recipes present concepts that can be used with any data source and provider, but they assume you are using the Northwind database that's included with SQL Server and its scaled-down relative, Microsoft Desktop Engine (MSDE). If you don't have access to SQL Server, you can use the local MSDE engine that's installed with Microsoft Visual Studio .NET or the .NET Framework SDK. Refer to the installation documentation included with that product for more information.

14.1 Use Connection Pooling

Problem

You want to maintain a pool of open connections to improve scalability for a large system.

Solution

Use connection pooling by configuring the connection string settings.

Discussion

Creating a database connection imposes a small but measurable overhead. In a large system where connections are continuously being acquired and released, this overhead can become a bottleneck that limits the overall throughput of the system. To prevent this problem, you can use *connection pooling*. With connection pooling, the system retains a pool of open connections that it can assign as needed. When you close a pooled connection, the underlying connection isn't actually released. Instead, it's moved to the connection pool. The next time a client tries to open a new connection, the existing connection is reused automatically, saving the overhead of creating and initializing a new connection.

You don't need to take any extra steps to implement connection pooling in ADO.NET. The SQL Server provider and the Oracle provider (included with .NET 1.1) both perform connection pooling automatically. However, you can configure connection pooling using connection string settings, as indicated in Table 14-1.

Table 14-1   Connection String Settings

Setting	Description
Connection Lifetime	Specifies the maximum amount of time that a connection can live in the pool (in seconds). Every time a connection is returned to the pool, its creation time is compared against this value. If it's older than the specified lifetime, it's destroyed. The default is 0, which specifies that all connections be retained for the life of the process.
Connection Reset	If *True*, the connection state is reset when a pooled connection is reused. State includes session-level *SET* statements and the currently selected database. This setting is recommended and is *True* by default.
Max Pool Size	The maximum number of connections allowed in the pool (100 by default). If the maximum pool size is reached and no connection is free, the request is queued and performance suffers.
Min Pool Size	The minimum number of connections always retained in the pool (0 by default). This number of connections is created when the first connection is created, leading to a minor delay for the first request.
Pooling	When *True* (the default), connection pooling is used.

Here's a basic example of how you can configure connection pooling:

```
' Create a pool that always retains at least 5 connections,
' and won't allow more than 10 simultaneous connections.
Dim ConnectionString As String = "Data Source=localhost;" & _
    "Integrated Security=SSPI;Min Pool Size=5;Max Pool Size=10"

Dim con As New SqlConnection(ConnectionString)

' Open the connection.
' If there is an existing connection in the pool, it will be reused.
' If this is the first time you have opened a connection,
' the basic pool of 5 connections will be created.
con.Open()

' This returns the connection to the connection pool so it can be reused.
con.Close()
```

> **Note** The OLE DB and ODBC providers also perform a more limited type of connection pooling. OLE DB session pooling is implemented automatically and cannot be configured. ODBC pooling is implemented at the driver level and can be configured through the ODBC Data Sources section of Control Panel. These forms of connection pooling are more limited than the connection pooling provided with the SQL Server and Oracle providers because they do not allow you to enforce pool minimums and maximums.

There are two factors that can cause connection pooling to behave differently than you expect.

- **Connection strings.** If there's any difference in the connection string used by different clients, the connections will be created and maintained in separate pools. Separate pools are used if the connection string specifies a different user for authentication or even if the connection string just has an extra space or changes the order of identical settings. Thus, it's recommended that you place the connection string in a configuration file to make sure it's always *exactly* the same.

- **The application process.** Connection pooling is tied to the application process. Thus, if you have multiple client applications running on separate computers, and they use a local database component, each client will have its own local pool, and connections won't be shared between clients. If, on the other hand, all these clients access the same database component through XML Web services or through .NET Remoting, the remote component can use connection pooling and a single server-side pool can serve all clients.

14.2 Retrieve the Unique ID for a New Record

Problem

You need to insert a record and retrieve its unique ID number, which is generated by the database.

Solution

Use a database stored procedure that returns this information in an output parameter.

Discussion

Many database tables use an ID or a GUID (globally unique identifier) field to uniquely identify records. This field is generated by the database when the record is created, not by the client. However, the client often needs to show this information to the user, and it might serve as a registration number or a confirmation number. To make it easy for the client to retrieve this information, it's recommended that you use a stored procedure that explicitly returns this information.

For example, the Northwind database includes a *Shippers* table. Every shipper is identified by a company name, a phone number, and a unique ID. A stored procedure that inserts this record and returns the new ID value would look like this:

```
CREATE Procedure AddShipper
(
    @CompanyName  nvarchar(40),
    @Phone        nvarchar(24),
    @ID           int OUTPUT
)
AS
  INSERT INTO Shippers
    (CompanyName, Phone)
  VALUES
    (@CompanyName, @Phone)

  SELECT @ID = @@Identity
GO
```

In this case, the stored procedure accepts two input parameters (the company name and phone number) and uses one output parameter. After the insert has been performed, the code uses the Transact-SQL global variable *@@Identity*, which provides the unique identity value that was just generated. This value is applied to the *@ID* output parameter. Here's a simple Console application that tests this stored procedure:

```
Public Module AutoIncrementInsert

    Private ConnectionString As String = "Data Source=localhost;" & _
        "Integrated Security=SSPI;Initial Catalog=Northwind"
```

```
Public Sub Main()
    ' Create the connection and command.
    Dim Con As New SqlConnection(ConnectionString)
    Dim Cmd As New SqlCommand("AddShipper", con)
    cmd.CommandType = CommandType.StoredProcedure

    ' Add the input parameters.
    Dim Param As SqlParameter = cmd.Parameters.Add("@CompanyName", _
      SqlDbType.NVarChar, 40)
    param.Value = "Test Company"

    Param = Cmd.Parameters.Add("@Phone", SqlDbType.NVarChar, 24)
    Param.Value = "(503) 555-9931"

    ' Add the output parameter.
    Param = cmd.Parameters.Add("@ID", SqlDbType.Int)
    Param.Direction = ParameterDirection.Output

    Try
        ' Execute the command.
        con.Open()
        cmd.ExecuteNonQuery()

        ' Display the returned ID
        Console.WriteLine("The record you inserted has ID " & _
          Param.Value.ToString())

    Catch Err As Exception
        Console.WriteLine(Err.ToString())

    Finally
        Con.Close()
    End Try

    Console.ReadLine()
End Sub

End Module
```

You can use a similar technique to retrieve GUID values. In this case, the stored procedure must first generate the GUID using the Transact-SQL function *NEWID*. It can then insert that value in the database, and return it to the user.

```
-- Create the GUID and assign it to the output parameter.
SELECT @GUID = NEWID()

-- (Now perform the insert using all the parameters.)
```

14.3 Retrieve the Unique ID for a New Record in a *DataSet*

Problem

When you perform an update with the *DataAdapter*, you want the ID numbers for newly added records to be inserted into the *DataSet*.

Solution

Use a database stored procedure that returns this information in an output parameter, and map the parameter to the appropriate column.

Discussion

Recipe 14.2 demonstrates how to return unique ID information with a stored procedure and configure the ADO.NET database command accordingly. This recipe shows how you can use this command with a *DataSet* so that the retrieved ID information is applied automatically to the appropriate field in the *DataSet*.

First you must map the parameters in the command to the fields in the *DataSet* by setting the *Parameter.SourceColumn* property to the corresponding field name. You also need to ensure that the *Command.UpdatedRowSource* property is set to *UpdateRowSource.OutputParameters* or *UpdateRow-Source.Both* (the default).

The following Console application uses the *AddShipper* stored procedure from recipe 14.2 to insert new records into the *Shippers* table of the Northwind database. The *DataSet* is updated automatically with the value from the identity field.

```
Public Module AutoIncrementInsert

    Private ConnectionString As String = "Data Source=localhost;" & _
    "Integrated Security=SSPI;Initial Catalog=Northwind"

    Public Sub Main()
        ' Create the connection.
        Dim Con As New SqlConnection(ConnectionString)

        ' Create the command for filling the DataSet.
        Dim CmdSelect As New SqlCommand("SELECT * FROM Shippers", Con)

        Dim Adapter As New SqlDataAdapter(CmdSelect)
        Dim Ds As New DataSet()
```

```vbnet
' Fill the DataSet.
Try
    Con.Open()
    Dim Rows As Integer = Adapter.Fill(Ds, "Shippers")
    Console.WriteLine("Retrieved " & Rows.ToString() & " rows.")
Catch Err As Exception
    Console.WriteLine(Err.ToString())
Finally
    Con.Close()
End Try

' Add a new row.
Dim Row As DataRow = Ds.Tables("Shippers").NewRow()
Row("CompanyName") = "Test Company"
Row("Phone") = "(503) 555-9931"
Ds.Tables("Shippers").Rows.Add(Row)

' Create the insert command.
Dim cmdInsert As New SqlCommand("AddShipper", Con)
cmdInsert.CommandType = CommandType.StoredProcedure

' Map the columns to the input parameters.
Dim Param As SqlParameter = cmdInsert.Parameters.Add("@CompanyName", _
  SqlDbType.NVarChar, 40, "CompanyName")
Param = cmdInsert.Parameters.Add("@Phone", SqlDbType.NVarChar, 24, _
  "Phone")

' Map the output parameter to the ID field.
Param = cmdInsert.Parameters.Add("@ID", SqlDbType.Int)
Param.SourceColumn = "ShipperID"
Param.Direction = ParameterDirection.Output

' Assign the command to the adapter.
Adapter.InsertCommand = cmdInsert

' Perform the insert.
Try
    ' Execute the command.
    Con.Open()

    Console.Write("ID before update: ")
    Console.WriteLine(Row("ShipperID"))

    Adapter.Update(Ds, "Shippers")
    Console.Write("ID after update: ")
    Console.WriteLine(Row("ShipperID"))

Catch Err As Exception
    Console.WriteLine(Err.ToString())
```

```
      Finally
          Con.Close()
      End Try

      Console.ReadLine()
   End Sub

End Module
```

14.4 Protect Against SQL Injection Attacks

Problem

You want to reduce the opportunity for attackers to submit malicious SQL code in command parameter values.

Solution

Use a parameterized query.

Discussion

Many applications build SQL commands dynamically by parsing the pieces together into a large string. This approach poses problems when dealing with binary data, and it also raises the possibility that an attacker can execute malicious SQL code by "injecting" it along with a parameter value. This malicious code could be used to tamper with information in the database or even launch another application on the server. You can read some frightening examples for different database servers on the Open Web Application Security Project Web site at *http://www.owasp.org/asac/input_validation/sql.shtml.*

To prevent this problem, you should validate user input, checking that it has the expected data type, is not unusually long, and so on. In addition, you should properly escape the input with delimiters. The easy way to perform this step is to use a parameterized query. The *Command* class will automatically escape all parameter values for you when you use a parameterized query.

Parameterized queries are used for all stored procedure calls, but you can also use them with dynamic SQL statements. In the latter case, you simply need to take an ordinary SQL statement and replace the dynamic values with parameters. (The result will look like the body of a simple stored procedure.) Here's an example parameterized SQL statement:

```
INSERT INTO Shippers (CompanyName, Phone) VALUES (@CompanyName, @Phone)
```

To use this statement, you need to add the corresponding *Parameter* objects to the *Command* object (with the appropriate values). In this case, two parameters (*@CompanyName* and *@Phone*) are required. The following Console application uses this parameterized query to add a new record to the *Shippers* table of the Northwind database.

```
Public Module ParameterizedQuery

    Private ConnectionString As String = "Data Source=localhost;" & _
        "Integrated Security=SSPI;Initial Catalog=Northwind"

    Public Sub Main()
        ' Create the connection and command.
        Dim Con As New SqlConnection(ConnectionString)
        Dim UpdateSQL As String = "INSERT INTO Shippers " & _
            "(CompanyName, Phone) VALUES (@CompanyName, @Phone)"
        Dim Cmd As New SqlCommand(UpdateSQL, Con)

        ' Add the input parameters.
        Dim Param As SqlParameter = Cmd.Parameters.Add("@CompanyName", _
            SqlDbType.NVarChar, 40)
        Param.Value = "Test Company"

        Param = Cmd.Parameters.Add("@Phone", SqlDbType.NVarChar, 24)
        Param.Value = "(503) 555-9931"

        Try
            ' Execute the command.
            Con.Open()
            Dim Rows As Integer = Cmd.ExecuteNonQuery()
            Console.WriteLine(Rows.ToString() & " row(s) affected.")
        Catch Err As Exception
            Console.WriteLine(Err.ToString())
        Finally
            Con.Close()
        End Try

        Console.ReadLine()
    End Sub

End Module
```

> **Note**   In most providers, parameterized queries use named parameters as shown earlier. However, in the OLE DB provider, you must use question mark (*?*) placeholders instead. When adding the *OleDbParameter* objects to *OleDbCommand*, the parameter name is not important. What is important is ensuring that you add the *OleDbParameter* objects in the same order as the question mark placeholders appear in the SQL statement.

14.5 Execute Multiple SQL Statements at Once

Problem

You want to execute more than one SQL statement without requiring multiple trips to the server.

Solution

Use a batch query, and separate your commands with a semicolon.

Discussion

Most ADO.NET providers support batch queries, which allow you to execute more than one SQL statement. To create a batch query, you simply separate the SQL statements using a semicolon, as shown here:

```
SELECT * FROM Products;SELECT * FROM Categories
```

In this example, both SQL statements are queries. If you to execute this statement using *Command.ExecuteReader*, you'll first retrieve the results from the first query (the list of products). Once you have read these results, you'll need to use the *DataReader.NextResult* method to move the *DataReader* to the next result set (the list of categories). If you use this batch query with a *DataAdapter*, as shown in the following example, the *DataAdapter* will actually add two tables to the *DataSet*, one for each result set.

```vb
Public Module BatchQuery

    Private ConnectionString As String = "Data Source=localhost;" & _
        "Integrated Security=SSPI;Initial Catalog=Northwind"

    Public Sub Main()
        ' Create the ADO.NET objects.
        Dim Con As New SqlConnection(ConnectionString)
        Dim BatchQuery As String = "SELECT * FROM Products;" & _
            "SELECT * FROM Categories"
        Dim Cmd As New SqlCommand(BatchQuery, Con)

        Dim Adapter As New SqlDataAdapter(Cmd)
        Dim Ds As New DataSet()

        ' Fill the DataSet.
        Try
            Con.Open()
            Dim Rows As Integer = Adapter.Fill(Ds)

            ' Display information about the retrieved tables.
            Console.WriteLine("The DataSet contains " & _
                Ds.Tables.Count.ToString() & " tables.")
            Dim Dt As DataTable, Dr As DataRow
            For Each Dt In Ds.Tables
                Console.WriteLine(Dt.TableName)

                ' Show the first column of each row in the table.
                For Each Dr In Dt.Rows
                    Console.WriteLine("   " & Dt.Columns(0).ColumnName & _
                        ": " & Dr(0))
                Next
                Console.WriteLine()
            Next

        Catch Err As Exception
            Console.WriteLine(Err.ToString())
        Finally
            Con.Close()
        End Try

        Console.ReadLine()
    End Sub

End Module
```

The output for this application looks like this:

```
The DataSet contains 2 tables.
Table
    ProductID: 1
    ProductID: 2
    ProductID: 3
    ProductID: 4
    . . .

Table1
    CategoryID: 1
    CategoryID: 2
    CategoryID: 3
    CategoryID: 4
    . . .
```

> **Note**   When adding multiple tables, the *DataAdapter* uses default names such as Table, Table1, Table2, and so on. You can modify these names after the fact, or you can use the table mapping approach shown in recipe 14.6 to map the automatically generated names to the real table names.

14.6 Use Column and Table Mappings

Problem

You want to map database column and table names to the names expected by your code for the *DataSet*.

Solution

Create *ColumnMapping* objects for each column and *DataTableMapping* objects for each table, and assign them to the *DataAdapter.TableMappings* collection.

Discussion

The *DataAdapter* provides a layer of indirection between the data source and the *DataSet*. Using the *DataAdapter*, you can configure table and column mappings so that code remains unchanged when the data source changes (or vice versa).

Column mappings link a field in the data source with a differently named field in the *DataSet*. The following example shows how you might modify names in the *Categories* table when filling a *DataSet*: Source fields like *ShipperID* and *Phone* are mapped to *ID* and *PhoneNumber* in the destination *DataTable*.

```
Public Module MappingTest

    Private ConnectionString As String = "Data Source=localhost;" & _
    "Integrated Security=SSPI;Initial Catalog=Northwind"

    Public Sub Main()
        ' Create the connection.
        Dim Con As New SqlConnection(ConnectionString)

        ' Create the command for filling the DataSet.
        Dim CmdSelect As New SqlCommand("SELECT * FROM Shippers", Con)

        Dim Adapter As New SqlDataAdapter(CmdSelect)
        Dim Ds As New DataSet()

        ' Map the default table name.
        Dim CustomerMap As System.Data.Common.DataTableMapping
        CustomerMap = Adapter.TableMappings.Add("Table", "Shippers")

        ' Add the column mappings to the table.
        CustomerMap.ColumnMappings.Add("ShipperID", "ID")
        CustomerMap.ColumnMappings.Add("CompanyName", "CompanyName")
        CustomerMap.ColumnMappings.Add("Phone", "PhoneNumber")

        ' Fill the DataSet.
        Adapter.Fill(Ds)

        ' Fill the DataSet.
        Try
            Con.Open()
            Dim Rows As Integer = Adapter.Fill(Ds, "Shippers")

            Console.WriteLine("The DataTable is named: " & _
              Ds.Tables(0).TableName)
            Console.Write("The column names are: ")
            Dim Col As DataColumn
```

```
            For Each Col In Ds.Tables(0).Columns
                Console.Write(Col.ColumnName & " ")
            Next

        Catch Err As Exception
            Console.WriteLine(Err.ToString())
        Finally
            Con.Close()
        End Try

        Console.ReadLine()
    End Sub

End Module
```

The great advantage of column mappings is that they are bidirectional. In other words, the *DataAdapter* applies the mappings both when reading data as part of a fill operation and when applying changes as part of an update operation.

14.7 Use Last-In-Wins Concurrency with the *DataAdapter*

Problem

You want to customize the *DataAdapter* update logic so that changes are allowed, even to records that have been modified by other users.

Solution

Customize the *UpdateCommand* so that is selects records based on a single unique field, instead of a combination of fields.

Discussion

The automatically generated update logic provided by the *CommandBuilder* selects records for an update by attempting to match each field in the *WHERE* clause. Here's an example update command for the *Shippers* table from the Northwind database:

```
UPDATE Shippers SET CompanyName=[NewVal]
  WHERE ShipperID=[LastVal] AND CompanyName=[LastVal] AND Phone=[LastVal] ...
```

This approach is usually inefficient because it increases the amount of data sent over the network. It's also more difficult for the database engine to optimize than a targeted query that matches only a single, indexed field. In addition, if any of the fields have changed since the *DataSet* was filled, the command won't be able to match the record. At this point an error will occur, and the update will fail.

There's more than one way to resolve this problem. If you want to increase *DataAdapter* performance but retain strict concurrency checking, you should use a timestamp, as described in recipe 14.8. If you want to optimize performance and allow looser "last-in-wins" concurrency, you can select records based on a single unique field. This way, even if the other fields in the record have been changed, the command will still find the record and update it without generating an error.

Here's an example that uses last-in-wins concurrency to match records from the *Shippers* table based on the *ShipperID*:

```
UPDATE Shippers SET CompanyName=[NewVal]
  WHERE ShipperID=[LastVal]
```

Custom update commands can be stored as procedure commands or parameterized commands. The following Console application demonstrates a parameterized command for updating the *Shippers* table.

```
Public Module LastInWinsConcurrency

    Private ConnectionString As String = "Data Source=localhost;" & _
    "Integrated Security=SSPI;Initial Catalog=Northwind"

    Public Sub Main()
        ' Create the ADO.NET objects.
        Dim Con As New SqlConnection(ConnectionString)
        Dim CmdSelect As New SqlCommand("SELECT * FROM Shippers", Con)
        Dim Adapter As New SqlDataAdapter(CmdSelect)
        Dim Ds As New DataSet()

        ' Fill the DataSet.
        Try
            Con.Open()
            Adapter.FillSchema(Ds, SchemaType.Mapped, "Shippers")
            Adapter.Fill(Ds, "Shippers")
        Catch Err As Exception
            Console.WriteLine(Err.ToString())
        Finally
            Con.Close()
        End Try

        ' Define a custom update command.
        Dim UpdateSQL As String = "UPDATE Shippers SET " & _
          "CompanyName=@Company, Phone=@Phone WHERE ShipperID=@ID"
        Dim CmdUpdate As New SqlCommand(UpdateSQL, Con)
```

```
    ' Map the DataSet fields to the parameter values.
    CmdUpdate.Parameters.Add("@Company", SqlDbType.VarChar, 40, _
      "CompanyName")
    CmdUpdate.Parameters.Add("@Phone", SqlDbType.VarChar, 24, "Phone")
    Dim Param As SqlParameter = CmdUpdate.Parameters.Add("@ID", _
      SqlDbType.Int, Nothing, "ShipperID")
    Param.SourceVersion = DataRowVersion.Original
    Adapter.UpdateCommand = CmdUpdate


    ' Apply a change to row with ShipperID 1 ("Speedy Express").
    ' Make the change using a duplicate DataSet.
    Dim DuplicateDs As DataSet = Ds.Copy()
    Dim Row As DataRow = DuplicateDs.Tables(0).Rows.Find(1)
    Row("CompanyName") = "Deluxe Express"
    Try
        Con.Open()
        Adapter.Update(DuplicateDs, "Shippers")
        Console.WriteLine("Successfully applied change from DuplicateDs.")
    Catch Err As Exception
        Console.WriteLine(Err.ToString())
    Finally
        Con.Close()
    End Try


    ' Now apply a conflicting change using the original DataSet.
    ' This simulates a concurrency problem, because the original
    ' values in the row are different than the information in the
    ' database.
    Row = Ds.Tables(0).Rows.Find(1)
    Row("CompanyName") = "Super Deluxe Express"
    Try
        Con.Open()

        ' This would fail with the auto-generated logic.
        Adapter.Update(Ds, "Shippers")
        Console.WriteLine("Successfully applied conflicting " & _
          "change from Ds.")
    Catch Err As Exception
        Console.WriteLine(Err.ToString())
    Finally
        Con.Close()
    End Try

    Console.ReadLine()
    End Sub

End Module
```

There is a significant limitation with last-in-wins concurrency: your changes will overwrite the changes of any other users that might have been made in the time between the query and updating the data source. If you update a record that has been modified by another user, all the values that are in your copy of the *DataRow* will be applied. In other words, this sequence of events can occur:

1. User A retrieves a *DataSet*.

2. User B retrieves a *DataSet*.

3. User A commits some changes to a row.

4. User B commits a change to a single field in the same row. At the same time, all the original values from the *DataRow* are applied, overwriting any changes User A made.

To resolve this problem, you need to use a type of changed-values-only concurrency. Unfortunately, though the *DataSet* tracks which rows have been modified and which rows have not, there's no way to create changed-values-only commands with ADO.NET. The only alternative is to create your own *DataAdapter* type of object, which steps through the rows in the *DataSet* and creates a new SQL *UPDATE* statement for each row based on its changed values.

14.8 Optimize *DataAdapter* Performance with a Timestamp

Problem

You want to use strict concurrency checking but optimize *DataAdapter* performance.

Solution

Add a timestamp field to your table, and create a custom update command that uses it.

Discussion

You can use the *CommandBuilder* to generate update logic for your database tables. However, the autogenerated SQL statements it creates are usually inefficient because they attempt to match every field in a table. As the number of columns increases in the *DataTable*, the number of columns in the *WHERE* clause of the query also increases.

To improve on this system, you can add a special timestamp field to your table. Most database systems support some kind of timestamp data type, which the data source updates automatically every time the row is changed. You never need to modify the timestamp column manually. However, you can examine it for changes and thereby determine whether another user has recently applied an update.

Note   In some databases, a timestamp column records the date and time of the last update. In the case of SQL Server, the timestamp column actually represents an increasing counter stored in binary format that's unique within the database (which is also referred to as a row version column). A SQL Server stored procedure can return the most recently generated timestamp value by retrieving the value from the *@@DBTS* global variable.

The advantage of using a timestamp is that you only need to examine one column to determine if any changes have been made, which shortens the SQL statement and simplifies the lookup logic.

The following example mirrors the example shown in recipe 14.7. The difference is that this example requires a timestamp column named *Version*. If any other user modifies any field in the record, the *Version* column will be modified as well. Before running this test, you'll need to add the *Version* timestamp column to the table.

```
Public Module TimestampUpdating

    Private ConnectionString As String = "Data Source=localhost;" & _
    "Integrated Security=SSPI;Initial Catalog=Northwind"

    Public Sub Main()
        ' Create the ADO.NET objects.
        Dim Con As New SqlConnection(ConnectionString)
        Dim CmdSelect As New SqlCommand("SELECT * FROM Shippers", Con)
        Dim Adapter As New SqlDataAdapter(CmdSelect)
        Dim Ds As New DataSet()

        ' Fill the DataSet.
        Try
```

```
        Con.Open()
        Adapter.FillSchema(Ds, SchemaType.Mapped, "Shippers")
        Adapter.Fill(Ds, "Shippers")
Catch Err As Exception
        Console.WriteLine(Err.ToString())
Finally
        Con.Close()
End Try


' Define a custom update command.
Dim UpdateSQL As UpdateSQL = "UPDATE Shippers SET " & _
    "CompanyName=@Company, Phone=@Phone WHERE ShipperID=@ID " & _
    "AND Version=@Version"
Dim CmdUpdate As New SqlCommand(UpdateSQL, Con)

' Map the DataSet fields to the parameter values.
CmdUpdate.Parameters.Add("@Company", SqlDbType.VarChar, 40, _
    "CompanyName")
CmdUpdate.Parameters.Add("@Phone", SqlDbType.VarChar, 24, "Phone")
Dim Param As SqlParameter = CmdUpdate.Parameters.Add("@ID", _
    SqlDbType.Int, Nothing, "ShipperID")
Param.SourceVersion = DataRowVersion.Original
Param = CmdUpdate.Parameters.Add("@Version", SqlDbType.Timestamp, _
    Nothing, "Version")
Adapter.UpdateCommand = CmdUpdate

' Apply a change to row with ShipperID 1 ("Speedy Express").
' Make the change using a duplicate DataSet.
Dim DuplicateDs As DataSet = Ds.Copy()
Dim Row As DataRow = DuplicateDs.Tables(0).Rows.Find(1)
Row("CompanyName") = "Deluxe Express"
Try
        Con.Open()
        Adapter.Update(DuplicateDs, "Shippers")
        Console.WriteLine("Successfully applied change from DuplicateDs.")
Catch Err As Exception
        Console.WriteLine(Err.ToString())
Finally
        Con.Close()
End Try

' Now apply a conflicting change using the original DataSet.
' This simulates a concurrency problem, because the original
' values in the row are different than the information in the
' database.
Row = Ds.Tables(0).Rows.Find(1)
Row("CompanyName") = "Super Deluxe Express"
Try
```

```
        Con.Open()

        ' This attempt will fail because the timestamp will not match.
        Adapter.Update(Ds, "Shippers")
        Console.WriteLine("Successfully applied conflicting change")
    Catch Err As Exception
        Console.WriteLine("Attempt to apply conflicting change failed.")
    Finally
        Con.Close()
    End Try

        Console.ReadLine()
    End Sub

End Module
```

> **Note** When crafting a custom update command with a timestamp,
> you should write the *WHERE* clause so that it attempts to match both
> the timestamp *and* some unique field. Technically, the timestamp field
> is unique in the database, and it could be used to uniquely match a
> row. However, a primary key will provide faster lookup because the pri-
> mary key column almost always has an index. You should never create
> an index on a timestamp value because it changes frequently.

14.9 Handle *DataAdapter* Concurrency Errors

Problem

You are performing an update that might fail because of a concurrency error.

Solution

Handle the *DataAdapter.RowUpdated* event and check for errors, or set the
DataAdapter.ContinueUpdateOnError property to *True*.

Discussion

If the *DataAdapter* executes an update command and detects that the number
of affected rows is 0, it throws a *DBConcurrencyException*. The entire update
operation will be aborted, and no further rows in the *DataSet* will be examined.

Usually, a *DBConcurrencyException* occurs for one of two reasons:

■ You have incorrectly written the SQL for a custom *UPDATE, INSERT,* or *DELETE* command.

■ The row can't be found because the information being used to find it doesn't match the current values. This problem signals that another user has changed the row since the last time you retrieved the information.

You can prevent concurrency errors using last-in-wins concurrency (as discussed in recipe 14.7). You can also handle concurrency errors on your own and act accordingly. For example, you might respond by informing the user, modifying the update command to allow the change to proceed, or querying the current information from the database.

There are two choices for handling the error. One option is to handle the *DataAdapter.RowUpdated* event that fires after a command has been executed but before an error has been raised. You can use this event handler to log problems, and programmatically instruct the *DataAdapter* to ignore the error and continue processing other errors. Here's an example that displays and skips all errors:

```
Private Sub OnRowUpdated(ByVal sender As Object, _
  e As SqlRowUpdatedEventArgs) Handles Adapter.RowUpdated

    ' Check how many records were affected.
    ' If no records were affected, there was an error.
    If e.RecordsAffected() = 0 Then
        ' The following statement retrieves a field from the row.
        Console.WriteLine("Error updating row: " & e.Row("ShipperID"))

        ' Statement types include DELETE, INSERT, UPDATE, and SELECT.
        Console.WriteLine(e.StatementType)

        Console.WriteLine(e.Errors.ToString())

        ' Don't throw an exception. Continue with following rows.
        e.Status = UpdateStatus.SkipCurrentRow
    End If

End Sub
```

Another, simpler choice is to set the *DataAdapter.ContinueUpdateOn-Error* property to *True*. Then, after the update is complete, you can investigate errors, log them, or display them to the user. The *DataAdapter* will attempt every change.

```
Adapter.ContinueUpdateOnError = True

' (Perform update here. Concurrency errors will be suppressed.)

' Display errors.
Dim Errors() As DataRow = Ds.Tables(0).GetErrors()
Dim RowError As DataRow
For Each RowError In Errors
    Console.WriteLine("Did not update row: " & RowError("ShipperID"))
Next
```

14.10 Use a Transaction with the *DataAdapter*

Problem

You want to ensure that *DataAdapter* changes are committed or rolled back as a whole.

Solution

Create a *Transaction* object, and assign it the *DataAdapter* commands that are used for deleting, updating, and inserting records.

Discussion

The *DataAdapter* does not expose a *Transaction* property. However, the *Command* objects that the *DataAdapter* uses do provide this property. The following application shows how you can ensure that all commands in a *DataAdapter* update operation are grouped into a single transaction:

```
Dim Con As New SqlConnection(ConnectionString)
Dim CmdSelect As New SqlCommand("SELECT * FROM Shippers", Con)
Dim Ds As New DataSet()
Dim Adapter As New SqlDataAdapter(CmdSelect)

' (Define the custom update, insert, and delete commands
' for the DataAdapter here.)

' Fill the DataSet.
Try
    Con.Open()
    Adapter.Fill(Ds, "Shippers")
Catch Err As Exception
    Console.WriteLine(Err.ToString())
Finally
```

```
        Con.Close()
    End Try

    ' (Make DataSet changes here.)

    Dim Tran As SqlTransaction
    Try
        Con.Open()

        ' Create a new transaction.
        Tran = Con.BeginTransaction()

        ' Enlist the DataAdapter commands in the transaction.
        Adapter.UpdateCommand.Transaction = Tran
        Adapter.InsertCommand.Transaction = Tran
        Adapter.DeleteCommand.Transaction = Tran

        ' Apply the update here.
        Adapter.Update(Ds, "Shippers")

        ' Commit the transaction.
        Tran.Commit()

    Catch Err As Exception
        Console.WriteLine(Err.ToString())

        ' Roll back the transaction.
        Tran.Rollback()

    Finally
        Con.Close()
    End Try
```

This approach is a little more difficult if you're using the *Command-Builder* object to automatically generate updating logic. The problem is that the *CommandBuilder* doesn't actually generate the updating logic when it's first created. In fact, the *CommandBuilder* will not actually build the updating logic until you call the *DataAdapter.Update* method. This poses a problem because the *CommandBuilder* retrieves metadata information from the database using the *DataAdapter.SelectCommand*. This command is not part of the transaction, so invoking it once the update has started and the transaction is underway will cause an exception.

To circumvent this problem, you can force the *CommandBuilder* to generate the logic early by calling a method such as *GetUpdateCommand* before you start the transaction. You can then enlist the insert, update, and delete commands. A complete Console application that demonstrates this approach is shown here:

```
Public Module DataAdapterTransaction

    Private ConnectionString As String = "Data Source=localhost;" & _
    "Integrated Security=SSPI;Initial Catalog=Northwind"

    Public Sub Main()
        Dim Con As New SqlConnection(ConnectionString)
        Dim CmdSelect As New SqlCommand("SELECT * FROM Shippers", Con)
        Dim Ds As New DataSet()
        Dim Adapter As New SqlDataAdapter(CmdSelect)
        Dim Builder As New SqlCommandBuilder(Adapter)

        ' Fill the DataSet.
        Try
            Con.Open()
            Adapter.Fill(Ds, "Shippers")
        Catch Err As Exception
            Console.WriteLine(Err.ToString())
        Finally
            Con.Close()
        End Try

        ' (Make DataSet changes here.)

        Dim Tran As SqlTransaction
        Try
            Con.Open()

            ' Call the GetUpdateCommand() method once so it
            ' retrieves the schema information it needs.
            Builder.GetUpdateCommand()

            ' Create a new transaction.
            Tran = Con.BeginTransaction()

            ' You can now enlist the commands in the transaction.
            Builder.GetUpdateCommand.Transaction = Tran
            Builder.GetInsertCommand.Transaction = Tran
            Builder.GetDeleteCommand.Transaction = Tran

            ' Apply the update here.
            Adapter.Update(Ds, "Shippers")

            ' Commit the transaction.
            Tran.Commit()
            Console.WriteLine("Transaction committed successfully.")

        Catch Err As Exception
            Console.WriteLine(Err.ToString())
```

```
                    ' Roll back the transaction.
                    Tran.Rollback()

              Finally
                    Con.Close()
              End Try
              Console.ReadLine()
        End Sub

    End Module
```

14.11 Read Large Binary Fields Efficiently with a *DataReader*

Problem

You want to read a large binary field without loading the entire row into memory at once.

Solution

Use the *CommandBehavior.SequentialAccess* option with the *DataReader* to use stream-based access to binary data.

Discussion

By default, the *DataReader* loads an entire row into memory every time you call the *Read* method. This approach is dangerously inefficient if your database records include extremely large fields—for example, binary data that might be tens of megabytes in size.

In this case, a better approach is to read the data in smaller blocks. This approach allows you to perform other processing as you read the data. For example, you might want to copy the data to the hard drive 1 KB at a time. To use this approach, you must pass the *CommandBehavior.SequentialAccess* value to the *Command.ExecuteReader* method. You can then read a block of bytes from the field using the *DataReader.GetBytes* method. To determine the total number of bytes in the field, pass a null reference (*Nothing*) to the *GetBytes* method.

The following example reads the binary data from a field in the *Categories* table and writes it to a file. No more than 1 KB of data is in memory at any one time. To use this example without modification, you must import the *System.IO* namespace along with the required *System.Data* namespaces.

```
Public Module StreamRead

    Private ConnectionString As String = "Data Source=localhost;" & _
        "Integrated Security=SSPI;Initial Catalog=Northwind"

    Public Sub Main()
        Dim Con As New SqlConnection(ConnectionString)
        Dim CmdSelect As New SqlCommand( _
            "SELECT CategoryID,Picture FROM Categories", Con)

        Try
            Con.Open()

            ' Open the reader in sequential mode.
            Dim Reader As SqlDataReader
            Reader = CmdSelect.ExecuteReader(CommandBehavior.SequentialAccess)

            ' Read all rows.
            Do While Reader.Read()

                ' Create a file where the binary data will be written.
                ' The filename is based on the first field (the CategoryID)
                Dim Filename As String = Reader.GetInt32(0).ToString() & _
                    ".bin"
                Console.WriteLine("Creating file " & Filename)

                Dim fs As New FileStream(Filename, _
                    FileMode.OpenOrCreate, FileAccess.Write)
                Dim w As New BinaryWriter(fs)

                ' Track the number of bytes read,
                ' and the position in the stream.
                Dim BytesRead As Integer
                Dim Offset As Integer = 0

                ' Read data in blocks of 1K.
                Dim Size As Integer = 1024
                Dim Bytes(1024) As Byte

                ' Write the data.
                Console.WriteLine("About to write " & _
                    Reader.GetBytes(1, 0, Nothing, 0, 0).ToString() & " bytes.")
                Console.WriteLine()

                Do
                    ' Open the second field (Picture) for sequential access.
                    BytesRead = Reader.GetBytes(1, Offset, Bytes, 0, Size)
```

```
                        w.Write(Bytes)
                        w.Flush()

                        Offset += BytesRead
                    Loop While (BytesRead <> 0)

                    ' Close the output file.
                    w.Close()
                    fs.Close()
                Loop
                Reader.Close()

            Catch Err As Exception
                Console.WriteLine(Err.ToString())
            Finally
                Con.Close()
            End Try

            Console.ReadLine()
        End Sub

    End Module
```

> **Note**   When using sequential access, you must read the fields in the
> same order that they are returned by the query. For example, if your
> query returns three columns, you must retrieve the values of the first
> and second fields before accessing the third field. If you access the
> third field first, you will not be able to access the first two fields. This is
> true regardless of whether the fields contain large binary data or sim-
> ple data types.

14.12 Select a Subset of Data from a *DataSet*

Problem

You want to find specific rows in a *DataSet*.

Solution

Use the *DataTable.Select* method or the *DataRowCollection.Find* method.

Discussion

You can use several approaches to find individual *DataRow* objects in a *DataSet*. The most obvious approach is to simply iterate through the collection of *DataRow* objects until you find one that matches the criteria you are looking for.

```
Dim MatchedRows() As New ArrayList

Dim Row As DataRow
For Each Row In Ds.Tables(0).Rows
    If Row(FieldName) = FieldValue Then
        MatchedRows.Add(Row)
    End If
Next
```

However, ADO.NET also provides two more-convenient approaches. First, you can use the *DataRowCollection.Find* method to find a single row based on its unique primary key. For example, if you're using the *Employees* table, you can find the row with a specific *EmployeeID* like this:

```
Dim MatchRow As DataRow
Dim EmployeeID As Integer = 1

' Retrieve the row with EmployeeID 1.
MatchRow = Ds.Tables("Employees").Rows.Find(EmployeeID)
```

For this approach to work, the *DataSet* must have some basic schema information about the data source, so it can identify the primary key. To add this information automatically, you can use the *DataAdapter.FillSchema* method before using the *DataAdapter.Fill* method when filling the *DataSet*.

A more powerful option is to use the *DataTable.Select* method, which allows you to retrieve an array of *DataRow* objects based on an SQL expression (and optionally a combination of *DataViewRowState* values). When calling *Select*, you must supply a text string that filters the rows according to specific field criteria. It plays the same role as the *WHERE* clause in an SQL *SELECT* statement.

For example, in the following code snippet, the *Select* method is used to find all Employees that are based in London:

```
Dim Filter As String = "City = 'London'"
Dim MatchRows() As DataRow = Ds.Tables("Employees").Select(Filter)

Console.WriteLine("Listing all the employees in London.")
Dim Row As DataRow
For Each Row In MatchRows
    Console.WriteLine(Row("FirstName").ToString() & _
        " " & Row("LastName").ToString())
Next
```

The *Select* method supports a rich subset of SQL, including the operators listed in Table 14-2. In addition, you can use some built-in functions to evaluate square roots, manipulate strings, and convert data types. These functions are described in detail in the MSDN reference, under the class library reference description for the *DataColumn.Expression* property.

Table 14-2 Operators That Can Be Used with *DataTable.Select*

Operator	Description
<, >, <=, >=, =, <>	Compares more than one value. If you use number data types, the comparisons will be numeric. If you use string data types, the comparisons will be alphabetic (and you must use apostrophes around all literal values).
AND	Combines multiple clauses. Records must match all criteria (for example, `EmployeeID = 10 AND FirstName='Jones'`).
OR	Combines multiple clauses. Records must match at least one of the specified criteria (for example, `EmployeeID = 10 OR First-Name='Jones'`).
NOT	Add before any expression to perform the reverse. (For example, `NOT EmployeeID = 10` finds all employees except those with an *EmployeeID* of 10.)
BETWEEN	Specifies an inclusive range. (For example, `Quantity BETWEEN 1 AND 10` selects rows that have a value in the *Quantity* column from 1 to 10.)
IS NULL	Tests the column for a null value (for example, `BirthDate IS NULL`).
LIKE	Performs limited pattern matching with string data types. You use the asterisk character (*) to specify zero or more characters. (So, `FirstName LIKE John*` will match Johnathan and any other name starting with John, and `ProductName LIKE *Toy*` will find products with the string *Toy* anywhere inside the name.)
+, -, *, /	Performs numeric addition, subtraction, multiplication, or division. The plus sign (+) can also be used to concatenate strings.
%	Finds the modulus (the remainder after one number is divided by another).

14.13 Create a Custom Record Browser

Problem

You want to synchronize multiple controls on a form.

Solution

Use data binding with the fields in a *DataTable*.

Discussion

Recipe 11.19 showed how you could use data binding to synchronize multiple controls on a Windows Form to a collection of custom objects. The same technique is possible with the *DataSet*.

As an example, consider the form shown in Figure 14-1. It includes four data-bound controls: a list box, two labels, and a text box. These controls are synchronized, so when you make a new selection in the list box, the other controls are updated with the data from the row. In addition, you can move from row to row using the Next and Prev buttons. Changes are supported for any editable control. For example, if the user types in a new price in the text box, that value will be applied to the *UnitPrice* field (assuming that the conversion can be made from a string to the SQL money type).

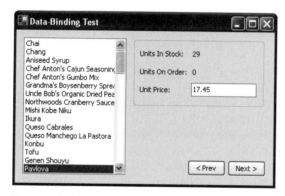

Figure 14-1   A data-bound form.

The form code is shown here:

```
Public Class BoundForm
    Inherits System.Windows.Forms.Form

    ' (Designer code omitted.)

    Private ConnectionString As String = "Data Source=localhost;" & _
        "Integrated Security=SSPI;Initial Catalog=Northwind"
    Private Ds As New DataSet()

    Private Sub BoundForm_Load(ByVal sender As System.Object, _
        ByVal e As System.EventArgs) Handles MyBase.Load
```

```
    Dim Con As New SqlConnection(ConnectionString)
    Dim CmdSelect As New SqlCommand("SELECT * FROM Products", Con)
    Dim Adapter As New SqlDataAdapter(CmdSelect)

    ' Fill the DataSet.
    Try
        Con.Open()
        Adapter.Fill(Ds, "Products")
    Catch Err As Exception
        Console.WriteLine(Err.ToString())
    Finally
        Con.Close()
    End Try

    ' Add the list box data binding.
    lstProductName.DataSource = Ds.Tables(0)
    lstProductName.DisplayMember = "ProductName"

    ' Connect three more controls using the DataBindings collection.
    txtUnitPrice.DataBindings.Add("Text", Ds.Tables(0), "UnitPrice")
    lblUnitsInStock.DataBindings.Add("Text", Ds.Tables(0), "UnitsInStock")
    lblUnitsOnOrder.DataBindings.Add("Text", Ds.Tables(0), "UnitsOnOrder")
End Sub

Private Sub cmdNext_Click(ByVal sender As System.Object, _
    ByVal e As System.EventArgs) Handles cmdNext.Click
        ' Look up the binding context for this data source,
        ' and increment the position by 1.
        Me.BindingContext(Ds.Tables(0)).Position += 1
End Sub

Private Sub cmdPrev_Click(ByVal sender As System.Object, _
    ByVal e As System.EventArgs) Handles cmdPrev.Click
        ' Look up the binding context for this data source,
        ' and decrement the position by 1.
        Me.BindingContext(Ds.Tables(0)).Position -= 1
End Sub

End Class
```

Remember, when using editable data-binding, you're simply allowing the user to modify the information in the disconnected *DataSet*. To apply changes, you'll need to pass the *DataSet* to the *DataAdapter.Update* method.

14.14 Filter or Sort Data with a *DataView*

Problem

You want to show a subset of data from a *DataTable* or sort that data.

Solution

Set a filter or sort rows using the *DataView.RowFilter* and *DataView.Sort* properties.

Discussion

When you bind a *DataTable* to a Windows control, you're actually making use of another type of object that acts as a mediator: the *DataView*. The *DataView* exposes the information from the *DataTable* and allows you to filter rows or apply a sort order.

You can create a *DataView* for a *DataTable* and bind the *DataView* to a control. However, it's more common to bind controls directly to a *DataTable*. In this case, the *DataView* referenced by the *DataTable.DefaultView* property is used automatically. Thus, if you want to configure sorting or filtering, you must modify the properties of the *DataTable.DefaultView*.

The *DataView.Sort* property works much like the *ORDER BY* clause in an SQL statement. If you want to sort according to a single column, set the *Sort* property to the column name. If you want to sort using multiple columns, set the *Sort* property to a list of column names, separated by commas. You can add *DESC* after a column name to perform a descending sort (with the smallest value first), instead of the default ascending sort. String columns are sorted alphabetically without regard to case. Numeric columns are ordered using a numeric sort. Columns that contain binary data can't be sorted.

Here's a code snippet that sorts data in reverse order, with the most recent dates first:

```
Ds.Tables(0).DefaultDataView.Sort = "OrderDate DESC"
```

The *DataView.RowFilter* property works like the *WHERE* clause in an SQL statement. You can filter rows based on any column expression. The *DataView.RowFilter* property supports the same syntax as the *DataTable.Select* method. Table 14-2, earlier in this chapter, lists supported operators.

Here's a code snippet that shows only products in a specific category:

```
Ds.Tables(0).DefaultDataView.RowFilter = "CategoryID = 10"
```

The following example (shown in Figure 14-2) shows two *DataGrid* controls in different binding contexts. Both *DataGrid* controls draw their data from the same underlying *DataTable*, but because they use different *DataView* objects, the sort and filter settings are different.

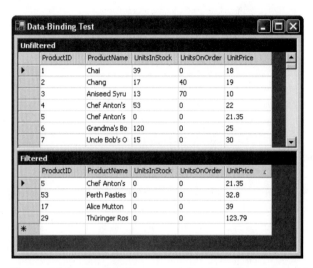

Figure 14-2   Binding the same data with different *DataView* objects.

```
Public Class BoundForm
    Inherits System.Windows.Forms.Form

    ' (Designer code omitted.)

    Private ConnectionString As String = "Data Source=localhost;" & _
      "Integrated Security=SSPI;Initial Catalog=Northwind"
    Private Ds As New DataSet()

    Private Sub BoundForm_Load(ByVal sender As System.Object, _
      ByVal e As System.EventArgs) Handles MyBase.Load
        Dim Con As New SqlConnection(ConnectionString)
        Dim CmdSelect As New SqlCommand("SELECT ProductID, " & _
          "ProductName, UnitsInStock, UnitsOnOrder, UnitPrice " & _
          "FROM Products", Con)
        Dim Adapter As New SqlDataAdapter(CmdSelect)

        ' Fill the DataSet.
        Try
```

```
        Con.Open()
        Adapter.Fill(Ds, "Products")
    Catch Err As Exception
        Console.WriteLine(Err.ToString())
    Finally
        Con.Close()
    End Try


    ' Bind the default DataView (which currently has no
    ' filters or sorts applied).
    gridUnfiltered.DataSource = Ds.Tables("Products")


    ' Create a new DataView and configure its filter and sorting.
    Dim View As New DataView(Ds.Tables("Products"))
    View.RowFilter = "UnitsInStock = 0 AND UnitsOnOrder = 0"
    View.Sort = "UnitPrice"


    ' Bind the new DataView.
    gridFiltered.DataSource = View
End Sub


End Class
```

Some controls also allow you to bind directly to the entire *DataSet*. (The *DataGrid* is one example.) In this case, the *DataViewManager* plays the role of intermediary. The *DataViewManager* contains a collection of *DataViewSetting* objects, one for each table in the *DataSet*. The *DataViewManager* creates *DataView* instances as needed to show the tables in a *DataSet*, using the settings from the corresponding *DataViewSetting* object. These settings provide the same information found in the *DataView* class, including the ever-important *Sort* and *RowFilter* properties.

Thus, to configure sorting or filtering when binding to a *DataSet*, you must modify the corresponding *DataViewSetting* in the *DataViewManager* that you're binding. Although you can create a *DataViewManager* by hand, every *DataSet* has a default *DataViewManager* that's referenced by the *DataSet.DefaultViewManager* property. Here's how your code might look:

```
' (Fill the DataSet.)

' Create a new DataViewManager.
Dim ViewManager As New DataViewManager(Ds)

' Customize the DataViewManager with a default filter and sort
' for the Products table.
ViewManager.DataViewSettings(Ds.Tables("Products")).RowFilter = _
  "UnitsInStock = 0 AND UnitsOnOrder = 0"
ViewManager.DataViewSettings(Ds.Tables("Products")).Sort = "UnitPrice"
```

```
' Bind the new DataViewManager.
gridFiltered.DataSource = ViewManager

' (When the Products table is selected, the ViewManager settings
' will be used to create the view.)
```

14.15 Create a Master-Details Form

Problem

You need to create a form that allows users to navigate a parent-child relationship.

Solution

React to the *CurrencyManager.PositionChanged* event for the parent table, and update the *DataView.RowFilter* used for the child table.

Discussion

You can create a master-details form using data binding and row filtering. In this case, you need to bind two separate tables. The row position will be tracked separately for each table. When a row is selected in the parent table, you can configure the child table to show only the related rows by modifying the corresponding *DataView.RowFilter* property (as introduced in recipe 14.14). Figure 14-3 shows an example with two *DataGrid* controls. The top-most *Data-Grid* shows a list of categories. The *DataGrid* under it shows the products in the currently selected category.

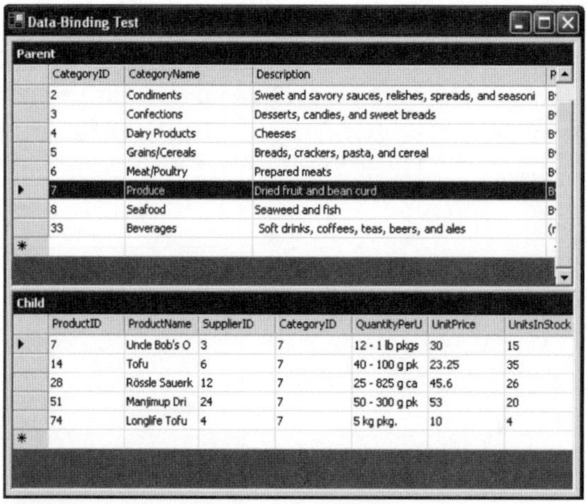

Figure 14-3   A master-details form.

The code for this form is fairly straightforward. The two tables are bound when the form first loads. In addition, the code connects an event handler that reacts to the *CurrencyManager.PositionChanged* event for the parent table. This event fires whenever the category row changes, whether the change is initiated by the user (for example, when the user chooses a new category in the *DataGrid*) or accomplished programmatically using the *CurrencyManager* properties (as shown in recipe 14.13). The event handler modifies the *RowFilter* property for the child table, which will affect all the controls that are bound to it. In this example, this changes the lists of products in the second *DataGrid*.

The complete form code is shown here:

```vb
Public Class BoundForm
    Inherits System.Windows.Forms.Form

    ' (Designer code omitted.)

    Private ConnectionString As String = "Data Source=localhost;" & _
      "Integrated Security=SSPI;Initial Catalog=Northwind"

    Private CategoriesTable As DataTable
    Private ProductsTable As DataTable

    Private Sub Form1_Load(ByVal sender As System.Object, _
      ByVal e As System.EventArgs) Handles MyBase.Load
        Dim Con As New SqlConnection(ConnectionString)
        Dim CmdSelect As New SqlCommand( _
          "SELECT * FROM Categories;SELECT * FROM Products", Con)
        Dim Adapter As New SqlDataAdapter(CmdSelect)
        Dim Ds As New DataSet()

        ' Fill the DataSet.
        Try
            Con.Open()
            Adapter.Fill(Ds)

            CategoriesTable = Ds.Tables(0)
            ProductsTable = Ds.Tables(1)
        Catch Err As Exception
            MessageBox.Show(Err.ToString())
        Finally
            Con.Close()
        End Try

        ' Bind the Categories table.
        gridCategories.DataSource = CategoriesTable

        ' Bind the Products table.
        gridProducts.DataSource = ProductsTable
```

```
            Dim Binding As BindingManagerBase = Me.BindingContext(CategoriesTable)
            AddHandler Binding.PositionChanged, AddressOf Binding_PositionChanged

            ' Invoke method once to update child table at startup.
            Binding_PositionChanged(Nothing, Nothing)
        End Sub

        Private Sub Binding_PositionChanged(ByVal sender As Object, _
          ByVal e As EventArgs)
            Dim Filter As String
            Dim SelectedRow As DataRow

            ' Find the current category row.
            Dim Index As Integer = Me.BindingContext(CategoriesTable).Position
            SelectedRow = CategoriesTable.Rows(Index)

            ' Create a filter expression using its CategoryID.
            Filter = "CategoryID='" & SelectedRow("CategoryID").ToString() & "'"

            ' Modify the view onto the product table.
            ProductsTable.DefaultView.RowFilter = Filter
        End Sub

    End Class
```

14.16 Format Data-Bound Fields

Problem

You want to apply specific formatting to certain fields in a database (for example, display numbers as currency strings, convert fixed constants to more descriptive text, and so on).

Solution

React to the *Parse* and *Format* data binding events, which allow you to "translate" values as they are retrieved from the *DataTable* and inserted back into the *DataTable*.

Discussion

In earlier versions of Microsoft Visual Basic, you had little ability to customize raw database values when displaying them through data binding. The data binding provided by Windows Forms improves on this situation with the *Parse* and *Format* events. The *Format* event fires just before a data value is displayed.

It allows you to format the information for display. The *Parse* event happens when a change is committed (usually when the user navigates to another control or another record). It allows you to take a formatted value and convert it into a value that's valid for the appropriate field in the *DataTable*.

To demonstrate how you use these two events, you can enhance the data-binding example from recipe 14.13 so that unit prices are formatted and parsed as needed. To do so, you'll need to replace this line of code

```
txtUnitPrice.DataBindings.Add("Text", Ds.Tables(0), "UnitPrice")
```

with the code segment shown here:

```
Dim PriceBinding As New Binding("Text", Ds.Tables(0), "UnitPrice")
AddHandler PriceBinding.Format, AddressOf DecimalToCurrencyString
AddHandler PriceBinding.Parse, AddressOf CurrencyStringToDecimal
txtUnitPrice.DataBindings.Add(PriceBinding)
```

The text box is still bound to the same database field, only now the code can receive the *Format* and *Parse* events for this binding. Be aware that data binding events are handled on a control-by-control basis. However, if you need to format several fields in an analogous way (for example, if you need to convert several different numeric values to currency strings), you can use the same event handlers for each set of binding events.

Finally you need to create the event handlers that perform the conversion. The *ConvertEventArgs.DesiredType* property indicates the type expected by the control (in the *Format* event handler) or by the *DataTable* field (in the *Parse* event handler). For example, the *Text* property of a text box requires a string data type. You convert the value provided in the *ConvertEventArgs.Value* property.

```
Private Sub DecimalToCurrencyString(ByVal sender As Object, _
  ByVal e As ConvertEventArgs)
    If e.DesiredType Is GetType(String) Then
        ' Use the ToString method to format the value as currency.
        e.Value = CType(e.Value, Decimal).ToString("c")
    End If
End Sub

Private Sub CurrencyStringToDecimal(ByVal sender As Object, _
  ByVal e As ConvertEventArgs)
    If e.DesiredType Is GetType(Decimal) Then
        ' Convert the string back to a decimal using the Parse method.
        e.Value = Decimal.Parse(e.Value.ToString, _
          Globalization.NumberStyles.Currency, Nothing)
    End If
End Sub
```

Figure 14-4 shows the formatted results.

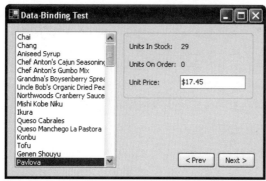

Figure 14-4 Formatting currency values.

14.17 Bind an Image Field to a *PictureBox*

Problem

You want to bind a *PictureBox* to a field that contains binary image data.

Solution

React to the *Format* data-binding event, and convert the binary data to an *Image* object.

Discussion

You can use data binding to bind any property from almost any control to a database field, including the *Image* property from the *PictureBox* control. However, the *Image* property requires an *Image* object—not just a byte array. Therefore, you need to perform some conversion to translate the binary data into an *Image* object.

You can use data-binding events to execute this conversion logic automatically. All you need to do is react to the *Format* event (first introduced in recipe 14.16) and create a new *Image* object using the supplied image field data. In the example shown in Figure 14-5, this technique allows an application to bind to the logo data contained in the *pub_info* table in the pubs database. (The Northwind databases also include some tables that use image data, but this image data is wrapped with the header information created by the Visual Basic 6 OLE Container control, and is thus more difficult to convert to pure image data.)

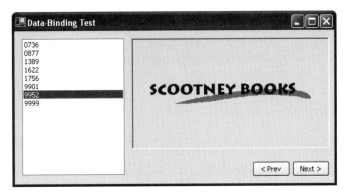

Figure 14-5   Binding to binary image data.

You can use the following code to bind the table to the list box and picture control when the form loads:

```
Private Sub BoundForm_Load(ByVal sender As System.Object, _
  ByVal e As System.EventArgs) Handles MyBase.Load

        Dim Con As New SqlConnection(ConnectionString)
        Dim CmdSelect As New SqlCommand("SELECT * FROM pub_info", Con)
        Dim Adapter As New SqlDataAdapter(CmdSelect)

        ' Fill the DataSet.
        Try
            Con.Open()
            Adapter.Fill(Ds, "pub_info")
        Catch Err As Exception
            MessageBox.Show(Err.ToString())
        Finally
            Con.Close()
        End Try

        ' Add the list box data binding.
        lstID.DataSource = Ds.Tables(0)
        lstID.DisplayMember = "pub_id"

        ' Add the picture box data binding.
        Dim LogoBinding As New Binding("Image", Ds.Tables(0), "logo")
        AddHandler LogoBinding.Format, AddressOf BindImage
        picLogo.DataBindings.Add(LogoBinding)

End Sub
```

The *BindImage* event handler converts the binary field data to an *Image* object.

```
Private Sub BindImage(ByVal sender As Object, ByVal e As ConvertEventArgs)

    If e.DesiredType Is GetType(Image) Then
        Dim ms As New System.IO.MemoryStream(CType(e.Value, Byte()))
        Dim Logo As Bitmap = Image.FromStream(ms)
        e.Value = Logo
    End If

End Sub
```

14.18 Bind a Field to a List Control, and Restrict It to the Values from Another Table

Problem

You want to fill a list control with allowed values from one table and use it to edit a field in another table.

Solution

Fill the list control with allowed values by setting the *DataSource*, *DisplayMember*, and *ValueMember* properties. Then bind the list control's *SelectedValue* to the field you want to edit using the *DataBindings* collection.

Discussion

List controls can play two roles in Windows data binding:

- **Record navigation.** In this case, you set the *DataSource*, *DisplayMember*, and *ValueMember* properties. For example, if you bind the list control in this way to the *ProductName* column in a *Products* table, the list will be filled with all the product names in the table. Every time you change the selection in the list box, you navigate to a different product record, and all other bound controls will be updated accordingly.

- **Single-value editing.** You can bind the *SelectedValue* or *Selected-Text* property of the list control to any field in a table using the *Dat-aBindings* collection. In this case, when you change the value in the list control, the corresponding field in the record is modified. For example, if you bind a combo box to the *ProductName* field in a *Products* table, every time the user changes the text in the combo box, the product record will be modified.

It's often useful to combine these two approaches, and use a list control to edit a field based on a list of allowed values. This approach is particularly useful when you need to deal with application-specific codes. For example, you might create an *Orders* table with a *Status* field. You can then create a *StatusValues* table that has all the allowed values for the *Status* field. You can fill the list control with the list of allowed *StatusValues* by setting the *DataSource* property, and you can bind the list control to the *Status* field in the *Orders* table using the *DataBindings* collection.

The Northwind sample database doesn't include any state tables. However, the same technique can be demonstrated with any two related tables. The following example shows how you can use this technique to edit the relation between territory and region records.

Figure 14-6 shows a custom record browser for editing territory records. Each territory is linked to a record in the *Region* table through a foreign *RegionID* field. In the custom record browser, the list control is pre-filled with the list of allowed region names. The *RegionID* field is used as the value for list control items, while the *RegionDescription* field is used for the display text. The user can change the selection in the list to link a territory to a different region.

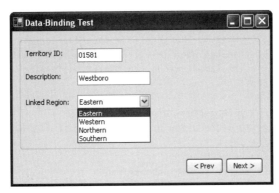

Figure 14-6   A record browser that allows you to modify a record relationship.

The full form code is shown here:

```
Public Class BoundForm
    Inherits System.Windows.Forms.Form

    ' (Designer code omitted.)

    Private ConnectionString As String = "Data Source=localhost;" & _
        "Integrated Security=SSPI;Initial Catalog=Northwind"

    Private dtRegions, dtTerritories As DataTable
```

```vb
Private Sub Form1_Load(ByVal sender As System.Object, _
  ByVal e As System.EventArgs) Handles MyBase.Load
    Dim Con As New SqlConnection(ConnectionString)
    Dim CmdRegions As New SqlCommand("SELECT * FROM Region", Con)
    Dim CmdTerritories As New SqlCommand("SELECT * FROM Territories", Con)
    Dim Adapter As New SqlDataAdapter(CmdRegions)
    Dim Ds As New DataSet()

    ' Fill the DataSet.
    Try
        Con.Open()
        Adapter.Fill(Ds, "Regions")
        Adapter.SelectCommand = CmdTerritories
        Adapter.Fill(Ds, "Territories")
    Catch Err As Exception
        MessageBox.Show(Err.Message)
        Return
    Finally
        Con.Close()
    End Try

    dtRegions = Ds.Tables("Regions")
    dtTerritories = Ds.Tables("Territories")

    ' Bind the two text boxes to the territory record information.
    txtTerritoryID.DataBindings.Add("Text", dtTerritories, "TerritoryID")
    txtTerritoryDescription.DataBindings.Add("Text", dtTerritories, _
      "TerritoryDescription")

    ' Fill the list box with region information.
    ' It will display the RegionDescription, but link to the RegionID
    ' through the value property.
    lstRegionID.DataSource = dtRegions
    lstRegionID.DisplayMember = "RegionDescription"
    lstRegionID.ValueMember = "RegionID"

    ' Bind the list control's SelectedValue property to the
    ' RegionID field in the Territories table.
    lstRegionID.DataBindings.Add("SelectedValue", dtTerritories, _
      "RegionID")
End Sub

Private Sub cmdNext_Click(ByVal sender As System.Object, _
  ByVal e As System.EventArgs) Handles cmdNext.Click
    Me.BindingContext(dtTerritories).Position += 1
End Sub
```

```
      Private Sub cmdPrev_Click(ByVal sender As System.Object, _
          ByVal e As System.EventArgs) Handles cmdPrev.Click
            Me.BindingContext(dtTerritories).Position -= 1
      End Sub
End Class
```

14.19 Create a Calculated Column That Uses a Relationship

Problem

You want to add a calculated column to a parent table that displays information from a child table.

Solution

Create a new *DataColumn* for the parent table. Set the *DataColumn.Expression* property to count or sum information from the related rows.

Discussion

You can create a simple calculated column by instantiating a new *DataColumn* object, setting its *Expression* property, and adding it the *DataTable.Columns* collection for the appropriate table. For example, the following code creates a column that multiplies the information from two other columns:

```
Dim Col As New DataColumn("InventoryValue", GetType(Decimal), _
  "UnitPrice * UnitsInStock")
Ds.Tables(0).Columns.Add(Col)
```

When writing the expression, you can use all the operators described in Table 14-2. They allow you to build a column that's based on any combination of values in the current row.

You can also create a calculated column that incorporates information from related rows. For example, you might add a column in a *Categories* table that indicates the number of related product rows. To create a calculated column that uses a relationship, you must first define the relationship with a *DataRelation* object. You'll also need to use one of the aggregate functions shown in Table 14-3. These functions allow you to calculate a single number from a series of values.

Table 14-3 Supported Aggregate Functions

Function	Description
Avg(fieldname)	Calculates the average of all values in a given numeric field
Sum(fieldname)	Calculates the sum of all values in a given numeric field
Min(fieldname) and *Max(fieldname)*	Finds the minimum or maximum value in a number field
Count(fieldname)	Returns the number of rows in the result set
Count(DISTINCT fieldname)	Returns the number of unique (and non-null) rows in the result set

The following example creates three calculated columns, all of which use a table relationship. These calculated columns provide the total number of products, the maximum price, and the total number of items in inventory for each category. The results are shown in a bound *DataGrid*. (See Figure 14-7.)

```
Public Class BoundForm
    Inherits System.Windows.Forms.Form

    ' (Designer code omitted.)

    Private ConnectionString As String = "Data Source=localhost;" & _
      "Integrated Security=SSPI;Initial Catalog=Northwind"

    Private Sub BoundForm_Load(ByVal sender As System.Object, _
      ByVal e As System.EventArgs) Handles MyBase.Load
        Dim Con As New SqlConnection(ConnectionString)
        Dim CmdSelect As New SqlCommand( _
          "SELECT CategoryID, CategoryName FROM Categories;" & _
          "SELECT * FROM Products", Con)
        Dim Adapter As New SqlDataAdapter(CmdSelect)
        Dim Ds As New DataSet()

        ' Fill the DataSet.
        Try
            Con.Open()
            Adapter.Fill(Ds)
        Catch Err As Exception
            MessageBox.Show(Err.ToString())
        Finally
            Con.Close()
        End Try

        ' Define a parent-child relationship between categories and products.
        Dim ParentCol As DataColumn = Ds.Tables(0).Columns("CategoryID")
```

```
    Dim ChildCol As DataColumn = Ds.Tables(1).Columns("CategoryID")
    Dim Relation As New DataRelation("Cat_Prod", ParentCol, ChildCol)
    Ds.Relations.Add(Relation)

    ' Create the calculated columns.
    Dim ColCount As New DataColumn("# Of Products", GetType(Integer), _
      "COUNT(Child(Cat_Prod).CategoryID)")
    Ds.Tables(0).Columns.Add(ColCount)

    Dim ColMax As New DataColumn("Max Price", GetType(Decimal), _
      "MAX(Child(Cat_Prod).UnitPrice)")
    Ds.Tables(0).Columns.Add(ColMax)

    Dim ColSum As New DataColumn("Total Inventory", GetType(Integer), _
      "SUM(Child(Cat_Prod).UnitsInStock)")
    Ds.Tables(0).Columns.Add(ColSum)

    ' Bind the table.
    grid.DataSource = Ds.Tables(0)
  End Sub

End Class
```

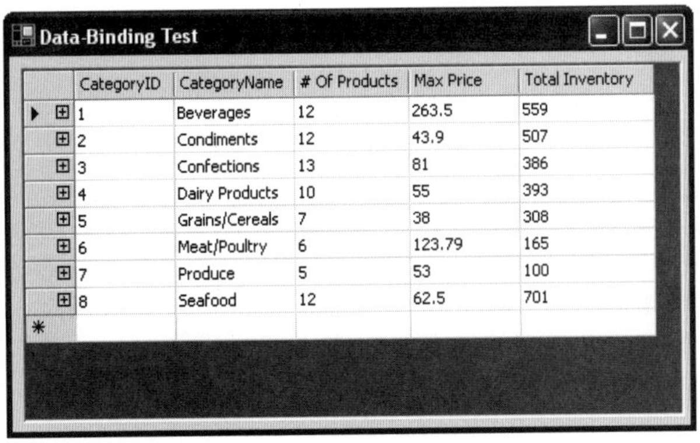

Data-Binding Test

	CategoryID	CategoryName	# Of Products	Max Price	Total Inventory
▶ ⊞	1	Beverages	12	263.5	559
⊞	2	Condiments	12	43.9	507
⊞	3	Confections	13	81	386
⊞	4	Dairy Products	10	55	393
⊞	5	Grains/Cereals	7	38	308
⊞	6	Meat/Poultry	6	123.79	165
⊞	7	Produce	5	53	100
⊞	8	Seafood	12	62.5	701
*					

Figure 14-7   Binding with calculated columns.

14.20 Create a Typed *DataSet*

Problem

You want to access table names and field values using strongly typed property names instead of field-name lookup.

Solution

Create a typed *DataSet* using Visual Studio .NET or the XSD.exe command-line utility.

Discussion

A strongly typed *DataSet* is actually a set of classes that inherit from the *DataSet*, *DataTable*, and *DataRow* classes. Although the basic *DataSet* can be used with any table structure, a strongly typed *DataSet* is designed for use with a specific set of tables. For example, you might create a strongly typed Northwind *DataSet* that includes a set of *DataTable* and *DataRow* classes customized for use with tables such as *Products*, *Employees*, *Categories*, *Shippers*, and so on. The strongly typed classes allow you to use named properties to retrieve tables and column values, and these classes include dedicated methods for navigating table relationships.

For example, with a strongly typed *DataSet* and *DataTable* based on the *Employees* table, you can replace code such as this

```
' Display the ID of the first row using string-lookup.
Console.WriteLine(ds.Tables("Employees").Rows(0)("EmployeeID"));
```

with this syntax:

```
' Display the ID of the first row using strongly typed properties.
Console.WriteLine(ds.Employees.Rows(0).EmployeeID);
```

This code is clearer and can be checked for name and data type errors at compile time. An error in string-based column lookup will generate a runtime error that might not be discovered until much later. The disadvantage of a strongly typed *DataSet* is that you need to manage and possibly distribute the assembly that contains the strongly typed classes.

There are two basic ways to create a typed *DataSet*:

■ Use Visual Studio .NET to generate it.

■ Use the XSD.exe command-line utility.

Both of these approaches require an XSD schema file describing the structure of the database. You can create this file using the *DataSet.WriteXmlSchema* method. Here's an example of the code you could use to create an XSD file that describes the structure of the *Categories* and *Products* tables:

```
Dim Con As New SqlConnection(ConnectionString)
Dim CmdProd As New SqlCommand("SELECT * FROM Products", Con)
Dim CmdCat As New SqlCommand("SELECT * FROM Categories", Con)
```

```
' (Define more SELECT commands here for all the tables you want to use.)

Dim Adapter As New SqlDataAdapter(CmdProd)
Dim Ds As New DataSet()

' Fill the DataSet.
Try
    Con.Open()
    Adapter.FillSchema(Ds, SchemaType.Mapped, "Products")

    ' Modify the command and re-execute it.
    Adapter.SelectCommand = cmdCat
    Adapter.FillSchema(Ds, SchemaType.Mapped, "Categories")

    ' (Repeat this process for all additional commands.)
Catch Err As Exception
    Console.WriteLine(Err.ToString())
Finally
    Con.Close()
End Try

' Save the XSD schema file.
Ds.WriteXmlSchema("Northwind.xsd")
```

You can now create a strongly typed *DataSet* in Visual Studio .NET. Open a project, right-click on the project in Solution Explorer, and choose Add Existing Item from the Add menu. Then browse to the XSD file you created.

Visual Studio .NET provides two display modes to examine and configure the XSD file: as XML or as a *DataSet*. The XML view allows you to edit the text of the XSD file with the benefit of a few IDE niceties such as automatic statement completion. The *DataSet* view provides a tabular diagram where you can easily modify data types and add relations. Figure 14-8 shows a portion of the *DataSet* view, with the *Categories* table definition. You'll notice that the *CategoryName* and *Description* fields have been created as special types with a character length restriction.

You can use the Visual Studio .NET designer to modify the type restrictions that will be applied to various fields. However, you shouldn't edit the column names because doing so will create a typed *DataSet* that references nonexistent fields.

You can also define relationships by right-clicking on the parent field and choosing New Relation from the Add menu. Figure 14-9 shows the custom Visual Studio .NET window that allows you to configure the relation and add the implied constraints. In this example, a relation is being defined between the *Categories* and *Products* tables.

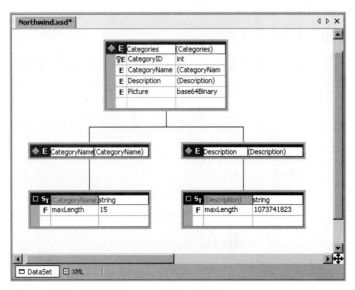

Figure 14-8   Configuring a *DataSet* schema.

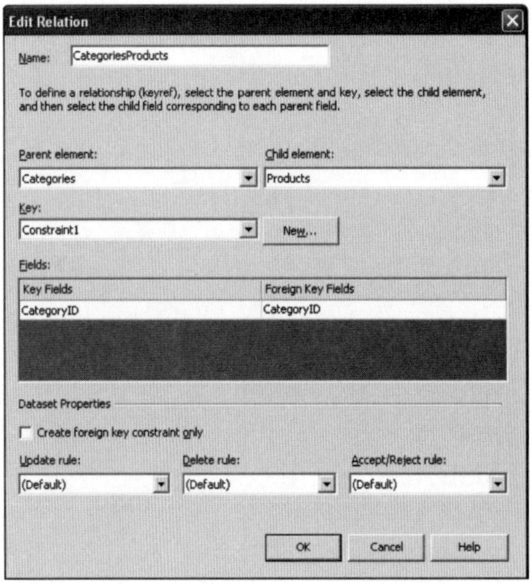

Figure 14-9   Adding a relationship.

Finally, to generate the *DataSet*, right-click on the designer window and select the Generate Dataset check box. (You can also select Preview Dataset to see the names, data types, and structures that will be used for the various data objects.) To actually see the strongly typed *DataSet* file, you'll need to select Show All Files from the Project menu. Then you'll find a Northwind.vb item under the Northwind.xsd node.

You can also create a typed *DataSet* from a schema file using the XSD.exe command-line utility that's included with the .NET Framework. To do so, use the following command at the command-line prompt:

```
xsd Northwind.xsd /d /l:VB /n:Northwind
```

The */d* switch specifies that you want source code for a *DataSet* to be created, and the */l* switch specifies that the utility should use the Visual Basic language. The */n* parameter specifies the namespace for the generated types. (The default is *Schemas*.) The resulting file will have the name Northwind.vb. You can add this file to an existing project or compile it to an assembly using the vbc.exe command-line compiler. MSDN describes all the parameters supported by the XSD.exe utility.

14.21 Read an Excel File with ADO.NET

Problem

You want to retrieve or insert data in a Microsoft Excel document using ADO.NET.

Solution

Use the ODBC provider in conjunction with the Microsoft Excel ODBC Driver.

Discussion

There's no managed provider or OLE DB provider for Excel. However, you can use the Microsoft Excel ODBC driver, which is installed by default with Excel, in conjunction with the ODBC .NET provider. The ODBC .NET provider is included with the .NET Framework 1.1 (and Visual Studio .NET 2003). If you are using .NET Framework 1.0, you can download the ODBC .NET provider as an add-on from the MSDN site at *http://msdn.microsoft.com/library /default.asp?url=/downloads/list/netdevframework.asp*.

In your connection string, you'll need to specify the driver you are using and the filename of the Excel file. Here's an example that points to a file named test.xls in the application's startup directory:

```
Private ConnectionString As String = _
  "Driver={Microsoft Excel Driver (*.xls)};DriverId=790;" & _
  "Dbq=" & Application.StartupPath & "\test.xls;"
```

After connecting, you can perform two types of operations: *SELECT* or *INSERT* commands. Instead of using tables, you select or insert using sheet names. Sheet names must end with a dollar sign ($) and be grouped in square brackets, or they'll generate a syntax error. You can also use page names or region names in your queries. Formatting is ignored, and the first row is automatically used for column names.

The following code example extracts and displays all the rows in Sheet1. The original Excel file is shown in Figure 14-10. The data is shown in a form in Figure 14-11.

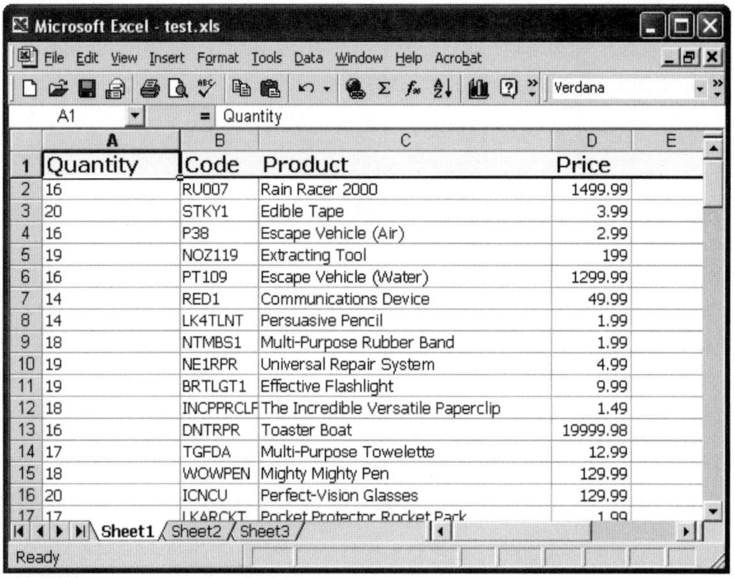

Figure 14-10   The Excel file.

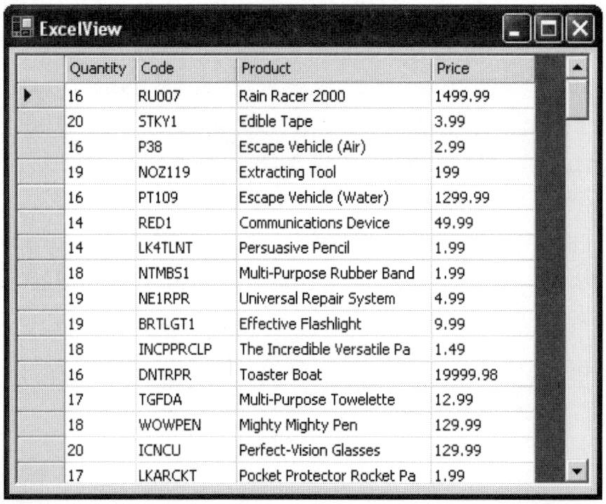

Figure 14-11   The Excel data in a .NET application.

Here's the code that queries the Excel file and binds the retrieved *DataSet* to the *DataGrid*:

```
Private Sub ExcelView_Load(ByVal sender As System.Object, _
  ByVal e As System.EventArgs) Handles MyBase.Load

    Dim Con As New OdbcConnection(ConnectionString)
    Dim CmdSelect As New OdbcCommand("SELECT * FROM [Sheet1$]", Con)
    Dim Adapter As New OdbcDataAdapter(CmdSelect)
    Dim Ds As New DataSet

    Try
        Con.Open()
        Adapter.Fill(Ds, "Sheet1")
    Catch Err As Exception
        MessageBox.Show(Err.ToString())
    Finally
        Con.Close()
    End Try

    grid.DataSource = Ds.Tables("Sheet1")

End Sub
```

> **Note** An alternate choice is to use Automation to "drive" Excel through the COM interfaces it exposes. This approach requires you to use COM Interop and the proprietary Excel objects, and it only works if you have Excel installed on the same computer. However, it exposes a richer set of functionality for interacting with spreadsheet data. Recipe 19.5 introduces this approach.

15

ASP.NET Web Applications

ASP.NET is a centerpiece of the .NET strategy—a new and unique platform for Web development that makes writing a dynamic Web page almost as easy as coding a Microsoft Windows application. However, despite that apparent similarity, ASP.NET developers frequently encounter challenges utterly unlike those faced in Windows applications. Examples include bridging the gap between requests in a stateless Web page (recipe 15.2), adding security and a login page (recipe 15.8), using validation code to prevent input errors (recipe 15.9), leveraging client-side JavaScript to extend your Web page interface (recipes 15.4 and 15.5), and using rich controls such as trees, toolbars, tab strips, and menus (recipes 15.16 and 15.17).

This chapter considers all these issues. In addition, it tackles advanced issues such as creating a dynamic interface with programmatically loaded controls (recipes 15.12 and 15.13), generating images such as pie charts on the fly (recipes 15.14 and 15.15), and using different caching techniques (recipes 15.10 and 15.11). These are some of the common techniques used when programming first-rate ASP.NET Web pages.

> **Note** Most of the Web pages in this chapter are held in one virtual directory, which is named VBCookbookWeb. To use the examples in the downloadable code, you can create the same virtual directory on your computer by following the instructions in the readme.txt file provided with the code download. Alternatively, you can add the Web pages directly to your own Web application projects, in which case they will be copied to an existing virtual directory.

15.1 Enable Web Site Debugging

Problem

When attempting to debug a Web application with Microsoft Visual Studio .NET, you receive an "unable to start debugging on the server" error.

Solution

Ensure that Internet Information Services (IIS) is installed correctly, that IIS was installed *before* the Microsoft .NET Framework, and that Integrated Windows authentication is enabled for the Web application directory.

Discussion

The "unable to start debugging" error signals that Visual Studio .NET was able to compile the Web application but can't execute it in debug mode. Unfortunately, this problem can result for countless different reasons, including:

■ IIS, the Windows component that hosts Web applications, is not installed or is installed incorrectly.

■ The user running Visual Studio .NET is not a member of the Debugger Users group for the Web server.

■ The user running Visual Studio .NET does not have permissions to debug the ASP.NET process. For example, if the ASP.NET process is running under the local system account, the user must have Administrator privileges to debug it.

■ The Web server is running a version of Windows that does not support debugging, such as Microsoft Windows NT and Windows XP Home Edition. (Windows 2000, Windows XP Professional, Windows XP Server, and Windows Server 2003 are all supported.)

■ The Web application does not have a web.config file, or the web.config file does not enable debugging.

■ You are running Visual Studio .NET, and you have not enabled Integrated Windows authentication for the virtual directory.

The first step that you should take when diagnosing why you can't debug a Web application is to check that IIS is installed on the Web server. To do so, open *http://localhost/localstart.asp* in your browser. (*localhost* is an alias for the current computer.) If the test page does not appear, IIS is not installed or is not enabled. You can also attempt to start your Web application without debugging by selecting Debug | Start Without Debugging from the Visual Studio .NET menu. If this test is successful, IIS is correctly installed.

If you installed IIS after you installed Visual Studio .NET or the .NET Framework, you might need to "repair" the .NET Framework using the original setup CD or DVD. To start this process, type in the following command at the command line (or in the Run window) using the Visual Studio .NET DVD. (It's split into two lines below because of page constraints, but it should be entered on a single line.)

```
<DVD Drive>:\wcu\dotNetFramework\dotnetfx.exe /t:c:\temp
  /c:"msiexec.exe /fvecms c:\temp\netfx.msi"
```

If you are using the CD version of Visual Studio .NET, use the following command line with the Windows Component Update disc:

```
<CD Drive>:\dotNetFramework\dotnetfx.exe /t:c:\temp
  /c:"msiexec.exe /fvecms c:\temp\netfx.msi"
```

If IIS is properly installed, the next step is to validate your Web application's web.config file. The web.config file should follow the structure shown here:

```
<configuration>
   <system.web>
      <compilation defaultLanguage="VB"
         debug="true" >

   <!-- Other settings omitted. -->

   </system.web>
</configuration>
```

By default, Visual Studio .NET adds the *compilation* tag to the automatically generated web.config file with the *debug* setting set to *true*.

The next step is to verify the IIS configuration. Problems will occur if you fail to create the required virtual application directory or if you try to run a Web application after you've removed or modified the virtual directory. To correct these problems, modify the virtual directory settings in IIS Manager by selecting Control Panel | Administrative Tools | Internet Information Services from the Start menu. Verify that the virtual application directory exists and that it is configured as a Web application. (You can see virtual directory settings by right-clicking on the directory and choosing Properties.) For example, in the screen shot shown in Figure 15-1, the virtual directory exists but is not configured as a Web application. To resolve this problem, you simply need to click the Create button in the Application Settings section.

Figure 15-1   A virtual directory that is not a Web application.

One other IIS configuration problem that can occur in Visual Studio .NET is a failure to authenticate. Visual Studio .NET attempts to access the local Web server using Integrated Windows authentication, even if you have anonymous authentication enabled for the virtual directory. This means that your virtual directory must allow both anonymous *and* Integrated Windows authentication. To allow both authentication methods, follow these steps:

1. In IIS Manager, right-click the virtual directory for your application, and choose Properties. (Alternatively, you can configure authentication for all directories if you right-click the Web Sites folder and choose Properties.)

2. Select the Directory Security tab.

3. In the Anonymous access and authentication control section, click the Edit button.

4. In the Authentication Methods dialog box, under Authenticated access, select Integrated Windows authentication, as shown in Figure 15-2.

5. Click OK to apply your changes.

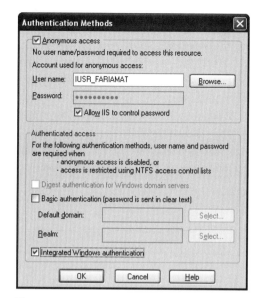

Figure 15-2   Enabling Integrated Windows authentication for debugging.

> **Note**   Microsoft describes these steps and some other troubleshooting steps for remote servers in a white paper at *http://msdn.microsoft.com/library/default.asp?url=/library/en-us/vsdebug/html/vxtbshttpservererrors.asp.*

15.2 Store Information Between Requests

Problem

You want to store some user-specific information in between page postbacks.

Solution

Use view state, query string arguments, session state, or a cookie, depending on your needs.

Discussion

ASP.NET is a stateless programming model. Every time a postback is triggered, your code loads into memory, executes, and is released from memory. If you want to keep track of information after your code has finished processing, you must use some form of state management.

ASP.NET provides several ways to store information, or *state*, in between requests. The type of state you use determines how long the information will live, where it will be stored, and how secure it will be. Table 15-1 lists the various state options provided by ASP.NET. This table doesn't include the *Cache* object, which provides temporary storage and is described in recipe 15.11. You can also use other custom approaches, like hidden fields or a back-end database.

Table 15-1   Types of State Management

Type of State	Allowed Data	Storage Location	Lifetime	Security
View State	All serializable .NET data types	A hidden field in the current Web page	Lost when the user navigates to another page.	By default, it is insecure. However, you can use page directives to enforce encryption and hashing to prevent data tampering.
Query String	String data only	The browser's URL string	Lost when the user enters a new URL or closes the browser. However, can be stored in a bookmark.	Clearly visible and easy for the user to modify.
Session State	All serializable .NET data types	Server memory	Times out after a pre-defined period (usually 20 minutes, but this period can be altered globally or programmatically).	Secure because data is never transmitted to the client.
Custom Cookies	String data only	The client's computer (in memory or a small text file, depending on its lifetime settings)	Set by the programmer. Can be used in multiple pages and can persist between visits.	Insecure, and can be modified by the user.
Application State	All serializable .NET data types	Server memory	The lifetime of the application (typically, until the server is rebooted). Unlike other methods, application data is global to all users.	Secure because data is never transmitted to the client.

Figure 15-3 shows a test page that allows you to store information in four different ways. A label control indicates the information that was found on the last postback.

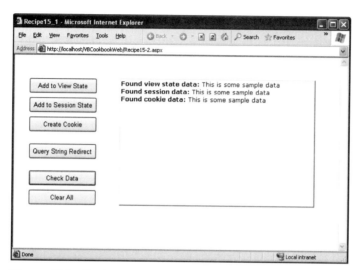

Figure 15-3   Storing state in several ways.

The button event handlers show how you can persist data in several different ways. In each case, the sample data is a string of text. The syntax for different data-storing methods is similar. Data is typically set or retrieved using string lookup with a collection.

```
Private Sub cmdViewState_Click(ByVal sender As System.Object, _
   ByVal e As System.EventArgs) Handles cmdViewState.Click
    Dim TestData As String = "This is some sample data"
    ViewState("TestData") = TestData
End Sub

Private Sub cmdSessionState_Click(ByVal sender As System.Object, _
   ByVal e As System.EventArgs) Handles cmdSessionState.Click
    Dim TestData As String = "This is some sample data"
    Session("TestData") = TestData

    ' (You can configure other Session object properties to
    ' programmatically change session timeout or abandon a session).
End Sub

Private Sub cmdQueryString_Click(ByVal sender As System.Object, _
   ByVal e As System.EventArgs) Handles cmdQueryString.Click
    Dim TestData As String = "This is some sample data"
    TestData = Server.UrlEncode(TestData)
```

```
        ' Query string data must be submitted in a URL,
        ' so a page redirect is required.
        ' This also has the effect of resetting the page and
        ' abandoning the view state information.
        ' Thus, the query string is commonly used to send data
        ' from one page to another
        Response.Redirect("Recipe15-2.aspx?TestData=" & TestData)
End Sub

Private Sub cmdAddCookie_Click(ByVal sender As System.Object, _
    ByVal e As System.EventArgs) Handles cmdAddCookie.Click
        Dim TestData As String = "This is some sample data"

        ' Check if the cookie already exists (named Recipe15-2).
        ' The cookie can store multiple strings, with different keys.
        If Request.Cookies("Recipe15-2") Is Nothing Then

            ' Create the cookie.
            Dim Cookie As New HttpCookie("Recipe15-2")
            Cookie("TestData") = TestData

            ' (You can modify additional Cookie properties to change
            '  the expiry date.)

            ' Attach the cookie to the response.
            ' It will be submitted with all future requests to this site
            ' until it expires.
            Response.Cookies.Add(Cookie)
        End If
End Sub
```

Every time the page is loaded or posted back, the *Page.Load* event fires. The event-handling code then checks for any stored data and updates a label control with information about what it has found.

```
Private Sub Page_Load(ByVal sender As System.Object, _
    ByVal e As System.EventArgs) Handles MyBase.Load

        ' This is the information that will be displayed in the label.
        Dim Message As String

        ' Check for information in view state.
        Dim Data As String
        Data = CType(ViewState("TestData"), String)
        If Not Data Is Nothing Then
            Message &= "<b>Found view state data:</b> " & Data & "<br>"
        End If
```

```
' Check for information in session state.
Data = CType(Session("TestData"), String)
If Not Data Is Nothing Then
    Message &= "<b>Found session data:</b> " & Data & "<br>"
End If


' Check for information in the query string.
Data = Request.QueryString("TestData")
If Not Data Is Nothing Then
    Data = Server.UrlDecode(Data)
    Message &= "<b>Found query string data:</b> " & Data & "<br>"
End If


' Check for information in a custom cookie.
Dim Cookie As HttpCookie = Request.Cookies("Recipe15-2")
If Not Cookie Is Nothing Then
    Data = Cookie("TestData")
    Message &= "<b>Found cookie data:</b> " & Data & "<br>"
End If


' Update the display.
lblDataFound.Text = Message

End Sub
```

To use this page (which is included with the online samples), click one of the buttons to store data and then click the Check Data button to trigger a second postback (at which point the label will be updated with the results). You'll notice that different types of state management behave differently—for example, the only way to submit values in the query string is to redirect the user to a new page, at which point any information in view state will be automatically lost.

The event handler for the Clear button demonstrates how to remove information from the various types of state.

```
Private Sub cmdClear_Click(ByVal sender As System.Object, _
  ByVal e As System.EventArgs) Handles cmdClear.Click

    ViewState("TestData") = Nothing
    Session("TestData") = Nothing
    ' (You can also use Session.Abandon to clear all session information.)

    ' To clear a cookie you must replace it with
    ' a cookie that has an expiration date that has already passed.
    Dim Cookie As New HttpCookie("Recipe15-2")
    Cookie.Expires = DateTime.Now.AddDays(-1)
    Response.Cookies.Add(Cookie)
```

```
' To remove the query string information you must redirect the user.
' (This also has the side effect of clearing all view state data.)
Response.Redirect("Recipe15-2.aspx")

End Sub
```

15.3 Add Line Breaks to a Label Control

Problem

You want to insert line breaks in the text of a Web control such as the *Label* control.

Solution

Add HTML markup to the string. For example, you can use *<p>* to denote paragraphs or *
* to divide a line.

Discussion

You can't use the carriage return character (or the *System.Environment.Newline* constant) to insert a line break in the text of a Web control. Instead, you must use HTML tags. For example, the following code snippet creates three lines of text:

```
lblMessage.Text = "This is line one.<br>"
lblMessage.Text &= "This is line two.<br>"
lblMessage.Text &= "This is line three."
```

Figure 15-4 shows the use of multiple lines in a Web control.

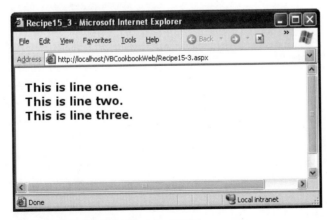

Figure 15-4 Multiple lines in a label.

15.4 Use JavaScript to Handle Key Presses, Mouse Movements, and More

Problem

You want to add client-side JavaScript code to a Web form.

Solution

Use the *Page.RegisterClientScriptBlock* method to add JavaScript functions to a page, and add control attributes that call the functions.

Discussion

ASP.NET includes a rich programming model. Unfortunately, once a page is rendered to HTML, you can't execute any more .NET code without first triggering a postback to the server. This limitation greatly reduces the effectiveness of validation code and other niceties that can lead to a more professional Web page.

Although .NET does not include any object interface for creating JavaScript, you can define a block of JavaScript code in a .NET string variable and instruct ASP.NET to insert it into the rendered Web form, where it can be used. You can then instruct a control to call a function in this block, without triggering a postback, when certain client-side JavaScript events occur. Events that are often useful include:

- *onFocus*   Occurs when a control receives focus

- *onBlur*   Occurs when focus leaves a control

- *onClick*   Occurs when the user clicks on a control

- *onChange*   Occurs when the user changes value of certain controls

- *onMouseOver*   Occurs when the user moves the mouse pointer over a control

The following example (shown in Figure 15-5) registers a JavaScript function that simply shows a message box and then connects the *onMouseOver* event of a text box to the function, all when the page first loads.

```
Private Sub Page_Load(ByVal sender As System.Object, _
    ByVal e As System.EventArgs) Handles MyBase.Load

    ' Define the JavaScript function.
    Dim Script As String = _
      "<script language=JavaScript> " & _
```

```
            "function ShowHello() {" & _
            "alert('Your mouse is on the control!');}" & _
            "</script>"

    ' Insert the function into the page (it will appear just after
    ' the <form runat= server> tag.
    ' Note that each script block is associated with a string name.
    ' This allows multiple controls to register the same script block,
    ' while ensuring it will only be rendered in the final page once.
    If Not Page.IsClientScripBlockRegistered("ScriptHello") Then
        Page.RegisterClientScriptBlock("ScriptHello", Script)
    End If

    ' Add the onMouseOver attribute to a text box.
    TextBox1.Attributes.Add("onMouseOver", "ShowHello()")

End Sub
```

The text box tag will be rendered like this:

```
<input name="TextBox1" type="text" id="TextBox1" onMouseOver="ShowHello()"
 ... />
```

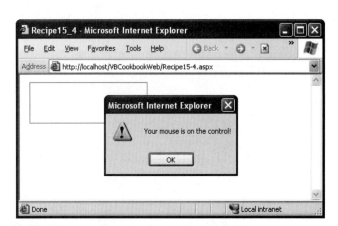

Figure 15-5   A JavaScript *onMouseOver*.

> **Note**   It's important to understand the security implications of Java-Script code. All JavaScript code is rendered directly in the HTML of the page. Therefore, you should assume that the user can examine it, and you should never include any secret algorithms or information in your code. Furthermore, you should use JavaScript validation code as a nicety, not as a way to prevent invalid actions because users might be able to disable or circumvent JavaScript in their browsers.

You can find numerous sites on the Internet that provide JavaScript tutorials and sample code. In addition, a full JavaScript reference is provided by Netscape at *http://developer.netscape.com/docs/manuals/index.html?content= javascript.html*.

15.5 Programmatically Set Control Focus

Problem

You want to specify that a specific control should be given focus when the page is rendered and sent to the user.

Solution

Create a JavaScript statement that sets the focus, and add it to the page using the *Page.RegisterStartupScript* method.

Discussion

The ASP.NET Web controls do not provide any way to programmatically set the focus. They do provide a *TabIndex* property that allows you to set the tab order, but this property only applies to Microsoft Internet Explorer and cannot be used to programmatically set the focus to the control of your choice. To overcome this limitation, you need to add a little snippet of JavaScript code.

The following subroutine generalizes this task. It accepts a reference to any control object, retrieves the associated client ID (which is the ID JavaScript code must use to refer to the control), and then builds and registers the startup script for setting the focus.

```
Private Sub SetFocus(ByVal ctrl As Control)

    ' Define a JavaScript statement that will move focus to
    ' the desired control.
    Dim SetFocus As String = "<script language='javascript'>" & _
        "document.getElementById(""" & ctrl.ClientID & _
        """).focus();</script>"

    ' Add the JavaScript code to the page.
    ctrl.Page.RegisterStartupScript("SetFocus", SetFocus)

End Sub
```

If you add this subroutine to a Web form, you can call *SetFocus* as needed. Here's an example that sets the focus when the page first loads:

```
Private Sub Page_Load(ByVal sender As System.Object, _
  ByVal e As System.EventArgs) Handles MyBase.Load

    If Not Me.IsPostBack Then
        ' Move to a specific text box the first time the page loads.
        SetFocus(TextBox3)
    End If

End Sub
```

15.6 Upload a File

Problem

You need to create a page that allows the user to upload a file.

Solution

Use the ASP.NET *HtmlFileInput* control.

Discussion

Because ASP.NET executes on the server, there is no way to access any of the resources on the client computer, including files. However, you can use the *HtmlFileInput* control to allow a user to upload a file. This control renders itself as the HTML *<input type="file">* element, which is displayed as a Browse button and a text box that contains a filename. The user clicks the Browse button and chooses a file. This step takes place automatically and requires no custom code. The user must then click another button (which you must create) to start the actual upload process.

Before you can create a working file upload page, you need to take these steps:

■ You must set the encoding type of the form to *"multipart/form-data"*. To make this change, find the *<form>* tag in your .aspx file and modify it as shown here:

```
<form id="Form1" enctype="multipart/form-data" runat="server">
```

- You need to add the *HtmlInputFile* control. In Visual Studio .NET, you'll find this control under the HTML tab of the Toolbox, with the name *File Field*. Once you've added this control, you must right-click on it and choose Run As Server Control, which creates the required `<input type="file" runat="server">` tag.

- You must add another button that actually starts the file transfer using the specified file by calling the *HtmlInputFile.PostedFile.SaveAs* method.

Figure 15-6 shows a sample page that allows file uploading. It includes an *HtmlInputFile* control and an Upload button with the following event handler:

```
Private Sub cmdUpload_Click(ByVal sender As System.Object, _
  ByVal e As System.EventArgs) Handles cmdUpload.Click

    If FileInput.PostedFile.FileName = "" Then
        ' No file was submitted.
        lblInfo.Text = "No file specified."

    Else
        Try
            If FileInput.PostedFile.ContentLength > 1048576 Then
                ' Forbid files larger than one megabyte.
                lblInfo.Text = "File is too large."
            Else

                ' The saved file will retain its original filename.
                Dim FileName As String = _
                  Path.GetFileName(FileInput.PostedFile.FileName)

                ' The ASP.NET process must have rights for the location where
                ' it is attempting to save the file, or an "access denied"
                ' exception will occur.
                FileInput.PostedFile.SaveAs(FileName)
                lblInfo.Text = "File " & FileName & " uploaded."
            End If

        Catch Err As Exception
            lblInfo.Text = Err.Message
        End Try
    End If

End Sub
```

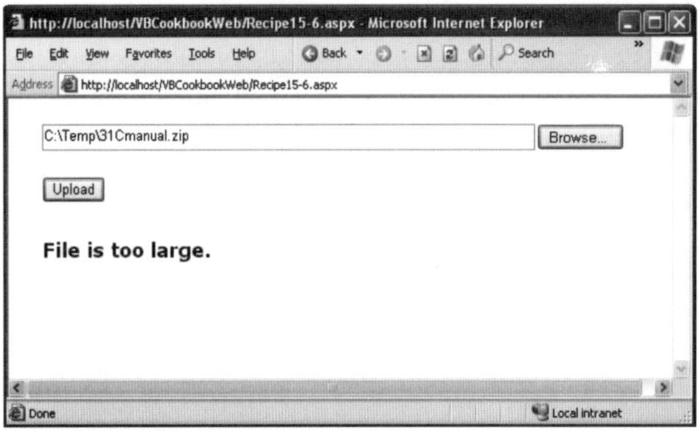

Figure 15-6 An upload test page.

The code can check various properties of the submitted file, including its size, before saving it, which allows you to prevent a denial of service attack that tricks an ASP.NET application into filling the hard disk with large files. However, this code doesn't prevent a user from submitting the file in the first place, which can still slow down the server and be used to launch a different type of denial of service attack—one that works by tying up all free ASP.NET worker threads. To prevent this type of attack, use the *<httpruntime>* tag in the web.config file to specify a maximum file size. Specify the maximum, in kilobytes, using the *maxRequestLength* attribute.

```
<?xml version="1.0" encoding="utf-8" ?>
<configuration>
  <system.web>

    <httpRuntime maxRequestLength="4096" />
    <!-- Other settings omitted. -->

  </system.web>
</configuration>
```

If you don't specify a maximum length, the default value of 4096 (4 megabytes) will apply. If the user attempts to submit a file that is too large, an exception will be thrown immediately when the page is posted back.

> **Note** There is another way to send files from a client to a Web server: use ASP.NET Web services, as described in recipe 16.8 in the next chapter. You simply need to develop a Windows application that allows the user to choose a file and then contacts a Web service to transmit the information.

15.7 Use Custom Error Pages

Problem

You want to show a custom error page when an unhandled exception or HTTP error occurs.

Solution

Specify a custom error page using the *<customErrors>* element in the web.config file for the application.

Discussion

Custom error pages allow you to specify a page that will be returned to the user if an unhandled .NET exception occurs in your page code. Custom error pages aren't a replacement for good error handling; they just allow your application to maintain its professional appearance in the event of an unexpected error. Custom error pages can also be used to catch HTTP errors (for example, if the user requests a page that does not exist) and return descriptive error pages.

You can define custom errors at the virtual directory level by adding the *<customErrors>* element to the web.config file. You have two options when using custom error pages. First, you can define a single error page that will respond to all error conditions, as shown here:

```
<configuration>
  <system.web>
    <customErrors defaultRedirect="DefaultError.aspx" />
  </system.web>
</configuration>
```

Second, you can create error pages targeted at specific types of HTTP errors. In this case, you must add an *<error>* subelement to the *<customErrors>* element. Each *<error>* element identifies the HTTP error code and the redirect page. The following example redirects requests for files that don't exist (HTTP error code 404):

```
<configuration>
  <system.web>
    <customErrors defaultRedirect="DefaultError.aspx">
    <error statusCode="404" redirect="404.aspx" />
    <customErrors>
  </system.web>
</configuration>
```

You can find (and customize) the default IIS error pages in the [Windows-Dir]\Help\iisHelp\common directory.

> **Note** Custom error pages that you define in the web.config file only come into effect if ASP.NET is handling the request. In other words, if you request the nonexistent page nopage.aspx, you'll be redirected according to the web.config error settings because the .aspx file extension is registered to the ASP.NET service. However, if you request the nonexistent page nopage.html, ASP.NET will not process the request and the default error settings specified in IIS will be used.

15.8 Use Forms Authentication

Problem

You want to prevent users from accessing certain pages unless they have first authenticated themselves with a custom login page.

Solution

Implement forms authentication. You must create the login page, but ASP.NET keeps track of a user's authentication status.

Discussion

Forms authentication is a flexible security model that allows you to prevent unauthenticated users from accessing certain pages. You write the code that performs the authentication, and ASP.NET uses a cookie to identify authenticated users. Users without the cookie are redirected to a login page when they try to access a secured page.

To implement forms authentication, you must take these steps:

- Configure forms authentication using the *<authentication>* tag in the application's web.config file.

- Restrict anonymous users from a specific page or directory using web.config settings.

- Create the login page, and add your authentication logic, which leverages the *FormsAuthentication* class from the *System.Web.Security* namespace.

The first step is to configure the web.config in the root application directory to enable forms authentication, as shown in the following code. You also need to specify your custom login page (where unauthenticated users will be redirected) and a timeout, after which the cookie will be removed. The authentication cookie is automatically renewed with each Web request.

```
<configuration>
  <system.web>

    <!-- Other settings omitted. -->

    <authentication mode="Forms">
      <forms loginUrl="login.aspx" timeout="30" />
    </authentication>

  </system.web>
</configuration>
```

Next you need to add an authorization rule denying anonymous users. The easiest way to secure pages is to create a subdirectory with its own web.config file. The web.config file should refuse access to anonymous users, as shown here:

```
<configuration>
  <system.web>

    <authorization>
        <deny users="?" />
    </authorization>

  </system.web>
</configuration>
```

Now ASP.NET will automatically forward unauthenticated requests for pages in this subdirectory to the custom login page. You need to create this page. (Figure 15-7 shows an example.) Your logic can authenticate the user using anything from a hard-coded password (suitable for simple tests) or a server-side database. Once the user has been successfully authenticated, call the shared *FormsAuthentication.RedirectFromLoginPage* method with the username. This method simultaneously sets the forms authentication cookie and redirects the user to the originally requested page.

Here's a rudimentary example that simply looks for a specific password when the user clicks a login button:

```
Private Sub cmdLogin_Click(ByVal sender As System.Object, _
  ByVal e As System.EventArgs) Handles cmdLogin.Click

    If txtPassword.Text.ToLower() = "secret" Then
```

```
        FormsAuthentication.RedirectFromLoginPage(txtName.Text, False)
    Else
        lblStatus.Text = "Try again."
    End If

End Sub
```

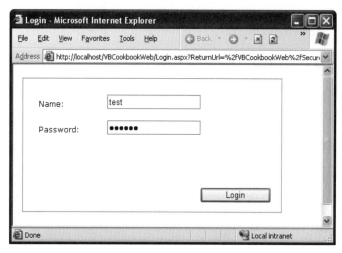

Figure 15-7 A custom login page.

To test this page with the online samples, request the Recipe15-8.aspx page, which is placed in a secured directory.

15.9 Validate User Input

Problem

You want to examine controls for invalid input before continuing.

Solution

Use one of the five validator controls included with ASP.NET.

Discussion

Web applications are frequently subject to input errors because all the information is entered on the client side. Unlike in Windows applications, you can't rely on events such as *KeyPress* to check input as it is entered. The only way to remedy these problems is to add your own JavaScript code for this purpose (as described in recipe 15.4) or use the validator controls.

The validator controls serve two purposes: they check control values for input errors, and they display messages describing these errors. In addition, validator controls emit Dynamic HTML (DHTML) code for up-level browsers that allows them to catch entry errors on the client side without requiring a postback.

ASP.NET provides five different validator controls, as listed in Table 15-2. Each validation control can be bound to a single input control. In addition, you can apply more than one validation control to the same input control to provide multiple types of validation. For example, if you use *RangeValidator*, *CompareValidator*, or *RegularExpressionValidator*, validation will automatically succeed if the input control is empty because there is no value to validate. If this is not the behavior that you want, you should add an additional *RequiredFieldValidator* to the control.

Every validator provides a basic set of properties, including *ControlToValidate* (which identifies the control that will be validated), *ErrorMessage*, *ForeColor*, and *Display*. The last three configure how the error message will be shown in the page.

Table 15-2   Validator Controls

Control Class	Description
RequiredFieldValidator	Validation succeeds as long as the input control does not contain an empty string.
RangeValidator	Validation succeeds if the input control contains a value within a specific numeric, alphabetic, or date range. You specify this information using the *MaximumValue*, *MinimumValue*, and *Type* properties.
CompareValidator	Validation succeeds if the input control contains a value that matches the value in another, specified input control. You specify this information using the *ControlToCompare*, *Operator*, *Type*, and *ValueToCompare* properties.
RegularExpressionValidator	Validation succeeds if the value in an input control matches a specified regular expression. You specify the regular expression using the *ValidationExpression* property. Recipe 1.17 provides several useful regular expressions for common types of data.
CustomValidator	Validation is performed by your own custom .NET code. You must handle the *ServerValidate* event to perform the validation at the server. In addition, you can use the *ClientValidationFunction* property to specify a JavaScript function that will be used for client-side validation on up-level browsers.

To add validation in Visual Studio .NET, you can add the required validator controls at design time, connect them to the appropriate input controls with
the *ControlToValidate* property, and then set the appropriate text in the
ErrorMessage property. Figure 15-8 shows a sample form that uses all five validation controls.

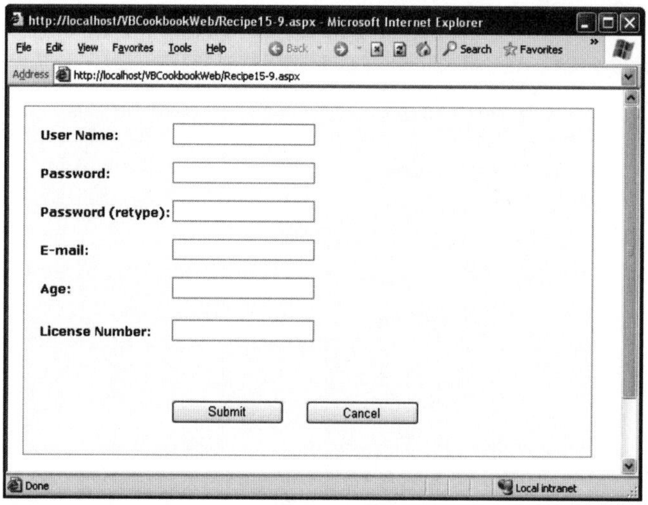

Figure 15-8   A form with several validators.

Here are the control tags from the .aspx file that show the settings of each
validator:

```
<asp:RequiredFieldValidator id="vldUserName" runat="server"
    ErrorMessage="You must enter a user name."
    ControlToValidate="txtUserName" />

<asp:RequiredFieldValidator id="vldPassword" runat="server"
    ErrorMessage="You must enter a password."
    ControlToValidate="txtPassword" />

<asp:CompareValidator id="vldRetype" runat="server"
    ErrorMessage="Your password does not match."
    ControlToCompare="txtPassword" ControlToValidate="txtRetype" />

<asp:RegularExpressionValidator id="vldEmail" runat="server"
    ErrorMessage="This email is missing the @ symbol."
    ValidationExpression=".+@.+" ControlToValidate="txtEmail" />

<asp:RangeValidator id="vldAge" runat="server"
    ErrorMessage="This age is not between 0 and 120." Type="Integer"
    MaximumValue="120" MinimumValue="0" ControlToValidate="txtAge" />
```

```
<asp:CustomValidator id="vldCode" runat="server"
    ErrorMessage="Try a string that starts with 025."
    ControlToValidate="txtCode" />
```

The only event handling code you need to add is for the custom validator, which checks that a value is divisible by five.

```
Private Sub vldCode_ServerValidate(ByVal source As System.Object, _
  ByVal e As System.Web.UI.WebControls.ServerValidateEventArgs) _
  Handles vldCode.ServerValidate

    ' Check if the first three digits are divisible by five.
    If Val(Left(e.Value, 3)) Mod 5 = 0 Then
        e.IsValid = True
    Else
        e.IsValid = False
    End If

End Sub
```

The page can be validated in two ways. If you are using an up-level browser and have configured the *EnableClientScript* property of your validator controls to *True*, the validation will be performed dynamically as the user moves from field to field. No postback is necessary. If *EnableClientScript* is *False* or the browser does not support DHTML and JavaScript, the validation will not be performed until the user clicks a button that has its *CausesValidation* property set to *True*. At this point, the entire page will be validated. Your code must check the state of the page and abort any additional action if validation has failed.

```
Private Sub cmdSubmit_Click(ByVal sender As System.Object, _
  ByVal e As System.EventArgs) Handles cmdSubmit.Click

    If Page.IsValid = False Then
        ' Do nothing. The returned page will show all the error information.
    Else
        ' The page is valid. You can continue with the expected action.
        ' For example, you might save values in the database,
        ' navigate to a new page, and so on.
        Response.Redirect("newpage.aspx")
    End If

End Sub
```

Be aware that this code will *never run* if you're using client-side validation on a supported browser. In this case, the user will be prevented from posting back the page until all input errors are resolved. However, you can't assume that the user will be using an up-level browser (or that the validation code hasn't somehow been circumvented), so you should always check whether the page is valid in your code before continuing. Figure 15-9 shows the same page after validation has failed.

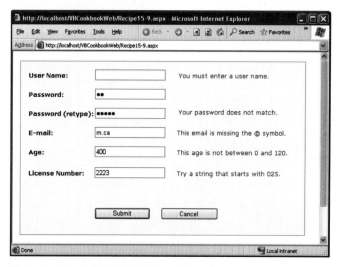

Figure 15-9   A failed validation attempt.

15.10 Use Page or Fragment Caching

Problem

You want to increase performance by caching completely rendered pages.

Solution

Add the *OutputCache* directive to a page or a user control, and specify how long the page should be kept in the cache.

Discussion

A modest use of caching can reduce bottlenecks such as database access and dramatically increase a Web site's overall performance. Caching has the greatest effect in a highly trafficked site. For example, consider what happens if you cache a page that displays the results of a database query. If you cache this page for one minute and ten requests are received for the page over that one-minute period, you'll reduce the database overhead by a factor of 10.

Implementing caching is easy. You simply add an *OutputCache* directive to the Web page. This directive must be added to the .aspx markup file, not to the .vb code-behind file. Here's an example that caches a page for 20 seconds:

```
<%@ OutputCache Duration="20" VaryByParam="None" %>
```

And here's an example that caches a page for 20 seconds but maintains separate cached copies depending on the value of query string arguments:

```
<%@ OutputCache Duration="20" VaryByParam="*" %>
```

You can test caching by using a page that displays the server date and time. You'll notice that subsequent requests for such a page will not cause it to be regenerated. Thus, the old time will be shown until the page expires.

Output caching is not effective in these situations:

- Your page needs to customize itself according to user-specific settings, such as user authentication information (the built-in *User* object) or state (the *Session* object). In this case, it doesn't make sense to reuse the same page for all users.

- Your page includes controls that post back and raise server-side events.

- Your page needs to perform another action (such as write to a log, enter some information in a database, or change an application variable). A cached page reuses the fully rendered HTML; all page code is bypassed.

- Your page includes data that must be generated with up-to-the-minute accuracy. This might be the case for a stock lookup, but it probably won't be the case for a product catalog.

In these cases, you might still be able to use a more flexible form of caching. You can use data caching, as described in recipe 15.11, to store a specific object. Or, you can use fragment caching to cache a portion of a page. To use fragment caching, create a user control that includes all the content that can be cached, and add the *OutputCache* directive to the user control. You can now use the user control in a Web page. The Web page code will still run, but the embedded user control can be cached.

15.11 Store Arbitrary Data in the ASP.NET Cache

Problem

You want to use caching, but you can't cache an entire page because it includes some code that must run or some content that must be generated dynamically.

Solution

Use the built-in *Cache* object to store most .NET data types.

Discussion

The *Cache* object allows you to store almost any .NET object using a string key, with the expiration policy you define. ASP.NET maintains the cache automatically, evicting objects when they expire or when memory becomes scarce.

There are two types of expiration policies that you can use when storing data in the cache. *Absolute expiration* invalidates cached items after a fixed period of time, much like output caching. Absolute expiration is the best approach if you need to store information that needs to be periodically refreshed (such as a product catalog).

```
' Store ObjectToCache under the key "Catalog" for 10 minutes.
' TimeSpan.Zero indicates that we won't use sliding expiration.
Cache.Insert("Catalog", ObjectToCache, Nothing, _
  DateTime.Now.AddMinutes(10), TimeSpan.Zero)
```

ASP.NET also supports a *sliding expiration* policy, which removes objects after a period of disuse. In this case, every time the object is accessed, its lifetime is reset. Sliding expiration works well when you have information that is always valid but is not always being used (such as historical data). This information doesn't need to be refreshed, but it shouldn't be kept in the cache if it isn't being used.

```
' Store ObjectToCache under the key "Catalog" as long as it is being used
' at least once every ten minutes.
' DateTime.MaxValue indicates that we won't use absolute expiration.
Cache.Insert("Catalog", ObjectToCache, Nothing, _
  DateTime.MaxValue, TimeSpan.FromMinutes(10))
```

When adding objects to the cache, the best design pattern is to create a separate function that can re-create the object as needed. For example, if you are storing a *DataSet*, create a function that checks the cache and requeries the database only if the *DataSet* cannot be found. The function below demonstrates this pattern. Be aware that when retrieving an item from the cache, you must always check first whether the item exists and then cast it to the desired type.

```
Private Function GetProductsDataSet() As DataSet

    ' Check for cached item.
    If Cache("Products") Is Nothing Then
        ' Show a debug message.
        lblInfo.Text &= "Creating DataSet...<br>"

        ' Re-create the item.
        Dim Products As New DataSet("ProductInfo")

        ' (You would now use a database query to fill the DataSet.)

        ' Store the item in the cache (for 30 seconds).
        Cache.Insert("Products", Products, Nothing, _
          DateTime.Now.AddSeconds(30), TimeSpan.Zero)

        ' Return the item.
        Return Products

    Else
        ' Show a debug message.
        lblInfo.Text &= "Retrieved DataSet from cache.<br>"

        ' Retrieve the item.
        Return CType(Cache("Products"), DataSet)
    End If

End Function
```

The *GetProductsDataSet* method is called every time the page is loaded. The *DataSet* is retrieved from the cache as long as you post back within the 30-second period. Once this period has expired, the *DataSet* must be re-created.

```
Private Sub Page_Load(ByVal sender As System.Object, _
  ByVal e As System.EventArgs) Handles MyBase.Load

    If Me.IsPostBack = True Then
        lblInfo.Text &= "Page posted back.<br>"
    Else
        lblInfo.Text &= "Page created.<br>"
    End If

    ' Retreive the DataSet from the cache or database,
    ' as required.
    Dim Products As DataSet = GetProductsDataSet()

    ' Display the name of the DataSet (to prove it has been successfully
    ' retrieved or reconstructed).
    lblInfo.Text &= "Using: " & Products.DataSetName & "<br><br>"

End Sub
```

The results of this simple test page are shown in Figure 15-10.

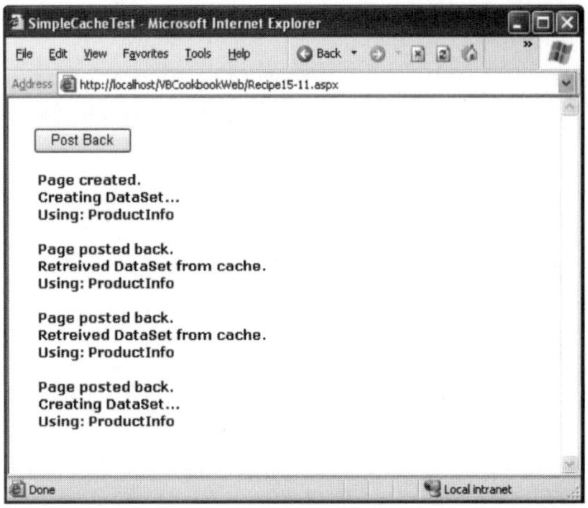

Figure 15-10   Storing a *DataSet* in the cache.

15.12 Add Controls to a Web Form Dynamically

Problem

You want to add a Web control to a Web page at run time and handle its events.

Solution

Create a control object, add it to the *Controls* collection of a container control, and use the *AddHandler* statement to connect any event handlers. You must create the control after every postback.

Discussion

You can use a similar technique to add Web controls to a Web page as you would use to add Windows controls to a form, but there are some differences, including:

■   Dynamically added controls will exist only until the next postback. If you need them, you must re-create them when the page is returned. This requirement does not prevent you from handling their events, however.

■   Dynamically added controls are not as easy to position. Typically, you will use literal controls containing HTML code (such as the line break *
*) to separate more than one dynamically created control.

- Dynamically created controls should be placed in a container control (such as a *Panel* or a *LiteralControl*) rather than directly on the page itself, which makes it easier to position them.

- If you want to interact with the control later, you should give it a unique ID. You can use this ID to retrieve the control from the *Controls* collection of its container.

The best place to generate new controls is in the *Page.Load* event handler, which ensures that the control will be created each time the page is served. In addition, if you are adding an input control that uses view state, the view state information will be restored to the control after the *Page.Load* event fires. That means a dynamically generated text box will retain its text over multiple postbacks, just like a text box that is defined in the .aspx file. Similarly, because the *Page.Load* event always fires before any other events take place, you can re-create a control that raises server-side events and its event-handling code will be triggered immediately after the *Page.Load* event. For example, this technique allows you to dynamically generate a button that can respond to user clicks.

The following example demonstrates all these concepts. It generates three dynamic server controls (two buttons and a text box) and positions them using literal controls that act as separators. The buttons are connected to distinct event handlers. The text box is given a unique identifier so that its text can be retrieved later, in response to the button clicks. Figure 15-11 shows the page in action.

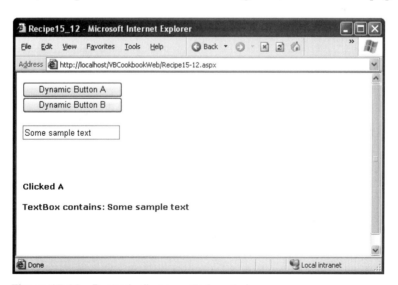

Figure 15-11   Dynamically generated controls.

The full code is shown here:

```vb
Public Class DynamicControlTest
    Inherits System.Web.UI.Page

    ' (Designer code omitted.)

    Private Sub Page_Load(ByVal sender As System.Object, _
        ByVal e As System.EventArgs) Handles MyBase.Load
        ' Create a dynamic button.
        Dim DynamicButton As New Button()
        DynamicButton.Text = "Dynamic Button A"

        ' Connect an event handler.
        AddHandler DynamicButton.Click, AddressOf cmdDynamicA_Click

        ' Add the button to a Panel.
        pnl.Controls.Add(DynamicButton)

        ' Add a line break separator.
        pnl.Controls.Add(New LiteralControl("<br>"))

        ' Create a second dynamic button.
        DynamicButton = New Button()
        DynamicButton.Text = "Dynamic Button B"
        AddHandler DynamicButton.Click, AddressOf cmdDynamicB_Click
        pnl.Controls.Add(DynamicButton)

        ' Add a line break separator.
        pnl.Controls.Add(New LiteralControl("<br><br>"))

        ' Create a dynamic text box.
        Dim DynamicText As New TextBox()
        pnl.Controls.Add(DynamicText)

        ' Assign a unique ID so the text box can be retrieved
        ' from the collection later.
        DynamicText.ID = "DynamicText"
    End Sub

    Private Sub cmdDynamicA_Click(ByVal sender As System.Object, _
        ByVal e As System.EventArgs)
        lblMessage.Text = "Clicked A"
        GetText()
    End Sub

    Private Sub cmdDynamicB_Click(ByVal sender As System.Object, _
        ByVal e As System.EventArgs)
```

```
        lblMessage.Text = "Clicked B"
        GetText()
    End Sub

    Private Sub GetText()
        lblMessage.Text &= "<br><br>"
        Dim ctrl As Control
        For Each ctrl In pnl.Controls
            If ctrl.ID = "DynamicText" Then
                lblMessage.Text &= "TextBox contains: " & _
                    CType(ctrl, TextBox).Text
            End If
        Next
    End Sub

End Class
```

If you need to dynamically create complex layouts that include some pre-built control "groups," you might prefer to use user controls and load them dynamically into a page. This technique is demonstrated in recipe 15.13.

15.13 Load User Controls Programmatically

Problem

You want to dynamically build the user interface of a page out of one or more user controls.

Solution

Use the *Page.LoadControl* method to load the control object from its .ascx file, and add it to the *Controls* collection of a container control.

Discussion

User controls are self-contained groups of controls. Like Web forms, user controls consist of a layout portion that defines the contained controls (.ascx file), and a code-behind portion with the event-handling logic (.vb file). User controls allow you to reuse common interface elements on multiple pages and build complex interfaces out of smaller building blocks. One useful characteristic of user controls is that they can be loaded programmatically, which allows you to create a highly configurable interface that you can tailor dynamically according to the user.

The next example demonstrates a dynamically loaded user control. The first step is to create the user control in Visual Studio .NET. In our example, we'll use a user control with one label. The code-behind class for the user control allows the host page to retrieve or change the text of a label through a user control property.

```
Public MustInherit Class CustomerUserControl
    Inherits System.Web.UI.UserControl

    ' (Designer code omitted.)

    Public Property LabelText() As String
        Get
            Return lblMessage.Text
        End Get
        Set(ByVal Value As String)
            lblMessage.Text = Value
        End Set
    End Property

End Class
```

The Web form loads this user control in the *Page.Load* event handler. The user control is placed in a *Panel* control container. The *LoadControl* method returns a generic *Control* object, which the code casts to the appropriate user control class.

```
Public Class UserControlHost
    Inherits System.Web.UI.Page

    ' (Designer code omitted.)

    Private Sub Page_Load(ByVal sender As System.Object, _
      ByVal e As System.EventArgs) Handles MyBase.Load

        Dim ctrl As Control = Page.LoadControl("CustomerUserControl1.ascx")
        Dim CustomCtrl As CustomerUserControl = CType(ctrl, CustomUserControl)
        CustomCtrl.LabelText = "A dynamic user control!"

        pnl.Controls.Add(ctrl)

    End Sub

End Class
```

When using Visual Studio .NET, the user control class is always available because classes are compiled into a single .dll assembly. If the user control is not a part of the project, however, you will not have the required user control class and you will not be able to access any of the user control's properties or methods. To remedy this problem, you can define a base class or an interface that defines the basic functionality you need to be able to access in any of your custom user controls.

> **Note**   For an excellent full-scale demonstration of this technique, download the IBuySpy portal case study from *www.ibuyspy.com*. It demonstrates a highly customizable layout that is built entirely out of dynamically loaded user controls.

15.14 Dynamically Generate an Image

Problem

You want to render dynamic graphics (perhaps to build the output for a chart or graph control).

Solution

Build the graphic using GDI+ and an in-memory *Bitmap* object, and then save it to the page output stream.

Discussion

You can draw dynamic graphics using the same GDI+ code in a Web application that you would use in a Windows application. The only difference is how you render the final graphic.

Dynamically generating an image imposes more of an overhead than using basic ASP.NET server controls. Therefore, these techniques are typically used only when you need to generate dynamic content. The following example creates the output for a pie chart based on the supplied data. The pie chart data is created as a series of *NumericDataItem* objects. Each data item constitutes a slice of the pie, with a caption and a numeric value.

The *NumericDataItem* class is shown in the following code. It's marked as serializable so that it can be stored in page view state if required.

```
<Serializable> _
Public Class NumericDataItem
    Private _DataValue As Single
    Private _Caption As String

    Public Property DataValue() As Single
        Get
            Return _DataValue
        End Get
        Set(ByVal Value As Single)
            _DataValue = Value
        End Set
    End Property

    Public Property Caption() As String
        Get
            Return _Caption
        End Get
        Set(ByVal Value As String)
            _Caption = Value
        End Set
    End Property

    Public Sub New(ByVal caption As String, ByVal dataValue As Single)
        Me.Caption = caption
        Me.DataValue = dataValue
    End Sub

    Public Overrides Function ToString() As String
        Return Caption & " (" & DataValue.ToString() & ")"
    End Function

End Class
```

When the page is loaded, the data is created. Then the data is evaluated and used to draw a pie chart with the GDI+ drawing functions. The page code is shown here:

```
Public Class DynamicDrawingTest
    Inherits System.Web.UI.Page

    ' (Designer code omitted.)

    Private Sub Page_Load(ByVal sender As System.Object, _
        ByVal e As System.EventArgs) Handles MyBase.Load
        ' Create the data you want to chart.
        Dim ChartData As New ArrayList()
```

```
ChartData.Add(New NumericDataItem("Col 1", 100))
ChartData.Add(New NumericDataItem("Col 2", 75))
ChartData.Add(New NumericDataItem("Col 3", 130))

' Create an in-memory bitmap where you will draw the image.
' The Bitmap is 300 pixels wide and 200 pixels high.
Dim Image As New Bitmap(300, 200)

' Get the graphics context for the bitmap.
Dim g As Graphics = Graphics.FromImage(Image)

' Set the background color and rendering quality.
g.Clear(Color.White)
g.SmoothingMode = Drawing.Drawing2D.SmoothingMode.AntiAlias

' Write some text to the image.
g.DrawString("Sample Chart", _
  New Font("Verdana", 18, FontStyle.Bold), _
  Brushes.Black, New PointF(5, 5))

' Calculate the total of all data values.
Dim Item As NumericDataItem
Dim Total As Single
For Each Item In ChartData
    Total += Item.DataValue
Next

' Draw the pie slices.
Dim CurrentAngle, TotalAngle As Double
Dim i As Integer
For Each Item In ChartData
    CurrentAngle = Item.DataValue / Total * 360
    g.FillPie(New SolidBrush(GetNextColor(i)), 10, 40, 150, 150, _
      CInt(TotalAngle), CInt(CurrentAngle))
    TotalAngle += CurrentAngle
    i += 1
Next

' Create a legend for the chart.
Dim ColorBoxPoint As PointF = New PointF(200, 83)
Dim TextPoint As PointF = New PointF(222, 80)

i = 0
For Each Item In ChartData
    g.FillRectangle(New SolidBrush(GetNextColor(i)), _
      ColorBoxPoint.X, ColorBoxPoint.Y, 20, 10)
    g.DrawString(Item.Caption, New Font("Tahoma", 10), _
      Brushes.Black, TextPoint)
```

```
            ColorBoxPoint.Y += 15
            TextPoint.Y += 15
            i += 1
    Next

    ' Render the image to the HTML output stream.
    Image.Save(Response.OutputStream, _
        System.Drawing.Imaging.ImageFormat.Gif)
End Sub

Private Function GetNextColor(ByVal index As Integer) As Color
    ' Support six different colors. This could be enhanced.
    If index > 5 Then
        index = index Mod 5
    End If

    Select Case index
        Case 0
            Return Color.Red
        Case 1
            Return Color.Blue
        Case 2
            Return Color.Yellow
        Case 3
            Return Color.Green
        Case 4
            Return Color.Orange
        Case 5
            Return Color.Purple
    End Select
End Function

End Class
```

The fully rendered chart is shown in Figure 15-12.

> **Note** When you save an image to the response stream, you replace any other output. Therefore, you can't use this technique with a page that also includes Web controls or static HTML content. If you want to use a page that combines dynamically generated images and Web controls, you need to wrap the dynamically generated image in a control. This technique is demonstrated in recipe 15.15.

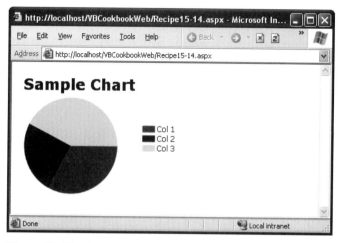

Figure 15-12   A dynamically generated image.

15.15 Dynamically Generate an Image on Part of a Page

Problem

You want to create a page that combines a dynamically generated image and ordinary Web controls.

Solution

Put the code that generates the dynamic image in a separate page, and create an *<img>* tag that references the page.

Discussion

The easiest way to use dynamically generated images with ASP.NET is to write them directly to the response stream. This means that a page that uses a dynamically generated image can't also use Web controls. One way to circumvent this problem is to create a full-blown custom Web control. Another, simpler option is to use an ordinary HTML *<img>* tag that references the form that generates the dynamic image.

Figure 15-13 shows one example. On the left are several Web controls that allow the user to specify the pie chart data. The pie chart itself is generated dynamically and presented in the image box on the right. In this case, the pie chart is an *Image* Web control. The *Image.ImageUrl* property is set to *Dynamic-Chart.aspx*, which is the form with the GDI+ drawing logic.

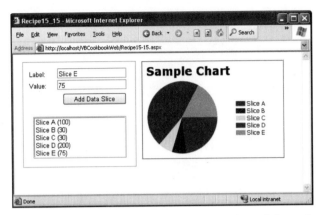

Figure 15-13   A Web form with Web controls and dynamic graphics.

The trick in this example is transferring the pie chart data from the main Web form to the dynamic image rendering form. There's no elegant way to solve this problem. You can use query string arguments, although they are easily tampered with and only support string information. Or you can use session state, as in this example. This approach works seamlessly, although it requires some server memory.

The following code creates the main Web form, which allows the user to define the pie chart data:

```
Public Class MainPage
    Inherits System.Web.UI.Page

    ' (Designer code omitted.)

    ' The data that will be used to create the pie chart.
    Private PieSlices As New ArrayList()

    Private Sub Page_Load(ByVal sender As System.Object, _
      ByVal e As System.EventArgs) Handles MyBase.Load
        ' Retrieve the pie slices that are defined so far.
        If Not Session("ChartData") Is Nothing Then
            PieSlices = CType(Session("ChartData"), ArrayList)
        End If
    End Sub

    Private Sub cmdAdd_Click(ByVal sender As System.Object, _
      ByVal e As System.EventArgs) Handles cmdAdd.Click
        ' Create a new pie slice.
```

```
        Dim PieSlice As New NumericDataItem(txtLabel.Text, _
          CType(Val(txtValue.Text), Single))
        PieSlices.Add(PieSlice)

        ' Bind the list box to the new data.
        lstPieSlices.DataSource = PieSlices
        lstPieSlices.DataBind()
    End Sub

    Private Sub Page_PreRender(ByVal sender As Object, _
      ByVal e As System.EventArgs) Handles MyBase.PreRender
        ' Before rendering the page, store the current collection
        ' of pie slices.
        Session("ChartData") = PieSlices
    End Sub

End Class
```

The code that renders the dynamic image in the DynamicChart.aspx page is adapted from the code in recipe 15-14 and is outlined here:

```
Private Sub Page_Load(ByVal sender As System.Object, _
  ByVal e As System.EventArgs) Handles MyBase.Load

    ' Create an in-memory bitmap where you will draw the image.
    Dim Image As New Bitmap(300, 200)
    Dim g As Graphics = Graphics.FromImage(Image)

    ' Set the background color and rendering quality.
    g.Clear(Color.White)
    g.SmoothingMode = Drawing.Drawing2D.SmoothingMode.AntiAlias

    ' Retrieve data.
    Dim ChartData As ArrayList
    If Session("ChartData") Is Nothing Then
        ' Display a blank image.
        Image.Save(Response.OutputStream, _
          System.Drawing.Imaging.ImageFormat.Gif)
        Return
    Else
        ChartData = CType(Session("ChartData"), ArrayList)
    End If

    ' (Remainder of drawing code omitted).

End Sub
```

15.16 Use the Internet Explorer Controls

Problem

You want to use *TreeView*, *Toolbar*, and *TabStrip* controls in a Web page.

Solution

Download the Internet Explorer controls, which include Web equivalents for four common Windows controls.

Discussion

The Internet Explorer controls include the following controls:

- *TabStrip* and *MultiPage*, which allow you to create a tabbed interface inside a single Web page

- *Toolbar*, which allows you to create a bar of text and image buttons

- *TreeView*, which allows you to display a hierarchical tree of items

The HTML generated by the Internet Explorer controls renders in all commonly used browsers. However, if the client is using Internet Explorer 5.5 or later, the controls will also use DHTML for a rich user experience. You can download the Internet Explorer controls from *http://msdn.microsoft.com/downloads /samples/internet/ASP_DOT_NET_ServerControls/WebControls/*. You can see the Internet Explorer Web control documentation at *http://msdn.microsoft.com /workshop/WebControls/webcontrols_entry.asp*.

The Internet Explorer Web controls include the C# source code for all controls. To use the controls, you must first run the build.bat batch file in the install directory (typically C:\Program Files\IE Web Controls). This compiles an assembly named Microsoft.Web.UI.WebControls.dll in the build subdirectory of the install directory. The easiest way to use this assembly is to add the Internet Explorer controls to your Toolbox. To do so, right-click the Toolbox and select Customize Toolbox (or Add/Remove Toolbox Items in Visual Studio .NET 2003). Select the .NET Framework Components tab, click Browse, and select the Microsoft.Web.UI.WebControls.dll assembly from the appropriate directory. The controls will be selected automatically, as shown in Figure 15-14. Click OK to add them to the Toolbox. When you drop them onto a Web page, the required assembly will be referenced automatically.

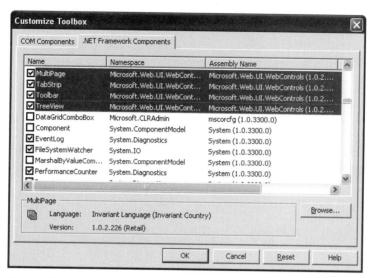

Figure 15-14   Adding the Internet Explorer controls to the Toolbox.

Note   The Internet Explorer controls are not officially supported by Microsoft. This means there is no guarantee that these controls will work with every release of the .NET Framework (although they do work with both versions 1.0 and 1.1), or that these controls won't be discontinued (possibly with some of the functionality being integrated into a future version of ASP.NET).

The *TabStrip* and *MultiPage* controls are the simplest of the four Internet Explorer controls. The *TabStrip* control is simply a row or column of tab buttons. The *MultiPage* control is a container that groups other controls into separate "pages" and displays a single page at a time.

To add tabs to a *TabStrip* control, you use the *Items* property. As with most of the Internet Explorer controls, you can configure this collection at design time using the Visual Studio .NET designer support included with the control. To add content to the *MultiPage* control, you must modify the .aspx layout manually. (You can do so in Visual Studio .NET using the HTML page view.) Each page is defined with a *<PageView>* tag, and each *<PageView>* can contain any other HTML content or ASP.NET controls.

Here's an example that defines three pages and places a separate line of text on each page:

```
<iewc:MultiPage id="MultiPage1" runat="server" >

 <iewc:PageView id="page1">
   <br><br><br>This is page one
 </iewc:PageView>
 <iewc:PageView id="page2">
   <br><br><br>This is page two
 </iewc:PageView>
 <iewc:PageView id="page3">
 <br><br><br>This is page three
 </iewc:PageView>


</iewc:MultiPage>
```

Usually, you will use the *TabStrip* and *MultiPage* controls in conjunction so that the *TabStrip* control is used to navigate among pages in the *MultiPage* control. Binding these controls together is easy: you simply need to set the *TabStrip.TargetID* property with the *ID* of the corresponding *MultiPage* control, and navigation will be performed automatically. Figure 15-15 shows the result.

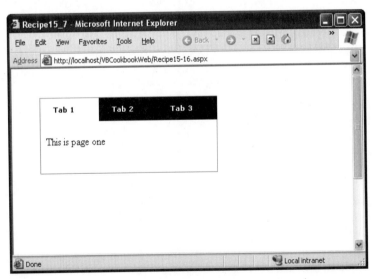

Figure 15-15   Linked *TabStrip* and *MultiPage* controls.

The *Toolbar* control also includes rich designer support that you can access through the *Items* property. The *Toolbar* control can hold various items, including buttons, separators, drop-down lists, text boxes, and more. A sample *Toolbar* control is shown in Figure 15-16.

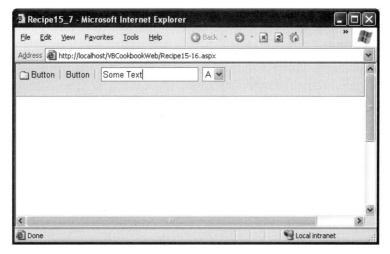

Figure 15-16   A *Toolbar* control.

You can respond to the *Toolbar.ButtonClick* event when a button is clicked. In this case, the sender will not be the *Toolbar* control, but the button in the *Toolbar* control that was clicked. You can identify the button using the *ID* property, as shown here:

```
Private Sub Toolbar1_ButtonClick(ByVal sender As Object, _
  ByVal e As System.EventArgs) Handles Toolbar1.ButtonClick

    ' Find the button that was clicked.
    Dim Button As ToolbarButton
    Button = CType(sender, ToolbarButton)
    lblMessage.Text = "You clicked: " & Button.ID

End Sub
```

Finally, the *TreeView* control is one of the most interesting of the Internet Explorer controls. It mimics the behavior of the Windows *TreeView* control, providing a hierarchical tree of nodes that can include text and images. Before populating the *TreeView* control, you can configure a set of node styles, which allows you to specify the images that will be used for each type of node. To configure node styles, modify the *TreeNodeType* property at design time.

Here's the .aspx code needed to define a *TreeView* control with a single node style that displays the image of a folder next to the node text:

```
<iewc:TreeView id="TreeView1" runat="server" >
  <iewc:TreeNodeType ImageUrl="folder.gif" Type="Folder"></iewc:TreeNodeType>
</iewc:TreeView>
```

Once you've set up the node styles, you can populate the *TreeView* control programmatically. The following example fills the *TreeView* control with a list of years and months:

```
Private Sub Page_Load(ByVal sender As System.Object, _
  ByVal e As System.EventArgs) Handles MyBase.Load

    ' Create the object needed to get month names.
    Dim Info As System.Globalization.DateTimeFormatInfo
    Info = System.Globalization.DateTimeFormatInfo.CurrentInfo()

    ' Populate the TreeView.
    Dim YearNum, MonthNum As Integer
    For YearNum = 1999 To 2004
        Dim YearNode As New TreeNode()
        YearNode.Text = YearNum.ToString()
        TreeView1.Nodes.Add(YearNode)
        For MonthNum = 1 To 12
            Dim MonthNode As New TreeNode()
            MonthNode.Text = Info.GetMonthName(MonthNum)
            YearNode.Nodes.Add(MonthNode)
        Next
    Next

End Sub
```

The resulting *TreeView* control is shown in Figure 15-17.

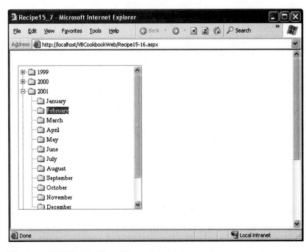

Figure 15-17 A *TreeView* control.

You can read the currently selected node from the *TreeView.Selected-NodeIndex* property. In addition, you can react to the *Collapse*, *Expand*, and *SelectedIndexChange* events.

15.17 Use a Dynamic Menu Control

Problem

You want to add a menu control to your Web pages.

Solution

Download a separate component, such as *RadMenu* from Telerik or the *Slide-Menu* from obout.

Discussion

The .NET Framework does not include any type of menu control. However, the Web is full of diverse examples of graphically rich menus built out of cascading style sheets and DHTML. Most controls are commercial and require some sort of licensing fee. However, there are at least two fully functional menu controls that can be downloaded for free, as shown in Figure 15-18.

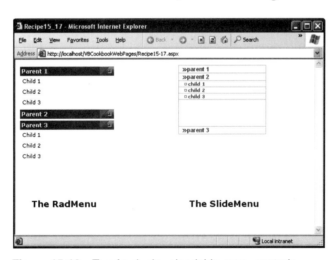

Figure 15-18   Two freely downloadable menu controls.

Both of these menus are designed as navigational aids that allow a user to move between multiple pages. As such, you don't directly handle a menu click event. Instead, you need to specify the URL where the user should be directed. If you want multiple menu items to trigger different actions on the same target page, you can pass query string arguments.

The *RadMenu* control from Telerik creates a menu that stacks numerous collapsible menu panes one after the other at the side of a Web page. You can download the Telerik *RadMenu* control from *www.telerik.com*. After installing the control, you can add the radmenu.dll assembly to the Visual Studio .NET Toolbox and then drop it on any form. The actual menu content must be entered into an XML file, which specifies the menu text, and assigns each menu entry a hyperlink. The following code is the XML used for the menu shown in Figure 15-18. The menu is bound to the control by setting the *RadMenu.Menu-File* property.

```
<Menu>
  <Group>
    <Item Label="Parent 1" ImagePosition="right"
     Image="img/corner.gif" ImageOver="img/cornerOver.gif">
      <Group>
        <Item Href="somepage.aspx" Label="Child 1"/>
        <Item Href="somepage.aspx" Label="Child 2"/>
        <Item Href="somepage.aspx" Label="Child 3"/>
      </Group>
    </Item>

    <Item Label="Parent 2" ImagePosition="Right"
     Image="img/corner.gif" ImageOver="img/cornerOver.gif">
      <Group>
        <Item Href="somepage.aspx" Label="Child 1"/>
        <Item Href="somepage.aspx" Label="Child 2"/>
        <Item Href="somepage.aspx" Label="Child 3"/>
      </Group>
    </Item>

    <Item Label="Parent 3" ImagePosition="Right"
     Image="img/corner.gif" ImageOver="img/cornerOver.gif">
      <Group>
        <Item Href="somepage.aspx" Label="Child 1"/>
        <Item Href="somepage.aspx" Label="Child 2"/>
        <Item Href="somepage.aspx" Label="Child 3"/>
      </Group>
    </Item>
  </Group>
</Menu>
```

The *SlideMenu* control from obout provides a similar collapsible menu with a different graphical appearance. You can download the control from *www.obout.com* and install the assembly to the virtual directory for the appropriate application. The *SlideMenu* does not include any control classes, so you can't add it to the Toolbox. Instead, you must add a reference to the appropriate assembly (obout_SlideMenu_NET.dll) and then create the menu programmatically. To display the menu on the page, you need to retrieve the HTML from the *HTML* property and assign it to another control (typically a *Label* control). Here's the code that creates the slide menu shown in Figure 15-18:

```
Private Sub Page_Load(ByVal sender As System.Object, _
  ByVal e As System.EventArgs) Handles MyBase.Load

    ' Create the menu.
    Dim Menu As New obout_SlideMenu_NET.Menu()
    Menu.Width = 185
    Menu.SubHeight = 95
    Menu.Speed_Step = 15

    ' Set menu images.
    Menu.Image_Child = "square_blue.gif"
    Menu.Image_ChildOver = "square_blue.gif"
    Menu.Image_ChildSelected = "square_blue.gif"
    Menu.Image_Parent = "arrow_red.gif"
    Menu.Image_ParentOver = "arrow_blue.gif"

    ' Create the menu items.
    Menu.AddParent("parent 1", Nothing, Nothing)
    Menu.AddParent("parent 2", Nothing, Nothing)
    Menu.AddChild("child 1", "somepage.aspx")
    Menu.AddChild("child 2", "somepage.aspx")
    Menu.AddChild("child 3", "somepage.aspx")
    Menu.AddParent("parent 3", Nothing, Nothing)

    ' Display the menu by copying its HTML to a control on the page.
    lblMenu.Text = Menu.HTML()

End Sub
```

You can download many .NET menu controls from the Microsoft ASP.NET Control Gallery at *http://www.asp.net/ControlGallery*, which includes free menu controls and free trials for commercial controls.

16

Web Services

Web services are the single most hotly hyped feature of the .NET platform, and it's no wonder—used properly, Web services can wrap legacy components, cross platform boundaries, and even Web-enable traditional rich desktop applications.

One of the most important details you should understand about Web services is that they use exactly the same Microsoft Visual Basic .NET code as any other .NET application. Therefore, you can use all the recipes from earlier chapters in a Web service to access files, connect to a database, process strings with regular expressions, and much more. The recipes in this chapter concentrate on .NET features that are unique to Web services. For example, you'll learn how to use caching with a Web service (recipes 16.2 and 16.3), how to use transactional Web methods (recipe 16.4), how to leverage Internet Information Services (IIS) authentication (recipe 16.6), and how to extend Web services with SOAP headers and a full-fledged SOAP extension (recipes 16.9 and 16.11).

> **Note**   All the Web services in this chapter are held in one virtual directory named VBCookbookWebServices. To use the examples in the downloadable code, you can create the same virtual directory (following the instructions in the included readme.txt file) or you can add the Web services to your own Web application projects. Many of the Web services in this chapter can be used without a dedicated client. Instead, you can use the simple Web service test page in a Web browser. For more advanced Web services, Microsoft Windows client applications are provided.

16.1 Avoid Hard-Coding the Web Service URL

Problem

You need to use a Web service whose URL might change.

Solution

Use a dynamic URL, which will be retrieved automatically from the client application's configuration file.

Discussion

By default, when you add a Web reference in Microsoft Visual Studio .NET, the Web service URL is hard-coded in the constructor of the proxy class.

```
Public Sub New()
    MyBase.New()
    Me.Url = "http://localhost/WebServices/MyService.asmx"
End Sub
```

You can override this setting in your code by manually modifying the *Url* property of the proxy class after you instantiate it. However, there's another option: configure the proxy class to use a dynamic URL endpoint. You can make this change by selecting the Web reference in the Visual Studio .NET Solution Explorer and changing the URL Behavior option in the Properties window, as shown in Figure 16-1.

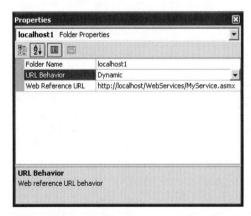

Figure 16-1 Configuring a dynamic Web service URL.

After you make this change, the Web service URL will be automatically added to the client application's configuration file. (The configuration file is named web.config for all Web applications and AppName.exe.config for all other applications, in which case the file appears in the design environment as simply App.config.) An example of the automatically generated configuration file setting is shown here:

```
<?xml version="1.0" encoding="utf-8"?>
<configuration>

  <appSettings>
    <add key="AppName.ServerName.ServiceName"
    value="http://localhost/WebServices/MyService.asmx"/>
  </appSettings>

</configuration>
```

In addition, the code in the proxy class is modified so that it attempts to read the URL from the configuration file. If it doesn't find the required value, it defaults to the URL that was used during development.

```
Public Sub New()
    MyBase.New()
    Dim urlSetting As String = _
       ConfigurationSettings.AppSettings("AppName.ServerName.ServiceName")

    If Not urlSetting Is Nothing Then
        Me.Url = urlSetting
    Else
        Me.Url = "http://localhost/WebServices/MyService.asmx"
    End If
End Sub
```

This approach allows you to modify the Web service URL after compiling and deploying the application, simply by editing the configuration file.

> **Note**   You can't modify the code for the proxy class constructor directly because your changes will be lost every time you regenerate the proxy class. Instead, you must change the URL Behavior setting so that Visual Studio .NET will automatically add the dynamic URL code.

16.2 Add Response Caching

Problem

You want to improve Web service performance by caching the return value of a Web method.

Solution

Use response caching by setting the *CacheDuration* property of the *WebMethod* attribute.

Discussion

ASP.NET Web services support response caching in much the same way as ASP.NET Web pages. When response caching is enabled, your code runs only once, and the return value of the Web method is stored for subsequent method invocations. With Web forms, caching is performed on a per-form basis. With Web services, caching is enabled and configured distinctly for each Web method.

For example, the following Web method returns the current date and time on the server. This information is cached for one minute, meaning that subsequent requests within this timeframe will receive the previously recorded date information. You can test this behavior using the Web service test page.

```
<WebMethod(CacheDuration:=60)> _
Public Function GetDate() As String
    Return DateTime.Now.ToString()
End Function
```

If your Web method accepts parameters, ASP.NET will only reuse the cached method result if it receives a request with the exact same parameters. If you have a method that accepts a wide range of values, caching might be ineffective or even wasteful because a great deal of information might be stored in the cache but rarely reused. For example, a Web method that performs a mathematical calculation based on numeric input is rarely a good choice for response caching. On the other hand, a Web method that accepts an ID referencing one of about a dozen different product items probably is. As always, response caching bypasses your code, making it unsuitable if your Web method needs to perform other actions (such as logging activity) or if your Web method depends on information that's not supplied through method parameters (such as user authentication information or session data).

> **Note**   One limitation of response caching with Web methods is that it only allows you to reuse data within the bounds of a single method. If you want to reuse specific data in different Web methods, data caching (described in recipe 16.3) will probably be more effective.

16.3 Add Data Caching

Problem

You want to improve Web service performance by caching some data, but you need to reuse cached data among several methods. Or, you want to run your Web method code but still use some cached information.

Solution

Store any object in the cache using the *Cache* object.

Discussion

Data caching with a Web service works almost exactly the same as the Web page data caching technique described in recipe 15.11. In fact, you can store data in the cache using Web page code and retrieve it in a Web service, or vice versa. Data caching supports two types of expiration policy: absolute expiration and sliding expiration. For more information, refer to recipe 15.11.

The only difference between caching in a Web service and caching in a Web page is that in the former case, you can't retrieve the *Cache* as a built-in property. Instead, you need to access the cache through the shared *HttpContext.Current* property.

The following example shows a Web service with two Web methods. The first Web method, *GetFullCustomerData*, returns a *DataSet* with a table of customer information. This *DataSet* is either retrieved from the cache or generated automatically (if required) using the private *GetCustomerDataSet* function. The second Web method, *GetCustomerNameList*, also uses the customer *DataSet* and the *GetCustomerDataSet* function. However, it retrieves a subset of the available information—a list of contact names—and returns it as a string. The end result is that both Web methods can use the same cached data, reducing the burden that is placed on the database.

The full Web service code is shown here:

```vb
<WebService()> _
Public Class DataCachingTest
    Inherits System.Web.Services.WebService

    <WebMethod()> _
    Public Function GetFullCustomerData() As DataSet
        ' Return the full customer table (from the cache if possible).
        Return GetCustomerDataSet()
    End Function

    <WebMethod()> _
    Public Function GetCustomerNameList() As String()
        ' Get the customer table (from the cache if possible).
        Dim Dt As DataTable = GetCustomerDataSet().Tables(0)

        ' Create an array that will hold the name of each customer.
        Dim Names() As String
        ReDim Names(Dt.Rows.Count - 1)

        ' Fill the array.
        Dim Row As DataRow
        Dim i As Integer
        For Each Row In Dt.Rows
            Names(i) = Row("ContactName").ToString()
            i += 1
        Next

        Return Names
    End Function

    Private Function GetCustomerDataSet() As DataSet
        Dim Cache As System.Web.Caching.Cache
        Cache = HttpContext.Current.Cache

        ' Check for cached item.
        If Cache("Customers") Is Nothing Then
            ' Recreate the item.
            Dim Customers As New DataSet("Customers")

            ' Create the connection. The connection string is retrieved
            ' from a setting in the web.config file.
            Dim Con As New SqlConnection( _
              ConfigurationSettings.AppSettings("DBCon"))

            ' Create the command for filling the DataSet.
            Dim CmdSelect As New SqlCommand("SELECT * FROM Customers", Con)
```

```
Dim Adapter As New SqlDataAdapter(CmdSelect)

' Fill the DataSet.
Try
    Con.Open()
    Adapter.Fill(Customers, "Customers")
Catch Err As Exception
    ' Throw a higher-level exception to mask any sensitive
    ' error information.
    Throw New ApplicationException("Database error.")
Finally
    Con.Close()
End Try

' Store the item in the cache (for 60 seconds).
Cache.Insert("Customers", Customers, Nothing, _
  DateTime.Now.AddSeconds(60), TimeSpan.Zero)

' Return the item.
Return Customers
        Else
            ' Retrieve the item.
            Return CType(Cache("Customers"), DataSet)
        End If
    End Function

End Class
```

16.4 Create a Transactional Web Method

Problem

You want to execute all the actions in a Web method within the context of a single COM+ transaction so that they all either fail or succeed as a unit.

Solution

Enable an automatic transaction using the *TransactionOption* property of the *WebMethod* attribute.

Discussion

.NET Web services include support for automatic transactions that can be enabled on a per-method basis. When enabled, any data source that supports COM+ transactions (which includes most databases) is automatically enlisted in the current transaction when it's used in your code. The transaction is automatically committed when the Web method completes. The transaction is rolled back if any unhandled exception occurs or if you explicitly call the *SetAbort* method of the *System.EnterpriseServices.ContextUtil* class.

To enable transaction support for a Web method, set the *TransactionOption* property of the *WebMethod* attribute to *RequiresNew*. For example, the transactional Web method shown in the following code takes two actions—it deletes records in a database and then tries to read from a file. However, if the file operation fails and the exception is not handled, the entire operation will be rolled back. To use this code, you must add a reference to the System.EnterpriseServices.dll assembly and import the *System.Enterprise-Services* namespace.

```
<WebMethod(TransactionOption:=TransactionOption.RequiresNew)> _
Public Sub UpdateDatabase()
    ' Create the connection.
    Dim Con As New SqlConnection(ConfigurationSettings.AppSettings("DBCon"))

    ' Create the command for filling the DataSet.
    Dim Cmd As New SqlCommand("DELETE * FROM Customers", Con)

    ' Apply the update. This will be registered as part of the transaction.
    Con.Open()
    Cmd.ExecuteNonQuery()

    ' Try to access a file.
    ' This generates an exception which is not handled.
    ' The Web method will be aborted and the changes will be rolled back.
    Dim fs As New System.IO.FileStream("does_not_exist.bin", IO.FileMode.Open)

    ' (If no errors have occurred, the database changes
    ' are committed here when the method ends).

End Sub
```

You can use the Component Services console to monitor this transaction. You can start the Component Services utility by selecting Component Services from the Administrative Tools section of the Control Panel. In the Component Services console, select the Distributed Transaction Coordinator for the current computer, and view the Transaction Statistics. Figure 16-2 shows how the display will look after running this code, which produces one failed transaction.

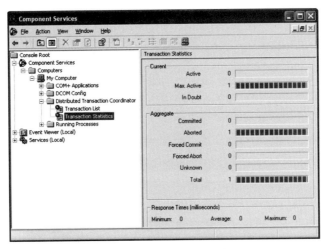

Figure 16-2   Monitoring a failed transaction.

Because of the stateless nature of the HTTP protocol, a Web service method can participate only as the root of a transaction, which means that you can't enlist more than one Web method in the same transaction. Although the *TransactionOption* property accepts all the standard *TransactionOption* values, the values don't have the expected meanings. For example, *Disabled*, *NotSupported*, and *Supported* all have the same effect: they disable transaction support. Similarly, *Required* and *RequiresNew* both enable transaction support and start a new transaction. I recommend that you use *RequiresNew* in your Web methods because its name most clearly matches the actual behavior.

> **Note**   COM+ transactions work seamlessly with most data sources because they provide compatible resource managers. But always remember, if you interact with a non-transactional resource, your code won't be rolled back. Some examples of actions that aren't transactional include writing a file, placing information into session state, and accessing a hardware device (such as a printer). On the other hand, data operations with most enterprise database systems (including SQL Server and Oracle) are COM+ compatible.

16.5 Create a One-Way Web Method

Problem

You want a Web method to perform a long task, and you don't want to force the client to wait while the Web service code executes.

Solution

Create a one-way Web method by applying the *SoapDocumentMethod* or *SoapRpcMethod* attribute and setting the *OneWay* property to *True*.

Discussion

With one-way Web methods, the client sends a request message, and the server responds immediately to indicate that the method began processing. This behavior has the following consequences:

- The client doesn't need to wait while the Web method code executes.

- The Web method can't return any information to the client, either through a return value or a *ByRef* parameter.

- If the Web method throws an unhandled exception, it won't be propagated back to the client.

To create a one-way Web method, you need to apply a *SoapDocumentMethod* attribute (from the *System.Web.Services.Protocols* namespace) to the appropriate method and set the *OneWay* property to *True*. Here's an example:

```
<SoapDocumentMethod(OneWay := True), _
  WebMethod()> _
Public Sub DoLongTask()
    ' (Start a long task that doesn't return
    ' information to the client.)
End Sub
```

This example assumes that your Web service and client are using SOAP document encoding (the default). If you're using RPC encoding, use the corresponding *SoapRpcMethod* attribute to mark a one-way method.

> **Note** One-way methods aren't the only way to remove client delays. You can also modify the client to call any Web method asynchronously. In this case, the client will wait for the Web service to complete, but it will wait on another thread, so the client application can continue with other work. Asynchronous method calls are described in recipe 7.1.

16.6 Set Authentication Credentials for a Web Service

Problem

You want a Web service client to submit logon credentials for IIS authentication.

Solution

Use the *Credentials* property of the proxy class. You can create a new *NetworkCredential* object or use the *CredentialCache* to retrieve the credentials for the current user.

Discussion

Web services, like Web pages, can be used in conjunction with IIS authentication. All you need to do is place your Web services in a virtual directory that restricts anonymous access.

Unlike Web pages, Web services have no built-in method for retrieving authentication information from the client because Web services are executed by other applications, not directly by the user. Thus, the application that's interacting with the Web service bears the responsibility for submitting any required authentication information. Furthermore, Web services must use a form of Windows authentication that maps user credentials to valid user accounts. Form-based authentication will not work.

To create a simple Web service test, enable both anonymous and Windows Integrated authentication for the virtual directory in IIS Manager. Make sure that the web.config file specifies that Windows authentication will be used and that anonymous users will be permitted.

```
<configuration>
  <system.web>

    <!-- Other settings omitted. -->

    <authentication mode="Windows" />

    <authorization>
        <allow users="*" />
    </authorization>

  </system.web>
</configuration>
```

Next create a new subdirectory. Add a web.config file that explicitly denies anonymous users, as shown here:

```
<configuration>
  <system.web>

    <authorization>
        <deny users="?" />
    </authorization>

  </system.web>
</configuration>
```

Unauthenticated calls to any Web services in this directory will fail. However, if the user can submit credentials that map to a valid user account, the user will be authenticated and you'll be able to retrieve the authentication information through the built-in *User* object.

> **Note**   Your Web service can access the *User* object as a built-in property, as long as you derive it from the *System.Web.WebServices.WebService* class. If you don't, you can still access the same user information through the shared *HttpContext.Current* property.

The following Web service provides a simple user authentication test. *GetIISUser* returns the user that was authenticated by IIS. If anonymous access is allowed, the result will be an empty string because no authentication will be performed. If anonymous access is denied, the result will be a string in the form

[DomainName]\[UserName] or [ComputerName]\[UserName]. You can use the role-based security techniques described in recipe 18.2 to examine the group membership of this authenticated user.

```
<WebService()> _
Public Class AuthenticationTest
    Inherits System.Web.Services.WebService

    ' Retrieves the authenticated IIS user.
    <WebMethod()> _
    Public Function GetIISUser() As String
        Return User.Identity.Name
    End Function

End Class
```

The final step is to create a client that can submit the authentication information. The credentials are submitted through the *Credentials* property of the *Proxy* class. If you are using Basic authentication, you must create a *NetworkCredential* object that specifies the user name and password information. If you are using Windows Integrated authentication, you can automatically use the credentials of the currently logged on user using the shared *CredentialCache.DefaultCredentials* property. Both the *CredentialCache* and *NetworkCredential* classes are found in the *System.Net* namespace.

Figure 16-3 shows a Windows client that tests both approaches to authentication and attempts an unauthenticated call.

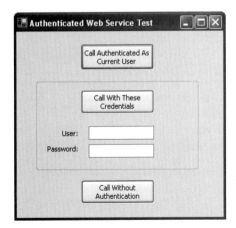

Figure 16-3   A client that tests authentication.

The full form code for the client is shown here:

```
Public Class AuthenticationClient
    Inherits System.Windows.Forms.Form

    ' (Designer code omitted.)

    Private Sub cmdNoAuthenticate_Click(ByVal sender As System.Object, _
      ByVal e As System.EventArgs) Handles cmdNoAuthenticate.Click
        ' Create the proxy.
        Dim Proxy As New localhost.AuthenticationTest()

        CallMethod(Proxy)
    End Sub

    Private Sub cmdAuthenticateCurrent_Click(ByVal sender As System.Object, _
      ByVal e As System.EventArgs) Handles cmdAuthenticateCurrent.Click
        ' Create the proxy.
        Dim Proxy As New localhost.AuthenticationTest()

        ' Assign the current user's credentials to the proxy class.
        ' This works for Windows Integrated authentication.
        Proxy.Credentials = System.Net.CredentialCache.DefaultCredentials

        CallMethod(Proxy)
    End Sub

    Private Sub cmdAuthenticateCustom_Click(ByVal sender As System.Object, _
      ByVal e As System.EventArgs) Handles cmdAuthenticateCustom.Click
        ' Create the proxy.
        Dim Proxy As New localhost.AuthenticationTest()

        ' Assign the credentials from the user name and password textboxes.
        ' This is required for Basic authentication.
        Proxy.Credentials = New System.Net.NetworkCredential( _
          txtUser.Text, txtPassword.Text)

        CallMethod(Proxy)
    End Sub

    Private Sub CallMethod(ByVal proxy As localhost.AuthenticationTest)
        Try
            MessageBox.Show("User: " & proxy.GetIISUser(), _
              "Authentication Succeeded")
        Catch Err As Exception
            MessageBox.Show(Err.Message, "Authentication Failed")
        End Try
    End Sub

End Class
```

16.7 Use Session State

Problem

You want to create a Web service that can store information in user-specific session state.

Solution

Avoid this option if possible because it leads to several complications. If it's absolutely necessary to use session state, set the *EnableSession* property of the *WebMethod* attribute to *True*, and initialize the *CookieContainer* property of the proxy class before calling the Web method.

Discussion

ASP.NET Web services can use session state to store objects in server-side memory. However, this approach has several consequences, including:

- Because session state must be tracked using a cookie with the session ID, the client must take additional steps to maintain the cookie. In addition, session state won't work over protocols other than HTTP.

- Cookies are maintained separately for each proxy class. Therefore, there's no easy way for multiple Web services to access the same session information for a client.

- Web services are usually designed as stateless classes. Creating a Web service that retains information between calls might lead to behavior the client does not expect. In addition, the lifetime of a session does not necessarily match the lifetime of the Web service proxy object.

- If you store a large amount of information in session state, server memory will become scarce and performance will suffer.

If you still decide to use session state, you must tweak both the Web service and the client code. On the Web service side, every Web method that needs access to the session state collection must set the *EnableSession* property of the *WebMethod* attribute to *True*. If you do not take this step, any existing session information will be preserved, but it will not be deserialized and made available to your Web method code.

The following Web service allows the remote user to store and retrieve a simple string:

```
<WebService()> _
Public Class SessionTest
    Inherits System.Web.Services.WebService

    <WebMethod(EnableSession:=True)> _
    Public Sub SetString(ByVal data As String)
        Session("Data") = data
    End Sub

    <WebMethod(EnableSession:=True)> _
    Public Function GetString() As String
        Return CType(Session("Data"), String)
    End Function

End Class
```

On the client side, you must create an empty cookie collection before you use the proxy. Otherwise, the proxy will not be able to accept the ASP.NET session cookie and a new session will be started for each method call. The client will need to maintain this instance of the proxy class (or at least its cookie collection) as long as it needs to access the same session.

Here's the code for a sample client that sends the data from a text box to the session-enabled Web service:

```
Public Class SessionClient
    Inherits System.Windows.Forms.Form

    ' (Designer code omitted.)

    Private Proxy As New localhost.SessionTest()

    Private Sub Form_Load(ByVal sender As System.Object, _
      ByVal e As System.EventArgs) Handles MyBase.Load
        ' Initialize the cookie container.
        Proxy.CookieContainer = New System.Net.CookieContainer()
    End Sub

    Private Sub cmdSet_Click(ByVal sender As System.Object, _
      ByVal e As System.EventArgs) Handles cmdSet.Click
        Proxy.SetString(txtData.Text)
        txtData.Text = ""
    End Sub

    Private Sub cmdGet_Click(ByVal sender As System.Object, _
      ByVal e As System.EventArgs) Handles cmdGet.Click
```

```
            txtData.Text = Proxy.GetString()
        End Sub

End Class
```

16.8 Upload or Download Large Binary Data

Problem

You want to transfer an image or a file to or from a Web service.

Solution

Submit or return the data as a byte array.

Discussion

Web services support only a carefully limited set of data types, an approach that's designed to ensure optimum cross-platform compatibility. However, you can transmit virtually anything if you convert it to binary first.

The following Web service accepts a byte array and saves it directly to disk. For this code to work, the ASP.NET process must have privileges to write to the appropriate directory. You should also import the *System.IO* namespace.

```
<WebService()> _
Public Class UploadData
    Inherits System.Web.Services.WebService

    <WebMethod()> _
    Public Sub UploadFile(ByVal originalName As String, _
      ByVal buffer As Byte())

        ' Canonicalize the originalName value so it just includes a filename.
        ' This strips out any path information, which a malicious user could
        ' submit to trick your application into writing in the wrong location.
        originalName = Path.GetFileName(originalName)

        ' Retrieve the save path from the configuration file.
        Dim SavePath As String
        SavePath = ConfigurationSettings.AppSettings("UploadDirectory")
        SavePath = Path.Combine(SavePath, originalName)

        ' Use CreateNew mode, so that an error will be raised if a file
        ' with the same name already exists.
        Dim fs As New FileStream(SavePath, FileMode.CreateNew)
```

```
        ' Write the file.
        fs.Write(buffer, 0, buffer.Length)
        fs.Close()

    End Sub

End Class
```

Here is a sample client that allows the user to select a file and submit it to the Web service:

```
Public Class UploadClient
    Inherits System.Windows.Forms.Form

    ' (Designer code omitted.)

    Private Sub cmdUpload_Click(ByVal sender As System.Object, _
      ByVal e As System.EventArgs) Handles cmdUpload.Click
        Me.Cursor = Cursors.WaitCursor

        ' Show a dialog that allows the user to choose a file.
        Dim dlgOpen As New OpenFileDialog()
        If dlgOpen.ShowDialog() = DialogResult.OK Then

            ' Read the file into a byte array.
            Dim fs As New FileStream(dlgOpen.FileName, FileMode.Open)
            Dim Buffer As Byte()
            ReDim Buffer(fs.Length)
            fs.Read(Buffer, 0, fs.Length)
            fs.Close()

            ' Submit the byte array to the Web service.
            Dim Proxy As New localhost.UploadData()
            Proxy.UploadFile(Path.GetFileName(dlgOpen.FileName), Buffer)
            MessageBox.Show("Upload complete.")

        End If

        Me.Cursor = Cursors.Default
    End Sub

End Class
```

Notice that this example doesn't take security into account. In a production-level application, you would want to authenticate the user before allowing him or her to write data to the server (using the technique shown in recipe 16.6). You might also limit the maximum accepted message size to prevent denial of service attacks that work by flooding the server with data.

You would also need to take additional steps to prevent name collision, which occurs when two files are uploaded with the same name. Name collision causes the first file to be overwritten or the second operation to fail, depending on the file access mode you use. To prevent name collision, you could create a new GUID with each Web method request and use this GUID as the file name. In this case, you would probably need to log some information in a database mapping the GUID to the original file name. Alternatively, you might want to use multiple user-specific directories and allow users to overwrite their own uploaded files.

> **Note**   Depending on the size of data and the speed of the connection, it might take some time to transmit large binary arrays. While the transfer is in process, the ASP.NET thread that's serving the request will not be able to respond to any other clients. So, if you need to create a system where users can frequently upload and download large amounts of data, you might want to use another approach, such as FTP.

16.9 Send Out-of-Band Data in a SOAP Header

Problem

You want to send some information to one or more Web methods without having to add it as a method parameter.

Solution

Create a custom SOAP header that encapsulates the additional information you need.

Discussion

Sometimes, you might need to submit information to a Web method that does not specifically relate to the method itself. This is most often the case when you are building your own custom authentication system or state management system, and you need to submit some type of credentials or tracking information every time you call the Web service. You can accommodate this information by inserting additional parameters into every method. However, this approach raises several problems, including:

- The client needs to track this information and remember to submit it with each request.

- The Web service method signatures are needlessly cluttered.

- If you change your custom authentication or tracking system, you must modify each and every method definition.

A better approach is to submit this data *out-of-band* as a SOAP header. In this case, the client needs to specify the information only once and it will be automatically added to every request message as needed.

For example, consider a Web service that uses *ticket-based authentication*. In this system, the user is authenticated only once and given a time-limited GUID ticket. This ticket is presented on subsequent method invocations, saving the effort of re-authenticating the user with each request. In ticket-based authentication, you might want to create a SOAP header that tracks the user's authenticated GUID ticket. The class would derive from *SoapHeader* in the *System.Web.Services.Protocols* namespace and would add a single public member variable.

```
Public Class TicketHeader
    Inherits SoapHeader

    Public Ticket As Guid

End Class
```

Now you must modify the Web service so that it includes a public *TicketHeader* member variable.

```
<WebService()> _
Public Class TicketTest
    Inherits System.Web.Services.WebService

    ' Holds the authentication SOAP header.
    Public Ticket As TicketHeader

    ' (Other code omitted.)

End Class
```

Web methods that need to use or set *TicketHeader* must include the *SoapHeader* attribute. This attribute provides the following two pieces of information:

- It indicates which member variable will be used to receive the header. This variable is defined as a string, but it must correspond to a public Web service member variable of the appropriate type.

■   It specifies the *Direction*, which indicates whether the Web method will receive the header from the client (*SoapHeaderDirection.In*), return a new header to the client (*SoapHeaderDirection.Out*), or need to be able to receive *and* modify the header (*SoapHeaderDirection.InOut*).

For example, the following *Login* Web method creates the authentication ticket if the user can be successfully authenticated. It uses *SoapHeaderDirection.Out* because it creates the SOAP header and returns it to the client.

```
<WebMethod(), _
 SoapHeader("Ticket", Direction:=SoapHeaderDirection.Out)> _
Public Function Login(ByVal userName As String, ByVal password As String) _
   As Boolean

    ' Typically, you would look up the user record in the database.
    ' In this case, authentication simply checks that the password is "test"
    If password = "test" Then
        ' Create the SOAP header.
        Ticket = New TicketHeader()
        Ticket.Ticket = Guid.NewGuid()

        ' Store the ticket in server memory to validate against later.
        Application(Ticket.Ticket.ToString()) = Ticket

        Return True
    Else
        Return False
    End If

End Function
```

> **Note**   The *Login* method assumes the user name and password are sent in clear text. Therefore, you should use Secure Socket Layer (SSL) encryption to ensure that this data is not visible to an eavesdropping attacker. See recipe 18.6 for more information.

The *Logout* method, on the other hand, uses *SoapHeaderDirection.InOut*, which means it automatically receives the SOAP header from the client (if it exists). In addition, any changes that are made to the SOAP header are propagated back to the client.

```
<WebMethod(), _
 SoapHeader("Ticket", Direction:=SoapHeaderDirection.InOut)> _
Public Sub Logout()
    If Not (Ticket Is Nothing) Then
        ' Remove the server-side ticket information.
        Application(Ticket.Ticket.ToString()) = Nothing

        ' Remove the ticket information from the SOAP header.
        Ticket.Ticket = Nothing
    End If

End Sub
```

All other methods can now receive the ticket header. The following *DoSomething* method is one example. It returns a string that indicates whether the ticket was found and could be authenticated. Usually, you would use these criteria to decide whether to carry on with a task or throw a *SecurityException*.

```
<WebMethod(), _
 SoapHeader("Ticket", Direction:=SoapHeaderDirection.In)> _
Public Function DoSomething() As String
    If IsAuthenticated() Then
        Return "Sucessful authentication"
    Else
        Return "Failed authentication"
    End If
End Function

Private Function IsAuthenticated() As Boolean
    ' Check first that the ticket exists.
    If Ticket Is Nothing Then Return False

    ' Now check if the ticket in the header corresponds to
    ' the ticket stored in server memory.
    If Application(Ticket.Ticket.ToString()) Is Nothing Then
        Return False
    Else
        Dim CachedTicket As TicketHeader
        CachedTicket = CType(Application(Ticket.Ticket.ToString()), _
          TicketHeader)

        ' (This is where you would add any expiration logic.)

        ' Verify the ticket values are the same.
        ' This is not really necessary, but it's a simple failsafe.
        If CachedTicket.Ticket.CompareTo(Ticket.Ticket) = 0 Then
            Return True
        Else
```

```
            Return False
        End If
    End If
End Function
```

Finally, consider the simple test code for a Windows client shown below. Notice that the client simply needs to call the *Login* method before using any other Web methods. The client does not need to interact with the ticket directly or even be aware that the ticket exists at all.

```
Dim Proxy As New localhost.TicketTest()
Dim Success As Boolean = Proxy.Login("Me", "test")
MessageBox.Show("Login result: " & Success.ToString())

' This succeeds.
Dim Result As String = Proxy.DoSomething()
MessageBox.Show("DoSomething result: " & Result)

Proxy.Logout()

' This fails, because the ticket information no longer exists.
Result = Proxy.DoSomething()
MessageBox.Show("DoSomething result: " & Result)
```

> **Note**   The examples in this recipe show a complete demonstration of how to use a SOAP header. However, if you want to use ticket-based authentication in your own application, you'll probably want to store information about when the ticket was created on the server so that you can expire tickets after a reasonable amount of time has passed. If an expired ticket is detected, you can throw a custom exception that the client can catch. The client can then log on again with the *Login* method.

16.10 Trace a SOAP Message Using the SOAP Toolkit

Problem

You want to see raw SOAP request and response messages, probably for debugging purposes.

Solution

Use the SOAP trace utility included with the Microsoft SOAP Toolkit, and forward all Web service request messages to port 8080.

Discussion

The SOAP Toolkit includes COM components that you can use to call Web services in non-.NET clients. However, even if you code exclusively in the .NET world, you'll still find that the trace utility can be quite useful.

You can download the latest version of the SOAP Toolkit from *http: //msdn.microsoft.com/library/default.asp?url=/downloads/list/websrv.asp*. You can then run the trace utility from the Start Menu icons created by the setup application. (Look for a shortcut named Trace Utility.)

To start a trace, select File | New | Formatted Trace from the menu in the trace utility. You can then use the defaults shown in Figure 16-4, in which case the trace utility will listen on port 8080 and forward all received messages to port 80 (which IIS uses to listen for all HTTP Web requests).

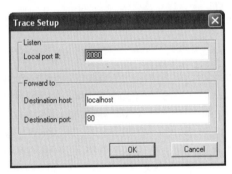

Figure 16-4   Configuring a SOAP trace.

To trace the messages sent in your application, you need to modify the client code so that SOAP requests are sent to the trace listener at port 8080. You can do so by modifying the Web service URL. For example, if your Web service is at *http://localhost/VBCookbookWebServices/Recipe16-7.asmx,* request *http: //localhost:8080/VBCookbookWebServices/Recipe16-7.asmx* instead. The following code shows how you can modify the URL of the proxy class using the *System.Uri* class, which allows you to insert the 8080 port into any URL.

```
' Retrieve the current URL for the proxy class.
Dim ProxyUri As New Uri(Proxy.Url)


' Insert the port 8080.
Proxy.Url = ProxyUri.Scheme & "://" & ProxyUri.Host & _
   ":8080" & ProxyUri.AbsolutePath
```

The trace listener will then forward your message to its destination (the Web service), intercept the response message, and forward it to your client. The full message trace will be displayed in the utility. Figure 16-5 shows an example using the Web service from recipe 16.7, with two messages.

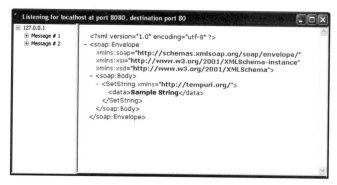

Figure 16-5   The results of a SOAP trace.

16.11 Log SOAP Messages with a SOAP Extension

Problem

You want to directly access or modify raw SOAP messages with .NET code.

Solution

Create a custom SOAP extension.

Discussion

ASP.NET allows you to access the raw SOAP messages that are transmitted to and from a Web service, but only by creating a special SOAP extension class. This class is triggered automatically as the SOAP message passes through the following four stages on the server:

- *SoapMessageStage.BeforeDeserialize* occurs immediately after the Web server receives the SOAP request message.

- *SoapMessageStage.AfterDeserialize* occurs after the raw SOAP message is translated to .NET data types but just before the Web method code runs.

- *SoapMessageStage.BeforeSerialize* occurs after the Web method code runs but before the return value is translated into a SOAP message.

■   *SoapMessageStage.AfterSerialize* occurs after the return data is serialized into a SOAP response message but before it is sent to the client.

Each time the message moves into a new stage, ASP.NET calls the *Process-Message* method of any attached SOAP extensions. Your SOAP extension can respond by inspecting and logging various information about the SOAP message. If the message is in the *BeforeDeserialize* or *AfterSerialize* stage, you can retrieve the full SOAP message text. This recipe presents the complete code for a SOAP extension that logs SOAP request and response messages to the Windows event log on the server.

All SOAP extensions consist of two ingredients: a custom class that derives from *System.Web.Services.Protocols.SoapExtension* and a custom attribute that you apply to a Web method to indicate that your SOAP extension should be used. The custom attribute is the simpler of the two ingredients. It needs to include two properties: *Priority* (which is seldom used) and *ExtensionType* (which returns a *Type* object that represents your custom *SoapExtension* class). You can also add additional properties that will be used to supply initialization information to your SOAP extension. The following example adds an *Event-Source* property, which stores the source string that will be used when writing event log entries:

```
<AttributeUsage(AttributeTargets.Method)> _
Public Class EventLogSoapExtensionAttribute
    Inherits SoapExtensionAttribute

    Private _Priority As Integer
    Private _EventSource As String

    ' The priority property allows you to configure the order that multiple
    ' SOAP extensions will execute in, if order is important.
    Public Overrides Property Priority() As Integer
        Get
            Return _Priority
        End Get
        Set(ByVal Value As Integer)
            _Priority = Value
        End Set
    End Property

    ' This is a custom piece of data used to configure event log entries.
    Public Property EventSource() As String
        Get
            Return _EventSource
        End Get
        Set(ByVal Value As String)
```

```
            _EventSource = Value
        End Set
    End Property


    ' Returns the type representing the SOAP extension class.
    ' In this case, the class is named EventLogSoapExtension.
    Public Overrides ReadOnly Property ExtensionType() As System.Type
        Get
            Return GetType(EventLogSoapExtension)
        End Get
    End Property

End Class
```

The *EventLogSoapExtension* class is much longer. Most of the code is basic boilerplate that you can copy into any SOAP extension. The custom logging logic is shown in bold text. All the lines that aren't bold are generic and will be a part of any SOAP extension you create.

```
Public Class EventLogSoapExtension
    Inherits SoapExtension

    ' These properties track the SOAP message as it is being
    ' serialized or deserialized.
    Private OldStream As Stream
    Private NewStream As Stream

    Public Overrides Function ChainStream(ByVal stream As Stream) As Stream
        OldStream = stream
        NewStream = New MemoryStream()
        Return NewStream
    End Function

    ' The source string that will be used when writing log entries.
    Private EventSource As String

    Public Overloads Overrides Function GetInitializer( _
      ByVal methodInfo As LogicalMethodInfo, _
      ByVal attribute As SoapExtensionAttribute) As Object
        ' Retrieve the EventSource property from the associated attribute.
        ' Use this information as the SOAP extension initializer.
        Return CType(attribute, EventLogSoapExtensionAttribute).EventSource
    End Function

    Public Overloads Overrides Function GetInitializer( _
      ByVal serviceType As Type) As Object
        ' The SOAP extension was loaded through a configuration file.
        ' Do not attempt to retrieve the initializer.
        Return ""
    End Function
```

```vb
Public Overrides Sub Initialize(ByVal initializer As Object)
    ' Apply the initializer every time the SOAP extension is executed.
    EventSource = CType(initializer, String)
    If EventSource = "" Then EventSource = "SOAPExtension"
End Sub

' This method is invoked as the SOAP message changes stages.
Public Overrides Sub ProcessMessage(ByVal message As SoapMessage)
    If message.Stage = SoapMessageStage.AfterSerialize Then
        ' The SOAP response message has just been created.
        ' We can log it.
        NewStream.Position = 0
        Dim LogData As New MemoryStream()
        CopyStream(NewStream, LogData)
        LogMessage(LogData, message)

        NewStream.Position = 0
        CopyStream(NewStream, OldStream)

    ElseIf message.Stage = SoapMessageStage.BeforeDeserialize Then
        CopyStream(OldStream, NewStream)
        NewStream.Position = 0

        ' The SOAP request message has not yet been deserialized.
        ' We can log it.
        Dim LogData As New MemoryStream()
        CopyStream(NewStream, LogData)
        LogMessage(LogData, message)

        NewStream.Position = 0
    End If

End Sub

Private Sub LogMessage(ByVal messageContent As Stream, _
  ByVal message As SoapMessage)
    ' Create a log message that includes data about the SOAP message,
    ' and the contents of the SOAP message itself.
    Dim LogMessage As String
    LogMessage &= "Message in: " & message.Stage.ToString() & vbNewLine
    LogMessage &= "Action: " & message.Action & vbNewLine
    LogMessage &= "URL: " & message.Url & vbNewLine
    LogMessage &= "Time: " & DateTime.Now.ToString()

    messageContent.Position = 0
    Dim r As New StreamReader(messageContent)
    LogMessage &= r.ReadToEnd()
```

```
        ' Create the EventLog source if needed.
        ' This action will only succeed if the ASP.NET worker process is
        ' running under an account that has been granted full control
        ' for the event log registry keys.
        If Not EventLog.SourceExists(EventSource) Then
            EventLog.CreateEventSource(EventSource, "Application")
        End If

        ' Log the message.
        Dim Log As New EventLog()
        Log.Source = EventSource
        Log.WriteEntry(LogMessage)
    End Sub

    Private Sub CopyStream(ByVal fromStream As Stream, _
      ByVal toStream As Stream)
        Dim r As New StreamReader(fromStream)
        Dim w As New StreamWriter(toStream)
        w.WriteLine(r.ReadToEnd())
        w.Flush()
    End Sub

End Class
```

Finally you need to apply the custom *EventLogSoapExtension* attribute to any method that will use the SOAP extension. At the same time, you can specify the event source that should be used for logging.

```
<WebMethod(), _
 EventLogSoapExtension(EventSource:="SOAPExtension")> _
Public Sub DoSomething()
    ' (No code needed.)
End Function
```

Now when a client invokes the *DoSomething* method, the *EventLogSoapExtension* will be invoked automatically and *ProcessMessage* will be called four times. Two messages will be logged to the Application event log, one for the request message (as shown in Figure 16-6) and one for the response message.

Note   To use the sample SOAP extension shown in this recipe, the ASP.NET worker process have must permission to access and modify the event log keys in the registry. Specific setup steps are provided in the readme.txt file with the code download. In addition, the SOAP extension will only execute if the Web method is invoked over SOAP. Therefore, a .NET client will trigger the SOAP extension, but the browser test page will not.

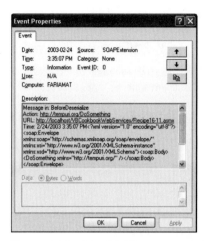

Figure 16-6   The SOAP message information in the event log.

16.12 Call a Web Service from a Visual Basic 6 Client

Problem

You need to invoke a .NET Web service from a Windows client written in Visual Basic 6.

Solution

Use the SOAP Toolkit, which provides this functionality through an easy-to-use COM library.

Discussion

The SOAP Toolkit includes a COM component that you can use to call any type of Web service that provides a valid Web Services Description Language (WSDL) document. Thus, the SOAP Toolkit supports .NET Web services and Web services created on other platforms. You can download the latest version of the SOAP Toolkit from *http://msdn.microsoft.com/library/default.asp?url= /downloads/list/websrv.asp*. In Visual Basic 6, you can add a reference to the SOAP Toolkit by selecting Project | References from the menu and adding a check mark next to the Microsoft Soap Type Library item, as shown in Figure 16-7.

To use the SOAP Toolkit, you need to know the location of the WSDL for the service you want to use. You must also know which Web methods the service provides. The SOAP Toolkit dynamically generates a proxy at run time, and it uses late binding to access the proxy methods. Therefore, no runtime checking is performed to ensure that you enter a valid Web method name or supply the right parameters and data types. To determine the available Web methods and correct method signatures, you must read the WSDL or any documentation that is provided with the service.

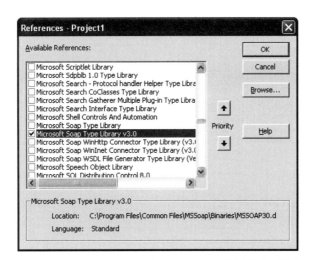

Figure 16-7   Adding a reference to the SOAP Toolkit in Visual Basic 6.

The following example shows a Visual Basic 6 client that calls the Web service presented in recipe 16.2 to determine the current date and time. In this case, the WSDL document is retrieved directly from the Web server. To improve performance, it's recommended that you save a local copy of the WSDL file and use it to configure the *SoapClient* object.

```
' (This is Visual Basic 6 code.)
Private Sub Form_Load()

    ' Create the SoapClient.
    Dim SoapClient As MSSOAPLib30.SoapClient30
    Set SoapClient = New MSSOAPLib30.SoapClient30

    ' Use the Init method to generate a proxy
    Dim WSDLPath As String
    WSDLPath = "http://localhost/VBCookbookWebServices/Recipe16-2.asmx?WSDL"
    Call SoapClient.MSSoapInit(WSDLPath)

    ' Call the GetDate web method to retrieve some information.
    MsgBox("Server returned: " & SoapClient.GetDate())

End Sub
```

17

Remoting and Enterprise Services

One of the most exciting developments in the Microsoft .NET Framework is the fact that all languages are equal. That means that a programmer can design an attractive interface for a Windows application in C# just as easily as in Microsoft Visual Basic .NET. Similarly, Visual Basic .NET can hold its weight with multi-threaded code, COM+, and the thorniest of distributed application issues.

This chapter considers some of the techniques that you'll use when designing large-scale enterprise applications. The first set of recipes (17.1 through 17.10) targets .NET Remoting, the new platform technology that allows objects to communicate across application and computer boundaries. The next set of recipes (17.11 through 17.14) considers enterprise services and the COM+ features for using transactions and object pooling. Finally, the chapter rounds up with a quick look at event logs (recipe 17.15), message queues (recipes 17.16 and 17.17), and performance counters (recipe 17.18).

> **Note**   Distributed application design is often the science (and art) of compromises. Though the recipes in this chapter teach some important techniques for using various enterprise services, they are no substitute for learning the underlying theory, design patterns, and best practices that can ensure application success (and avoid common pitfalls). For more information about .NET Remoting, you can refer to the dedicated book *Microsoft .NET Remoting* (Microsoft Press, 2002). For a solid grounding on distributed programming, consult my own *Microsoft .NET Distributed Applications* (Microsoft Press, 2003).

17.1 Make an Object Remotable

Problem

You want to create a class that can be accessed from another application or another computer on the network.

Solution

Make the class remotable by deriving from *System.MarshalByRefObject*, and create a component host that registers the class with the .NET Remoting infrastructure.

Discussion

Remoting allows you to make an object accessible across process and machine boundaries. To use .NET Remoting, you need the following ingredients, each of which must reside in a separate assembly:

■ **A remotable object.** This object can be accessed from other applications and computers and must derive from the *System.MarshalByRefObject*.

■ **A component host.** This application registers the remotable type with the .NET Remoting infrastructure using the *RemotingConfiguration* class from the *System.Runtime.Remoting* namespace. As long as the component host is running, remote clients can create instances of the remotable object.

■ **A client application.** This application can create instances of the remotable class in the component host process and interact with them. The client uses the *RemotingConfiguration* class to register the types it wants to access remotely.

Figure 17-1 shows how these three parts interact. In this example, there is only one client. However, it's also possible for multiple clients to create instances of the remotable class at the same time. In this case, each client will have its own remotable object instance, and all the objects will reside in the application domain of the component host.

Figure 17-1 Using a remotable class.

The first step is to create the remotable class. A simple example is shown here, with a remotable class that returns a *DataSet*. This approach allows a remote client to retrieve database information without needing to connect directly to the server-side database. The remotable class gains the ability to be invoked remotely because it derives from *MarshalByRefObject*.

```
Public Class RemoteObject
    Inherits MarshalByRefObject

    Public Function GetCustomerDs() As DataSet
        Dim ds As New DataSet("Customers")

        ' (Fill the DataSet by performing a DataBase query.)

        Return ds
    End Function

    ' This method allows you to verify that remoting is working.
    Public Function GetLocation() As String
        Return AppDomain.CurrentDomain.FriendlyName
    End Function

End Class
```

This class is defined in a class library assembly named RemoteObjects.dll.

Note Ideally, the remote object won't retain any state. This allows you to use *single-call activation*, in which object instances are created at the beginning of each method call and released at the end, much like a Web service. This ensures optimum performance and saves you from the added complexity of implementing a lease policy to configure object lifetime.

Next you must create the component host—the server-side application that hosts all instances of the remote class. You can use any type of long-running .NET application for a component host (including Windows applications, Windows services, and Console applications). Here is the form code for a simple Windows component host. In order to use the code as written, you must import the *System.Runtime.Remoting* namespace.

```
Public Class ComponentHostForm
    Inherits System.Windows.Forms.Form

    ' (Desginer code omitted.)

    Private Sub Form_Load(ByVal sender As System.Object, _
      ByVal e As System.EventArgs) Handles MyBase.Load
        ' Register the remotable classes.
        RemotingConfiguration.Configure("SimpleServer.exe.config")

        ' (As long as this application is running, the remote objects
        ' will be accessible.)
    End Sub

End Class
```

The component host uses a configuration file to configure the classes it will support, the ports it will support for network communication, and the Uniform Resource Identifier (URI) that the client will use to access the object. Following is a simple configuration file that registers the *RemoteObjects.RemoteObject* class from the RemoteObjects.dll assembly, and provides network access through TCP/IP on the port 9080. This assembly must be in the global assembly cache (GAC) or in the same directory as the server application. The configuration file also configures the remote object to use single-call activation.

```
<configuration>
  <system.runtime.remoting>
    <application>

      <!-- Define the remotable object. -->
      <service>
        <wellknown
            mode = "SingleCall"
            type="RemoteObjects.RemoteObject, RemoteObjects"
            objectUri="RemoteObject" />
      </service>

      <!-- Define the protocol used for network access.
```

```
                   You can use tcp or http channels. -->
        <channels>
          <channel ref="tcp" port="9080" />
        </channels>

    </application>
  </system.runtime.remoting>
</configuration>
```

The component host never interacts with the remotable objects directly. All it does is register the appropriate types with the .NET Remoting infrastructure. After this point, clients can create object instances, and the server application can continue with other tasks. However, when the component host is closed, any remotable objects will be destroyed, and no more objects can be created.

The client application uses a similar configuration file that indicates the URL of the remote object and its type. The URL takes this form:

```
[Protocol]://[Server]:[PortNumber]/[ObjectURI]
```

Here is the complete client configuration file:

```
<configuration>
  <system.runtime.remoting>
    <application>

        <!-- Define the object this application will access remotely. -->
        <client>
          <wellknown type="RemoteObjects.RemoteObject, RemoteObjects"
             url="tcp://localhost:9080/RemoteObject" />
        </client>

        <!-- Define the protocol used for network access.
             The protocol must match the component host, but any port is valid.
             A port of 0 means "dynamically choose an available port." -->
        <channels>
          <channel ref="tcp" port="0" />
        </channels>

    </application>
  </system.runtime.remoting>
</configuration>
```

The client application uses the *RemotingConfiguration.Configure* method to register the objects it wants to call. Once this step is taken, the client can create the object exactly as it would create a local object. However, the object will actually be created in the component host application domain. You can verify this with the simple Windows client shown here on the following page.

```
Public Class ClientForm
    Inherits System.Windows.Forms.Form

    ' (Desginer code omitted.)

    Private Sub Form_Load(ByVal sender As System.Object, _
        ByVal e As System.EventArgs) Handles MyBase.Load
        ' Register the classes that will be accessed remotely.
        RemotingConfiguration.Configure("SimpleClient.exe.config")
        ' (Now any attempts to instantiate the RemoteObjects.RemoteObject
        ' class will actually create a proxy to a remote instance.)

        ' Interact with the remote object through a proxy.
        Dim Proxy As New RemoteObjects.RemoteObject()
        MessageBox.Show("Object executing in: " & Proxy.GetLocation())
        ' (This displays the name of the component host application domain,
        ' where the object executes.)

        MessageBox.Show("Retrieved DataSet: " & _
            Proxy.GetCustomerDs.DataSetName)
    End Sub

End Class
```

In order to instantiate a remote object, the client needs to have a reference to the assembly where the class is defined. This presents an additional deployment step, which you can avoid by using an interface that defines the supported functionality, as explained in recipe 17.5.

> **Note** In order to transmit data to and from a remote object, the types you use for parameters and return values must be serializable. All basic types (such as strings, numbers, and so on) are serializable. If you want to use custom classes to transmit data to or from a remote object, you must make sure these classes are also serializable using the *Serializable* attribute, as described in recipe 4.8.

17.2 Register All the Remotable Classes in an Assembly

Problem

You want to register all the remotable classes that are defined in an assembly without having to specify them in a configuration file.

Solution

Load the assembly with the remotable classes using reflection. Loop through all its types, and use the *RemotingConfiguration.RegisterWellKnownServiceType* to register every remotable class.

Discussion

.NET makes it equally easy to register remotable classes through a configuration file or programmatically with code. For example, consider the example from recipe 17.1. To use programmatic registration, you would first remove the class declarations from the configuration file and leave it as shown here:

```
<configuration>
  <system.runtime.remoting>
    <application>

      <channels>
        <channel ref="tcp" port="9080" />
      </channels>

    </application>
  </system.runtime.remoting>
</configuration>
```

Now you can combine reflection with the *RegisterWellKnownServiceType* method to programmatically register all remotable objects.

```
Private Sub Form_Load(ByVal sender As System.Object, _
  ByVal e As System.EventArgs) Handles MyBase.Load

    ' Use the configuration file to define networking options.
    RemotingConfiguration.Configure("SimpleServer.exe.config")

    ' Create a System.Reflection.Assembly representing the assembly
    ' where remotable classes are defined.
    Dim RemoteAsm As System.Reflection.Assembly
    RemoteAsm = System.Reflection.Assembly.LoadFrom("RemoteObjects.dll")

    ' Process all the types in this namespace.
    Dim Obj As Type
    For Each Obj In RemoteAsm.GetTypes()
        ' Check if the type is remotable.
        If Obj.IsSubclassOf(GetType(MarshalByRefObject)) Then
            ' Register each type using the type name as the URI
            ' (like RemoteObject).
```

```
                RemotingConfiguration.RegisterWellKnownServiceType( _
                    Obj, Obj.Name, WellKnownObjectMode.SingleCall)
            End If
        Next

    End Sub
```

> **Note** This code determines whether or not a class is remotable by examining if it derives from *MarshalByRefObject*. This approach always works, but it could lead you to expose some types that you don't want to make remotable. For example, the *System.Windows.Forms.Form* object derives indirectly from *MarshalByRefObject*. That means that if your remote object library contains any forms, they will be exposed remotely.
>
> To avoid this problem, do not include remotable types in your assembly unless you want to make them publicly available. Or, identify the types you want to register with a custom attribute. You could then check for this attribute before registering a type. This technique is demonstrated in recipe 9.9.

You can even remove the configuration file entirely and register channels programmatically. Here is the code you would need to replace the current configuration file settings. You'll also need to add a reference to the System.Runtime.Remoting.dll assembly and import the *System.Runtime.Remoting.Channels* and *System.Runtime.Remoting.Channels.Tcp* namespaces.

```
' Define the channel on port 9080.
Dim Channel As New TcpServerChannel(9080)

' Register the channel.
ChannelServices.RegisterChannel(Channel)
```

17.3 Host a Remote Object in IIS

Problem

You want to create a remotable object in IIS (perhaps so that you can use SSL or IIS authentication) instead of a dedicated component host.

Solution

Place the configuration file and assembly in a virtual directory, and modify the object URI so it ends in .rem or .soap.

Discussion

Instead of creating a dedicated component host, you can host a remotable class in Internet Information Services (IIS). This allows you to ensure that the remotable classes will always be available, and it allows you to use IIS features such as SSL encryption and Integrated Windows authentication.

In order to host a remotable class in IIS, you must first create a virtual directory. The virtual directory will contain two things: a configuration file that registers the remotable classes, and a bin directory where you must place the corresponding class library assembly (or install the assembly in the GAC).

The configuration file for hosting in IIS is quite similar to the configuration file you use with a custom component host. However, you must follow several additional rules:

- You must use the HTTP channel (although you can use the binary formatter for smaller message sizes).

- You can't specify a port number for listening. IIS listens on all the ports you have configured in the IIS Manager. Typically, this will be ports 80 and 443 (for secure SSL communication).

- The object URI must end with .rem or .soap.

- The configuration file must be named web.config, or it will be ignored.

Here's an example web.config file that registers the remote class shown in recipe 17-1:

```
<configuration>
  <system.runtime.remoting>
    <application>
      <service>
        <wellknown mode="SingleCall"
            type="RemoteObjects.RemoteObject, RemoteObjects"
            objectUri="RemoteObject.rem" />
      </service>

      <channels>
        <channel ref="http">
```

```
    <!-- Uncomment the following tags to use the binary formatter
         instead of the default SOAP formatter. -->
    <!--
      <serverProviders>
        <formatter ref="binary"/>
      </serverProviders>
      -->

    </channel>
  </channels>

  </application>
 </system.runtime.remoting>
</configuration>
```

A client can use an object hosted in IIS in the same way as an object hosted in a custom component host. However, the virtual directory name will become part of the object URI. For example, if the web.config file shown in the preceding code is hosted in the virtual directory *http://localhost/RemoteObjects*, the full URL will be *http://localhost/RemoteObjects/RemoteObject.rem*.

17.4 Fire an Event over a Remoting Channel

Problem

You need to create a client that can receive an event fired by a remote object.

Solution

Make sure you are using bidirectional channels. Create a remotable object on the client side that can receive the event from the server.

Discussion

Although the event-handling syntax doesn't change when you use .NET Remoting, it takes additional steps to create a client that can handle an event from a remote object. There are three key requirements:

■   The remotable class must use client-activated or singleton activation mode (not single-call). This ensures that the object remains alive in between method calls, allowing it to fire an event to the client.

■   The client must use a bidirectional channel so that it can receive connections initiated by the server.

■   The *EventArgs* object for the event must be serializable so that it can be transmitted across application domain boundaries.

■   The client must use a remotable "listener" object to receive the event. This listener will then raise a local event that can be handled by the client. The remote object cannot fire the event directly to an ordinary class because ordinary classes aren't accessible from other application domains.

■   In addition, if you are using .NET 1.1, you must modify the client and server configuration files to explicitly allow full serialization.

Here's a sample remotable class that you might use to fire an event to the client. It provides a single public method—*StartTask*. This method starts a timer, which fires after a short delay (about 10 seconds). When the timer fires, the remotable object raises a *TaskComplete* event.

```
Public Class RemoteObject
    Inherits MarshalByRefObject

    Public Event TaskComplete(ByVal sender As Object, _
      ByVal e As TaskCompleteEventArgs)

    Private WithEvents tmrCallback As New System.Timers.Timer()

    Public Sub StartTask()
        tmrCallback.Interval = 10000
        tmrCallback.Start()
    End Sub

    Private Sub tmrCallback_Elapsed(ByVal sender As System.Object, _
      ByVal e As System.Timers.ElapsedEventArgs) Handles tmrCallback.Elapsed
        tmrCallback.Enabled = False
        RaiseEvent TaskComplete(Me, _
          New TaskCompleteEventArgs("Task completed on server"))
    End Sub

    ' Uncomment these lines to allow the object to live forever.
    ' Otherwise, it will be destroyed after five minutes (by default).
    ' Public Overrides Function InitializeLifetimeService() As Object
    '     Return Nothing
    ' End Function

End Class
```

```
<Serializable()> _
Public Class TaskCompleteEventArgs
    Inherits EventArgs

    Public Result As String

    Public Sub New(ByVal result As String)
        Me.Result = result
    End Sub
End Class
```

The next step is to define a remotable class that runs on the client and can receive this event. This class can then contact the client. The *EventListener* class shown in the following code provides one such example—it simply raises a second event, which the client can handle directly. As with all remotable objects, it will only be accessible remotely for five minutes, unless you explicitly modify the lifetime lease policy (as described in recipe 17.6). One approach is to simply override the *InitializeLifetimeService* method to allow the object to live forever, as shown here.

```
Public Class EventListener
    Inherits MarshalByRefObject

    Public Event TaskComplete(ByVal sender As Object, _
      ByVal e As RemoteObjects.TaskCompleteEventArgs)

    ' Handle the remote event.
    Public Sub TaskCompleted(ByVal sender As Object, _
      ByVal e As RemoteObjects.TaskCompleteEventArgs)
        ' Now raise the event to a local listener.
        RaiseEvent TaskComplete(sender, e)
    End Sub

    ' Ensures that this object will be accessible remotely as long as the
    ' client application is running.
    Public Overrides Function InitializeLifetimeService() As Object
        Return Nothing
    End Function

End Class
```

The event listener must be defined in a separate assembly so that it can be referenced by the client application and the remotable class, which both need to interact with it.

Now the client application can start the asynchronous task through the *RemoteObject* class and handle the event through the *EventListener*. The following form code shows a simple client that displays a message box when the event is received.

```
Public Class ClientForm
    Inherits System.Windows.Forms.Form

    ' (Designer code omitted.)

    ' You can define a RemoteObject as a member variable, but you
    ' must not create it until after you have called
    ' RemotingConfiguration.Configure.
    ' Otherwise, you will instantiate the object locally.
    Private RemoteObj As RemoteObjects.RemoteObject
    Private WithEvents Listener As New EventListener.EventListener()

    Private Sub Form_Load(ByVal sender As System.Object, _
      ByVal e As System.EventArgs) Handles MyBase.Load
        RemotingConfiguration.Configure("SimpleClient.exe.config")
        RemoteObj = New RemoteObjects.RemoteObject()
    End Sub

    Private Sub cmdTest_Click(ByVal sender As System.Object, _
      ByVal e As System.EventArgs) Handles cmdTest.Click
        AddHandler RemoteObj.TaskComplete, AddressOf Listener.TaskCompleted
        RemoteObj.StartTask()
        MsgBox("Task has been started.")
    End Sub

    Private Sub RemoteObj_TaskComplete(ByVal sender As Object, _
      ByVal e As RemoteObjects.TaskCompleteEventArgs) _
      Handles Listener.TaskComplete
        ' This event fires on one of the remoting listener threads.
        MessageBox.Show("Event received: " & e.Result)
    End Sub

End Class
```

In order for this to work, you must make sure that the client is using bidirectional channels. Thus, the channel tag in the configuration file should look like this:

```
<channel ref="tcp" port="0" />
```

On the other hand, here's an example of a client-only channel tag, which cannot receive events:

```
<channel ref="tcp client" />
```

In addition, if you are using .NET 1.1 (the version of the .NET Framework that's included with Visual Studio .NET 2003), you must explicitly enable support for full serialization. Otherwise, the server will not be allowed to receive a delegate for the *Listener.TaskCompleted* method, and it won't be able to connect the remote event handler.

To enable full serialization support on the server, you need to modify the component host configuration file as shown here:

```xml
<?xml version="1.0" encoding="utf-8" ?>
<configuration>
  <system.runtime.remoting>
    <application name="SimpleServer" >

      <service>
        <activated type="RemoteObjects.RemoteObject, RemoteObjects"/>
      </service>

      <channels>
        <channel ref="tcp" port="9080">
          <serverProviders>
            <formatter ref="binary" typeFilterLevel="Full" />
          </serverProviders>
        </channel>
      </channels>

    </application>
  </system.runtime.remoting>
</configuration>
```

To enable full serialization support on the client, you need to modify the client configuration file:

```xml
<?xml version="1.0" encoding="utf-8" ?>
<configuration>
  <system.runtime.remoting>
    <application>

      <client url="tcp://localhost:9080/SimpleServer">
        <activated type="RemoteObjects.RemoteObject, RemoteObjects"/>
      </client>

      <channels>
        <channel ref="tcp" port="0">
          <serverProviders>
            <formatter ref="binary" typeFilterLevel="Full" />
          </serverProviders>
        </channel>
      </channels>

    </application>
  </system.runtime.remoting>
</configuration>
```

These changes aren't required for applications running under .NET 1.0 because it doesn't impose this additional layer of security. The downloadable code for this recipe includes two solutions, one for each version of .NET.

> **Note**   In this example, the event handler executes on one of the remoting listener threads provided by .NET, not the main application thread. That means that you might need to take additional steps to ensure thread-safety. In particular, if you need to interact with a control on a window, you should marshal your code to the correct thread, as described in recipe 7.9.

17.5 Access a Remote Object Through an Interface

Problem

You want a client to be able to create a remote object without requiring a reference to the assembly that defines it.

Solution

Create an interface that defines the methods the client needs to access, and distribute an assembly that contains only the interface.

Discussion

One of the limitations with .NET Remoting is that the client needs a local copy of the assembly with the code for the remote object in order to determine what methods are available. This not only poses an additional distribution headache, but it also can compromise security if you don't want the client to be able to examine the code or create local instances of the classes it contains.

The solution is to create an interface that declares the supported methods. The remote object will then implement the interface. This gives you the freedom to modify the remote object without affecting the client, as long as the interface remains unchanged.

As an example, consider the following interface, which defines the two methods used for the remote class introduced in recipe 17.1.

```
Public Interface IRemoteObject

    Function GetCustomerDs() As DataSet
    Function GetLocation() As String

End Interface
```

The *RemoteObject* class implements this interface:

```
Public Class RemoteObject
    Inherits MarshalByRefObject
    Implements RemoteObjectInterfaces.IRemoteObject

    Public Function GetCustomerDs() As DataSet _
      Implements RemoteObjectInterfaces.IRemoteObject.GetCustomerDs
        Dim ds As New DataSet("Customers")
        Return ds
    End Function

    Public Function GetLocation() As String _
      Implements RemoteObjectInterfaces.IRemoteObject.GetLocation
        Return AppDomain.CurrentDomain.FriendlyName
    End Function

End Class
```

> **Note** Remember, in order to be able to distribute the interface independently, you must place it in a separate class library assembly. If your remote object uses any custom structures or classes to transmit data, or if it uses any custom exceptions or events, these should be defined in the same assembly.

The component host needs no changes—it will still register the *RemoteObject* class directly from the RemoteObjects.dll assembly. The client, however, needs two small changes. Because the client activates the remote object through an interface, it can no longer create it directly by using the *New* keyword. Instead, it needs to use the *System.Activator* class, which provides a shared *GetObject* method. The *GetObject* method accepts two parameters: a *Type* object that indicates the type of class you are activating, and a URL that specifies its exact location:

```
Obj = Activator.GetObject( _
  GetType(RemoteObjectInterfaces.IRemoteObject), _
  "tcp://localhost:9080/RemoteObject")
```

This shift forces the client to hard-code information that would normally be placed in the configuration file. To overcome this limitation and retain the ability to modify the location without recompiling the client, you can store the URL in a custom application setting value in the configuration file.

```
<?xml version="1.0" encoding="utf-8" ?>
<configuration>

  <appSettings>
    <add key="RemoteObjUrl"
    value="tcp://localhost:9080/RemoteObject" />
  </appSettings>

  <system.runtime.remoting>
    <application>
      <channels>
        <channel ref="tcp" port="0" />
      </channels>
    </application>
  </system.runtime.remoting>

</configuration>
```

Here's the code the client calls to create the object through its interface and access a method:

```
' Configure the network channel.
RemotingConfiguration.Configure("SimpleClient.exe.config")

' Register the object using the interface and a URL defined
' in the <appSettings> section of the configuration file.
Dim Obj As Object
Obj = Activator.GetObject( _
  GetType(RemoteObjectInterfaces.IRemoteObject), _
  ConfigurationSettings.AppSettings("RemoteObjUrl"))

' Access the remote object through the interface.
RemoteObj = CType(Obj, RemoteObjectInterfaces.IRemoteObject)

MessageBox.Show("Object executing in: " & RemoteObj.GetLocation)
```

> **Note**   One of the benefits of interface-based programming is that it's impossible for the client to accidentally instantiate a local copy of the remoted object. This mistake is prevented because the client no longer has access to the remote object's code.

17.6 Control the Lifetime of a Remote Object

Problem

You want to configure how long a singleton or client-activated object lives while not in use.

Solution

Configure a lease policy by using configuration file settings, overriding the *InitializeLifetimeService* method, or implementing a custom lease provider.

Discussion

If an object uses single-call activation, it will be automatically destroyed at the end of each method call. This behavior changes with client-activated and singleton objects, which are given a longer lifetime dictated by a *lifetime lease*. With the default settings, a remote object will be automatically destroyed if it's inactive for two minutes, provided it has been in existence for at least five minutes.

The component host, client, and remote object each have the opportunity to change lifetime settings.

- The component host can specify different lease lifetime defaults in the configuration file. These settings will apply to all the objects it hosts.

- The client can call the *MarshalByRefObject.GetLifetimeService* method with a specific remote object to retrieve an *ILease* instance. The client can then call the *ILease.Renew* method to specify a minimum amount of time the object should be kept alive.

- The remote class can override its *GetLifetimeService* method to modify its initial lease settings using the provided *ILease* object.

You can create a simple client that periodically checks the lifetime of a remote object. Figure 17-2 shows an example of one such application, which uses a timer that continually polls the settings of the remote object's *ILease*. Using this application, you can watch the lifetime lease gradually tick down, you can access the object through your code (at which point its lifetime will be renewed automatically), or you can renew the object's lifetime manually, specifying that it should be given five minutes of life. (If the remote object already has at least five minutes of lifetime left, this renewal will have no effect.)

Figure 17-2   Monitoring the lifetime of a remote object.

The full client code is shown here:

```
Public Class ClientForm
    Inherits System.Windows.Forms.Form

    ' (Designer code omitted.)

    Private RemoteObj As RemoteObjects.RemoteObject
    Private Lease As System.Runtime.Remoting.Lifetime.ILease

    Private Sub Form_Load(ByVal sender As System.Object, _
      ByVal e As System.EventArgs) Handles MyBase.Load
        RemotingConfiguration.Configure("SimpleClient.exe.config")
        RemoteObj = New RemoteObjects.RemoteObject()

        ' Start the timer that checks the lease.
        tmrCheckLease.Interval = 1000
        tmrCheckLease.Start()

        ' Retrieve the lease with information about the remote object.
        ' This lease is actually stored in the component host application
        ' domain. To communicate with it, you use remoting and a proxy.
        Lease = RemoteObj.GetLifetimeService()
    End Sub

    Private Sub tmrCheckLease_Tick(ByVal sender As System.Object, _
      ByVal e As System.EventArgs) Handles tmrCheckLease.Tick
        ' Check the lease information.
        Try
            ' The Lease will be nothing if the remote object has
            ' overridden InitializeLifetimeService and given itself
            ' an infinite lifespan.
            If Not (Lease Is Nothing) Then
                lblLease.Text = "Current State: "
                lblLease.Text &= Lease.CurrentState.ToString() & vbNewLine
```

```
                      lblLease.Text &= "Initial Time Allocation: "
                      lblLease.Text &= Lease.InitialLeaseTime.ToString() & vbNewLine
                      lblLease.Text &= "Time Remaining: "
                      lblLease.Text &= Lease.CurrentLeaseTime.ToString()
               End If
          Catch err As RemotingException
               ' An error will occur if the object is no longer alive.
               lblLease.Text = err.ToString()
               tmrCheckLease.Stop()
          End Try
     End Sub

     Private Sub cmdRenew_Click(ByVal sender As System.Object, _
       ByVal e As System.EventArgs) Handles cmdRenew.Click
          ' Give the remote object five minutes of life.
          Lease.Renew(TimeSpan.FromMinutes(5))
     End Sub

     Private Sub cmdAccess_Click(ByVal sender As System.Object, _
       ByVal e As System.EventArgs) Handles cmdAccess.Click
          ' When this method is called, the object lifetime is automatically
          ' renewed according to the default renewal settings.
          Dim Test As String = RemoteObj.GetLocation()
     End Sub

End Class
```

Another way to configure lifetime is through the component host config-uration file using the *<lifetime>* tag. These lease settings apply to all the remote objects created by the component host. Use a trailing *M* for minutes or an *S* to indicate seconds.

Here's an example that gives remote objects an initial lifetime of 10 min-utes. When a client accesses the object, its lifetime is automatically renewed to at least three minutes.

```
<configuration>
  <system.runtime.remoting>
    <application>

      <service>
        <wellknown
            mode = "Singleton"
            type="RemoteObjects.RemoteObject, RemoteObjects"
            objectUri="RemoteObject" />
      </service>

      <channels>
```

```
        <channel ref="tcp" port="9080" />
      </channels>

      <lifetime leaseTime = "10M"
                renewOnCallTime = "3M" />

    </application>
  </system.runtime.remoting>
</configuration>
```

Finally, a remote object can override *InitializeLifetimeService* to take control of its own destiny. This is most commonly the case if you are creating a singleton object that needs to run independently (and permanently), even if clients aren't currently using it.

The following code shows the code you could add to a remote class to give it a default 10-minute lifetime and 5-minute renewal time. If you wanted the object to have an unlimited lifetime, simply return a null reference (*Nothing*) instead of an *ILease* object.

```
Public Overrides Function InitializeLifetimeService() As Object
    Dim Lease As ILease = MyBase.InitializeLifetimeService()

    ' Lease can only be configured if it is in an initial state.
    If Lease.CurrentState = LeaseState.Initial Then
        Lease.InitialLeaseTime = TimeSpan.FromMinutes(10)
        Lease.RenewOnCallTime = TimeSpan.FromMinutes(5)
    End If

    Return Lease

End Function
```

17.7 Use a Sponsor to Keep Remote Objects Alive

Problem

You want to keep a remote object alive while it's in use, but you don't want to be forced to periodically call the *ILease.Renew* method from your client.

Solution

Create and register a lease sponsor that will automatically renew the remote object.

Discussion

.NET Remoting introduces the ideas of lifetime leases and lease sponsors. A *lease sponsor* is remotable object that runs in the client's application domain. It has a single purpose—to keep the remote objects your application is using alive.

The lease sponsor doesn't interact with the remote object directly. Instead, it waits for the .NET Remoting infrastructure to initiate communication. Whenever a remote object is about to expire, .NET will contact every registered lease sponsor. These lease sponsors are given the opportunity to renew the object, keeping it alive. Once .NET finds a lease sponsor that's willing to renew the life of an object, it ends its search. This approach ensures that leasing is a very bandwidth-friendly approach to lifetime management.

You can create your own custom lease sponsor by implementing the *System.Runtime.Remoting.Lifetime.ISponsor* interface. However, a simpler option is just to use the prebuilt *ClientSponsor* class from the *System.Runtime.Remoting.Lifetime* namespace. This class provides a single property—*RenewalTime*—which indicates the lease time that will be given to the remote object on renewal. The *ClientSponsor* class also provides *Register* and *Unregister* methods, which you use to specify the remote objects it should sponsor.

The following code rewrites the client presented in recipe 17.6 so that it uses a lease sponsor. Now, the object will be renewed automatically, as long as the client application is running.

```
Private Sponsor As New System.Runtime.Remoting.Lifetime.ClientSponsor()

Private Sub Form_Load(ByVal sender As System.Object, _
  ByVal e As System.EventArgs) Handles MyBase.Load
    RemotingConfiguration.Configure("SimpleClient.exe.config")
    RemoteObj = New RemoteObjects.RemoteObject()
    Lease = RemoteObj.GetLifetimeService()

    ' Start the timer that checks the lease.
    tmrCheckLease.Interval = 1000
    tmrCheckLease.Start()

    ' Register the remote object with the lease sponsor.
    Sponsor.RenewalTime = TimeSpan.FromMinutes(5)
    Sponsor.Register(RemoteObj)
End Sub
```

For lease sponsors to work, you must use bidirectional channels. Otherwise, the .NET Remoting infrastructure won't be able to initiate a connection to your lease sponsor. Also, if you are using version 1.1 of the .NET Framework, you will need to add an additional section to the *<channel>* element of the client and component host configuration files to enable support for full serialization. Here's the modified component host configuration file, with the new lines highlighted:

```
<configuration>
  <system.runtime.remoting>
    <application>

      <service>
        <wellknown
            mode = "Singleton"
            type="RemoteObjects.RemoteObject, RemoteObjects"
            objectUri="RemoteObject" />
      </service>

      <channels>
        <channel ref="tcp" port="9080" >
          <serverProviders>
            <formatter ref="binary" typeFilterLevel="Full" />
          </serverProviders>
        </channel>
      </channels>

    </application>
  </system.runtime.remoting>
</configuration>
```

Remember, you can make these changes only if you are using .NET 1.1 (as included with Visual Studio .NET 2003). These settings won't be recognized (and aren't required) for .NET 1.0 applications.

17.8 Control Versioning for Remote Objects

Problem

You want to create a component host that can host more than one version of the same object.

Solution

Install all versions of the object into the GAC, and explicitly register each version at a different URI endpoint.

Discussion

.NET Remoting does not include any intrinsic support for versioning. When a client creates a remote object, the component host automatically uses the version in the local directory or, in the case of a shared assembly, the latest version from the GAC. To support multiple versions, you have three choices:

- Create separate component host applications. Each component host will have a different version of the remote object assembly and will register its version with a different URI. This approach forces you to run multiple component host applications at once and is most practical if you are using IIS hosting (as described in recipe 17.3).

- Create an entirely new remote object assembly (instead of simply changing the version). You can then register the classes from both assemblies at different URIs, using the same component host.

- Install all versions of the remote object assembly in the GAC. You can now create a component host that maps different URIs to specific versions of the remote object assembly.

The last option is the most flexible in cases where you need to support multiple versions. For example, consider the following configuration file, which registers two versions of the *RemoteObjects* assembly at two different endpoints. Notice that you need to include the exact version number and public key token when using assemblies from the GAC. You can find this information by viewing the assembly in the Windows Explorer GAC plug-in (browse to C:\[WindowsDir]\Assembly).

```
<configuration>
  <system.runtime.remoting>
    <application>
      <service>
        <!-- The type information is split over two lines to accommodate the
             bounds of the page. In the configuration file, this information
             must all be placed on a single line. -->

        <wellknown mode="SingleCall"
          type="RemoteObjects.RemoteObject, RemoteObjects, Version 1.0.0.1,
              Culture=neutral, PublicKeyToken=8b5ed84fd25209e1"
          objectUri="RemoteObj" />

        <wellknown mode="SingleCall"
          type="RemoteObjects.RemoteObject, RemoteObjects, Version 2.0.0.1,
              Culture=neutral, PublicKeyToken=8b5ed84fd25209e1"
          objectUri="RemoteObj_2.0" />
```

```
        </service>
        <channels>
          <channel ref="tcp server" port="9080" />
        </channels>
      </application>
    </system.runtime.remoting>
</configuration>
```

The client configuration file won't change at all (aside from updating the URI, if required). The client "chooses" the version it wants to use by using the corresponding URI.

17.9 Use a One-Way Method

Problem

You want a method in a remote object to perform a long task, and you don't want to force the client to wait while the method code executes.

Solution

Create a one-way method by applying the *OneWay* attribute from the *System.Runtime.Remoting.Messaging* namespace.

Discussion

With one-way methods, the client sends a request message, and the remote object responds immediately to indicate it has begun processing. This has several consequences:

- The client doesn't need to wait while the method code executes.

- The method can't return any information to the client, either through a return value or *ByRef* parameter.

- If the method throws an unhandled exception, it won't be propagated back to the client.

To create a one-way method, you need to apply a *OneWay* attribute (from the *System.Runtime.Remoting.Messaging* namespace) to the appropriate method. The following example shows a remote object that provides two methods, each of which causes a 10-second delay. One of the two methods uses the *OneWay* attribute, and therefore it won't stall the client.

```
Public Class RemoteObject
    Inherits MarshalByRefObject

    <System.Runtime.Remoting.Messaging.OneWay()> _
    Public Sub DoLongTask()
        ' (Start a long task, that doesn't return
        ' information to the client.)
        Delay(10)
    End Sub

    Public Sub DoLongTaskWithWait()
        ' (Start a long task, but force the client
        ' to wait while processing takes place.)
        Delay(10)
    End Sub

    Private Sub Delay(ByVal seconds As Integer)
        Dim CurrentTime As DateTime = DateTime.Now
        Do
        Loop Until DateTime.Now.Subtract(CurrentTime).TotalSeconds > seconds
    End Sub

End Class
```

> **Note** One-way methods aren't the only way to remove client delays. You can also modify the client to call any method asynchronously. In this case, the client will wait for the method to complete, but it will wait on another thread, so the client application can continue with other work. Asynchronous method calls are described in recipe 7.1.

17.10 Track Multiple Clients with a Singleton

Problem

You want to allow multiple clients to communicate with each other through a single server.

Solution

Create a server-side singleton object that tracks all the currently available clients on the network. The server should store a proxy object for each client in an in-memory collection.

Discussion

When you create a remote object that uses singleton activation mode, only a single instance of it will be created. All the clients that use this remote object will access the same instance. This means that the remote object can store some information that will be shared among all users (such as a list of connected clients). It also means that you'll need to craft thread-safe code using the techniques presented in Chapter 7 because more than one client will be able to access the remote object at the same time.

> **Note**   This recipe incorporates bidirectional communication (from recipe 17.4), interface-based remoting (from recipe 17.5), and one-way messages (from recipe 17.9). You might want to review these recipes before applying this one.

One useful example is a simple coordinator object that allows clients to log on, log off, and broadcast messages. In order for this type of communication system to work, both the coordinator and the client must include a remotable object. You can define the basic interfaces for the system as follows:

```
' IClient simply defines the functionality needed
' to receive a message from the server.
Public Interface IClient
    Sub ReceiveMessage(ByVal message As String)
End Interface


' IServer simply defines the functionality needed
' to register users and allow any user to request
' that a message be delivered to all other users.
Public Interface IServer
    Sub AddUser(ByVal user As IClient)
    Sub RemoveUser(ByVal user As IClient)
    Sub BroadcastMessage(ByVal message As String)
End Interface
```

The server object tracks all the currently connected clients. It also allows any one client to broadcast a message to all clients through the *BroadcastMessage* method. The full code is shown here, with the required synchronization code to prevent errors from occurring if multiple threads attempt to modify the *Clients* collection at the same time.

```
Public Class Server
    Inherits MarshalByRefObject
    Implements RemoteObjectInterfaces.IServer

    Private Users As New ArrayList()

    Public Sub AddUser(ByVal user As RemoteObjectInterfaces.IClient) _
      Implements RemoteObjectInterfaces.IServer.AddUser
        SyncLock Users
            Users.Add(user)
        End SyncLock
    End Sub

    Public Sub RemoveUser(ByVal user As RemoteObjectInterfaces.IClient) _
      Implements RemoteObjectInterfaces.IServer.RemoveUser
        SyncLock Users
            Users.Remove(user)
        End SyncLock
    End Sub

    ' This is a one-way method. There is no need for the client to
    ' wait while all users are contacted with the message.
    <System.Runtime.Remoting.Messaging.OneWay()> _
    Public Sub BroadcastMessage(ByVal message As String) _
      Implements RemoteObjectInterfaces.IServer.BroadcastMessage
        ' Create a copy of the client collection. This way, the collection
        ' doesn't need to be locked while messages are being delivered.
        Dim Recipients As ArrayList
        SyncLock Users
            Recipients = Users.Clone()
        End SyncLock

        Dim Recipient As RemoteObjectInterfaces.IClient
        For Each Recipient In Recipients
            Dim ReceiveDelegate As New _
              RemoteObjectInterfaces.ReceiveMessageDelegate( _
              AddressOf Recipient.ReceiveMessage)
            ReceiveDelegate.BeginInvoke(message, Nothing, Nothing)
        Next
    End Sub

End Class
```

The client application includes a *Client* class that can receive broadcasted messages. Notice that the client does not need to register this class with the .NET Remoting infrastructure because the client will provide a proxy to the remote object by calling the *AddUser* method.

```
Public Class Client
    Inherits MarshalByRefObject
    Implements RemoteObjectInterfaces.IClient

    ' This is the local event that will alert the client application
    ' that the server sent a broadcast message.
    Public Event MessageReceived(ByVal sender As Object, _
      ByVal e As MessageEventArgs)

    ' This is a one-way method. There is no need for the server to wait
    ' while the client deals with the message it has received.
    <System.Runtime.Remoting.Messaging.OneWay()> _
    Public Sub ReceiveMessage(ByVal message As String) _
      Implements RemoteObjectInterfaces.IClient.ReceiveMessage
        RaiseEvent MessageReceived(Me, New MessageEventArgs(message))
    End Sub

End Class

Public Class MessageEventArgs
    Inherits EventArgs

    Private _Message As String

    Public Property Message() As String
        Get
            Return _Message
        End Get
        Set(ByVal Value As String)
            _Message = Value
        End Set
    End Property

    Public Sub New(ByVal message As String)
        MyBase.New()
        Me.Message = message
    End Sub

End Class
```

When a message is received, a local event is fired, which the client handles directly. In this case, the client simply displays a message box:

```
Private WithEvents Client As New Client()

Private Sub Client_MessageReceived(ByVal sender As Object, _
  ByVal e As SimpleClient.MessageEventArgs) Handles Client.MessageReceived
    MessageBox.Show("Received: " & e.Message)
End Sub
```

When the client first starts, it creates a local instance of the *Client* class, registers the remote object it wants to access, and then calls the remote *AddUser* method. The remote object receives a proxy to the remotable *Client* class, which it stores in the collection so that it can contact the client later.

```
Private Server As RemoteObjectInterfaces.IServer

Private Sub Form_Load(ByVal sender As System.Object, _
  ByVal e As System.EventArgs) Handles MyBase.Load
    RemotingConfiguration.Configure("SimpleClient.exe.config")

    Dim Obj As Object Obj = Activator.GetObject( _
      GetType(RemoteObjectInterfaces.IServer), _
      ConfigurationSettings.AppSettings("RemoteObjUrl"))
    Server = CType(Obj, RemoteObjectInterfaces.IServer)

    ' Register the client with the server.
    Server.AddUser(Client)
End Sub
```

The client can then call *BroadcastMessage* to send a message to all clients. Here's an example that fires a message in response to a button click:

```
Private Sub cmdTest_Click(ByVal sender As System.Object, _
  ByVal e As System.EventArgs) Handles cmdTest.Click
    Server.BroadcastMessage("This is a test")
End Sub
```

If you're writing this application using the .NET Framework 1.1, you'll need to explicitly enable full serialization, or the client reference won't be able to cross application boundaries. To make this change, you'll need to modify the *<channel>* tag in the client and server configuration files, as shown here:

```
<channels>
  <channel ref="tcp" port="0" >
    <serverProviders>
      <formatter ref="binary" typeFilterLevel="Full" />
    </serverProviders>
  </channel>
</channels>
```

The downloadable code includes two versions of this recipe—one for each version of the .NET Framework.

> **Note**   Currently, the *BroadcastMessage* method does not incorporate any error-handling logic. In a production-level application, you would check for an error that might occur if the client cannot be contacted. (This might occur if the client is disconnected or shut down without calling the *RemoveUser* method.) In response to this error, you would remove the client from the collection and then continue contacting the remaining clients.

17.11 Create a COM+ Serviced Component

Problem

You want to create a component that can use COM+ services such as distributed transactions and object pooling.

Solution

Derive your component from the *ServicedComponent* class, give your assembly a strong name, and register it in the COM+ catalog using the regsvcs.exe utility.

Discussion

To use COM+ services (as described in recipes 17.13 and 17.14), you must create your component as a class library assembly and add a reference to the System.EnterpriseServices.dll assembly. You can then add one or more classes that derive from *System.EnterpriseServices.ServicedComponent*. These classes do not need any additional COM-specific code. They gain the ability to use a wide range of COM+ services that you can configure using the attributes in the *System.EnterpriseServices* namespace.

To test a component that uses COM+ services, you must register it and create a test application. Registering a serviced component takes several steps. The recommended approach is as follows:

1.   Generate a key pair using the sn.exe command-line utility included with Microsoft .NET. Here's an example that saves a key pair to a file named AssemblyKey.snk:

```
sn -k AssemblyKey.snk
```

2. Add an *AssemblyKeyFile* attribute to your class library project, identifying the file with the key pair. This ensures that when your assembly is compiled, it will have a unique strong name and can be added to the GAC.

```
<Assembly: AssemblyKeyFile("AssemblyKey.snk")>
```

3. Compile the assembly, and place it in the GAC. You can perform this step by pasting the file into the C:\[WindowsDir]\Assembly directory using the Windows Explorer GAC shell extension, or you can use the GACUtil.exe command-line utility.

```
gacutil /i mydll.dll
```

4. Register the component using the Regsvcs command-line utility. This creates a COM+ application entry in the COM+ catalog, using the root namespace, and adds all *ServicedComponent* classes to the application.

```
regsvcs mydll.dll
```

5. To view your classes in the COM+ catalog, select Component Services from the Administrative Tools section of the Control Panel. The COM+ Explorer is shown in Figure 17-3.

Figure 17-3   The COM+ catalog.

> **Note**   The steps described in this recipe are the recommended best practice. However, you can avoid manual registration and use a .NET feature known as *dynamic registration*, which will register a COM+ serviced component as soon as it's instantiated by a client. Dynamic registration is completely transparent and convenient while testing. However, it can cause problems if the user running the client doesn't have administrative privileges, or if you update the component code without changing the version number.

17.12 Prevent Duplicate Entries for Serviced Components

Problem

When you update a serviced component, it's registered in the COM+ catalog with a different type library and component GUID.

Solution

Specify the version number of your assembly and GUID of your classes using attributes.

Discussion

By default, every time you register a serviced component, a new type library will be generated, and all the classes it contains will be given new GUIDs. This leads to duplicate entries in the COM+ catalog, which can cause significant confusion. Fortunately, resolving these problems is easy.

The first step is to fix the version number of your assembly. Microsoft Visual Studio .NET creates all applications with the following attribute in the AssemblyInfo.vb file:

```
<Assembly: AssemblyVersion("1.0.*")>
```

This attribute indicates that the assembly should be given a new (incrementally updated) version number starting with 1.0 each time it's compiled. COM+ versioning requires that different versions of the same component have different type libraries. But if you are creating multiple builds during the development and testing process, you'll want to fix the version number so that the type library is not regenerated with each modification. Here's one possible example:

```
<Assembly: AssemblyVersion("1.0.0.2")>
```

However, the classes in your assembly will still be assigned new GUIDs each time you register the component. To prevent this behavior, you must choose a GUID for each class and specify it using the *Guid* attribute from the *System.Runtime.InteropServices* namespace.

```
<Guid("00E1160C-1040-471e-912D-1F5DAB449364")> _
Public Class MyServiceClass
    Inherits ServicedComponent
    ' (Code omitted.)
End Class
```

17.13 Create a Pooled Component

Problem

You want to use COM+ object pooling to maintain a pool of preinitialized objects.

Solution

Derive your class from *ServicedComponent*, add the *ObjectPooling* attribute, and override the *CanBePooled* method.

Discussion

With object pooling, a "pool" of available, instantiated objects is retained permanently. When a client creates an object, COM+ provides a preinitialized object from the pool. When a client releases an object, it isn't destroyed, but is instead returned to the object pool, where it remains ready to serve another client. Object pooling is most often used for one of two reasons in a distributed application:

■   **To reduce the cost of creating an expensive object.**   Most objects can be created quite quickly and easily. But if an object performs a significant amount of work in its constructor, object pooling can improve performance.

- **To set a maximum number of allowed objects.** Object pools can enforce minimums and maximums. You might want to establish a maximum if an object wraps a limited resource. That way, it will be impossible to create more objects than can be supported by the system.

To use object pooling, you must create a serviced component, as described in recipe 17.11. Then add the *System.EnterpriseServices.ObjectPooling* attribute to the declaration for the class you want to pool. In the attribute constructor, you can specify both the minimum size of the pool and the maximum. The minimum size specifies the number of available objects that should always be in the pool. The maximum size specifies the maximum number objects that can be created at any one time, including those that are in use and those that are available in the pool.

Consider the following example:

```
<ObjectPooling(5, 10)> _
Public Class MyClass
    ' (Code omitted.)
End Class
```

This class exhibits the following behavior:

- The first time a client creates an instance of *MyClass*, five additional *MyClass* objects are created and added to the pool.

- Every time a client creates a new instance of *MyClass*, the client receives one of the preinitialized objects in the pool. At almost the same time, a new instance will be generated and added to the pool to ensure that there are always five free objects available.

- If there are 10 instances of *MyClass* in use, the pool will be empty and it won't be possible to create any new instances. If a client attempts to create a new instance, a timeout error will occur.

In addition, when creating a pooled object, you must override the *CanBe-Pooled* method. This method is called whenever the object is disposed, and it must return *True* if you want the object to be placed in the pool. Otherwise, the object will be destroyed. You can also override the *Activate* and *Deactivate* methods to configure the object immediately after it's fetched from the pool and just before it's returned to the pool.

Here's a sample component that demonstrates object pooling. It performs some time-consuming logic in the constructor when it's first created. The first time the object is created, there will be noticeable delay. On subsequent use, the object will be retrieved almost instantaneously from the pool.

```vb
<ObjectPooling(5, 10)> _
Public Class PooledObject
    Inherits ServicedComponent

    Private _CreatedTime As DateTime

    Public ReadOnly Property CreatedTime() As DateTime
        Get
            Return _CreatedTime
        End Get
    End Property

    Public Sub New()
        ' Simulate a time-consuming operation.
        Dim i, j As Integer
        For i = 1 To 100000
            For j = 1 To 10000
            Next
        Next

        _CreatedTime = DateTime.Now
    End Sub

    ' Allow this object to be pooled unless it is five minutes old.
    Protected Overrides Function CanBePooled() As Boolean
        If DateTime.Now.Subtract(CreatedTime).TotalMinutes < 5 Then
            Return True
        Else
            Return False
        End If
    End Function

End Class
```

The *PooledObject* class tracks the time that it was created and provides this information through a public *CreatedTime* property. This allows the object to decide not to return to the pool if a certain amount of time has elapsed (in this example, five minutes). In addition, it allows the client to determine when a specific instance was first created.

Here's how the client would interact with the *PooledObject* class:

```vb
' Create the object.
Dim Obj As New TestComponent.PooledObject()

' Check when this instance of the object was created.
MessageBox.Show("Object created at: " & Obj.CreatedTime.ToLongTimeString())

' Release the object (possibly to the pool).
Obj.Dispose()
```

> **Note**   In Windows 2000, COM+ pooled components are created in a default application domain and shared among all clients machine-wide. In Windows XP, pooled components are limited to the application domain where they were created (therefore, pools can't be shared even between two applications on the same computer). If you want to pool objects among multiple clients, you must add an additional layer between the pooled object and the client. For example, you could create a Web service or a .NET Remoting component that runs on a server and uses pooled components.

17.14 Use a COM+ Distributed Transaction

Problem

You want to perform multiple operations with different data sources, and you want these operations to either fail or succeed as a unit.

Solution

Derive your class from *ServicedComponent*, specify the type of transactional behavior you want by adding the *Transaction* attribute to the class declaration, and add the *AutoComplete* attribute to all methods.

Discussion

COM+ allows you to create classes that have set transaction requirements. When a client uses a method in a transactional class, a transaction will be started automatically, and committed when the code completes. Coding transactions in this way is easy and transparent. It also allows you to flexibly tie multiple methods together in a single transaction at runtime. However, COM+ transactions require the Distributed Transaction Coordinator (DTC) service on the computer to coordinate all transactions using a two-stage commit process. This is inherently slower than a simple database-initiated transaction. For that reason, COM+ transactions are most often used when you need to create a transaction that spans multiple data sources (such as an Oracle database and a SQL Server database).

To use distributed transactions, you must first create a serviced component, as described in recipe 17.11. Then, add the *System.EnterpriseServices.Transaction* attribute to the class that will run inside the transaction and specify a value from the *TransactionOption* enumeration. Supported values include

- **Required**   This object must run in a transaction. If the caller has already started a transaction, this object participates inside that transaction. Otherwise, a new transaction is created.

- **RequiresNew**   This object must run in a transaction. If the caller has already started a transaction, a new and completely independent transaction is created for this object.

- **Supported**   This object can run in a transaction and is enlisted in the caller's transaction if it exists. Otherwise, this object doesn't run in a transaction.

- **NotSupported**   This object doesn't participate in a transaction. If the caller has a current transaction, this object can't vote on it.

- **Disabled**   The object doesn't have any transaction requirements. This is the default value. In .NET, this value is equivalent to *NotSupported*.

In a COM+ transaction, every participating object must vote to commit or abort the transaction. If any object votes to abort, the entire transaction is rolled back. Your object can vote by setting the shared *ContextUtil.MyTransactionVote* property. However, a simpler approach is to add the *AutoComplete* attribute to all methods. In this case, the transaction will be automatically committed if the code completes successfully and aborted if an unhandled exception is encountered.

The following class provides an *AttemptChanges* method that modifies a SQL Server database. However, before the method completes, an unhandled exception is thrown, and the entire transaction is rolled back.

```
<Transaction(TransactionOption.Required)> _
Public Class TransactionTest
    Inherits ServicedComponent

    Private ConnectionString As String = "Data Source=localhost;" & _
      "Integrated Security=SSPI;Initial Catalog=Northwind"

    <AutoComplete()> _
    Public Sub AttemptChanges()
        ' Delete records from SQL Server.
        Dim Con As New SqlConnection(ConnectionString)
        Dim Cmd As New SqlCommand("DELETE * FROM Customers", Con)
        Try
            Con.Open()
```

```
        Cmd.ExecuteNonQuery()
    Finally
        Con.Close()
    End Try

    ' (Access another data source here.)

    ' This unhandled exception will cause all transactional
    ' operations to be rolled back.
    ' You could also set the vote manually using
    ' ContextUtil.MyTransactionVote = TransactionVote.Abort
    ' ContextUtil.DeactivateOnReturn = True
    Throw New ApplicationException("Task aborted.")
End Sub

End Class
```

> **Note**   If a data source supports COM+ transactions, it will automatically be enlisted in the current transaction. However, some operations (such as writing a file to disk) are inherently not transactional. That means that these operations won't be rolled back if the transaction fails.

17.15 Write to the Windows Event Log

Problem

You need to write a log entry to the Windows event log on the current computer.

Solution

Register the event source and create the log if required. Write the message using the *System.Diagnostics.EventLog* class.

Discussion

The *EventLog* class makes it easy to write and retrieve event log entries. You create an *EventLog* instance that wraps a specific log—typically the all-purpose Application log or a custom log that's used by your application.

```
' Access the Application log.
Dim Log As New EventLog("Application")
```

You can also supply an additional argument to the *EventLog* constructor to specify a computer name. This allows you to access an event log defined on another computer on the network.

```
' Access the Application log.
Dim Log As New EventLog("Application", "ComputerName")
```

To retrieve log entries, use the *EventLog.Entries* property, which provides a collection of *EventLogEntry* instances. To write a log entry, call the *Event-Log.WriteEntry* method, specifying a text message and optionally other information, including an event log type (error, warning information, or security audit). However, before you attempt to write a message, you should make sure the current application is registered to write in the log, and you should call the *EventLog.CreateEventSource* method if it's not.

Here's an example Console application that writes a single log entry into a custom log and the displays all the entries in the log:

```
Public Module EventLogTest

    Public Sub Main()
        ' Register the event source if needed.
        If Not EventLog.SourceExists("MyApp1") Then
            ' This registers the event source and creates the custom log,
            ' if needed.
            EventLog.CreateEventSource("MyApp1", "MyNewLog")
        End If

        ' Create a log instance.
        Dim Log As New EventLog("MyNewLog")
        Log.Source = "MyApp1"

        ' Write a message.
        Log.WriteEntry("This is a test message.", _
          EventLogEntryType.Information)

        ' Display all messages.
        Dim Entry As EventLogEntry
        For Each Entry In Log.Entries
            Console.WriteLine("Message: " & Entry.Message)
            Console.WriteLine("Written By: " & Entry.Source)
            Console.WriteLine("Written At: " & Entry.TimeWritten.ToString())
            Console.WriteLine("Type: " & Entry.EntryType.ToString())
            Console.WriteLine()
        Next

        Console.ReadLine()
    End Sub

End Module
```

This code will work only it if executes under an account that has permission to modify the event log. To grant this permission to an account that lacks it, you must use regedt32.exe and find the HKEY_Local_Machine\SYSTEM\CurrentControlSet\Services\EventLog key. Then right-click the EventLog key, and select Permissions. Any account that is granted Full Control of this folder will be able to write to the event log.

17.16 Find All the Message Queues on a Computer

Problem

You need to retrieve a list of the public queues in Active Directory or the private queues on a given computer.

Solution

Use the *GetPublicQueues* or *GetPrivateQueuesByMachine* methods of the *System.Messaging.MessageQueue* class.

Discussion

.NET allows you to examine and administer message queues and the messages they contain using the classes in the *System.Messaging* namespace. You can create a *MessageQueue* class that wraps a specific message queue by specifying the queue path in the constructor.

```
' Check if a queue named MyQueue exists on the current computer.
If MessageQueue.Exists(".\MyQueue") Then
    ' Show its name.
    Dim Queue As New MessageQueue(".\MyQueue")
    Console.WriteLine(Queue.QueueName)
End If
```

In addition, you can retrieve all the queues in Active Directory using the shared *MessageQueue.GetPublicQueues* method, or you can retrieve the private queues on a given machine using the shared *MessageQueue.GetPrivateQueuesByMachine* method, in which case you must specify a computer name, or a period (.) to indicate the current computer.

The following code shows a simple Console application that enumerates all the queues on the current machine and displays the messages they contain. In order to use this code, you must add a reference to the System.Messaging.dll assembly and import the *System.Messaging* namespace.

```
Public Module GetQueues

    Public Sub Main()
        Dim Queue, Queues() As MessageQueue

        ' Get the private queues for the current machine.
        Queues = MessageQueue.GetPrivateQueuesByMachine(".")

        For Each Queue In Queues
            Console.WriteLine("Name: " & Queue.QueueName)
            Console.WriteLine("Path: " & Queue.Path)

            ' Get a snapshot of all messages (without removing them.)
            Console.WriteLine("Contains:")
            Dim Message, Messages() As Message
            Messages = Queue.GetAllMessages()
            For Each Message In Messages
                Console.WriteLine(Message.Id.ToString())
                Console.WriteLine(Message.Body.ToString())
            Next
            Console.WriteLine()
        Next

        Console.ReadLine()
    End Sub

End Module
```

> **Note** You can add, remove, and administer message queues using the Computer Management console. Expand the Message Queuing node under the Services And Application node. You can right-click on a queue category folder to create a new queue for your application.

17.17 Send a Custom *Message* Object Through Message Queuing

Problem

You want to send a custom object to another application via a message queue.

Solution

Create a serializable class that has a zero-argument constructor and includes no read-only properties. Wrap an instance of this class in a *Message* object and pass the *Message* object to the *MessageQueue.Send* method.

Discussion

Message queues accept simple text messages and custom .NET objects. In order to use a custom object, it must satisfy three criteria:

- The class must have a public constructor with no arguments. .NET uses this constructor to re-create the object when the message is received.

- The class must be marked with the *Serializable* attribute.

- All class properties must be readable and writable. Read-only properties won't be serialized because .NET won't be able to restore the property values when re-creating the object.

Here's an example of a class that can be serialized and sent in the body of a message:

```
<Serializable()> _
Public Class OrderMessage

    Private _OrderCode As String
    Private _ClientName As String

    Public Property OrderCode()
        Get
            Return _OrderCode
        End Get
        Set(ByVal Value)
            _OrderCode = Value
        End Set
    End Property

    Public Property ClientName() As String
        Get
            Return _ClientName
        End Get
        Set(ByVal Value As String)
            _ClientName = Value
        End Set
    End Property
```

```
Public Sub New()
    ' No actions are required in the default constructor.
End Sub

Public Sub New(ByVal code As String, ByVal client As String)
    OrderCode = code
    ClientName = client
End Sub

End Class
```

The following example shows the full code for a simple test form that sends and receives instances of the *OrderMessage* object. Sending the object is effortless—you simply need to wrap it in a *Message* object and pass the *Message* object to the *MessageQueue.Send* method. Retrieving the message is equally easy, provided you make sure to specify the expected object types in the constructor for the *XmlMessageFormatter*. If you attempt to deserialize an unrecognized object (one that you have not configured through the *MessageQueue.AllowedTypes* property), an exception will be thrown.

```
Public Class QueueForm
    Inherits System.Windows.Forms.Form

    ' (Designer code omitted.)
    Private QueuePath As String = ".\Private$\OrderQueue"
    Private Queue As MessageQueue

    Private Sub Form_Load(ByVal sender As System.Object, _
      ByVal e As System.EventArgs) Handles MyBase.Load
        ' Create the queue if needed.
        If MessageQueue.Exists(QueuePath) Then
            Queue = New MessageQueue(QueuePath)
        Else
            Queue = MessageQueue.Create(QueuePath)
        End If

        ' Messages are formatted using XML (not binary) encoding.
        Queue.Formatter = New XmlMessageFormatter()
    End Sub

    Private Sub cmdSend_Click(ByVal sender As System.Object, _
      ByVal e As System.EventArgs) Handles cmdSend.Click
        Dim Ord As New OrderMessage(Guid.NewGuid().ToString(), "Test Client")
        Dim Msg As New Message(Ord)

        ' (Configure other Message properties here.)
        Msg.Label = "Test Order"
```

```
        Queue.Send(Msg)
    End Sub

    Private Sub cmdReceive_Click(ByVal sender As System.Object, _
      ByVal e As System.EventArgs) Handles cmdReceive.Click
        Me.Cursor = Cursors.WaitCursor

        Dim ReceivedMessage As Message

        ' Specify all the allowed object types in an array.
        Dim AllowedTypes() As Type = {GetType(OrderMessage)}
        Queue.Formatter = New XmlMessageFormatter(AllowedTypes)

        Try
            ' If no message is found after five seconds, an exception occurs.
            ' You can also explicitly retrieve all messages from the queue
            ' using the Queue.GetAllMessages method.
            ReceivedMessage = Queue.Receive(TimeSpan.FromSeconds(5))

            ' Check if it is the expected type.
            If TypeOf ReceivedMessage.Body Is OrderMessage Then
                ' Process message here.
                Dim ReceivedOrder As OrderMessage
                ReceivedOrder = CType(ReceivedMessage.Body, OrderMessage)
                MessageBox.Show("Received order: " & ReceivedOrder.OrderCode)
            End If
        Catch Err As MessageQueueException
            MessageBox.Show("No messages.")
        End Try

        Me.Cursor = Cursors.Default
    End Sub

End Class
```

In order to use this code as written, you must add a reference to the System.Messaging.dll assembly and import the *System.Messaging* namespace.

17.18 Use a Custom Performance Counter

Problem

You want to gauge the performance of an application with a custom business-specific counter.

Solution

Create the counters using the *PerformanceCounterCategory* and *CounterCreationDataCollection* classes. Increment the counters using the *PerformanceCounter* class.

Discussion

.NET includes performance counters that allow you to monitor the performance of the common language runtime, Microsoft ADO.NET, .NET Remoting, and Microsoft ASP.NET. In addition, you can create your own custom counters using the classes in the *System.Diagnostics* namespace.

Before using a custom counter, you need to create it. You can create custom counters using the Visual Studio .NET Server Explorer or programmatically in code. You also need to create a new category for your counters (unless you want to use an existing category). Once the counter category and counters have been created, you can create instances of the counter using the *PerformanceCounter* class and call the *Increment* method to add one to the counter value.

There are several different types of counters. Two of the most common are *total counters* (which simply keep track of the total number of times they have been incremented), and *rate counters* (which track the number of times they are incremented in a given unit of time). When recording totals, you can use the *NumberOfItems32* and *NumberOfItems64* counter types (depending on whether you want to store the counter as a 32-bit or 64-bit value). When recording rates, you can use *RateOfCountsPerSecond32* and *RateOfCountsPerSecond64*. In addition, you can calculate the average time for an operation using *AverageTimer32*. These represent the five most commonly used counter types.

The Console application shown here creates a new counter category and adds a total and rate counter. The application then creates instances of each counter and increments them.

```
Public Module CounterTest

    Public Sub Main()
        ' Create the counters if needed
        CreateCounters()

        ' Create an instance of each counter.
        ' The instance name is "CounterTest". If you use the same
        ' counters in other applications, you could use a different
        ' instance name so as not to confuse them.
        Dim LoginCounter As New PerformanceCounter("MyApp Counters", _
```

```vb
        "TotalLogins", "CounterTest", False)
    Dim DBCounter As New PerformanceCounter("MyApp Counters", _
        "DatabaseOperations", "CounterTest", False)

    Console.WriteLine("Counters created.")
    Console.WriteLine("You can add them to the Performance Monitor now.")

    ' Increment both of the counters 10 times.
    ' You can monitor the effect of this code in Performance Monitor.
    Console.WriteLine("Press Enter to increment 10 times, " & _
        "or type exit to end.")
    Do Until Console.ReadLine().ToLower() = "exit"
        Dim i As Integer
        For i = 1 To 10
            LoginCounter.Increment()
            DBCounter.Increment()
        Next
        Console.WriteLine("Press Enter to increment 10 times, " & _
          "or type exit to end.")
    Loop

    ' Remove the counters.
    DBCounter.RemoveInstance()
    LoginCounter.RemoveInstance()
End Sub

Private Sub CreateCounters()
    If Not (PerformanceCounterCategory.Exists("MyApp Counters")) Then
        Dim Counters As New CounterCreationDataCollection()

        ' Create a simple counter that records a total value.
        Dim CountCounter As New CounterCreationData()
        CountCounter.CounterName = "TotalLogins"
        CountCounter.CounterHelp = "Total number of user logins."
        CountCounter.CounterType = PerformanceCounterType.NumberOfItems32

        ' Create a rate counter that records a per second value.
        Dim RateCounter As New CounterCreationData()
        RateCounter.CounterName = "DatabaseOperations"
        RateCounter.CounterHelp = "Number of database operations " & _
          "performed by MyApp per second"
        RateCounter.CounterType = _
          PerformanceCounterType.RateOfCountsPerSecond32

        ' Add both counters to the collection.
        Counters.Add(CountCounter)
        Counters.Add(RateCounter)
```

```
                    ' Create the custom category.
                    PerformanceCounterCategory.Create("MyApp Counters", _
                      "Counters for MyApp", Counters)
             End If
      End Sub

End Module
```

You can view the results using Performance Monitor (select Performance from the Administrative Tools section of the Control Panel). The rate counter will fall off dramatically when the counter is not being incremented. The total counter will remain fixed, rising proportionately as it's incremented. The results of a simple test are shown in Figure 17-4.

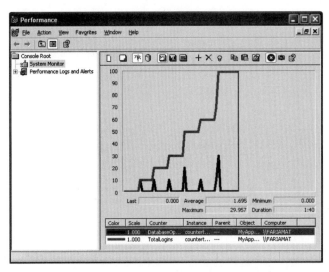

Figure 17-4   Custom performance counters in the Performance Monitor.

18

Security and Cryptography

Security is a broad field that encompasses everything from scrambling data with encryption to locking the server room door. To write secure code, it's essential to conduct risk analysis and threat assessment studies, make use of industrial-strength security standards such as Secure Sockets Layer (SSL) and Kerberos, and have everything reviewed by a security expert. There are several excellent books that can help you come to terms with essential security concepts. You can refer to Bruce Schneier's *Applied Cryptography*, Second Edition (John Wiley & Sons, 1995) for an introduction to cryptographic concepts; Microsoft's own *Writing Secure Code,* Second Edition (Microsoft Press, 2003) for an introduction to a wide range of security concepts; and Eric Lippert's *Visual Basic .NET Code Security Handbook* (Wrox Press, 2002) for a comprehensive overview of the code access security infrastructure that's built into the .NET Framework.

Remember, writing code that deals with some aspect of security is fairly easy. Writing *secure code* is a much more subtle and complex issue.

This chapter considers common tasks in several areas of security programming. Recipes 18.1 to 18.5 consider the Windows security system, and how you can retrieve information about the current user, check group membership, get lists of users and groups, and even log on to a different account programmatically. Recipes 18.6 to 18.18 deal with cryptography, and they form the bulk of this chapter. In these recipes, you'll learn how to use symmetric and asymmetric encryption to hide data, how to use hash codes and digital signatures to prevent data tampering, how to securely store a password in a database, and how to generate cryptographically secure random numbers. For most of these recipes, you'll need to import the *System.Security.Cryptography* and *System.IO* namespaces. Finally, recipes 18.19 and 18.20 consider how to display assembly evidence and limit assembly permissions using code access security.

18.1 Retrieve Information About the Current Windows User

Problem

You need to retrieve information about the current user's Windows account.

Solution

Use the *WindowsIdentity.GetCurrent* method to retrieve a *WindowsIdentity* object representing the current user.

Discussion

The *WindowsIdentity* class in the *System.Security.Principal* namespace represents basic information about a Windows user account. You can use the shared *GetCurrent* method to retrieve a *WindowsIdentity* object that represents the account under which your code is executing.

The following code example uses *GetCurrent* to retrieve a *WindowsIdentity*, and then displays all the available information. To use this example as written, you must import the *System.Security.Principal* namespace.

```
Public Module WindowsSecurityTest

    Public Sub Main()
        ' Retrieve the identity of the current user.
        Dim Identity As WindowsIdentity
        Identity = WindowsIdentity.GetCurrent()

        ' Display some information about the identity.
        Console.WriteLine("Authenticated: " & Identity.IsAuthenticated)
        Console.WriteLine("Anonymous: " & Identity.IsAnonymous)
        Console.WriteLine("Guest: " & Identity.IsGuest)
        Console.WriteLine("System: " & Identity.IsSystem)
        Console.WriteLine("Authentication: " & Identity.AuthenticationType)
        Console.WriteLine("User Name: " & Identity.Name)
        Console.WriteLine("Token: " & Identity.Token.ToString())

        Console.ReadLine()
    End Sub

End Module
```

The *WindowsIdentity.Name* property takes the format Computer-Name\UserName or DomainName\UserName. *WindowsIdentity.Token* is a memory reference to the account token (technically, an *IntPtr* instance). Here's an example of the sample output that will be displayed in the Console window:

```
Authenticated: True
Anonymous: False
Guest: False
System: False
Authentication: NTLM
User Name: FARIAMAT\Matthew
Token: 280
```

On its own, the *WindowsIdentity* class doesn't allow you to test the roles that a user belongs to. For this task, you need a *WindowsPrincipal* object, as described in recipe 18.2.

18.2 Use Windows Role-Based Security

Problem

You want to determine application privileges based on group membership.

Solution

Create a *WindowsPrincipal* object from the current *WindowsIdentity*, and call the *IsInRole* method.

Discussion

The Windows operating system allows you to place users in groups and give these groups different permissions for accessing resources such as files and the registry. In addition, you can create application-specific groups (such as Sales-Managers, Contractors, and so on), examine these in your code, and then configure the behavior of your application accordingly. To configure groups and group members, select Computer Management from the Control Panel. Figure 18-1 shows the Computer Management console with some common groups.

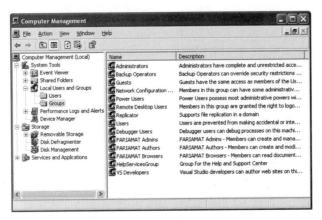

Figure 18-1   Managing users and groups.

To access group membership information in your code, you must use the *WindowsPrincipal* class. The *WindowsPrincipal* class contains two members: an *Identity* property that returns the associated *WindowsIdentity* and an *IsInRole* method that allows you to determine whether the account is in a specific group.

You can retrieve a *WindowsPrincipal* object in two ways. The first way is to retrieve it from the current thread by using the *Thread.CurrentPrincipal* shared property. For this technique to work, you must first call the *AppDomain.SetPrincipalPolicy* method. This method instructs Windows to associate the current principal (which encapsulates the current user identity) with the application thread. Here's the code you'll need:

```
' Associate the authentication information for the current user with
' the current thread.
AppDomain.CurrentDomain.SetPrincipalPolicy(PrincipalPolicy.WindowsPrincipal)

' Retrieve the current principal.
Dim Principal As WindowsPrincipal
Principal = CType(Thread.CurrentPrincipal, WindowsPrincipal)
```

Another option is to create a *WindowsPrincipal* object manually and pass the associated *WindowsIdentity* object in the constructor:

```
' Retrieve the identity of the current user.
Dim Identity As WindowsIdentity
Identity = WindowsIdentity.GetCurrent()

' Create the corresponding principal.
Dim Principal As New WindowsPrincipal(Identity)
```

Once you have the *WindowsPrincipal*, you can call *IsInRole* to determine group membership. There are three overloaded versions of the *IsInRole* method, allowing you to specify a numeric role ID, a role name, or a value from the *WindowsBuiltInRoles* enumeration. If you use a string, you must use the format ComputerName\RoleName or DomainName\RoleName. If you're using a built-in role, you can use the *WindowsBuiltInRoles* enumeration or the syntax BuiltIn\RoleName. Built-in roles include

- Account Operators
- Administrators
- Backup Operators
- Guests
- Power Users
- Print Operators
- Replicators
- System Operators
- Users

The following example demonstrates a simple Console application that tests group membership. To use this example, you must import the *System.Security.Principal* namespace.

```
Public Module WindowsSecurityTest

    Public Sub Main()
        ' Retrieve the identity of the current user.
        Dim Identity As WindowsIdentity
        Identity = WindowsIdentity.GetCurrent()
        Console.WriteLine("User Name: " & Identity.Name)

        ' Create the corresponding principal.
        Dim Principal As New WindowsPrincipal(Identity)

        ' Testing for a custom role you have defined.
        ' If this group doesn't exist no error will be raised.
        ' IsInRole will simply return False.
        Console.WriteLine("Member of Managers: " & _
            Principal.IsInRole("Managers"))

        ' Testing for a built-in role.
        Console.WriteLine("Member of Administrators: " & _
            Principal.IsInRole("BUILTIN\Administrators"))
```

```
        ' Using the WindowsBuiltInRole enumeration.
        Console.WriteLine("Member of Administrators: " & _
          Principal.IsInRole(WindowsBuiltInRole.Administrator))

        Console.ReadLine()
    End Sub

End Module
```

18.3 Retrieve a List of All Windows Accounts or Groups

Problem

You need to retrieve a list of all users on the current computer or on a network domain.

Solution

Perform a query using the *Win32_UserAccount* or *Win32_Group* Windows Management Instrumentation (WMI) class.

Discussion

The Microsoft .NET Framework doesn't include any classes that allow you to retrieve a list of Windows accounts. However, there's no need to delve into the intricacies of the Win32 API—instead, you can access this information by performing a simple WMI query.

To use the WMI objects, you must import the *System.Management* namespace and add a reference to the System.Management.dll assembly. You can then retrieve a list of users by domain, by computer name, or by using a combination of other criteria. Each user account exposes the same properties you can view in the Computer Management console, including user account name, full name, password expiry settings, unique identifier, and so on. You can also retrieve a list of groups, each of which has a name and a description.

The following Console application retrieves all the users and groups for a computer or domain you specify.

```
Public Module WindowsSecurityTest

    Public Sub Main()
        Console.Write("Enter a domain or computer name: ")
        Dim Domain As String = Console.ReadLine()
        Console.WriteLine()
```

```
    ' Retrieve the user list.
    Dim UserQuery As String = "SELECT * FROM Win32_UserAccount " & _
      "WHERE Domain='" & Domain & "'"
    Dim Query As New ManagementObjectSearcher(UserQuery)

    Console.WriteLine(New String("*"c, 60))
    Console.WriteLine(" USERS")
    Console.WriteLine(New String("*"c, 60))
    Dim User As ManagementObject
    For Each User In Query.Get()
        Console.WriteLine("User name: " & User("Name").ToString())
        Console.WriteLine("Full name: " & User("FullName").ToString())
        Console.WriteLine("SID: " & User("SID").ToString())
        Console.WriteLine()
    Next

    ' Retrieve the group list.
    Console.WriteLine()
    Dim GroupQuery As String = "SELECT * FROM Win32_Group WHERE " & _
      "Domain='" & Domain & "'"
    Query = New ManagementObjectSearcher(GroupQuery)

    Console.WriteLine(New String("*"c, 60))
    Console.WriteLine(" GROUPS")
    Console.WriteLine(New String("*"c, 60))
    Dim Group As ManagementObject
    For Each Group In Query.Get()
        Console.WriteLine("Group name: " & Group("Name").ToString())
        Console.WriteLine("Group description: " & _
          Group("Description").ToString())
        Console.WriteLine("SID: " & Group("SID").ToString())
        Console.WriteLine()
    Next

    Console.ReadLine()
  End Sub

End Module
```

A sample run of this program produces the following (shortened) output:

```
Enter a domain or computer name: fariamat

************************************************************
 USERS
************************************************************
User name: ACTUser
Full name: Application Center Test Account
SID: S-1-5-21-507921405-1383384898-1708537768-1018
```

```
User name: Administrator
Full name: Administrator
SID: S-1-5-21-507921405-1383384898-1708537768-500

User name: ASPNET
Full name: aspnet_wp account
SID: S-1-5-21-507921405-1383384898-1708537768-1011
. . .


**********************************************************
 GROUPS
**********************************************************
Group name: Administrators
Group description: Administrators have complete and unrestricted access to the
computer/domain
SID: S-1-5-32-544

Group name: Guests
Group description: Guests have the same access as members of the Users group
by default, except for the Guest account which is further restricted
SID: S-1-5-32-546
```

18.4 Log In to Another Account Programmatically

Problem

You want part of your code to execute under a different user account than that of the current user.

Solution

Log in to the new account with the unmanaged *LogonUser* function, and use the *WindowsIdentity.Impersonate* method.

Discussion

By default, your code executes under the Windows identity of the current user. That means that your code has the ability to perform any action the user can and it will be prevented if it attempts any action that's forbidden to the user. In some cases, however, you might want to allow your code to execute with different permissions than the current user account. For example, you might create an application that runs permanently on a shared kiosk in an organization. Before a user can perform certain operations (such as reading a file), you'll want the application to temporarily assume that user's identity so that the appropriate file rights and restrictions are applied. Or you might want to create an application that can run under an "administrator" and a "user" mode. In either case, you'll want your application to temporarily assume another Windows identity—a process called *impersonation*.

To use impersonation in a .NET application, you need to take five steps:

1. Log on with the new account using the unmanaged *LogonUser* function from the Windows API (the advapi32.dll file). This function returns a memory reference to the user's security token.

2. Duplicate the token using the unmanaged *DuplicateToken* function (also defined in the advapi32.dll file).

3. Use the token to create a new *WindowsIdentity* object by passing the token to the constructor.

4. Call the *WindowsIdentity.Impersonate* method to assume the new identity. This method returns a *WindowsImpersonationContext* object.

5. At this point, you can execute code statements under the new account. To stop impersonating the user, call the *Undo* method of the *WindowsImpersonationContext* object.

The following Console application demonstrates these steps. To use the code as written, you must import the *System.Security.Principal* namespace.

```
Public Module WindowsSecurityTest

    ' This API function gets the security token for a user.
    Private Declare Auto Function LogonUser Lib "advapi32.dll" _
        (ByVal lpszUsername As String, ByVal lpszDomain As String, _
        ByVal lpszPassword As String, ByVal dwLogonType As Integer, _
        ByVal dwLogonProvider As Integer, ByRef phToken As IntPtr) As Integer

    Private Enum Logon
        Interactive = 2
        NetworkCleartext = 8
    End Enum

    Private Enum Provider
        [Default] = 0
        WindowsNT35 = 1
        WindowsNT40 = 2
        Windows2000 = 3
    End Enum
```

```
' This API function duplicates a security token so you can use it.
Private Declare Auto Function DuplicateToken Lib "advapi32.dll" _
  (ByVal ExistingTokenHandle As IntPtr, _
  ByVal ImpersonationLevel As Integer, _
  ByRef DuplicateTokenHandle As IntPtr) As Integer

Public Sub Main()
    Console.WriteLine("*** Current User ***")
    DisplayIdentityInfo()

    ' Get the login information from the user.
    Console.WriteLine("Enter the information for the user " & _
      "you want to impersonate.")
    Dim UserName, Domain, Password As String
    Console.Write("Domain: ")
    Domain = Console.ReadLine()
    Console.Write("User Name: ")
    UserName = Console.ReadLine()
    Console.Write("Password: ")
    Password = Console.ReadLine()

    ' Log the new identity in.
    Dim NewIdentity As WindowsIdentity
    NewIdentity = GetWindowsIdentity(UserName, Domain, Password)
    Console.WriteLine()

    If NewIdentity Is Nothing Then
        Console.WriteLine("Invalid credentials.")
    Else
        ' Impersonate the new identity.
        Dim NewContext As WindowsImpersonationContext
        NewContext = NewIdentity.Impersonate()

        Console.WriteLine("*** Starting Impersonation ***")
        DisplayIdentityInfo()

        ' Revert to the original identity.
        NewContext.Undo()

        Console.WriteLine("*** Ending Impersonation ***")
        DisplayIdentityInfo()
    End If

    Console.ReadLine()
End Sub

' This function displays information about the current user.
Private Sub DisplayIdentityInfo()
```

```
    Dim Identity As WindowsIdentity = WindowsIdentity.GetCurrent()
    Console.WriteLine("This application is executing as " & Identity.Name)
    Console.WriteLine()
End Sub


' This function uses the Win32 API functions to return a WindowsIdentity
' object for a given user.
Private Function GetWindowsIdentity(ByVal UserName As String, _
  ByVal Domain As String, ByVal Password As String) As WindowsIdentity
    Dim SecurityToken, TokenDuplicate As IntPtr

    If LogonUser(UserName, Domain, Password, _
      Logon.Interactive, Provider.Default, SecurityToken) > 0 Then
        DuplicateToken(SecurityToken, 2, TokenDuplicate)
        Return New WindowsIdentity(TokenDuplicate)
    Else
        ' Invalid user information.
        Return Nothing
    End If
End Function


End Module
```

Here's the output of a sample test run:

```
*** Current User ***
This application is executing as FARIAMAT\Matthew

Enter the information for the user you want to impersonate.
Domain: fariamat
User Name: test
Password: test

*** Starting Impersonation ***
This application is executing as FARIAMAT\test

*** Ending Impersonation ***
This application is executing as FARIAMAT\Matthew
```

> **Note**   Windows XP imposes some restrictions on the use of blank
> passwords to prevent network-based attacks. As a result of these
> restrictions, you won't be able to use the *LogonUser* function to imper-
> sonate an account with a blank password.

18.5 Impersonate the IIS User with ASP.NET

Problem

You want to impersonate the Internet Information Services (IIS) authenticated user in your Web page or Web service code.

Solution

Retrieve a *WindowsIdentity* object that represents the authenticated user from the built-in *User* object. You can use this identity to perform impersonation with the *WindowsIdentity.Impersonate* method.

Discussion

In an ASP.NET application, all code runs under a special worker or local system account that has the necessary privileges for running Web page and Web service code. In some situations, however, it might be useful to run part of the application logic under a user-specific account. For example, if you have a file-lookup service, you might want to use Windows access control lists (ACLs) to determine whether a given user can retrieve a specific file. Without impersonation, you have to write all the security code yourself, and your service can be tricked into accessing a file it shouldn't if the code contains an error. If you use impersonation, however, you don't have to write any security code. If the code attempts to access a disallowed file, an exception will be thrown automatically when the operating system refuses access.

You can use the technique shown in recipe 18.4 to perform impersonation. However, this approach is less ideal if you need to retrieve the authentication credentials (such as a username and password) from a remote user. A better approach is to use IIS to perform the authentication automatically using the most secure standard that's supported in your environment. You can then use the IIS-authenticated identity to perform impersonation.

To use IIS authentication, you must disable anonymous access for the corresponding virtual directory. Start IIS Manager (by selecting Internet Information Services from the Administrative Tools section of the Control Panel), right-click on a virtual directory, and select Properties. Then choose the Directory Security tab, and click Edit in the Anonymous Access And Authentication Control section. You can then enable the appropriate authentication method, as shown in Figure 18-2.

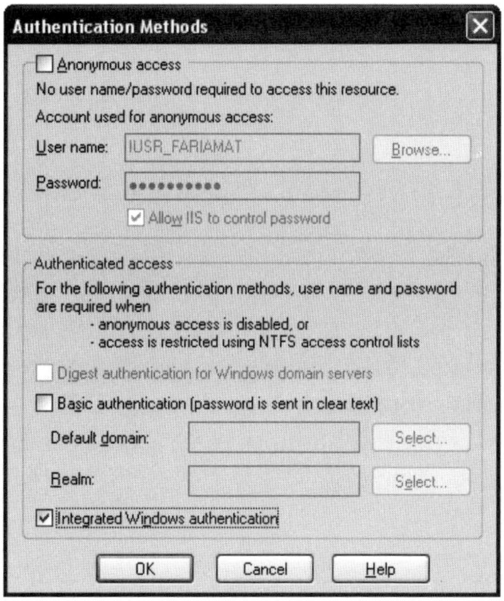

Figure 18-2   IIS virtual directory authentication settings.

Once you've taken these steps, users will be required to authenticate themselves. In a Web page, the browser will perform the authentication automatically, either by retrieving the current user information (for Windows Integrated authentication) or by displaying a login dialog to the user. In a Web service, the client application must supply the credentials programmatically (as demonstrated in recipe 16.6). However, your Web page or Web service code will still run under the local ASP.NET account. To change this behavior, you need to add code that retrieves the IIS-authenticated identity and impersonates it.

Here's a code snippet that uses impersonation with the IIS user identity:

```
If Not User.GetType() Is WindowsPrincipal
    ' User was not authenticated with Windows authentication.
    Throw New SecurityException( _
      "Windows authentication was not performed.")

Else
    ' Retrieve the identity object.
    Dim Identity As WindowsIdentity
    Identity = CType(User.Identity, WindowsIdentity)

    ' Impersonate the identity.
    Dim ImpersonateContext As WindowsImpersonationContext
    ImpersonateContext = Identity.Impersonate()
```

```
        ' (Perform tasks under the impersonated account.)

        ' Revert to the original ID.
        ImpersonateContext.Undo()
    End If
```

> **Note** You can also enable impersonation with a configuration file setting. However, this approach is much less flexible because it ensures that *all* your Web page or Web service code runs under the IIS account. In this case, you must make sure that the account has the additional permissions required for executing ASP.NET applications. For example, the account will require read/write access to the Temporary ASP.NET Files directory, where the compiled ASP.NET files are stored.

18.6 Use SSL Encryption with ASP.NET

Problem

You want to ensure that communication between the server and a remote client is encrypted to ensure privacy.

Solution

Install a server certificate, and configure the virtual directory to require SSL.

Discussion

Secure Sockets Layer (SSL) technology is used to encrypt communication between a client and a Web server. You can use SSL automatically with a Web service or Web site—all you need to do is configure IIS accordingly.

Before a Web server can support SSL connections, it must have an X.509 digital certificate. This certificate indicates that the server identity is registered with a valid certificate authority (CA). You can generate your own certificate for testing (using Certificate Server from Windows 2000 Server or Windows 2003 Server). When creating a public application, however, you'll probably want to use a genuine certificate authority such as VeriSign. (See, for example, *http://www.verisign.com*.)

> **Note**   Certificates are used to establish trust. They indicate that a certificate authority vouches for the server's identity. The client makes the decision, "I will trust this server because the CA vouches that it is Amazon.com," not "I trust this server because it claims to be Amazon.com." To support this model, every computer is preconfigured with a list of trusted certificate authorities. You can modify this list using a tool such as certmgr.exe, which is installed with the .NET Framework. Certificates also contain a small set of identifying information, including the holder's name, organization, and address; the holder's public key; validation dates; and a unique serial number.

One of the easiest ways to purchase a certificate is to create and e-mail a certificate request to the appropriate certificate authority. IIS Manager allows you to create a certificate request automatically by following these steps:

1.   Expand the Web Sites group, right-click on your Web site (often called Default Web Site), and choose Properties.

2.   In the Directory Security tab, click the Server Certificate button. This starts the IIS Certificate Wizard, which requests some basic organization information and generates a request file.

3.   Complete all steps of the wizard. Figure 18-3 shows one step, in which you must choose the Web site name and key length. The longer the bit length, the stronger the key.

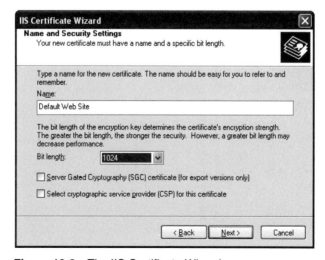

Figure 18-3   The IIS Certificate Wizard.

4. E-mail the generated request file (which is automatically encrypted using the CA's public key) to the CA.

5. You'll receive a certificate that you can install in IIS to complete the request, along with additional step-by-step instructions from the CA.

6. Once the certificate is installed, you can force individual virtual directories to use secure communication. Simply right-click on a virtual directory, and select Properties. Then choose the Directory Security tab, and click Edit in the Secure Communications section.

> **Note** You can read much more information about certificate requests and how to use certificates with IIS in the online IIS help (*http://localhost/iisHelp*).

18.7 Symmetrically Encrypt a File

Problem

You want to use symmetric encryption to prevent a malicious user from viewing the contents of a file.

Solution

Wrap the *FileStream* with a *CryptoStream* that encrypts data as it's being written to disk (or decrypts it as it's being read).

Discussion

Symmetric encryption renders data indecipherable using a secret value. To decrypt the data, you need the same secret value (or key) that was used to encrypt the data. For that reason, symmetric encryption is often described as *shared secret* encryption.

Several classes provide symmetric encryption services in the *System.Security.Cryptography* namespace. These classes all derive from the base *System.Security.SymmetricAlgorithm* class, and they work almost identically. The difference is that each class implements a different encryption algorithm. Table 18-1 lists all of your choices and indicates the supported key sizes (in bits). As a general rule, the larger the key size, the stronger the encryption scheme is against a brute force attack. In addition, symmetric encryption algorithms use a random *initialization vector* (IV), which ensures that the encrypted ciphertext will vary even when encrypting the same source data.

Table 18-1   Symmetric Algorithm Classes

Algorithm	Implementation Class	Valid Key Sizes	Default Key Size
DES	*DESCryptoServiceProvider*	64	64
TripleDES	*TripleDESCryptoServiceProvider*	128, 192	192
RC2	*RC2CryptServiceProvider*	40–128 (in 8-bit increments)	128
Rijndael	*RijndaelManaged*	128, 192, 256	256

The *RijndaelManaged* class is implemented entirely in managed code, and it supports a range of strong key sizes. For that reason, it's commonly used for symmetric encryption.

The easiest way to use a symmetric encryption class is in conjunction with *CryptoStream*. *CryptoStream* is a stream object that can wrap any other stream, including those that represent files, network connections, memory buffers, and so on. *CryptoStream* uses the symmetric algorithm class to perform encryption or decryption. For example, you can wrap a *CryptoStream* over a *FileStream* to seamlessly encrypt data as it's being written or decrypt it as it's being read.

The following Windows application (shown in Figure 18-4) demonstrates encryption and decryption with a file.

When the application is first started, a new *RijndaelManaged* object is created. This object encapsulates the key data and the IV. The key data is saved to a file for future reference.

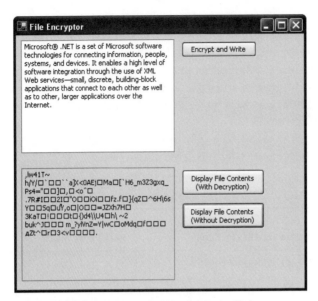

Figure 18-4 Encrypting and decrypting a file.

```
Private Rijndael As New RijndaelManaged()

Private Sub Form_Load(ByVal sender As System.Object, _
  ByVal e As System.EventArgs) Handles MyBase.Load

    ' Check for file with key data.
    If File.Exists("key.bin") Then
        ' There is a key file. Read the key data.
        Dim fs As New FileStream("key.bin", FileMode.Open)
        Dim Key() As Byte
        ReDim Key(Rijndael.Key.Length - 1)
        fs.Read(Key, 0, Key.Length)
        Rijndael.Key = Key
        fs.Close()
    Else
        ' There is no key file. Use the randomly generated key,
        ' and write it to a file for future use.
        Dim fs As New FileStream("key.bin", FileMode.CreateNew)
        fs.Write(Rijndael.Key, 0, Rijndael.Key.Length)
        fs.Close()
    End If

End Sub
```

The encryption opens a file and wraps it with a *CryptoStream*. The *CryptoStream* uses an encryptor that's created from the *RijndaelManaged* object using the *CreateEncryptor* method. A *StreamWriter* wraps the *CryptoStream*, providing an easy way to convert the string data in the text box to a series of bytes. The IV is also written directly to the file without performing any encryption.

```
Private Sub cmdEncrypt_Click(ByVal sender As System.Object, _
  ByVal e As System.EventArgs) Handles cmdEncrypt.Click

    ' Create the transform for Rijndael encryption.
    Dim Transform As ICryptoTransform = Rijndael.CreateEncryptor()

    ' Open a file for writing.
    Dim fs As New FileStream("testfile.bin", FileMode.Create)

    ' Write the random initialization vector without encryption.
    ' This helps strengthen the encryption against certain
    ' types of attacks, because each file will be encrypted
    ' slightly differently.
    fs.Write(Rijndael.IV, 0, Rijndael.IV.Length)

    ' Create a cryptographic stream in write mode.
    ' This stream will encode binary data just before it reaches
    ' the file stream and is written to disk.
    Dim cs As New CryptoStream(fs, Transform, CryptoStreamMode.Write)

    ' Create a text writer.
    ' This text writer will convert our text into binary data.
    Dim w As New StreamWriter(cs)
    w.Write(txtSource.Text)
    w.Flush()

    ' The CryptoStream encrypts data one block at a time.
    ' At the end of your operation, you must pad the final
    ' partial block with zeros, and then write it to the file.
    cs.FlushFinalBlock()

    ' Close the file.
    w.Close()

End Sub
```

To view the encrypted contents of the file, your code simply needs to open the file, skip over the IV, and convert the remaining information to a string (which will appear as meaningless gibberish):

```
Private Sub cmdDisplay_Click(ByVal sender As System.Object, _
  ByVal e As System.EventArgs) Handles cmdDisplay.Click
```

```
' Open a file for reading.
Dim fs As New FileStream("testfile.bin", FileMode.Open)

' Skip over the IV.
fs.Seek(Rijndael.IV.Length, SeekOrigin.Begin)

' Create a text reader. This will convert the
' data from a series of bytes into a string.
' Note that no decryption is performed.
Dim r As New StreamReader(fs)
txtFileContents.Text = r.ReadToEnd()
r.Close()

End Sub
```

Finally the decryption process mirrors the encryption process. The only difference is that the *CryptoStream* now uses a decryptor (which is created from the same *RijndaelManaged* object), and the *CryptoStream* operates in read mode, not write mode.

```
Private Sub cmdDecrypt_Click(ByVal sender As System.Object, _
  ByVal e As System.EventArgs) Handles cmdDecrypt.Click

    ' Open a file for reading.
    Dim fs As New FileStream("testfile.bin", FileMode.Open)

    ' Retrieve the IV that was used (in conjunction with the secret key)
    ' to encrypt this file.
    Dim IV As Byte()
    ReDim IV(Rijndael.IV.Length - 1)
    fs.Read(IV, 0, IV.Length)
    Rijndael.IV = IV

    ' Create the transform for Rijndael decryption.
    Dim Transform As ICryptoTransform = Rijndael.CreateDecryptor()

    ' Create a cryptographic stream in read mode.
    ' This stream will decode binary data just after
    ' it is read from the file.
    Dim cs As New CryptoStream(fs, Transform, CryptoStreamMode.Read)

    ' Create a text reader. This will convert the decrypted
    ' data from a series of bytes into a string.
    Dim r As New StreamReader(cs)
    txtFileContents.Text = r.ReadToEnd()
    r.Close()

End Sub
```

To decrypt a block of data, you must use the same secret key that was used to encrypt it. In the preceding example, this key is generated automatically when the *RijndaelManaged* class is created the first time the program is started, and the byte sequence is saved to another file. The key is read from this file for subsequent tests. This is suitable for a demonstration, but it's impractical in a professional application. In a real-world scenario, you would house the key in a secure location (like a piece of hardware or a protected database). Remember, most attackers defeat encryption not by attempting a brute force attack but because they somehow obtain the secret key.

The key weakness of symmetric encryption is that both the writer and the reader of the document must share the same secret value. You can't transmit this value in any obvious way (for example, over a network connection) because a malicious user can intercept it. In scenarios in which no shared secret is available, you might be able to use asymmetric encryption instead. (See recipe 18.10.)

> **Note**   If you don't want to generate a random key, you can derive this information from a string password. To do this securely, you need to use the *PasswordDeriveBytes* class and the technique presented in recipe 18.9.

18.8 Symmetrically Encrypt Any Data

Problem

You need to symmetrically encrypt data that isn't stream-based, such as a series of variables.

Solution

Write these variables to a *MemoryStream*, and wrap this with a *CryptoStream*.

Discussion

All symmetric encryption is stream-based. If you need to convert data that's stored in ordinary variables such as integers and strings, you must write this data to an in-memory stream.

The following Console application demonstrates this approach.

```vbnet
Public Module EncryptionTest

    Public Sub Main()
        ' Declare the data.
        Dim Name As String = "Joe Tester"
        Dim Age As Integer = 28

        ' Create the in-memory stream.
        Dim ms As New System.IO.MemoryStream()

        ' Create the cryptographic object.
        Dim Rijndael As New RijndaelManaged()

        ' Write and encrypt the data using a CryptoStream
        ' and BinaryWriter.
        Dim cs As New CryptoStream(ms, Rijndael.CreateEncryptor(), _
            CryptoStreamMode.Write)
        Dim w As New System.IO.BinaryWriter(cs)
        w.Write(Name)
        w.Write(Age)

        ' Pad the final block with zeroes and encrypt it.
        cs.FlushFinalBlock()

        ' Move to the start of the stream.
        ms.Position = 0

        ' Decrypt the data using a CryptoStream and BinaryReader.
        cs = New CryptoStream(ms, Rijndael.CreateDecryptor, _
            CryptoStreamMode.Read)
        Dim r As New System.IO.BinaryReader(cs)
        Console.WriteLine(r.ReadString())          ' Displays "Joe Tester".
        Console.WriteLine(r.ReadInt32)             ' Displays 28.

        Console.ReadLine()
    End Sub

End Module
```

You can also perform encryption on an entire object by serializing the object to an encrypted memory stream. Simply use the technique outlined in recipe 4.10, but instead of using a *MemoryStream* object, serialize the object to a *CryptoStream* that wraps a *MemoryStream*. This approach is shown in recipe 18-12.

18.9 Derive a Key from a Password

Problem

You want to change a string into a series of bytes suitable for use with symmetric encryption.

Solution

Use the *CryptDeriveKey* method of the *PasswordDeriveBytes* class.

Discussion

You can convert a string to a series of bytes using the techniques described in Chapter 1 and Chapter 2. However, this approach is insufficient for cryptography. For example, most passwords are relatively short and use a limited set of characters (alphabetic characters and numerals). This dramatically reduces the number and strength of the keys that you can generate.

You can, however, use a string value to seed a cryptographically strong random number generator, which can then generate a cryptographically strong sequence of bytes that you can use as a key. The .NET Framework allows you to perform this operation with the *PasswordDeriveBytes* class. When you create a *PasswordDeriveBytes* object, you supply the password and a salt value to the constructor.

> **Note** The *salt* is a random series of bytes. It's combined with the password when generating the key. If you use a nonzero salt value, you can protect against *dictionary attacks*, where attackers derive a key for every word in the dictionary and try to use this list of pregenerated keys to decrypt your data. The trick is that attackers generate their key lists by assuming that there is no salt. When you use a salt value, the attacker needs to discover it and then regenerate the full key list. If you use different salt values for different data documents, the attacker will need to generate a different key list for each document, which dramatically reduces the effectiveness of the dictionary attack.
>
> Although salt helps protect your data against these automated attacks, it can also make your application logic a little more complicated. The problem is that if you use a nonzero salt value, you need to record it so you can use it when regenerating the key for decryption.

To create a key, you call the *PasswordDeriveBytes.CryptDeriveKey* method to create the key, specifying the type of encryption and hashing algorithms to use when creating the key sequence. The most important piece of information is the third parameter, which indicates the size of the desired key:

```
' Create a key that is 128 bits long.
Dim Key() As Byte = PDB.CryptDeriveKey("RC2", "SHA", 128, Salt)
```

The following Console application demonstrates how to create a sample key.

```
Public Module PasswordToKey

    Public Sub Main()
        ' Get a password.
        Console.Write("Enter a password: ")
        Dim Password As String = Console.ReadLine()

        ' In this example, we use a blank salt value.
        Dim Salt(7) As Byte

        ' To use random value for the salt (which is recommended for
        ' maximum protection), uncomment the following lines.
        ' Dim Random As New RNGCryptoServiceProvider()
        ' Random.GetBytes(Salt)

        Dim Rijndael As New RijndaelManaged()

        ' Use the password to create a key.
        Dim PDB As New PasswordDeriveBytes(Password, Salt)
        Dim Key() As Byte
        Key = PDB.CryptDeriveKey("RC2", "SHA", 128, Salt)

        ' Display the key bytes.
        Console.WriteLine(BitConverter.ToString(Key))

        ' Apply the key to a symmetric encryption object.
        Rijndael.Key = Key

        Console.ReadLine()
    End Sub

End Module
```

You can combine this technique with the examples in recipe 18.8 or 18.7 to encrypt data or a file using an ordinary password. However, to ensure the best security, you should use a password that for an attacker is difficult to guess. Ideally, this password will include mixed case, be at least eight characters, and include numeric and special characters.

18.10 Asymmetrically Encrypt Data

Problem

You need to encrypt data in situations in which there is no shared secret key.

Solution

Use asymmetric encryption with the *RSACryptoServiceProvider* class.

Discussion

Asymmetric encryption allows you to exchange encrypted data between two parties without requiring a shared secret value. Asymmetric encryption introduces the concept of key pairs. The basic concept is that every user has both a private and a public key. Information encrypted with the public key can be decrypted only with the private key. The public key is made available to the whole world and can be transmitted freely over unsecured connections such as the Internet. The private key is carefully guarded. Thus, any user can make use of another user's public key to encrypt a message. The only person that can decrypt such a message is the intended recipient, who holds the matching private key.

To asymmetrically encrypt data in .NET, you use the *RSACryptoServiceProvider* class, which supports key sizes from 384 to 16,384 bits (in 8-bit increments). The default key size is 1024 bits. As a general rule of thumb, the larger the key size, the stronger the encryption. However, asymmetric key sizes don't correlate directly to symmetric key sizes. In fact, it's estimated that a 1024-bit RSA key is roughly equivalent to a 75-bit symmetric key.

The following example uses two Console applications to demonstrate this concept. These applications communicate using .NET Remoting (and assume that you've imported the *System.Runtime.Remoting* namespace in addition to the *System.Security.Cryptography* namespace). The configuration files used are similar to those in recipe 17.1, with one difference. The remote object needs to be configured as a singleton, so that it stays alive in between client requests. This ensures that it retains the same random symmetric key for the duration of the test.

```
<?xml version="1.0" encoding="utf-8" ?>
<configuration>
  <system.runtime.remoting>
    <application>
```

```
<!-- Define the remotable object. -->
<service>
  <wellknown
     mode = "Singleton"
     type="RemoteObjects.RemoteObject, RemoteObjects"
     objectUri="RemoteObject" />
</service>

<!-- Define the protocol used for network access.
     You can use tcp or http channels. -->
<channels>
  <channel ref="tcp" port="9080" />
</channels>

    </application>
  </system.runtime.remoting>
</configuration>
```

Following is the code for the remote object. The remote object provides two methods: one for transmitting the public portion of the key to the client (*GetPublicKey*), and one for receiving encrypted data (*ReceiveSecretData*). The data is displayed in the Console window of the component host as soon as it is received.

```
Public Class RemoteObject
    Inherits MarshalByRefObject

    ' Create a key pair.
    Private Key As New RSACryptoServiceProvider()

    Public Function GetPublicKey() As String
        ' Export only the public portion of the key.
        Return Key.ToXmlString(False)
        ' (To export both parts, you would supply True.
        '  You could use that approach to save a key pair
        '  in some secure location for later use.)
    End Function

    Public Sub ReceiveSecretData(ByVal data() As Byte)
        ' Decrypt the received data.
        Dim DecryptedData As String
        DecryptedData = System.Text.Encoding.UTF8.GetString( _
          Key.Decrypt(data, False))
        Console.WriteLine("RECEIVED: " & DecryptedData)
    End Sub

End Class
```

The client begins by requesting the remote object's public key. The client then enters a loop, requesting information from the current user. Every time the user types in text, the client uses the key to encrypt the data and then sends it to the remote object. Here's the complete code used for the client:

```
Public Module Startup

    Public Sub Main()
        ' Create the proxy that references the remote object.
        RemotingConfiguration.Configure("SimpleClient.exe.config")
        Dim RemoteObj As New RemoteObjects.RemoteObject()

        ' Construct a key object using the public portion of the key.
        ' The client will be able to encrypt, but not decrypt information.
        Dim Key As New RSACryptoServiceProvider()
        Key.FromXmlString(RemoteObj.GetPublicKey())

        Console.WriteLine("Press Enter to exit, or type some text to send.")
        Console.Write("> ")
        Dim Text As String = Console.ReadLine()
        Do Until Text = ""
            ' Encrypt the text.
            Dim EncryptedData As Byte()
            EncryptedData = Key.Encrypt( _
              System.Text.Encoding.UTF8.GetBytes(Text), False)

            ' Send the data to the server.
            RemoteObj.ReceiveSecretData(EncryptedData)
            Console.WriteLine("Sent encrypted data.")
            Console.WriteLine()
            Console.WriteLine("Press Enter to exit, " & _
              "or type some text to send.")
            Console.Write("> ")
            Text = Console.ReadLine()
        Loop
    End Sub

End Module
```

Asymmetric encryption is not nearly as convenient as symmetric encryption. It doesn't use the same stream-based model, and it forces you to encrypt data in small blocks. If you try to encrypt data that's larger than a single block without first subdividing it, an error will occur. To resolve this problem, you can combine asymmetric encryption with judicious use of symmetric encryption, as described in recipe 18.11.

> **Note** On its own, asymmetric encryption is not enough to secure communication in a distributed system. The problem is that there is no easy way to validate the identity of other users. For example, John might believe he's talking to Lucy but actually be communicating with the malicious user Sam. He'll send an encrypted message to Sam, but because the message is encrypted using Sam's public key, the malicious user will be able to decipher it easily. To avoid this type of problem, it's recommended that you use a prebuilt security infrastructure for mission-critical applications, such as SSL. SSL incorporates digital certificates, which are used to establish identity.

18.11 Combine Asymmetric and Symmetric Encryption

Problem

You want to use symmetric encryption (perhaps because you need to encrypt a large amount of data, or performance is very important), but there is no shared secret that you can use.

Solution

Create a random symmetric key, and use this key to encrypt your data symmetrically. Then encrypt the random key asymmetrically.

Discussion

Asymmetric encryption is typically 1000 times slower than symmetric encryption, and the encrypted data it creates is several times larger. You can avoid these limitations by generating a random symmetric key, and using it to encrypt the bulk of your data. The trick is to encrypt the random key using asymmetric encryption with the recipient's public key, and then add it to the encrypted document. The recipient can retrieve the encrypted symmetric key, decrypt it using his or her private key, and then use it to decrypt the remainder of the document. This technique is commonly used; two examples are SSL (which negotiates a symmetric session key for each interaction) and the Windows Encrypting File System (which generates a random symmetric key for each file it encrypts).

The following example rewrites the code from recipe 18.7 to use this technique.

```
Public Class FileEncryptor
    Inherits System.Windows.Forms.Form

    Private RSA As New RSACryptoServiceProvider()

    Private Sub Form_Load(ByVal sender As System.Object, _
      ByVal e As System.EventArgs) Handles MyBase.Load
        ' Check for file with key data.
        ' This file will contain the full public and private key pair.
        If File.Exists("key.bin") Then
            Dim fs As New FileStream("key.bin", FileMode.Open)
            Dim r As New StreamReader(fs)
            RSA.FromXmlString(r.ReadToEnd())
            fs.Close()
        Else
            Dim fs As New FileStream("key.bin", FileMode.CreateNew)
            Dim w As New StreamWriter(fs)
            w.Write(RSA.ToXmlString(True))
            w.Flush()
            fs.Close()
        End If
    End Sub

    Private Sub cmdEncrypt_Click(ByVal sender As System.Object, _
      ByVal e As System.EventArgs) Handles cmdEncrypt.Click
        ' Open a file for writing.
        Dim fs As New FileStream("testfile.bin", FileMode.Create)

        ' Create a new (random) symmetric key.
        Dim Rijndael As New RijndaelManaged()

        ' Encrypt the symmetric key and IV using the RSA public key.
        Dim EncryptedKey() As Byte = RSA.Encrypt(Rijndael.Key, False)
        Dim EncryptedIV() As Byte = RSA.Encrypt(Rijndael.IV, False)

        ' Write the asymmetrically encrypted key and IV to the file.
        fs.Write(EncryptedKey, 0, EncryptedKey.Length)
        fs.Write(EncryptedIV, 0, EncryptedIV.Length)

        ' Write the remainder of the file using symmetric encryption.
        Dim Transform As ICryptoTransform = Rijndael.CreateEncryptor()
        Dim cs As New CryptoStream(fs, Transform, CryptoStreamMode.Write)
        Dim w As New StreamWriter(cs)
        w.Write(txtSource.Text)
        w.Flush()

        cs.FlushFinalBlock()
        w.Close()
    End Sub
```

```
Private Sub cmdDecrypt_Click(ByVal sender As System.Object, _
    ByVal e As System.EventArgs) Handles cmdDecrypt.Click
    ' Open a file for reading.
    Dim fs As New FileStream("testfile.bin", FileMode.Open)

    ' The key size is measured in bits. 8 bits = 1 byte.
    ' The amount of bytes in an encrypted block of data is always
    ' the same as the key size.
    Dim EncryptedBlockSize As Integer = CType(RSA.KeySize / 8, Integer)

    ' Retrieve the encrypted key and IV.
    Dim Rijndael As New RijndaelManaged()
    Dim EncryptedKey(EncryptedBlockSize - 1) As Byte
    Dim EncryptedIV(EncryptedBlockSize - 1) As Byte
    fs.Read(EncryptedKey, 0, EncryptedKey.Length)
    fs.Read(EncryptedIV, 0, EncryptedIV.Length)
    Rijndael.KeySize = EncryptedBlockSize
    Rijndael.Key = RSA.Decrypt(EncryptedKey, False)
    Rijndael.IV = RSA.Decrypt(EncryptedIV, False)

    ' Use the symmetric key to read the remainder of the file.
    Dim Transform As ICryptoTransform = Rijndael.CreateDecryptor()
    Dim cs As New CryptoStream(fs, Transform, CryptoStreamMode.Read)
    Dim r As New StreamReader(cs)
    txtFileContents.Text = r.ReadToEnd()
    r.Close()
End Sub

End Class
```

18.12 Encrypt an Object

Problem

You want to use encryption on an entire object, not just individual pieces of data.

Solution

Use .NET serialization to convert the object to a stream of bytes, and encrypt the serialized data.

Discussion

Recipes 4.9, 4.11, and 4.12 demonstrated different ways to serialize an object to a stream of bytes. You can use this technique in conjunction with symmetric or asymmetric encryption to encrypt the contents of a serializable object. If you're using asymmetric encryption, you'll need to convert the object to an array of bytes and then encrypt these bytes one block at a time. If you're using symmetric encryption, you can serialize and encrypt the data in one operation by using a *CryptoStream*.

For example, consider the serializable *Person* class shown here:

```
<Serializable()> _
Public Class Person

    Private _FirstName As String
    Private _LastName As String

    Public Property FirstName() As String
        Get
            Return _FirstName
        End Get
        Set(ByVal Value As String)
            _FirstName = Value
        End Set
    End Property

    Public Property LastName() As String
        Get
            Return _LastName
        End Get
        Set(ByVal Value As String)
            _LastName = Value
        End Set
    End Property

    Public Sub New(ByVal firstName As String, ByVal lastName As String)
        Me.FirstName = firstName
        Me.LastName = lastName
    End Sub

End Class
```

The following Console application shows how to encrypt and decrypt a *Person* object. It begins by creating three objects: a *Person*, a *BinaryFormatter* that can serialize the *Person*, and a *MemoryStream* where the serialized data will be placed. It then wraps the destination *MemoryStream* with a *CryptoStream*. The code serializes the data to the *CryptoStream* instead of using the *MemoryStream* directly. This way, the data will be encrypted just before it's placed into the *MemoryStream*.

```
Public Module EncryptObject

    Public Sub Main()
        Dim Person As New Person("Henrick", "Digali")

        ' Construct a formatter.
        Dim Formatter As New BinaryFormatter()

        ' Create the cryptographic object.
        Dim Rijndael As New RijndaelManaged()

        ' Serialize the object to memory and encrypt it.
        Dim ms As New MemoryStream()
        Dim cs As New CryptoStream(ms, Rijndael.CreateEncryptor(), _
          CryptoStreamMode.Write)
        Formatter.Serialize(cs, Person)
        cs.FlushFinalBlock()

        ' Display the encrypted data.
        ms.Position = 0
        Dim r As New StreamReader(ms)
        Console.Write("Encrypted Data: ")
        Console.WriteLine(r.ReadToEnd())
        Console.WriteLine()

        ' Decrypt and deserialize the object.
        ms.Position = 0
        cs = New CryptoStream(ms, Rijndael.CreateDecryptor, _
          CryptoStreamMode.Read)
        Person = CType(Formatter.Deserialize(cs), Person)
        Console.Write("Decrypted Data: ")
        Console.WriteLine(Person.FirstName & " " & Person.LastName)

        Console.ReadLine()
    End Sub

End Module
```

In order to use this code as written, you need to import the *System.Runtime.Serialization.Formatters.Binary* and *System.IO* namespaces, in addition to the *System.Security.Cryptography* namespace.

Here's an example of the output this test produces:

```
Encrypted Data: 5d|-J\)nlZL^!"?ZYMAi}P?4*?R$yYjga*Bii3ZMgn-
Decrypted Data: Henrick Digali
```

If you are creating a custom class, you might want to create dedicated methods in the class for serialization and deserialization. For example, if you are creating a *Person* class, you might add a shared *Person.Decrypt* method that accepts a stream of encrypted data, decrypts it, and returns the deserialized *Person* object. Similarly, you might add a *Person.Encrypt* method that returns the serialized and encrypted data for the current *Person* as a stream or byte array. This approach can make it easier to keep encryption code out of your application logic.

18.13 Verify That Data Hasn't Changed

Problem

You want to ensure that a file or combination of data files cannot be undetectably altered.

Solution

Use a *HashAlgorithm* class to create a hash code based on the data, and store this hash code to use for future comparisons.

Discussion

Encryption prevents malicious users from reading your data, but it doesn't stop them from tampering with it. Instead, you need a way to validate data and detect whether it has been altered. This is the role played by hash codes.

A hash code algorithm generates a small (typically about 20-byte) binary fingerprint for any data that can be represented as a sequence of bytes. Hash codes are cryptographically secure, which means that it's extremely difficult for a malicious user to create a document that will generate a given hash code. It's also impossible for an attacker to determine any information about the original data by looking at the hash code. And while it is possible for different data to generate the same hash codes, it's statistically unlikely. In fact, even a minor change (for example, modifying a single bit in the source data) has a 50 percent chance of independently changing each bit in the hash code.

Table 18-2 lists the hash code algorithms provided in the *System.Security.Cryptography* namespace. They all inherit from the base *HashAlgorithm* class and provide a *ComputeHash* method that takes a byte array of a stream and returns a byte array with the hash data. Like encryption algorithms, the smaller the hash size, the less protection a hash code algorithm provides (and the easier it is for an attacker to find another set of data that generates an identical hash code).

Table 18-2   Hash Algorithm Classes

Algorithm	Default Implementation Class	Hash Size (in Bits)
MD5	*MD5CryptoServiceProvider*	128
SHA-1	*SHA1CryptoServiceProvider*	160
SHA-256	*SHA256Managed*	256
SHA-384	*SHA384Managed*	384
SHA-512	*SHA512Managed*	512

The following code demonstrates a simple Console application that computes and compares the hash codes of a test file, both before and after a simple change. The code includes a helper function that tests byte arrays for equality by iterating through all the values.

```
Public Module HashTest

    Public Sub Main()
        ' Create a new file.
        Dim fs As New FileStream("testfile.bin", FileMode.Create)

        ' Write some data.
        Dim w As New StreamWriter(fs)
        w.WriteLine("This is the first line.")
        w.WriteLine("This is the second line.")
        w.Flush()

        ' Calculate a 512 bit (64 byte) hash for the file.
        Dim SHA As New SHA512Managed()
        fs.Position = 0
        Dim HashA() As Byte = SHA.ComputeHash(fs)

        ' Display the hash.
        Console.WriteLine(BitConverter.ToString(HashA))
        Console.WriteLine()

        ' Add another value to the file and calculate the hash.
        w.Write("!")
        w.Flush()
        fs.Position = 0
        Dim HashB() As Byte = SHA.ComputeHash(fs)
        fs.Close()
```

```
' Display the hash.
Console.WriteLine(BitConverter.ToString(HashB))
Console.WriteLine()

' Compare the hashes.
If CompareByteArray(HashA, HashB) Then
    Console.WriteLine("Hash codes match.")
Else
    Console.WriteLine("No match.")
End If

Console.ReadLine()
End Sub

Private Function CompareByteArray(ByVal BytesA() As Byte, _
    ByVal BytesB() As Byte) As Boolean
    If Not BytesA.Length = BytesB.Length Then Return False

    Dim i As Integer
    For i = 0 To BytesA.Length - 1
        If Not BytesA(i) = BytesB(i) Then Return False
    Next
    Return True
End Function

End Module
```

To ensure data integrity, you should store the hash code in a secure location (such as a protected database). Otherwise, an attacker will be able to tamper with the document and simply generate a new hash code that can be used to replace the original hash code. If you need to store the hash code in an unsecured location or with the data itself, you should create a tamper-proof hash code, as explained in recipe 18.14.

18.14 Create a Tamper-Proof Hash Code

Problem

You want to create a hash code that can't be replaced by a malicious user.

Solution

Combine hashing with encryption, either by using a keyed hash code or a digital signature.

Discussion

Hash codes have one obvious limitation: unless you store the hash code in a secure location, there is nothing to stop an attacker from tampering with your data and generating a new hash code that matches the altered data. In this scenario, it would be impossible to detect that any change has taken place. This is a common problem in distributed applications, which use hash codes to validate messages that are sent over a network.

The solution is to create a hash code that an attacker won't be able to recreate. For example, you can encrypt the hash code using a secret key that the attacker won't know. This is called a *keyed hash algorithm*. The .NET Framework includes two keyed hash algorithms (shown in Table 18-3), both of which derive from the base *KeyedHashAlgorithm* class in the *System.Security.Cryptography* namespace. The prime difference between these classes and the ordinary hash algorithm classes is that they provide a *Key* property in which you store the secret key (sequence of bytes) that will be used to generate the hash.

Table 18-3 Keyed Hash Algorithm Classes

Algorithm	Default Implementation Class	Hash Size (Bits)	Key Size
HMAC-SHA1	*HMACSHA1*	160	64 (recommended)
MAC-3DES-CBC	*MACTripleDES*	64	8, 16, or 24

The following code snippet computes a keyed hash for the same data using two different key values. Note that the resulting hash codes will not be the same.

```
' Create a new file.
Dim fs As New FileStream("testfile.bin", FileMode.Create)

' Write some data.
Dim w As New StreamWriter(fs)
w.WriteLine("This is the first line.")
w.WriteLine("This is the second line.")
w.Flush()

' Calculate a keyed hash for the file.
Dim HMACSHA As New HMACSHA1()
fs.Position = 0
Dim HashA() As Byte = HMACSHA.ComputeHash(fs)

' Display the hash.
Console.WriteLine(BitConverter.ToString(HashA))
Console.WriteLine()
```

```
' Calculate a keyed hash with the same algorithm and same
' data, but using a different key.
fs.Position = 0
HMACSHA = New HMACSHA1()
Dim HashB() As Byte = HMACSHA.ComputeHash(fs)

' Display the hash.
Console.WriteLine(BitConverter.ToString(HashB))
Console.WriteLine()

fs.Close()

' Compare the hashes.
If CompareByteArray(HashA, HashB) Then
    Console.WriteLine("Hash codes match.")
Else
    Console.WriteLine("No match.")
End If
```

Another choice is to encrypt a hash algorithm using a private key from an asymmetric key pair. This ensures that any other user will be able to validate the hash code (using the corresponding public key) but no other user will be able generate a new hash code because no other user has the private key. This type of hash code is called a *digital signature*, and it can be generated using the *RSACryptoServiceProvider* or *DSACryptoServiceProvider* asymmetric algorithm class. When using theses classes, you don't need to call a *ComputeHash* method and compare the byte arrays manually. Instead, you use the *SignData* and *VerifyData* methods with a stream or array of bytes, as shown in the following code snippet.

```
' Create two signature objects.
Dim DsaKeyPair As New DSACryptoServiceProvider()
Dim DsaPublicKeyOnly As New DSACryptoServiceProvider()

' Copy the public key from DsaKeyPair to DsaPublicKeyOnly.
DsaPublicKeyOnly.FromXmlString(DsaKeyPair.ToXmlString(False))
' You need the full key pair to sign the data, because the
' private key is used. However, to verify the data, you only
' require the public key. This example uses DsaKeyPair to
' sign the data, and DsaPublicKeyOnly to verify it.

' Create some data.
Dim Data As String = "This is some tamper-proof data."
Dim DataBytes() As Byte = System.Text.Encoding.UTF8.GetBytes(Data)

' Create a signed hash for the data.
Dim Signature() As Byte = DsaKeyPair.SignData(DataBytes)
```

```
' Verify the data.
If DsaPublicKeyOnly.VerifyData(DataBytes, Signature) Then
    Console.WriteLine("Signature authenticated.")
Else
    Console.WriteLine("Invalid signature.")
End If
```

> **Note** If you want to ensure data integrity *and* confidentiality, you'll need to combine encryption and hashing. Typically, it will be easiest to encrypt the data and then calculate the hash (so that the hash can be verified without requiring that the recipient decrypt the data first).

18.15 Create an XML Digital Signature

Problem

You need to sign part of an XML document according the XML Signatures standard.

Solution

Use the classes in the *System.Security.Cryptography.Xml* namespace.

Discussion

You can apply the hashing and signing techniques in recipe 18.12 and 18.13 to encrypt XML content in a file or a byte array, just as you would create a hash for any other type of data. However, this approach introduces several limitations:

■ There's no easy way to create a hash code and then make the resulting document (XML source and hash code) into a valid XML document.

■ Minor differences in XML documents (such as the addition of white space) will change the hash code, even though they have no effect on how the XML data is parsed. This can be a particular problem if you need to create a hash code on one system and validate it using an application written in another programming language or using different XML tools.

■ There's no easy way to sign just part of an XML document (or sign different parts with signatures from different users).

The solution to all of these problems has been provided by the XML Signatures W3C recommendation, which is described at *http://www.w3.org/TR/xmldsig-core*. XML Signatures defines a standard way of signing XML documents and a canonical representation of XML, so that identical documents will always generate identical signatures. However, the XML Signatures standard uses the same signing algorithms as any other type of data.

The .NET Framework provides an XML Signatures implementation with the types in the *System.Security.Cryptography.Xml* namespace. To access these types, you need to add a reference to the System.Security.dll assembly.

XML signatures can be of three types:

- **Detached signatures.** The signature is stored as a separate XML fragment that uses a Uniform Resource Identifier (URI) to refer to the signed document.

- **Enveloping signatures.** The signature wraps the XML document.

- **Enveloped signatures.** The signature is inserted into the original XML document that contains the information it is signing.

You can create all of these signature types in .NET. The following example presents a Windows application that creates and verifies enveloped signatures. The original XML document is shown here:

```
<Orders>
  <Order>
    <ID>1</ID>
    <Name>Toaster Oven</Name>
    <Price>400.99</Price>
  </Order>
</Orders>
```

The signed XML is shown in Figure 18-5. This document includes the original XML data and a signature with the signature value and information about the algorithm that was used to create the signature as well as the public key needed to validate it.

The code for signing and verifying the signature takes place in two button event handlers. The form code is shown here:

```
Public Class SignXml
    Inherits System.Windows.Forms.Form

    ' (Form code omitted.)

    Private Sub cmdEnveloped_Click(ByVal sender As System.Object, _
      ByVal e As System.EventArgs) Handles cmdEnveloped.Click
        ' Load the XML data that you want to sign.
```

```
            Dim Doc As New XmlDocument()
            Doc.Load("doc.xml")

            ' Create XML signature.
            Dim SignedXml As New SignedXml(Doc)

            ' Sign the data in the entire document.
            ' You could tailor this XPath expression to point to a single element.
            Dim Reference As New Reference()
            Reference.Uri = "#xpointer(/)"
            SignedXml.AddReference(Reference)

            ' Use a transform required for enveloped signatures.
            Reference.AddTransform(New XmlDsigEnvelopedSignatureTransform())

            ' Use the RSA algorithm to create the signature.
            Dim Rsa As New RSACryptoServiceProvider()

            ' Add the key details to the signature.
            SignedXml.SigningKey = Rsa
            Dim KeyInfo As New KeyInfo()
            KeyInfo.AddClause(New RSAKeyValue(Rsa))
            SignedXml.KeyInfo = KeyInfo

            ' Calculate the signature.
            SignedXml.ComputeSignature()

            ' Get the XML representation of the signature.
            Dim XmlSignature As XmlElement = SignedXml.GetXml()

            ' Insert the XML signature into the document.
            Dim Node As XmlNode = Doc.ImportNode(XmlSignature, True)
            Dim Root As XmlNode = Doc.DocumentElement
            Root.InsertAfter(Node, Root.FirstChild)

            ' Save the XML document with the enveloped signature.
            Doc.Save("SignedDoc.xml")

            ' Display the full document with signature.
            txtXml.Text = Doc.OuterXml
        End Sub

        Private Sub cmdVerify_Click(ByVal sender As System.Object, _
          ByVal e As System.EventArgs) Handles cmdVerify.Click
            ' Load the signed XML document.
            Dim Doc As New XmlDocument()
            Doc.Load("SignedDoc.xml")
```

```
    ' Create a SignedXml object for verification.
    Dim SignedXml As New SignedXml(Doc)

    ' Find the first signature.
    Dim Node As XmlNode = Doc.GetElementsByTagName("Signature", _
        "http://www.w3.org/2000/09/xmldsig#")(0)
    SignedXml.LoadXml(Node)

    ' Verify the signature.
    If SignedXml.CheckSignature() Then
        MessageBox.Show("Signature authenticated.")
    Else
        MessageBox.Show("Invalid signature.")
    End If
End Sub

End Class
```

Figure 18-5   Creating enveloped XML signatures.

18.16 Store a Salted Password Hash in a Database

Problem

You want to store password information in a database, but you want to make sure the passwords aren't clearly visible.

Solution

Instead of storing a plain text password, store a salted hash of the password in the database as a binary field. This password hash is still suitable for authentication, but much more difficult for an attacker to reverse engineer.

Discussion

Many applications authenticate users by comparing a supplied username and password with information stored in a back-end database. Often, the password information is stored in the database as plain text, which raises a serious security risk. If a malicious user can gain access to the database server, even for only a few minutes, the attacker will be able to retrieve a comprehensive unencrypted password list. This password list can form the basis for other attacks in the future—it might even be used to attack user accounts on another system.

A better approach is to limit the damage of a security breach by storing encrypted password information in the database. In fact, in an ideal scenario, you won't store the password at all—instead, you'll store a *salted hash* that has been generated from the password. Because it's a hash, the attacker won't be able to reverse engineer the information to determine the original password. If an attack occurs, you simply need to force all users to submit new passwords. The stolen password hashes will then become worthless.

The password hash approach is a common one—for example, it's used to safeguard user accounts in UNIX. For maximum security, all password hashes should also be *salted*, which means the hash should incorporate a short random series of bytes (the "salt"). In a table of passwords, each password would have a different salt value. This reduces the ability of attackers to use automated brute force attacks such as a dictionary attack. Because each password hash has a different salt value, each password hash must be attacked separately.

To use salted password hashes in this recipe, we'll use the following steps:

1. Convert the password to a byte array, and calculate a hash for the password.

2. Generate a random salt, and add it to the password hash. Hash the resulting byte array a second time.

3. Add the random salt to the new hash, and store the final result in a binary field in a database.

Figure 18-6 diagrams this process of creating a new salted password hash.

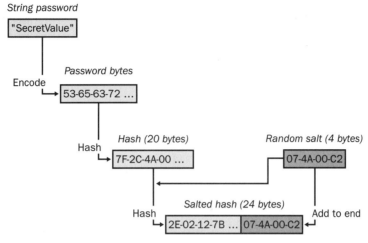

Figure 18-6   Creating a salted password hash.

To authenticate a user with a password hash, you need to follow these steps:

1. Look up the corresponding user record, and retrieve the salted password hash from the database.

2. Extract the salt from the salted hash.

3. Use the salt value to calculate the salted password hash with the user-supplied password.

4. Verify that this salted hash matches the value in the database.

The *HashHelper* class shown below encapsulates these two tasks. The *CreateDBPassword* method is used to generate a salted hash, which you can store in the database. The *ComparePasswords* method is used to compare the salted password hash in the database to a user-supplied password.

```
Public Class HashHelper

    Private Const SaltLength As Integer = 4

    ' This function returns a salted password hash,
    ' which is suitable for storage in the database.
```

```vb
' It uses a randomly generated salt value.
Public Function CreateDBPassword(ByVal password As String) As Byte()
    ' Create the unsalted password hash.
    Dim UnsaltedPassword() As Byte = CreatePasswordHash(password)

    ' Generate a random salt value.
    Dim SaltValue(SaltLength - 1) As Byte
    Dim Rng As New RNGCryptoServiceProvider()
    Rng.GetBytes(SaltValue)

    ' Create the salted hash.
    Return CreateSaltedPassword(SaltValue, UnsaltedPassword)
End Function

' This function returns a password hash
' that hasn't been salted.
Private Function CreatePasswordHash(ByVal password As String) As Byte()
    Dim Sha1 As New SHA1Managed()
    Return Sha1.ComputeHash(System.Text.Encoding.UTF8.GetBytes(password))
End Function

' This function accepts the password hash, and
' salts it with the given salt value.
Private Function CreateSaltedPassword(ByVal saltValue As Byte(), _
  ByVal unsaltedPassword() As Byte) As Byte()
    ' Add the salt to the hash.
    Dim RawSalted(unsaltedPassword.Length + saltValue.Length - 1) As Byte
    unsaltedPassword.CopyTo(RawSalted, 0)
    saltValue.CopyTo(RawSalted, unsaltedPassword.Length)

    ' Create the salted hash.
    Dim Sha1 As New SHA1Managed()
    Dim SaltedPassword() As Byte = Sha1.ComputeHash(RawSalted)

    ' Add the salt value to the salted hash.
    Dim DbPassword(SaltedPassword.Length + saltValue.Length - 1) As Byte
    SaltedPassword.CopyTo(DbPassword, 0)
    saltValue.CopyTo(DbPassword, SaltedPassword.Length)

    Return DbPassword
End Function

' This function compares a hashed password against the
' hashed and salted password from the database.
' It returns true if authentication succeeds.
Public Function ComparePasswords(ByVal storedPassword() As Byte, _
  ByVal suppliedPassword As String) As Boolean
```

```
    ' Extract the salt value from the salted hash.
    Dim SaltValue(SaltLength - 1) As Byte
    Dim SaltOffset As Integer = storedPassword.Length - SaltLength
    Dim i As Integer
    For i = 0 To SaltLength - 1
        SaltValue(i) = storedPassword(SaltOffset + i)
    Next

    ' Convert the password supplied by the user
    ' to a salted password, using the salt value
    ' from the database record.
    Dim HashedPassword As Byte() = CreatePasswordHash(suppliedPassword)
    Dim SaltedPassword As Byte() = CreateSaltedPassword(SaltValue, _
      HashedPassword)

    ' Compare the two salted hashes.
    ' If they are the same, authentication has succeeded.
    Return CompareByteArray(storedPassword, SaltedPassword)
End Function

' This helper function compares two byte arrays, and returns
' true if they contain the same series of bytes.
Private Function CompareByteArray(ByVal arrayA() As Byte, _
  ByVal arrayB() As Byte) As Boolean
    ' Make sure the arrays are the same size.
    If arrayA.Length <> arrayB.Length Then Return False

    ' Compare each byte in the two arrays.
    Dim i As Integer
    For i = 0 To arrayA.Length - 1
        If Not arrayA(i).Equals(arrayB(i)) Then Return False
    Next

    ' Both tests succeeded. The arrays match.
    Return True
End Function

End Class
```

The following example shows a simple Console client that tests the *Hash-Helper* class. It generates a salted and hashed password value using *CreateDB-Password*, and then uses *ComparePasswords* to validate against it.

```
Public Module Startup

    Public Sub Main()
        Dim HashHelper As New HashHelper()
```

```
        Console.WriteLine("Enter the password you want to hash and salt.")
        Console.WriteLine("This password will be used for authentication.")

        Console.Write("Enter the new password: ")
        Dim Password As String = Console.ReadLine()

        ' Hash and salt the password.
        Dim SaltedPasswordHash As Byte()
        SaltedPasswordHash = HashHelper.CreateDBPassword(Password)

        Console.WriteLine()
        Console.WriteLine("Now you can perform authentication.")

        Dim Success As Boolean
        Console.Write("Enter the password (or press Enter to exit): ")
        Password = Console.ReadLine()
        Do Until Password = ""
            ' Try to authenticate with this password.
            Success = HashHelper.ComparePasswords( _
              SaltedPasswordHash, Password)

            If Success Then
                Console.WriteLine("Authentication succeeded.")
            Else
                Console.WriteLine("Authentication failed.")
            End If
            Console.WriteLine()

            Console.Write("Enter the password (or press Enter to exit):")
            Password = Console.ReadLine()
        Loop
    End Sub

End Module
```

In this example, the salted password hash is stored only in memory, and each time you run the test program you need to create it. To store the password hash in a database, you simply need to create a binary field of sufficient length. In this example, that field would be 24 bytes, because the hash is 20 bytes in size and the appended salt is 4 bytes long. Figure 18-7 shows the database table you might want to create. In addition, you would probably want to create stored procedures that handle the work of adding and retrieving user records. (You can refer to recipes that deal with stored procedures and ADO.NET code in Chapter 14.)

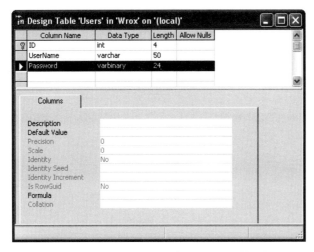

Figure 18-7   A database table for password hashes.

18.17 Generate a Secure Random Number

Problem

You want to generate a random number that can't be reverse-engineered (or predicted) by a malicious user.

Solution

Use the *RNGCryptoServiceProvider* class in the *System.Security.Cryptography* namespace instead of the *System.Random* class.

Discussion

Computers are designed to be deterministic. As a result, they aren't often a good source of random numbers. The numbers you generate with the *System.Random* class are *statistically random*, which means that they follow a random distribution and are suitable for modeling, simulations, computer games, and so on. However, these generators aren't suitable for cryptographic purposes. With knowledge of the algorithm, a malicious user can look at the random numbers you generate, determine how the seed value is calculated (typically it's drawn from the system clock), and then be able to predict future "random" values. In fact, pseudorandom numbers have been the basis of several infamous attacks, including one that exploited a time-dependent random number generator in an early version of Netscape Navigator, which compromised the key used for SSL connections. (See *http://www.cs.berkeley.edu/~daw/papers/ddj-netscape.html* for a complete description of this vulnerability.)

The solution is to use a *cryptographically strong* random number. These numbers are seeded using multiple values, including system and user data such as the process ID and the thread ID, the system clock, the system time, the system counter, the number of free disk clusters, the latency between mouse or keyboard actions, and the hashed user environment block. This value is then used in conjunction with a cryptographic algorithm to create a stream of truly unpredictable random data.

The following Console application demonstrates this technique to create a series of random numbers.

```
Public Module RandomGenerator

    Public Sub Main()
        Dim RandomByte(0) As Byte
        Dim Random As New RNGCryptoServiceProvider()
        Dim Input As String

        Do
            ' Fill the byte array with random bytes. In this case,
            ' the byte array holds only a single byte.
            Random.GetBytes(RandomByte)

            ' Display the random byte value.
            Console.WriteLine(RandomByte(0).ToString())

            ' Convert the random byte into a decimal from 1 to 10.
            Console.WriteLine(Int(RandomByte(0) / 256 * 10) + 1)

            Console.WriteLine("Type 'exit' to stop " & _
              "or press Enter to continue.")
            Input = Console.ReadLine()
        Loop While Input <> "exit"
    End Sub

End Module
```

It takes approximately ten times longer to create a cryptographically secure random number. That means it might not be suitable if you need to rapidly generate millions of random numbers.

18.18 Generate a Secure Random GUID

Problem

You want to create a cryptographically secure, random globally unique identifier (GUID).

Solution

Use the *RNGCryptoServiceProvider* class to create 16 random bytes, and then use these to create a new GUID by passing them to the *Guid* constructor.

Discussion

The random GUIDs you create with the *Guid.NewGuid* method are not known to be cryptographically secure. Thus, it's theoretically possible for a user to predict a GUID value that you generate for another user or task and use this to exploit weaknesses in your system. To prevent this possibility, you can create a cryptographically secure GUID using the *RNGCryptoServiceProvider* class. Here's the code you need:

```
Public Module RandomGuidGenerator

    Public Sub Main()
        ' A GUID is essentially a 16-byte (or 128-bit) number.
        ' So we must create a byte array with 16 byte elements.
        Dim RandomBytes(15) As Byte

        ' Fill the byte array with random bytes.
        Dim Random As New RNGCryptoServiceProvider()
        Random.GetBytes(RandomBytes)

        ' Create the GUID using these bytes.
        Dim MyGuid As New Guid(randomBytes)
        Console.WriteLine(MyGuid.ToString())

        Console.ReadLine()
    End Sub

End Module
```

18.19 Determine the Evidence Associated with an Assembly

Problem

You want to determine the evidence that the .NET security infrastructure uses to determine the permissions of a piece of code.

Solution

Create a *System.Reflection.Assembly* object, and walk through all the items in the *Evidence* collection.

Discussion

It's often useful to be able to read the evidence that .NET attaches to an assembly. This is particularly important when debugging code access security settings with a distributed application that uses reflection to load assemblies from the Internet. (See recipe 9-7 for a specific example.)

You can retrieve the evidence for any assembly through the *Assembly.Evidence* property. This property returns a *System.Security.Policy.Evidence* object. You can walk through the items of evidence, and display the associated XML, by calling *Evidence.GetHostEnumerator*.

The following Console application displays the evidence for the current executing assembly.

```
Public Module ShowAssemblyEvidence

    Public Sub Main()
        ' Retrieve an object representing the current code assembly.
        Dim Asm As System.Reflection.Assembly
        Asm = System.Reflection.Assembly.GetExecutingAssembly()

        ' Get an enumerator that allows us to walk through the
        ' host evidence.
        Dim Enumerator As IEnumerator
        Enumerator = Asm.Evidence.GetHostEnumerator()

        Do While Enumerator.MoveNext()
            ' Show the current piece of evidence.
            Console.WriteLine(Enumerator.Current.ToString())
            Console.WriteLine()
        Loop

        Console.ReadLine()
    End Sub

End Module
```

Following is an example of the typical output this code produces (in a slightly abbreviated form). The evidence includes the zone from which the code was loaded, the corresponding URL, and a hash of the assembly file.

```
<System.Security.Policy.Zone version="1">
  <Zone>MyComputer</Zone>
</System.Security.Policy.Zone>

<System.Security.Policy.Url version="1">
  <Url>file://C:/Code/Chapter 18/Recipe 18-18/bin/Recipe 18-18.exe</Url>
</System.Security.Policy.Url>

<System.Security.Policy.Hash version="1">
  <RawData>4D5A9000030000000400000...</RawData>
</System.Security.Policy.Hash>
```

18.20 Programmatically Restrict Code Permissions

Problem

You want to dynamically load an assembly using reflection but prevent it from having the same permissions as your application.

Solution

Create a custom piece of evidence, and attach it to the dynamically loaded assembly. Give assemblies with this evidence lowered permissions.

Discussion

The .NET Framework uses code access security to give assemblies different permissions, depending on several factors. In some cases, you might want to lower these permissions for certain assemblies. For example, you might create an extensible application with a plug-in framework that allows extra functionality to be added by supplying a new assembly. Your code can instantiate the classes in this assembly through .NET reflection, and, presuming these classes implement some known interface, your code can use them to perform a task at runtime. To ensure that this extensibility model isn't exploited to introduce malicious code, you can reduce the permission set granted to dynamically loaded code, perhaps giving it only the permission to execute and return values, not the permission to write files, read the registry, or present the user interface.

The first step is to create an evidence class that you'll attach to dynamically loaded assemblies. This class doesn't actually contain any code.

```
<Serializable()> _
Public NotInheritable Class SandboxEvidence
End Class
```

The next step is to create an *IMembershipCondition* class that allows the .NET Framework to test whether *SandboxEvidence* is present in a given assembly. This class implements a *Check* method that scans a collection of evidence and returns *True* if it finds an instance of *SandboxEvidence*. Because this membership condition is never stored, it isn't necessary to implement all the methods—you can simply throw a *NotImplementedException* from those methods that aren't needed.

```
<Serializable()> _
Public NotInheritable Class SandboxMembershipCondition
    Implements IMembershipCondition

    Public Function Check(ByVal ev As Evidence) As Boolean _
      Implements IMembershipCondition.Check

        Dim Evidence As Object
        For Each Evidence In ev
            If TypeOf Evidence Is SandboxEvidence Then
                Return True
            End If
        Next
        Return False

    End Function

    Public Function Copy() As IMembershipCondition _
      Implements IMembershipCondition.Copy
        Return New SandboxMembershipCondition()
    End Function

    Public Overloads Overrides Function Equals(ByVal obj As Object) _
      As Boolean Implements IMembershipCondition.Equals
        Return (obj Is Me)
    End Function

    Public Overloads Overrides Function ToString() As String _
      Implements IMembershipCondition.ToString
        Return "SandboxMembershipCondition"
    End Function
```

```
Public Sub FromXml(ByVal e As SecurityElement) _
  Implements ISecurityEncodable.FromXml
    Throw New NotImplementedException()
End Sub

Public Function ToXml() As SecurityElement _
  Implements ISecurityEncodable.ToXml
    Throw New NotImplementedException()
End Function

Public Sub FromXml(ByVal e As SecurityElement, _
ByVal Level As PolicyLevel) Implements ISecurityPolicyEncodable.FromXml
    Throw New NotImplementedException()
End Sub

Public Function ToXml(ByVal Level As PolicyLevel) As SecurityElement _
  Implements ISecurityPolicyEncodable.ToXml
    Throw New NotImplementedException()
End Function
```

```
End Class
```

You can now sandbox dynamically loaded assemblies as demonstrated in the following Console application. You simply need to choose the permissions that should be granted to the assemblies and set the security policy.

```
Public Module SandboxTest

    Public Sub Main()
        ' Define permissions for dynamically loaded assemblies.
        ' In this case, we grant Execute permission only.
        Dim SandBoxPerms As New NamedPermissionSet("Sandbox", _
          PermissionState.None)
        SandBoxPerms.AddPermission( _
          New SecurityPermission(SecurityPermissionFlag.Execution))

        ' Create a security policy that uses this permission set.
        Dim Policy As PolicyLevel = PolicyLevel.CreateAppDomainLevel()
        Policy.AddNamedPermissionSet(SandBoxPerms)

        ' Code is matched to a permission set based on its code group.
        ' Code groups are determined based on membership conditions.
        Dim SandboxCondition As New SandboxMembershipCondition()
        Dim AllCondition As New AllMembershipCondition()
        Dim All, None As NamedPermissionSet
        None = Policy.GetNamedPermissionSet("Nothing")
        All = Policy.GetNamedPermissionSet("Everything")
        Dim RootCodeGroup As New FirstMatchCodeGroup(AllCondition, _
```

```
          New PolicyStatement(None))
Dim SandboxCodeGroup As New UnionCodeGroup(SandboxCondition, _
          New PolicyStatement(SandBoxPerms))
Dim AllCodeGroup As New UnionCodeGroup(AllCondition, _
          New PolicyStatement(All))
RootCodeGroup.AddChild(SandboxCodeGroup)
RootCodeGroup.AddChild(AllCodeGroup)
Policy.RootCodeGroup = RootCodeGroup

' Set this policy into action for the current application.
AppDomain.CurrentDomain.SetAppDomainPolicy(Policy)

' You can now dynamically load an assembly, and
' supply the evidence that will force it to be sandboxed.
Dim Evidence As New Evidence()
Evidence.AddHost(New SandboxEvidence())

Dim Asm As System.Reflection.Assembly
Asm = System.Reflection.Assembly.LoadFrom("myfile.dll", Evidence)
Dim MyClass As IMyInterface
MyClass = CType(Asm.CreateInstance("ClassName"), IMyInterface)

' (Now MyClass only has Execute permissions.)

Console.ReadLine()
    End Sub

End Class
```

You can test this example using the downloadable code for this recipe. It dynamically loads two classes, each of which provides a single method. One class performs numerical calculations, while the other tries to create a file. The method in the first class can always be executed successfully. However, if you try to use the second class after applying the restricted permission set, a *SecurityException* will be thrown.

Note This dynamic sandbox approach is used in the .NET learning game Terrarium, which can be downloaded from *http://www.gotdotnet.com*. You can read an interview about how Terrarium implements dynamically loaded assemblies (with C# code samples) at *http://msdn.microsoft.com/theshow/episode021/TranscriptText.asp*.

19

Useful COM Interop

As expansive as the Microsoft .NET Framework is, it would be unrealistic to expect it to duplicate all the features available in COM components today. In the previous chapters of this book, you've already seen how you can extend the functionality of .NET by leveraging features from the Win32 API, WMI, and COM components like the Windows Script Host. This chapter considers a few more useful features from the world of unmanaged code, including ADO classic (recipe 19.1), components for Web pages with Microsoft Internet Explorer (recipes 19.2 and 19.3), components for automating Microsoft Word and Excel (recipes 19.4 and 19.5), and ActiveX controls for animated movies and masked text boxes (recipes 19.7 and 19.8). And best of all, even though these controls and components exist outside the .NET class library, the .NET Framework's support for COM interoperability makes using them seamless.

19.1 Use ADO Classic

Problem

You want to use the ADO data access libraries for interoperability with an existing application or (rarely) to access some functionality that isn't available in Microsoft ADO.NET, like dynamic server-side cursors.

Solution

Use the ADO interop assembly ADODB.dll, which is included with the .NET Framework.

Discussion

Even though the .NET Framework is tailored for the new disconnected data access model of ADO.NET, you can still use the original ADO COM objects if required. You simply need to add a reference to the Microsoft ActiveX Data Objects 2.7 Library (msado15.dll) by right-clicking your project, selecting Add Reference, and choosing the COM tab. A reference will be added to the primary interop assembly ADODB.dll, which is included with the .NET Framework and installed in the global assembly cache (GAC). All the ADO objects are contained in a namespace named *ADODB*.

The ADO objects always connect through OLE DB, and thus you must use the OLE DB syntax for connection strings. You can manipulate *Connection*, *Command*, and *Recordset* objects directly, and you can even copy the data from a connected *Recordset* into a disconnected ADO.NET *DataSet* using the *OleDb-DataAdapter*. The following Console application demonstrates this technique.

```
Public Module ADOTest

    ' Note that the connection string must use OLE DB syntax.
    Private ConnectionString As String = "Provider=SQLOLEDB;" & _
        "Data Source=localhost;Integrated Security=SSPI;" & _
        "Initial Catalog=Northwind"

    Public Sub Main()
        ' Create the ADO classic objects.
        Dim ADOCon As New ADODB.Connection()
        ADOCon.ConnectionString = ConnectionString
        Dim SQL As String = "SELECT * FROM Customers"
        Dim Rs As ADODB.Recordset

        ' Create the ADO.NET adapter that will transfer the Recordset
        ' data to a table in the DataSet. Note that only the OLE DB
        ' provider exposes this functionality.
        Dim Adapter As New System.Data.OleDb.OleDbDataAdapter()
        Dim Ds As New DataSet()

        Try
            ' Open the Recordset.
            ADOCon.Open()
            Rs = ADOCon.Execute(SQL)

            ' Copy the Recordset to the DataSet.
            Adapter.Fill(Ds, Rs, "Customers")
        Catch Err As Exception
```

```
                Console.WriteLine(Err.ToString())
            Finally
                ADOCon.Close()
            End Try

            Console.WriteLine("Retrieved " & Ds.Tables(0).Rows.Count & " rows.")
            Console.ReadLine()
        End Sub

    End Module
```

19.2 Display a Web Page with Internet Explorer

Problem

You want to display an HTML page (or another type of document supported by Internet Explorer) in a Windows application.

Solution

Use the Web browser ActiveX control included with Internet Explorer.

Discussion

The .NET Framework does not include any controls for rendering HTML content. However, this functionality would be useful, either to display some local HTML content (like a rich help document) or some information from the Web (for example, a Web page that lists downloads a user might use to update an application).

To show an HTML page, you can add an Internet Explorer window to your Windows applications. This window not only supports HTML, it also supports JavaScript and Visual Basic Scripting Edition (VBScript) code, ActiveX controls, and various plug-ins depending on your system configuration (including Word, Excel, and Adobe Acrobat Reader). In fact, you can even use the Web browser control to browse the folders on a local drive or show the files on an FTP site.

To add the Web browser to a project, right-click the Toolbox and choose Customize Toolbox. Then select the COM Components tab, and check the Microsoft Web Browser control (shdocvw.dll). This will add the Explorer control to your Toolbox. When you drop this control onto a form, the necessary interop assemblies will be generated and added to your project.

When using the Web browser, you'll commonly use these methods:

- *Navigate* redirects the page to the URL you specify.

- *GoBack* and *GoForward* navigate to pages in the history list.

- *GoHome* navigates to the home page set on the current computer, and *GoSearch* shows the search page.

In addition, the user will be able to trigger page navigation by clicking page links (if they exist). You can retrieve the current URL from the *Location-URL* property and determine if the control is still rendering the page by examining the *Busy* property. In addition, you can react to a variety of events, including ones that fire when navigation starts and stops.

Figure 19-1 shows a simple test application that allows the user to visit two pages (and follow any links they provide).

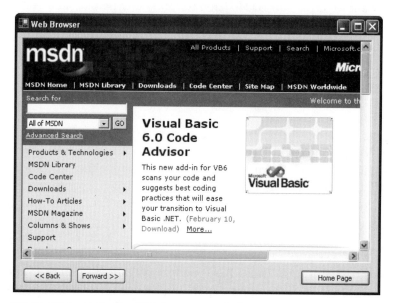

Figure 19-1   Using the Web browser control.

```
Public Class Form1
    Inherits System.Windows.Forms.Form

    ' (Designer code omitted.)

    Private Sub Form1_Load(ByVal sender As System.Object, _
      ByVal e As System.EventArgs) Handles MyBase.Load
        Explorer.Navigate2("http://www.prosetech.com")
    End Sub
```

```
Private Sub cmdBack_Click(ByVal sender As System.Object, _
  ByVal e As System.EventArgs) Handles cmdBack.Click
    Try
        Explorer.GoBack()
    Catch
        MessageBox.Show("Already on first page.")
    End Try
End Sub

Private Sub cmdForward_Click(ByVal sender As System.Object, _
  ByVal e As System.EventArgs) Handles cmdForward.Click
    Try
        Explorer.GoForward()
    Catch
        MessageBox.Show("Already on last page.")
    End Try
End Sub

Private Sub cmdHome_Click(ByVal sender As System.Object, _
  ByVal e As System.EventArgs) Handles cmdHome.Click
    Explorer.GoHome()
End Sub

End Class
```

19.3 Drive Internet Explorer

Problem

You want to show a separate Internet Explorer window, but retain control over that window.

Solution

Use Automation and the Microsoft Internet Explorer control to drive Internet Explorer.

Discussion

Microsoft provides more than one way to access the functionality of Internet Explorer. You can host an Internet Explorer browser window directly on a form, as shown in recipe 19.2, or you can use Automation to drive a standalone Internet Explorer window. In either case, the object model is virtually identical.

To use Automation with Internet Explorer, you must first add a reference to the necessary COM library. Right-click your project in the Solution Explorer, select Add Reference, and choose the COM tab. Find the Microsoft Internet Controls (shdocvw.dll) item in the list, and add it. The necessary interop assemblies will be generated and added to your project immediately.

As with the Web browser control, you can direct the window to various URLs and handle navigation events. In addition, you can control whether or not the window is visible (by setting the *Visible* property), and you can close the window by calling *Quit*.

The following Console application launches a standalone Internet Explorer window to show the indicated URL. It then handles the *NavigateComplete2* event, displaying new URLs as the user accesses them. You can close the Internet Explorer window by pressing Enter in the Console window.

```
Public Module IETest

    Public Sub Main()
        ' Create the IE instance.
        Dim IE As New SHDocVw.InternetExplorer()

        ' Connect an event handler that responds after navigations.
        AddHandler IE.NavigateComplete2, AddressOf IE_NavigateComplete2

        ' Navigate to a new page.
        IE.Navigate("http://www.prosetech.com")

        ' Show the window.
        IE.Visible = True

        Console.WriteLine("Press any key to exit.")
        Console.ReadLine()

        Console.WriteLine("Closing the IE window.")
        IE.Quit()
    End Sub

    Public Sub IE_NavigateComplete2(ByVal pDisp As Object, _
      ByRef URL As Object)
        Console.WriteLine("Visited: " & URL.ToString())
    End Sub

End Module
```

19.4 Drive Microsoft Word

Problem

You want to interact with Microsoft Word, either to automate a business task or to read and write Word documents.

Solution

Use the Word Automation objects included with Microsoft Office.

Discussion

Microsoft provides a rich object model that you can use to interact with Word and other Office applications. You can use these objects to create and read Word documents, automate complex or repetitive batch tasks, and even access Word features like the spelling dictionary.

To use Automation with Microsoft Word, you must first add a reference to the necessary COM library. Right-click your project in the Solution Explorer, select Add Reference, and choose the COM tab. Find the Microsoft Word Object Library item in the list, and add it. The exact name of the Automation objects depends on the version of Word you have installed. With Word 2000, the library is version 9.0, whereas Word 2002 (included with Office XP) uses version 10. The necessary interop assemblies will be added to your project immediately. The objects are located in a *Word* namespace.

Note   You can download primary interop assemblies for Office XP directly from Microsoft at *http://msdn.microsoft.com/library/default.asp?url=/downloads/list/office.asp*. These .NET assemblies wrap the Office COM components and include certain refinements that make the Office object model easier to use in a .NET application. Once you have downloaded the assemblies and installed them in the global assembly cache, they will be used automatically when you add a reference to any of the Office COM components.

The following Console application uses the Word Automation objects in several ways. It creates a document in the background, accesses the spelling checker, displays some document information, displays a print preview, and programmatically prints a document.

```
Public Module DriveWord

    Public Sub Main()
        ' Start Word in the background.
        Dim App As New Word.Application()
        App.DisplayAlerts = Word.WdAlertLevel.wdAlertsNone

        ' Create a new document (this is not visible to the user).
        Dim Doc As Word._Document = App.Documents.Add()

        Console.WriteLine()
        Console.WriteLine("Creating new document.")
        Console.WriteLine()

        ' Add a heading and two lines of text.
        Dim Range As Word.Range = Doc.Paragraphs.Add().Range
        Range.InsertBefore("Test Document")
        Range.Style = "Heading 1"

        Range = Doc.Paragraphs.Add().Range
        Range.InsertBefore("Line one." & vbCrLf & "Line two.")
        Range.Font.Bold = True

        ' Use Word as a dictionary.
        Console.Write("Enter a word to look up: ")
        Dim TestWord As String = Console.ReadLine()
        If App.CheckSpelling(TestWord) = False Then
            Console.WriteLine(TestWord & " is not in the dictionary.")

            Console.WriteLine("Suggestions include:")
            Dim Suggestion As Word.SpellingSuggestion
            For Each Suggestion In App.GetSpellingSuggestions(TestWord)
                Console.WriteLine(Suggestion.Name)
            Next
        Else
            Console.WriteLine(TestWord & " is in the dictionary.")
        End If
        Console.WriteLine()

        ' Save and close the current document.
        Doc.SaveAs(App.StartupPath & "\test.doc")
        Doc.Close()
        Doc = Nothing
```

```
' Now open the document again, show a print preview, and make
' Word visible.
Doc = App.Documents.Open(App.StartupPath & "\test.doc")
Doc.PrintPreview()
App.Visible = True

' Display some document information
Dim Words As Integer
Words = Doc.ComputeStatistics(Word.WdStatistic.wdStatisticWords)
Console.WriteLine("This document has " & Words.ToString() & " words.")

' Attempt to convert to a PDF file using Adobe Acrobat Distiller
' printing. This fails if you do not have the full Adobe Acrobat
' installed.
Try
    App.ActivePrinter = "Acrobat Distiller"

    Console.WriteLine("Press any key to print this document.")
    Console.ReadLine()
    Doc.PrintOut()
Catch
    Console.WriteLine("Printer not found.")
End Try

' Close and quit Word.
Console.WriteLine()
Console.WriteLine("Closing Word.")
Doc.Close()
CType(App, Word._Application).Quit()
End Sub

End Module
```

Here's an example of this application's output. The generated Word document is shown in Figure 19-2.

```
Creating new document.

Enter a word to look up: huggly
huggly is not in the dictionary.
Suggestions include:
hugely
ugly
haggle
haggy

This document has 6 words.
Press any key to print this document.

Closing Word.
```

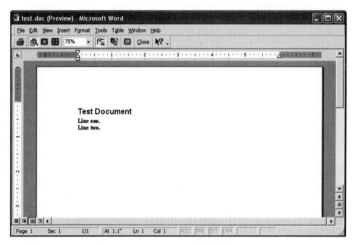

Figure 19-2 Generating a Word document programmatically.

> **Note** It's usually easiest to debug with the Word window fully visible, by setting *Word.Application.Visible* to *True*. When you have perfected your code, you can hide the window so that the user can't interfere with it.

19.5 Drive Microsoft Excel

Problem

You want to interact with Microsoft Excel, either to automate a business task or to read and write Excel documents.

Solution

Use the Excel Automation objects included with Microsoft Office.

Discussion

Microsoft provides a rich object model you can use to interact with Excel, allowing you to read and write spreadsheets and manipulate charts and other advanced Excel features. To use Automation with Microsoft Excel, you must first add a reference to the necessary COM library. Right-click your project in the Solution Explorer, select Add Reference, and choose the COM tab. Find the Microsoft Excel Object Library item in the list, and add it. The exact name of the Automation objects depends on the version of Excel you have installed. With Excel 2000, the library is version 9.0, whereas Excel 2002 (included with Office XP) uses version 10. The necessary interop assemblies will be added to your project immediately. If you've installed the primary interop assemblies for Office XP (available at *http://msdn.microsoft.com/library/default.asp?url= /downloads/list/office.asp*), they will be used automatically. Otherwise, a new interop assembly will be generated. The objects you need to use are located in an *Excel* namespace.

The following Console application creates a new Excel document, adds some data, generates a chart, and copies the chart data into a Windows Form. These steps are all performed with the Excel window fully visible, although you could change this behavior by setting the *Excel.Application.Visible* property to *False*.

```
Public Class DriveExcelForm
    Inherits System.Windows.Forms.Form

    ' (Designer code omitted.)

    Private Sub Form_Load(ByVal sender As System.Object, _
      ByVal e As System.EventArgs) Handles MyBase.Load
        ' Start and show Excel.
        Dim App As New Excel.Application()
        App.Visible = True

        ' Create a new document.
        Dim Doc As Excel.Workbook = App.Workbooks.Add()
        Dim Sheet As Excel.Worksheet = Doc.Sheets(1)

        ' Format the table headings.
        Sheet.Range("A1").Value = "Month"
        Sheet.Range("B1").Value = "Number of Days"

        ' The range expression 1:1 selects all cells in the first row.
        Sheet.Range("1:1").Font.Size = 12
        Sheet.Range("1:1").Font.Bold = True
        Sheet.Range("1:1").RowHeight = 20

        ' The range expression A:A selects all cells in the first column.
        Sheet.Range("A:A").ColumnWidth = 20
        Sheet.Range("B:B").ColumnWidth = 20

        ' Populate the sheet with some tabular data.
```

```
        Dim Days As Integer
        Dim i As Integer
        For i = 1 To 12
            Days = DateTime.DaysInMonth(DateTime.Now.Year, i)
            Sheet.Range("A" & (i + 1)).Value = _
              DateTimeFormatInfo.CurrentInfo.GetMonthName(i)
            Sheet.Range("B" & (i + 1)).Value = Days
        Next

        ' Create and format a new 3D column chart.
        Dim Chart As Excel.Chart = Doc.Charts.Add(, Sheet)
        Chart.ChartType = Excel.XlChartType.xl3DColumn
        Chart.SetSourceData(Sheet.Range("A1:B13"))

        ' Copy the chart to a PictureBox on this form, using the clipboard.
        Chart.ChartArea.Select()
        Chart.ChartArea.Copy()

        ' Retrieve the picture.
        Dim ChartImage As Image = _
          CType(Clipboard.GetDataObject().GetData(DataFormats.Bitmap), Bitmap)

        ' Shrink the picture to fit the form.
        Dim ScalingRatio As Single = PictureBox1.Width / ChartImage.Width
        ChartImage = ChartImage.GetThumbnailImage( _
          ChartImage.Width * ScalingRatio, ChartImage.Height * ScalingRatio, _
          Nothing, Nothing)

        PictureBox1.Image = ChartImage

        ' Modify the chart so it appears alongside the Excel table,
        ' instead of in a separate window.
        Chart.Location(Excel.XlChartLocation.xlLocationAsObject, "Sheet1")
    End Sub

End Class
```

Figure 19-3 shows the automatically generated Excel data and chart. Figure 19-4 shows the chart after it has been copied into the Windows application.

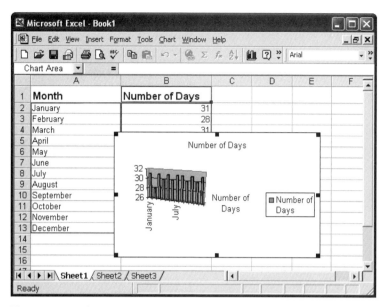

Figure 19-3   Generating an Excel document with a chart.

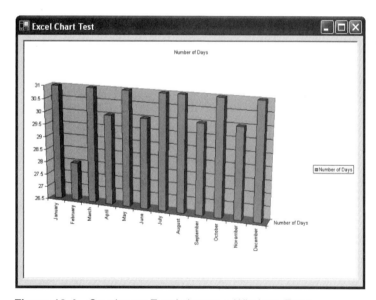

Figure 19-4   Copying an Excel chart to a Windows Form.

19.6 Use MAPI to Send E-Mail Messages

Problem

You want to send an e-mail message, but you don't have a Simple Mail Transfer Protocol (SMTP) mail server configured for the computer.

Solution

Use the MAPI (Message Application Programming Interface) COM component, which interacts with the mail account configured on the current computer.

Discussion

MAPI is an interface that allows you to interact with the mailing features that are integrated into the Windows operating system. You can use MAPI (either through its unmanaged API, or through the MAPI COM component) to interact with the default mail client (usually Microsoft Outlook or Outlook Express). Tasks include retrieving contact information from the address box, retrieving the messages in the Inbox, and programmatically composing and sending messages. You should note that the MAPI control is not included with .NET—it's installed with earlier versions of Visual Studio, such as Visual Basic 6. Although you can redistribute the MAPI ActiveX control with applications that use it, you'll need to have a product such as Visual Basic 6 in order to develop with it.

To use MAPI, right-click your project in the Solution Explorer, select Add Reference, and choose the COM tab. Find the Microsoft MAPI Controls 6.0 (msmapi32.ocx) item in the list, and add it. The necessary interop assemblies will be added to your project immediately. The objects are located in an *MSMAPI* namespace.

Figure 19-5 shows a simple e-mail client that uses MAPI to download a list of messages in the local Inbox and send a test message.

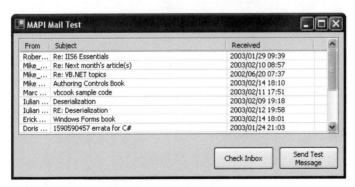

Figure 19-5 A simple MAPI e-mail client.

The code simply creates and logs into a MAPI session using a *MAPISession* object, and then accesses mail services through a *MAPIMessagesClass* object.

```vb
Public Class EmailClient
    Inherits System.Windows.Forms.Form

    ' (Designer code omitted.)

    Private Sub cmdSend_Click(ByVal sender As System.Object, _
        ByVal e As System.EventArgs) Handles cmdSend.Click
        ' Start a new session.
        Dim Session As New MSMAPI.MAPISession()

        ' You can disable the user interface, provided you have
        ' already configured the account correctly.
        Session.LogonUI = False

        ' Do not retrieve mail from the mail server.
        Session.DownLoadMail = False

        ' Start a session.
        Session.SignOn()

        ' Create a new message.
        Dim Messages As New MSMAPI.MAPIMessagesClass()
        Messages.SessionID = Session.SessionID
        Messages.Compose()

        ' Specify some message information.
        Messages.RecipDisplayName = "matthew@prosetech.com"
        Messages.MsgNoteText = "Hey this is great the MAPI code works fine :)"
        Messages.Send(False)

        ' End the session.
        Session.SignOff()
    End Sub

    Private Sub cmdReceive_Click(ByVal sender As System.Object, _
        ByVal e As System.EventArgs) Handles cmdReceive.Click
        ' Start a new session.
        Dim Session As New MSMAPI.MAPISession()
        Session.LogonUI = False

        ' Do not retrieve mail from the mail server.
        Session.DownLoadMail = False

        ' Start a session.
        Session.SignOn()
```

```
' Fetch the e-mail in the Inbox.
Dim Messages As New MSMAPI.MAPIMessagesClass()
Messages.SessionID = Session.SessionID
Messages.Fetch()

' Add all the messages to the ListView control.
Dim i As Integer
For i = 0 To Messages.MsgCount - 1
    Messages.MsgIndex = i
    Dim lvItem As New ListViewItem(Messages.MsgOrigDisplayName)
    lvItem.SubItems.Add(Messages.MsgSubject)
    lvItem.SubItems.Add(Messages.MsgDateReceived)
    lstInbox.Items.Add(lvItem)
Next

' End the session.
Session.SignOff()
End Sub

End Class
```

19.7 Play Media Files

Problem

You want to play movie video (for example, MPEG files) or MP3 audio files.

Solution

Add the ActiveX MCI control for multimedia, and connect it to a *PictureBox* control if you need to display video.

Discussion

The .NET Framework does not include any classes for playing multimedia such as sounds, videos, or MIDI files. Recipe 10.14 described how you can use the Win32 API to play WAV files. Even more functionality is available if you use the MCI ActiveX control. However, the MCI ActiveX control is not included with .NET—it's installed with earlier versions of Visual Studio, such as Visual Basic 6. Although you can redistribute the MCI ActiveX control with applications that use it, you'll need to have a product such as Visual Basic 6 in order to develop with it.

To add the MCI control to a project, right-click the Toolbox and choose Customize Toolbox. Then select the COM Components tab, and check the Microsoft Multimedia Control 6.0 (mci32.ocx) item. This will add the MMControl to your Toolbox. When you drop this control onto a form, the necessary interop assemblies will be generated and added to your project.

The MCI control appears on a form as a bar of playback controls. Usually, these controls will be hidden from the user. Your application code can interact with the MCI control to start and stop playback. You perform actions such as opening a file, playing it, and so on, by setting the control's *Command* property with an action string like *Open* or *Play*.

Figure 19-6 shows a simple demonstration of the MCI control that adds two custom playback buttons.

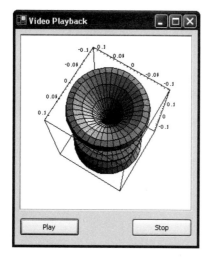

Figure 19-6   Video playback with the MCI control.

When the form loads, a sample MPEG file is opened, and a *PictureBox* is bound to the control. The code then uses the *Command* property to start and stop playback.

```
Public Class VideoForm
    Inherits System.Windows.Forms.Form

    ' (Designer code omitted.)

    Private Sub Form_Load(ByVal sender As System.Object, _
        ByVal e As System.EventArgs) Handles MyBase.Load
        ' Open the file.
        MMC.FileName = Application.StartupPath & "\test.mpg"
```

```
            MMC.Command = "Open"

            ' Hide the playback bar.
            MMC.Visible = False

            ' Show video in the PictureBox pic.
            MMC.hWndDisplay = pic.Handle.ToInt32()
    End Sub

    Private Sub cmdPlay_Click(ByVal sender As System.Object, _
      ByVal e As System.EventArgs) Handles cmdPlay.Click
            ' Rewind to the beginning.
            MMC.Command = "Prev"

            ' Start playback.
            MMC.Command = "Play"
    End Sub

    Private Sub cmdStop_Click(ByVal sender As System.Object, _
      ByVal e As System.EventArgs) Handles cmdStop.Click
            ' Stop playback.
            MMC.Command = "Stop"
    End Sub

End Class
```

> **Note**   If you need more extensive multimedia capabilities, you might want to use the Windows Media Player 9 Series Software Development Kit, which can be downloaded from *http://www.microsoft.com /downloads*. Microsoft also provides a managed DirectX toolkit for more ambitious multimedia development.

19.8 Use Masked Text Boxes

Problem

You want to have a fine-grained control over user text entry.

Solution

Use the masked ActiveX edit control, which can restrict and format data according to an input mask.

Discussion

The masked edit control looks like the text box control, but it includes enhancements for masked input and formatted output. If you don't use an input mask, the masked edit control behaves like a standard text box.

To define an input mask, you set the *Mask* property with a string. The mask can include two types of characters: *placeholders*, which map to user supplied characters, and *literal characters*, which are entered automatically as the user types. The literal characters serve as visual cues that indicate the type of input that is being entered (such as the parentheses around the area code portion of a telephone number). The placeholders provide input validation. If the user attempts to enter a character that conflicts with the input mask, the control generates a *ValidationError* event, and the character won't appear. Table 19-1 indicates the placeholders you can use. To retrieve the formatted text that's currently in the control, you use the *Text* property.

Table 19-1   Masked Edit Control Placeholders

Mask character	Description
#	Digit placeholder.
.	Decimal placeholder. The actual character used is the one specified as the decimal placeholder in your international settings. This character is treated as a literal for masking purposes.
,	Thousands separator. The actual character used is the one specified as the thousands separator in your international settings. This character is treated as a literal for masking purposes.
:	Time separator. The actual character used is the one specified as the time separator in your international settings. This character is treated as a literal for masking purposes.
/	Date separator. The actual character used is the one specified as the date separator in your international settings. This character is treated as a literal for masking purposes.
\	Treat the next character in the mask string as a literal. This allows you to include the #, &, A, and ? characters in the mask. This character is treated as a literal for masking purposes.
&	Character placeholder. Valid values for this placeholder are ANSI characters in the following ranges: 32–126 and 128–255.
>	Convert all the characters that follow to uppercase.
<	Convert all the characters that follow to lowercase.

Table 19-1   Masked Edit Control Placeholders   *(continued)*

Mask character	Description
A	Alphanumeric character placeholder (entry required). For example: a–z, A–Z, or 0–9.
a	Alphanumeric character placeholder (entry optional).
9	Digit placeholder (entry optional). For example: 0–9.
C	Character or space placeholder (entry optional). This operates exactly like the *&* placeholder, and ensures compatibility with Microsoft Access.
?	Letter placeholder. For example: a–z or A–Z.

To add the masked text box control to a project, right-click the Toolbox and choose Customize Toolbox. Then select the COM Components tab, and check the Microsoft Masked Edit Control (msmask32.ocx). This will add the MaskedEdBox to your Toolbox. When you drop this control onto a form, the necessary interop assemblies will be generated and added to your project.

This code snippet assigns a masked code that consists of numbers and automatically capitalized letters, separated by hyphens:

```
' This box holds data like 123-ABC-abc.
EditBox.Mask = "###->???-<???"
```

The control, with some partially entered data, is shown in Figure 19-7.

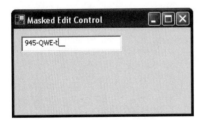

Figure 19-7   A masked text box.

Index

Symbols

+ (addition) metacharacter, 27
+ (addition) operator, joining strings, 3
& (and) operator, joining strings, 3
* (asterisk) metacharacter, 27
^ (caret) metacharacter, 27
$ (dollar =) metacharacter, 27
| metacharacter, 27
( ) (parentheses) metacharacter, 27. (period)
    metacharacter, 27
? (question mark) metacharacter, 27
[ ] (square brackets) metacharacter, 27

A

Abort method, 233, 247–249
About boxes, creating dynamically, 299–301
absolute expiration, storing data in a cache, 570
access
    control lists. *See* ACLs (access control lists)
    Desktop, 336–338
    FTP sites, 291–297
    Start menu, 336–338
    Windows registry, 330–332
    Windows Script Host, 338–341
ACLs (access control lists), 684
Active Directory, retrieving public queues, 665–666
ActiveX controls (HTML page), displaying in Windows
    applications, 729–731
    edit controls, masked text boxes, 744–746
    MCI controls, displaying media files, 742–744
Add Installer link, 478
AddHandler statements, connecting event handlers, 572
Addition (+) metacharacter, 27
AddRange method, copying from arrays into
    ArrayLists, 87
addresses, IP. *See* IP addresses
AddText method, 244
ADO.NET
    connection pooling, 491–494
    data access libraries, 727–729
    reading Excel files, 541–543
algorithms
    classes, 689
        HashAlgorithm, 705
        KeyedHashAlgorithm, 708
    Luhn's credit card validation, 37–38
    SoundEx, string comparisons, 39–42

ALLUSERSPROFILE environment variable, 337
And keyword, bitwise arithmetic, 158–159
And (&) operation, 232
APIs (Application Programming Interfaces), Win32, 330
AppDomain.SetPrincipalPolicy method, 676
AppDomain.UnhandledException event, 366
Append method, StringBuilder class, 20
Application.Run method, starting applications, 341–343
applications
    configuration settings
        custom settings, 180–182
        reading, 178–180
    file associations, 371–374
    instances, 352–353
    sending keystrokes, 354–356
    starting
        Application.Run method, 341-343
        Main method, 341–343
        registered file types, 346–347
    Web applications (ASP.NET), 545–591
        adding controls to a Web form, 572–575
        applying JavaScript, 555–557
        caching, 568–572
        custom error pages, 561–562
        dynamically generating images, 577–583
        enabling Web site debugging, 546–548
        forms authentication, 562–564
        inserting line breaks to a Label control, 554
        Internet Explorer controls, 584–589
        loading user controls programmatically, 575–577
        menu controls, 589–591
        programmatically setting control focus, 557–558
        state management, 549–553
        uploading files, 558–560
        validating user input, 564–568
arbitrary data storage, ASP.NET caching, 570–572
arguments, retrieving command-line arguments, 344–
    345
arithmetic
    bitwise arithmetic, file attributes, 158–159
    Mod 11, ISBN validation, 38–39
Array class, reversing strings with Reverse method, 16
Array.CreateInstance method
    jagged arrays, 83–85
    non-bounded at zero arrays, 82–83
ArrayList class
    copying from arrays into ArrayLists, 87-89
    dynamic arrays lists, 85–86
    methods, 85

M

About the Author

Matthew MacDonald is the author of several popular programming books, including *Microsoft .NET Distributed Applications*, *The Book of VB .NET*, and *ASP.NET: The Complete Reference*. He writes a column for *Inside Visual Basic* and is a regular contributor to *ASPToday*, *C#Today*, *Hardcore Visual Basic*, and other periodicals. A Microsoft Certified Solution Developer with a passion for emerging technologies, Matthew spends his time writing, developing, and teaching.